# Fuzzy Sets, Fuzzy Logic and Their Applications 2021

# Fuzzy Sets, Fuzzy Logic and Their Applications 2021

Editor

**Michael Voskoglou**

MDPI

Basel • Beijing • Wuhan • Barcelona • Belgrade • Novi Sad • Cluj • Manchester

*Editor*
Michael Voskoglou
University of Peloponnese
(Ex Graduate Technological
Educational Institute of
Western Greece)
Patras, Greece

*Editorial Office*
MDPI
St. Alban-Anlage 66
4052 Basel, Switzerland

This is a reprint of articles from the Special Issue published online in the open access journal *Mathematics* (ISSN 2227-7390) (available at: https://www.mdpi.com/si/mathematics/fuzzy_2021).

For citation purposes, cite each article independently as indicated on the article page online and as indicated below:

| Lastname, A.A.; Lastname, B.B. Article Title. *Journal Name* **Year**, *Volume Number*, Page Range. |
|---|

**ISBN 978-3-0365-7374-8 (Hbk)**
**ISBN 978-3-0365-7375-5 (PDF)**
**doi.org/10.3390/books978-3-0365-7375-5**

# Contents

**About the Editor** . . . . . . . . . . . . . . . . . . . . . . . . . . . . . . . . . . . . . . . . . . . . . . . **vii**

**Preface** . . . . . . . . . . . . . . . . . . . . . . . . . . . . . . . . . . . . . . . . . . . . . . . . . . . . . **ix**

**Shuling Wang and Haitao Li**
Resolution of Fuzzy Relational Inequalities with Boolean Semi-Tensor Product Composition
Reprinted from: *Mathematics* **2021**, *9*, 937, doi:10.3390/math9090937 . . . . . . . . . . . . . . . . . **1**

**Andrei Alexandru and Gabriel Ciobanu**
Fuzzy Results for Finitely Supported Structures
Reprinted from: *Mathematics* **2021**, *9*, 1651, doi:10.3390/math9141651 . . . . . . . . . . . . . . . . **19**

**Hesham Alhumade, Hegazy Rezk, Abdulrahim A. Al-Zahrani, Sharif F. Zaman and Ahmed Askalany**
Artificial Intelligence Based Modelling of Adsorption Water Desalination System
Reprinted from: *Mathematics* **2021**, *9*, 1674, doi:10.3390/math9141674 . . . . . . . . . . . . . . . . **43**

**Amir Masoud Rahmani, Saqib Ali, Mohammad Sadegh Yousefpoor, Efat Yousefpoor, Rizwan Ali Naqvi, Kamran Siddique and Mehdi Hosseinzadeh**
An Area Coverage Scheme Based on Fuzzy Logic and Shuffled Frog-Leaping Algorithm (SFLA) in Heterogeneous Wireless Sensor Networks
Reprinted from: *Mathematics* **2021**, *9*, 2251, doi:10.3390/math9182251 . . . . . . . . . . . . . . . . **57**

**Siukai Choy, Tszching Ng, Carisa Yu and Benson Lam**
Fuzzy Bit-Plane-Dependence Region Competition
Reprinted from: *Mathematics* **2021**, *9*, 2392, doi:10.3390/math9192392 . . . . . . . . . . . . . . . . **99**

**Pedro J. Correa-Caicedo, Horacio Rostro-González, Martin A. Rodriguez-Licea, Óscar Octavio Gutiérrez-Frías, Carlos Alonso Herrera-Ramírez, Iris I. Méndez-Gurrola, et al.**
GPS Data Correction Based on Fuzzy Logic for Tracking Land Vehicles
Reprinted from: *Mathematics* **2021**, *9*, 2818, doi:10.3390/math9212818 . . . . . . . . . . . . . . . . **119**

**Shuker Khalil, Ahmed Hassan, Haya Alaskar, Wasiq Khan and Abir Hussain**
Fuzzy Logical Algebra and Study of the Effectiveness of Medications for COVID-19
Reprinted from: *Mathematics* **2021**, *9*, 2838, doi:10.3390/math9222838 . . . . . . . . . . . . . . . . **137**

**Hennie Husniah and Asep K. Supriatna**
Computing the Number of Failures for Fuzzy Weibull Hazard Function
Reprinted from: *Mathematics* **2021**, *9*, 2858, doi:10.3390/math9222858 . . . . . . . . . . . . . . . . **149**

**Susana Díaz-Vázquez, Emilio Torres-Manzanera, Irene Díaz, Susana Montes**
On the Search for a Measure to Compare Interval-Valued Fuzzy Sets
Reprinted from: *Mathematics* **2021**, *9*, 3157, doi:10.3390/math9243157 . . . . . . . . . . . . . . . . **169**

**Ibtesam Alshammari, Mani Parimala, Cenap Ozel, Muhammad Riaz and Rania Kammoun**
New MCDM Algorithms with Linear Diophantine Fuzzy SoftTOPSIS, VIKOR and Aggregation Operators
Reprinted from: *Mathematics* **2022**, *10*, 3080, doi:10.3390/math10173080 . . . . . . . . . . . . . . . **199**

**Georgios Souliotis, Yousif Alanazi and Basil Papadopoulos**
Construction of Fuzzy Numbers via Cumulative Distribution Function
Reprinted from: *Mathematics* **2022**, *10*, 3350, doi:10.3390/math10183350 . . . . . . . . . . . . . . . **221**

# About the Editor

**Michael Voskoglou**

Michael Gr. Voskoglou (B.Sc., M.Sc., M.Phil. and Ph.D. in Mathematics) is an Emeritus Professor of the Graduate Technological Educational Institute (T. E. I.) of Western Greece in Patras. He was a full-time Professor at the same institute from 1987 to 2010, was an instructor at the Hellenic Open University, as well as in the Mathematics Department of the University of Patras and at the Schools of Primary and Secondary In—Service Teachers' Training in Patras, as well as was a teacher of mathematics in Greek public secondary education (1972–1987). Michael Gr. Voskoglou was also a Visiting Researcher at the Bulgarian Academy of Sciences (1997–2000), at the University of Warsaw (2009), at the University of Applied Sciences in Berlin (2010) and at the National Institute of Technology of Durgapur (2016). He is the author/editor of 18 books and of about 600 papers, with more than 2000 citations. He has been the reviewer of the American Mathematical Society and the Editor of many mathematical journals, as well as the supervisor of many student dissertations and an external examiner of Ph.D. dissertations at universities in Egypt, India and Saudi Arabia. His research interests include algebra, fuzzy logic, Markov chains, artificial intelligence and mathematics education.

# Preface

This book, containing 13 from the total of 40 submitted articles that were accepted and published in the Special Issue "Fuzzy Sets, Fuzzy Logic and Their Applications, 2021" of the MDPI "Mathematics" journal, is the third volume of a successful series that began with the Special Issue "Fuzzy Sets, Fuzzy Logic and Their Applications" (2019, 20 papers) and was followed by the Special Issue "Fuzzy Sets, Fuzzy Logic and Their Applications, 2020" (24 papers).

The 13 articles in the present book, which appear in the order that they were accepted and published in "Mathematics", cover a wide range of topics connected to the theory and applications of fuzzy sets and systems, of fuzzy logic and of their extensions/generalizations.

More explicitly, the first paper, written by Shuling Wang and Haitao Lipaper, studies the resolution of a kind of FRI with a Boolean semi-tensor product composition.

The second paper, by Andrei Alexandru and Gabriel Ciobanu, presents a survey of some results recently published by the authors regarding the fuzzy aspects of finitely supported structures.

The third paper, by Hesham Alhumade, Hegazy Rezk, Abdulrahim A. Al-Zahrani, Sharif F. Zaman and Ahmed Askalany, models the output performance of an adsorption water desalination system (AWDS) in terms of switching and cycle time using artificial intelligence.

The fourth paper, by Amir Masoud Rahmani, Saqib Ali, Mohammad Sadegh Yousefpoor, Efat Yousefpoor, Rizwan Ali Naqvi, Kamran Siddique and Mehdi Hosseinzadeh, develops an area coverage scheme based on fuzzy logic and a shuffled frog-leaping algorithm (SFLA) in heterogeneous wireless sensor networks.

The fifth paper, by Siukai Choy, Tszching Ng, Carisa Yu and Benson Lam, presents a novel variational model based on fuzzy region competition and statistical image variation modeling for image segmentation.

The sixth paper, by Pedro J. Correa-Caicedo, Martin A. Rodriguez-Licea, Óscar Octavio Gutiérrez-Frías, Óscar Octavio Gutiérrez-Frías, Carlos Alonso Herrera-Ramírez, Iris I. Méndez-Gurrola, Miroslava Cano-Lara and Alejandro I. Barranco-Gutiérrez, proposes an intelligent system based on fuzzy logic, which takes the information from the sensors and corrects the vehicle's absolute position according to its latitude and longitude.

Shuker Khalil, Ahmed Hassan, Haya Alaskar, Wasiq Khan and Abir Hussain investigate in the seventh paper the new types of cubic soft algebras and they study their applications.

In the next paper, Hennie Husniah and Asep K. Supriatna compute the number of failures for a system which has Weibull failure distribution with a fuzzy shape parameter.

Susana Díaz-Vázquez, Emilio Torres-Manzanera, Irene Díaz and Susana Montes revisit in the next paper the axioms that a measure of the difference between two interval-valued fuzzy sets should satisfy, paying special attention to the condition of monotonicity in the sense that the closer the intervals are, the smaller the measure of difference between them is.

In the tenth paper, Ibtesam Alshammar, Ibtesam Alshammar, Ibtesam Alshammar, Cenap Oze, Muhammad Riaz and Rania Kammoun focus on several ideas associated with linear Diophantine fuzzy soft sets, along with their algebraic structure.

In the next paper, Georgios Souliotis, Yousif Alanazi and Basil Papadopoulos present a construction of fuzzy numbers via the cumulative distribution function.

In a review paper, Michael Gr. Voskoglou details the main steps that were laid from Zadeh's fuzziness and Atanassov's intuitionistic fuzzy sets, to Smarandache's indeterminacy and Molodstov's soft sets.

The last paper, by Muhammad Bilal Khan, Hakeem A. Othman, Michael Gr. Voskoglou, Lazim Abdullah and Alia M. Alzubaidi, studies the Aumann and fuzzy Aumann integrals which are the most significant interval and fuzzy operators that allow the classical theory of integrals to be generalized.

It is hoped that this book will be interesting and useful for those working in the areas of fuzzy sets, fuzzy systems and fuzzy logic, as well as for those with a proper mathematical background and those willing to become familiar with the recent advances in fuzzy mathematics and fuzzy logic.

As the Guest Editor of the present Special Issue, I am grateful to the authors of the papers for their quality contributions, to the reviewers for their valuable comments toward improvements in the submitted works and to the administrative staff of MDPI for the support in completing this project. Special thanks are due to the Managing Editor of the three Special Issues (2019, 2020 and 2021) Ms. Grace Du for her excellent collaboration and valuable assistance during all of these years.

**Michael Voskoglou**
*Editor*

*mathematics*

MDPI

*Article*

# Resolution of Fuzzy Relational Inequalities with Boolean Semi-Tensor Product Composition

**Shuling Wang and Haitao Li ***

School of Mathematics and Statistics, Shandong Normal University, Jinan 250014, China; 2018020496@stu.sdnu.edu.cn

* Correspondence: lihaitao@sdnu.edu.cn or haitaoli09@gmail.com

**Abstract:** Resolution of fuzzy relational inequalities (FRIs) plays a significant role in decision-making, image compression and fuzzy control. This paper studies the resolution of a kind of FRIs with Boolean semi-tensor product composition. First, by resorting to the column stacking technique, the equivalent form of FRIs with Boolean semi-tensor product composition is obtained, which is a system of FRIs (SFRIs) with max–min composition. Second, based on the semi-tensor product method, all the solutions to FRIs with Boolean semi-tensor product composition are obtained by finding all possible parameter set solutions. Finally, a general procedure is developed for the resolution of FRIs with Boolean semi-tensor product composition. Two illustrative examples are worked out to show the effectiveness of the obtained new results.

**Keywords:** fuzzy relational inequality; Boolean semi-tensor product composition; column stacking; semi-tensor product of matrices

**Citation:** Wang, S.; Li, H. Resolution of Fuzzy Relational Inequalities with Boolean Semi-Tensor Product Composition. *Mathematics* **2021**, *9*, 937. https://doi.org/10.3390/math9090937

Academic Editors: Michael Voskoglou and Salvatore Sessa

Received: 14 March 2021
Accepted: 21 April 2021
Published: 23 April 2021



## 1. Introduction

Resolution of fuzzy relational equations (FREs) and fuzzy relational inequalities (FRIs) has wide applications in several research fields including decision-making, image compression, fuzzy control and so on [1–4]. E. Sanchez initiated the resolution theory of FREs and applied it to medical research [5]. Since then, the resolution of FREs (FRIs) has become a heated topic [6–8]. The resolution of FREs with max-product composition was considered in [9–11]. Cornejo et al. [12,13] investigated the solvability of bipolar max-product FREs. Several effective alternatives for solving fuzzy nonlinear equations were proposed in [14–16]. An algorithm for solving FREs with max-T composition was established in [17]. The resolution of FREs with max–min composition was investigated in [18–20]. Besides the study of FREs and FRIs, the resolution of system of fuzzy relational equations (SFREs) and system of fuzzy relational inequalities (SFRIs) has also been widely studied [21,22].

Recently, the semi-tensor product of matrices has been put forward by Cheng [23], which has been widely applied to the analysis and control of finite-value dynamical systems, including controllability [24,25], observability [26], stability and stabilization [27–29], optimal control [30], synchronization [31], game theory [32–36] and so on [37,38]. Lu et al. [39] presented a detailed survey on the applications of semi-tensor product of matrices to finite-value dynamical systems. In particular, the semi-tensor product method has also been applied to the modeling of fuzzy systems [40,41] and resolution of FREs and FRIs [42,43]. Cheng et al. [44] first applied the semi-tensor product method to the resolution of FREs with max–min composition. Based on the semi-tensor product of matrices, Li and Wang [45] studied the resolution of FRIs with max–min composition. Several kinds of FRIs and SFRIs with max–min composition were considered in [46] by virtue of a column stacking approach.

In the past decade, dimension-varying systems have received intensive attention due to the wide applications in spacecrafts, vehicle clutch systems and biological systems [47]. When considering dimension-varying fuzzy systems, it is significant to deal with fuzzy relations with incompatible dimensions. However, all the existing results on the resolution of FREs and FRIs just considered the case where fuzzy matrices have compatible dimensions (see Definition 2 below). When the dimensions of two fuzzy matrices are not compatible, we call it Boolean semi-tensor product composition. Therefore, it is meaningful to investigate the resolution of FREs and FRIs with Boolean semi-tensor product composition, and apply the obtained results to the study of dimension-varying fuzzy systems. It is easy to see that the max–min composition is a special case of Boolean semi-tensor product composition.

This paper focuses on the resolution of FRIs (see (11) below) and SFRIs (see (12) below) with Boolean semi-tensor product composition, and aims to propose a general procedure to obtain all the solutions. The main contributions of this paper are two-fold. On one hand, we investigate the basic theory of Boolean semi-tensor product. Compared with semi-tensor product, we find that some important properties of semi-tensor product such as associative law, pseudo commutativity, and the properties of swap matrix and transpose operator still hold for Boolean semi-tensor product. On the other hand, we establish a general procedure for the resolution of FRIs and SFRIs with Boolean semi-tensor product composition, which facilitates the application of fuzzy theory in dimension-varying systems.

The remainder of this paper is organized as follows. In Section 2, we recall some necessary preliminaries. Section 3 formulates the problems studied in this paper and studies the equivalent forms of FRIs and SFRIs with Boolean semi-tensor product composition. In Section 4, a general procedure is established for the resolution of the considered FRIs and SFRIs. Two numerical examples are given to support our new results in Section 5, which is followed by a brief conclusion in Section 6.

## 2. Preliminaries

### 2.1. Semi-Tensor Product of Matrices

In this part, we present some necessary preliminaries on the semi-tensor product of matrices. For details, please refer to [23,44].

**Definition 1.** *Let $P \in \mathcal{M}_{m\times n}$, $Q \in \mathcal{M}_{s\times t}$. Denote the least common multiple of $n$ and $s$ by $\alpha = lcm(n,s)$. Then, the semi-tensor product of $P$ and $Q$ is*

$$P \ltimes Q = (P \otimes I_{\frac{\alpha}{n}})(Q \otimes I_{\frac{\alpha}{s}}), \tag{1}$$

*where $\otimes$ is the Kronecker product.*

**Lemma 1.** *Let $X \in \mathcal{M}_{s\times 1}$ be a column vector and $P \in \mathcal{M}_{m\times n}$. Then*

$$X \ltimes P = (I_s \otimes P) \ltimes X. \tag{2}$$

Denote $\mathcal{D}_k := \{0, \frac{1}{k-1}, \cdots, \frac{k-2}{k-1}, 1\}$. When $k=\infty$, $\mathcal{D}_\infty := [0,1]$. Define $\Delta_s := \{\delta_s^i : i = 1,2,\cdots,s\}$, where $\delta_s^i$ denotes the $i$-th column of identity matrix $I_s$. Identify $\frac{i}{k-1}$ as $\delta_k^{k-i}$, $i = 0,1,\cdots,k-1$. Then, one can see that $\mathcal{D}_k \sim \Delta_k$. $\delta_k^{k-i}$ is called the vector form of $\frac{i}{k-1}$ and we do not distinguish $\delta_k^{k-i}$ and $\frac{i}{k-1}$ if no confusion arises in the sequel. For any $a, b \in \mathcal{D}_k$, $a \vee_k b = \max\{a,b\}$, $a \wedge_k b = \min\{a,b\}$. When $k=\infty$, $a \vee b := a \vee_\infty b$ and $a \wedge b := a \wedge_\infty b$.

**Lemma 2.** *Let $x$, $y \in \mathcal{D}_k$. Then*

*(i)*

$$x \vee_k y = M_d^k \ltimes x \ltimes y, \tag{3}$$

*where $M_d^k = \delta_k[P_1\ P_2\ \cdots\ P_k]$, and $P_r = [1\ 2\ \cdots\ r-1\ \underbrace{r\ \cdots\ r}_{k-r+1}]$, $r = 1,2,\cdots,k$;*

*(ii)*

$$x \wedge_k y = M_c^k \ltimes x \ltimes y, \tag{4}$$

where $M_c^k = \delta_k[Q_1\ Q_2\ \cdots\ Q_k]$, and $Q_r = [\underbrace{r\ \cdots\ r}_{r}\ r+1\ r+2\ \cdots\ k]$, $r = 1, 2, \cdots, k$.

*2.2. Boolean Semi-Tensor Product Composition*

To formulate the problem considered in this paper, we introduce some necessary operators. Denote the set of $s \times t$ matrices with their entries in $\mathcal{D}_k$ by $\mathcal{D}_k^{s\times t}$.

**Definition 2.** *Let $P = (p_{i,j}) \in \mathcal{D}_\infty^{m\times n}$, $Q = (q_{i,j}) \in \mathcal{D}_\infty^{n\times s}$. Then, the max–min composition operator, denoted by "$\circ$", is defined as*

$$R = (r_{i,j}) = P \circ Q \in \mathcal{D}_\infty^{m\times s},$$

*where $r_{i,j} = \vee_{k=1}^{n}(p_{i,k} \wedge q_{k,j})$.*

**Definition 3.** *Let $P = (p_{i,j}) \in \mathcal{D}_\infty^{m\times n}$, $Q = (q_{i,j}) \in \mathcal{D}_\infty^{s\times t}$. Then, the Boolean Kronecker product of $P$ and $Q$, denoted by $P \otimes_{\mathcal{B}} Q \in \mathcal{D}_\infty^{ms\times nt}$, is*

$$P \otimes_{\mathcal{B}} Q = \begin{bmatrix} p_{1,1} \otimes_{\mathcal{B}} Q & \cdots & p_{1,n} \otimes_{\mathcal{B}} Q \\ \vdots & & \vdots \\ p_{m,1} \otimes_{\mathcal{B}} Q & \cdots & p_{m,n} \otimes_{\mathcal{B}} Q \end{bmatrix},$$

*where*

$$p_{i,j} \otimes_{\mathcal{B}} Q = \begin{bmatrix} p_{i,j} \wedge q_{1,1} & \cdots & p_{i,j} \wedge q_{1,t} \\ \vdots & & \vdots \\ p_{i,j} \wedge q_{s,1} & \cdots & p_{i,j} \wedge q_{s,t} \end{bmatrix}.$$

Similar to the ordinary Kronecker product, one can obtain the following properties of Boolean Kronecker product.

**Proposition 1.** *(i) Let $P$, $Q$, $R$ be three real matrices with arbitrary dimensions. Then*

$$P \otimes_{\mathcal{B}} Q \otimes_{\mathcal{B}} R = P \otimes_{\mathcal{B}} (Q \otimes_{\mathcal{B}} R). \tag{5}$$

*(ii) Let $P \in \mathcal{M}_{m\times n}$, $Q \in \mathcal{M}_{s\times t}$. Then*

$$(P \otimes_{\mathcal{B}} Q)^\top = P^\top \otimes_{\mathcal{B}} Q^\top. \tag{6}$$

**Definition 4.** *Let $P = (p_{i,j}) \in \mathcal{D}_\infty^{m\times n}$, $Q = (q_{i,j}) \in \mathcal{D}_\infty^{s\times t}$. Then, the Boolean semi-tensor product composition operator, denoted by "$\ltimes_{\mathcal{B}}$", is defined as*

$$P \ltimes_{\mathcal{B}} Q = (P \otimes_{\mathcal{B}} I_{\frac{\alpha}{n}}) \circ (Q \otimes_{\mathcal{B}} I_{\frac{\alpha}{s}}), \tag{7}$$

*where $\alpha = lcm(n, s)$.*

**Remark 1.** *One can easily see from Definition 4 that $P \ltimes_{\mathcal{B}} Q = P \circ Q$ holds for $n = s$.*

Next, we present some important properties of Boolean semi-tensor product composition.

**Proposition 2.** *Let $P$, $Q$, $R$ be three real matrices with arbitrary dimensions. Then*

$$P \ltimes_{\mathcal{B}} Q \ltimes_{\mathcal{B}} R = P \ltimes_{\mathcal{B}} (Q \ltimes_{\mathcal{B}} R). \tag{8}$$

**Proposition 3.** *Let $P \in \mathcal{M}_{m\times n}$, $Q \in \mathcal{M}_{s\times t}$. Then*

$$(P \ltimes_{\mathcal{B}} Q)^\top = Q^\top \ltimes_{\mathcal{B}} P^\top. \tag{9}$$

**Proof of Proposition 3.** A simple calculation shows that

$$\begin{aligned}(P \ltimes_{\mathcal{B}} Q)^{\top} &= [(P \otimes_{\mathcal{B}} I_{\frac{\alpha}{n}}) \circ (Q \otimes_{\mathcal{B}} I_{\frac{\alpha}{s}})]^{\top} \\ &= (Q \otimes_{\mathcal{B}} I_{\frac{\alpha}{s}})^{\top} \circ (P \otimes_{\mathcal{B}} I_{\frac{\alpha}{n}})^{\top} \\ &= (Q^{\top} \otimes_{\mathcal{B}} I_{\frac{\alpha}{s}}) \circ (P^{\top} \otimes_{\mathcal{B}} I_{\frac{\alpha}{n}}) \\ &= Q^{\top} \ltimes_{\mathcal{B}} P^{\top},\end{aligned}$$

where $\alpha = \text{lcm}(n, s)$. □

**Proposition 4.** *Let $X \in \mathcal{D}_{\infty}^{s\times 1}$ and $Y \in \mathcal{D}_{\infty}^{t\times 1}$ be two column vectors. Then*

$$W_{[s,t]} \ltimes_{\mathcal{B}} X \ltimes_{\mathcal{B}} Y = Y \ltimes_{\mathcal{B}} X, \tag{10}$$

*where $W_{[s,t]} := [I_t \otimes \delta_s^1 \ I_t \otimes \delta_s^2 \ \cdots \ I_t \otimes \delta_s^s]$.*

**Proof of Proposition 4.** Set $X = [x_1 \, x_2 \, \cdots \, x_s]^{\top}$ and $Y = [y_1 \, y_2 \, \cdots \, y_t]^{\top}$. Then, it holds that

$$\begin{aligned}X \ltimes_{\mathcal{B}} Y &= (X \otimes_{\mathcal{B}} I_t) \circ Y \\ &= [x_1 \wedge y_1 \ \ x_1 \wedge y_2 \cdots x_1 \wedge y_t \ \ x_2 \wedge y_1 \ \ x_2 \wedge y_2 \cdots x_2 \wedge y_t \\ &\quad \cdots x_s \wedge y_1 \ \ x_s \wedge y_2 \cdots x_s \wedge y_t]^{\top}.\end{aligned}$$

Thus,

$$\begin{aligned}W_{[s,t]} \ltimes_{\mathcal{B}} X \ltimes_{\mathcal{B}} Y &= W_{[s,t]} \ltimes_{\mathcal{B}} (X \ltimes_{\mathcal{B}} Y) \\ &= [x_1 \wedge y_1 \ \ x_2 \wedge y_1 \cdots x_s \wedge y_1 \ \ x_1 \wedge y_2 \ \ x_2 \wedge y_2 \cdots x_s \wedge y_2 \\ &\quad \cdots x_1 \wedge y_t \ \ x_2 \wedge y_t \cdots x_s \wedge y_t]^{\top} \\ &= Y \ltimes_{\mathcal{B}} X.\end{aligned}$$

□

## 3. Problem Formulation

In this paper, we consider the following two problems:

- Problem 1: Solve the following FRI:

$$G \leqslant A \ltimes_{\mathcal{B}} X \leqslant H, \tag{11}$$

where $X \in \mathcal{D}_{\infty}^{p\times q}$ is an unknown matrix, $A \in \mathcal{D}_{\infty}^{m\times n}$, $G, \ H \in \mathcal{D}_{\infty}^{\frac{\alpha m}{n} \times \frac{\alpha q}{p}}$ are known matrices, and $\alpha = \text{lcm}(n, p)$.
- Problem 2: Solve the following SFRIs:

$$\begin{cases} G_1 \leq A_1 \ltimes_{\mathcal{B}} X \leq H_1, \\ G_2 \leq A_2 \ltimes_{\mathcal{B}} X \leq H_2, \\ \qquad \vdots \\ G_N \leq A_N \ltimes_{\mathcal{B}} X \leq H_N, \end{cases} \tag{12}$$

where $X \in \mathcal{D}_{\infty}^{p\times q}$ is an unknown matrix, $A_i \in \mathcal{D}_{\infty}^{m_i\times n_i}$, $G_i, \ H_i \in \mathcal{D}_{\infty}^{\frac{\alpha_i m_i}{n_i} \times \frac{\alpha_i q}{p}}$ are known matrices, $\alpha_i = \text{lcm}(n_i, p), i = 1, 2, \cdots, N$, and $N \in \mathbb{Z}_+, N \geq 2$.

Let $A = (a_{i,j}) \in \mathcal{M}_{s\times t}$. Then, the column stacking form of $A$, denoted by $V_c(A) \in \mathcal{M}_{st\times 1}$, is defined as

$$V_c(A) = [a_{1,1} \, a_{2,1} \cdots a_{s,1} \cdots a_{1,t} \, a_{2,t} \cdots a_{s,t}]^{\top}.$$

Using column stacking operator, we present the equivalent forms of FRI (11) and SFRIs (12) successively.

**Proposition 5.** *Let* $A \in \mathcal{D}_\infty^{m\times n}$, $B \in \mathcal{D}_\infty^{n\times p}$. *Then*

$$V_c(A \circ B) = (I_p \otimes_{\mathcal{B}} A) \circ V_c(B). \tag{13}$$

**Proof of Proposition 5.** A direct calculation shows that

$$\begin{aligned} V_c(A \circ B) &= V_c\Big([A \circ Col_1(B) \;\; A \circ Col_2(B) \cdots A \circ Col_p(B)]\Big) \\ &= \begin{bmatrix} A \circ Col_1(B) \\ A \circ Col_2(B) \\ \vdots \\ A \circ Col_p(B) \end{bmatrix} = \begin{bmatrix} A & \mathbf{0} & \cdots & \mathbf{0} \\ \mathbf{0} & A & \cdots & \mathbf{0} \\ \vdots & & & \vdots \\ \mathbf{0} & \mathbf{0} & \cdots & A \end{bmatrix} \circ \begin{bmatrix} Col_1(B) \\ Col_2(B) \\ \vdots \\ Col_p(B) \end{bmatrix} \\ &= (I_p \otimes_{\mathcal{B}} A) \circ V_c(B), \end{aligned}$$

where $Col_i(B)$ denotes the $i$-th column of $B$, $i = 1, 2, \cdots, p$. □

**Proposition 6.** *Let* $A \in \mathcal{D}_\infty^{p\times q}$. *Then*

$$V_c(A \otimes_{\mathcal{B}} I_s) = T^s_{p,q} \circ V_c(A), \tag{14}$$

*where*

$$T^s_{p,q} = W_{[s,q]} \ltimes_{\mathcal{B}} W_{[pq,s]} \ltimes_{\mathcal{B}} W_{[s^2,pq]} \ltimes_{\mathcal{B}} (V_c(I_s) \otimes_{\mathcal{B}} I_{pq}).$$

**Proof of Proposition 6.** Let

$$\begin{aligned} \xi_i^j &= [a_{1,i} \wedge (\delta_s^j)^\top \; a_{2,i} \wedge (\delta_s^j)^\top \; \cdots \; a_{p,i} \wedge (\delta_s^j)^\top],\; i = 1, 2, \cdots, q,\; j = 1, 2, \cdots, s; \\ \zeta_{i,j} &= [a_{i,j} \wedge (\delta_s^1)^\top \; a_{i,j} \wedge (\delta_s^2)^\top \; \cdots \; a_{i,j} \wedge (\delta_s^s)^\top],\; i = 1, 2, \cdots, p,\; j = 1, 2, \cdots, q. \end{aligned}$$

By Definition 4, it is easy to obtain that

$$V_c(A) \ltimes_{\mathcal{B}} V_c(I_s) = [\zeta_{1,1} \; \zeta_{2,1} \; \cdots \; \zeta_{p,1} \; \zeta_{1,2} \; \zeta_{2,2} \; \cdots \zeta_{p,2} \; \cdots \; \zeta_{1,q} \; \zeta_{2,q} \; \cdots \; \zeta_{p,q}]^\top.$$

Then, we have

$$\begin{aligned} & W_{[s,q]} \ltimes_{\mathcal{B}} W_{[pq,s]} \ltimes_{\mathcal{B}} V_c(A) \ltimes_{\mathcal{B}} V_c(I_s) \\ =\; & W_{[s,q]} \ltimes_{\mathcal{B}} [\xi_1^1 \; \xi_2^1 \; \cdots \; \xi_q^1 \; \xi_1^2 \; \xi_2^2 \; \cdots \xi_q^2 \; \cdots \; \xi_1^s \; \xi_2^s \; \cdots \; \xi_q^s]^\top \\ =\; & [\xi_1^1 \; \xi_1^2 \; \cdots \; \xi_1^s \; \xi_2^1 \; \xi_2^2 \; \cdots \xi_2^s \; \cdots \; \xi_q^1 \; \xi_q^2 \; \cdots \; \xi_q^s]^\top \\ =\; & V_c(A \otimes_{\mathcal{B}} I_s), \end{aligned}$$

which together with (8) and (10) shows that

$$\begin{aligned} V_c(A \otimes_{\mathcal{B}} I_s) &= W_{[s,q]} \ltimes_{\mathcal{B}} W_{[pq,s]} \ltimes_{\mathcal{B}} V_c(A) \ltimes_{\mathcal{B}} V_c(I_s) \\ &= W_{[s,q]} \ltimes_{\mathcal{B}} W_{[pq,s]} \ltimes_{\mathcal{B}} W_{[s^2,pq]} \ltimes_{\mathcal{B}} V_c(I_s) \ltimes_{\mathcal{B}} V_c(A) \\ &= [W_{[s,q]} \ltimes_{\mathcal{B}} W_{[pq,s]} \ltimes_{\mathcal{B}} W_{[s^2,pq]} \ltimes_{\mathcal{B}} (V_c(I_s) \otimes_{\mathcal{B}} I_{pq})] \circ V_c(A) \\ &= T^s_{p,q} \circ V_c(A). \end{aligned}$$

□

**Remark 2.** *Precisely, for (14), we have*

$$
\begin{aligned}
T^s_{p,q} &= W_{[s,q]} \ltimes_{\mathcal{B}} W_{[pq,s]} \ltimes_{\mathcal{B}} W_{[s^2,pq]} \ltimes_{\mathcal{B}} (V_c(I_s) \otimes_{\mathcal{B}} I_{pq}) \\
&= \Big[ \underbrace{\delta^1_{pq}\, \mathbf{0} \cdots \mathbf{0}}_{s} \cdots \underbrace{\delta^p_{pq}\, \mathbf{0} \cdots \mathbf{0}}_{s}\ \underbrace{\mathbf{0}\, \delta^1_{pq}\, \mathbf{0} \cdots \mathbf{0}}_{s} \cdots \underbrace{\mathbf{0}\, \delta^p_{pq}\, \mathbf{0} \cdots \mathbf{0}}_{s} \cdots \underbrace{\mathbf{0} \cdots \mathbf{0}\, \delta^1_{pq}}_{s} \cdots \\
&\quad \underbrace{\mathbf{0} \cdots \mathbf{0}\, \delta^p_{pq}}_{s}\ \underbrace{\delta^{p+1}_{pq}\, \mathbf{0} \cdots \mathbf{0}}_{s} \cdots \underbrace{\delta^{2p}_{pq}\, \mathbf{0} \cdots \mathbf{0}}_{s}\ \underbrace{\mathbf{0}\, \delta^{p+1}_{pq}\, \mathbf{0} \cdots \mathbf{0}}_{s} \cdots \underbrace{\mathbf{0}\, \delta^{2p}_{pq}\, \mathbf{0} \cdots \mathbf{0}}_{s} \cdots \\
&\quad \underbrace{\mathbf{0} \cdots \mathbf{0}\, \delta^{p+1}_{pq}}_{s} \cdots \underbrace{\mathbf{0} \cdots \mathbf{0}\, \delta^{2p}_{pq}}_{s} \cdots \underbrace{\delta^{(q-1)p+1}_{pq}\, \mathbf{0} \cdots \mathbf{0}}_{s} \cdots \underbrace{\delta^{qp}_{pq}\, \mathbf{0} \cdots \mathbf{0}}_{s} \\
&\quad \underbrace{\mathbf{0}\, \delta^{(q-1)p+1}_{pq}\, \mathbf{0} \cdots \mathbf{0}}_{s} \cdots \underbrace{\mathbf{0}\, \delta^{qp}_{pq}\, \mathbf{0} \cdots \mathbf{0}}_{s} \cdots \underbrace{\mathbf{0} \cdots \mathbf{0}\, \delta^{(q-1)p+1}_{pq}}_{s} \cdots \\
&\quad \underbrace{\mathbf{0} \cdots \mathbf{0}\, \delta^{qp}_{pq}}_{s} \Big]^\top \in \mathcal{D}^{s^2pq \times pq}_\infty.
\end{aligned}
$$

**Proposition 7.** *Let $A \in \mathcal{D}^{m\times n}_\infty$, $B \in \mathcal{D}^{p\times q}_\infty$. Then*

$$V_c(A \ltimes_{\mathcal{B}} B) = K \circ V_c(B), \tag{15}$$

*where $K = (I_{\frac{\alpha q}{p}} \otimes_{\mathcal{B}} A \otimes_{\mathcal{B}} I_{\frac{\alpha}{n}}) \circ T^{\frac{\alpha}{p}}_{p,q} \in \mathcal{D}^{\frac{\alpha^2 mq}{np} \times pq}_\infty$ and $\alpha = lcm(n,p)$.*

**Proof of Proposition 7.** By Definition 4, Propositions 5 and 6, one can obtain that

$$
\begin{aligned}
V_c(A \ltimes_{\mathcal{B}} B) &= V_c((A \otimes_{\mathcal{B}} I_{\frac{\alpha}{n}}) \circ (B \otimes_{\mathcal{B}} I_{\frac{\alpha}{p}})) \\
&= [I_{\frac{\alpha q}{p}} \otimes_{\mathcal{B}} (A \otimes_{\mathcal{B}} I_{\frac{\alpha}{n}})] \circ V_c(B \otimes_{\mathcal{B}} I_{\frac{\alpha}{p}}) \\
&= (I_{\frac{\alpha q}{p}} \otimes_{\mathcal{B}} A \otimes_{\mathcal{B}} I_{\frac{\alpha}{n}}) \circ (T^{\frac{\alpha}{p}}_{p,q} \circ V_c(B)) \\
&= [(I_{\frac{\alpha q}{p}} \otimes_{\mathcal{B}} A \otimes_{\mathcal{B}} I_{\frac{\alpha}{n}}) \circ T^{\frac{\alpha}{p}}_{p,q}] \circ V_c(B).
\end{aligned}
$$

□

**Remark 3.** *The matrix $K$ in (15) can be represented as the following block matrix:*

$$
K = \begin{bmatrix} K' & \mathbf{0} & \cdots & \mathbf{0} \\ \mathbf{0} & K' & \cdots & \mathbf{0} \\ \vdots & \vdots & & \vdots \\ \mathbf{0} & \mathbf{0} & \cdots & K' \end{bmatrix},
$$

*where $K' = \delta^{1\top}_q \ltimes_{\mathcal{B}} \left[(I_{\frac{\alpha q}{p}} \otimes_{\mathcal{B}} A \otimes_{\mathcal{B}} I_{\frac{\alpha}{n}}) \circ T^{\frac{\alpha}{p}}_{p,q}\right] \ltimes_{\mathcal{B}} \delta^1_q \in \mathcal{D}^{\frac{\alpha^2 m}{np} \times p}_\infty$.*

Next, we present an example to illustrate Proposition 7.

**Example 1.** *Given $A = \begin{bmatrix} 0.1 & 0.5 & 0.7 & 0.2 \\ 1 & 0.3 & 0.2 & 0.6 \\ 0 & 0.2 & 0.4 & 0.3 \end{bmatrix} \in \mathcal{D}^{3\times 4}_\infty$, and assume that $X = (x_{i,j}) \in \mathcal{D}^{2\times 3}_\infty$ is an unknown matrix.*

By Proposition 7, we have

$$V_c(A \ltimes_{\mathcal{B}} X) = [(I_6 \otimes_{\mathcal{B}} A) \circ T^2_{2,3}] \circ V_c(X),$$

where

$$I_6 \otimes_{\mathcal{B}} A = \begin{bmatrix} A & \cdots & \mathbf{0} \\ \vdots & & \vdots \\ \mathbf{0} & \cdots & A \end{bmatrix} \in \mathcal{D}_\infty^{18\times 24}$$

and $T^2_{2,3} = [\delta_6^1\ \mathbf{0}\ \delta_6^2\ \mathbf{0}\ \mathbf{0}\ \delta_6^1\ \mathbf{0}\ \delta_6^2\ \delta_6^3\ \mathbf{0}\ \delta_6^4\ \mathbf{0}\ \mathbf{0}\ \delta_6^3\ \mathbf{0}\ \delta_6^4\ \delta_6^5\ \mathbf{0}\ \delta_6^6\ \mathbf{0}\ \mathbf{0}\ \delta_6^5\ \mathbf{0}\ \delta_6^6]^\top$. Thus,

$$V_c(A \ltimes_{\mathcal{B}} X) = K \circ \begin{bmatrix} x_{1,1} & x_{2,1} & x_{1,2} & x_{2,2} & x_{1,3} & x_{2,3} \end{bmatrix}^\top,$$

where $K = \begin{bmatrix} K' & \mathbf{0} & \mathbf{0} \\ \mathbf{0} & K' & \mathbf{0} \\ \mathbf{0} & \mathbf{0} & K' \end{bmatrix}$, and $K' = \begin{bmatrix} 0.1 & 0.6 & 0.6 & 1 & 0.3 & 0.1 \\ 0.6 & 1 & 0.1 & 0.6 & 0.1 & 0.3 \end{bmatrix}^\top$.

Based on Proposition 7 and Remark 3, we have the following equivalent form of FRI (11).

**Theorem 1.** *FRI (11) is equivalent to the following SFRIs composed of FRIs with the max–min composition:*

$$\begin{cases} \mathbf{g}^1 \le K' \circ \mathbf{x}^1 \le \mathbf{h}^1, \\ \mathbf{g}^2 \le K' \circ \mathbf{x}^2 \le \mathbf{h}^2, \\ \quad\vdots \\ \mathbf{g}^q \le K' \circ \mathbf{x}^q \le \mathbf{h}^q, \end{cases} \tag{16}$$

*where*

$$\begin{aligned} \mathbf{g} &= V_c(G) = [(\mathbf{g}^1)^\top\ (\mathbf{g}^2)^\top\ \cdots\ (\mathbf{g}^q)^\top]^\top \in \mathcal{D}_\infty^{\frac{\alpha^2 mq}{np}\times 1},\ \mathbf{g}^j \in \mathcal{D}_\infty^{\frac{\alpha^2 m}{np}\times 1},\ j = 1,2,\cdots,q; \\ \mathbf{h} &= V_c(H) = [(\mathbf{h}^1)^\top\ (\mathbf{h}^2)^\top\ \cdots\ (\mathbf{h}^q)^\top]^\top \in \mathcal{D}_\infty^{\frac{\alpha^2 mq}{np}\times 1},\ \mathbf{h}^j \in \mathcal{D}_\infty^{\frac{\alpha^2 m}{np}\times 1},\ j = 1,2,\cdots,q; \\ \mathbf{x} &= V_c(X) = [(\mathbf{x}^1)^\top\ (\mathbf{x}^2)^\top\ \cdots\ (\mathbf{x}^q)^\top]^\top \in \mathcal{D}_\infty^{pq\times 1},\ \mathbf{x}^j \in \mathcal{D}_\infty^{p\times 1},\ j = 1,2,\cdots,q; \end{aligned}$$

*and*

$$\begin{aligned} K &= (I_{\frac{\alpha q}{p}} \otimes_{\mathcal{B}} A \otimes_{\mathcal{B}} I_{\frac{\alpha}{n}}) \circ T^{\frac{\alpha}{p}}_{p,q} = \begin{bmatrix} K' & \mathbf{0} & \cdots & \mathbf{0} \\ \mathbf{0} & K' & \cdots & \mathbf{0} \\ \vdots & \vdots & & \vdots \\ \mathbf{0} & \mathbf{0} & \cdots & K' \end{bmatrix} \in \mathcal{D}_\infty^{\frac{\alpha^2 mq}{np}\times pq}, \\ K' &= \delta_q^{1\top} \ltimes_{\mathcal{B}} \left[ (I_{\frac{\alpha q}{p}} \otimes_{\mathcal{B}} A \otimes_{\mathcal{B}} I_{\frac{\alpha}{n}}) \circ T^{\frac{\alpha}{p}}_{p,q} \right] \ltimes_{\mathcal{B}} \delta_q^1 \in \mathcal{D}_\infty^{\frac{\alpha^2 m}{np}\times p}. \end{aligned}$$

**Proof of Proposition 1.** The proof of this theorem is based on a straightforward calculation, and thus we omit it here. □

**Example 2.** *Recall Example 1 and given*

$$G = \begin{bmatrix} 0.1 & 0.2 & 0.4 & 0.3 & 0.2 & 0.3 \\ 0.2 & 0.1 & 0.3 & 0.1 & 0 & 0.2 \\ 0 & 0.1 & 0.2 & 0.2 & 0 & 0.2 \end{bmatrix},\ H = \begin{bmatrix} 0.3 & 0.5 & 1 & 0.5 & 0.4 & 0.5 \\ 0.4 & 0.4 & 0.6 & 0.3 & 0.4 & 0.5 \\ 0.3 & 0.2 & 0.5 & 0.3 & 0.3 & 1 \end{bmatrix}.$$

*Then, according to Theorem 1, FRI*

$$G \le A \ltimes_{\mathcal{B}} X \le H \tag{17}$$

*is equivalent to the following SFRIs composed of FRIs with the max–min composition:*

$$\begin{cases} \mathbf{g}^1 \leq K' \circ \mathbf{x}^1 \leq \mathbf{h}^1, \\ \mathbf{g}^2 \leq K' \circ \mathbf{x}^2 \leq \mathbf{h}^2, \\ \mathbf{g}^3 \leq K' \circ \mathbf{x}^3 \leq \mathbf{h}^3, \end{cases} \tag{18}$$

*where* $\mathbf{x}^i \in \mathcal{D}_\infty^{2\times 1}$, $\mathbf{g}^i$, $\mathbf{h}^i \in \mathcal{D}_\infty^{6\times 1}$, $i = 1,2,3$ *satisfy* $V_c(X) = [(\mathbf{x}^1)^\top\ (\mathbf{x}^2)^\top\ (\mathbf{x}^3)^\top]^\top$, $V_c(G) = [(\mathbf{g}^1)^\top\ (\mathbf{g}^2)^\top\ (\mathbf{g}^3)^\top]^\top$ *and* $V_c(H) = [(\mathbf{h}^1)^\top\ (\mathbf{h}^2)^\top\ (\mathbf{h}^3)^\top]^\top$*, respectively, and* $K'$ *is given in Example 1.*

Similar to Theorem 1, we can also present the equivalent form of SFRIs (12).

**Theorem 2.** *SFRIs (12) is equivalent to the following SFRIs composed of FRIs with the max–min composition:*

$$\begin{cases} \mathbf{g}^{1,1} \leq K^{1'} \circ \mathbf{x}^1 \leq \mathbf{h}^{1,1}, \\ \mathbf{g}^{1,2} \leq K^{1'} \circ \mathbf{x}^2 \leq \mathbf{h}^{1,2}, \\ \quad\vdots \\ \mathbf{g}^{1,q} \leq K^{1'} \circ \mathbf{x}^q \leq \mathbf{h}^{1,q}, \\ \quad\vdots \\ \mathbf{g}^{N,1} \leq K^{N'} \circ \mathbf{x}^1 \leq \mathbf{h}^{N,1}, \\ \mathbf{g}^{N,2} \leq K^{N'} \circ \mathbf{x}^2 \leq \mathbf{h}^{N,2}, \\ \quad\vdots \\ \mathbf{g}^{N,q} \leq K^{N'} \circ \mathbf{x}^q \leq \mathbf{h}^{N,q}, \end{cases} \tag{19}$$

*where*

$$\begin{aligned} \mathbf{g}^i &= V_c(G_i) = [(\mathbf{g}^{i,1})^\top\ (\mathbf{g}^{i,2})^\top \cdots (\mathbf{g}^{i,q})^\top]^\top \in \mathcal{D}_\infty^{\frac{\alpha_i^2 m_i q}{n_i p}\times 1},\ \mathbf{g}^{i,j} \in \mathcal{D}_\infty^{\frac{\alpha_i^2 m_i}{n_i p}\times 1}; \\ \mathbf{h}^i &= V_c(H_i) = [(\mathbf{h}^{i,1})^\top\ (\mathbf{h}^{i,2})^\top \cdots (\mathbf{h}^{i,q})^\top]^\top \in \mathcal{D}_\infty^{\frac{\alpha_i^2 m_i q}{n_i p}\times 1},\ \mathbf{h}^{i,j} \in \mathcal{D}_\infty^{\frac{\alpha_i^2 m_i}{n_i p}\times 1}; \\ \mathbf{x} &= V_c(X) = [(\mathbf{x}^1)^\top\ (\mathbf{x}^2)^\top \cdots (\mathbf{x}^q)^\top]^\top \in \mathcal{D}_\infty^{pq\times 1},\ \mathbf{x}^j \in \mathcal{D}_\infty^{p\times 1}; \end{aligned}$$

$$\begin{aligned} K^i &= (I_{\frac{\alpha_i q}{p}} \otimes_{\mathcal{B}} A_i \otimes_{\mathcal{B}} I_{\frac{\alpha_i}{n_i}}) \circ T_{p,q}^{\frac{\alpha_i}{p}} = \begin{bmatrix} K^{i'} & 0 & \cdots & 0 \\ 0 & K^{i'} & \cdots & 0 \\ \vdots & \vdots & & \vdots \\ 0 & 0 & \cdots & K^{i'} \end{bmatrix} \in \mathcal{D}_\infty^{\frac{\alpha_i^2 m_i q}{n_i p}\times pq}, \\ K^{i'} &= \delta_q^{1\top} \ltimes_{\mathcal{B}} \left[ (I_{\frac{\alpha_i q}{p}} \otimes_{\mathcal{B}} A_i \otimes_{\mathcal{B}} I_{\frac{\alpha_i}{n_i}}) \circ T_{p,q}^{\frac{\alpha_i}{p}} \right] \ltimes_{\mathcal{B}} \delta_q^1 \in \mathcal{D}_\infty^{\frac{\alpha_i^2 m_i}{n_i p}\times p}, \end{aligned}$$

*and* $i = 1,2,\cdots,N$, $j = 1,2,\cdots,q$.

**Example 3.** *Recall Examples 1 and 2. Given*

$$A_1 = [0.3\ 1\ 0.2\ 0.7],\ G_1 = [0.2\ 0.6\ 0\ 0.7\ 0.2\ 0.1],\ H_1 = [0.4\ 0.5\ 0.2\ 1\ 0.3\ 0.4].$$

*Then, according to Theorem 2, SFRI*

$$\begin{cases} G \leq A \ltimes_{\mathcal{B}} X \leq H, \\ G_1 \leq A_1 \ltimes_{\mathcal{B}} X \leq H_1, \end{cases}$$

*is equivalent to the following SFRIs composed of FRIs with the max–min composition:*

$$\begin{cases} \mathbf{g}^1 \le K' \circ \mathbf{x}^1 \le \mathbf{h}^1, \\ \mathbf{g}^2 \le K' \circ \mathbf{x}^2 \le \mathbf{h}^2, \\ \mathbf{g}^3 \le K' \circ \mathbf{x}^3 \le \mathbf{h}^3, \\ \mathbf{g}^{1,1} \le K^{1'} \circ \mathbf{x}^1 \le \mathbf{h}^{1,1}, \\ \mathbf{g}^{1,2} \le K^{1'} \circ \mathbf{x}^2 \le \mathbf{h}^{1,2}, \\ \mathbf{g}^{1,3} \le K^{1'} \circ \mathbf{x}^3 \le \mathbf{h}^{1,3}, \end{cases}$$

*where* $K^{1'} = \begin{bmatrix} 0.3 & 0.2 \\ 1 & 0.7 \end{bmatrix}$, $\mathbf{g}^{1,i}$, $\mathbf{h}^{1,i} \in \mathcal{D}_\infty^{2\times 1}$, $i = 1,2,3$ *satisfy* $V_c(G_1) = [(\mathbf{g}^{1,1})^\top\ (\mathbf{g}^{1,2})^\top\ (\mathbf{g}^{1,3})^\top]^\top$ *and* $V_c(H_1) = [(\mathbf{h}^{1,1})^\top\ (\mathbf{h}^{1,2})^\top\ (\mathbf{h}^{1,3})^\top]^\top$, *respectively,* $K'$ *is given in Example 1, and* $\mathbf{x}^i$, $\mathbf{g}^i$, $\mathbf{h}^i$, $i = 1,2,3$ *are given in Example 2.*

**Remark 4.** *From Theorems 1 and 2, one can see that both FRI (11) and SFRIs (12) are equivalent to SFRIs composed of FRIs with the max–min composition. Thus, the column stacking technique unifies the resolution of (11) and (12), and converts Problems 1 and 2 into the resolution of FRIs with the max–min composition. Therefore, one just needs to study the resolution of the following FRI with the max–min composition:*

$$\mathbf{u} \le W \circ \mathbf{x} \le \mathbf{v}, \tag{20}$$

*where* $\mathbf{u} = [u_1\ u_2\ \cdots\ u_m]^\top$, $\mathbf{v} = [v_1\ v_2\ \cdots\ v_m]^\top \in \mathcal{D}_\infty^{m\times 1}$, $W = (w_{i,j}) \in \mathcal{D}_\infty^{m\times n}$ *and* $\mathbf{x} = [x_1\ x_2\ \cdots\ x_n]^\top \in \mathcal{D}_\infty^{n\times 1}$.

## 4. Resolution of FRI (20)

In this section, we investigate the resolution of FRI (11) and SFRIs (12) via solving FRI (20). To this end, we recall some results on the resolution of FRI (20). For details, please refer to [42,44,45].

**Definition 5.** *Denote the solution set of FRI (20) by* $X(W, \mathbf{u}, \mathbf{v}) \subseteq \mathcal{D}_\infty^{n\times 1}$.

*(i)* *If* $\overline{\mathbf{x}} \ge \mathbf{x}$ *holds for any* $\mathbf{x} \in X(W, \mathbf{u}, \mathbf{v})$, *then* $\overline{\mathbf{x}} \in X(W, \mathbf{u}, \mathbf{v})$ *is called the maximum solution;*

*(ii)* *If for any* $\mathbf{x} \in X(W, \mathbf{u}, \mathbf{v})$, $\mathbf{x} \le \underline{\mathbf{x}}$ *implies* $\mathbf{x} = \underline{\mathbf{x}}$, *then* $\underline{\mathbf{x}} \in X(W, \mathbf{u}, \mathbf{v})$ *is called a minimal solution.*

Denote the solution set of FRI (20) by $\Omega$. It was pointed out in [45] that the solution set of FRIs with max–min composition can be characterized by the unique maximum solution and finite minimal solutions. More specifically, it holds that

$$\Omega = \bigcup_{i=1}^{s} \begin{bmatrix} \underline{x}_1^i \le x_1 \le \overline{x}_1 \\ \underline{x}_2^i \le x_2 \le \overline{x}_2 \\ \vdots \\ \underline{x}_n^i \le x_n \le \overline{x}_n \end{bmatrix}, \tag{21}$$

where $\underline{x}^i = [\underline{x}_1^i\ \underline{x}_2^i\ \cdots\ \underline{x}_n^i]^\top$, $i = 1,2,\cdots,s$ are all the minimal solutions to (20), and $\overline{x} = [\overline{x}_1\ \overline{x}_2\ \cdots\ \overline{x}_n]^\top$ is the unique maximum solution to (20). In addition, it shows that all the minimal solutions and the unique maximum solution are within the set of parameter set solutions. Keeping these points in mind, we calculate the set of parameter set solutions to FRI (20) based on semi-tensor product of matrices.

Denote the parameter set of FRI (20) by $\Phi = \{\varphi_1, \varphi_2, \cdots, \varphi_l\}$, and identify $\varphi_i \sim \frac{i-1}{l-1} \sim \delta_l^{l-i+1}$, $\varphi_i \in \Phi$, $i = 1, 2, \cdots, l$. Then, we have $\Phi \sim \mathcal{D}_l \sim \Delta_l$. We say $\delta_l^{l-i_1+1} \leq \delta_l^{l-i_2+1}$, if $\varphi_{i_1} \geq \varphi_{i_2}$.

Then, for the $i$-th inequality of (20), i.e.,

$$u_i \leq (w_{i,1} \wedge x_1) \vee (w_{i,2} \wedge x_2) \vee \cdots \vee (w_{i,n} \wedge x_n) \leq v_i, \tag{22}$$

by Lemma 1, we can convert the middle part of (22) into the following form:

$$\begin{aligned} & (w_{i,1} \wedge x_1) \vee (w_{i,2} \wedge x_2) \vee \cdots \vee (w_{i,n} \wedge x_n) \\ = \; & (M_d^l)^{n-1} \ltimes_{t=1}^{n} [I_{l^{t-1}} \otimes (M_c^l \ltimes w_{i,t})] \ltimes_{j=1}^{n} x_j \\ = \; & N_i \ltimes x, \end{aligned}$$

where $N_i = (M_d^l)^{n-1} \ltimes_{t=1}^{n} [I_{l^{t-1}} \otimes (M_c^l \ltimes w_{i,t})]$, $x = \ltimes_{j=1}^{n} x_j$, and $M_d^l$, $M_c^l$ are given in Lemma 2. Then, (22) becomes

$$u_i \geq N_i \ltimes x \geq v_i, \tag{23}$$

where $N_i$ is a logical matrix, $x \in \Delta_{l^n}$ and $u_i, v_i \in \Delta_l$.

Noting that $N_i \ltimes \delta_{l^n}^k = Col_k(N_i)$, then we can obtain the following result.

**Lemma 3.** $\mathbf{x} = [x_1\ x_2\ \cdots\ x_n]^\top \in \mathcal{D}_\infty^{n\times 1}$ *with* $x = \ltimes_{j=1}^{n} x_j = \delta_{l^n}^k$ *is a parameter set solution to FRI (22), if and only if*

$$u_i \geq Col_k(N_i) \geq v_i.$$

The following proposition is crucial for the resolution of FRI (22), which can be obtained by Lemma 3.

**Lemma 4.** *Assume that* $K_i = \{k : u_i \geq Col_k(N_i) \geq v_i\}$, $i = 1, 2, \cdots, m$. *Then, the set of parameter set solutions to FRI (22), denoted by* $\Lambda_i$, *is*

$$\Lambda_i = \{\mathbf{x} = [x_1\ x_2\ \cdots\ x_n]^\top \in \mathcal{D}_\infty^{n\times 1} \text{ with } \ltimes_{j=1}^{n} x_j = \delta_{l^n}^k : k \in K_i\}.$$

*Thus, the set of parameter set solutions to (20) is*

$$\Lambda = \cap_{i=1}^{m} \Lambda_i.$$

*Moreover, if* $\Lambda = \emptyset$, *then FRI (20) has no solution.*

To sum up, we have the following procedure (Table 1) on the resolution of FRI (11) and SFRIs (12). Figure 1 presents the flowchart of the procedure given in Table 1.

**Remark 5.** *Since* $A \ltimes_{\mathcal{B}} X \geq G$ *and* $A \ltimes_{\mathcal{B}} X \leq H$ *can be converted into* $G \leq A \ltimes_{\mathcal{B}} X \leq \mathbf{1}$ *and* $\mathbf{0} \leq A \ltimes_{\mathcal{B}} X \leq H$, *respectively, Table 1 can also be applied to the resolution of these two kinds of FRIs. When* $G = H$, *FRI (11) becomes an FRE. Thus, Table 1 can be used to solve FRE* $A \ltimes_{\mathcal{B}} X = G$.

**Table 1.** Procedure on the resolution of FRI (11) and SFRIs (12).

| |
|---|
| To obtain all the solutions to FRI (11) (resp. SFRIs (12)), one can proceed by the following steps: |
| (1) Calculate the equivalent form of FRI (11) (resp. SFRIs (12)) by Theorem 1 (resp. Theorem 2);<br>(2) Construct the parameter set $\Phi^j$ of the $j$-th FRI in SFRIs (16) (resp. (19)), and give the vector form of every element in $\Phi^j$;<br>(3) Calculate $\Lambda^j$ by Lemma 4;<br>(4) Obtain all the minimal solutions and the unique maximum solution to the $j$-th FRI in (16) (resp. (19)) by comparing the finite number of elements in $\Lambda^j$;<br>(5) Obtain the solution set $\Omega^j$ of the $j$-th FRI in (16) (resp. (19)) by (21);<br>(6) Obtain the solution set $\Omega$ of FRI (11) (resp. SFRIs (12)). |

**Remark 6.** *One can convert* $\tilde{G} \le X \ltimes_B \tilde{A} \le \tilde{H}$ *into* $\tilde{G}^\top \le \tilde{A}^\top \ltimes_B X^\top \le \tilde{H}^\top$ *by (9), which has the same form with FRI (11). Therefore, Table 1 is also applicable to finding all the solutions to this kind of FRI.*

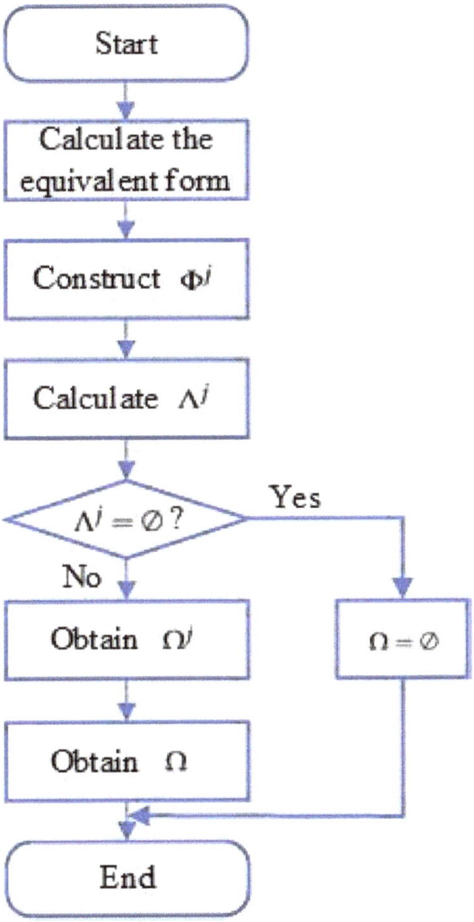


**Figure 1.** Flowchart of obtaining all the solutions to FRI (11) (resp. SFRIs (12)).

## 5. Illustrative Examples

In this section, we give two examples to illustrate the main results.

**Example 4.** *Recall Example 2 and consider the resolution of FRI (17).*

In Example 2, we have obtained the equivalent form of FRI (17), i.e., SFRIs (18). In the following, we solve every FRI in (18).

To obtain the solution set of the first FRI in (18), we first find the following parameter set:

$$\Phi^1 = \{0, 0.1, 0.2, 0.3, 0.4, 0.5, 0.6, 1\},$$

and identify each element of $\Phi^1$ by vector form as

$$0 \sim \delta_8^8, 0.1 \sim \delta_8^7, 0.2 \sim \delta_8^6, 0.3 \sim \delta_8^5, 0.4 \sim \delta_8^4, 0.5 \sim \delta_8^3, 0.6 \sim \delta_8^2, 1 \sim \delta_8^1.$$

Next, we calculate all the parameter set solutions to the first FRI in (18).

For the following first inequality of the first FRI in (18):

$$0.1 \leq (0.1 \wedge x_{1,1}) \vee (0.6 \wedge x_{2,1}) \leq 0.3,$$

by Lemmas 1 and 2, we obtain its algebraic form as follows:

$$\delta_8^7 \geq M^{1,1} \ltimes x^1 \geq \delta_8^5,$$

where

$$M^{1,1} = M_d^8 \ltimes_{t=1}^2 [I_{8^{t-1}} \otimes (M_c^8 \ltimes k'_{1,t})] = \delta_8[2\,2\,3\,4\,5\,6\,7\,7 \cdots 2\,2\,3\,4\,5\,6\,7\,8]$$

and $x^1 = x_{1,1} \ltimes x_{2,1}$. Then, according to Lemma 4, the set of parameter set solutions to the first inequality of the first FRI in (18) is

$$\begin{aligned} \Lambda^{1,1} = \{ & \delta_{64}^5, \cdots, \delta_{64}^8, \delta_{64}^{13}, \cdots, \delta_{64}^{16}, \delta_{64}^{21}, \cdots, \delta_{64}^{24}, \delta_{64}^{29}, \cdots, \delta_{64}^{32}, \\ & \delta_{64}^{37}, \cdots, \delta_{64}^{40}, \delta_{64}^{45}, \cdots, \delta_{64}^{48}, \delta_{64}^{53}, \cdots, \delta_{64}^{56}, \delta_{64}^{61}, \cdots, \delta_{64}^{63}\}. \end{aligned}$$

Similarly, we can respectively convert other inequalities of the first FRI in (18) into the following algebraic forms:

$$\delta_8^6 \geq M^{1,2} \ltimes x^1 \geq \delta_8^4,\ \delta_8^8 \geq M^{1,3} \ltimes x^1 \geq \delta_8^5,$$
$$\delta_8^6 \geq M^{1,4} \ltimes x^1 \geq \delta_8^3,\ \delta_8^7 \geq M^{1,5} \ltimes x^1 \geq \delta_8^4,$$
$$\delta_8^7 \geq M^{1,6} \ltimes x^1 \geq \delta_8^6,$$

where

$$\begin{aligned} M^{1,2} &= M_d^8 \ltimes_{t=1}^2 [I_{8^{t-1}} \otimes (M_c^8 \ltimes k'_{2,t})] = \delta_8[1\,2\,2\,2\,2\,2\,2\,2 \cdots 1\,2\,3\,4\,5\,6\,7\,8], \\ M^{1,3} &= M_d^8 \ltimes_{t=1}^2 [I_{8^{t-1}} \otimes (M_c^8 \ltimes k'_{3,t})] = \delta_8[2\,2\,2\,2\,2\,2\,2\,2 \cdots 7\,7\,7\,7\,7\,7\,7\,8], \\ M^{1,4} &= M_d^8 \ltimes_{t=1}^2 [I_{8^{t-1}} \otimes (M_c^8 \ltimes k'_{4,t})] = \delta_8[1\,1\,1\,1\,1\,1\,1\,1 \cdots 2\,2\,3\,4\,5\,6\,7\,8], \\ M^{1,5} &= M_d^8 \ltimes_{t=1}^2 [I_{8^{t-1}} \otimes (M_c^8 \ltimes k'_{5,t})] = \delta_8[5\,5\,5\,5\,5\,5\,5\,5 \cdots 7\,7\,7\,7\,7\,7\,7\,8], \\ M^{1,6} &= M_d^8 \ltimes_{t=1}^2 [I_{8^{t-1}} \otimes (M_c^8 \ltimes k'_{6,t})] = \delta_8[5\,5\,5\,5\,5\,6\,7\,7 \cdots 5\,5\,5\,5\,5\,6\,7\,8]. \end{aligned}$$

Then, the corresponding set of parameter set solutions to each inequality is

$$\begin{aligned}
\Lambda^{1,2} &= \{\delta_{64}^{28}, \cdots, \delta_{64}^{32}, \delta_{64}^{36}, \cdots, \delta_{64}^{40}, \delta_{64}^{44}, \cdots, \delta_{64}^{48}, \delta_{64}^{52}, \cdots, \delta_{64}^{54}, \delta_{64}^{60}, \cdots, \delta_{64}^{62}\}, \\
\Lambda^{1,3} &= \{\delta_{64}^{33}, \delta_{64}^{34} \cdots, \delta_{64}^{64}\}, \\
\Lambda^{1,4} &= \{\delta_{64}^{19}, \cdots, \delta_{64}^{24}, \delta_{64}^{27}, \cdots, \delta_{64}^{32}, \delta_{64}^{35}, \cdots, \delta_{64}^{40}, \delta_{64}^{43}, \cdots, \delta_{64}^{48}, \delta_{64}^{51}, \cdots, \delta_{64}^{54}, \\
&\quad \delta_{64}^{58}, \cdots, \delta_{64}^{62}\}, \\
\Lambda^{1,5} &= \{\delta_{64}^{1}, \delta_{64}^{2} \cdots, \delta_{64}^{63}\}, \\
\Lambda^{1,6} &= \{\delta_{64}^{6}, \cdots, \delta_{64}^{8}, \delta_{64}^{14}, \cdots, \delta_{64}^{16}, \delta_{64}^{22}, \cdots, \delta_{64}^{24}, \delta_{64}^{30}, \cdots, \delta_{64}^{32}, \delta_{64}^{38}, \cdots, \delta_{64}^{40}, \\
&\quad \delta_{64}^{46}, \cdots, \delta_{64}^{48}, \delta_{64}^{54}, \cdots, \delta_{64}^{56}, \delta_{64}^{62}, \cdots, \delta_{64}^{63}\}.
\end{aligned}$$

Thus, by resorting to Lemma 4, the set of parameter set solutions to the first FRI in (18) is

$$\begin{aligned}
\Lambda^{1} &= \Lambda^{1,1} \cap \Lambda^{1,2} \cap \Lambda^{1,3} \cap \Lambda^{1,4} \cap \Lambda^{1,5} \cap \Lambda^{1,6} \\
&= \{\delta_{64}^{38}, \cdots, \delta_{64}^{40}, \delta_{64}^{46}, \cdots, \delta_{64}^{48}, \delta_{64}^{54}, \delta_{64}^{62}\}.
\end{aligned}$$

Comparing all the parameter set solutions to the first FRI in (18), we obtain the maximum solution to it as

$$\delta_{64}^{38} = \delta_8^5 \ltimes \delta_8^6 \sim [0.3 \;\; 0.2]^\top,$$

and the minimal solutions as

$$\begin{aligned}
\delta_{64}^{48} &= \delta_8^6 \ltimes \delta_8^8 \sim [0.2 \;\; 0]^\top, \\
\delta_{64}^{62} &= \delta_8^8 \ltimes \delta_8^6 \sim [0 \;\; 0.2]^\top.
\end{aligned}$$

Therefore, by (21), the solution set of the first FRI in (18) is

$$\Omega^1 = \begin{bmatrix} 0.2 \le x_{1,1} \le 0.3 \\ 0 \le x_{2,1} \le 0.2 \end{bmatrix} \bigcup \begin{bmatrix} 0 \le x_{1,1} \le 0.3 \\ 0.2 \end{bmatrix}.$$

Similar to the resolution of the first FRI in (18), all the parameter set solutions to the second and third FRIs in (18) can be successively obtained as

$$\begin{aligned}
\Lambda^{2} &= \{\delta_{64}^{19}, \delta_{64}^{20}, \delta_{64}^{27}, \delta_{64}^{28}, \delta_{64}^{35}, \delta_{64}^{36} \delta_{64}^{43}, \delta_{64}^{44}\}, \\
\Lambda^{3} &= \{\delta_{64}^{36}, \delta_{64}^{37}, \delta_{64}^{38}, \delta_{64}^{44}, \delta_{64}^{45}\}.
\end{aligned}$$

Then, we can obtain their solution sets as

$$\begin{aligned}
\Omega^2 &= \begin{bmatrix} 0.2 \le x_{1,2} \le 0.5 \\ 0.4 \le x_{2,2} \le 0.5 \end{bmatrix}, \\
\Omega^3 &= \begin{bmatrix} 0.3 \\ 0.2 \le x_{2,3} \le 0.4 \end{bmatrix} \bigcup \begin{bmatrix} 0.2 \le x_{1,3} \le 0.3 \\ 0.3 \le x_{2,3} \le 0.4 \end{bmatrix}.
\end{aligned}$$

To sum up, the solution set of (17) is

$$\begin{aligned}
\Omega &= \begin{bmatrix} 0.2 \le x_{1,1} \le 0.3 & 0.2 \le x_{1,2} \le 0.5 & 0.3 \\ 0 \le x_{2,1} \le 0.2 & 0.4 \le x_{2,2} \le 0.5 & 0.2 \le x_{2,3} \le 0.4 \end{bmatrix} \\
&\bigcup \begin{bmatrix} 0.2 \le x_{1,1} \le 0.3 & 0.2 \le x_{1,2} \le 0.5 & 0.2 \le x_{1,3} \le 0.3 \\ 0 \le x_{2,1} \le 0.2 & 0.4 \le x_{2,2} \le 0.5 & 0.3 \le x_{2,3} \le 0.4 \end{bmatrix} \\
&\bigcup \begin{bmatrix} 0 \le x_{1,1} \le 0.3 & 0.2 \le x_{1,2} \le 0.5 & 0.3 \\ 0.2 & 0.4 \le x_{2,2} \le 0.5 & 0.2 \le x_{2,3} \le 0.4 \end{bmatrix} \\
&\bigcup \begin{bmatrix} 0 \le x_{1,1} \le 0.3 & 0.2 \le x_{1,2} \le 0.5 & 0.2 \le x_{1,3} \le 0.3 \\ 0.2 & 0.4 \le x_{2,2} \le 0.5 & 0.3 \le x_{2,3} \le 0.4 \end{bmatrix}.
\end{aligned}$$

Consider the entry in the first row and second column of $H$. In fact, for any $0 < |\varepsilon| < 0.1$, we have

$$0.4 < 0.5 + \varepsilon < 0.6,$$

which implies that $\Phi^1$ is unchangeable. Thus, the solution set of the first FRI in (18) is unchangeable and the solution set of (17) is unchangeable.

**Example 5.** *Solve the following latticized linear programming:*

$$\min\ z = \begin{bmatrix} 0.2 & 1 \end{bmatrix} \circ \begin{bmatrix} x_1 \\ x_2 \end{bmatrix} \tag{24}$$

$$s.t.\ \begin{bmatrix} 0 & 0.1 \\ 0.1 & 0 \\ 0.3 & 0.1 \end{bmatrix} \leq \begin{bmatrix} 0.1 & 0.2 & 0.7 & 0.5 \\ 0.4 & 0.2 & 0.3 & 0.1 \\ 0.2 & 0.7 & 0.4 & 0.3 \end{bmatrix} \ltimes_{\mathcal{B}} \begin{bmatrix} x_1 \\ x_2 \end{bmatrix} \leq \begin{bmatrix} 0.3 & 0.4 \\ 0.7 & 0.2 \\ 1 & 0.4 \end{bmatrix}. \tag{25}$$

Step 1: Solve FRI constraint (25).

The equivalent form of (25) is

$$\begin{bmatrix} 0 & 0.1 & 0.3 & 0.1 & 0 & 0.1 \end{bmatrix}^\top \leq K' \circ \begin{bmatrix} x_1 & x_2 \end{bmatrix}^\top \leq \begin{bmatrix} 0.3 & 0.7 & 1 & 0.4 & 0.2 & 0.4 \end{bmatrix}^\top, \tag{26}$$

where $K' = \begin{bmatrix} 0.1 & 0.4 & 0.2 & 0.2 & 0.2 & 0.7 \\ 0.7 & 0.3 & 0.4 & 0.5 & 0.1 & 0.3 \end{bmatrix}^\top := (k'_{i,j}),\ i = 1,2,\cdots,6,\ j = 1,2.$

The parameter set of (26) is

$$\Phi = \{0, 0.1, 0.2, 0.3, 0.4, 0.5, 0.7, 1\},$$

and each element in $\Phi$ can be identified by vector form as

$$0 \sim \delta_8^8, 0.1 \sim \delta_8^7, 0.2 \sim \delta_8^6, 0.3 \sim \delta_8^5, 0.4 \sim \delta_8^4, 0.5 \sim \delta_8^3, 0.7 \sim \delta_8^2, 1 \sim \delta_8^1.$$

Then, the inequalities of (26) can be respectively converted into the following algebraic forms:

$$\begin{aligned} &\delta_8^8 \geq M_1 \ltimes x \geq \delta_8^5,\ \delta_8^7 \geq M_2 \ltimes x \geq \delta_8^2, \\ &\delta_8^5 \geq M_3 \ltimes x \geq \delta_8^1,\ \delta_8^7 \geq M_4 \ltimes x \geq \delta_8^4, \\ &\delta_8^8 \geq M_5 \ltimes x \geq \delta_8^6,\ \delta_8^7 \geq M_6 \ltimes x \geq \delta_8^4, \end{aligned}$$

where

$$\begin{aligned} M_1 &= M_d^8 \ltimes_{t=1}^2 [I_{8^{t-1}} \otimes (M_c^8 \ltimes k'_{1,t})] = \delta_8[2\,2\,3\,4\,5\,6\,7\,7 \cdots 2\,2\,3\,4\,5\,6\,7\,8], \\ M_2 &= M_d^8 \ltimes_{t=1}^2 [I_{8^{t-1}} \otimes (M_c^8 \ltimes k'_{2,t})] = \delta_8[4\,4\,4\,4\,4\,4\,4\,4 \cdots 5\,5\,5\,5\,5\,6\,7\,8], \\ M_3 &= M_d^8 \ltimes_{t=1}^2 [I_{8^{t-1}} \otimes (M_c^8 \ltimes k'_{3,t})] = \delta_8[4\,4\,4\,4\,5\,6\,6\,6 \cdots 4\,4\,4\,4\,5\,6\,7\,8], \\ M_4 &= M_d^8 \ltimes_{t=1}^2 [I_{8^{t-1}} \otimes (M_c^8 \ltimes k'_{4,t})] = \delta_8[3\,3\,3\,4\,5\,6\,6\,6 \cdots 3\,3\,3\,4\,5\,6\,7\,8], \\ M_5 &= M_d^8 \ltimes_{t=1}^2 [I_{8^{t-1}} \otimes (M_c^8 \ltimes k'_{5,t})] = \delta_8[6\,6\,6\,6\,6\,6\,6\,6 \cdots 7\,7\,7\,7\,7\,7\,7\,8], \\ M_6 &= M_d^8 \ltimes_{t=1}^2 [I_{8^{t-1}} \otimes (M_c^8 \ltimes k'_{6,t})] = \delta_8[2\,2\,2\,2\,2\,2\,2\,2 \cdots 5\,5\,5\,5\,5\,6\,7\,8], \end{aligned}$$

and $x = x_1 \ltimes x_2$. Thus, one can obtain the set of parameter solutions to (26), denoted by $\Lambda$.

Comparing all the elements in $\Lambda$, we obtain the maximum solution to (26) as

$$\delta_{64}^{29} = \delta_8^4 \ltimes \delta_8^5 \sim [0.4\ \ 0.3]^\top,$$

and the minimal solution as

$$\delta_{64}^{61} = \delta_8^8 \ltimes \delta_8^5 \sim [0\ \ 0.3]^\top.$$

Therefore, according to (21), it is easy to obtain the solution set of FRI (26) as

$$\Omega = \begin{bmatrix} 0 \leq x_1 \leq 0.4 \\ 0.3 \end{bmatrix}.$$

Step 2: Calculate the optimal value of the objective function $z$.
The optimal value of $z$ can be calculated as

$$z_{\min} = \begin{bmatrix} 0.2 & 1 \end{bmatrix} \circ \begin{bmatrix} 0 \\ 0.3 \end{bmatrix} = 0.3.$$

Step 3: Solve the following FRE:

$$\begin{bmatrix} 0.2 & 1 \end{bmatrix} \circ \begin{bmatrix} x_1 \\ x_2 \end{bmatrix} = 0.3. \tag{27}$$

To obtain all the optimal solutions to (24) and (25), we just need to solve FRE (27) in $\Omega$. The parameter set of (27) is

$$\Phi' = \{0, 0.2, 0.3, 1\},$$

and each element in $\Phi'$ is identified by

$$0 \sim \delta_4^4, 0.2 \sim \delta_4^3, 0.3 \sim \delta_4^2, 1 \sim \delta_4^1.$$

Next, we calculate the parameter set solutions to (27).
By Lemma 1, one can obtain the following algebraic form of (27):

$$M' \ltimes x_1 \ltimes x_2 = \delta_4^2,$$

where

$$M' = M_d^4 \ltimes M_c^4 \ltimes \delta_4^3 \ltimes [I_4 \otimes (M_c^k \ltimes \delta_4^1)] = \delta_4[1\ 2\ 3\ 3\ 1\ 2\ 3\ 3\ 1\ 2\ 3\ 3\ 1\ 2\ 3\ 4].$$

Then, by Lemma 4, we can obtain all the parameter set solutions to (27), denoted by $\Lambda'$.

Comparing all the elements in $\Lambda'$, we find the maximum solution to (27) as

$$\delta_{16}^2 = \delta_4^1 \ltimes \delta_4^2 \sim [1\ \ 0.3]^\top,$$

and the minimal solution as

$$\delta_{16}^{14} = \delta_4^4 \ltimes \delta_4^2 \sim [0\ \ 0.3]^\top.$$

Therefore, according to (21), the solution set of (27) is

$$\Omega' = \begin{bmatrix} 0 \leq x_1 \leq 1 \\ 0.3 \end{bmatrix}.$$

Step 4: Calculate the optimal solution set of latticized linear programming (24) and (25).
The optimal solution set of (24) and (25) is

$$\begin{aligned} Y &= \Omega \cap \Omega' \\ &= \begin{bmatrix} 0 \leq x_1 \leq 0.4 \\ 0.3 \end{bmatrix} \bigcap \begin{bmatrix} 0 \leq x_1 \leq 1 \\ 0.3 \end{bmatrix} \\ &= \begin{bmatrix} 0 \leq x_1 \leq 0.4 \\ 0.3 \end{bmatrix}. \end{aligned}$$

## 6. Conclusions

In this paper, we have investigated the resolution of a kind of FRIs with the Boolean semi-tensor product composition. By using the column stacking operator, we have obtained the equivalent column stacking form of FRIs with Boolean semi-tensor product composition, which has the form of SFRIs with max–min composition. Based on the semi-tensor product of matrices, we have obtained the solution set of FRIs with Boolean semi-tensor product composition by finding all possible parameter set solutions, and a general procedure has been developed. It should be pointed out that when fuzzy matrices in FRIs are with compatible dimension, the Boolean semi-tensor product composition coincides with max–min composition. As a result, Boolean semi-tensor product composition is a generalization of max–min composition. Although this paper has obtained all the solutions for FRIs with Boolean semi-tensor product composition, the computational complexity may limit the application of the method proposed in this paper.

Fuzzy relation-based fuzzy control is an important research topic [48]. In the future, we will investigate the fuzzy controller design based on the resolution of FRIs with Boolean semi-tensor product composition. In addition, the sensitivity analysis of FRIs with Boolean semi-tensor product composition is another interesting research topic.

**Author Contributions:** S.W. and H.L. obtained the solution set of a kind of FRIs with the Boolean semi-tensor product composition, and S.W. drafted the paper. All authors have read and agreed to the published version of the manuscript.

**Funding:** The work was supported by the National Natural Science Foundation of China under grants 62073202 and 61873150, the Young Experts of Taishan Scholar Project under grant tsqn201909076, and the Natural Science Fund for Distinguished Young Scholars of Shandong Province under grant JQ201613.

**Institutional Review Board Statement:** Not applicable.

**Informed Consent Statement:** Not applicable.

**Data Availability Statement:** Not applicable.

**Conflicts of Interest:** The authors declare no conflict of interest.

## References

1. Ghodousian, A.; Khorram, E. Fuzzy linear optimization in the presence of the fuzzy relation inequality constraints with max-min composition. *Inf. Sci.* **2008**, *178*, 501–519. [CrossRef]
2. Nobuhara, H.; Pedrycz, W.; Hirota, K. Fast solving method of fuzzy relational equation and its application to lossy image compression/reconstruction. *IEEE Trans. Fuzzy Syst.* **2000**, *8*, 325–334. [CrossRef]
3. Passion, K.; Yurkovich, S. *Fuzzy Control*; Addision-Wesley: Boston, MA, USA, 2002.
4. Verbruggen, H.; Babuska, R. *Fuzzy Logic Control: Advances in Applications*; World Scientific: Singapore, 1999.
5. Sanchez, E. Resolution of composite fuzzy relation equations. *Inf. Control* **1976**, *30*, 38–48. [CrossRef]
6. Fang, S.; Li, G. Solving fuzzy relation equations with a linear objective function. *Fuzzy Sets Syst.* **1999**, *103*, 107–113. [CrossRef]
7. Pedrycz, W. An identification algorithm in fuzzy relation systems. *Fuzzy Sets Syst.* **1984**, *13*, 153–167. [CrossRef]
8. Shieh, B. Solutions of fuzzy relation equations based on continuous t-norms. *Inf. Sci.* **2007**, *177*, 4208–4215. [CrossRef]
9. Bourke, M.; Fisher, D. Solution algorithm for fuzzy relational equations with max-product composition. *Fuzzy Sets Syst.* **1998**, *94*, 61–69. [CrossRef]
10. Li, J.; Hu, G. An algorithm for fuzzy relation equations with max-product composition. *Adv. Fuzzy Sets Syst.* **2009**, *4*, 1–21.
11. Loetamonphong, J.; Fang, S. An efficient solution procedure for fuzzy relation equations with max-product composition. *IEEE Trans. Fuzzy Syst.* **1999**, *7*, 441–445. [CrossRef]
12. Cornejo, M.; Lobo, D.; Medina, J. On the solvability of bipolar max-product fuzzy relation equations with the product negation. *J. Comput. Appl. Math.* **2018**, *354*, 520–532. [CrossRef]
13. Cornejo, M.; Lobo, D.; Medina, J. On the solvability of bipolar max-product fuzzy relation equations with the standard negation. *Fuzzy Sets Syst.* **2021**, *410*, 1–18. [CrossRef]
14. Waziri, M.; Aisha, H.; Mamat, M. A Newton's-like method with extra updating strategy for solving singular fuzzy nonlinear equations. *Appl. Math. Sci.* **2014**, *8*, 7047–7057. [CrossRef]
15. Waziri, M.; Majid, Z. A new approach for solving dual fuzzy nonlinear equations using Broyden's and Newton's methods. *Adv. Fuzzy Syst.* **2012**, *2012*, 682087. [CrossRef]

16. Waziri, M.; Moyi, A. An alternative approach for solving dual fuzzy nonlinear equations. *Int. J. Fuzzy Syst.* **2016**, *18*, 103–107. [CrossRef]
17. Molai, A.; Khorram, E. An algorithm for solving fuzzy relation equations with max-T composition operator. *Inf. Sci.* **2008**, *178*, 1293–1308. [CrossRef]
18. Ignjatovic, J.; Ciric, M.; Damljanovic, N.; Jancic, I. Weakly linear systems of fuzzy relation inequalities: The heterogeneous case. *Fuzzy Sets Syst.* **2012**, *199*, 64–91. [CrossRef]
19. Li, P.; Fang, S. On the unique solvability of fuzzy relational equations. *Fuzzy Optim. Decis. Mak.* **2011**, *10*, 115–124. [CrossRef]
20. Yeh, C. On the minimal solutions of max-min fuzzy relational equations. *Fuzzy Sets Syst.* **2008**, *159*, 23–39. [CrossRef]
21. Perfilieva, I. Fuzzy function as an approximate solution to a system of fuzzy relation equations. *Fuzzy Sets Syst.* **2004**, *147*, 363–383. [CrossRef]
22. Perfilieva, I.; Noskova, L. System of fuzzy relation equations with inf-$\rightarrow$ composition: Complete set of solutions. *Fuzzy Sets Syst.* **2008**, *159*, 2256–2271. [CrossRef]
23. Cheng, D.; Qi, H. *Analysis and Control of Boolean Networks: A Semi-Tensor Product Approach*; Springer: London, UK, 2011.
24. Li, H.; Wang, S.; Li, X.; Zhao, G. Perturbation analysis for controllability of logical control networks. *SIAM J. Control Optim.* **2020**, *58*, 3632–3657. [CrossRef]
25. Meng, M.; Xiao, G.; Zhai, C.; Li, G. Controllability of Markovian jump Boolean control networks. *Automatica* **2019**, *106*, 70–76. [CrossRef]
26. Zhang, K.; Johansson, K. Efficient verification of observability and reconstructibility for large Boolean control networks with special structures. *IEEE Trans. Autom. Control* **2020**, *65*, 5144–5158. [CrossRef]
27. Guo, Y.; Li, Z.; Liu, Y.; Gui, W. Asymptotical stability and stabilization of continuous-time probabilistic logic networks. *IEEE Trans. Autom. Control* **2021**. [CrossRef]
28. Li, F.; Tang, Y. Set stabilization for switched Boolean control networks. *Automatica* **2017**, *78*, 223–230. [CrossRef]
29. Wang, L.; Liu, Y.; Wu, Z.; Lu, J.; Yu, L. Stabilization and finite-time stabilization of probabilistic Boolean control networks. *IEEE Trans. Syst. Man Cybern. Syst.* **2021**, *51*, 1559–1566. [CrossRef]
30. Wu, Y.; Sun, X.; Zhao, X.; Shen, T. Optimal control of Boolean control networks with average cost: A policy iteration approach. *Automatica* **2019**, *100*, 378–387. [CrossRef]
31. Chen, H.; Liang, J. Local synchronization of interconnected Boolean networks with stochastic disturbances. *IEEE Trans. Neural Netw. Learn. Syst.* **2020**, *31*, 452–463. [CrossRef]
32. Cheng, D.; He, F.; Qi, H.; Xu, T. Modeling, analysis and control of networked evolutionary games. *IEEE Trans. Autom. Control* **2015**, *60*, 2402–2415. [CrossRef]
33. Li, C.; Xing, Y.; He, F.; Cheng, D. A strategic learning algorithm for state-based games. *Automatica* **2020**, *113*, 108615. [CrossRef]
34. Liu, T.; Wang, J.; Zhang, X.; Cheng, D. Game theoretic control of multiagent systems. *SIAM J. Control Optim.* **2019**, *57*, 1691–1709. [CrossRef]
35. Liu, X.; Zhu, J. On potential equations of finite games. *Automatica* **2016**, *68*, 245–253. [CrossRef]
36. Zhu, B.; Xia, X.; Wu, Z. Evolutionary game theoretic demand-side management and control for a class of networked smart grid. *Automatica* **2016**, *70*, 94–100. [CrossRef]
37. Li, R.; Chu, T.; Wang, X. Bisimulations of Boolean Control Networks. *SIAM J. Control Optim.* **2018**, *56*, 388–416. [CrossRef]
38. Zhong, J.; Yu, Z.; Li, Y.; Lu, J. State estimation for probabilistic Boolean networks via outputs observation. *IEEE Trans. Neural Netw. Learn. Syst.* **2021**. [CrossRef]
39. Lu, J.; Li, H.; Liu, Y.; Li, F. A survey on semi-tensor product method with its applications in logical networks and other finite-valued systems. *IET Control Theory Appl.* **2017**, *11*, 2040–2047. [CrossRef]
40. Lyu, H.; Wang, W.; Liu, X.; Wang, Z. Modeling of multivariable fuzzy systems by semitensor product. *IEEE Trans. Fuzzy Syst.* **2020**, *28*, 228–235. [CrossRef]
41. Lyu, H.; Wang, W.; Liu, X. Universal approximation of fuzzy relation models by semitensor product. *IEEE Trans. Fuzzy Syst.* **2020**, *28*, 2972–2981. [CrossRef]
42. Fan, H.; Feng, J.; Meng, M. Solutions to fuzzy relation inequality $A \circ X \circ B \leq C$. *Control Theory Appl.* **2016**, *33*, 694–700.
43. Yan, Y.; Chen, Z.; Liu, Z. Solving type-2 fuzzy relation equations via semi-tensor product of matrices. *Control Theory Technol.* **2014**, *12*, 173–186. [CrossRef]
44. Cheng, D.; Feng, J.; Lv, H. Solving fuzzy relational equations via semi-tensor product. *IEEE Trans. Fuzzy Syst.* **2012**, *20*, 390–396. [CrossRef]
45. Li, H.; Wang, Y. A matrix approach to latticized linear programming with fuzzy-relation inequality constraints. *IEEE Trans. Fuzzy Syst.* **2013**, *21*, 781–788. [CrossRef]
46. Wang, S.; Li, H. Column stacking approach to resolution of systems of fuzzy relational inequalities. *J. Frankl. Inst.* **2019**, *356*, 3314–3332. [CrossRef]
47. Cheng, D.; Xu, Z.; Shen, T. Equivalence-based model of dimension-varying linear systems. *IEEE Trans. Autom. Control* **2020**, *65*, 5444–5449. [CrossRef]
48. Feng, J.; Lv, H.; Cheng, D. Multiple fuzzy relation and its application to coupled fuzzy control. *Asian J. Control* **2013**, *15*, 1313–1324. [CrossRef]

mathematics MDPI

Article

# Fuzzy Results for Finitely Supported Structures

**Andrei Alexandru [1] and Gabriel Ciobanu [2,*]**

[1] Institute of Computer Science, Romanian Academy, 700505 Iaşi, Romania; andrei.alexandru@iit.academiaromana-is.ro
[2] Faculty of Computer Science, Alexandru Ioan Cuza University, 700506 Iaşi, Romania;
* Correspondence: gabriel@info.uaic.ro

**Abstract:** We present a survey of some results published recently by the authors regarding the fuzzy aspects of finitely supported structures. Considering the notion of finite support, we introduce a new degree of membership association between a crisp set and a finitely supported function modelling a degree of membership for each element in the crisp set. We define and study the notions of invariant set, invariant complete lattices, invariant monoids and invariant strong inductive sets. The finitely supported (fuzzy) subgroups of an invariant group, as well as the $L$-fuzzy sets on an invariant set (with $L$ being an invariant complete lattice) form invariant complete lattices. We present some fixed point results (particularly some extensions of the classical Tarski theorem, Bourbaki–Witt theorem or Tarski–Kantorovitch theorem) for finitely supported self-functions defined on invariant complete lattices and on invariant strong inductive sets; these results also provide new finiteness properties of infinite fuzzy sets. We show that apparently, large sets do not contain uniformly supported, infinite subsets, and so they are invariant strong inductive sets satisfying finiteness and fixed-point properties.

**Keywords:** invariant set; $L$-fuzzy set; $T$-fuzzy set; invariant complete lattice; invariant strong inductive set; fixed points; $S$-finite support principle; uniformly supported set

**MSC:** AMS 2020 Subject Classification; 03E30; 03E72; 08A72

**Citation:** Alexandru, A.; Ciobanu, G. Fuzzy Results for Finitely Supported Structures. *Mathematics* **2021**, *9*, 1651. https://doi.org/10.3390/math9141651

Academic Editor: Michael Voskoglou

Received: 31 May 2021
Accepted: 7 July 2021
Published: 13 July 2021



## 1. Introduction

### 1.1. General Aspects

Lotfi Zadeh published in 1965 his pioneering article[1] that has over 100,000 citations today. The theory of fuzzy sets was introduced in Zermelo–Fraenkel set theory (ZF) as a framework for studying the concepts of vagueness and uncertainty. Each element of a fuzzy set has a certain degree of membership belonging to the real interval $[0,1]$. Fuzzy aspects can be applied in various fields of mathematics and computer science such as algebra, logic, analysis, operational research, control theory, decision theory, artificial intelligence and expert systems [2].

We extended the classical approach of fuzzy theory to characterise fuzzy sets over finitely supported structures. The finitely supported sets and structures are related to permutation models from Zermelo–Fraenkel set theory with atoms (ZFA) and to admissible sets (particularly to hereditary finite sets) described in [3]. They were originally introduced by Fraenkel, Lindenbaum and Mostowski during the period 1922–1938 in order to prove the independence of the axiom of choice and the other axioms in ZFA. The axioms of the recently introduced Fraenkel–Mostowski set theory are precisely the axioms of ZFA set theory together with an additional axiom for finite support. They are involved in the (hierarchical) construction of finitely supported sets; hereditary finitely supported sets are the sets constructed with respect to Fraenkel–Mostowski axioms over an infinite family of basic elements called atoms.

### 1.2. Motivation and Novelties

The motivation for studying finitely supported sets comes from the idea of dealing in a discrete manner with infinite algebraic structures (hierarchically constructed from atoms) by analysing their finite supports. Even thoughwe admit the existence of infinite atomic sets for such a structure, we are focused only on a finite family of its elements (namely, its 'finite support', a set which is able to characterise the entire structure).

The finitely supported structures can be described both in the ZF framework and in the ZFA framework. We follow the approach presented in [4] as an alternative to the Fraenkel–Mostowski set theory, and work over the classical ZF set theory. We define invariant sets as ZF sets equipped with actions of the group of all permutations of a certain fixed set $A$ (formed by elements whose internal structure is ignored, called atoms) satisfying a certain finite support requirement. The related requirement states that any element of an invariant set is left unchanged under the effect of each permutation of $A$ that fixes pointwise, finitely,many atoms. Finitely supported sets are defined as finitely supported elements in the powerset of an invariant set. Finitely supported structures are finitely supported sets endowed with finitely supported internal laws (that are supported as functions, i.e., as subsets in a Cartesian product of invariant set); more details can be found in [5,6]. The theory of finitely supported sets allows the computational study of structures which may be infinite, but contain enough symmetries such that they can be concisely represented [6].

Finitely supported sets include ZF sets that are trivial invariant sets. However, translating ZF results in the framework of finitely supported sets is not an easy task because the family of finitely supported sets is not closed under subset constructions (there exist subsets of finitely supported sets that fail to be finitely supported; for instance, the ZF infinite and coinfinite subsets of the set $A$ of all atoms). In order to prove results for the finitely supported sets, we cannot use results from ZF without reformulating them with respect to the finite support requirement. As a consequence, there exist results which are valid in ZF, but fail to be valid for finitely supported sets (e.g., choice principles and Stone duality) [6].

Our main purpose is to analyse whether a non-atomic ZF result can be adequately reformulated by replacing 'non-atomic ZF element/set/structure' with 'atomic, finitely supported element/set/structure'. A proof of a result in the framework of finitely supported structures should involve only finitely supported constructions even in the intermediate steps. The meta-theoretical techniques for the translation of a result from non-atomic structures to finitely supported atomic structures are based on a refinement of the finite support principle from [4], presented in [6] and called the '$S$-finite support principle' claiming that 'for any finite set $S \subseteq A$, anything that is definable under the rules in higher-order logic from $S$-supported structures by involving only $S$-supported constructions is also $S$-supported'. The formal use of this principle implies a hierarchical construction of the support of a structure by employing, step-by-step, the supports of the substructures of a related structure.

Here, we present an overview of results dealing with fuzzy aspects of finitely supported structures (fss). Essentially, by employing the notion of 'finite support', we extend the fuzzy aspects from a finite framework to a (finitely supported) infinite one. Using specific proof techniques that are extensively presented in [5,6], we obtain new algebraic properties of the fuzzy sets over fss, including some that cannot be obtained in ZF set theory. We introduce a new (infinite) fss degree of membership association, and connect it to the notions of invariant monoids and invariant complete lattices. We also show that the family of finitely supported (fuzzy) subgroups of an invariant group forms an invariant complete lattice, and that the family of finitely supported fuzzy normal subgroups forms an invariant modular lattice. We present some fixed point theorems for finitely supported structures that are preserving the validity the classical fixed point theorems, but also some fixed point properties of the finitely supported algebraic structures without corresponding results in ZF set theory. As applications of the fixed point theorems, we present some examples of finitely supported ordered structures for which these results can be used; in particular, properties of $L$-fuzzy and $T$-fuzzy sets defined in the framework of finitely supported structures, where $L$ is an invariant complete lattice and $T$ is an invariant strong inductive set.

## 2. Finitely Supported Sets: Preliminaries

We consider a fixed infinite ZF set $A$ without involving any internal structure for its elements. As usual, a *transposition* is a function $(x\,y) : A \to A$ defined by $(x\,y)(x) = y$, $(x\,y)(y) = x$ and $(x\,y)(z) = z$ for $z \neq x, y$. The *permutations* of $A$ are bijections of $A$ generated by finitely composing many transpositions, i.e., bijections of $A$ leaving unchanged all but the finiteelements of $A$. The set of all permutations of $A$ is denoted by $S_A$. We proved in [5] that any finitely supported bijection of $A$ should be necessarily a permutation of $A$, i.e., it should be expressed as a finite composition of transpositions. Thus, the notions 'bijection of $A$' and 'permutation of $A$' coincide in finitely supported structures.

**Definition 1.** *Let $X$ be a ZF set.*

1. *An* $S_A$-action *on $X$ is a group action of $S_A$ on $X$. An* $S_A$-set *is a pair $(X, \cdot)$, where $X$ is a ZF set and $\cdot : S_A \times X \to X$ is an $S_A$-action on $X$.*
2. *Let $(X, \cdot)$ be an $S_A$-set. We say that $S \subset A$* supports *$x$ (or $x$ is $S$-supported) if for each $\pi \in Fix(S)$ we have $\pi \cdot x = x$, where $Fix(S) = \{\pi \mid \pi(a) = a$ for all $a \in S\}$. An element which is supported by a finite subset of atoms is called* finitely supported.
3. *Let $(X, \cdot)$ be an $S_A$-set. We say that set $X$ is an* invariant set *whenever for each $x \in X$ there is a finite set $S_x \subset A$ supporting $x$.*
4. *Let $X$ be an $S_A$-set, and $x \in X$. If there is a finite set supporting $x$, then a least finite set $supp(x)$ supporting $x$ [5], defined as the intersection of all sets supporting $x$, which is called* the support of $x$. *An empty supported element is* equivariant; *$z \in X$ is equivariant if and only if $\pi \cdot z = z$ for all $\pi \in S_A$.*

Let $(X, \cdot)$ and $(Y, \diamond)$ be $S_A$-sets. According to [6], the set $A$ of atoms is an invariant set with the $S_A$-action $\cdot : S_A \times A \to A$ defined by $\pi \cdot a := \pi(a)$ for all $\pi \in S_A$ and $a \in A$. Moreover, $supp(a) = \{a\}$ for each $a \in A$. If $\pi \in S_A$ and $x \in X$ is finitely supported, then $\pi \cdot x$ is finitely supported and $supp(\pi \cdot x) = \{\pi(u) \mid u \in supp(x)\} := \pi(supp(x))$. The Cartesian product $X \times Y$ is an $S_A$-set with the $S_A$-action $\otimes$ defined by $\pi \otimes (x, y) = (\pi \cdot x, \pi \diamond y)$ for all $\pi \in S_A$ and all $x \in X$, $y \in Y$. For $(X, \cdot)$ and $(Y, \diamond)$ invariant sets, $(X \times Y, \otimes)$ is also an invariant set. The powerset $\wp(X) = \{Z \mid Z \subseteq X\}$ is an $S_A$-set with the $S_A$-action $\star : S_A \times \wp(X) \to \wp(X)$ defined by $\pi \star Z := \{\pi \cdot z \mid z \in Z\}$ for all $\pi \in S_A$ and $Z \subseteq X$. For an invariant set $(X, \cdot)$, $\wp_{fs}(X)$ denotes the set formed from those subsets of $X$ that are finitely supported in the sense of Definition 1(2) as elements in $\wp(X)$ with respect to the action $\star$; $(\wp_{fs}(X), \star|_{\wp_{fs}(X)})$ is also an invariant set, where $\star|_{\wp_{fs}(X)}$ represents the action $\star$ restricted to $\wp_{fs}(X)$. Non-atomic sets are trivially invariant, i.e., they are equipped with the action $(\pi, x) \mapsto x$.

A subset $Z$ of an invariant set $(X, \cdot)$ is called *finitely supported* if and only if $Z \in \wp_{fs}(X)$, i.e., if and only if $Z$ is finitely supported as an element of the $S_A$-set $\wp(X)$ with respect to the action $\star$ defined on $\wp(X)$. A subset $Z$ of $X$ is *uniformly supported* if all of its elements are supported by the same finite set of atoms (elements of $A$). Certainly, a finite subset of an invariant set should be uniformly supported (by the union of the supports of its elements), but there may exist invariant sets that do not contain uniformly supported, infinite subsets, as we will prove below.

Let us notice that not any subset of an invariant set is finitely supported. For instance, if $X \subset A$ and $X$ is finite, then it is finitely supported with $supp(X) = X$. If $Y \subseteq A$ and $Y$ is cofinite (i.e., its complement is finite), then it is finitely supported with $supp(Y) = A \setminus Y$. Whenever $Z \subseteq A$ is neither finite nor cofinite, then $Z$ is not finitely supported. It is proven that a subset of $A$ is finitely supported if and only if it is either finite or cofinite [7]. Moreover, if $\pi$ is a permutation of $A$ and $X$ is a subset of an $S_A$-set $Y$, then $\pi \star X = X$ if and only if $\pi \star X \subseteq X$, considering $\star$ defined on $\wp(Y)$. As a consequence of the previous definitions, a subset $Z$ of an invariant set $(X, \cdot)$ is supported by a finite set $S \subseteq A$ if and only if $\pi \star Z \subseteq Z$ for all $\pi \in Fix(S)$, i.e., if and only if $\pi \cdot z \in Z$ for all $z \in Z$ and $\pi \in Fix(S)$ (this happens because permutations of atoms are of a finite order). If $X$ is an invariant set, its finite powerset $\wp_{fin}(X)$ (namely, the set of all finite subsets of $X$) and its cofinite powerset $\wp_{cofin}(X)$ (namely, the set of all cofinite subsets of $X$) are equivariant subsets of $\wp_{fs}(X)$, meaning that they are themselves invariant sets having the restrictions of the action $\star$ on $\wp_{fs}(X)$. In [6], we proved that $supp(X) = \bigcup_{x \in X} supp(x)$ whenever $X$ is a uniformly supported subset of an invariant set.

As functions are specific relations (i.e., subsets of a Cartesian product of two sets), for two invariant sets $(X, \cdot)$ and $(Y, \diamond)$, $Z$, a finitely supported subset of $X$, and $T$, a finitely supported subset of $Y$, we say that a function $f : Z \to T$ is *finitely supported* if $f \in \wp_{fs}(X \times Y)$. Note that $Y^X$ is an $S_A$-set with the $S_A$-action $\widetilde{\star} : S_A \times Y^X \to Y^X$ defined by $(\pi \widetilde{\star} f)(x) = \pi \diamond (f(\pi^{-1} \cdot x))$ for all $\pi \in S_A$, $f \in Y^X$ and $x \in X$. A function $f : X \to Y$ is finitely supported (in the sense of the above definition) if and only if it is finitely supported with respect to the permutation action $\widetilde{\star}$. The set of all finitely supported functions from $Z$ to $T$ is denoted by $T^Z_{fs}$. As an immediate characterisation, a function $f : Z \to T$ is supported by a finite set $S \subseteq A$ if and only if for all $x \in Z$ and all $\pi \in Fix(S)$ we have $\pi \cdot x \in Z$, $\pi \diamond f(x) \in T$ and $f(\pi \cdot x) = \pi \diamond f(x)$.

An *invariant, partially ordered set (invariant poset)* is an invariant set $(P, \cdot, \sqsubseteq)$ equipped with an equivariant partial order relation $\sqsubseteq$ on $P$. A *finitely supported, partially ordered set* is a finitely supported subset $Q$ of an invariant set together with a finitely supported partial order relation. An *invariant complete lattice* is an invariant partially ordered set $(L, \cdot, \sqsubseteq)$ such that every finitely supported subset $X \subseteq L$ has a least upper bound with respect to the order relation $\sqsubseteq$. It is proven [6] that in an invariant complete lattice, every finitely supported subset $X \subseteq L$ has a greatest upper bound with respect to the order relation $\sqsubseteq$. A *finitely supported complete lattice* is a finitely supported subset $L$ of an invariant set, equipped with a finitely supported order $\sqsubseteq$ such that every finitely supported subset of $L$ has a least upper bound with respect to $\sqsubseteq$.

In both [5,6], several examples of invariant/finitely supported partially ordered sets are presented. For example, if $X$ is an invariant/finitely supported set, then $(\wp_{fs}(X), \star, \subseteq)$ is an invariant/finitely supported complete lattice. Here, we focus on the fuzzy theory over invariant sets, mainly presenting the results of [6–10].

## 3. Fuzziness over Invariant Sets

Let us consider a set $U$ called the universal set (or the universe of discourse). Recall that a crisp set $Z$ in the universe of discourse $U$ can be described by mentioning all of its members or by specifying the properties that have to be be satisfied by its members. The theory of fuzzy sets is a generalisation of this classical view: a fuzzy set is represented by a subset $Z$ of the universal set $U$ which has associated a related membership function generalising the characteristic function from the classical set theory. More exactly, the membership function associated to $Z$ could take any values in the interval [0,1] (modelling a certain degree of membership), while the classical characteristic function of $Z$ can only take two values: 0 (for non-membership) and 1 (for membership). Fuzzy sets over infinite invariant sets were introduced and studied first in [8], and then extended in [9].

**Definition 2.** *A fuzzy set over the invariant set $(U, \cdot)$ is a finitely supported subset $Z$ of $(U, \cdot)$ together with a finitely supported membership function $\mu_Z : U \to [0, 1]$.*

We say simply that $(Z, \mu_Z)$ is a fuzzy set over $(U, \cdot)$. In our approach, a fuzzy set over the invariant set $U$ is a (finitely supported) element in the invariant set $(\wp_{fs}(U) \times [0,1]^U_{fs}, \otimes)$. It is easy to see that in such a Cartesian pair, there is no precise fss association between the crisp finitely supported subset of $U$ and the related finitely supported function belonging to $[0,1]^U_{fs}$. Therefore, we allow more than one finitely supported membership function to be associated with the same finitely supported subset of $U$.

We decided to not yet define such an fss association because it is not necessary to assume the existence of an explicit finitely supported relation on $\wp_{fs}(U)$ and $[0,1]^U_{fs}$ for proving the properties of fuzzy sets for fss. On the other hand, the case when certain fss relations are defined between $\wp_{fs}(U)$ and $[0,1]^U_{fs}$ is analysed later in Section 4.

In the theory of fuzzy sets in ZF, we have two useful notions: *α-cut* and *fuzzy support*. For fss, an *α-cut* of a fuzzy set $(Z, \mu_Z)$ over the invariant set $(U, \cdot)$ is a crisp set $Z_\alpha$ containing all the elements in $U$ with membership values greater than or equal to $\alpha$, i.e., $Z_\alpha = \{z \in U \mid \mu_Z(z) \geq \alpha\}$.

**Proposition 1.** *Any α-cut $Z_\alpha$ of a fuzzy set $(Z, \mu_Z)$ over the invariant set $(U, \cdot)$ is a finitely supported subset of $U$ with the property that $supp(Z_\alpha) \subseteq supp(\mu_Z)$.*

**Definition 3.** *The* fuzzy support *of a fuzzy set $(Z, \mu_Z)$ over the invariant set $(U, \cdot)$ (also called the* algebraic support *of $\mu_Z$) is a crisp set $FZS(Z, \mu_Z)$ containing all the elements in $U$ with membership values greater than 0, i.e., $FZS(Z, \mu_Z) = \{z \in U \mid \mu_Z(z) > 0\}$.*

We prove (similar to Proposition 1) that the fuzzy support $FZS(Z, \mu_Z)$ of a fuzzy set $(Z, \mu_Z)$ over the invariant set $(U, \cdot)$ is a finitely supported subset of $U$ with the property that $supp(FZS(Z, \mu_Z)) \subseteq supp(\mu_Z)$. Moreover, in the particular case when the fuzzy support $FZS(Z, \mu_Z)$ is finite, we have the following result that presents a relationship between the (fuzzy) support and the atomic support of a fuzzy set.

**Proposition 2.** *Considering the fuzzy set $(Z, \mu_Z)$ over the invariant set $(U, \cdot)$, if $FZS(Z, \mu_Z)$ is finite, then $supp(FZS(Z, \mu_Z)) = supp(\mu_Z)$. Particularly, if $(Z, \mu_Z)$ is a fuzzy set over the invariant set $A$ of atoms and $FZS(Z, \mu_Z)$ is finite, then we have $FZS(Z, \mu_Z) = supp(\mu_Z)$.*

More generally, finitely supported functions from the set of atoms $A$ to a non-atomic ZF set $Z$ (e.g., $Z$ can be the unit interval [0,1] have the following property which allows to connect our notion of support with the classical notion of algebraic support.

**Theorem 1.** *Let $(Z, \diamond)$ be an infinite non-atomic ZF set and $f : A \to Z$ a function.*

1. *If $f$ is finitely supported, then there is $z_0 \in Z$ such that $\{a \in A \mid f(a) \neq z_0\}$ is finite.*
2. *If there is $z_0 \in Z$ such that $\{a \in A \mid f(a) \neq z_0\}$ is finite, then $f$ is finitely supported and $supp(f) = \{a \in A \mid f(a) \neq z_0\}$.*

For the fuzzy sets over invariant sets, we define operations similarly to those in ZF.

**Lemma 1.** *Let $(X, \mu_X)$ and $(Y, \mu_Y)$ be fuzzy sets over the invariant set $(U, \cdot)$.*

1. *Then $X \cup Y$ is finitely supported, and the function $x \mapsto max[\mu_X(x), \mu_Y(x)]$ defined on $U$ is also finitely supported.*
2. *Then $X \cap Y$ is finitely supported and, furthermore, the function $x \mapsto min[\mu_X(x), \mu_Y(x)]$ defined on $U$ is also finitely supported.*
3. *Both the complementary of $X$ (denoted by $C_X$) and the function $x \mapsto 1 - \mu_X(x)$ defined on $U$ are finitely supported.*

According to Lemma 1, the following definition is valid for fss.

**Definition 4.** *Let $(X, \mu_X)$ and $(Y, \mu_Y)$ be two fuzzy sets over the invariant set $(U, \cdot)$.*

1. *The* union *of two fuzzy sets $X$ and $Y$ is a fuzzy set over the invariant set $U$ given by the finitely supported subset $X \cup Y$ of $U$ with the finitely supported membership function $\mu_{X \cup Y} : U \to [0,1]$ defined by $\mu_{X \cup Y}(x) = max[\mu_X(x), \mu_Y(x)]$ for all $x \in U$.*
2. *The* intersection *of two fuzzy sets $X$ and $Y$ is a fuzzy set over the invariant set $U$ given by the finitely supported subset $X \cap Y$ of $U$ with the finitely supported membership function $\mu_{X \cap Y} : U \to [0,1]$ defined by $\mu_{X \cap Y}(x) = min[\mu_X(x), \mu_Y(x)]$ for all $x \in U$.*

3. *The* complement *of a fuzzy set X is a fuzzy set over the invariant set U given by the finitely supported subset $C_X$ of U together with the finitely supported membership function $\mu_{C_X}: U \to [0,1]$ defined by $\mu_{C_X}(x) = 1 - \mu_X(x)$ for all $x \in U$.*

**Proposition 3.** *Let $(X, \mu_X)$ and $(Y, \mu_Y)$ be fuzzy sets over the invariant set $(U, \cdot)$. Then, we have the following relations:*

1. $C_{(X,\mu_X)\cap(Y,\mu_Y)} = C_{(X,\mu_X)} \cup C_{(Y,\mu_Y)}$;
2. $C_{(X,\mu_X)\cup(Y,\mu_Y)} = C_{(X,\mu_X)} \cap C_{(Y,\mu_Y)}$.

**Lemma 2.** *Let $\mathcal{F} = (Z_i, \mu_{Z_i})_{i\in I}$ be a family of fuzzy sets over the invariant set $(U, \cdot)$ which is finitely supported as a subset of $(\wp_{fs}(U) \times [0,1]^U_{fs}, \otimes)$. Then, $\bigcup_{i\in I} Z_i$ is finitely supported by $supp(\mathcal{F})$, and the function $z \mapsto \bigvee_{i\in I}\{\mu_{Z_i}(z) \mid i \in I\}$ defined on U is finitely supported by $supp(\mathcal{F})$, where $\vee$ represents the notation for supremum (least upper bound).*

**Lemma 3.** *Let $\mathcal{F} = (Z_i, \mu_{Z_i})_{i\in I}$ be a family of fuzzy sets over the invariant set $(U, \cdot)$ which is finitely supported as a subset of $(\wp_{fs}(U) \times [0,1]^U_{fs}, \otimes)$. Then, $\bigcap_{i\in I} Z_i$ is finitely supported by $supp(\mathcal{F})$, and the function $z \mapsto \bigwedge_{i\in I}\{\mu_{Z_i}(z) \mid i \in I\}$ defined on U is also finitely supported by $supp(\mathcal{F})$, where $\wedge$ represents the notation for infimum (greatest lower bound).*

Due to Lemmas 2 and 3, the next definition is also valid for finitely supported structures.

**Definition 5.** *Let $\mathcal{F} = (Z_i, \mu_{Z_i})_{i\in I}$ be a family of fuzzy sets over the invariant set $(U, \cdot)$ which is finitely supported as a subset of $(\wp_{fs}(U) \times [0,1]^U_{fs}, \otimes)$.*

1. *The* arbitrary union *of the fuzzy sets $(Z_i, \mu_{Z_i})_{i\in I}$ is a fuzzy set over the invariant set U represented by the finitely supported subset $\bigcup_{i\in I} Z_i$ of U together with the finitely supported function $\mu_{\bigcup_{i\in I} Z_i}: U \to [0,1]$ defined by $\mu_{\bigcup_{i\in I} Z_i}(z) = \bigvee_{i\in I}\{\mu_{Z_i}(z) \mid i \in I\}$.*
2. *The* arbitrary intersection *of the family of fuzzy sets $(Z_i, \mu_{Z_i})_{i\in I}$ is a fuzzy set over the invariant set U represented by the finitely supported subset $\bigcap_{i\in I} Z_i$ of U together with the finitely supported function $\mu_{\bigcap_{i\in I} Z_i}: U \to [0,1]$ defined by $\mu_{\bigcap_{i\in I} Z_i}(z) = \bigwedge_{i\in I}\{\mu_{Z_i}(z) \mid i \in I\}$.*

According to the extension principle in the classical theory of fuzzy sets, the domain of a function to be extended from crisp points in the universe $U$ to fuzzy sets in $U$ is allowed. More precisely, let $f : U \to V$ be a function from a crisp set $U$ to a crisp set $V$. Suppose that we have a given fuzzy set $Z$ in $U$, and want to determine a fuzzy set $Y$ in $V$ induced by $f$ (i.e., $Y = f(Z)$). In general, the membership function for $Y$ is defined by $\mu_Y(y) = \bigvee_{z\in f^{-1}(y)} \mu_Z(z)$, where $y \in V$ and $f^{-1}(y) = \{z \in U \mid f(z) = y\}$.

**Theorem 2.** *Let $(U, \cdot)$ and $(V, \diamond)$ be two invariant sets, and consider a finitely supported function $f : U \to V$. If $(Z, \mu_Z)$ is a fuzzy set over the invariant set $(U, \cdot)$; then, $Y = f(Z)$ is a fuzzy set over the invariant set $(V, \diamond)$ with the finitely supported membership function $\mu_Y : V \to [0,1]$ defined as follows:*

$$\mu_Y(y) = \begin{cases} \bigvee_{z\in f^{-1}(y)} \mu_Z(z) & \text{for } y \in V, f^{-1}(y) \neq \emptyset \\ 0 & \text{for } y \in V, f^{-1}(y) = \emptyset \end{cases}.$$

*Moreover, we have $supp(Y) \subseteq supp(f) \cup supp(Z)$, and $supp(\mu_Y) \subseteq supp(f) \cup supp(\mu_Z)$.*

**Theorem 3.** *Let $(U_1, \cdot_1), \ldots, (U_n, \cdot_n)$ and $(V, \diamond)$ be invariant sets, and a finitely supported function $f : U_1 \times \ldots \times U_n \to V$. If $(Z_i, \mu_{Z_i})$ is a fuzzy set over the invariant set $(U_i, \cdot_i)$ for all $i \in \{1, \ldots n\}$, then $Y = f(Z_1 \times \ldots \times Z_n)$ is a fuzzy set over the invariant set $(V, \diamond)$ with the finitely supported membership function $\mu_Y : V \to [0,1]$ defined as follows:*

$$\mu_Y(y) = \bigvee_{y=f(z_1,\ldots,z_n)} [min(\mu_{Z_1}(z_1),\ldots,\mu_{Z_n}(z_n))]$$
$$\text{for } y \in V \text{ and } f^{-1}(y) \neq \emptyset;$$
$$\mu_Y(y) = 0 \qquad \text{for } y \in V \text{ and } f^{-1}(y) = \emptyset.$$

*Moreover, we have that* $supp(Y) \subseteq supp(f) \cup supp(Z_1) \cup \ldots \cup supp(Z_n)$*, and* $supp(\mu_Y) \subseteq supp(f) \cup supp(\mu_{Z_1}) \cup \ldots \cup supp(\mu_{Z_n})$.

## 4. Degree of Membership Association for Invariant Sets

A fuzzy set is an element of the invariant set $(\wp_{fs}(U) \times [0,1]^U_{fs}, \diamond)$. In such a Cartesian pair, we have not yet required the existence of an fss association between the crisp finitely supported subset of $U$ and the related finitely supported function in $[0,1]^U_{fs}$; such a firm fss association should itself preserve the finite support requirement, and for the previous results, such a condition was not mandatory. We now analyse the case when such an relationship between $\wp_{fs}(U)$ and $[0,1]^U_{fs}$ is defined.

**Definition 6.** *Let us consider the invariant set* $(U,\cdot)$*. A fss degree of membership association over* $U$ *is an equivariant binary relation* $R$ *on* $\wp_{fs}(U)$ *and* $[0,1]^U_{fs}$*, i.e., an equivariant (i.e., empty supported) subset* $R$ *of* $\wp_{fs}(U) \times [0,1]^U_{fs}$*.*

**Lemma 4.** *Let* $Y$ *be a finitely supported subset of an invariant set* $(U,\cdot)$*, and* $\chi_Y$ *be the characteristic function on* $Y$*, i.e.,*

$$\chi_Y(y) \overset{def}{=} \begin{cases} 1 & for\ y \in Y \\ 0 & for\ y \in U \setminus Y \end{cases}.$$

*Then* $\chi_Y : U \to [0,1]$ *is a finitely supported function for any* $Y \in \wp_{fs}(U)$*, and the function* $Z \mapsto \chi_Z$ *defined on* $\wp_{fs}(U)$ *is equivariant.*

Let $algsup(f) \overset{def}{=} \{z \in U \mid f(z) > 0\}$ be the *algebraic support* of $f$, where $(U,\cdot)$ is an invariant set and $f : U \to [0,1]$ a finitely supported function.

**Lemma 5.** *The algebraic support* $algsup(f)$ *is a finitely supported subset of* $U$*. Moreover, the function* $f \mapsto algsup(f)$ *defined on* $[0,1]^U_{fs}$ *is equivariant.*

We provide some examples of fss degree of membership associations.

**Example 1.** *Let* $(U,\cdot)$ *be an invariant set.*

1. *We define* $R = \{(Y,\chi_Y) \mid Y \in \wp_{fs}(U)\}$*, where* $\chi_Y$ *represents the characteristic function of* $Y$*. According to Lemma 4,* $R$ *is equivariant, and so* $R$ *is a fss degree of membership association over* $U$*.*
2. *We define* $R = \{(algsup(f), f) \mid f \in [0,1]^U_{fs}\}$*, where* $algsup(f)$ *represents the algebraic support of* $f$*. According to Lemma 5,* $R$ *is equivariant, and so* $R$ *is a fss degree of membership association over* $U$*.*

**Definition 7.** *Let* $(U,\cdot)$ *be an invariant set. A full fss degree of membership association over the invariant set* $U$ *is an equivariant binary relation* $F$ *on* $\wp_{fs}(U)$ *and* $[0,1]^U_{fs}$ *(i.e., an equivariant subset* $F$ *of the invariant set* $\wp_{fs}(U) \times [0,1]^U_{fs}$*) satisfying the following conditions:*

1. $F$ *is a left-total binary relation; namely, for any finitely supported subset* $Z$ *of* $U$*, a finitely supported function* $f : U \to [0,1]$ *called F-degree of membership function of* $Z$ *such that* $(Z,f) \in F$*.*
2. $F$ *is an onto binary relation; namely, for every finitely supported function* $f : U \to [0,1]$*,* $Z \in \wp_{fs}(U)$ *such that* $(Z,f) \in F$*.*

The conditions in Definition 7 correspond to our intuition of how a full fss degree of membership association over an invariant set should be defined.

1. The first condition in Definition 7 means that for each element in $\wp_{fs}(U)$, we should find at least one associated fss degree of membership function which models the degree of membership in $X$ for each element in $U$ (at least the characteristic function of $X$ is such a finitely supported function).
2. The second condition in Definition 7 means that any element of $[0,1]^U_{fs}$ should be a fss degree of membership function associated with a certain element of $\wp_{fs}(U)$. For each $f \in [0,1]^U_{fs}$, we could consider that $f$ is associated to at least its algebraic support.

**Example 2.** *Let $(U, \cdot)$ be an invariant set.*
*Let $F = \{(Y, \chi_Y) \mid Y \in \wp_{fs}(U)\} \cup \{(algsup(f), f) \mid f \in [0,1]^U_{fs}\}$, where $\chi_Y$ represents the characteristic function of $Y$ and $algsup(f)$ represents the algebraic support of $f$. Then $F$ is equivariant. Furthermore, $F$ is a full fss degree of membership association over $U$.*

**Proposition 4.**

1. *Let $(U, \cdot)$ be an invariant set such that there is a fss degree of membership association $F$ over it. Then the set of all F-degree of membership functions of $U$, i.e., $\wp^F_{fuzzy}(U) \stackrel{def}{=} \{f \in [0,1]^U_{fs} \mid \exists Z \in \wp_{fs}(U), (Z, f) \in F\} = Im(F)$ is an equivariant subset of $([0,1]^U_{fs}, \widetilde{\star})$, where $\widetilde{\star}$ is the standard $S_A$-action on $[0,1]^U_{fs}$.*
2. *Let $(U, \cdot)$ be an invariant set such that there is a full fss degree of membership association $F$ over it. Then the set of all F-degrees of membership functions defined on $U$, namely, $\wp^F_{fuzzy}(U)$, is an invariant set that coincides with $([0,1]^U_{fs}, \widetilde{\star})$.*

**Theorem 4.** *Let $(U, \cdot)$ be an invariant set such that there is a full fss degree of membership association $F$ over the invariant set $U$. Then $(\wp^F_{fuzzy}(U), \widetilde{\star}, \sqsubseteq)$ is an invariant complete lattice, where $\sqsubseteq$ is an equivariant order relation on $\wp^F_{fuzzy}(U) = \{f \in [0,1]^U_{fs} \mid \exists Z \in \wp_{fs}(U), (Z, f) \in F\}$ defined by: $f \sqsubseteq g$ is and only if $f(x) \le g(x)$ for all $x \in U$.*

To prove Theorem 4, when $\mathcal{F} = (f_i)_{i \in I}$ is a finitely supported family of elements from $[0,1]^U_{fs}$, we define $\underset{i\in I}{\sqcup} f_i : U \to [0,1]$ by $(\underset{i\in I}{\sqcup} f_i)(x) = \underset{i\in I}{supremum}\{f_i(x) \mid i \in I\}$ for all $x \in U$, where by *supremum* we denoted the least upper bounds in the set of real numbers. Using the fact that, whenever $\pi \in Fix(supp(\mathcal{F}))$, for any $i \in I$ there is a unique $j \in I$ such that $f_i = \pi^{-1} \widetilde{\star} f_j$ (where $\widetilde{\star}$ is the $S_A$-action on $[0,1]^U_{fs}$), we obtain that for each $i \in I$ there is a unique $j \in I$ such that $f_i(x) = f_j(\pi \cdot x)$ for all $x \in U$. Then we concluded that $\underset{i\in I}{supremum}\{f_i(\pi \cdot x) \mid i \in I\} = \underset{i\in I}{supremum}\{f_i(x) \mid i \in I\}$ for all $x \in U$ and all $\pi \in Fix(supp(\mathcal{F}))$, from which we obtained that $supp(\mathcal{F})$ supports $\underset{i\in I}{\sqcup} f_i$, which means $\underset{i\in I}{\sqcup} f_i$ is the least upper bound of $\mathcal{F}$ in $[0,1]^U_{fs} = \wp^F_{fuzzy}(U)$ (for the last relation we used Proposition 4(2)).

Several properties of $(\wp^F_{fuzzy}(U), \widetilde{\star}, \sqsubseteq)$ are obtained from the general properties of invariant complete lattices [6].

**Corollary 1.** *Let $(U, \cdot)$ be an invariant set such that there is a full fss degree of membership association $F$ over $U$.*

1. *Let $\varphi : \wp^F_{fuzzy}(U) \to \wp^F_{fuzzy}(U)$ be a finitely supported order preserving function over $(\wp^F_{fuzzy}(U), \widetilde{\star}, \sqsubseteq)$. Then there is a greatest $f \in \wp^F_{fuzzy}(U)$ such that $\varphi(f) = f$, as well as a least $g \in \wp^F_{fuzzy}(U)$ such that $\varphi(g) = g$.*

2. *Let $\varphi : \wp^F_{fuzzy}(U) \to \wp^F_{fuzzy}(U)$ be a finitely supported order-preserving function over $(\wp^F_{fuzzy}(U), \widetilde{\star}, \sqsubseteq)$. Let $P$ be the set of fixed points of $\varphi$. Then $(P, \widetilde{\star}, \sqsubseteq)$ is a finitely supported (by $supp(\varphi)$) complete lattice.*

It is worth noting that we obtain properties that cannot be obtained with standard fuzzy techniques in ZF. For instance, there exist lattices that are invariant complete, but fail to be complete in the ZF framework. A related example is presented in [11], where we proved that the set of those subsets of $A$ which are either finite or cofinite is an invariant complete lattice (with the classical inclusion order), but it fails to be a complete lattice in ZF. Another such example is presented in Proposition 4.

**Proposition 5.** *Let us assume that there is a full fss degree of membership association $F$ over the invariant set of atoms $A$. Then $(\wp^F_{fuzzy}(A), \widetilde{\star}, \sqsubseteq)$ is an invariant complete lattice, but it fails to be a complete lattice in ZF framework when $A$ is considered as a set in ZF.*

In order to prove Proposition 5, we considered $P$ to be a fixed ZF simultaneously infinite and coinfinite subset of $A$. For each $a \in A$ we defined $\varphi_a : A \to [0,1]$ by $\varphi_a(b) = \begin{cases} 1 & \text{for } b = a \\ 0 & \text{for } b \in A \setminus \{a\} \end{cases}$. Any function $\varphi_a$ is supported by $supp(a)$. Moreover, we proved that the function $j : A \to [0,1]^A_{fs}$ defined by $j(a) = \varphi_a$ for all $a \in A$ is equivariant. We considered the infinite family $\mathcal{F}$ from $[0,1]^A_{fs}$ defined by $\mathcal{F} = \{\varphi_a \mid a \in P\}$. The only possible least upper bound of $\mathcal{F}$ would have been the function $\psi : A \to [0,1]$ defined by $\psi(x) = \begin{cases} 1 & \text{for } x \in P \\ 0 & \text{for } x \in A \setminus P \end{cases}$. Since $P$ is not finitely supported, it followed that $\psi$ is not finitely supported, and so $\mathcal{F}$ does not have a least upper bound in $[0,1]^A_{fs}$.

Since the construction of $\wp^F_{fuzzy}(A) = [0,1]^A_{fs}$ makes sense in ZF, the previous result shows that $\wp^F_{fuzzy}(A)$ is a lattice which is not complete in ZF, but is the only invariantcomplete. This aspect emphasises one benefit of this approach: even though we have only a refined form of completeness (namely, the invariant completeness) in ZF for $\wp^F_{fuzzy}(A)$, we can provide new properties of $\wp^F_{fuzzy}(A)$ derived from the general properties of the invariant complete lattices (presented in [6]).

Invariant monoids were introduced in [12] as invariant sets equipped with equivariant internal monoid laws. More exactly, $(M, +, \cdot)$ is an invariant monoid if $(M, \cdot)$ is an invariant set and $(M, +, 0)$ is a monoid having the properties that $\pi \cdot (x + y) = (\pi \cdot x) + (\pi \cdot y)$, $\pi \cdot 0 = 0$ for all $x, y \in M$ and $\pi \in S_A$.

**Theorem 5.** *Let $(U, \cdot)$ be an invariant set such that there is a full fss degree of membership association $F$ over it. Then $\wp^F_{fuzzy}(U)$ can be organised as an invariant monoid in the following two forms:*

1. *$(\wp^F_{fuzzy}(U), \otimes, \widetilde{\star})$ is an invariant commutative monoid, where $\widetilde{\star}$ is the $S_A$-action on $[0,1]^U_{fs}$, and $f \otimes g : U \to [0,1]$ is defined by the relation $(f \otimes g)(x) = f(x)g(x)$ for all $x \in U$. The neutral element is the equivariant function $1_U : U \to [0,1]$ defined by $1_U(x) = 1$ for all $x \in U$.*
2. *$(\wp^F_{fuzzy}(U), \sqcup, \widetilde{\star})$ is an invariant commutative monoid, where $\widetilde{\star}$ is the $S_A$-action on $[0,1]^U_{fs}$, and $f \sqcup g : U \to [0,1]$ is defined by the relation $(f \sqcup g)(x) = supremum\{f(x), g(x)\}$ for all $x \in U$. The neutral element is the equivariant function $0_U : U \to [0,1]$ defined by $0_U(x) = 0$ for all $x \in U$.*

The general properties of invariant monoids presented in [12] lead to new properties of $\wp^F_{fuzzy}(U)$ (equipped with one of the two internal laws defined in Theorem 5). Some of them are related to the invariant isomorphism theorems, to invariant universality theorems or to Cayley monoids theorem. We present here an fss Cayley-type embedding theorem for $\wp^F_{fuzzy}(U)$ which follows from Theorem 7 in [12].

**Theorem 6.** *Let $(U, \cdot)$ be an invariant set with the property that there is a full fss degree of membership association $F$ over it. Then there is an equivariant isomorphism between $\wp^F_{fuzzy}(U)$ and an invariant submonoid of the invariant monoid formed by the finitely supported elements of $\wp^F_{fuzzy}(U)^{\wp^F_{fuzzy}(U)}$.*

The universality properties for invariant monoids [12] allow us to establish connectivity results between the set of all fuzzy sets over an invariant set $U$, the free monoid over $U$ and the set of all extended multisets over $U$.

Let $(U, \cdot)$ be an invariant set such that there is a full fss degree of membership association $F$ over it. Let $\mathbb{N}_{ext}(U)$ be the set of all extended multisets over $U$ (defined as functions $f : U \to \mathbb{N}$ with finite algebraic supports, which are proved to be finitely supported by their algebraic supports, where $\mathbb{N}$ is the set of all positive integers). Then, $\mathbb{N}_{ext}(U)$ endowed with the classical pointwise sum of extended multisets is an invariant monoid with the same $S_A$-action as $\mathbb{N}^U_{fs}$. If $U^*$ is the free monoid on $U$, then $U^*$ endowed with the classical juxtaposition of words is an invariant monoid with the $S_A$ action $\diamond$ defined by $\pi \diamond x_1 \ldots x_n = (\pi \cdot x_1) \ldots (\pi \cdot x_n)$ for all $\pi \in S_A$, $x_1 \ldots x_n \in U^* \setminus \{1\}$, and $\pi \diamond 1 = 1$ for all $\pi \in S_A$ (where 1 is the empty word).

**Theorem 7.** *Let $U, V$ be invariant sets with the property that there is a full fss degree of membership association with $V$. Let $j : U \to \mathbb{N}_{ext}(U)$ be the function which maps each $x \in U$ into the characteristic function $\chi_{\{x\}}$. If $\phi : U \to \wp^F_{fuzzy}(V)$ is an arbitrary finitely supported function, then there is a unique finitely supported homomorphism of invariant commutative monoids $\psi : \mathbb{N}_{ext}(U) \to \wp^F_{fuzzy}(V)$ with $\psi \circ j = \phi$, i.e., $\psi(\chi_{\{x\}}) = \phi(x)$ for all $x \in U$. Furthermore, $supp(\psi) \subseteq supp(\phi)$.*

**Theorem 8.** *Let $U, V$ be invariant sets with the property that there is a full fss degree of membership association with $V$. Let $i : U \to U^*$ be the standard inclusion of $U$ into $U^*$ which maps each element $x \in U$ into the word $x$. If $\phi : U \to \wp^F_{fuzzy}(V)$ is an arbitrary finitely supported function, then there is a unique finitely supported homomorphism of invariant monoids $\psi : U^* \to \wp^F_{fuzzy}(V)$ with $\psi \circ i = \phi$. Furthermore, $supp(\psi) \subseteq supp(\phi)$.*

The following isomorphism theorem can be proved from the general properties of invariant monoids [5]. For its corollaries, we involve Theorem 5 and the fact that the function $f \mapsto FZS(X, f)$ is an equivariant homomorphism between $(FAS(X), \sqcup, \tilde{\star})$ and $(\wp_{fin}(X), \cup, \star)$ with the notations in Corollary 3.

**Theorem 9.** *Let $(M, +_M, \cdot)$ and $(N, +_N, \diamond)$ be invariant monoids and let $f : M \to N$ be an equivariant homomorphism. On $M$ we define the relation $\sim_f$ by: $m_1 \sim_f m_2$ if $f(m_1) = f(m_2)$. Then $\sim_f$ is an equivariant equivalence relation and there is an equivariant isomorphism $\varphi$ between the invariant factor monoid $(M/\sim_f, +, \star)$ and the invariant monoid $Im(f)$, defined by $\varphi([m]) = f(m)$ for all $m \in M$, whereby $[m]$ we denoted the equivalence class of $m$ modulo $\sim_f$; the internal law $+$ is defined by : $[m] + [m'] = [m +_M m']$ for all $[m], [m'] \in M/\sim_f$ and the $S_A$-action $\star$ is defined by $\pi \star [m] = [\pi \cdot m]$ for all $[m] \in M/\sim_f$.*

**Corollary 2.** *Let $(X, \cdot)$ be an invariant set with the property that there is a full fss degree of membership association with $X$, and let $(N, +_N, \diamond_N)$ be an invariant monoid. Let $\psi : \wp^F_{fuzzy}(X) \to N$ be an equivariant homomorphism. On $\wp^F_{fuzzy}(X)$ (equipped with the internal laws $\otimes$ or $\sqcup$), we define the relation $\sim_\psi$ by: $f_1 \sim_\psi f_2$ if $\psi(f_1) = \psi(f_2)$. Then $\sim_\psi$ is an equivariant equivalence relation and there is an equivariant isomorphism $\varphi$ between the invariant monoid $\wp^F_{fuzzy}(X)/\sim_\psi$*

*and the invariant monoid $Im(\psi)$, defined by $\varphi([f]) = \psi(f)$ for all $f \in \wp^F_{fuzzy}(X)$, whereby $[f]$ we denoted the equivalence class of $f$ modulo $\sim_\psi$.*

**Corollary 3.** *Let $(X, \cdot)$ be an invariant set with the property that there is a full fss degree of membership association with $X$. Let $FAS(X) = \{f : X \to [0,1] \mid FZS(X, f) \text{ is finite}\}$. On $FAS(X)$ we define the relation $\sim$ by: $f \sim g$ if and only if $FZS(X, f) = FZS(X, f)$. Then $FAS(X)$ is an equivariant submonoid of $(\wp^F_{fuzzy}(X), \sqcup, \tilde{\star})$ and there is an equivariant isomorphism $\varphi$ between the invariant factor monoid $FAS(X)/\sim$ and the invariant monoid $(\wp_{fin}(X), \cup, \star)$ defined by $\varphi([f]) = FZS(X, f)$ for all $f \in FAS(X)$, whereby $[f]$ we denoted the family of functions from $X$ to $[0,1]$ having the same algebraic support as $f$.*

## 5. $L$-Fuzzy Sets and Invariant Complete Lattices

We present the notion of $L$-fuzzy set and several fixed point properties in this framework. By now on, we implicitly assume that the invariant sets we involve are endowed with a full fss degree of membership associations. Therefore, for an invariant algebraic structure $P$, the $P$-fuzzy sets over an invariant set $U$ will be defined as finitely supported functions from $U$ to $P$.

**Definition 8.** *Let $(L, \cdot, \sqsubseteq)$ be an invariant complete lattice and $(U, \diamond)$ an invariant set.*

- *An L-fuzzy set over $U$ is a finitely supported function $\mu : U \to L$.*
- *The algebraic support of a function $f : U \to L$ is the crisp set $FZS(U, f) = \{x \in U \mid 0 \sqsubset f(x)\}$.*

**Example 3.**

- *Let $U$ be an invariant set. The function $f : U \to \wp_{fs}(A)$ defined by $f(x) = supp(x)$ for all $x \in U$ is an equivariant L-fuzzy set over $U$. This is because $\wp_{fs}(A)$ is an invariant complete lattice and, for all $\pi \in S_A$, we have $supp(\pi \cdot x) = \pi(supp(x)) = \pi \star supp(x)$ for all $x \in X$.*
- *Let $(X, \cdot)$ be an invariant set. Let $\varphi : [0,1]^X_{fs} \to \wp_{fs}(X)$, $\varphi(f) = FZS(X, f)$. For $\pi \in S_A$ we verify that $\pi \star FZS(X, f) = FZS(X, \pi\tilde{\star}f)$ for all $f \in [0,1]^X_{fs}$. Fix $f$ and let $z \in \pi \star FZS(X, f)$. Then $z = \pi \cdot x$ with $x \in FZS(X, f)$, and hence $(\pi\tilde{\star}f)(z) = f(\pi^{-1} \cdot z) = f(x) > 0$, i.e., $z \in FZS(X, \pi\tilde{\star}f)$. Conversely, let $z \in FZS(X, \pi\tilde{\star}f)$. It follows that $f(\pi^{-1} \cdot z) > 0$. Thus, $z = \pi \cdot (\pi^{-1} \cdot z)$ with $\pi^{-1} \cdot z \in FZS(X, f)$, and so $z \in \pi \star FZS(X, f)$. Thus, since $\wp_{fs}(X)$ is an invariant complete lattice, we have that $\varphi$ is an equivariant L-fuzzy set over $[0,1]^X_{fs}$.*

**Theorem 10.** *Let $(L, \cdot, \sqsubseteq)$ be an invariant complete lattice and $(U, \diamond)$ an invariant set. Any function $f : U \to L$ has the following properties:*

1. *If $f$ is an L-fuzzy set over $U$, then $FZS(U, f)$ is finitely supported, and:*
    - *$supp(FZS(U, f)) \subseteq supp(f)$;*
    - *$supp(f(FZS(U, f))) \subseteq supp(FZS(U, f)) \cup supp(f)$;*
2. *If the algebraic support of $f$ is finite, then $f$ is an L-fuzzy set over $U$ (i.e., $f$ is finitely supported) and $supp(f) \subseteq supp(FZS(U, f)) \cup supp(f(FZS(U, f)))$.*
3. *If the algebraic support of $f$ is finite, then $supp(f(FZS(U, f))) \setminus supp(FZS(U, f)) = supp(f) \setminus supp(FZS(U, f))$.*

The $L$-fuzzy sets are characterised by the following property.

**Theorem 11.** *Let $(U, \diamond)$ be an invariant set and $(L, \cdot, \sqsubseteq)$ an invariant complete lattice.*

- *The family of those finitely supported functions $f : U \to L$ (i.e., the family $L^U_{fs}$ of all L-fuzzy sets over the invariant set $U$) is an invariant complete lattice with the order relation $\leq$ defined by $f \leq g$ if and only if $f(x) \sqsubseteq g(x)$ for all $x \in U$.*

- *Furthermore, if $\mathcal{F} = (f_i)_{i \in I}$ is a finitely supported family of L-fuzzy sets over the invariant set U, its least upper bound with respect to $\leq$ is $\bigvee_{i \in I} f_i : U \to L$ defined by $(\bigvee_{i \in I} f_i)(x) = \bigsqcup_{i \in I} \{f_i(x) \mid i \in I\}$ for all $x \in U$, whereby $\sqcup$ we denoted least upper bounds in L with respect to $\sqsubseteq$.*

The requirement that $L$ is invariant complete in Theorem 11 is necessary. For example, let us fix an element $a \in A$; the family $(f_n)_{n \in \mathbb{N}}$ of functions from $A$ to $\mathbb{N}$ defined by $f_i(b) = \begin{cases} i & \text{for } b = a \\ 0 & \text{for } b \in A \setminus \{a\} \end{cases}$ for all $i \in \mathbb{N}$ is finitely supported (each $f_i$ is supported by the same set $\{a\}$), but it does not have a supremum modulo $\sqsubseteq$.

It is worth noting that some ZF structures are not finitely supported. The family of finitely supported functions from $U$ to $L$ makes sense in ZF, but it is an invariant complete lattice and not a *fully* ZF complete lattice in respect with all atomic sets.

According to Theorem 11, the following fixed point results can provide properties of finitely supported $L$-fuzzy sets over an invariant set. We chose to present the results in the general case, making them also applicable for other finitely supported structures (not only for finitely supported $L$-fuzzy sets).

In this section, we present fixed point theorems of Tarski's type in the framework of finitely supported structures. Tarski's theorem plays an important role in the theory of abstract interpretation of programming languages reformulated in the world of finitely supported structures [11].

**Theorem 12** (Strong Tarski Theorem for fss). *Let $(L, \cdot, \sqsubseteq)$ be an invariant complete lattice and $f : L \to L$ a finitely supported, order-preserving function. Let F be the set of all fixed points of f. Then $(F, \cdot, \sqsubseteq)$ is itself a non-empty, finitely supported (by $supp(f)$), complete lattice.*

In terms of $L$-fuzzy sets, this result states that, if $(L, \cdot, \sqsubseteq)$ is an invariant complete lattice and $f$ is an order-preserving $L$-fuzzy set over the invariant set $L$, then the set of fixed points of $f$ is itself a non-empty finitely supported (by $supp(f)$) complete lattice.

**Corollary 4.** *Let $(L, \cdot, \sqsubseteq)$ be an invariant complete lattice and $f : L \to L$ a finitely supported, order-preserving function. Then f has a least-fixed point defined as $\sqcap\{x \in L \mid f(x) \sqsubseteq x\}$ and a greatest-fixed point defined as $\sqcup\{x \in L \mid x \sqsubseteq f(x)\}$, which are both supported by $supp(f)$.*

**Corollary 5.** *Let $(L, \cdot, \sqsubseteq)$ be an invariant complete lattice and $f : L \to L$ an equivariant order-preserving function. Let F be the set of all fixed points of f. Then $(F, \cdot, \sqsubseteq)$ is itself an invariant complete lattice.*

According to Theorem 13, Tarski's fixed-point theorem can be applied for finitely supported self-functions on the family of those finitely supported subsets of an invariant set [9].

**Theorem 13.** *If $(X, \cdot)$ is an invariant set, then $(\wp_{fs}(X), \star, \subseteq)$ is an invariant complete lattice.*

Theorem 12 can be extended. We were able to prove the existence of fixed points of a finitely supported, order preserving self-function on an invariant partially ordered set, by imposing the existence condition of least upper bounds only for those uniformly supported subsets of the invariant, partially ordered set, and not for all finitely supported subsets of the related invariant, partially ordered set [10].

**Theorem 14.** *Let $(X, \cdot, \sqsubseteq)$ be a non-empty invariant partially ordered set having the additional property that every uniformly supported subset of X has a least upper bound. Let $f : X \to X$ be a finitely supported, order-preserving function with the property that there is $x_0 \in X$ such that $x_0 \sqsubseteq f(x_0)$. Then there is $u \in X$ with $x_0 \sqsubseteq u$ such that $f(u) = u$.*

From Theorems 11 and 12, we obtain the following fixed point result for $L$-fuzzy sets over invariant sets.

**Theorem 15.** *Let $(U, \diamond)$ be an invariant set, $(L, \cdot, \sqsubseteq)$ an invariant complete lattice and $\varphi : L^U_{fs} \to L^U_{fs}$ a finitely supported, order-preserving function over $L^U_{fs}$. Let $F$ be the set of fixed points of $\varphi$. Then $(F, \widetilde{\star}, \leq)$ is a non-empty, finitely supported (by $supp(f)$) complete lattice, where $\widetilde{\star}$ is the induced $S_A$-action on the function space $L^U_{fs}$, and $\leq$ is the order relation of the family $L^U_{fs}$ of all $L$-fuzzy sets over the invariant set $U$ defined by $f \leq g$ if and only if $f(x) \sqsubseteq g(x)$ for all $x \in U$.*

## 6. Fuzzy Subgroups of an Invariant Group

Rosenfeld introduced the notion of a fuzzy group and proved that many concepts of group theory can naturally be extended in order to develop the theory of fuzzy groups [13]. A survey of the development of fuzzy group theory can be found in [14].
Let us recall some results of the classical Zermelo–Fraenkel theory of fuzzy groups.

**Definition 9.** *Let $(G, \cdot, 1)$ be a group. On the family $\{\nu \mid \nu : G \to [0,1]\}$ of all fuzzy sets on $G$ we define a partial order relation $\sqsubseteq$, called fuzzy sets inclusion by $\eta \sqsubseteq \mu$ if and only if $\eta(x) \leq \mu(x)$ for all $x \in G$.*

**Definition 10.** *Let $(G, \cdot, 1)$ be a group. A fuzzy set $\eta$ over the group $G$ (i.e., a function $\eta : G \to [0,1]$) is called* fuzzy subgroup *of $G$ if the following conditions are satisfied:*

- *$\eta(x \cdot y) \geq min\{\eta(x), \eta(y)\}$ for all $x, y \in G$;*
- *$\eta(x^{-1}) \geq \eta(x)$ for all $x \in G$.*

**Definition 11.** *Let $(G, \cdot, 1)$ be a group. A fuzzy subgroup $\mu$ of $G$ that satisfies the additional condition $\mu(x \cdot y) = \mu(y \cdot x)$ for all $x, y \in G$ is called a fuzzy normal subgroup of $G$.*

**Theorem 16.** *Let $(G, \cdot, 1)$ be a group.*

- *The set $FL(G)$ formed by all fuzzy subgroups of $G$ is a complete lattice with respect to fuzzy sets inclusion.*
- *The set $FN(G)$ formed by all fuzzy normal subgroups of $G$ is a modular lattice with respect to fuzzy sets inclusion.*

We translate the above results in the framework of finitely supported structures, proving their consistency within the new framework.

**Definition 12.** *An* invariant group *is a triple $(G, \cdot, \diamond)$ with the property that the following conditions are satisfied:*

- *$G$ is a group with the internal law $\cdot$;*
- *$G$ is a non-trivial invariant set with the $S_A$-action $\diamond$;*
- *for each $\pi \in S_A$ and each $x, y \in G$ we have $\pi \diamond (x \cdot y) = (\pi \diamond x) \cdot (\pi \diamond y)$, meaning that the internal law on $G$ is equivariant.*

**Proposition 6.** *$(G, \cdot, \diamond)$ be an invariant group. We have the following properties:*

1. *$\pi \diamond e = e$ for all $\pi \in S_A$, where $e$ is the neutral element of $G$.*
2. *$\pi \diamond x^{-1} = (\pi \diamond x)^{-1}$ for all $\pi \in S_A$ and $x \in G$.*

We provide the following examples of invariant groups.

**Example 4.**

1. *The group $(S_A, \circ, \cdot)$ is an invariant group, where $\circ$ is the composition of permutations and $\cdot$ is the $S_A$-action on $S_A$ defined by $\pi \cdot \sigma := \pi \circ \sigma \circ \pi^{-1}$ for all $\pi, \sigma \in S_A$. Since the composition*

*of functions is associative, it is easy to verify that* $\pi \cdot (\sigma \circ \tau) = (\pi \cdot \sigma) \circ (\pi \cdot \tau)$ *for all* $\pi, \sigma, \tau \in S_A$.

2. *The free group* $(F(X), \top, \widetilde{\star})$ *over an invariant set* $(X, \diamond)$ *(formed by those equivalence classes* $[w]$ *of words* $w$*, where two words are in the same equivalence class if one can be obtained from another by repeatedly inserting or cancelling terms of the form* $u^{-1}u$ *or* $uu^{-1}$ *for* $u \in X$*) is an invariant group, where* $\widetilde{\star} : S_A \times F(X) \to F(X)$ *is defined by* $\pi \widetilde{\star} [x_1^{\varepsilon_1} x_2^{\varepsilon_2} \dots x_l^{\varepsilon_l}] = [(\pi \diamond x_1)^{\varepsilon_1} \dots (\pi \diamond x_l)^{\varepsilon_l}]$*, and* $[x_1^{\varepsilon_1} x_2^{\varepsilon_2} \dots x_n^{\varepsilon_n}] \top [y_1^{\delta_1} y_2^{\delta_2} \dots y_m^{\delta_m}] = [x_1^{\varepsilon_1} x_2^{\varepsilon_2} \dots x_n^{\varepsilon_n} y_1^{\delta_1} y_2^{\delta_2} \dots y_m^{\delta_m}]$.
3. *Given an invariant set* $(X, \diamond)$*, any function* $f : X \to \mathbb{Z}$ *(where* $\mathbb{Z}$ *is the set of all integers) with the property that* $S_f \overset{def}{=} \{x \in X \mid f(x) \neq 0\}$ *is finite is called an extended generalised multiset over X. The set of all extended generalised multisets over X is denoted by* $\mathbb{Z}_{ext}(X)$*. Each function* $f \in \mathbb{Z}_{ext}(X)$ *is finitely supported with* $supp(f) = supp(S_f)$*. The set* $(\mathbb{Z}_{ext}(X), +, \widetilde{\star})$ *is an invariant commutative group, where* $f+g: X \to \mathbb{Z}$ *is defined pointwise by* $(f+g)(x) = f(x) + g(x)$ *for all* $x \in X$ *and* $\widetilde{\star}$ *is the standard* $S_A$*-action on* $\mathbb{Z}_{fs}^X$.

**Definition 13.** *Let* $(G, \cdot, \diamond)$ *be an invariant group. A* finitely supported subgroup *of G is a subgroup of G, which is also an element of* $\wp_{fs}(G)$.

**Example 5.**

1. *Let* $(G, \cdot, \diamond)$ *be an invariant group. The centre of G (namely,* $C(G) := \{g \in G \mid g \cdot u = u \cdot g$ *for all* $u \in G\}$*) is a finitely supported subgroup of G, and it is itself an invariant group because it is empty-supported as an element of* $\wp(G)$.
2. *Let X be a finitely supported subset of G. The subgroup of G generated by X (denoted by* $[X]$*) is a finitely supported (by* $supp(X)$*) subgroup of G, but not itself an invariant group.*

If $(G, \cdot, \diamond)$ is an invariant group, we denote by $L_{fs}(G)$ the family of all finitely supported subgroups of $G$ ordered by inclusion.

**Theorem 17.**

- *Let* $(G, \cdot, \diamond)$ *be an invariant group. Then* $(L_{fs}(G), \star, \subseteq)$ *is an invariant complete lattice, where* $\subseteq$ *represents the classical inclusion relation on* $\wp(G)$ *and* $\star$ *is the* $S_A$*-action on* $\wp(G)$.
- *Furthermore, if* $\mathcal{F} = (H_i)_{i \in I}$ *is a finitely supported family of finitely supported subgroups of G, then its least upper bound is* $[\bigcup_{i \in I} H_i]$ *which is supported by* $supp(\mathcal{F})$.

From Tarski's theorem (Theorem 12), we obtain the next result.

**Corollary 6.** *Let* $(G, \cdot, \diamond)$ *be an invariant group and* $f : L_{fs}(G) \to L_{fs}(G)$ *a finitely supported, order-preserving function. The set of all fixed points of f is itself a finitely supported (by* $supp(f)$*) complete lattice.*

**Definition 14.** *Let* $(G, \cdot, \diamond)$ *be an invariant group. A fuzzy set* $\eta$ *over the invariant set G (i.e., a finitely supported function* $\eta : G \to [0, 1]$*) is called a* finitely supported fuzzy subgroup *of G if the following conditions are satisfied:*

- $\eta(x \cdot y) \geq min\{\eta(x), \eta(y)\}$ *for all* $x, y \in G$;
- $\eta(x^{-1}) \geq \eta(x)$ *for all* $x \in G$.

**Example 6.** *Let* $(F(A), \top, \widetilde{\star})$ *be the invariant free group over the set A of atoms defined as in Example 4(2). For an element* $[w] = [x_1^{\varepsilon_1} x_2^{\varepsilon_2} \dots x_k^{\varepsilon_k}]$ *in* $F(A)$*, we define* $sum([w]) = \varepsilon_1 + \varepsilon_2 + \dots + \varepsilon_k$*. Whenever* $[w] = [w']$*, we have* $sum([w]) = sum([w'])$*, and so sum is well defined. It can be proved that sum is an equivariant (empty-supported) group homomorphism between the invariant groups* $F(A)$ *and* $\mathbb{Z}$ *(the set of all integers being a trivial invariant group).*

*Let us consider* $\eta_A : F(A) \to [0, 1]$ *defined by*

$$\eta_A([w]) = \begin{cases} 0, & \text{if } sum([w]) \text{ is an odd integer;} \\ 1 - \frac{1}{n}, & \text{if } sum([w]) = m \cdot 2^n \text{ where } m \text{ is an odd integer and } n \in \mathbb{N}; \\ 1, & \text{if } sum([w]) = 0\,. \end{cases}$$

*It can be proved that $\mu_A$ is a finitely supported fuzzy subgroup of $F(A)$.*

**Theorem 18.** *Let $(G, \cdot, \diamond)$ be an invariant group. The set $FL_{fs}(G)$ consisting of all finitely supported fuzzy subgroups of $G$ forms an invariant complete lattice with respect to fuzzy sets inclusion.*

In order to prove Theorem 18, the construction of least upper bounds for finitely supported subsets of $FL_{fs}(G)$ follows the next steps [9]:

- First, we proved that $FL_{fs}(G)$ is itself an invariant set; that is, we verified that $\pi \widetilde{\star} \mu$ is a finitely supported fuzzy subgroup of $G$ for all $\pi \in S_A$ and $\mu \in FL_{fs}(G)$ (it satisfies the conditions in Definition 14), where $\widetilde{\star}$ is the $S_A$-action on $[0,1]^G_{fs}$.
- We remarked that the inclusion relation $\sqsubseteq$ on $FL_{fs}(G)$, defined by $\mu \sqsubseteq \eta$ if and only if $\mu(x) \leq \eta(x)$ for all $x \in G$, is equivariant.
- For each $\alpha \in [0,1]$ and each $\nu \in [0,1]^G_{fs}$, we defined $G^\nu_\alpha = \{x \in G \mid \nu(x) \geq \alpha\}$ (which corresponds to the concept of $\alpha$-cut). We obtained that each $G^\nu_\alpha$ is finitely supported by $supp(\nu)$.
- As in Example 5(2), we obtained that each subgroup $[G^\nu_\alpha]$ generated by $G^\nu_\alpha$ is finitely supported by $supp(\nu)$.
- For any finitely supported function $\mu : G \to [0,1]$, we defined the function $\mu^* : G \to [0,1]$ by $\mu^*(x) = supremum\{\alpha \in [0,1] \mid x \in [G^\mu_\alpha]\}$ for any $x \in G$, whereby *supremum* we denoted the least upper bounds in the set of real numbers. We proved that $\mu^*$ is supported by $supp(\mu)$.
- If $\mathcal{F} = (\mu_i)_{i \in I}$ is a finitely supported family of elements from $FL_{fs}(G)$, we defined $\bigsqcup_{i \in I} \mu_i : G \to [0,1]$ by $\bigsqcup_{i \in I} \mu_i(x) = supremum_{i \in I}\{\mu_i(x) \mid i \in I\}$ for all $x \in G$. Since $[0,1]$ is a ZF (trivial invariant) complete lattice, from Theorem 11 we have that $supp(\mathcal{F})$ supports $\bigsqcup_{i \in I} \mu_i$. Therefore, we have that $(\bigsqcup_{i \in I} \mu_i)^*$ is finitely supported by $supp(\bigsqcup_{i \in I} \mu_i) \subseteq supp(\mathcal{F})$.
- As in the standard fuzzy groups theory, we found that $(\bigsqcup_{i \in I} \mu_i)^*$ is a fuzzy subgroup of $G$ (in the sense of Definition 14) and it is the least upper bound of $\mathcal{F}$ in $FL_{fs}(G)$ with respect to the order relation $\sqsubseteq$.

From Tarski's theorem (Theorem 12), the next result follows.

**Corollary 7.** *Let $(G, \cdot, \diamond)$ be an invariant group and $f : FL_{fs}(G) \to FL_{fs}(G)$ a finitely supported, order-preserving function. The set of all fixed points of $f$ is itself a finitely supported (by $supp(f)$) complete lattice.*

**Theorem 19.** *Let $(G, \cdot, \diamond)$ be an invariant group. The set $FN_{fs}(G)$ consisting of all finitely supported fuzzy normal subgroups of $G$ forms an invariant modular lattice with respect to fuzzy sets inclusion.*

## 7. $T$-Fuzzy Sets and Invariant Strong Inductive Sets

We introduce the concept of the $T$-fuzzy set, where $T$ is an invariant partially ordered set having the property that every finitely supported totally ordered subset of $T$ has a least upper bound in $T$. We present some fixed point results in a more general framework; they can be also applied to $T$-fuzzy sets.

**Definition 15.**

1. *An invariant strong inductive set is an invariant partially ordered set* $(T, \cdot, \sqsubseteq)$ *with the property that every finitely supported totally ordered subset (i.e., every finitely supported chain) of* $T$ *has a least upper bound in* $T$.
2. *Let* $(X, \cdot_X, \sqsubseteq_X)$ *and* $(Y, \cdot_Y, \sqsubseteq_Y)$ *be two invariant partially ordered sets. A finitely supported function* $f : X \to Y$ *is* c-continuous *if and only if for each finitely supported, countable sequence* $(u_n)_{n\in\mathbb{N}}$ *in* $X$ *which has a least upper bound, we have that* $f((u_n)_{n\in\mathbb{N}})$ *has a least upper bound in* $Y$ *and* $f(\bigsqcup_{n\in\mathbb{N}} u_n) = \bigsqcup_{n\in\mathbb{N}}(f(u_n))$.

**Definition 16.** *Let* $(T, \cdot, \sqsubseteq)$ *be an invariant strong inductive set and* $(U, \diamond)$ *an invariant set. A T-fuzzy set over* $U$ *is a finitely supported function* $\mu : U \to T$.

The $T$-fuzzy sets are characterised by the following property.

**Theorem 20.**

- *Let* $(U, \diamond)$ *be an invariant set and* $(T, \cdot, \sqsubseteq)$ *an invariant strong inductive set. The family of those finitely supported functions* $f : U \to T$ *(i.e., the family of all finitely supported T-fuzzy sets over U) is an invariant strong inductive set with the order relation* $\leq$ *defined by* $f \leq g$ *if and only if* $f(x) \sqsubseteq g(x)$ *for all* $x \in U$.
- *Furthermore, if* $\mathcal{F} = (f_i)_{i\in I}$ *is a finitely supported, totally ordered family of T-fuzzy sets over the invariant set U, its least upper bound with respect to* $\leq$ *is* $\bigvee_{i\in I} f_i : U \to T$ *defined by* $(\bigvee_{i\in I} f_i)(x) = \bigsqcup_{i\in I}\{f_i(x) \mid i \in I\}$ *for all* $x \in U$*, whereby* $\sqcup$ *we denoted least upper bounds in T of finitely supported totally ordered subsets (with respect to* $\sqsubseteq$*).*

The following theorem connects the concept of a 'uniformly supported set' with the concept of a 'invariant strong inductive set'.

**Theorem 21.**

- *An invariant partially ordered set* $(T, \cdot, \sqsubseteq)$ *with the property that every uniformly supported subset of T has a least upper bound in T is an invariant strong inductive set.*
- *An invariant partially ordered lattice (not necessarily complete)* $(T, \cdot, \sqsubseteq)$ *with the property that T does not contain a uniformly supported, infinite subset is an invariant strong inductive set.*

The following result presents a hierarchical construction of invariant sets containing no uniformly supported, infinite subsets [6,7]. We were able to prove this property for apparently large finitely supported sets that are presented as functions spaces.

**Theorem 22.**

1. *Let* $A^{\leq n} = \{(a_1, \ldots, a_k) \mid a_1, \ldots, a_k \in A, k \leq n\}$*. Let T be a finitely supported subset of an invariant set such that T does not contain a uniformly supported, infinite subset. The function space* $T_{fs}^{A^{\leq n}}$ *does not contain a uniformly supported, infinite subset, whenever* $n \in \mathbb{N}$.
2. *Let* $\wp_{\leq n}(A) = \{Z \in \wp_{fin}(A) \mid Z \in \wp_m(A)$ *for some* $m \leq n\}$*, where* $\wp_m(A)$ *is the family of all m-sized subsets of A. Let T be a finitely supported subset of an invariant set such that T does not contain a uniformly supported, infinite subset. The function space* $T_{fs}^{\wp_{\leq n}(A)}$ *does not contain a uniformly supported, infinite subset, whenever* $n \in \mathbb{N}$.

**Corollary 8.** *Let T be a finitely supported subset of an invariant set such that T does not contain a uniformly supported, infinite subset. For any* $n \in \mathbb{N}$,

1. *The function space* $T_{fs}^{A^n}$ *does not contain a uniformly supported, infinite subset;*
2. *The function space* $T_{fs}^{\wp_n(A)}$ *does not contain a uniformly supported, infinite subset.*

**Corollary 9.** *Let $P$ be an invariant set (in particular, $P$ could be an invariant complete lattice or an invariant strong inductive set) that does not contain a uniformly supported, infinite subset. Let $X$ be one of the sets $A^n, A^{\leq n}, \wp_n(A), \wp_{\leq n}(A)$ for some $n \in \mathbb{N}$. The set of all $P$-fuzzy sets over the invariant set $X$ does not contain a uniformly supported, infinite subset.*

The following four results are specific to finitely supported sets, i.e., they do not have ZF correspondents. We present some examples of finite powersets that are invariant strong inductive sets. Such a result does not hold in ZF since a ZF set could admit an unbounded countable ascending chain of finite subsets.

**Theorem 23.** *Let $(T, \cdot)$ be an invariant set such that $T$ does not contain a uniformly supported, infinite subset. Then $(\wp_{fin}(T), \star, \subseteq)$ does not contain a uniformly supported, infinite subset, and so it is an invariant strong inductive set.*

**Corollary 10.** *Let $(T, \cdot)$ be an invariant set such that $T$ does not contain a uniformly supported, infinite subset. Then $(\wp_{fin}(T_{fs}^{A^n}), \star, \subseteq)$ is an invariant strong inductive set, $n \in \mathbb{N}$.*

**Corollary 11.** *Let $(T, \cdot)$ be an invariant set such that $T$ does not contain a uniformly supported, infinite subset. Then $(\wp_{fin}(T_{fs}^{\wp_n(A)}), \star, \subseteq)$ is an invariant strong inductive set, $n \in \mathbb{N}$.*

**Corollary 12.** *Let $(T, \cdot)$ be an invariant set such that $T$ does not contain a uniformly supported, infinite subset. Then $(\wp_{fin}(\wp_{fs}(A^n)), \star, \subseteq)$ is an invariant strong inductive set, $n \in \mathbb{N}$.*

**Example 7.**

- *Let $X$ be an invariant set. The function $f : X \to \wp_{fin}(A)$ defined by $f(x) = supp(x)$ for all $x \in X$ is an equivariant $T$-fuzzy set over $X$. This is because $(\wp_{fin}(A), \star, \subseteq)$ is an invariant strong inductive set according to Theorem 23 and, for all $\pi \in S_A$, we have $supp(\pi \cdot x) = \pi(supp(x)) = \pi \star supp(x)$.*
- *Let $(X, \cdot)$ be an invariant set which does not contain an infinite uniformly supported subset. According to Theorem 23, $(\wp_{fin}(X), \star, \subseteq)$ is an invariant, strong inductive set. Let $FAS(X) = \{f : X \to [0,1] \mid FZS(X, f) \text{ is finite}\}$. Since $[0,1]$ is a trivial invariant complete lattice, according to Theorem 10(2), every function $f \in FAS(X)$ is finitely supported. As in Example 3(2), for all $\pi \in S_A$, we have $FZS(X, \pi\tilde{\star}f) = \pi \star FZS(X, f)$ for all $f \in FAS(X)$, and so $FAS(X)$ is an invariant set. The equivariant function $\psi$ between the invariant set $FAS(X)$ and the invariant set $(\wp_{fin}(X), \star)$ defined by $\psi(f) = FZS(X, f)$ for all $f \in FAS(X)$ is a $T$-fuzzy set over $FAS(X)$.*
- *Let $(X, \cdot)$ be an invariant set which does not contain an infinite uniformly supported subset. On $FAS(X)$ we define the relation $\sim$ by: $f \sim g$ if and only if $FZS(X, f) = FZS(X, g)$. Then, according to Corollary 3, since equivariant isomorphisms of monoids are also equivariant functions, we know that there is an equivariant function $\varphi$ between the invariant set $FAS(X)/\sim$ and the invariant set $(\wp_{fin}(X), \star)$ defined by $\varphi([f]) = FZS(X, f)$ for all $f \in FAS(X)$, where by $[f]$ we denoted the family of functions from $X$ to $[0,1]$ having the same algebraic support as $f$. Thus, $\varphi$ is a $T$-fuzzy set over $FAS(X)/\sim$.*

From Theorem 20, Theorem 23, Corollary 10, Corollary 11 and Theorem 22, the following property of $T$-fuzzy sets can be presented.

**Theorem 24.** *Let $(U, \diamond)$ be an invariant set.*

1. *Let $T$ be an invariant set such that $T$ does not contain a uniformly supported, infinite subset. The family of all $\wp_{fin}(T)$-fuzzy sets over the invariant set $U$ is an invariant strong inductive set with the order relation $\leq$ defined by $f \leq g$ if and only if $f(x) \subseteq g(x)$ for all $x \in U$.*
2. *Let $(T, \cdot)$ be an invariant set such that $T$ does not contain a uniformly supported, infinite subset. For each $n \in \mathbb{N}$, the family of all $\wp_{fin}(T_{fs}^{A^n})$-fuzzy sets over the invariant set $U$ is*

*an invariant strong inductive set with the order relation $\leq$ defined by $f \leq g$ if and only if $f(x) \subseteq g(x)$ for all $x \in U$.*

3. *Let $(T, \cdot)$ be an invariant set such that $T$ does not contain a uniformly supported, infinite subset. For each $n \in \mathbb{N}$, the family of all $\wp_{fin}(T_{fs}^{\wp_n(A)})$-fuzzy sets over the invariant set $U$ is an invariant strong inductive set with the order relation $\leq$ defined by $f \leq g$ if and only if $f(x) \subseteq g(x)$ for all $x \in U$.*

According to Theorem 20, the following fixed point results can provide properties of finitely supported $T$-fuzzy sets over an invariant set. We chose to present the results in the general case, making them applicable also for other finitely supported structures.

The Bourbaki–Witt theorem is an important fixed-point result in mathematics. Its ZF formulation is used to define recursive data types (e.g., linked lists in domain theory). Other applications can be found in logic or in the theory of computable functions. This theorem is also valid for finitely supported progressive self-functions on invariant sets.

**Theorem 25** (Bourbaki–Witt Theorem for fss). *Let $(T, \cdot, \sqsubseteq)$ be an invariant strong inductive set. Let $f : T \to T$ be a finitely supported function having the additional property that $x \sqsubseteq f(x)$ for all $x \in T$. Then there is $u \in T$ such that $f(u) = u$.*

In terms of $T$-fuzzy sets, this result states that, if $(T, \cdot, \sqsubseteq)$ is an invariant strong inductive set and $f$ is a $T$-fuzzy set over the invariant set $T$ with the additional property that $x \sqsubseteq f(x)$ for all $x \in T$, then $f$ has a fixed point.

**Corollary 13.** *Let $(T, \cdot, \sqsubseteq)$ be an invariant strong inductive set. Let $f : T \to T$ be a finitely supported function having the additional property that $x \sqsubseteq f(x)$ for all $x \in T$. Then for any $y \in T$, there is $u \in T$ such that $f(u) = u$ and $y \sqsubseteq u$.*

If in the statement of Theorem 25 we impose the requirement regarding the existence of least upper bounds for all uniformly supported subsets of an invariant set (instead of for all finitely supported totally ordered subsets of an invariant set), we obtain the following result of Bourbaki–Witt type [6,10].

**Theorem 26.** *Let $(T, \cdot, \sqsubseteq)$ be a non-empty invariant partially ordered set with the property that every uniformly supported subset of $T$ has a least upper bound. Let $f : T \to T$ be a finitely supported function having the additional property that $x \sqsubseteq f(x)$ for all $x \in T$. Then there is $u \in T$ such that $f(u) = u$.*

We proved in [6] that the existence of fixed points for a finitely supported, order-preserving function is possible even in the case when the related function is defined on an invariant strong inductive set (instead on an invariant complete lattice).

**Theorem 27** (Tarski—Extended Theorem for fss). *Let $(T, \cdot, \sqsubseteq)$ be an invariant strong inductive set. Let $f : T \to T$ be a finitely supported, order preserving function having the additional property that there is $x_0 \in T$ such that $x_0 \sqsubseteq f(x_0)$. Then there is $u \in T$ such that $f(u) = u$.*

In terms of $T$-fuzzy sets, this result states that, if $(T, \cdot, \sqsubseteq)$ is an invariant strong inductive set and $f$ is an order-preserving $T$-fuzzy set over the invariant set $T$ having the additional property that $x_0 \in T$ with $x_0 \sqsubseteq f(x_0)$ exists, then $f$ has a fixed point.

From Theorems 20, 25 and 27 we obtain the following fixed point result for $T$-fuzzy sets.

**Theorem 28.** *Let $(U, \diamond)$ be an invariant set and $(T, \cdot, \sqsubseteq)$ an invariant strong inductive set.*

1. *Let $\varphi : T_{fs}^U \to T_{fs}^U$ be a finitely supported function with the property that $f \leq \varphi(f)$ for all $f \in T_{fs}^U$, where $\leq$ is the order relation on the family of all $T$-fuzzy sets over the invariant set*

*$U$ defined by $f_1 \leq f_2$ if and only if $f_1(x) \sqsubseteq f_2(x)$ for all $x \in U$. Then there is $g \in T^U_{fs}$ such that $\varphi(g) = g$.*

2. *Let $\varphi : T^U_{fs} \to T^U_{fs}$ be a finitely supported, order-preserving function with the property that $f_0 \in T^U_{fs}$ exists such that $f_0 \leq \varphi(f_0)$, where $\leq$ is the order relation on the family of all $T$-fuzzy sets over the invariant set $U$ defined by $f_1 \leq f_2$ if and only if $f_1(x) \sqsubseteq f_2(x)$ for all $x \in U$. Then $g \in T^U_{fs}$ is with $f_0 \sqsubseteq g$ such that $\varphi(g) = g$.*

In ZF, the following two fixed point theorems (known as the Tarski–Kantorovitch theorem and Scott theorem, respectively) have applications in domain theory, in formal semantics of programming languages, in the theory of iterated function systems and in abstract interpretation. We adequately reformulate them for finitely supported sets.

**Theorem 29** (Tarski–Kantorovitch Theorem for fss). *Let $(T, \cdot, \sqsubseteq)$ be an invariant partially ordered set and $f : T \to T$ a finitely supported c-continuous function. Assume that $x_0 \in T$, having the following properties:*

- *$x_0 \sqsubseteq f(x_0)$;*
- *Every finitely supported countable chain in $\uparrow_{x_0} = \{x \in T \mid x_0 \sqsubseteq x\}$ has a least upper bound in $T$.*

*Then $f$ has a fixed point $u = \underset{n\in\mathbb{N}}{\sqcup} f^n(x_0)$ with the property that $supp(u) \subseteq supp(f) \cup supp(x_0)$.*

**Corollary 14** (Scott Theorem for fss). *Let $(T, \cdot, \sqsubseteq, 0)$ be an invariant, partially ordered set with a least element $0$ and with the additional property that any finitely supported countable ascending chain in $T$ has a least upper bound. Every finitely supported c-continuous function $f : T \to T$ has a least fixed point $u = \underset{n\in\mathbb{N}}{\sqcup} f^n(0)$ with the property that $supp(u) \subseteq supp(f)$.*

**Corollary 15.** *Let $(T, \cdot, \sqsubseteq, 0)$ be an invariant strong inductive set with a least element $0$. Every finitely supported c-continuous function $f : T \to T$ has a least fixed point $u = \underset{n\in\mathbb{N}}{\sqcup} f^n(0)$ with the property that $supp(u) \subseteq supp(f)$.*

From Corollary 15 we conclude that if $(T, \cdot, \sqsubseteq, 0)$ is an invariant strong inductive set with a least element $0$ and $f$ is an $c$-continuous $T$-fuzzy set over the invariant set $T$, then $\underset{n\in\mathbb{N}}{\sqcup} f^n(0)$ is the least fixed point of $f$.

Theorem 29 was generalised in [10] to the following result.

**Theorem 30.** *Let $(T, \cdot, \sqsubseteq)$ be an invariant partially ordered set with the property that every uniformly supported subset has a least upper bound. If $f : T \to T$ is a finitely supported c-continuous function having the additional property that $x_0 \in T$ and $k \in \mathbb{N}^*$ such that $x_0 \sqsubseteq f^k(x_0)$, then $\underset{n\in\mathbb{N}}{\sqcup} f^n(x_0)$ is a fixed point of $f$.*

**Proposition 7.** *Let $(T, \cdot, \sqsubseteq)$ be an invariant partially ordered set containing no uniformly supported, infinite subset and $f : T \to T$ a finitely supported, order-preserving function over $T$.*

- *If the set $X = \{x \in T \mid x \sqsubseteq f(x)\}$ is non-empty and totally ordered, then $f$ has the greatest fixed point defined as $\mathrm{gfp}(f) = \sqcup X$.*
- *If the set $X' = \{x \in T \mid f(x) \sqsubseteq x\}$ is non-empty and totally ordered, then $f$ has the least fixed point defined as $\mathrm{lfp}(f) = \sqcap X'$.*

*In either of the above cases, $f$ only has many finitely fixed points that form a finitely supported complete lattice.*

We presented above examples of invariant partially ordered sets that do not contain uniformly supported, infinite subsets. For these sets, some fixed point properties hold.

**Theorem 31.** *Let $(T, \cdot, \sqsubseteq)$ be an invariant partially ordered set that does not contain a uniformly supported, infinite subset. Let $f : T \to T$ be a finitely supported function having the additional property that $x \sqsubseteq f(x)$ for all $x \in T$. Then for each $x \in T$ $n \in \mathbb{N}$ exists, such that $f^k(x)$ is a fixed point of $f$ for all $k \geq n$.*

**Theorem 32.** *Let $(T, \cdot, \sqsubseteq)$ be an invariant, partially ordered set that does not contain a uniformly supported, infinite subset. Let $f : T \to T$ be a finitely supported, order-preserving function having the additional property that there is $x_0 \in T$ such that $x_0 \sqsubseteq f(x_0)$. Then there is $n \in \mathbb{N}$ such that $f^k(x_0)$ is a fixed point of $f$ for all $k \geq n$.*

From Theorems 22, 23, 31 and 32, we obtain the following corollaries.

**Corollary 16.** *Let $(T, \cdot)$ be an invariant set such that $T$ does not contain a uniformly supported, infinite subset. Let $f : \wp_{fin}(T) \to \wp_{fin}(T)$ be a $\wp_{fin}(T)$-fuzzy set over the invariant set $\wp_{fin}(T)$ and let $T_0 \in \wp_{fin}(T)$ such that $T_0 \subseteq f(T_0)$. If $f$ is order-preserving or progressive (i.e., $f$ has the property that $Y \subseteq f(Y)$ for all $Y \in \wp_{fin}(T)$), then $n \in \mathbb{N}$ exists, such that $f^k(T_0)$ is a fixed point of $f$ for all $k \geq n$.*

**Corollary 17.** *Let $(T, \cdot)$ be an invariant set such that $T$ does not contain a uniformly supported, infinite subset. Let $f$ be a $\wp_{fin}(T_{fs}^{A^n})$-fuzzy set over the invariant set $\wp_{fin}(T_{fs}^{A^n})$ having the additional property that $f$ is a progressive function. Then $T_0 \in \wp_{fin}(T_{fs}^{A^n})$ such that $f(T_0) = T_0$.*

**Corollary 18.** *Let $(T, \cdot)$ be an invariant set such that $T$ does not contain a uniformly supported, infinite subset. Let $f$ be a $\wp_{fin}(T_{fs}^{A^n})$-fuzzy set over the invariant set $\wp_{fin}(T_{fs}^{A^n})$ which is order-preserving. Then a least $T_0 \in \wp_{fin}(T_{fs}^{A^n})$ supported by $supp(f)$ such that $f(T_0) = T_0$.*

**Corollary 19.** *Let $(T, \cdot)$ be an invariant set such that $T$ does not contain a uniformly supported, infinite subset. Let $f$ be a $\wp_{fin}(T_{fs}^{\wp_n(A)})$-fuzzy set over the invariant set $\wp_{fin}(T_{fs}^{\wp_n(A)})$ having the additional property that $f$ is a progressive function. Then $T_0 \in \wp_{fin}(T_{fs}^{\wp_n(A)})$ such that $f(T_0) = T_0$.*

**Corollary 20.** *Let $(T, \cdot)$ be an invariant set such that $T$ does not contain a uniformly supported, infinite subset. Let $f$ be a $\wp_{fin}(T_{fs}^{\wp_n(A)})$-fuzzy set over the invariant set $\wp_{fin}(T_{fs}^{\wp_n(A)})$ which is order-preserving. Then there is a least $T_0 \in \wp_{fin}(T_{fs}^{\wp_n(A)})$ supported by $supp(f)$ such that $f(T_0) = T_0$.*

For a particular class of $T$-fuzzy sets, i.e., for those $\wp_{fin}(A)$-fuzzy sets over the invariant set $\wp_{fin}(A)$ (which are actually finitely supported self-functions defined on the finite powerset of atoms) that satisfy some additional conditions such as injectivity, surjectivity, monotony or progressivity, we were able to prove stronger fixed point properties than in the general case; we mention some of them here.

**Proposition 8.** *Let $f$ be a $\wp_{fin}(A)$-fuzzy set over the invariant set $\wp_{fin}(A)$ which is strictly order-preserving (i.e., $f$ has the property that $U \subsetneq V$ implies $f(U) \subsetneq f(V)$). Then we have $Z \setminus supp(f) = f(Z \setminus supp(f))$ for all $Z \in \wp_{fin}(A)$.*

**Proposition 9.** *Let $f$ be a $\wp_{fin}(A)$-fuzzy set over the invariant set $\wp_{fin}(A)$ with the property that $Y \subseteq f(Y)$ for all $Y \in \wp_{fin}(A)$. There are infinitefixed points of $f$, namely, those finite subsets of $A$ containing all the elements of $supp(f)$.*

**Proposition 10.** *Let $f$ be a $\wp_{fin}(A)$-fuzzy set over the invariant set $\wp_{fin}(A)$ which is injective. For each $Y \in \wp_{fin}(A)$ we have $Y \setminus supp(f) \neq \emptyset$ if and only if $f(Y) \setminus supp(f) \neq \emptyset$. Furthermore, $Y \setminus supp(f) = f(Y) \setminus supp(f)$.*

**Proposition 11.** *Let $f$ be a $\wp_{fin}(A)$-fuzzy set over the invariant set $\wp_{fin}(A)$ which is surjective. For each $Y \in \wp_{fin}(A)$ we have $Y \setminus supp(f) \neq \emptyset$ if and only if $f(Y) \setminus supp(f) \neq \emptyset$. Furthermore, $Y \setminus supp(f) = f(Y) \setminus supp(f)$.*

**Proposition 12.** *Let $f$ be a $\wp_{fin}(A)$-fuzzy set over the invariant set $\wp_{fin}(A)$ having the properties that $f(Y) \subseteq Y$ for all $Y \in \wp_{fin}(A)$ and $f(Y) \neq \emptyset$ for all $Y \neq \emptyset$. Then $f(Z) = Z$ for all $Z \in \wp_{fin}(A)$ with $Z \cap supp(f) = \emptyset$.*

From Theorems 20 and 14 we obtain the following fixed point result for $T$-fuzzy sets.

**Theorem 33.** *Let $(U, \diamond)$ be an invariant set and $(T, \cdot, \sqsubseteq)$ an invariant, strong inductive set with a least element 0. Let $\varphi : T^U_{fs} \to T^U_{fs}$ be a finitely supported, c-continuous function defined on the family of all T-fuzzy sets over the invariant set U. Then a least $g \in T^U_{fs}$ with the property that $\varphi(g) = g$. Furthermore, $g = \bigvee_{n \in \mathbb{N}} \varphi^n(0_U)$, whereby $\vee$ we denoted the least upper bounds in $T^U_{fs}$ with respect to the relation $\leq$ defined by $f_1 \leq f_2$ if and only if $f_1(x) \sqsubseteq f_2(x)$ for all $x \in U$, and $0_U : U \to T$, $0_U(x) = 0$ for all $x \in U$.*

## 8. Conclusions

This article represents an overview of the properties of $L$-fuzzy sets and $T$-fuzzy sets over possibly infinite universes, properties presented in a discrete manner by involving the notion of finite support. We presented a relationship between the algebraic support and the finite support of an ($L$-)fuzzy set over an invariant set. We translated several concepts from the framework of classical ZF fuzzy sets (such as $\alpha - cut$, operations with fuzzy sets, fuzzy extension principles, fuzzy subgroups) into the framework of finitely supported structures, and proved the consistency of their related results in the new framework of finitely supported structures.

Several fixed-point theorems for partially ordered sets (that can be particularly applied to the families of $L$-fuzzy sets and $T$-fuzzy sets over invariant sets) are adequately reformulated in the framework of finitely supported sets; they can also be generalised by imposing requirements only for uniformly supported subsets. Also presented are other fixed point properties for functions defined on invariant sets containing no uniformly supported, infinite subsets. Specific properties of self-functions defined on finite powersets are presented as corollaries of some general results. We presented even stronger fixed-point properties for order preserving, injective, surjective or progressive self-functions defined on the finite powerset of atoms. We introduced and described lattices and inductive sets in the framework of finitely supported structures. We connected the concept of $L$-fuzzy set with the concept of invariant complete lattice, and the concept of $T$-fuzzy set with the concept of invariant strong inductive set. Some particular invariant complete lattices were studied. We mentioned the finitely supported subsets of an invariant set, the finitely supported functions from an invariant set to an invariant complete lattice (i.e., the finitely supported $L$-fuzzy sets with $L$ being an invariant complete lattice) and the finitely supported (fuzzy) subgroups of an invariant group. For these particular invariant complete lattices, the theorems presented in this article can provide new properties. We also presented some examples of invariant strong inductive sets, such as the finite powerset of a set containing no uniformly supported, infinite subset. For the finitely supported self-functions on invariant strong inductive sets, some fixed point properties are mentioned. The related fixed-point properties (presented in the general case) lead to applications in the theory of $L$-fuzzy sets and $T$-fuzzy sets over invariant sets (e.g., Theorems 15, 28 and 33). According to Examples 3 and 7, the functions which associate with any classical fuzzy set on an invariant set means its algebraic support or its finite support are fss $L$-fuzzy sets, and in some cases, fss $T$-fuzzy sets. In this way, we can discretely model the infinite classical fuzzy sets over invariant sets in terms of finite supports or algebraic supports using the properties of fss $L$-fuzzy sets or fss $T$-fuzzy sets, respectively.

## 9. Future Research

We mention below some future work directions.

- Finitely supported monoids can be used to describe automata and languages over infinite alphabets. A relaxed notion of 'finite' called 'orbit finite' is defined; it means 'having a finite number of orbits (equivalence classes) under a certain group action' [15]. A future goal is to describe and study finitely supported $M$-fuzzy sets, where $M$ is a finitely supported monoid (similarly to finitely supported $T$-fuzzy sets) and finitely supported fuzzy submonoids (similarly to finitely supported fuzzy sugbroups). For these fuzzy structures, we would provide embedding theorems, isomorphism properties, universality theorems and applications in automata theory and programming languages.
- The study of fixed points is important since they can encode recursion or model inductive reasoning. Other applications can be found in the theory of computable functions, in logic, in abstract interpretation to prove the existence of least fixed points for specific mappings (defined on chain complete sets of properties) modelling the transitions between properties of programming languages, in formal semantics of programming languages and in the theory of iterated function systems. A fixed-point induction technique in the framework of finitely supported structures could be presented, to prove even stronger properties than those that would lead to usual replacement of 'non-atomic structure' with 'atomic, finitely supported structure' in a related ZF result. For example, a fixed-point theorem of Knaster–Tarski type claims that a finitely supported, monotone self-function defined on a finitely supported partially ordered set having the property that any finitely supported subset has a least upper bound is valid in fss if we require the existence of least upper bounds only for uniformly supported subsets, and not for all finitely supported subsets of the domain of the related function.
- We intend to present some examples of apparently large sets (such as finite powersets or functions spaces) that satisfy some Dedekind-finiteness properties and for which the fss fixed-point properties can provide a certain form of stability. We particularly mention $\wp_{fin}(X)$, $\wp_{fin}(X_{fs}^{A^{\leq n}})$, $\wp_{fin}(X_{fs}^{\wp_{\leq n}(A)})$ that are proved to be fss Dedekind finite whenever $X$ is a finitely supported Dedekind finite set (i.e., whenever $X$ has the property that every finitely supported injection $f : X \to X$ is also surjective). Many other pair-wise, non-equivalent forms of infinity such as Levy infinity, Tarski infinity, Kuratowski infinity, Mostowski infinity, ascending infinity, etc. can be defined and compared; for functions on sets satisfying these forms of infinity, new calculability and stability properties could be presented.
- Uncertainty is an inherent property of all living systems. P systems are models used in membrane computing inspired by the behaviour of living cells [16]. There have been a few defined fuzzy P systems: fuzzy cell-like P systems and fuzzy reasoning spiking neural P systems. Fuzzy aspects have been used to handle the uncertainty in the number of copies of the reactants, imperfectness of objects in membranes and approximate copies of reactants used in reactions. A possible future work is to continue the existing development by introducing fss $L$-fuzzy sets in membrane computing, and studying them together with the natural finiteness properties.

**Author Contributions:** All authors contributed equally to this work. All authors have read and agreed to the published version of the manuscript.

**Funding:** This research received no external funding.

**Conflicts of Interest:** The authors declare no conflict of interest.

## References


1. Zadeh, L.A. Fuzzy sets. *Inf. Control* **1965**, *8*, 338–353. [CrossRef]
2. Zimmermann, H.J. *Fuzzy Set Theory and Its Applications*; Springer: Dordrecht, The Netherlands, 2001.
3. Barwise, J. *Admissible Sets and Structures: An Approach to Definability Theory*; Perspectives in Math. Logic; Springer: Berlin/Heidelberg, Germany, 1975; Volume 7.
4. Pitts, A.M. *Nominal Sets Names and Symmetry in Computer Science*; Cambridge University Press: Cambridge, UK, 2013.
5. Alexandru, A.; Ciobanu, G. *Finitely Supported Mathematics: An Introduction*; Springer: Cham, Switzerland, 2016.
6. Alexandru, A.; Ciobanu, G. *Foundations of Finitely Supported Structures: A Set Theoretical Viewpoint*; Springer: Cham, Switzerland, 2020.
7. Alexandru, A.; Ciobanu, G. Properties of the atoms in finitely supported structures. *Arch. Math. Logic* **2020**, *59*, 229–256. [CrossRef]
8. Alexandru, A.; Ciobanu, G. Fuzzy sets within finitely supported mathematics. *Fuzzy Sets Syst.* **2018**, *339*, 119–133. [CrossRef]
9. Alexandru, A.; Ciobanu, G. Fixed point results for finitely supported algebraic structures. *Fuzzy Sets Syst.* **2020**, *397*, 1–27. [CrossRef]
10. Alexandru, A.; Ciobanu, G. Uniformly supported sets and fixed points properties. *Carpath. J. Math.* **2020**, *36*, 351–364. [CrossRef]
11. Alexandru, A.; Ciobanu, G. Abstract interpretations in the framework of invariant sets. *Fundam. Inf.* **2016**, *144*, 1–22. [CrossRef]
12. Alexandru, A.; Ciobanu, G. Mathematics of multisets in the Fraenkel-Mostowski framework. *Bull. Math. Soc. Sci. Math. Roumanie* **2015**, *58*, 3–18.
13. Rosenfeld, A. Fuzzy groups. *J. Math. Anal. Appl.* **1971**, *35*, 512–517. [CrossRef]
14. Mordeson, J.N.; Bhutan, K.R.; Rosenfeld, A. *Fuzzy Group Theory*; Studies in Fuzziness and Soft Computing 182; Springer: Berlin/Heidelberg, Germany, 2005.
15. Bojanczyk, M.; Klin, B.; Lasota, S. Automata with group actions. In Proceedings of the 26th Symposium on Logic in Computer Science, Toronto, ON, Canada, 21–24 June 2011; pp. 355–364.
16. Păun, G.; Rozenberg, G.; Salomaa, A. (Eds.) *Handbook of Membrane Computing*; Oxford University Press: Oxford, UK, 2010.

mathematics

MDPI

Article

# Artificial Intelligence Based Modelling of Adsorption Water Desalination System

**Hesham Alhumade [1,2,*], Hegazy Rezk [3,4], Abdulrahim A. Al-Zahrani [1], Sharif F. Zaman [1] and Ahmed Askalany [5]**

1 Chemical and Materials Engineering Department, Faculty of Engineering, King Abdulaziz University, Jeddah 21589, Saudi Arabia; azahrani@kau.edu.sa (A.A.A.-Z.); sfzaman@kau.edu.sa (S.F.Z.)
2 Center of Excellence in Desalination Technology, King Abdulaziz University, Jeddah 21589, Saudi Arabia
3 College of Engineering at Wadi Addawaser, Prince Sattam Bin Abdulaziz University, Al-Kharj 11911, Saudi Arabia; hegazy.hussien@mu.edu.eg
4 Electrical Engineering Department, Faculty of Engineering, Minia University, 61517 Minia, Egypt
5 Mechanical Engineering Department, Faculty of Industrial Education, Sohag University, Sohag 82524, Egypt; ahmed_askalany3@yahoo.com
* Correspondence: halhumade@kau.edu.sa

**Abstract:** The main target of this research work is to model the output performance of adsorption water desalination system (AWDS) in terms of switching and cycle time using artificial intelligence. The output performance of the ADC system is expressed by the specific daily water production (SDWP), the coefficient of performance (COP), and specific cooling power (SCP). A robust Adaptive Network-based Fuzzy Inference System (ANFIS) model of SDWP, COP, and SCP was built using the measured data. To demonstrate the superiority of the suggested ANFIS model, the model results were compared with those achieved by Analysis of Variance (ANOVA) based on the maximum coefficient of determination and minimum error between measured and estimated data in addition to the mean square error (MSE). Applying ANOVA, the average coefficient-of-determination values were 0.8872 and 0.8223, respectively, for training and testing. These values are increased to 1.0 and 0.9673, respectively, for training and testing thanks to ANFIS based modeling. In addition, ANFIS modelling decreased the RMSE value of all datasets by 83% compared with ANOVA. In sum, the main findings confirmed the superiority of ANFIS modeling of the output performance of adsorption water desalination system compared with ANOVA.

**Keywords:** artificial intelligence; modelling based ANFIS; adsorption desalination

**Citation:** Alhumade, H.; Rezk, H.; Al-Zahrani, A.A.; Zaman, S.F.; Askalany, A. Artificial Intelligence Based Modelling of Adsorption Water Desalination System. *Mathematics* **2021**, *9*, 1674. https://doi.org/10.3390/math9141674

Academic Editor: Michael Voskoglou

Received: 16 June 2021
Accepted: 10 July 2021
Published: 16 July 2021



## 1. Introduction

It has become evident that the energy and water dilemmas are escalating day by day to the point where they threaten the lives of many people and fuel conflicts between societies [1]. And that the two problems have become so intertwined that they cannot be separated, because if you want to save water, you must consume the scarce energy in the first place. It is also noticeable that the areas that suffer from severe water shortages are mostly desert areas and have untapped solar energy available [2]. Therefore, researchers in this field should think about how to link the parties to this puzzle and use that wasted energy to provide the required water, especially in light of the availability of seawater and wells that are not suitable for drinking [3]. The researchers have improved in this way and made a great effort until they presented many ideas that can be built upon and developed. Among these ideas was the idea to use the phenomenon of adsorption to desalinate water with solar energy or waste energy. This idea went through many stages until prototypes were built and work was carried out to improve its performance in several ways, including improving the properties of the used materials. One of these methods is to improve the properties of the used materials, and also to improve the working cycle and try to make it work efficiently at lower temperatures, which was a great challenge. The strength of adsorption desalination systems is that they are suitable for being run with solar energy or waste energy, but they have a weak point, which is their low productivity compared to widespread systems such as reverse osmosis systems (RO) [4]. Hence, researches were conducted theoretically and experimentally on improving and promoting the system performance. Different ways of researches had been followed like presenting new adsorbents and merging this technology with others like RO. Among these research ways were attempts to improve the performance by controlling cycle time and heating and cooling times.

Heat recovery has been presented by Ng et al. [5] between evaporator and condenser to produce a SDWP of about 27 $m^3$/ton per day of silica gel every day. Also, heat recovery between the adsorption beds has been examined by Ma et al. [6] reaching SDWP 4.69 $m^3$/ton of silica gel and COP of 0.766. Four adsorption beds connected to two evaporators have been studied theoretically by Ali et al. [7]. SDWP of 8.84 $m^3$/ton/day has been reached in this study at a COP of 0.52 employing 95 °C driving temperature. At 80 °C driving temperature, the AD cycle showed its ability to be work as shown by Olkis et al. [8] experimentally where the studied AD system produced a SDWP of 10.9 $m^3$/ton/day. The effect of the temperatures of the condenser and the evaporator on the AD productivity has been studied numerically by Youssef et al. [9] to optimize the system performance. SDWP of 10 $m^3$/ton/day has been recorded at a condenser temperature of 10 °C and an evaporator temperature of 30 °C.

Using heat and mass recovery, the performance of a 2-bed AD system has been studied by Amirfakhraei et al. [10]. The theoretical study showed that the cycle could reach a SDWP of 9.58 $m^3$/ton of silica gel daily by using heating and cooling temperatures of 95 °C and 30 °C, respectively. Zhang et al. [11] presented an experimental optimization study for an AD system by operating conditions. Desalinated water of 191.3 kg/h has been reached at a heating temperature of 80 °C. Another optimization study has been presented by Rezk et al. [12] using a model optimization method to declare the optimal operating conditions of solar-driven AD cycle. The optimal cycle could produce a SDWP of about 6.9 $m^3$/ton silica gel/day, a SCP of 191 W/kg, and a COP of 0.961.

Based on the above, it becomes clear to us that many efforts are being made to improve and raise the performance of the adsorption desalination systems; however, these efforts must be continued. It is worth mentioning here that there is something that can be added in this area if the operating cycle is well examined and modeled to extract the highest possible productivity without changing the construction or the content of the system, only by reaching the best-operating conditions. The model has been presented here employing artificial intelligence (AI) based on an experimental dataset to save money, effort, and time. Artificial intelligence tools conquered many fields of applications. Systems modeling is one of these fields [13,14]. The choice of the AI modeling tool depends mainly on the nature of the application and the available dataset. Fuzzy Logic (FL) and Artificial Neural Networks (ANN) are two popular and efficient AI techniques. Therefore, the main target of this research work is to model the output performance of adsorption water desalination system (AWDS) in terms of switching and cycle time using an Adaptive Network-based Fuzzy Inference System (ANFIS). The output performance of the SADC system is expressed by the specific daily water production (SDWP), the coefficient of performance (COP) and specific cooling power (SCP). A robust ANFIS model of SDWP, COP, and SCP was built using the measured data. To demonstrate the superiority of the suggested ANFIS model, the model results were compared with those achieved by Analysis of Variance (ANOVA) based on the maximum coefficient of determination and minimum error between measured and estimated data. AVOVA has been used in several applications such as a bioelectrochemical desalination process [15], biodesalination of Seawater [16] and desalination by reverse osmosis [17]. Therefore, it has been used as a benchmark for the problem under study.

The rest of the paper is organized as follows. Section 2 briefly presents the experimental work. The proposed methodology is explained in Section 3. Section 4 presents the discussion of the obtained results. Finally, the main finding and future work are outlined in Section 5.

## 2. Experimental Work

An adsorption water desalination system has been built of two adsorption beds containing metal-organic framework MOF (CPO-27(Ni)). The system has a condenser and evaporator as shown in Figure 1. The system works in a semi-continuous mode where Bed1 and Bed 2 work interchangeably. When Bed1 is in adsorption mode, Bed2 is in the desorption mode. During the adsorption mode, the bed is cooled down by using cold water and during the desorption mode, the bed has been heated up using hot water. This system has been presented elsewhere and it is still under review. The condenser and the evaporator are connected to perform internal heat recovery which improves the performance of the system by raising the produced desalinated water. The operating conditions such as driving temperature, cooling temperature, switching time, and cycle time have been studied.

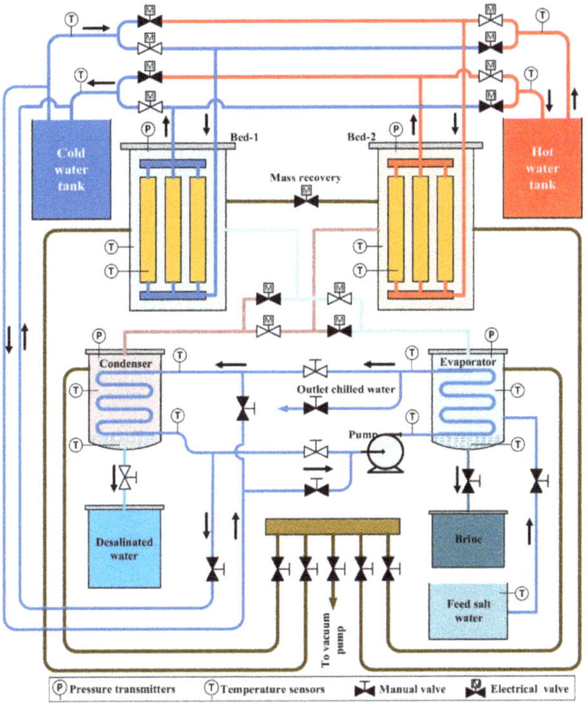


**Figure 1.** Schematic diagram of the adsorption water desalination system.

## 3. Methodology

In this work, both ANOVA and ANFIS are considered. ANOVA is nominated in many experimental applications [15–17]. ANOVA mathematically quantifies the relationship between the output and inputs based on linear regression. The significance of every factor is considered based on its significant value, $p$-value. For input to be significant, its $p$-value must be lower than 5%.

ANFIS is featured with the advantages of FL and ANN. Modeling by ANFIS involves three phases. The first phase consists of fuzzifying the values of the input signals. This is performed by mapping the crisp values, through their corresponding membership functions (MFs), to fuzzy values. This phase is called fuzzification. These MFs can take either Gaussian or triangular shapes, depending on the application. The fuzzified inputs are logically processed to obtain the fuzzy output according to the pre-set fuzzy rules [14,18]. The second phase is the fuzzy inference system. In this phase, the fuzzy output is then passed to the defuzzification in order to return the output to its crisp values. There are two common methods of fuzzification: center of gravity and weighted average. Unlike mathematical modeling, which formulates the relation between the inputs and the corresponding output as a mathematical equation, fuzzy modeling describes this relationship via a set of IF (premise) THEN (consequence) rules. These rules are generally created based on experimental datasets. An example of a fuzzy rule statement, for a two-input single-output system, simply takes the form:

IF a is MFa and b is MFb, THEN c is MFc,

where MFa and MFb denote the fuzzy membership functions of the two inputs a and b, respectively, and MFc is the fuzzy membership function of the output c.

## 4. Results and Discussion

### *4.1. Modelling Based ANOVA*

Tables 1–3 present the ANOVA results for modeling COP, SCP, and SDWP, respectively. Considering Table 1, for the first output response, the Model F-value of 60.33 implies the model is significant. There is only a 0.01% chance that an F-value this large could occur due to noise. The $p$-values less than 0.05 indicate model terms are significant. In this case $A$, $A^2$ are significant model terms. Values greater than 0.1 indicate the model terms are not significant. The following relation in terms of actual factors can be used to make predictions about the first output response.

$$X_{COP} = -0.15017 + 0.00249A + 0.00071B + 9.132 \times 10^{-07} A \times B - 2.336 \times 10^{-06} A^2 - 0.000018B^2 \quad (1)$$

**Table 1.** ANOVA table for first output response (COP).

| Source | Sum of Squares | df | Mean Square | F-Value | $p$-Value | |
|---|---|---|---|---|---|---|
| Model | 0.0706 | 5 | 0.0141 | 60.33 | <0.0001 | significant |
| A | 0.0558 | 1 | 0.0558 | 238.62 | <0.0001 | |
| B | 0.0005 | 1 | 0.0005 | 1.98 | 0.1932 | |
| AB | 0.0000 | 1 | 0.0000 | 0.1686 | 0.6910 | |
| $A^2$ | 0.0253 | 1 | 0.0253 | 108.04 | <0.0001 | |
| $B^2$ | 0.0001 | 1 | 0.0001 | 0.2279 | 0.6445 | |
| Residual | 0.0021 | 9 | 0.0002 | | | |
| Cor Total | 0.0727 | 14 | | | | |

**Table 2.** ANOVA table for second output response (SCP).

| Source | Sum of Squares | df | Mean Square | F-Value | $p$-Value | |
|---|---|---|---|---|---|---|
| Model | 6463.77 | 5 | 1292.75 | 12.94 | 0.0007 | significant |
| A | 524.94 | 1 | 524.94 | 5.25 | 0.0476 | |
| B | 735.63 | 1 | 735.63 | 7.36 | 0.0239 | |
| AB | 65.40 | 1 | 65.40 | 0.6546 | 0.4393 | |
| $A^2$ | 4458.14 | 1 | 4458.14 | 44.62 | <0.0001 | |
| $B^2$ | 6.53 | 1 | 6.53 | 0.0654 | 0.8039 | |
| Residual | 899.16 | 9 | 99.91 | | | |
| Cor Total | 7362.93 | 14 | | | | |

**Table 3.** ANOVA table for third output response (SDWP).

| Source | Sum of Squares | df | Mean Square | F-Value | *p*-Value | |
|---|---|---|---|---|---|---|
| Model | 42.93 | 5 | 8.59 | 25.35 | <0.0001 | significant |
| A | 15.84 | 1 | 15.84 | 46.76 | <0.0001 | |
| B | 0.9132 | 1 | 0.9132 | 2.70 | 0.1350 | |
| AB | 0.0012 | 1 | 0.0012 | 0.0035 | 0.9543 | |
| $A^2$ | 18.49 | 1 | 18.49 | 54.59 | <0.0001 | |
| $B^2$ | 0.0106 | 1 | 0.0106 | 0.0314 | 0.8632 | |
| Residual | 3.05 | 9 | 0.3388 | | | |
| Cor Total | 45.98 | 14 | | | | |

Regarding the second output response, the AVOVA data shown in Table 2, the Model F-value of 12.94 indicates the model is significant. There is only a 0.07% chance that an F-value this large could occur due to noise. The *p*-values less than 0.05 show model terms are significant. In this case, $A$, $B$, $A^2$ are significant model terms. Values greater than 0.1000 indicate the model terms are not significant. The next relation in terms of actual factors can be used to make predictions about the second output response.

$$X_{SCP} = 70.54652 + 0.894124A - 0.641050B - 0.001176A \times B - 0.000981A^2 + 0.006222B^2 \quad (2)$$

Regarding the third output response, the AVOVA data shown in Table 3, the Model F-value of 25.35 indicates the model is significant. There is only a 0.01% chance that an F-value this large could occur due to noise. The *p*-values less than 0.05 indicate model terms are significant. In this case $A$, $A^2$ are significant model terms. Values greater than 0.1 indicate the model terms are not significant. The next relation in terms of actual factors can be used to make predictions about the second output response.

$$X_{SDWP} = 0.054238 + 0.049419A - 0.001139B + 4.98791 \times 10^{-06} A \times B - 0.000063A^2 - 0.000251B^2 \quad (3)$$

The statical analysis of different ANOVA models are presented in Table 4. For COP model, the predicted $R^2$ of 0.9399 is in reasonable agreement with the adjusted $R^2$ of 0.9549; i.e., the difference is less than 0.2. The value of RMSE is 0.6552. The adequate precision measures the signal to noise ratio. It compares the range of the predicted values at the design points to the average prediction error. Ratios greater than 4 indicate adequate model discrimination [19]. For COP model, the ratio of 20.228 indicates an adequate signal. This model can be used to navigate the design space.

**Table 4.** Statical analysis of the ANOVA model.

| First ANOVA Model of COP | | | | Second ANOVA Model of SCP | | | |
|---|---|---|---|---|---|---|---|
| **Std. Dev.** | **0.0153** | **$R^2$** | **0.9710** | **Std. Dev.** | **10.00** | **$R^2$** | **0.8779** |
| MSE | 0.4293 | Adjusted $R^2$ | 0.9549 | MSE | 213.93 | Adjusted $R^2$ | 0.8100 |
| C.V.% | 3.56 | Predicted $R^2$ | 0.9399 | C.V.% | 4.67 | Predicted $R^2$ | 0.6760 |
| RMSE | 0.6552 | Adeq Precision | 20.2281 | RMSE | 14.6263 | Adeq Precision | 11.6747 |
| Third ANOVA model of SDWP | | | | | | | |
| | Std. Dev. | 0.582 | | $R^2$ | | 0.9337 | |
| | MSE | 7.88 | | Adjusted $R^2$ | | 0.8969 | |
| | C.V.% | 7.38 | | Predicted $R^2$ | | 0.8512 | |
| | RMSE | 2.8071 | | Adeq Precision | | 13.8258 | |

For SCP, the predicted $R^2$ of 0.6760 is in reasonable agreement with the adjusted $R^2$ of 0.8100. The value of RMSE is 14.6263. Also, the adequate precision (11.675) is greater than 4 is desirable that indicates an adequate signal. This model can be used to navigate the design space. Finally, for SDWP, the predicted $R^2$ of 0.8512 is in reasonable agreement with the adjusted $R^2$ of 0.8969. The value of RMSE is 2.8071. The signal to noise of 13.826 indicates an adequate signal. This model can be used to navigate the design space. In sum, the average value of RMSE for the three models is 8.607.

Figure 2 illustrates the 3-D surface plots for the three output response models. The red-filled circles show the response values above the predicted values, and the pink-filled circles show the values below the predicted one. The yellow curvature lines show the high output performances. As demonstrated in Figure 3, the actual values are the measured response, and the predicted response is determined by using the approximate function values to evaluate the model. Most of the results of both models are close to the diagonal, indicating an excellent correlation between the expected and the actual values.

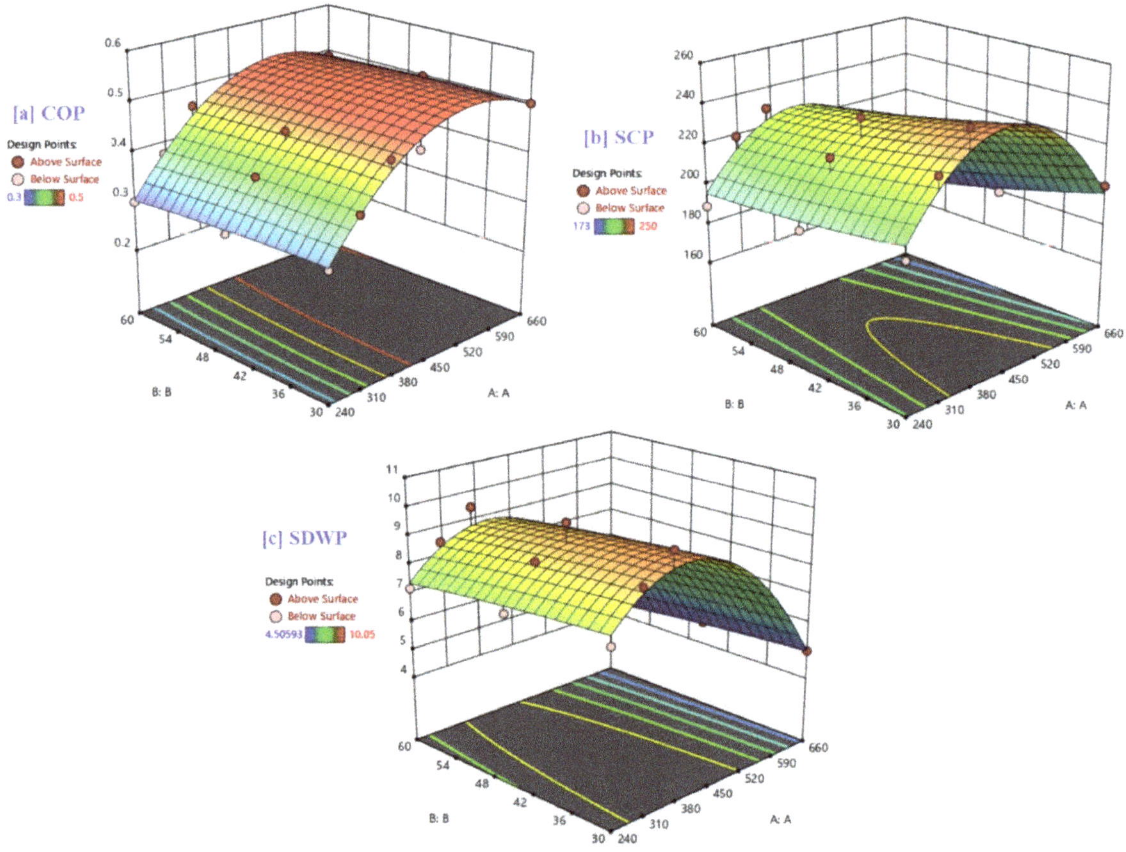


**Figure 2.** 3-D response surface plots for output responses (**a**) COP; (**b**) SCP, and (**c**) SDWP.

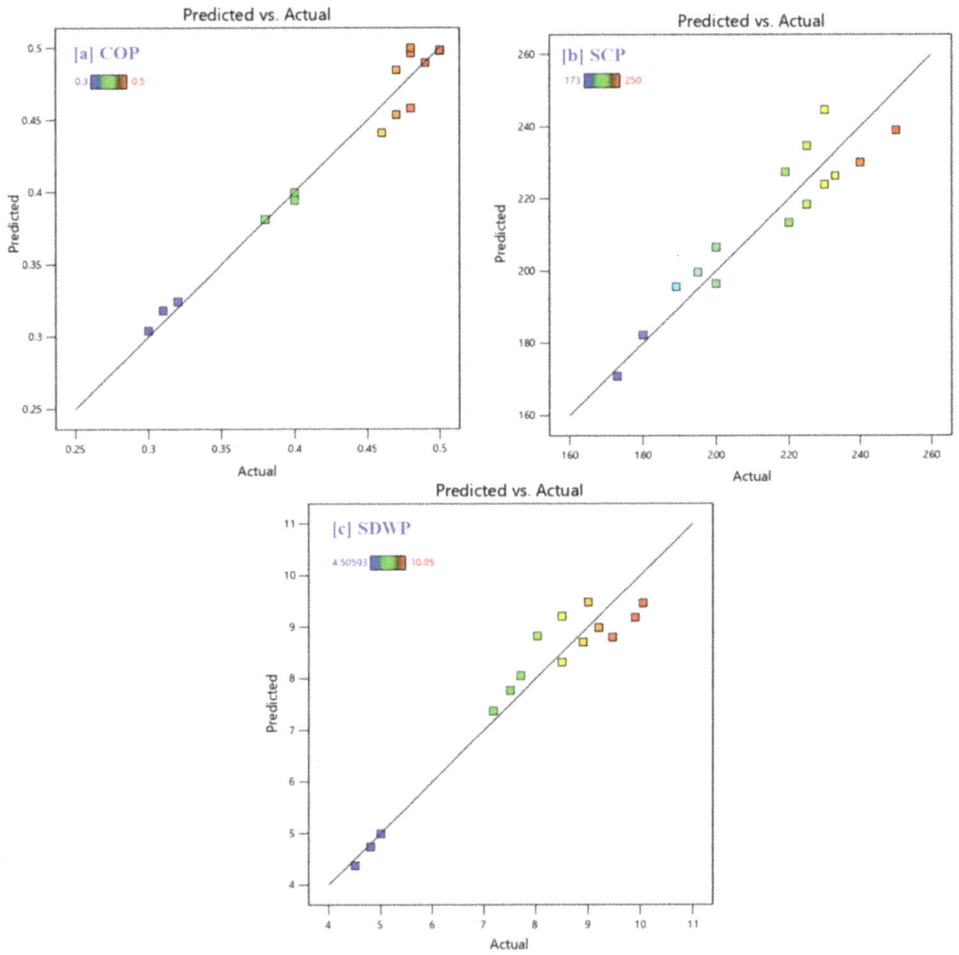


**Figure 3.** Comparison of the predicted values of output response (**a**) COP; (**b**) SCP, and (**c**) SDWP.

### *4.2. Modelling Based ANFIS*

Based on the experimental dataset, a model based ANFIS has been created to simulate the output performance of AWDS in terms of switching and cycle time. Three ANFIS models respectively for COP, SCP, and SDWP are created. The experimental dataset (15 experiments) was divided into two parts with a ratio of 70:30 for the training (10 experiments) and testing (5 experiments) stages. In the current model modeling, the Takagi-Sugeno ANFIS is adopted because of its ability to track the nonlinear data precisely. Also, the subtractive clustering method has been applied to build the fuzzy rules. The number of fuzzy rules is 9, 9, and 10, respectively, for COP, SCP, and SDWP. The minimum, maximum, and Wavg were used for the implication, aggregation, and defuzzification methods, respectively. Additionally, the inputs' MFs were chosen as the Gaussian shape for the fuzzification procedure, and only 10 epochs were found to be enough for the training. The MSE, RMSE, and the coefficient of determination ($R^2$) between the measured data and estimated data are used to evaluate the accuracy of the ANFIS model. The statistical assessment of the ANFIS models of COP, SCP, and SDWP is presented in Table 5. Applying ANOVA, the average coefficient-of-determination values were 0.8872 and 0.8223, respectively, for training and testing. These values are increased to 1.0 and 0.9673, respectively, for training and testing thanks to ANFIS based modeling. In addition, RMSE values using ANFIS were 0.00117, 2.5201 and 1.46 respectively, for training, testing and all datasets. Compared with ANOVA, the average RMSE value based on all datasets is decreased from 8.607 (ANOVA) to 1.46 by using ANFIS. This means ANFIS modelling decreased the RMSE of all datasets by 83% compared with ANOVA.

**Table 5.** Statistical assessment of the ANFIS models of COP, SCP, and SDWP.

| **MSE** | | | **RMSE** | | | **Coefficient of Determination ($R^2$)** | | |
|---|---|---|---|---|---|---|---|---|
| **Train** | **Test** | **All** | **Train** | **Test** | **All** | **Train** | **Test** | **All** |
| | | | | First fuzzy model of **COP** | | | | |
| $2.71 \times 10^{-10}$ | 0.0002 | 0.0001 | 0 | 0.0154 | 0.0089 | 1 | 0.9751 | 0.9867 |
| | | | | Second fuzzy model of **SCP** | | | | |
| $1.14 \times 10^{-5}$ | 49.0493 | 16.3498 | 0.0034 | 7.0035 | 4.0435 | 1 | 0.9916 | 0.9791 |
| | | | | Third fuzzy model of **SDWP** | | | | |
| $5.29 \times 10^{-9}$ | 0.2934 | 0.0978 | 0.0001 | 0.5416 | 0.3127 | 1 | 0.9352 | 0.9712 |
| | | | | Average | | | | |
| $3.80 \times 10^{-6}$ | $1.64 \times 10^{1}$ | **5.480** | 0.000117 | 2.52 | 1.46 | 1 | 0.967 | 0.979 |

Figure 4 demonstrates the fuzzification phase in establishing an ANFIS model, in which the ANFIS model has two inputs (switching and cycle time) and one output for each model. The 3-D surface plot of the three output responses with varying input is shown in Figure 5. Whereas Figure 6. illustrates the input and the output membership functions of the fuzzy system for COP, SCP, and SDWP.

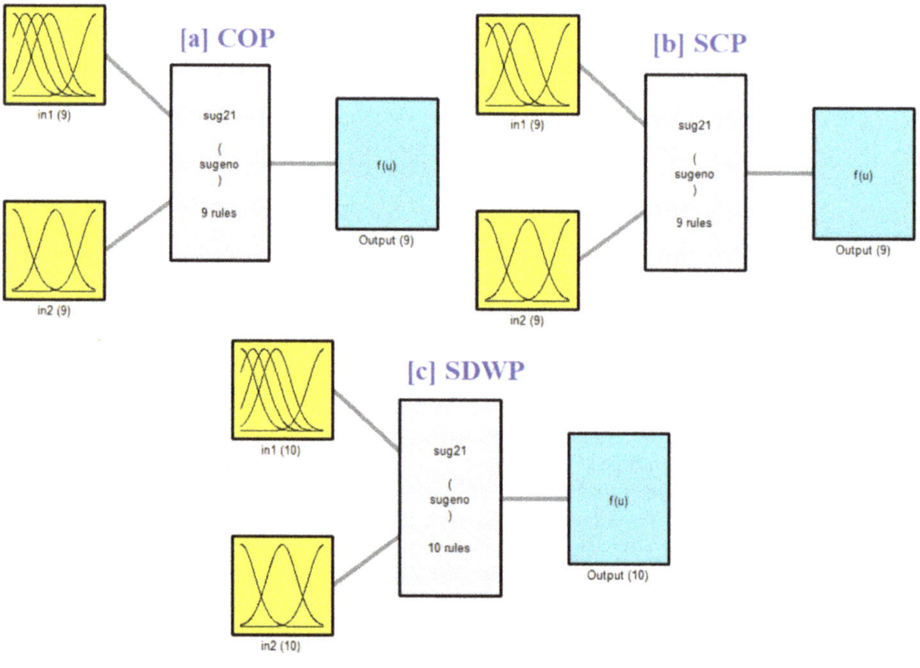


**Figure 4.** Inputs and outputs of ANFIS model (**a**) COP; (**b**) SCP, and (**c**) SDWP.

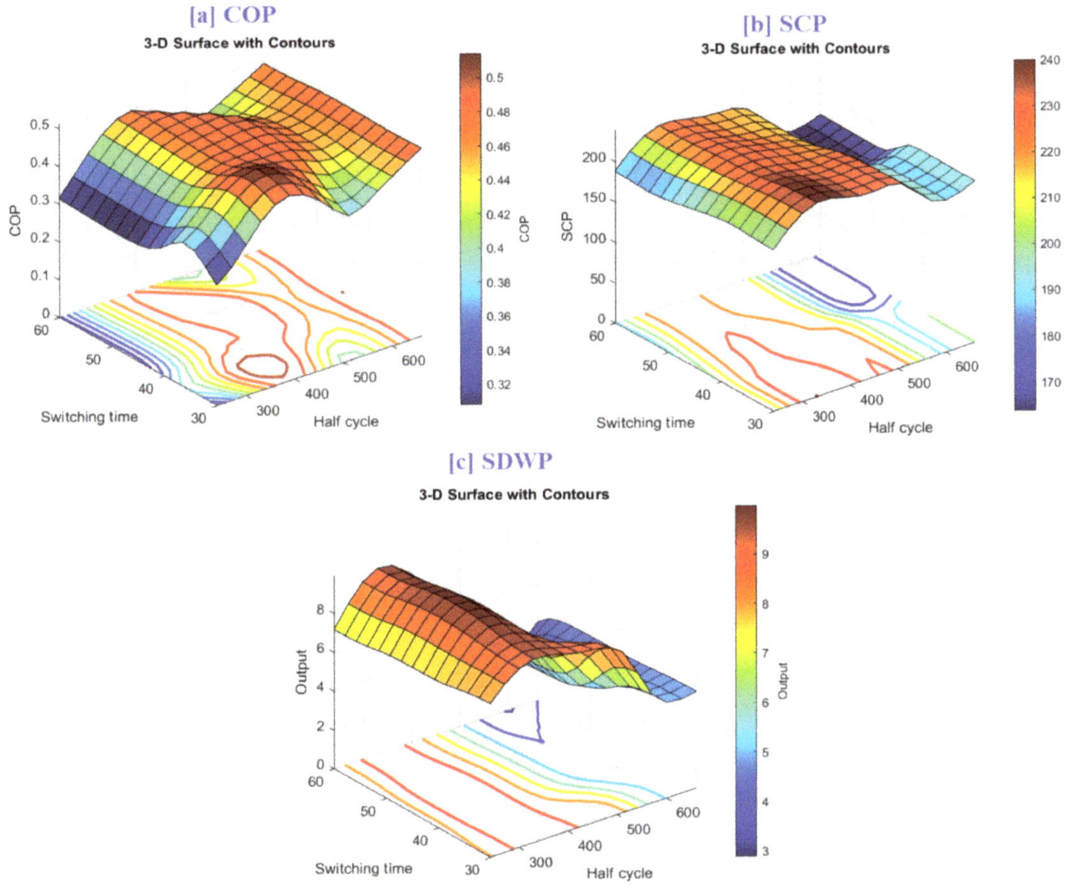


**Figure 5.** 3-D surface plot of output performance changing values related to input parameters (**a**) COP; (**b**) SCP, and (**c**) SDWP.

The main goal of this research and this technique is that we can study many cases and study the effect of changing many factors at the same time, which saves a lot of time and effort. It would be difficult to study these factors together in a laboratory, so this study explores what we can do and summarizes many practical experiments to bring us to the best-operating conditions as shown in Figure 5. The figure shows the effect of cycle time and switching time on the performance parameters of the systems which are COP, SCP, and SDWP. The COP could be reached up to 0.5 by increasing the cycle time were changing the switching time has a marginally effect on the COP. By longing the cycle time more amount of pure water is generated which raises the COP.

The effect of changing cycle time is very clear when dealing with SDWP as shown in Figure 5c. Increasing half-cycle time up to 300 s has a good impact on the SDWP however behind this limit, the SDWP shows a drop. This indicates that however, the desalinated water amount may increase by increasing cycle time, the benefits of this are dissipated because of the decrease in the number of cycles that can be performed per day with the increase in cycle time.

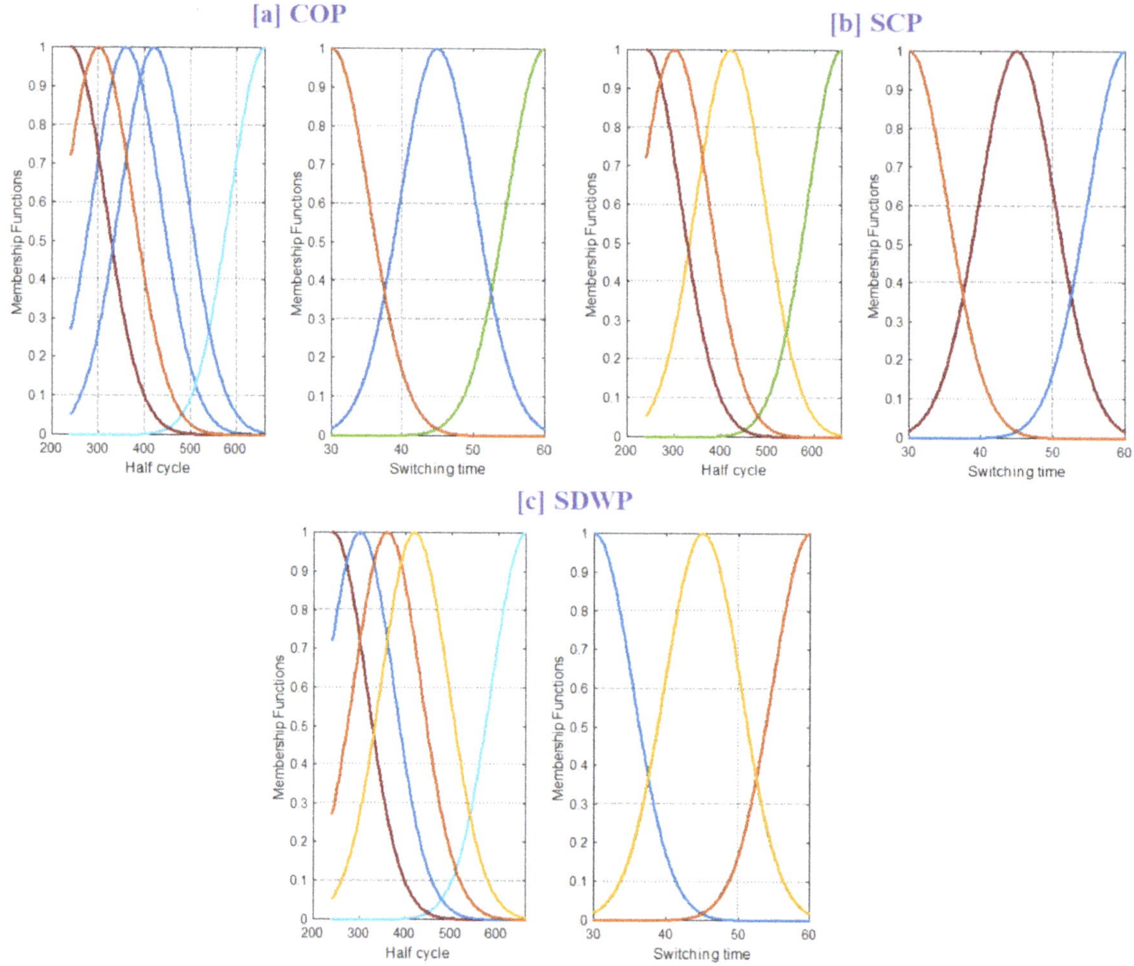


**Figure 6.** Inputs membership functions of the fuzzy system (**a**) COP; (**b**) SCP, and (**c**) SDWP.

A significant measure to assess the model's prediction precision is to plot these predictions versus their corresponding targets. Consequently, Figure 7 presents the accuracy plots of COP, SCP, and SDWP models. Considering Figure 7, it is clear that for COP, SCP, and SDWP models, the training and the testing predictions are distributed closer to the one hundred percent accuracy line that matches with the obtained high values of the $R^2$.

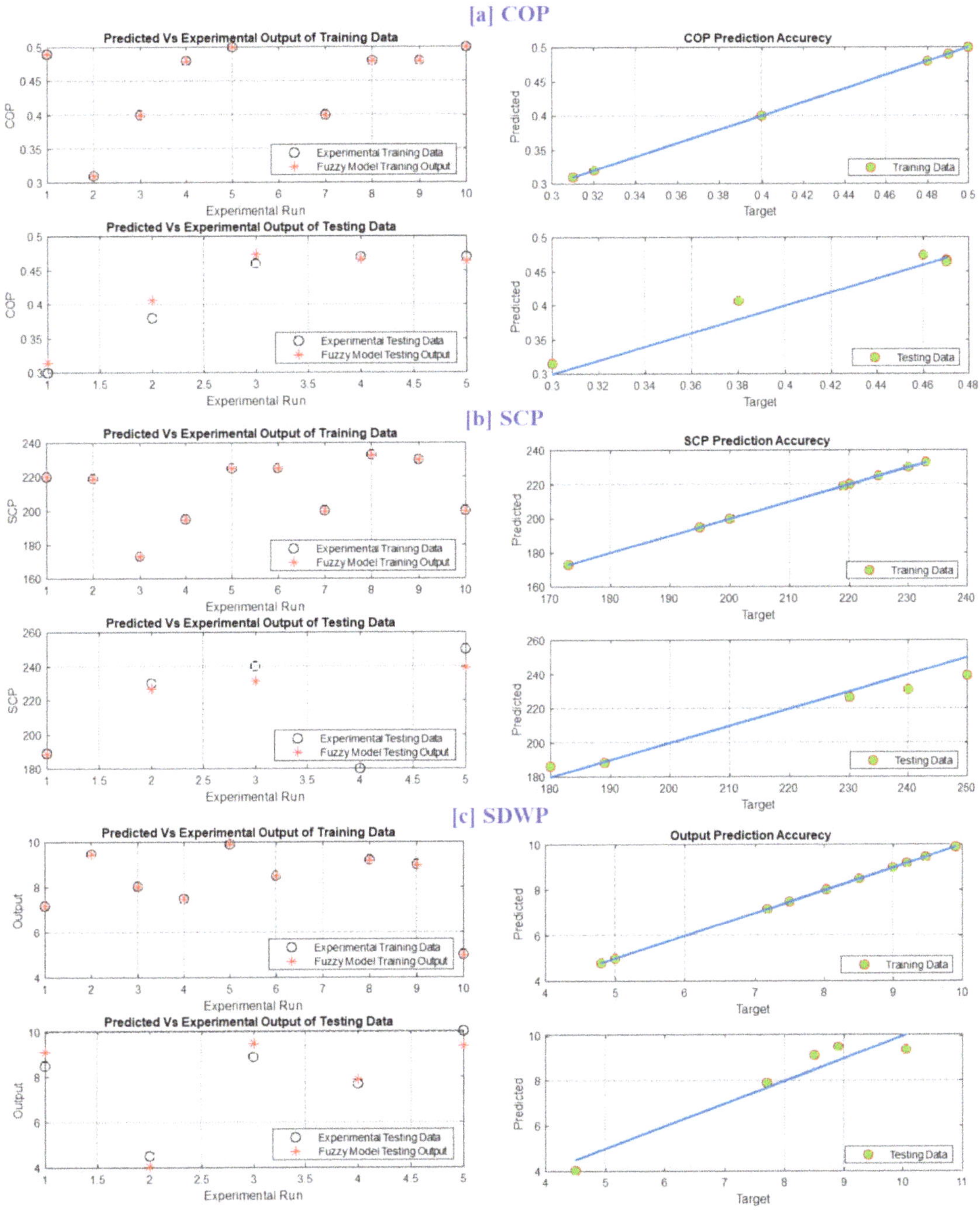


**Figure 7.** Comparison of the training and testing data (**a**) COP; (**b**) SCP, and (**c**) SDWP.

## 5. Conclusions

Based on the measured data of adsorption water desalination system (AWDS), an accurate model has been created to simulate the specific daily water production (SDWP), the coefficient of performance (COP), and specific cooling power (SCP) in terms of switching and cycle time. Adaptive Network-based Fuzzy Inference System (ANFIS) is selected to do this job because it is the beneficial product of the combination between fuzzy logic and artificial neural networks. For comparison purposes, an ANOVA model was also created. Applying ANOVA, the average coefficient-of-determination values were 0.8872 and 0.8223, respectively, for training and testing. These values are increased to 1.0 and 0.9673, respectively, for training and testing thanks to ANFIS based modeling. In addition, RMSE values using ANFIS were 0.00117, 2.5201 and 1.46 respectively, for training, testing and all data. Compared with ANOVA, the average RMSE value based on all datasets is decreased from 8.607 (ANOVA) to 1.46 by using ANFIS. This means ANFIS modelling decreased the RMSE of all datasets by 83% compared with ANOVA. In sum, the main findings confirmed the superiority of ANFIS modeling of the output performance of AWDS compared with ANOVA. In future work, modern optimization algorithms will be integrated with ANFIS modeling to identify the best operating parameters AWDS.

**Author Contributions:** Data curation, H.A. and A.A.; Formal analysis, A.A.A.-Z. and A.A.; Funding acquisition, H.A.; Investigation, H.A., H.R. and S.F.Z.; Methodology, H.R. and A.A.; Resources, A.A.A.-Z.; Software, S.F.Z.; Supervision, H.A.; Visualization, A.A.; Writing—original draft, H.A., H.R. and A.A. All authors have read and agreed to the published version of the manuscript.

**Funding:** This research received funding from the Institutional Fund Projects under grant no. (IFPRC-038-135-2020) supported by the Ministry of Education and King Abdulaziz University, Deanship of Scientific Research (DSR), Jeddah, Saudi Arabia.

**Institutional Review Board Statement:** Not applicable.

**Informed Consent Statement:** Not applicable.

**Data Availability Statement:** No new data were created or analyzed in this study.

**Acknowledgments:** This research work was funded by the Institutional Fund Projects under grant no. (IFPRC-038-135-2020). Therefore, authors gratefully acknowledge technical and financial support from the Ministry of Education and King Abdulaziz University, DSR, Jeddah, Saudi Arabia.

**Conflicts of Interest:** The authors declare no conflict of interest.

## References


1. Rashid, K. Design, Economics, and Real-Time Optimization of a Solar/Natural Gas Hybrid Power Plant. Doctoral Dissertation, The University of Utah, Salt Lake City, UT, USA, 2019.
2. Rashid, K.; Safdarnejad, S.M.; Powell, K.M. Dynamic simulation, control, and performance evaluation of a synergistic solar and natural gas hybrid power plant. *Energy Convers. Manag.* **2019**, *179*, 270–285. [CrossRef]
3. Rezk, H.; Al-Dhaifallah, M.; Hassan, Y.B.; Ziedan, H.A. Optimization and energy management of hybrid photovoltaic-diesel-battery system to pump and desalinate water at isolated regions. *IEEE Access* **2020**, *8*, 102512–102529. [CrossRef]
4. Rezk, H.; Sayed, E.T.; Al-Dhaifallah, M.; Obaid, M.; Abou Hashema, M.; Abdelkareem, M.A.; Olabi, A.G. Fuel cell as an effective energy storage in reverse osmosis desalination plant powered by photovoltaic system. *Energy* **2019**, *175*, 423–433. [CrossRef]
5. Ng, K.C.; Thu, K.; Hideharu, Y.; Saha, B.B.; Chakraborty, A.; Al-Ghasham, T. Apparatus and Method for Improved Desalination. Patent SG 170810, 2009.
6. Ma, H.; Zhang, J.; Liu, C.; Lin, X.; Sun, Y. Experimental investigation on an adsorption desalination system with heat and mass recovery between adsorber and desorber beds. *Desalination* **2018**, *446*, 42–50. [CrossRef]
7. Ali, S.M.; Haider, P.; Sidhu, D.S.; Chakraborty, A. Thermally driven adsorption cooling and desalination employing multi-bed dual-evaporator system. *Appl. Therm. Eng.* **2016**, *106*, 1136–1147. [CrossRef]
8. Olkis, C.; Brandani, S.; Santori, G. Cycle and performance analysis of a small-scale adsorption heat transformer for desalination and cooling applications. *Chem. Eng. J.* **2019**, *378*, 122104. [CrossRef]
9. Youssef, P.; Mahmoud, S.M.; Al-Dadah, R. Numerical simulation of combined adsorption desalination and cooling cycles with integrated evaporator/condenser. *Desalination* **2016**, *392*, 14–24. [CrossRef]
10. Amirfakhraei, T.Z.; Khorshidi, J. Performance improvement of adsorption desalination system by applying mass and heat recovery processes. *Therm. Sci. Eng. Progress* **2020**, *18*, 100516. [CrossRef]
11. Zhang, H.; Ma, H.; Liu, S.; Wang, H.; Sun, Y.; Qi, D. Investigation on the operating characteristics of a pilot-scale adsorption desalination system. *Desalination* **2020**, *473*, 114196. [CrossRef]
12. Rezk, H.; Alsaman, A.S.; Aldhaifallah, M.; Askalany, A.; Abdelkareem, M.A.; Nassef, A.M. Identifying optimal operating conditions of solar-driven silica gel based adsorption desalination cooling system via modern optimization. *Sol. Energy* **2019**, *181*, 475–489. [CrossRef]

13. Tanveer, W.H.; Rezk, H.; Nassef, A.; Abdelkareem, M.A.; Kolosz, B.; Karuppasamy, K.; Aslam, J.; Gilani, S.O. Improving fuel cell performance via optimal parameters identification through fuzzy logic based-modeling and optimization. *Energy* **2020**, *204*, 117976. [CrossRef]
14. Yousef, B.A.A.; Rezk, H.; Abdelkareem, M.A.; Olabi, A.G.; Nassef, A.M. Fuzzy modeling and particle swarm optimization for determining the optimal operating parameters to enhance the bio-methanol production from sugar cane bagasse. *Int. J. Energy Res.* **2020**, *44*, 8964–8973. [CrossRef]
15. Stuart-Dahl, S.; Martinez-Guerra, E.; Kokabian, B.; Gude, V.G.; Smith, R.; Brooks, J. Resource recovery from low strength wastewater in a bioelectrochemical desalination process. *Eng. Life Sci.* **2019**, *20*, 54–66. [CrossRef] [PubMed]
16. Sani, F.S.; Azmi, A.S.; Ali, F.; Mel, M. Interactive effect of temperature, pH and light intensity on biodesalination of seawater by synechococcus sp. PCC 7002 and on the cyanobacteria growth. *J. Adv. Res. Fluid Mech. Therm. Sci.* **2018**, *52*, 85–93.
17. Khayet, M.; Cojocaru, C.; Essalhi, M. Artificial neural network modeling and response surface methodology of desalination by reverse osmosis. *J. Membr. Sci.* **2011**, *368*, 202–214. [CrossRef]
18. Rahman, S.M.A.; Nassef, A.M.; Rezk, H.; Assad, M.E.H.; Hoque, E. Experimental investigations and modeling of vacuum oven process using several semi-empirical models and a fuzzy model of cocoa beans. *Heat Mass Transf.* **2021**, *57*, 175–188. [CrossRef]
19. Dritsa, V.; Rigas, F.; Doulia, D.; Avramides, E.J.; Hatzianestis, I. Optimization of Culture Conditions for the Biodegradation of Lindane by the Polypore Fungus Ganoderma australe. *Water Air Soil Pollut.* **2009**, *204*, 19–27. [CrossRef]

*mathematics*

MDPI

*Article*

# An Area Coverage Scheme Based on Fuzzy Logic and Shuffled Frog-Leaping Algorithm (SFLA) in Heterogeneous Wireless Sensor Networks

**Amir Masoud Rahmani [1,†], Saqib Ali [2], Mohammad Sadegh Yousefpoor [3], Efat Yousefpoor [3], Rizwan Ali Naqvi [4,†], Kamran Siddique [5,*] and Mehdi Hosseinzadeh [6,*]**

1 Future Technology Research Center, National Yunlin University of Science and Technology, Douliou 64002, Yunlin, Taiwan; rahmania@yuntech.edu.tw
2 Department of Information Systems, College of Economics and Political Science, Sultan Qaboos University, Muscat P.C.123, Oman; saqib@squ.edu.om
3 Department of Computer Engineering, Dezful Branch, Islamic Azad University, Dezful 73210, Iran; ms.yousefpoor@iaud.ac.ir (M.S.Y.); eyousefpoor@iaud.ac.ir (E.Y.)
4 Department of Intelligent Mechatronics Engineering, Sejong University, Seoul 05006, Korea; rizwanali@sejong.ac.kr
5 Department of Information and Communication Technology, Xiamen University Malaysia, Sepang 43900, Malaysia
6 Pattern Recognition and Machine Learning Lab, Gachon University, 1342 Seongnamdaero, Sujeanggu, Seongnam 13120, Korea
* Correspondence: kamran.siddique@xmu.edu.my (K.S.); mehdi@gachon.ac.kr (M.H.)
† Amir Masoud Rahmani and Rizwan Ali Naqvi have contributed equally to this work.

**Citation:** Rahmani, A.M.; Ali, S.; Yousefpoor, M.S.; Yousefpoor, E.; Naqvi, R.A.; Siddique, K.; Hosseinzadeh, M. An Area Coverage Scheme Based on Fuzzy Logic and Shuffled Frog-Leaping Algorithm (SFLA) in Heterogeneous Wireless Sensor Networks. *Mathematics* **2021**, *9*, 2251. https://doi.org/10.3390/math9182251

Academic Editor: Michael Voskoglou

Received: 5 August 2021
Accepted: 31 August 2021
Published: 14 September 2021



**Abstract:** Coverage is a fundamental issue in wireless sensor networks (WSNs). It plays a important role in network efficiency and performance. When sensor nodes are randomly scattered in the network environment, an ON/OFF scheduling mechanism can be designed for these nodes to ensure network coverage and increase the network lifetime. In this paper, we propose an appropriate and optimal area coverage method. The proposed area coverage scheme includes four phases: (1) Calculating the overlap between the sensing ranges of sensor nodes in the network. In this phase, we present a novel, distributed, and efficient method based on the digital matrix so that each sensor node can estimate the overlap between its sensing range and other neighboring nodes. (2) Designing a fuzzy scheduling mechanism. In this phase, an ON/OFF scheduling mechanism is designed using fuzzy logic. In this fuzzy system, if a sensor node has a high energy level, a low distance to the base station, and a low overlap between its sensing range and other neighboring nodes, then this node will be in the ON state for more time. (3) Predicting the node replacement time. In this phase, we seek to provide a suitable method to estimate the death time of sensor nodes and prevent possible holes in the network, and thus the data transmission process is not disturbed. (4) Reconstructing and covering the holes created in the network. In this phase, the goal is to find the best replacement strategy of mobile nodes to maximize the coverage rate and minimize the number of mobile sensor nodes used for covering the hole. For this purpose, we apply the shuffled frog-leaping algorithm (SFLA) and propose an appropriate multi-objective fitness function. To evaluate the performance of the proposed scheme, we simulate it using NS2 simulator and compare our scheme with three methods, including CCM-RL, CCA, and PCLA. The simulation results show that our proposed scheme outperformed the other methods in terms of the average number of active sensor nodes, coverage rate, energy consumption, and network lifetime.

**Keywords:** wireless sensor networks (WSNs); coverage; fuzzy logic; metaheuristic algorithms; Internet of Things (IoT)

## 1. Introduction

Today, wireless sensor networks (WSNs) have been transformed into an attractive research field for many researchers in industry and academia. These networks include a large number of sensor nodes, which are randomly or deterministically deployed in the network environment without any infrastructure [1,2]. Sensor nodes have been tasked to monitor the Region of Interest (RoI).

WSNs are applied in many applications, such as industry [3], agriculture [3], military [4], medicine [3,5], and Internet of Things (IoT) [4]. Today, micro-electro-mechanical systems have grown dramatically. As a result, many low-cost and robust sensor nodes have been produced [6]. Each sensor node is a multi-functional device including a sensing unit, processing unit, memory unit, communication unit, energy unit, and so on [7,8]. They can sense a target or phenomenon that occurs in their sensing range, they then process the data received from the environment, and finally forward their data packets to the base station (BS) in a single-hop or multi-hop manner [9,10].

Sensor nodes have small sensing and communication ranges. Furthermore, they have limited energy resources [11,12]. In WSNs, quality of service (QoS) and resource management are two critical issues that must be addressed. QoS is measured based on connectivity and coverage [13,14]. Thus, appropriate coverage and maintenance of connectivity play a important role in the network performance.

Coverage is defined as the area/point covered or monitored by the sensor nodes deployed in the network area. If an area/point is inside the sensing range of at least one active sensor node; then, it can be said that this area/point have been covered or monitored [15,16]. In general, coverage is classified into several groups according to what exactly is monitored:

- **Area coverage:** In this coverage, the main goal is to cover or monitor the RoI so that any point in this area should be covered [17,18]. See this coverage type in Figure 1. Area coverage is divided into two categories based on the desired application, including partial and full coverage:

  Partial coverage

  In this coverage, the area is partially covered to guarantee the efficient and acceptable coverage degree according to the desired application. In partial coverage, the goal is to cover the $P$ percentage of the area. This coverage type is also called $P$-coverage. Partial coverage can save energy of sensor nodes and increase network lifetime. Moreover, it requires a less number of sensor nodes compared to the full coverage [18]. For example, it is sufficient to achieve 80% area coverage in applications, such as environment monitoring, calculating the environment temperature, and forest fire detection during rainy seasons.

  Full coverage

  When it is necessary to cover the entire area, the full coverage is applied. In the full coverage, any point of RoI should be monitored by at least one sensor node. Full area coverage is very costly because it requires a large number of sensor nodes [19]. In addition, the coverage degree is defined based on the application requirements. In some applications, simple coverage is required, i.e., one sensor node is sufficient to cover each point of RoI. However, in other applications, at least $k$ sensor nodes ($k > 1$) must cover any point of RoI. In this case, the network is fault-tolerant, and, if a sensor node dies, then the network will continue its normal performance with the $k - 1$ sensor nodes; however, this is impossible in simple coverage.
- **Point coverage:** In this coverage, it is sufficient to monitor some points of RoI depending on the application. It has a low-cost network deployment because fewer sensor nodes are used to cover the target points [20,21]. Figure 2 shows the point coverage.
- **Barrier coverage:** In this coverage, the purpose is to create a barrier using sensor nodes deployed in the network. When sensor nodes sense some subversive activ-

ities of attackers at this barrier, they transmit their sensed data to the base station. Barrier coverage is applied in some applications, such as creating infrastructure margins or monitoring important areas, such as country borders, coastlines, battlefield boundaries, and so on [18]. This coverage is shown in Figure 3.

- **Sweep coverage:** In this coverage, some points of RoI must be monitored periodically, i.e., target points are covered at a certain time interval. Therefore, it is better to cover the target points using a minimum number of mobile sensor nodes [19,22]. Sweep coverage should not be done using static sensor nodes because they have weak performance and additional overhead. This coverage is illustrated in Figure 4.

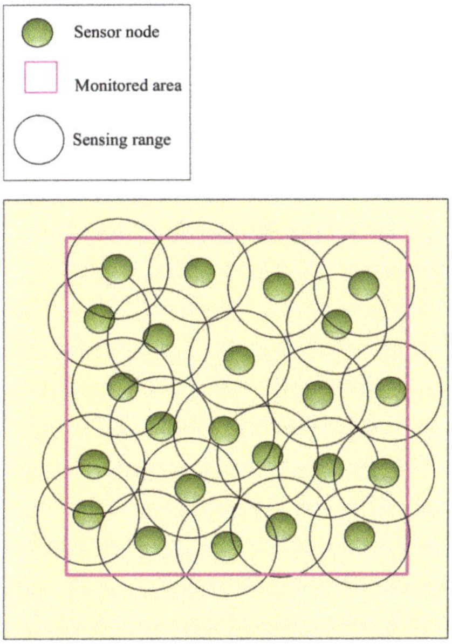


**Figure 1.** Area coverage.

On the other hand, coverage methods are classified into two categories: centralized coverage schemes and distributed (decentralized) coverage schemes. In centralized coverage methods, only the base station is tasked to manage the coverage process in the network. Whereas, in distributed coverage methods, sensor nodes also participate in this process. In large-scale WSNs, distributed coverage schemes are more efficient because they do not require global information of all sensor nodes in the network, and each sensor node manages the coverage process based on local information received from its neighboring nodes. Coverage methods can be categorized into static and dynamic classes.

In static coverage schemes, the best replacement strategy of sensor nodes is first determined in the network so that proper coverage rate is ensured. Then, this strategy is fixed throughout the network lifetime. However, in dynamic coverage methods, this strategy is always not fixed and updated periodically or when an event occurs [23]. Dynamic coverage methods are more suitable for WSNs due to their limited resources, failure of sensor nodes, and establishing holes.

In most engineering and science problems, it is important to find the maximum or minimum value of a function with different variables. In some cases, there are algorithms based on applied analysis, such as linear programming, that can be used to find the global optimum solution. However, in hybrid or discrete optimization problems, there is no efficient algorithm to find the optimum solution. In the real world, optimization problems are very complex, high dimensions, and highly dynamic.

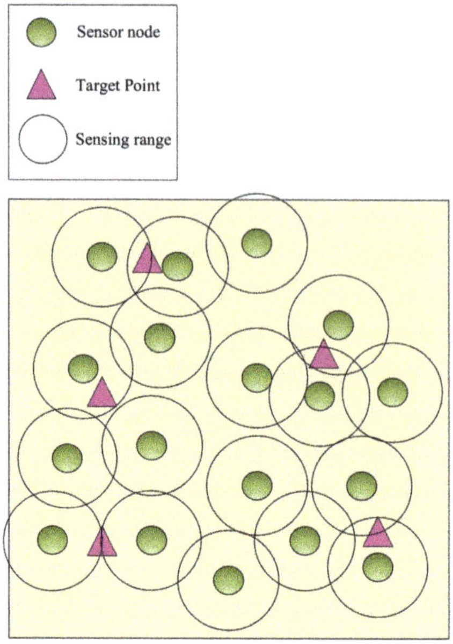


**Figure 2.** Point coverage.

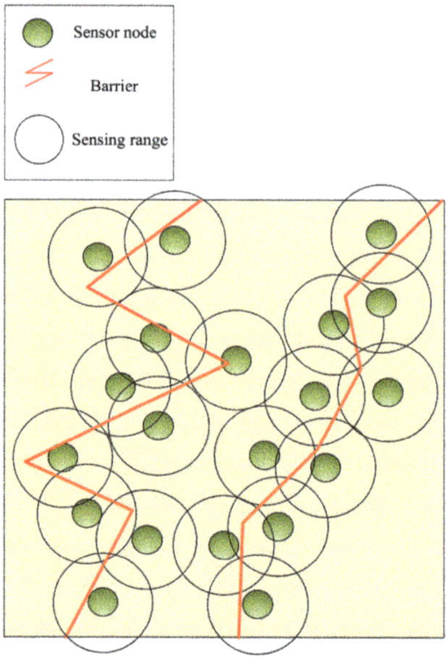


**Figure 3.** Barrier coverage.

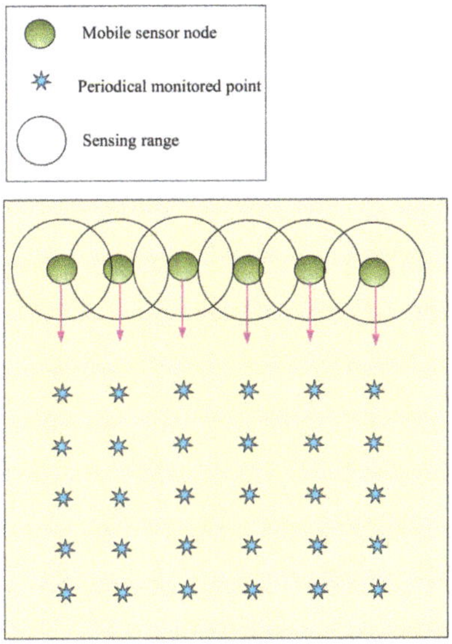


**Figure 4.** Sweep coverage.

As a result, it is necessary to use heuristic or metaheuristic methods as algorithms, such as dynamic programming or divide and conquer, have a lot of computational overhead. Today, the metaheuristic algorithms are dramatically becoming popular because they can find acceptable solutions for NP-Hard and nonlinear optimization problems. Metaheuristic algorithms provide a general framework for solving complex optimization problems [24].

These methods are generally inspired by a natural phenomenon. Today, many biological algorithms have been invented or improved. They have successfully been used to solve hybrid and numerical optimization problems—for example, ant colony optimization (ACO) [25], particle swarm optimization (PSO) [26], artificial bee colony (ABC) algorithm [27], shuffled frog-leaping algorithm (SFLA) [28], and artificial immune system (AIS) [29].

Many studies have been presented to solve the coverage problem in WSNs. Coverage techniques focus on several issues: designing a replacement strategy for sensor nodes in the network environment, designing a scheduling mechanism for sensor nodes, and selecting a subset of nodes for full coverage. We review a number of papers related to the research subject in Section 2 and express their strengths and weaknesses.

Most of these methods do not consider the energy of the sensor nodes in the network. They have a lot of communication overhead, which threatens the network lifetime. Moreover, they are often centralized and static schemes and propose no useful strategy for reconstructing holes created in the network. These problems reduce their scalability and network lifetime. Therefore, it is necessary to design an efficient area coverage method, which schedules the activity of sensor nodes in the network intelligently.

We design an appropriate strategy for reconstructing holes in the network. Furthermore, it is important and critical to calculate the overlap of nodes to select the lowest number of active sensor nodes in the network. However, calculating the overlap between the sensing ranges of sensor nodes is a complicated, time-consuming, and difficult task due to limited resources and low energy of sensor nodes.

In this paper, we present a simple, efficient, and distributed method to calculate the overlap between sensor nodes. The purpose of this paper is to present a suitable area coverage scheme for heterogeneous WSNs, and thus this method can balance the energy consumption of sensor nodes in the network and improve network lifetime. We attempt to increase the coverage quality in the network. The main contributions of the paper are expressed as follows:

- In the first phase, each sensor node estimates the overlap between its sensing range and sensing ranges of neighboring nodes using a distributed method based on geometric mathematics. Calculating the overlap between the sensing range of a sensor node and its neighboring nodes is a complex operation with a lot of computational overhead and high time complexity. In the proposed method, we attempt to reduce computational overhead and introduce a new, efficient and distributed method based on a digital matrix to calculate the overlap.
- In the second phase, the goal is to design an ON/OFF scheduling mechanism based on fuzzy logic. This fuzzy system has three inputs: the overlap between sensing range of a sensor node and sensing ranges of its neighboring nodes, the residual energy, and the distance between a sensor node and BS. The fuzzy system output is the activity time of each sensor node (ON time). In this fuzzy system, if the overlap between the sensing range of a sensor node and sensing ranges of neighboring nodes is low and its energy level is high and the distance between this node and BS is low, then this node stays at the ON state for more time slots.
- In the third phase, we attempt to present a suitable method that predicts the death time of sensor nodes and prevents possible holes in the network, and thus there is no interruption in the data transmission process to the base station.
- In the fourth phase, the goal is to find the best replacement strategy for mobile nodes to maximize the coverage rate and minimize the number of mobile nodes applied for covering holes. For this purpose, we use the shuffled frog-leaping algorithm (SFLA) and present a suitable and multi-objective fitness function.

The rest of paper is organized as follows: In Section 2, some recent studies are reviewed in the coverage field for WSNs. In Section 3, the basic concepts used in the proposed scheme, namely the fuzzy logic and the shuffled frog-leaping algorithm (SFLA), are described briefly. In Section 4, we present the system model in the proposed method. This model includes the network model, energy model, sensing model, and communication model. In Section 5, we define the problem studied in this paper. In Section 6, the proposed scheme is described in detail. In Section 7, the simulation results of the proposed scheme are presented and compared with some coverage methods. Finally, our conclusions are presented in Section 8.

## 2. Related Works

Coverage is one of the most important and fundamental issues in WSNs, because it has a direct effect on the energy consumption of sensor nodes and network lifetime. Generally, coverage is defined as monitoring on the network environment effectively and efficiently. Today, many papers have been published in the coverage field in WSNs. These papers often focus on three concepts: deploying sensor nodes in a predetermined manner, designing a scheduling mechanism, and selecting a subset of sensor nodes for ensuring full coverage. In the following, we briefly introduce some coverage methods .

Sharma et al. [30] suggested the coverage connectivity maintenance based on reinforcement learning (CCM-RL) protocol in wireless sensor networks. The purpose of this method is to achieve the maximum coverage rate, maintain connectivity, and save energy efficiently. In this scheme, the learning algorithm is implemented in each sensor node. This algorithm allows them to automatically learn their optimal activity. The purpose of this algorithm is that only subsets of sensor nodes are activated in each scheduling round to minimize energy consumption, maximize the coverage rate, and maintain network connectivity.

In addition, CCM-RL presents a sensing range customization mechanism for removing coverage redundancy. After executing the learning algorithm, active sensor nodes, which overlap with each other, should customize their sensing range using this mechanism to maintain network resources, such as energy and memory, reduce duplicated data packets, and lower network congestion. CCM-RL is a dynamic and distributed coverage method, that is, the sensor nodes participate in the scheduling process.

As a result, CCM-RL is a scalable scheme. However, CCM-RL schedules sensor nodes based on only two parameters, including distance and coverage rate. It ignores energy parameters in this process. Furthermore, CCM-RL may have a lot of delay. This method does not provide any mechanism for detecting or reconstructing coverage holes in the network.

Yu et al. [31] presented two centralized and distributed protocols based on the coverage contribution area (CCA) concept to solve the $K$-coverage problem in homogeneous wireless sensor networks. The purpose of this method is to achieve $K$-coverage with a minimum number of sensor nodes and improve network lifetime. CCA presents a scheduling process to activate a subset of sensor nodes for covering the RoI. This process is based on two criteria, including energy and distance. After implementing this algorithm, nodes are in two modes, including ON (active) or OFF (inactive).

Yu et al. introduced the centralized $k$-coverage protocol in two dynamic and static modes. However, the dynamic scheme has a higher delay than the static method; but it provides better coverage. In general, the centralized CCA is not scalable. As a result, it is not suitable for the large scale WSN. As the sink node requires global information of all sensor nodes in the network. The distributed CCA is scalable and solves the problem of the centralized CCA method, but it has high communication overhead. CCA presents no detection and reconstruction mechanism for repairing network holes.

Mostafaei et al. [32] offered a partial coverage with learning automata (PCLA) scheme in WSNs. The main purpose of this method is to minimize the number of sensor nodes required for covering RoI and maintain connectivity. PCLA uses the learning automata (LA) for scheduling sensor nodes. This scheme provides a probabilistic framework to select the subset of the sensor nodes to create a backbone to improve the coverage rate and guarantee network connectivity.

PCLA has two phases: (1) The learning phase. In this phase, subsets of sensor nodes are selected to create a backbone in the network so that network connectivity is guaranteed. (2) The partial coverage phase. If the selected subset in the first phase cannot provide a suitable coverage rate of the RoI, additional nodes are added to this subset to satisfy the appropriate coverage level. PCLA is a distributed, dynamic and scalable method. However, it has a lot of communication overhead. Moreover, PCLA does not present any mechanism for detecting and reconstructing network holes.

Hanh et al. [33] proposed an area coverage method based on genetic algorithm (GA) called MIGA in heterogeneous WSNs. MIGA is an improved version of IGA. In this method, a stable and reliable fitness function was presented to evaluate the area coverage approximately.

MIGA has five phases: (1) Individual representation. In this phase, each genotype is divided into $k$ sections corresponding to $k$ sensor types and each section has several genes. (2) Population initialization. In this phase, population initialization is not random. In fact, it is done based on a heuristic algorithm. (3) Genetic operators. In MIGA, two crossover operators are used, namely Laplace crossover ($LX$) and Arithmetic crossover method ($AMXO$). Then, generated individuals are sorted based on location of sensor nodes in the network. (4) Designing the fitness function. In MIGA, an integral-based fitness function has been proposed to evaluate the RoI coverage. (5) VFA Optimization.

When the MIGA algorithm is stopped, the best solution can be improved using Virtual Force Algorithm (VFA) to maximize area coverage. In this phase, the overlapping sensor nodes are slightly spaced apart to reduce their overlap. As a result, each sensor node executes a local search with neighboring nodes to optimize the final solution. MIGA has several advantages: achieving a stable and quality solution and maximizing area coverage.

Furthermore, this method has certain disadvantages: (1) The integral-based fitness function is not comprehensive and cannot cover all different cases that two sensor nodes may overlap with each other. However, this method introduce a new idea for calculating the overlap between different sensor nodes and can be improved. (2) In this MIGA, the authors attempted to reduce the computational overhead, but they achieved little success.

(3) In this method, a centralized area coverage scheme was presented. Therefore, it was not scalable.

Luo et al. [34] introduced the maximum coverage sets scheduling (MCSS) problem in WSNs. The purpose of this scheme is to find the optimal scheduling strategy for coverage sets to maximize the network lifetime. In this method, two algorithms, called greedy-MCSS and MCSSA, were presented to solve this problem. This method has the advantages: (1) acceptable time complexity, (2) appropriate computational complexity, and (3) improving the network lifetime through the proper scheduling of coverage sets.

However, this method also has disadvantages: (1) It is assumed that the coverage sets are predetermined (the coverage set represents a subset of sensor nodes in the network that can cover the entire network). However, it is important to define these sets. However, the authors ignored this problem. (2) Furthermore, it is assumed that the time slots required for the activity of sensor nodes are already known, whereas this is a false hypothesis that can limit the application of this method. (3) The MCSSA algorithm is a centralized method. As a result, it is not scalable and cannot be desirable for large-scale WSNs. (4) The authors only considered the activity time of the sensor nodes for solving the MCSS problem. However, this is an important weakness because other parameters, such as the energy and distance of nodes from each other, are critical.

Benahmed et al. [35] presented an optimal barrier coverage method that minimizes the number of sensor nodes and maximizes the coverage rate in homogeneous WSNs. This method can calculate the minimum number of sensor nodes that cover a 2D area completely. Moreover, a geometric mathematics-based formula was proposed for calculating the coverage value. In this method, the minimum number of sensor nodes was calculated based on the distance and angle between two neighboring nodes that have overlap.

In addition, the authors presented an algorithm to reduce overlap between sensor nodes as much as possible so that appropriate distance between two sensor nodes is obtained based on the optimal number of nodes and the maximum coverage rate. They proposed a mechanism for detecting failed nodes and reconstructing holes created in the network. The most important advantage of this method is the appropriate coverage rate with the minimum number of sensor nodes.

On the other hand, the geometric mathematical model presented in this method is a novel and attractive solution that can be improved. This method takes into account parameters, like the distance and the overlap between the sensor nodes, to determine the coverage rate of the network. This method can be improved by considering more parameters, such as the energy of the sensor nodes.

One of the disadvantages of this scheme is that it applied a reactive mechanism for detecting failed nodes and reconstructing holes in the network, i.e., when a failed node or hole is identified, then this mechanism is executed to repair it. This can disrupt network performance and increase delay in the data transmission process to BS. Therefore, it is better to use predictive methods to detect nodes that may be damaged in the near future.

Saha et al. [36] introduced a suitable and rapid scheme to approximate the area covered in homogeneous WSNs. This approach utilizes digital geometry to approximate a real circle (i.e., sensing range of each sensor node) using a digital circle. The authors argue that their proposed algorithm has less computational complexity and lower time complexity than geometric mathematics-based operations executed on a real circle.

In addition, each digital circle is estimated using two squares: (1) the largest square inside the circle and (2) the smallest square outside the circle. As a result, this method can estimate the area covered by each sensor node with an acceptable error rate and appropriate time complexity. The authors proposed a fast, simple and distributed algorithm, which has low computational overhead, to estimate the total area covered in the network. As a result, it is suitable for energy-limited WSN.

However, the authors added some points to improve the performance of this method: (1) In this method, a suitable scheduling mechanism was not designed to adjust the activity time of nodes. Moreover, it is important to take into account various parameters, such as the node energy for modeling this mechanism. (2) This method ignores a reconstruction and detection mechanism to repair holes created in the network due to the death of some sensor nodes. (3) This method is a static area coverage scheme, whereas, WSNs have a dynamic topology and are more compatible with dynamic schemes.

Binh et al. [37] proposed two nature-based algorithms, including improved cuckoo search (ICS) and chaotic flower pollination algorithm (CFPA), to improve area coverage in heterogeneous WSNs. The purpose of this method is to reduce energy consumption of sensor nodes. This method has several steps, including individual representation, initialization and fitness function, and updating individuals. Refer to [37] for more details.

The proposed fitness function in these algorithms is based on the overlap between sensing range of sensor nodes. Obviously, if the overlap between sensor nodes is reduced, then they can cover a larger area. ICS and CFPA algorithms can reduce computational complexity and generate high quality responses. Another advantage of these algorithms is their simplicity and high convergence speed.

However, these two algorithms also have disadvantages: (1) The fitness function considers only one parameter, namely the overlap between the sensor nodes. However, it can improve with considering more parameters. (2) This method is a static area coverage. It searches for the best replacement strategy for sensor nodes. However, it does not provide a reconstruction and detection mechanism to resolve problems related to death of some sensor nodes and hole establishment in the network.

Binh et al. [38] proposed two meta-heuristic algorithms, namely genetic algorithm (GA) and particle swarm optimization (PSO) to maximize the area coverage in a heterogeneous WSN. It is assumed that network includes a number of obstacles, which block communications between sensor nodes. Therefore, the authors have defined the maximum area coverage problem in a network having obstacles and have proposed two algorithms GA and PSO to solve this problem.

In this method, a novel fitness function was designed based on the overlap between sensing ranges of the sensor nodes with respect to obstacles in the network. The purpose of these algorithms is to reduce the overlap between sensor nodes in the network. Refer to [38] for more details. These algorithms have an important advantage: maximizing the area coverage with acceptable computational overhead.

However, this method also has disadvantages: (1) It considers only one parameter i.e., the overlap for designing fitness function. (2) In this method, the aim is maximum area coverage. However, the maximum network lifetime is also important. If the residual energy of the sensor nodes has been considered in the fitness function, then it can also improve network lifetime. (3) This is a static and centralized area coverage method. Thus, it has low scalability.

Li et al. [39] presented a reasonable mathematical model to solve the weak coverage problem in WSNs. The area coverage algorithm can adjust movement direction of the sensor nodes toward low-density areas, and thus that the area coverage is maximized. As a result, sensor nodes are almost distributed in the network uniformly. The authors improved the virtual force algorithm. Refer to [39] for more details.

This method has several advantages: (1) maximizing the network coverage rate and (2) a low computational complexity. However, this method also has some disadvantages: (1) It is a centralized area coverage method, whereas distributed area coverage schemes are more desirable for WSNs. (2) This method does not take into account the network lifetime. Considering energy of the nodes is important in WSNs. (3) This area coverage method is static. This can weaken its efficiency.

Kashi et al. [40] proposed a heterogeneous distributed precise coverage rate (HDPCR) mechanism, which calculates the area coverage in a distributed manner. This method can detect the network boundaries, holes, and stains using simple mathematical calculations and compute the entire area covered in the network exactly. This process is locally done and each sensor node participates in it. This method includes several important advantages:

(1) a low computational overhead and (2) a distributed area coverage method that is more suitable for WSNs than for centralized schemes.

However, it suffers from several major weaknesses: (1) High communication overhead. (2) This method only calculates the area covered in the network. It does not describe the purpose of these operations. Generally, the main purposes of an area coverage method are searching for the best replacement strategy for sensor nodes in the network, obtaining the best area coverage quality with the minimum sensor nodes, achieving the maximum network lifetime, designing suitable scheduling schemes, and so on.

Therefore, calculating the area covered in the network alone is not the main goal of an area coverage method. (3) In this approach, the covered area is locally calculated through the sensor nodes in the network. If one of the sensor nodes performs its calculations incorrectly, then the final result will not be accurate.

Miao et al. [41] introduced a grey wolf optimizer with enhanced hierarchy (GWO-EH) that improved the grey wolf optimizer (GWO) algorithm. The authors claimed that GWO-EH can solve certain weaknesses of GWO, such as the low convergence speed and becoming trapped in local optimum. They solved the convergence rate by improving the weight coefficients. To balance global and local searches, they improve the position updating equation. Then, they applied GWO-EH to solve the area coverage problem in homogeneous WSNs.

The experiments indicate that this method has a suitable convergence rate. However, this method also has some disadvantages: (1) In this scheme, if the number of sensor nodes in the network is increased, then the convergence rate will be reduced. Therefore, this method is not scalable. (2) Its computational complexity is high. (3) This is a centralized area coverage method. (4) It is a static coverage scheme and cannot provide a suitable reconstruction and detection mechanism for covering holes established in the network.

Table 1 lists the advantages and disadvantages of different coverage schemes, which were briefly reviewed in this section.

## 3. Basic Concepts

In this section, we illustrate some the basic concepts, including fuzzy logic and the shuffled frog-leaping algorithm (SFLA). These concepts have been applied in the proposed scheme.

### 3.1. Fuzzy Logic

Based on the research studies, it can be deduced that measuring, modeling, and controlling real and complex processes are not accurate because there are uncertainties, such as incompleteness, randomness and data loss. Fuzzy logic (FL) is a mathematical technique [42]. Its aim is to describe approximately human thinking. Unlike classical set theory, in which the outputs are either true or false, fuzzy logic generates partial values based on inference rules and linguistic variables.

**Table 1.** Various coverage methods.

| Number | Scheme | Purpose | Advantages | Disadvantages |
|---|---|---|---|---|
| 1 | [30] | Achieving energy-efficient coverage, and maintaining connectivity | Scalability, designing the dynamic and distributed coverage method, presenting the sensing range customization mechanism, low network congestion, low energy consumption, high coverage rate | High delay, ignoring energy of nodes in the scheduling process, not designing a detection and reconstruction mechanism for covering holes |
| 2 | [31] | Solving the $K$-coverage problem with the minimum sensor nodes | Scalability, appropriate computational overhead, considering energy of nodes in the scheduling process, presenting a dynamic and distributed $K$-coverage scheme, improving network lifetime | High delay, high communication overhead, not designing a detection and reconstruction mechanism for covering holes |

**Table 1.** *Cont.*

| Number | Scheme | Purpose | Advantages | Disadvantages |
|---|---|---|---|---|
| 3 | [32] | Minimizing the number of sensor nodes required for partial area coverage and network connectivity maintenance | Scalability, presenting a dynamic and distributed coverage scheme, guaranteeing network connectivity, achieving an appropriate coverage level of the RoI | High communication overhead, not designing a detection and reconstruction mechanism for covering holes |
| 4 | [33] | Maximizing area coverage | Achieving a high quality and appropriate solution, increasing area coverage | Incomplete fitness function for evaluating area covered, high computational overhead, a centralized area coverage, low scalability |
| 5 | [34] | Finding the optimal scheduling strategy for coverage sets and maximizing network lifetime | Acceptable time complexity, appropriate computational complexity, improving network lifetime using a suitable scheduling mechanism | Not designing a mechanism for determining coverage sets, considering predetermined time slots for sensor node activity, presenting a centralized algorithm, low scalability, ignoring parameters, such as the distance between sensor nodes and energy |
| 6 | [35] | Designing a barrier coverage method with minimum sensor nodes and maximizing the coverage rate | Achieving a suitable coverage rate with a minimum number of sensor nodes, presenting a novel scheme for calculating coverage rate based on geometric mathematics | Considering insufficient parameters for calculating the coverage rate, designing a reactive detection and reconstruction mechanism for repairing network holes, making interruption and delay in the network performance |
| 7 | [36] | Presenting a fast and efficient method for estimating area covered | Appropriate time complexity, acceptable computational complexity, low error rate (high accuracy), introducing a distributed method for estimating the total area covered in the network | Not designing a proper scheduling mechanism, not designing a detection and reconstruction mechanism for covering holes, presenting a static area coverage method |
| 8 | [37] | Maximizing area coverage in the network | Appropriate computational complexity, generating high quality solutions, simplicity and appropriate convergence rate | Not considering various parameters in the fitness function, proposing a static area coverage method |
| 9 | [38] | Maximizing area coverage in a network with obstacles | Achieving the maximum area coverage rate, appropriate computational overhead | Not considering various parameters in the fitness function, not considering the maximization network lifetime, proposing a static area coverage method, low scalability |
| 10 | [39] | Improving area coverage and reducing the distance traveled by mobile nodes | Maximizing coverage rate, very low computational complexity | Presenting a static and centralized area coverage scheme, not considering the node energy for improving the network lifetime |
| 11 | [40] | Calculating coverage rate in a distributed manner | Low computational overhead, introducing a distributed area coverage scheme | High communication overhead, not designing a suitable coverage mechanism, high error rate for calculating the coverage rate |
| 12 | [41] | Maximizing area coverage | Proper convergence rate, ability for finding optimal solution | Low scalability, high computational complexity, providing a centralized and static area coverage method |

Today, fuzzy inference mechanisms are widely applied in various applications. In the following, we refer to some applications. Vilela et al. in [43] combined fuzzy logic with the Value of Information (VoI) assessment system. This scheme has been developed to evaluate the oil and gas subsurface. Nguyen et al. [44] presented the Fuzzy Q-Charging method to determine the optimal amount of energy charging for sensor nodes using fuzzy logic.

Bayrakdar in [45] used the fuzzy logic technique to select the lowest number of sensor nodes for monitoring the agricultural environment. Peng et al. [46] used fuzzy logic to design a transmission power allocation strategy (TPA) to maximize the lifetime of WSN. Baradaran and Navi in [47] proposed the HQCA clustering method, which uses fuzzy logic to choose the cluster head nodes in WSNs. We used fuzzy logic in our paper to design a scheduling mechanism for sensor nodes in the network. Two well-known fuzzy inference mechanisms are *Mamdani fuzzy inference* and *Sugeno fuzzy inference (TSK)*.

A fuzzy system has four main modules: fuzzification, defuzzification, a fuzzy rule base, and a fuzzy inference engine. A fuzzy system is shown in Figure 5. The fuzzification module maps the system inputs to the fuzzy sets and determines their fuzzy membership degree. These fuzzy values are simulated using an inference engine that uses fuzzy rules stored as IF-THEN rules. The results of the inference system are in the fuzzy form, which are transformed into crisp values using a defuzzification module, such as an averaging scheme and the centroid scheme [42].

Today, fuzzy inference mechanisms are widely applied in various applications. In the following, we refer to some applications. Vilela et al. in [43] combined fuzzy logic with the Value of Information (VoI) assessment system. This scheme has been developed to evaluate the oil and gas subsurface. Nguyen et al. [44] presented the Fuzzy Q-Charging method to determine the optimal amount of energy charging for sensor nodes using fuzzy logic.

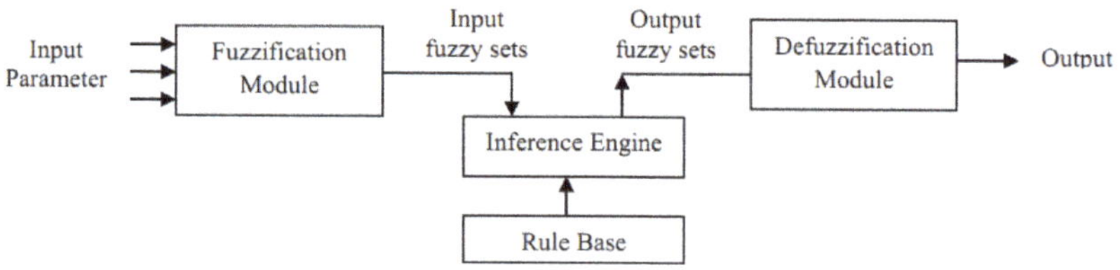


**Figure 5.** Fuzzy system model.

### 3.2. *Shuffled Frog-Leaping Algorithm (SFLA)*

The shuffled frog-leaping algorithm (SFLA) is a metaheuristic algorithm inspired by the foraging behavior of frogs. Eusuff et al. [28] introduced the SFLA in 2006. This algorithm has two elements, including local search and global information exchange. In SFLA, an initial population of frogs is divided into several groups called *memeplexes*. In general, there are two search methods: (1) local search, which searches the optimal position in each group, and (2) Global search, in which information is exchanged between different groups.

In the local search process, each memeplex is partitioned into a number of *sub-memeplexes*. Then, frogs are evaluated based on a fitness function and are sorted in descending order according to their fitness values to determine the best and worst frogs in each the sub-memeplex, which are described as $P_B$ and $P_w$, respectively. Then, the position of the worst frog ($P_w$) is improved toward the best frog ($P_B$) using Equation (1):

$$U(q) = P_w + S_i \tag{1}$$

where $U(q)$ is the new position frog, $S_i$ indicates the step size, and thus $S_{\min} \leq S_i \leq S_{\max}$.

$$S_i = Rand \times (P_B - P_w) \tag{2}$$

where *Rand* is a random number in $[0, 1]$. If the fitness value of the new position is better than the old position, then the new position is replaced with the old position. Otherwise, the new position is removed, and a new position is calculated based on Equation (3):

$$S_i = Rand \times (P_X - P_w) \tag{3}$$

where $P_X$ represents the best position in the memeplex. If the new position is better than the old position, then it is replaced with the old position. Otherwise, the new position is deleted. Then, a new solution is randomly calculated according to Equation (4) and is replaced with the old position:

$$U(q) = r \tag{4}$$

where $r$ is a new frog, which was randomly generated.

We used SFLA in our proposed method because this algorithm has many advantages, including simplicity, low number of parameters, high global search capability, and easy implementation.

## 4. System Model

This section includes four sub-sections, including the network model, the energy model, the sensing model, and the communication model. In the following, we explain each of these models in detail.

### 4.1. Network Model

In the proposed method, the wireless sensor network includes $N$ heterogeneous sensor nodes. Sensor nodes are different in terms of energy source, sensing range, and communication range. These nodes are randomly scattered in the network environment. Each sensor node $SN_i$ (where $i = 1, 2, ..., N$) knows its spatial coordinates $(x_i, y_i)$ in the network at any time using a positioning system, like GPS.

Furthermore, all sensor nodes are aware of the spatial coordinates of the base station $(x_{BS}, y_{BS})$ in the network. In addition, they are aware of their residual energy ($E_{residual}$) at any time. A sensor node can communicate directly with other sensor nodes in its communication range using a wireless communication channel. In this model, the network includes a BS, $N_{Static}$ static sensor nodes, and $N_{Dynamic}$ mobile sensor nodes, where $N_{Static} + N_{Dynamic} = N$ and $N_{Dynamic} \leq N_{Static}$. Figure 6 depicts the network model used in our proposed method. In the following, we describe the tasks of each sensor node:

- **Base station (BS):** It is responsible for processing the data received from sensor nodes in the network.
- **Static sensor nodes:**These nodes are tasked to sense the RoI and send the sensed data to BS. It is assumed that these sensor nodes completely cover the entire RoI and may overlap with each other.
- **Mobile sensor nodes:**These sensor nodes are tasked to reconstruct the holes created in the network. Thus, the data transmission process will not be disrupted. The number of these nodes is limited, and they have been scattered in the network.

### 4.2. Energy Model

In WSNs, the sensor nodes have extremely limited energy. As a result, one of the most important issues is energy conservation in these networks. Each sensor node is a multifunctional device, which includes a sensing unit, processing unit, memory unit, communication unit, energy unit, and so on.

The communication unit consumes the most energy compared to other units, because it is responsible for sending and receiving data. Based on energy model, if the sensor node $SN_i$ transmits $k$ bits to the sensor node $SN_j$, where the distance between them is equal to $d$. Then, the energy consumed by the sensor node $SN_i$ is calculated using Equation (5):

$$E_{TX}(k,d) = \begin{cases} E_{elec} \times k + E_{fs} \times k + d^2, & d < d_0 \\ E_{elec} \times k + E_{mp} \times k + d^4, & d \geq d_0 \end{cases} \tag{5}$$

In addition, the energy consumed by $SN_j$ is calculated based on Equation (6):

$$E_{RX}(k,d) = E_{elec} \times k \tag{6}$$

where $E_{elec}$ is the energy consumed by the transmitter/receiver circuitry. Moreover, $E_{fs}$ and $E_{mp}$ indicate the energy consumed by the transmitter amplifier for the free space model and multipath model, respectively. Furthermore, $d_0$ is the threshold transmission distance, and thus $d_0 = \sqrt{\frac{E_{fs}}{E_{mp}}}$.

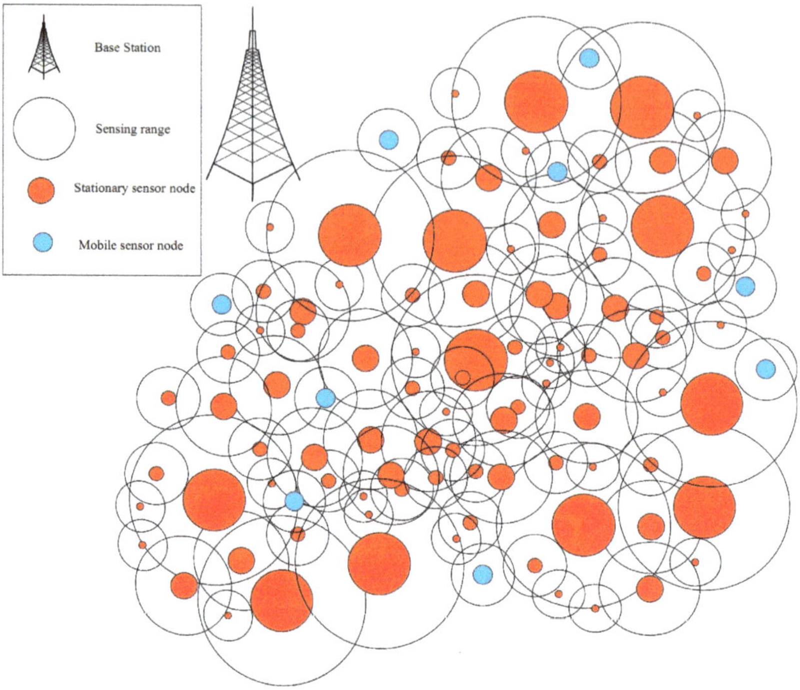


**Figure 6.** Network model in the proposed scheme.

### 4.3. Sensing Model

In the proposed scheme, we apply the binary sensing model (0/1 model). This model is shown in Figure 7. In this model, each sensor node $SN_i$ can sense a circle with radius $RS_i$. Assume that $P = (x_p, y_p)$ is a point in RoI. According to this model, if the *Euclidean distance* between $SN_i$ and $P$ is less than $RS_i$, then $SN_i$ senses this point because $P$ is within its sensing range. Otherwise, $SN_i$ cannot sense $P$. This is stated in Equation (7):

$$C(S, P) = \begin{cases} 1 & d(SN_i, P) \leq RS_i \\ 0 & d(SN_i, P) > RS_i \end{cases} \tag{7}$$

where

$$d(SN_i, P) = \sqrt{(x_i - x_p)^2 + (y_i - y_p)^2} \tag{8}$$

where $d(SN_i, P)$ represents the *Euclidean distance* between $SN_i$ and $P$. $(x_i, y_i)$ and $(x_p, y_p)$ represent the spatial coordinates of $SN_i$ and $P$, respectively.

### 4.4. Communication Model

The communication model used in the proposed method is the binary disk model. In this model, the communication radius $(RC)$ is defined as the upper bound, in which a sensor node can communicate with other nodes in the network. Therefore, if two sensor nodes are within the communication range of each other, then they can communicate directly with each other. See Figure 8. The sensing radius $(RS)$ is smaller than the communication radius $(RC)$, and thus:

$$RS < RC \tag{9}$$

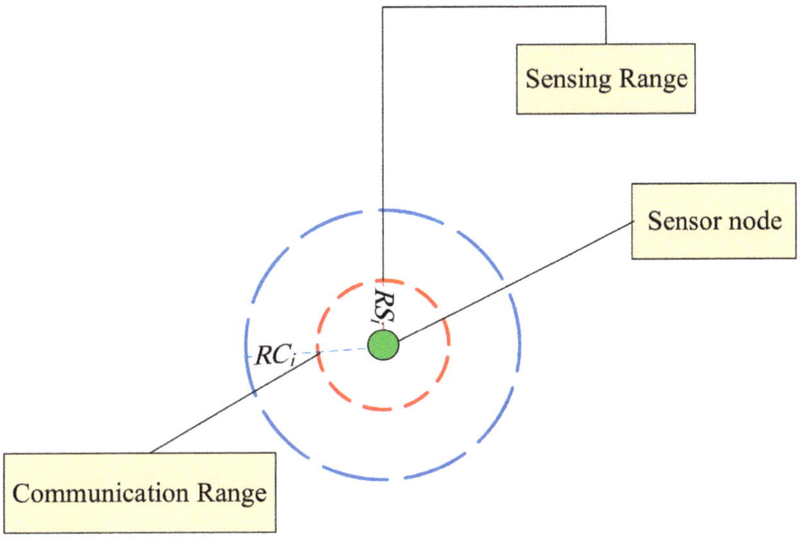


**Figure 7.** Sensing model in the proposed scheme.

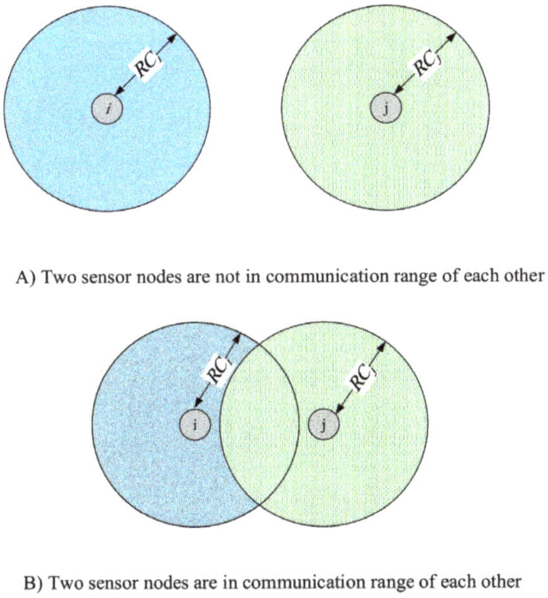


**Figure 8.** Communication range in the proposed method.

## 5. Problem Definition

In this paper, the problem is to maximize network lifetime by designing an appropriate ON/OFF scheduling mechanism for sensor nodes in a heterogeneous WSN. Therefore, a 2D area is considered as $R : X \times Y$. The network consists of $N$ heterogeneous sensor nodes.

We assume that sensor nodes are $T$ different types in the network, and thus each sensor node has its own initial energy, communication range, and sensing range. The purpose of the problem is to set the activity time of the sensor nodes ($Time_{ON}$) in the network so that the entire area is covered and the maximum network lifetime is achieved. In general, this problem is formulated as follows:

**Inputs:**

- The Region of Interest (RoI) in area coverage problem is:

$$R : X \times Y \tag{10}$$

- Sensor nodes are $T$ different types, and the total number of them is $N$:

$$\begin{cases} Type1 : SN_1, SN_2, \ldots, SN_{n_1}, \; Sensing\,radius = RS_1 \\ Type2 : SN_1, SN_2, \ldots, SN_{n_2}, \; Sensing\,radius = RS_2 \\ \vdots \\ TypeT : SN_1, SN_2, \ldots, SN_{n_T}, \; Sensing\,radius = RS_T \end{cases} \tag{11}$$

where $n_1 + n_2 + \ldots + n_T = N$.

**Output:**

- Designing a mechanism to schedule the activity of sensor nodes in the network (ON/OFF mechanism).

**Objective:**

- The activity time of the sensor nodes ($Time_{ON}$) in the network is adjusted so that the entire area is covered and the maximum network lifetime is achieved.

In Table 2, we introduce some symbols used in the proposed method.

**Table 2.** Symbols used in the proposed scheme.

| Symbols | Definition |
|---|---|
| $N$ | The number of sensor nodes in the network |
| $SN_i$ | Sensor node $i$ |
| BS | The base station |
| $(x_i, y_i)$ | The spatial coordinates of $SN_i$ |
| $(x_{BS}, y_{BS})$ | The spatial coordinates of BS |
| $E_{residual}$ | The residual energy of $SN_i$ |
| $N_{Static}$ | The number of static sensor nodes |
| $N_{Dynamic}$ | The number of mobile sensor nodes |
| $RS_i$ | The sensing radius of $SN_i$ |
| $RC_i$ | The communication radius of $SN_i$ |
| $Time_{ON}$ | The activity time of the sensor nodes |
| $C_i$ | The sensing range of $SN_i$ |
| $n$ | The number of circle sectors |
| $s\widehat{e}c_p$ | Circle sector $p$ |
| $\Delta\theta$ | The angle of each circle sector |
| $m$ | The number of small circles ($c_q$) |
| $c_q$ | Small circle $q$, which partitions $C_i$ |
| $\Delta R$ | The radius of smallest $c_q$ (i.e., $c_m$) |
| $r_q$ | The radius of each circle $c_q$ |

**Table 2.** *Cont.*

| Symbols | Definition |
|---|---|
| $DigitC_i$ | Digital matrix corresponding to $C_i$ |
| $a_{qp}$ | Matrix element corresponding to the row $c_q$ and the column $\widehat{sec}_p$ |
| $ID_i$ | The identifier of $SN_i$ |
| $Table_{neighbor}$ | The neighborhood table of sensor nodes |
| $d_{ij}$ | Euclidean distance between $SN_i$ and $SN_j$ |
| $\alpha$ | The angle of the center of the circle $C_j$ with respect to $SN_i$ |
| $\gamma_q$ | The overlapping area between $c_q$ and $C_j$ |
| $Overlap_i$ | The overlap between the sensing range of $SN_i$ and the sensing range of its neighboring nodes |
| $A_{qp}$ | Rectangular area of $C_i$ corresponding to $c_q$ and $\widehat{sec}_p$ |
| $D_{i-BS}$ | Distance between $SN_i$ and BS |
| $Priority_i$ | The importance degree of $SN_i$ |
| $Packet_{size_i}$ | The number of data packets in the buffer of $SN_i$ |
| $Buffer_{size_i}$ | Buffer capacity of $SN_i$ |
| $s_i$ | Mobile sensor nodes $i$ |
| $\overline{RS}$ | The mean sensing radius of sensor nodes |

## 6. Proposed Method

The purpose of this paper is to present an appropriate area coverage scheme to balance the energy consumption of sensor nodes in the network and improve network lifetime. We seek to increase and optimize the network coverage quality. The proposed method includes four phases:

- Calculating the overlap between sensing ranges of sensor nodes in the network.
- Designing a fuzzy scheduling mechanism.
- Predicting node replacement time.
- Reconstructing and covering of holes created in the network.

In the following, we explain each of these phases in detail.

### 6.1. Phase 1, Calculating the Overlap between Sensing Ranges of Sensor Nodes in the Network

In this phase, we propose a distributed scheme based on geometric mathematics so that each sensor node can estimate the overlap between its sensing range and the sensing ranges of neighboring nodes. In this scheme, the sensing range of a sensor node is represented using a *digital matrix*. This scheme is a simple and efficient solution to calculate the overlap between the sensing range of a sensor node and sensing ranges of its neighboring nodes.

Accurate calculation of the overlap is not easy, because it is not clear what nodes overlap with a sensor node and it is in what form. Therefore, calculating the overlap is a complex and time-consuming operation with high computational overhead. In the following, we describe how to calculate the overlap between the sensing range of a sensor node and the sensing ranges of its neighboring nodes using a 0/1 matrix. This matrix is called the *digital matrix*. This process includes the following steps:

#### 6.1.1. Transforming the Sensing Range of a Sensor Node into a Digital Matrix

In this section, we describe how to transform the sensing range of a sensor node ($SN_i$) into a *digital matrix*. First, $SN_i$ is assumed as the center of a coordinate axis. In this paper, the sensing range of $SN_i$ is represented as $C_i$ that has the sensing radius $RS_i$. Then, we divide the area $C_i$ into $n$ circle sectors ($s\widehat{ec}_p$) where $p = 1, 2, \ldots, n$; so that $n = \frac{2\pi}{\Delta\theta}$. The angle of each circle sector ($s\hat{e}c_p$) is equal to $\Delta\theta$. This is expressed in Equation (12):

$$C_i = \begin{cases} s\widehat{ec}_1 : \theta \le s\hat{e}c_1 \le \theta + \Delta\theta \\ s\widehat{ec}_2 : \theta + \Delta\theta \le s\hat{e}c_2 \le \theta + 2\Delta\theta \\ \vdots \\ s\widehat{ec}_n : \theta + (n-1)\Delta\theta \le s\hat{e}c_n \le \theta + n\Delta\theta \end{cases} \tag{12}$$

Then, we partition the area $C_i$ into $m$ smaller circles ($c_q$), where their center is $SN_i$, and thus $q = 1, 2, \ldots, m$ and $m = \frac{RS_i}{\Delta R}$. The radius of each circle $c_q$ is equal to $r_q$, which has been stated in Equation (13):

$$C_i = \begin{cases} c_1 : r_1 = m\Delta R \\ c_2 : r_2 = (m-1)\Delta R \\ \vdots \\ c_m : r_m = \Delta R \end{cases} \tag{13}$$

This process has been illustrated in Figure 9. As shown in Figure 9, the sensing range of the sensor node $SN_i$ is divided into 16 sectors and 8 smaller circles. Two parameters, $\Delta\theta$ and $\Delta R$, are adjustable. If the value of these parameters is close to zero, then the results will be more accurate. However, the memory and computational overhead are also increased.

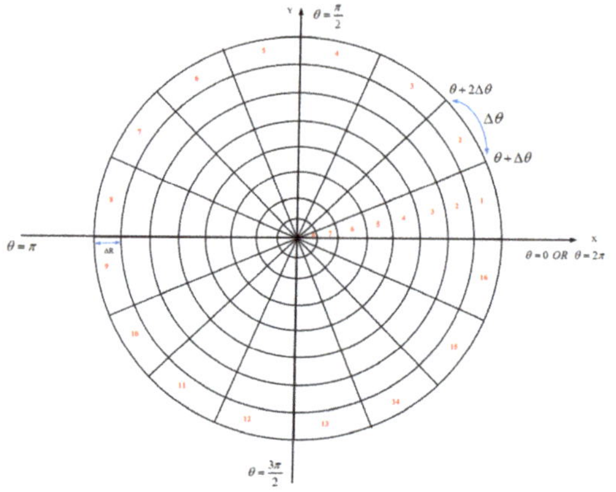


**Figure 9.** Partitioning the sensing range of the sensor node $SN_i$.

Finally, the circle $C_i$ is divided into almost rectangular areas. We simulate this circle using a *digital matrix* ($DigitC_i$), where its size is equal to $m \times n$. Furthermore, its rows represent small circles ($c_q$) and its columns represent sectors ($s\widehat{ec}_p$). $DigitC_i$ is shown in Equation (14):

$$DigitC_i = \begin{pmatrix} a_{11} & \cdots & a_{1n} \\ \vdots & \ddots & \vdots \\ a_{m1} & \cdots & a_{mn} \end{pmatrix}_{m \times n} \tag{14}$$

In the example presented in Figure 9, the dimensions of the matrix are equal to $m = 8$ and $n = 16$. Each matrix element ($a_{qp}$) corresponds to a rectangular area, such that $q = 1, \ldots, m$ and $p = 1, \ldots, n$. Moreover, each matrix element can be zero or one. If a rectangular area is covered by the sensing range of at least one of the neighboring nodes, then corresponding matrix element is equal to one. Otherwise, its value is equal to zero.

$$a_{qp} = \begin{cases} 1, & If\ C_i\ ovrlaps\ with\ other\ its\ neighbor \\ 0, & otherwise \end{cases} \tag{15}$$

The pseudocode of this process is expressed in Algorithm 1. According to this algorithm, it can be deduced that its time complexity is $O(nm)$.

---

**Algorithm 1** Transforming $C_i$ into digital matrix ($DigitC_i$)

---

**Input:** $(x_i, y_i)$, $RS_i$, $\Delta\theta$, $\Delta R$
**Output:** $DigitC_i$
  **Begin**
$n = \frac{2\pi}{\Delta\theta}$; {*n is the number of circle sectors.*}
$m = \frac{RS_i}{\Delta R}$; {*m is the number of small circles.*}
Create an $m \times n$ digital matrix that is called $DigitC_i$;
**for** $q = 1$ to $m$ **do**
  **for** $p = 1$ to $n$ **do**
    **if** ($C_i$ overlaps with its neighbors) **then**
      $a_{qp} = 1$; {*$DigitC_i$ matrix elements.*}
    **else**
      $a_{qp} = 0$; {*$DigitC_i$ matrix elements.*}
    **end if**
  **end for**
**end for**
  **End**

---

### 6.1.2. Digital Matrix Initialization Process

In this section, we present an example to illustrate how to quantify the matrix $DigitC_i$. Assume that the sensing range of the sensor node $SN_i$ (i.e., the circle $C_i$ with center $(x_i, y_i)$) overlaps with the sensing ranges of two sensor nodes $SN_j$ and $SN_k$, see Figure 10. The values corresponding to the elements of the matrix $DigitC_i$ are plotted on the rectangular areas. As shown in Figure 10, if a rectangular area is not completely covered by the sensing ranges of neighboring nodes, the corresponding matrix element is equal to zero. We believe that it is a simple and intelligent estimation scheme, which can accurately calculate overlapping areas. It should be remembered that traditional methods for calculating the overlap have high computational complexity.

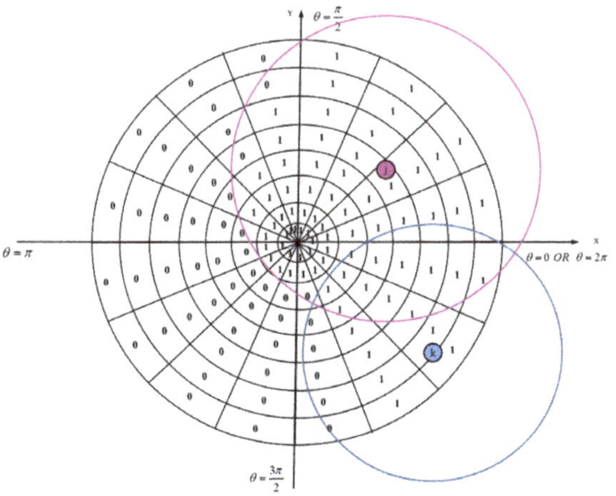


**Figure 10.** Overlap between $SN_i$ and two sensor nodes $SN_j$ and $SN_k$.

In the following, we explain the initialization process of the matrix elements in detail. First, we calculate the overlap between the sensing ranges of $SN_i$ and $SN_j$ in detail. A similar process is executed to calculate the overlap between $SN_i$ and other neighboring nodes. This process includes the following steps:

- Each sensor node ($SN_i$, and thus $i = 1, 2, ..., N$) broadcasts a *Hello message* to its neighbors. This message includes its ID ($ID_i$), its spatial coordinates $(x_i, y_i)$, its residual energy $(E_{Residual_i})$, and its sensing radius $(RS_i)$. This message is only broadcast to single-hop neighboring nodes. Therefore, it requires low energy for sending.
- The sensor node $SN_i$ ($i = 1, 2, ..., N$) records information of the neighboring nodes in its own neighborhood table ($Table_{neighbor}$). This information is applied to quantify the matrix $DigitC_i$. The information inserted into $Table_{neighbor}$ is listed in Table 3.

**Table 3.** $Table_{neighbor}$ corresponding to $SN_i$.

| Number | Node ID | Spatial Coordinates | Sensing Range | Residual Energy |
|---|---|---|---|---|
| 1 | $ID_j$ | $(x_j, y_j)$ | $RS_j$ | $E_{residual_j}$ |
| 2 | $ID_k$ | $(x_k, y_k)$ | $RS_k$ | $E_{residual_k}$ |

- Assume that the sensing range and sensing radius of the sensor node $SN_j$ are displayed as $C_j$ and $RS_j$, respectively. The sensing range and sensing radius of $SN_i$ are considered as $C_i$ and $RS_i$, respectively.
- As stated in Section 6.1.1, the radii of smaller circles ($c_q$) are calculated based on Equation (13). The radii of $c_1, \ldots, c_8$ are equal to $r_1, \ldots, r_8$, respectively.
- Then, $SN_i$ calculates the *Euclidean distance* between itself and $SN_j$ (i.e., its neighboring node in $Table_{neighbor}$) using Equation (16):

$$d_{ij} = \sqrt{(x_i - x_j)^2 + (y_i - y_j)^2} \tag{16}$$

  where $(x_i, y_i)$ is spatial coordinates of $SN_i$ and $(x_j, y_j)$ indicates spatial coordinates of $SN_j$.
- According to Figure 11, if Mode 2 is met, then the two nodes $SN_i$ and $SN_j$ do not overlap within their sensing ranges. As a result, all the elements of the matrix $DigitC_i$ are equal to zero. If Mode 1 or Mode 3 is met, then the two nodes overlap within their sensing ranges. If Mode 1 is met, then all the elements of the matrix $DigitC_i$ will be equal to one. Otherwise, if Mode 3 is satisfied, then the angle of the center of the circle $C_j$ with respect to a coordinates axis with center $SN_i$ is calculated using Equation (17):

$$\alpha = \arctan\left(\frac{x_j - x_i}{y_j - y_i}\right), \quad 0 \leq \alpha \leq 2\pi \tag{17}$$

  Then, the process of calculating the overlap between $SN_i$ and $SN_j$ (quantifying the elements of the matrix $DigitC_i$) follows the following rules.
  - If $d_{ij} \geq R_j + r_q$; where $1 \leq q \leq 8$ (Mode 2 in Figure 11), then the circle $c_q$ and all the circles, which are smaller than $c_q$ (i.e., $c_{q+1}, \ldots, c_8$), are outside the circle $C_j$. As a result, the matrix elements in the rows $c_q, c_{q+1}, \ldots, c_8$ are zero.
  - If $d_{ij} \leq R_j - r_q$; where $1 \leq q \leq 8$ (Mode 1 in Figure 11), then the circle $c_q$ and all the circles, which are smaller than $c_q$ (i.e., $c_{q+1}, \ldots, c_8$), are inside the circle $C_j$. Thus, the matrix elements in rows $c_q, c_{q+1}, \ldots, c_8$ are equal to one (see, for example, circles $c_7$ and $c_8$ (gray circles) in Figure 13).

| Mode | Condition | Status | Description |
|---|---|---|---|
| 1 | $d_{ij} \leq RS_j - RS_i$ | 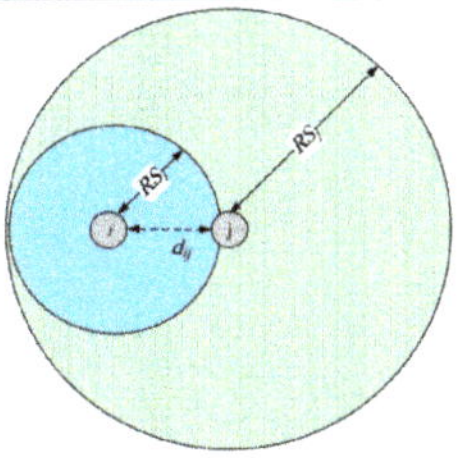 | In this mode, the sensing range of node i is completely inside the sensing range of node j. |
| 2 | $d_{ij} \geq RS_i + RS_j$ | 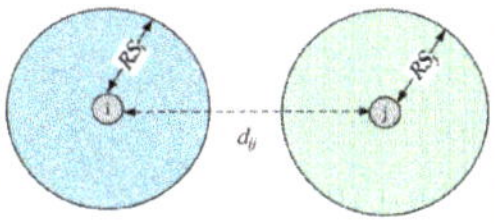 | In this mode, the sensing range of node i and the sensing range of node j have no overlap. |
| 3 | $RS_i - RS_j < d_{ij} < RS_i + RS_j$ | 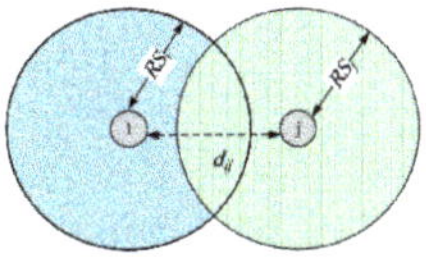 | In this mode, the sensing range of node i and the sensing range of node j overlap slightly. |

**Figure 11.** Different modes of two sensor nodes.

See Figure 12.

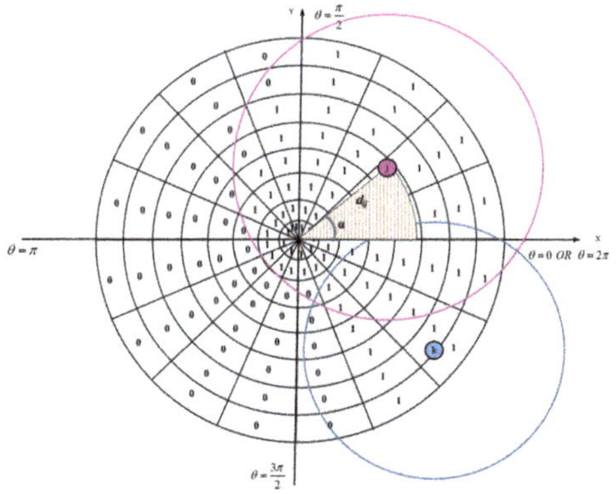


**Figure 12.** Calculating the angle of $SN_j$ with respect to $SN_i$.

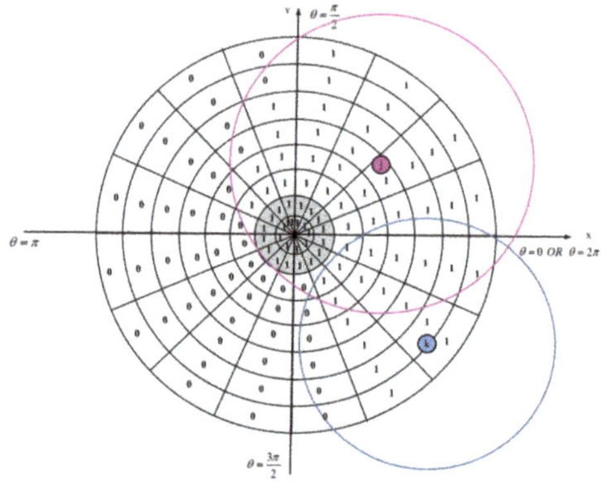


**Figure 13.** Filling process of the matrix $DigitC_i$.

- If $R_j - r_q < d_{ij} < R_j + r_q$; where $1 \le q \le 8$ (Mode 3 in Figure 11), it means that the circle $c_q$ and the circle $C_j$ intersect with each other (see, for example, the circle $c_6$ (blue circle) in Figure 14). The overlapping area between these two circles is calculated as follows:
  - Draw a triangle including three vertices $(x_i, y_i)$, $(x_j, y_j)$, and the intersection point of the circles $c_q$ and $C_j$. This triangle is shown in Figure 14.
  - We can easily obtain the length of three sides of this triangle. Therefore, we apply the law of cosines to calculate the angle $\theta_1 = \theta_2$:

$$R_j^2 = r_q^2 + d_{ij}^2 - 2r_q d_{ij} \cos\theta_1 \tag{18}$$

Therefore, we have:

$$\theta_1 = \arccos\left(\frac{r_q^2 + d_{ij}^2 - R_j^2}{2r_q d_{ij}}\right), \quad 0 \le \theta_1 \le \pi \tag{19}$$

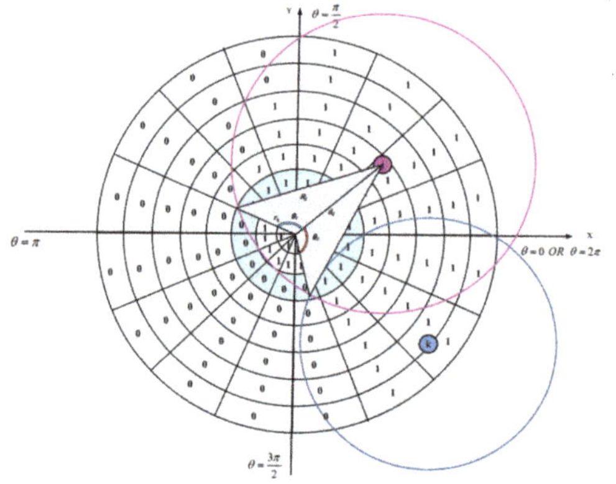


**Figure 14.** Calculating the overlapping area between $c_6$ (the blue circle) and $C_j$.

  - The overlapping area between these two circles $c_q$ and $C_j$ ($\gamma_q$) is calculated using Equation (20):

$$\alpha - \theta_1 \le \gamma_q \le \alpha + \theta_1, \quad 0 \le \gamma_q \le 2\pi \tag{20}$$

- In the matrix $DigitC_i$, the matrix element corresponding to the row $c_q$ and the column $s\widehat{e}c_p$ is determined based on Equation (21).

$$a_{qp} = \begin{cases} 1, & IF \begin{cases} R_j - r_q < d_{ij} < R_j + r_q \\ AND \\ \alpha - \theta_1 \leq s\hat{e}c_p \leq \alpha + \theta_1 \end{cases} \\ 0, & otherwise \end{cases} \tag{21}$$

This process is repeated for all intersecting circles to determine all elements of the matrix $DigitC_i$. Figure 15 shows the triangles formed between the circles $c_1, \ldots, c_8$ and the circle $C_j$. Algorithm 2 illustrates the pseudocode of the filling process of matrix $DigitC_i$. According to Algorithm 2, it can be deduced that the time complexity of this algorithm is $O(\eta mn)$.

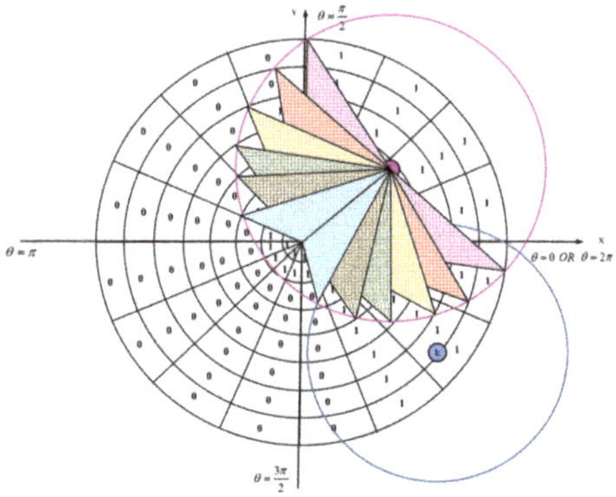

**Figure 15.** Triangles formed between the circles $c_1, \ldots, c_8$ and the circle $C_j$.

### 6.2. Phase 2, Designing Fuzzy Scheduling Mechanism

In this phase, the purpose is to design a fuzzy logic-based scheduling mechanism to determine the appropriate time slots to put a sensor node in ON state so that the network lifetime is maximized and energy is saved. In our proposed method, we used the Mamdani fuzzy inference system. The proposed fuzzy system includes three main parts: fuzzy inputs, fuzzy system outputs, and the rule base. In the following, these parts are introduced in detail.

#### 6.2.1. Fuzzy System Inputs

Our proposed fuzzy system includes three inputs:

- ***The overlap between the sensing range of a sensor node and the sensing range of its neighboring nodes (Overlap$_i$):*** This parameter was selected as a fuzzy input to be taken into account the density of sensor nodes in the network when designing the ON/OFF mechanism for them. If the density of the sensor nodes in the network is high, then they overlap with each other extremely. As a result, they should be in the OFF state for more time. Therefore, their energy will be saved.

**Algorithm 2** The digital matrix filling process

**Input:** $\Delta\theta, \Delta R, m, n,$
$\quad N$ {$N$ is the number of sensor nodes in the network.}
$\quad SN_i: DigitC_i, (x_i, y_i), RS_i, C_i$
$\quad SN_j: (x_j, y_j), RS_j, C_j$
$\quad SN_k: (x_k, y_k), RS_k, C_k$

**Output:** $DigitC_i$

Begin
1: **for** $i = 1$ to $N$ **do**
2: $\quad SN_i$: Broadcast a *HELLO message* for its neighbors;
3: **end for**
4: $\eta = number_{neighbor}$ {$\eta$ is the number of neighbors of $SN_i$. In this example, $\eta = 2$.}
5: **while** $\eta \neq 0$ **do**
6: $\quad SN_i$: Compute *Euclidean distance* $(d_{i,\eta})$ between $SN_i$ and $SN_\eta$;
$\quad$ {In the following, it is examined whether the two nodes are in the communication range of each other or not.}
7: $\quad$ **if** $(d_{i,\eta} < RS_i + RS_\eta)$ **then**
8: $\quad\quad SN_i$: Compute the angle $\alpha$ using Equation (17);
9: $\quad\quad$ **for** $q = 1$ to $m$ **do**
10: $\quad\quad\quad$ **if** $(d_{i,\eta} \geq RS_\eta + r_q)$ **then**
11: $\quad\quad\quad\quad$ **for** $p = 1$ to $n$ **do**
12: $\quad\quad\quad\quad\quad a_{qp} = 0;$
13: $\quad\quad\quad\quad$ **end for**
14: $\quad\quad\quad$ **else if** $(d_{i,\eta} \leq RS_\eta - r_q)$ **then**
15: $\quad\quad\quad\quad$ **for** $p = 1$ to $n$ **do**
16: $\quad\quad\quad\quad\quad a_{qp} = 1;$
17: $\quad\quad\quad\quad$ **end for**
18: $\quad\quad\quad$ **else if** $(RS_\eta - r_q < d_{i,\eta} < RS_\eta + r_q)$ **then**
19: $\quad\quad\quad\quad SN_i$: Compute the angle $\theta_1$ based Equation (19);
20: $\quad\quad\quad\quad$ **for** $p = 1$ to $n$ **do**
21: $\quad\quad\quad\quad\quad$ **if** $(\alpha - \theta_1 \leq s\hat{e}c_p \leq \alpha + \theta_1)$ **then**
22: $\quad\quad\quad\quad\quad\quad a_{qp} = 1;$
23: $\quad\quad\quad\quad\quad$ **else**
24: $\quad\quad\quad\quad\quad\quad a_{qp} = 0;$
25: $\quad\quad\quad\quad\quad$ **end if**
26: $\quad\quad\quad\quad$ **end for**
27: $\quad\quad\quad$ **end if**
28: $\quad\quad$ **end for**
29: $\quad$ **end if**
30: $\quad \eta = \eta - 1;$
31: **end while**
End

In Phase 1, we expressed how to transform the sensing range of a sensor node into a digital matrix. After accurately calculating the matrix $DigitC_i$ corresponding to $SN_i$ (so that $i = 1, 2, ..., N$ and $N$ is the number of sensor nodes in the network), its overlap area (i.e., digital matrix elements that are equal to one) are calculated as follows. First, we calculate the rectangular area $A_{qp}$ (gray rectangular area), which is shown in Figure 16, according to Equation (22):

$$A_{qp} = Area_{Circle\ sector_{qp}} - Area_{Circle\ sector_{(q-1)p}} \qquad (22)$$

where $Area_{Circle\ sector_{qp}}$ represents the circle sector area $p$ of the circle $c_q$, which is obtained using Equation (23):

$$Area_{Circle\ sector_{qp}} = \frac{1}{2}r_q^2\Delta\theta \qquad (23)$$

We place Equation (23) in Equation (22):

$$A_{qp} = \frac{1}{2}r_q^2\Delta\theta - \frac{1}{2}r_{q-1}^2\Delta\theta = \frac{1}{2}\Delta\theta\left(r_q^2 - r_{q-1}^2\right) \tag{24}$$

According to Equation (13), we have:

$$\begin{aligned} r_q &= (m-(q-1))\Delta R \\ r_{q-1} &= (m-(q-2))\Delta R \end{aligned} \tag{25}$$

Therefore, $A_{qp}$ is calculated using Equation (26):

$$\begin{aligned} A_{qp} &= \tfrac{1}{2}\Delta\theta\,\Delta R^2\left((m-(q-1))^2 - (m-(q-2))^2\right) \\ &= \tfrac{1}{2}\Delta\theta\,\Delta R^2(2(q-m)-3) \end{aligned} \tag{26}$$

As a result, the total area of the overlap ($Overlap_i$) is obtained according to Algorithm 3. The time complexity of this algorithm is $O(mn)$, and thus $m$ and $n$ represent the dimensions of the matrix $DigitC_i$. The normalization process of this parameter is expressed in Equation (27):

$$Overlap_{norm} = \frac{Overlap_i}{Area_{C_i}} \tag{27}$$

where $Area_{C_i}$ is the area of the sensing range of $SN_i$.

$$Area_{C_i} = \pi RS_i^2 \tag{28}$$

where $RS_i$ is the sensing radius of $SN_i$.

This fuzzy parameter ($Overlap_{norm}$) consists of three modes (low, medium, and high). Figure 17 illustrates its fuzzy membership function.

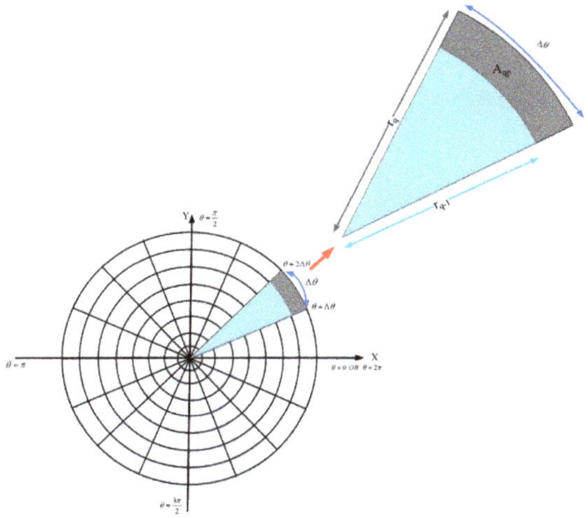

**Figure 16.** Calculating the area of $A_{qp}$.

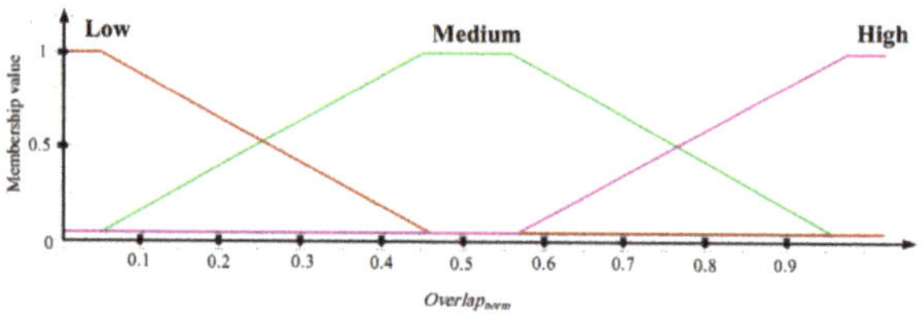


**Figure 17.** Diagram of the fuzzy membership function corresponding to the parameter $Overlap_{norm}$.

- ***Residual energy ($E_{residual}$):*** This parameter was selected as a fuzzy input because it helps sensor nodes with more energy to be at the ON state for more time. Low-energy nodes perform their activities at shorter time slots. Hence, their lifetime will be increased. As a result, this parameter can balance the energy consumption in the network. Sensor nodes are aware of their own residual energy at any time. This parameter is normalized using Equation (29).

$$E_{norm-residual} = \frac{E_{residual}}{E_{\max}} \tag{29}$$

where $E_{\max}$ is the maximum energy of a sensor node in the network. This fuzzy parameter includes three modes (low, medium, and high). The fuzzy membership function diagram of $E_{norm-residual}$ is shown in Figure 18.

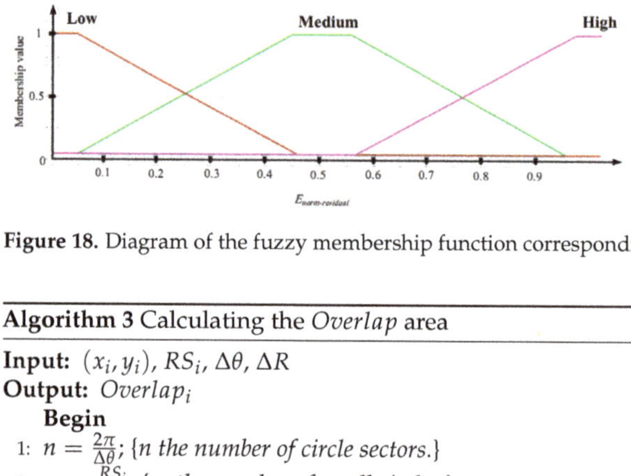


**Figure 18.** Diagram of the fuzzy membership function corresponding to the parameter $E_{norm-residual}$.

---

**Algorithm 3** Calculating the $Overlap$ area

---

**Input:** $(x_i, y_i)$, $RS_i$, $\Delta\theta$, $\Delta R$
**Output:** $Overlap_i$
**Begin**
$n = \frac{2\pi}{\Delta\theta}$; {*n the number of circle sectors.*}
$m = \frac{RS_i}{\Delta R}$; {*m the number of small circles.*}
**for** $q = 1$ to $m$ **do**
  **for** $p = 1$ to $n$ **do**
    $Overlap_i = Overlap_i + (a_{qp})\frac{1}{2}\Delta\theta\,\Delta R^2(2(q-m)-3)$ {$a_{qp}$ *is the matrix element that is equal to* 0 *or* 1.}
  **end for**
**end for**
**return** $Overlap_i$;
**End**

---

- ***Distance between a sensor node and the base station ($D_{i-BS}$):*** This parameter was selected as a fuzzy input to help the nodes close to the BS to be at ON state for more time slots because these nodes are more active than other nodes in the network.

Therefore, these nodes require more time to perform their activities. This parameter is calculated based on the *Euclidean distance* between node $SN_i$ and the base station.

$$D_{i-BS} = \sqrt{(x_i - x_{BS})^2 + (y_i - y_{BS})^2} \tag{30}$$

Moreover, this parameter is normalized based on Equation (31):

$$D_{norm-i-BS} = \frac{D_{i-BS}}{D_{\max}} \tag{31}$$

where $D_{\max}$ represents the maximum distance in the network. For example, assume that the network is a rectangular area with dimensions $X \times Y$, and, as a result, $D_{\max}$ is obtained using Equation (32):

$$D_{\max} = \sqrt{X^2 + Y^2} \tag{32}$$

Figure 19 illustrates the fuzzy membership function diagram of $D_{norm-i-BS}$. This fuzzy parameter includes three modes (low, medium, and high).

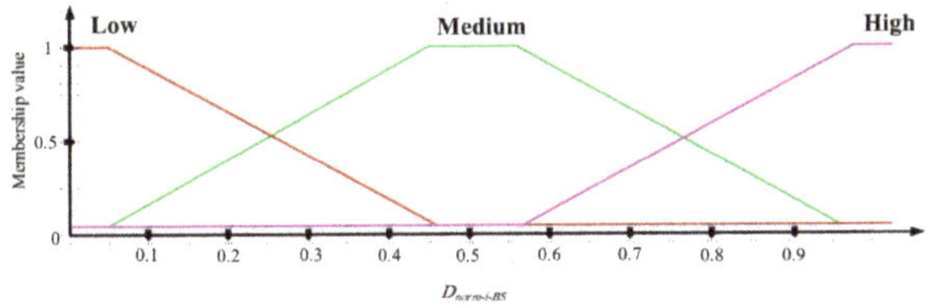


**Figure 19.** Diagram of the fuzzy membership function corresponding to the parameter $D_{norm-i-BS}$.

### 6.2.2. Fuzzy System Output

In the proposed fuzzy system, the fuzzy output is the activity time of each sensor node ($Time_{ON}$). In this fuzzy system, if a sensor node has the low overlap with neighboring nodes, and its energy level is high, and its distance from BS is low, it stays at the ON state for more time slots. This fuzzy output includes seven modes, including very very low, very low, low, medium, high, very high, and very very high. The fuzzy membership function diagram is shown in Figure 20.

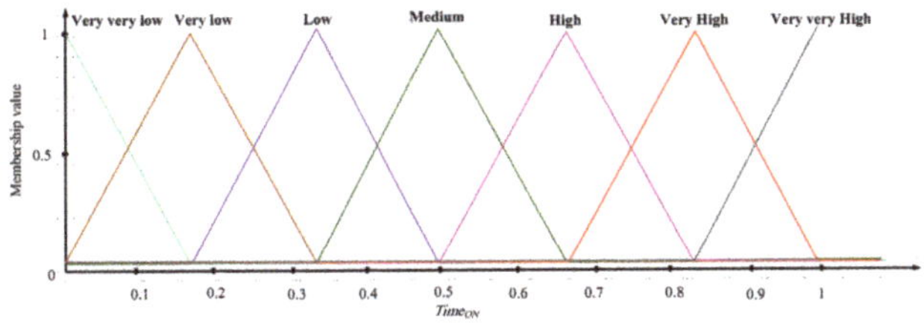


**Figure 20.** Diagram of the fuzzy membership function corresponding to the parameter $Time_{ON}$.

### 6.2.3. Rule Base

Our proposed fuzzy system consists of 27 fuzzy rules listed in Table 4. For example, rule 1 is expressed as follows:

**Rule1: IF** $Overlap_{norm}$ is *low* **AND** $E_{norm-residual}$ is *low* **AND** $D_{norm-i-BS}$ is *low* **THEN** $Time_{ON}$ is *high*.

**Table 4.** Rule base in the proposed fuzzy system.

| Number | Fuzzy System Inputs | | | Fuzzy System Output |
|---|---|---|---|---|
| | $Overlap_{norm}$ | $E_{norm-residual}$ | $D_{Norm-I-Bs}$ | $Time_{ON}$ |
| 1 | Low | Low | Low | High |
| 2 | Low | Low | Medium | Medium |
| 3 | Low | Low | High | Low |
| 4 | Low | Medium | Low | Very high |
| 5 | Low | Medium | Medium | High |
| 6 | Low | Medium | High | Medium |
| 7 | Low | High | Low | Very very high |
| 8 | Low | High | Medium | Very high |
| 9 | Low | High | High | High |
| 10 | Medium | Low | Low | Medium |
| 11 | Medium | Low | Medium | Low |
| 12 | Medium | Low | High | Very low |
| 13 | Medium | Medium | Low | High |
| 14 | Medium | Medium | Medium | Medium |
| 15 | Medium | Medium | High | Low |
| 16 | Medium | High | Low | Very high |
| 17 | Medium | High | Medium | High |
| 18 | Medium | High | High | Medium |
| 19 | High | Low | Low | Low |
| 20 | High | Low | Medium | Very low |
| 21 | High | Low | High | Very very low |
| 22 | High | Medium | Low | Medium |
| 23 | High | Medium | Medium | Low |
| 24 | High | Medium | High | Very low |
| 25 | High | High | Low | High |
| 26 | High | High | Medium | Medium |
| 27 | High | High | High | Low |

Algorithm 4 describes the pseudocode of the proposed fuzzy system. The time complexity of this algorithm is $O(mn)$.

*6.3. Phase 3, Predicting the Node Replacement Time*

Once the network is running, the sensor nodes start their activities, such as sensing the environment, processing data, sending/receiving data, etc., based on the time slots determined in Section 6.2. These activities reduce the energy of the sensor nodes. In WSNs, the energy required for each node is supplied by a small battery, which cannot be recharged or replaced. These nodes are scattered in undesirable and inaccessible areas. Therefore, when their battery is discharged, they die. As a result, a hole is created in the network. The purpose of this phase is to provide a suitable solution to predict the death time of sensor nodes to prevent the hole establishment in the network. Therefore, it helps sensor nodes to continue data transmission operations without any interruption.

In this phase, the sensor node $SN_i$ calculates a parameter called $Priority_i$, which is updated periodically. This parameter expresses the importance degree of this sensor node. The parameter is calculated according to Equation (33):

$$Priority_i = \left(1 - \frac{Overlap_i}{\pi RS_i^2}\right) + \left(\frac{Packet_{size_i}}{Buffer_{size_i}}\right) \tag{33}$$

where $\left(1 - \frac{Overlap_i}{\pi RS_i^2}\right)$ is the part of the sensing range of the node $SN_i$, which does not overlap with any neighboring node. $Overlap_i$ indicates the overlap between the sensing range of $SN_i$ and sensing ranges of its neighboring nodes. In Section 6.2, we described how to calculate this parameter. Moreover, $RS_i$ represents the sensing radius of $SN_i$. $\left(\frac{Packet_{size_i}}{Buffer_{size_i}}\right)$ is used to evaluate the coming traffic of $SN_i$. $Packet_{size_i}$ indicates the number of data packets in the buffer of $SN_i$ at a time period. $Buffer_{size_i}$ also indicates the buffer capacity of $SN_i$. All parameters are normalized in Equation (33). The purpose of the normalization process is to place the parameters in $[0,1]$ to have the same effect on the $Priority_i$.

**Algorithm 4** Fuzzy system

**Input:** $(x_i, y_i)$, $(x_{BS}, y_{BS})$, $E_{residual_i}$, $DigitC_i$
**Output:** $Time_{ON}$
**Begin**
**$SN_i$:** Calculate $Overlap_i$ using Algorithm 3;
**$SN_i$:** Normalize $Overlap_i$ based on Equation (27);
**$SN_i$:** Normalize $E_{residual_i}$ based on Equation (29);
**$SN_i$:** Calculate $D_{i-BS}$ based on Equation (30);
**$SN_i$:** Normalize $D_{i-BS}$ based on Equation (31);
**$SN_i$:** Calculate $Time_{ON}$ using proposed fuzzy system;
**return** $Time_{ON}$;
**End**

When the energy level of $SN_i$ is less than a threshold, this node sends an *Alert message* including $Priority_i$ to the base station. After receiving this message, the BS checks $Priority_i$ to decide whether to replace this node. As mentioned, $Priority_i$ indicates the importance degree of this sensor node in the network. The base station compares this parameter with a threshold value ($P_{Threshold} > 0$). $P_{Threshold}$ is a constant number.

- If $Priority_i > P_{Threshold}$, then this node is important in the network and its death can jeopardize the normal operation of the network. Therefore, the base station sends a *Coverage message* to the nearest mobile node to be replaced with $SN_i$. The *Coverage message* includes the spatial coordinates of $SN_i$.
- If $Priority_i \leq P_{Threshold}$, then the death of this node does not affect the normal operation of the network and can be ignored.

Algorithm 5 describes the pseudocode related to this process. The time complexity of this algorithm is $O(1)$. If several sensor nodes die at the same time in one part of the network, then a hole will be created in this part. As a result, the base station must apply several mobile nodes to reconstruct this hole. The exact number of mobile sensor nodes and their new location for repairing the hole are discussed in Section 6.4.

### 6.4. Phase 4, Reconstructing, and Covering of Holes Created in the Network

As stated in Section 6.3, the death of sensor nodes can create holes in the network. We seek to use mobile nodes to repair such holes. In this phase, we assume that there are a number of sensor nodes, which may die soon, in the area $H$ of the network with dimensions $H : X' \times Y'$. Upon receiving the *Alert message* from these nodes, the base station should find the best replacement strategy of the mobile nodes in the area $H$ to maximize the coverage rate and minimize the number of mobile nodes used for repairing the area $H$.

First, the base station checks the mobile sensor nodes around this area. For example, assume that there are $t$ mobile nodes around this area. In this case, the BS utilizes SFLA to search for the best node replacement strategy in the $H$-area. Then, it advertises the new spatial coordinates of the mobile nodes using a *Coverage message*. We illustrate this process with an example to understand it easily. In the following, we present some hypotheses for this problem:

**Algorithm 5** Replacing sensor nodes

**Input:** $Overlap_i$, $Packet_{size_i}$, $Buffer_{size_i}$
**Output:** *Covering a hole*

**Begin**
**$SN_i$:** Calculate $Priority_i$ using Equation (33);
**if** ($E_{residual_i}$ < *Treshold*) **then**
  **$SN_i$:** Send an *alert message* to the BS;
**end if**
**BS:** Receive the *alert message*;
**BS:** Extract $Priority_i$ from the *alert message*;
**if** ($Priority_i > P_{Threshold}$) **then**
  **BS:** Send a *Coverage message* to the nearest mobile node;
**end if**
**End**

- Figure 21 shows the coordinates of the area $H$ in the network. According to this figure, the spatial coordinates of the mobile sensor nodes ($s_i$) must be expressed based on Equation (34) to cover this area:

$$s_i = \{(x, y)|RS_i \leq x \leq RS_i + X', RS_i \leq y \leq RS_i + Y'\} \tag{34}$$

  In this equation, $RS_i$ represents the sensing radius of $s_i$, and $(X', Y')$ is the dimensions of the area $H$.
- In this example, assume that the initial population of frogs is 12. Moreover, each frog represents a solution to the problem, i.e., the new spatial coordinates of the mobile nodes for covering the area $H$ in the network.
- It is assumed that the number of mobile sensor nodes $s_i$ is equal to 10 (so that, $i = 1, \ldots, 10$).

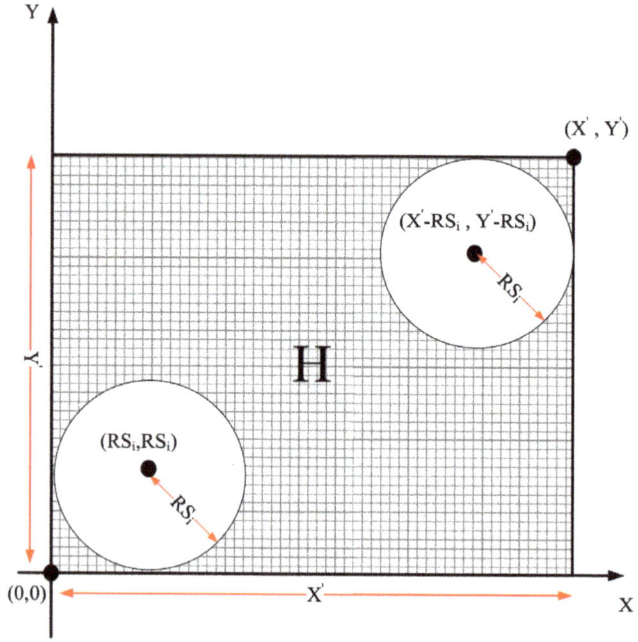


**Figure 21.** Coordinates of the area $H$ in the network.

To find the best solution for this problem (i.e., the best replacement strategy of mobile nodes in the area $H$) using SFLA, we perform the following steps:

**Step 1- Frog representation**

Each frog represents a solution for this problem, that is the new spatial coordinates of the mobile sensor nodes ($s_i$) in the network. Each frog is depicted as a two-dimensional array so that its length is equal to the total number of mobile nodes (in this example, the length is 10). In this array, each column corresponds to a mobile node. The first row indicates the number of mobile nodes used to cover the area $H$ so that its elements can be *zero* or *one*.

If an element is equal to *one*, then the corresponding node ($s_i$) has been applied for covering $H$. Otherwise, if its value is equal to *zero*, then the corresponding node ($s_i$) is not in the solution. The second row also represents the spatial coordinates of the mobile nodes ($s_i$) for covering the area $H$. Figure 22 shows an example of the frog representation. In this example, the frog (i.e., solution of this problem) includes several nodes, including $s_3$, $s_4$, $s_6$, $s_7$, $s_8$, and $s_{10}$, and their spatial coordinates are $(5,8)$, $(1,4)$, $(6,8)$, $(3,9)$, $(1,10)$, and $(2,8)$, respectively.

| 1 | 2 | 3 | 4 | 5 | 6 | 7 | 8 | 9 | 10 |
|---|---|---|---|---|---|---|---|---|---|
| 0 | 0 | 1 | 1 | 0 | 1 | 1 | 1 | 0 | 1 |
| (5,1) | (2,5) | (5,8) | (1,4) | (2,5) | (6,8) | (3,9) | (1,10) | (10,10) | (2,8) |

**Figure 22.** Frog representation.

**Step 2- Initial population establishment**

In this step, the population of frogs is randomly initialized. This process is done in such a way that the coordinates of each sensor node must be in the area $H$ (according to Equation (34)).

In the previous example, the initial population establishment process is shown in Figure 23.

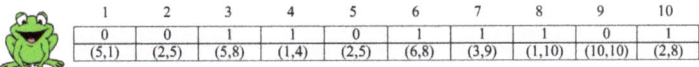

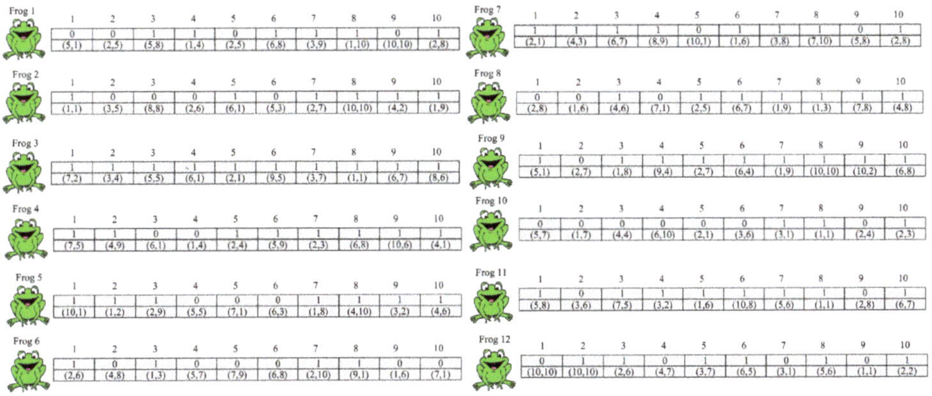

| Frog | | 1 | 2 | 3 | 4 | 5 | 6 | 7 | 8 | 9 | 10 |
|---|---|---|---|---|---|---|---|---|---|---|---|
| Frog 1 | | 0 | 0 | 1 | 1 | 0 | 1 | 1 | 1 | 0 | 1 |
| | | (5,1) | (2,5) | (5,8) | (1,4) | (2,5) | (6,8) | (3,9) | (1,10) | (10,10) | (2,8) |
| Frog 2 | | 1 | 0 | 0 | 0 | 1 | 0 | 1 | 1 | 1 | 1 |
| | | (1,1) | (3,5) | (8,8) | (2,6) | (6,1) | (5,3) | (2,7) | (10,10) | (4,2) | (1,9) |
| Frog 3 | | 1 | 1 | 1 | 1 | 1 | 1 | 1 | 1 | 1 | 1 |
| | | (7,2) | (3,4) | (5,5) | (6,1) | (2,1) | (9,5) | (3,7) | (1,1) | (6,7) | (8,6) |
| Frog 4 | | 1 | 1 | 0 | 0 | 1 | 1 | 1 | 1 | 1 | 1 |
| | | (7,5) | (4,9) | (6,1) | (1,4) | (2,4) | (5,9) | (2,3) | (6,8) | (10,6) | (4,1) |
| Frog 5 | | 1 | 1 | 1 | 0 | 0 | 0 | 1 | 1 | 1 | 1 |
| | | (10,1) | (1,2) | (2,9) | (5,5) | (7,1) | (6,3) | (1,8) | (4,10) | (3,2) | (4,6) |
| Frog 6 | | 1 | 0 | 1 | 0 | 0 | 0 | 1 | 1 | 0 | 0 |
| | | (2,6) | (4,8) | (1,3) | (5,7) | (7,9) | (6,8) | (2,10) | (9,1) | (1,6) | (7,1) |
| Frog 7 | | 1 | 1 | 1 | 1 | 0 | 1 | 1 | 1 | 0 | 1 |
| | | (2,1) | (4,3) | (6,7) | (8,9) | (10,1) | (1,6) | (3,8) | (7,10) | (5,8) | (2,8) |
| Frog 8 | | 0 | 0 | 1 | 0 | 1 | 1 | 1 | 1 | 1 | 1 |
| | | (2,8) | (1,6) | (4,6) | (7,1) | (2,5) | (6,7) | (1,9) | (1,3) | (7,8) | (4,8) |
| Frog 9 | | 1 | 0 | 1 | 1 | 1 | 1 | 1 | 1 | 1 | 1 |
| | | (5,1) | (2,7) | (1,8) | (9,4) | (2,7) | (6,4) | (1,9) | (10,10) | (10,2) | (6,8) |
| Frog 10 | | 0 | 0 | 0 | 0 | 0 | 0 | 1 | 1 | 0 | 1 |
| | | (5,7) | (1,7) | (4,4) | (6,10) | (2,1) | (3,6) | (3,1) | (1,1) | (2,4) | (2,3) |
| Frog 11 | | 1 | 0 | 1 | 1 | 1 | 1 | 1 | 1 | 0 | 1 |
| | | (5,8) | (3,6) | (7,5) | (3,2) | (1,6) | (10,8) | (5,6) | (1,1) | (2,8) | (6,7) |
| Frog 12 | | 0 | 1 | 1 | 0 | 1 | 1 | 0 | 1 | 0 | 1 |
| | | (10,10) | (10,10) | (2,6) | (4,7) | (3,7) | (6,5) | (3,1) | (5,6) | (1,1) | (2,2) |

**Figure 23.** The initial population establishment process.

**Step 3- Ranking the frogs**

In this step, we present a fitness function to evaluate each frog. Finally, the frogs are sorted based on its fitness value in descending order. The proposed fitness function is a multi-objective function that is expressed in Equation (35):

$$F = w_1 f_1 + w_2 f_2 \tag{35}$$

where $f_1$ is a function for evaluating the coverage of the $H$ area that has dimensions equal to $X' \times Y'$. The first goal of this optimization problem is to maximize the area coverage. Moreover, $f_2$ is a function that calculates the number of mobile sensor nodes ($s_i$) used in solution. The second goal of this problem is to find the solution with the minimum number of sensor nodes for covering the area $H$.

In addition, $w_1$ and $w_2$ are the weight coefficients, and thus $w_1 + w_2 = 1$, and $w_1 = w_2 = \frac{1}{2}$. $f_1$ and $f_2$ are normalized, and their values are in the range $[0, 1]$ to have the same effect on the fitness function. If $f_1$ approaches one, then it means a better area coverage, and therefore the fitness value of solution approaches one. If $f_2$ approaches one, it means that this solution has used the optimal number of mobile sensor nodes to cover the area $H$. As a result, $F$ approaches one. This is expressed in Equation (36):

$$\textbf{IF}\ \ f_1 \to 1\ \ \textbf{AND}\ \ f_2 \to 1\ \ \textbf{THEN}\ \ F \to 1 \tag{36}$$

To design the function $f_1$, we calculate the difference between the *Euclidean distance* of the two nodes $i$ and $j$ ($d_{ij}$) and the sum of the sensing radii of them ($RS_i + RS_j$).

$$f_1 = 1 - \left( \frac{\sqrt{\frac{2}{n(n-1)} \sum_{i=1}^{n-1} \sum_{j=i+1}^{n} \left(d_{ij} - (RS_i + RS_j)\right)^2}}{\frac{2}{n(n-1)} \sum_{i=1}^{n-1} \sum_{j=i+1}^{n} (RS_i + RS_j)} \right) \tag{37}$$

where $n > 0$ indicates the total number of mobile sensor nodes used to cover the $H$ area.

$f_2$ is a function that evaluates the number of mobile sensor nodes in the solution. It is remembered that our goal is to minimize the number of sensor nodes and maximize the area coverage. $f_2$ is obtained using Equation (38):

$$f_2 = \begin{cases} 1, & \min \le num_i \le \max \\ 1 - \left( \frac{|num_i - \min|}{\min} \right), & 0 \le num_i < \min \\ 1 - \left( \frac{|num_i - \max|}{\max} \right), & \max < num_i \le t \end{cases} \tag{38}$$

where $t$ represents the total number of mobile sensor nodes. $\min > 0$ indicates the minimum number of nodes that can cover the area $H$. When the minimum distance between sensor nodes with each other is equal to $2RS$, they have the least overlap with each other; where $RS$ indicates the sensing radius of the mobile nodes. We know that sensor nodes are heterogeneous. Therefore, we use the mean sensing radius ($\overline{RS}$) in the proposed method. $\overline{RS}$ is calculated using Equation (39):

$$\overline{RS} = \frac{1}{n} \sum_{i=1}^{n} RS_i \tag{39}$$

where $n$ is the number of mobile nodes used in the solution. $RS_i$ indicates the sensing range of $s_i$. Hence, we have:

$$\min = n_x \times n_y \tag{40}$$

where

$$n_x = \left\lfloor \frac{X'}{2\overline{RS}} \right\rfloor \qquad n_y = \left\lfloor \frac{Y'}{2\overline{RS}} \right\rfloor \tag{41}$$

$(X', Y')$ are dimensions of the area $H$ and $\overline{RS}$ is the mean sensing radius of mobile nodes. $\max > 0$ represents the maximum number of nodes required for covering the area $H$. According to [48], we know that the best coverage for nodes in the network is when they overlap slightly and all parts of the area $H$ are covered by at least one sensor node. In this case, the distance between sensor nodes is equal to $\sqrt{3}RS$. As mentioned, we have used the mean sensing radius ($\overline{RS}$) in Equation (43) because the sensor nodes are heterogeneous and have different sensing radii. As a result, we have:

$$\max = n'_x \times n'_y \tag{42}$$

where

$$\begin{aligned} n'_x &= \left\lceil \frac{X' - \overline{RS}}{\sqrt{3}\overline{RS}} \right\rceil + 1 \\ n'_y &= \left\lceil \frac{Y' - \overline{RS}}{\sqrt{3}\overline{RS}} \right\rceil + 1 \end{aligned} \tag{43}$$

**Step 4- Partitioning the frogs and creating memeplexes**

After evaluating the frogs, we sort them based on their fitness value in descending order. Then, the frogs are divided into $m$ memeplexes. This process is shown in Figure 24. According to this figure, the initial population of frogs is equal to 12. We divide it into three memeplexes, and each memeplex consists of 4 frogs.

**Step 5- Formation of sub-memeplexes**

In this step, each memeplex is divided into $n$ sub-complexes, which are shown in Figure 25.

**Step 6- Evolution of each sub-memeplex**

In this step, each sub-complex evolves based on the local exploration phase presented in SFLA, and thus the position of the worst frog $(x_w, y_w)$ in each sub-complex is improved according to Equation (44).

$$\begin{aligned} x_{new} &= x_w + S_{ix} \\ y_{new} &= y_w + S_{iy} \end{aligned} \tag{44}$$

where $(x_{new}, y_{new})$ is the new position of the frog. Moreover, $S_{ix}$ and $S_{iy}$ indicate the step size in the direction of the $x$ and $y$ axes, respectively; so that, $S_{\min} \leq S_{ix} \leq S_{\max}$ and $S_{\min} \leq S_{iy} \leq S_{\max}$.

$$\begin{aligned} S_{ix} &= Rand \times (x_B - x_w) \\ S_{iy} &= Rand \times (y_B - y_w) \end{aligned} \tag{45}$$

where $Rand$ is a random number in the range $[0, 1]$ and $(x_B, y_B)$ indicates position of the best frog in the submemeplex. If the new position is better than the old position, then the new position replaces the old position. Otherwise, the new position is deleted, and another new position is calculated based on Equation (46):

$$\begin{aligned} S_{ix} &= Rand \times (x_X - x_w) \\ S_{iy} &= Rand \times (y_X - y_w) \end{aligned} \tag{46}$$

where $(x_X, y_X)$ is the position of the best frog in the memeplex. If the new position is better than the old position, then it replaces the old position. Otherwise, the new position is removed and another new position is randomly calculated based on Equation (47) and replaces the old position:

$$\begin{aligned} x_{new} &= x_r \\ y_{new} &= y_r \end{aligned} \tag{47}$$

where $(x_r, y_r)$ is the position of a new frog that is generated randomly.

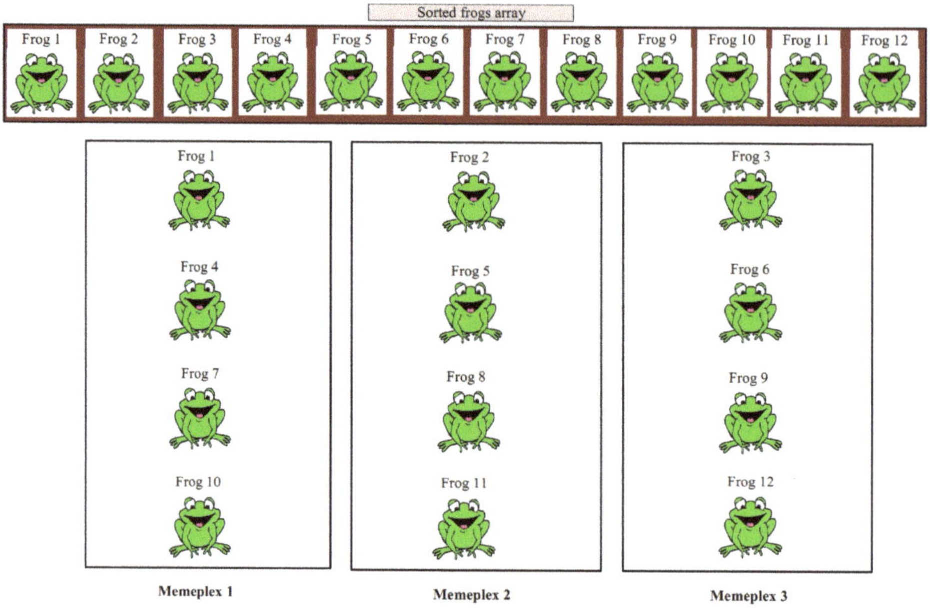


**Figure 24.** The formation of memeplexes.

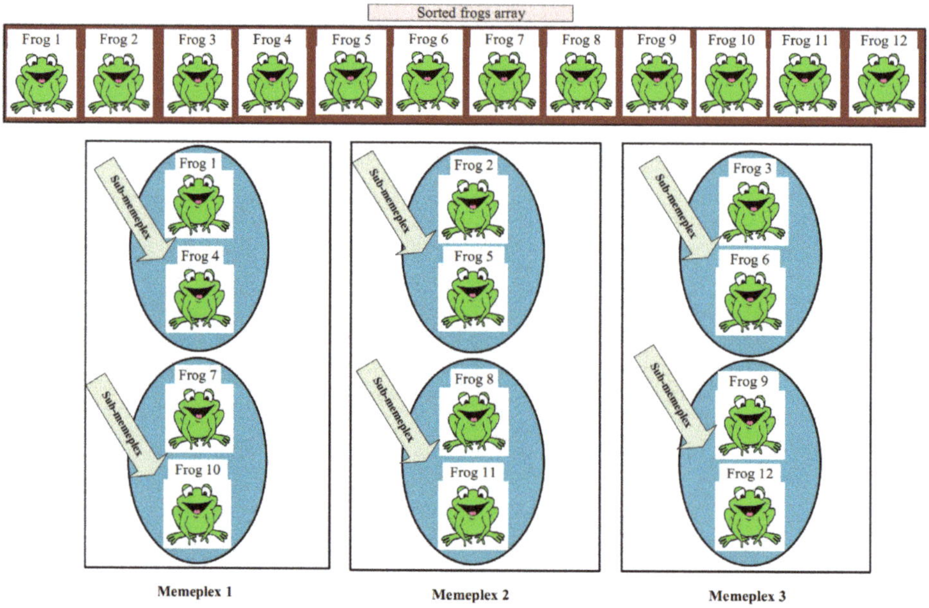


**Figure 25.** Partitioning memeplexes into sub-memeplexes.

**Step 7- Convergence checking**

In this step, the stop condition of SFLA is checked. If the stop condition is met, the algorithm is completed and the best solution will be returned as output. In our proposed method, the stop condition of the algorithm is that the number of iterations reaches $\lambda > 0$.

Algorithm 6 describes the pseudocode of the process of finding the best replacement strategy for mobile nodes in the area $H$ using SFLA.

---

**Algorithm 6** Covering a hole
---
**Input:** $S = \{s_1, s_2, \ldots, s_t\}$ {A set of mobile sensor nodes. In this example, $t = 10$.}
  $H : X' \times Y'$ {Hole area}
  $Population_{Size} = 12$ {This indicates the population size of frogs.}
  $Set_{Solution} = \{Frog_1, Frog_2, \ldots, Frog_{12}\}$
  $m$ {This is the number of memeplexes.}
  $n$ {This indicates the number of sub-memeplexes.}
  $P_G$ {This indicates the best frog in $Set_{Solution}$.}
  $(x_w, y_w)$ {This indicates the worst frog in each sub-memeplex.}
  $(x_B, y_B)$ {This indicates the best frog in each sub-memeplex.}
  $(x_X, y_X)$ {This indicates the best frog in each memeplex.}
**Output:** New position of mobile sensor nodes
  **Begin**
1: **BS:** Initialize $Set_{Solution}$ randomly;
2: **while** Convergence criteria is not met **do**
3:   **BS:** Evaluate frogs in $Set_{Solution}$ using the proposed fitness function in Equation (35);
4:   **BS:** Sort frogs in descending order based on their fitness value;
5:   **BS:** $P_G = Frog_1$;
6:   **BS:** Classify frogs in $m$ memeplexes;
7:   $Mem = \begin{cases} Mem_1, Mem_2, \ldots, Mem_m | \\ Frog1 \in Mem_1, Frog_2 \in Mem_2, \ldots, Frog_m \in \\ Mem_m, Frog_{m+1} \in Mem_1, \ldots \end{cases}$
8:   **for** $i = 1$ to $m$ **do**
9:     **BS:** Divide $Mem_i$ into $n$ sub-memplexes;
10:  **end for**
11:  **for** $i = 1$ to $m$ **do**
12:    **for** $j = 1$ to $n$ **do**
13:      **BS:** Improve $(x_w, y_w)$ based on Equation (44) and Equation (45);
14:      **if** (($x_{new}, y_{new}$) is not better than $(x_w, y_w)$) **then**
15:        **BS:** Remove $(x_{new}, y_{new})$;
16:        **BS:** Calculate a new position $(x_{new}, y_{new})$ based on Equation (44) and Equation (46);
17:        **if** (($x_{new}, y_{new}$) is not better than $(x_w, y_w)$) **then**
18:          **BS:** Remove $(x_{new}, y_{new})$;
19:          **BS:** Calculate a random position based on Equation (47);
20:        **end if**
21:      **end if**
22:    **end for**
23:  **end for**
24: **end while**
25: **BS:** Evaluate frogs in $Set_{Solution}$ using the proposed fitness function in Equation (35);
26: **BS:** Extract the best frog in $Set_{Solution}$ ($P_G$);
27: **BS:** Send a *Coverage message* based on $P_G$ to the mobile nodes;
  **End**

## 7. Simulation and Evaluation of Results

In this section, we simulate the proposed area coverage scheme using the NS2 software in a system with CPU 4GB Intel Core i4 2.40 GHz, RAM 4GB, and OS Ubuntu 15.04 LTS to evaluate its performance. Then, we compare its simulation results with three methods, including CCM-RL [30], CCA [31], and PCLA [32]. When simulating the proposed scheme, it is assumed that the network size is $1000 \times 1000$ m$^2$, and thus the sensor nodes are randomly distributed in this network. The number of nodes in the network varies between $250 \leq N \leq 2000$. 250 nodes are added to the network at each step. In the simulation process, it is assumed that sensor nodes have different sensing ranges, including, 25, 30, and 35 m. Moreover, they have different communication ranges, including 50, 60, and 70 m.

In addition, it is assumed that the amount of energy consumed by nodes is equal to 57 mA and 0.40 $\mu$A in ON and OFF modes, respectively. In Table 5, simulation parameters are presented briefly. We compare the proposed method with three methods, including CCM-RL [30], CCA [31], and PCLA [32] in terms of the average number of active sensor nodes, coverage rates, energy consumption, and network lifetime.

**Table 5.** Simulation parameters.

| Parameter | Value |
|---|---|
| Simulator | NS2 |
| Netwok size ($m^2$) | $1000 \times 1000$ |
| Number of nodes | $250 \leq N \leq 2000$ |
| Simulation time ($min$) | 20 |
| Sensing ranges ($m$) | $25, 30, 35$ |
| Communication ranges ($m$) | $50, 60, 70$ |
| Initial energy of sensor nodes ($J$) | 100 |
| Energy consumed by sensor nodes in ON mode ($mA$) | 57 |
| Energy consumed by sensor nodes in OFF mode ($\mu A$) | 0.40 |

### *7.1. The Average Number of Active Sensor Nodes*

The number of active sensor nodes indicates a subset of sensor nodes, which are selected to be in ON mode, for covering the RoI. An appropriate area coverage scheme should achieve a proper coverage rate with the minimum number of active sensor nodes. As shown in Figure 26, the proposed scheme has the lowest number of active sensor nodes at a scheduling round. On average, our scheme improves this value by 3.64%, 5.9%, and 8.81% compared to CCM-RL [30], CCA [31], and PCLA [32], respectively. This is because we use a fuzzy logic-based scheduling mechanism in the proposed method.

This fuzzy system determines the activity time of a sensor node based on three parameters, including the overlap between the sensing range of the sensor node and its neighboring nodes, residual energy, and distance between the sensor node and the base station. On the other hand, we calculate the overlap between a sensor node and its neighbor nodes using the digital matrix. This method helps the fuzzy system to calculate the activity time of sensor nodes based on their density in the network.

As a result, the proposed method activates the minimum sensor nodes in the dense regions. In addition, as shown in Figure 26, in all methods, when the number of sensor nodes increases in the network, the number of active nodes increases. When the number of nodes in the network is low, it means that the network density is also low. In this case, a coverage scheme cannot activate all sensor nodes (ON mode), because these sensor nodes consume high energy in this case.

As a result, the network lifetime will decrease. Therefore, all sensor nodes cannot be in ON mode at the same time. As a result, active nodes cannot properly cover the whole area. In contrast, when the network density is high, each of the coverage schemes can activate the more number of nodes. This improves the coverage quality of the RoI.

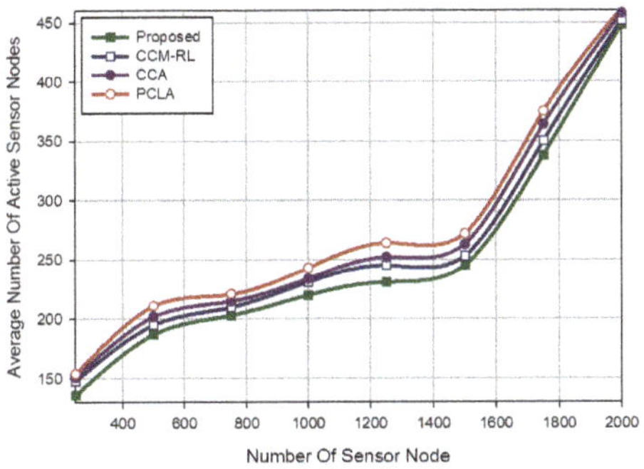


**Figure 26.** Comparison of different methods in terms of the average number of active sensor nodes.

## 7.2. Coverage Rate

The coverage rate represents the percentage of the area covered by the number of active nodes. As shown in Figure 27, our proposed scheme has the best performance compared to other schemes in terms of coverage rate. On average, it increases the coverage rate by 4.17%, 17.01%, and 21.88% compared to CCM-RL [30], CCA [31], and PCLA [32], respectively. The reason for this is that our scheme can calculate the overlap of the sensor nodes using the digital matrix (i.e., $DigitC_i$).

This helps the fuzzy system to activate nodes that have the lowest overlapping with each other. As a result, the proposed method can succeed for the best coverage rate with the minimum active nodes compared to other methods. On the other hand, the proposed method presents an SFLA-based detection and reconstruction mechanism for covering network holes; whereas, other schemes do not consider such a mechanism. This mechanism uses mobile nodes to rebuild the network holes.

As a result, the proposed method can ensure an appropriate coverage rate even if some sensor nodes die in the network. As shown in Figure 27, when increasing the number of active nodes in the network, the coverage rate increases in all methods. Our proposed method can achieve a coverage rate equal to 88% using 350 active sensor nodes.

Afterward, if the number of active sensor nodes increases, this coverage rate will be constant. CCM-RL [30] has a weaker function than our method. In this scheme, the coverage rate is not constant and rises with increasing the number of active sensor nodes. In the CCA [31] method, when the number of active nodes is 300, the coverage rate is fixed and equal to 77%. PCLA [32] has the weakest performance compared to other schemes in terms of coverage rate. When the number of active nodes in the network is 350, PCLA [32] can achieve a coverage rate equal to 73%.

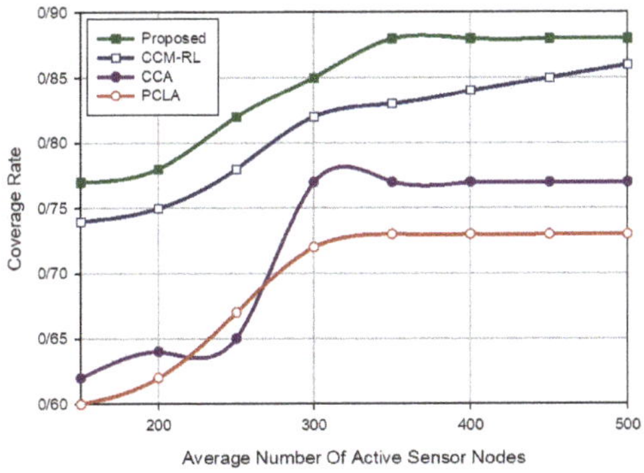


**Figure 27.** Comparison of different methods in terms of the coverage rate.

### 7.3. Energy Consumption

In Figure 28, different coverage schemes are compared with each other in terms of energy consumption. As shown in this figure, our proposed scheme has the lowest energy consumption compared with other methods. On average, it improves the energy consumption by 33.34%, 59.01% and 45.45% compared to CCM-RL [30], CCA [31] and PCLA [32], respectively. We consider the residual energy of sensor nodes in the proposed fuzzy scheduling mechanism. In this process, low-energy nodes are in OFF mode for more time to consume less energy.

This helps our scheme to balance the energy consumption in the network and reduce the energy consumption. As shown in Figure 28, CCM-RL [30] has the second rank compared to other methods in terms of energy consumption. This scheme uses the sensing range customization mechanism in the network. This mechanism helps sensor nodes to consume energy efficiently. In PCLA [32], the energy consumption is relatively high, which is due to the communication overhead and the coverage redundancy. Due to the high communication overhead, CCA [31] has the worst performance compared to others in terms of the energy consumption.

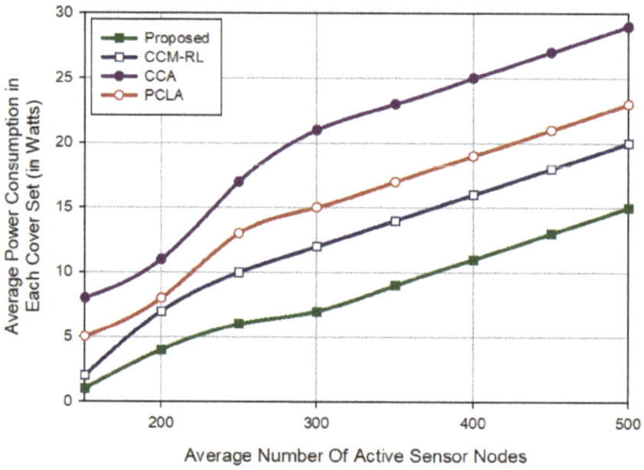


**Figure 28.** Comparison of different methods in terms of the average energy consumption.

### 7.4. Network Lifetime

In Figure 29, different methods are compared with each other in terms of the network lifetime. In this experiment, it is assumed that the number of alive sensor nodes in the network is equal to 200. These nodes lose their energy over time. When all nodes die, the network cannot continue its operations. As shown this figure, our proposed scheme has the highest network lifetime in comparison with other methods.

On average, it improves the network lifetime by 21.45%, 24.43% and 20.41% compared with CCM-RL [30], CCA [31] and PCLA [32], respectively. This shows that our method can distribute the energy consumption evenly between sensor nodes in the network. As the proposed method takes into account the residual energy of the sensor nodes in the scheduling mechanism based on fuzzy logic.

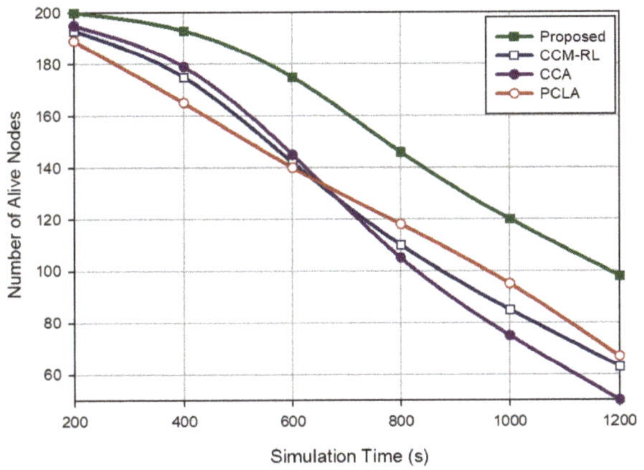


**Figure 29.** Comparison of different methods in terms of the network lifetime.

## 8. Conclusions

In this paper, an area coverage method was presented for heterogeneous wireless sensor networks. The purpose of this method is to balance the energy consumption of sensor nodes in the network, improve the network lifetime, and maximize the coverage rate in the network. To achieve these purposes, in the first phase, we presented a new, efficient and distributed method based on the digital matrix (i.e., $DigitC_i$) to calculate the overlap of each sensor node with its neighboring nodes accurately.

Then, in the second phase, we designed a fuzzy scheduling mechanism to determine the activity time of each sensor node ($Time_{ON}$) based on three parameters, including the overlap of each node with neighboring nodes, the residual energy and distance between each node and the base station. In the third phase, a strategy was presented to recognize early the death of sensor nodes and prevent the hole creation in the network. Finally, in the fourth phase, we proposed a SFLA-based solution to find the best placement strategy of mobile nodes in order to maximize the coverage rate of holes created in the network.

To evaluate the performance of the proposed scheme, we simulated it and compared our scheme with three methods, including CCM-RL [30], CCA [31], and PCLA [32]. Simulation results indicate that our proposed method outperformed the others. Our scheme can cover ROI with the lowest number of active sensor nodes. The important advantage of the proposed method is to simultaneously achieve the highest coverage rate and the lowest energy consumption compared to CCM-RL [30], CCA [31], and PCLA [32].

As a result, it improves the network lifetime compared to other methods. This show that our method can uniformly distribute energy consumption in the network. In the future, we seek to improve the efficiency of our method using machine learning techniques (ML) and metaheuristic algorithms.

**Author Contributions:** Conceptualization, M.S.Y., E.Y. and M.H.; Formal analysis, A.M.R. and S.A.; Funding acquisition, K.S.; Investigation, A.M.R.; Methodology, M.S.Y. and E.Y.; Project administration, A.M.R. and R.A.N.; Resources, K.S. and M.H.; Software, S.A.; Supervision, M.H.; review and editing, R.A.N. All authors have read and agreed to the published version of the manuscript.

**Funding:** This research was supported by Xiamen University Malaysia Research Fund (Grant No: XMUMRF/2019-C3/IECE/0006).

**Institutional Review Board Statement:** Not applicable.

**Informed Consent Statement:** Not applicable.

**Conflicts of Interest:** The authors declare no conflict of interest.

## References


1. Yousefpoor, E.; Barati, H.; Barati, A. A hierarchical secure data aggregation method using the dragonfly algorithm in wireless sensor networks. *Peer-Peer Netw. Appl.* **2021**, 14, 1–26. [CrossRef]
2. Yousefpoor, M.S.; Barati, H. Dynamic key management algorithms in wireless sensor networks: A survey. *Comput. Commun.* **2019**, *134*, 52–69. [CrossRef]
3. Goyal, P.; Sahoo, A.K.; Sharma, T.K.; Singh, P.K. Internet of Things: Applications, security and privacy: A survey. *Mater. Today Proc.* **2021**, *34*, 752–759. [CrossRef]
4. Saputro, N.; Tonyali, S.; Aydeger, A.; Akkaya, K.; Rahman, M.A.; Uluagac, S. A review of moving target defense mechanisms for internet of things applications. *Model. Des. Secur. Internet Things* **2020**, 15, 563–614. [CrossRef]
5. Sepasgozar, S.; Karimi, R.; Farahzadi, L.; Moezzi, F.; Shirowzhan, S.; Ebrahimzadeh, S.M.; Hui, F.; Aye, L. A systematic content review of artificial intelligence and the Internet of things applications in smart home. *Appl. Sci.* **2020**, *10*, 3074. [CrossRef]
6. Yousefpoor, M.S.; Yousefpoor, E.; Barati, H.; Barati, A.; Movaghar, A.; Hosseinzadeh, M. Secure data aggregation methods and countermeasures against various attacks in wireless sensor networks: A comprehensive review. *J. Netw. Comput. Appl.* **2021**, *190*, 103118 [CrossRef]
7. Yousefpoor, M.S.; Barati, H. DSKMS: A dynamic smart key management system based on fuzzy logic in wireless sensor networks. *Wirel. Netw.* **2020**, *26*, 2515–2535. [CrossRef]
8. Fahmy, H.M.A. *Wireless Sensor Networks: Energy Harvesting and Management for Research and Industry*; Springer Nature: Berlin, Germany, 2020. [CrossRef]
9. Mesbahi, M.R.; Rahmani, A.M.; Hosseinzadeh, M. Highly reliable architecture using the 80/20 rule in cloud computing datacenters. *Future Gener. Comput. Syst.* **2017**, *77*, 77–86. [CrossRef]
10. Javaheri, D.; Hosseinzadeh, M.; Rahmani, A.M. Detection and elimination of spyware and ransomware by intercepting kernel-level system routines. *IEEE Access* **2018**, *6*, 78321–78332. [CrossRef]
11. Golsorkhtabar, M.; Kaviani Nia, F.; Hosseinzadeh, M.; Vejdanparast, Y. The Novel Energy Adaptive Protocol for heterogeneous wireless sensor networks. In Proceedings of the 2010 3rd International Conference on Computer Science and Information Technology. Chengdu, China, 9–11 July 2010; Volume 2, pp. 178–182. [CrossRef]
12. Nikravan, M.; Movaghar, A.; Hosseinzadeh, M. A lightweight defense approach to mitigate version number and rank attacks in low-power and lossy networks. *Wirel. Pers. Commun.* **2018**, *99*, 1035–1059. [CrossRef]
13. Priyadarshi, R.; Gupta, B.; Anurag, A. Deployment techniques in wireless sensor networks: A survey, classification, challenges, and future research issues. *J. Supercomput.* **2020**, 76, 7333–7373. [CrossRef]
14. Shivalingegowda, C.; Jayasree, P. Hybrid gravitational search algorithm based model for optimizing coverage and connectivity in wireless sensor networks. *J. Ambient. Intell. Humaniz. Comput.* **2021**, *12*, 2835–2848. [CrossRef]
15. Wu, W.; Zhang, Z.; Lee, W.; Du, D. *Optimal Coverage in Wireless Sensor Networks*; Springer: Berlin/Heidelberg, Germany, 2020. [CrossRef]
16. Farsi, M.; Elhosseini, M.A.; Badawy, M.; Ali, H.A.; Eldin, H.Z. Deployment techniques in wireless sensor networks, coverage and connectivity: A survey. *IEEE Access* **2019**, *7*, 28940–28954. [CrossRef]
17. Chakraborty, S.; Goyal, N.K.; Soh, S. On area coverage reliability of mobile wireless sensor networks with multistate nodes. *IEEE Sens. J.* **2020**, *20*, 4992–5003. [CrossRef]
18. Elhabyan, R.; Shi, W.; St-Hilaire, M. Coverage protocols for wireless sensor networks: Review and future directions. *J. Commun. Netw.* **2019**, *21*, 45–60. [CrossRef]
19. Maheshwari, A.; Chand, N. A survey on wireless sensor networks coverage problems. In *Proceedings of the 2nd International Conference on Communication, Computing and Networking*; Springer: Berlin/Heidelberg, Germany, 2019; pp. 153–164. [CrossRef]
20. Yarinezhad, R.; Hashemi, S.N. A sensor deployment approach for target coverage problem in wireless sensor networks. *J. Ambient. Intell. Humaniz. Comput.* **2020**, *10*, 1–16. [CrossRef]
21. Keshmiri, H.; Bakhshi, H. A new 2-phase optimization-based guaranteed connected target coverage for wireless sensor networks. *IEEE Sens. J.* **2020**, *20*, 7472–7486. [CrossRef]
22. Khedr, A.M.; Al Aghbari, Z.; Pravija Raj, P. Coverage aware face topology structure for wireless sensor network applications. *Wirel. Netw.* **2020**, *26*, 4557–4577. [CrossRef]
23. Hajjej, F.; Hamdi, M.; Ejbali, R.; Zaied, M. A distributed coverage hole recovery approach based on reinforcement learning for Wireless Sensor Networks. *Ad Hoc Netw.* **2020**, *101*, 102082. [CrossRef]
24. Harizan, S.; Kuila, P. Evolutionary algorithms for coverage and connectivity problems in wireless sensor networks: A study. In *Design Frameworks for Wireless Networks*; Springer: Berlin/Heidelberg, Germany, 2020; pp. 257–280. [CrossRef]
25. Dorigo, M.; Birattari, M.; Stutzle, T. Ant colony optimization. *IEEE Comput. Intell. Mag.* **2006**, *1*, 28–39. [CrossRef]
26. Marini, F.; Walczak, B. Particle swarm optimization (PSO). A tutorial. *Chemom. Intell. Lab. Syst.* **2015**, *149*, 153–165. [CrossRef]
27. Karaboga, D.; Ozturk, C. A novel clustering approach: Artificial Bee Colony (ABC) algorithm. *Appl. Soft Comput.* **2011**, *11*, 652–657. [CrossRef]
28. Eusuff, M.; Lansey, K.; Pasha, F. Shuffled frog-leaping algorithm: A memetic meta-heuristic for discrete optimization. *Eng. Optim.* **2006**, *38*, 129–154. [CrossRef]
29. De Castro, L.N.; Timmis, J. Artificial immune systems: A novel approach to pattern recognition. In *Artificial Neural Networks in Pattern Recognition*; University of Paisley: Glasgow, UK, 2002; pp. 67–84.

30. Sharma, A.; Chauhan, S. A distributed reinforcement learning based sensor node scheduling algorithm for coverage and connectivity maintenance in wireless sensor network. *Wirel. Netw.* **2020**, *26*, 4411–4429. [CrossRef]
31. Yu, J.; Wan, S.; Cheng, X.; Yu, D. Coverage contribution area based *k*-coverage for wireless sensor networks. *IEEE Trans. Veh. Technol.* **2017**, *66*, 8510–8523. [CrossRef]
32. Mostafaei, H.; Montieri, A.; Persico, V.; Pescapé, A. A sleep scheduling approach based on learning automata for WSN partialcoverage. *J. Netw. Comput. Appl.* **2017**, *80*, 67–78. [CrossRef]
33. Hanh, N.T.; Binh, H.T.T.; Hoai, N.X.; Palaniswami, M.S. An efficient genetic algorithm for maximizing area coverage in wireless sensor networks. *Inf. Sci.* **2019**, *488*, 58–75. [CrossRef]
34. Luo, C.; Hong, Y.; Li, D.; Wang, Y.; Chen, W.; Hu, Q. Maximizing network lifetime using coverage sets scheduling in wireless sensor networks. *Ad Hoc Netw.* **2020**, *98*, 102037. [CrossRef]
35. Benahmed, T.; Benahmed, K. Optimal barrier coverage for critical area surveillance using wireless sensor networks. *Int. J. Commun. Syst.* **2019**, *32*, e3955. [CrossRef]
36. Saha, D.; Pal, S.; Das, N.; Bhattacharya, B.B. Fast estimation of area-coverage for wireless sensor networks based on digital geometry. *IEEE Trans. Multi-Scale Comput. Syst.* **2016**, *3*, 166–180. [CrossRef]
37. Binh, H.T.T.; Hanh, N.T.; Dey, N. Improved cuckoo search and chaotic flower pollination optimization algorithm for maximizing area coverage in wireless sensor networks. *Neural Comput. Appl.* **2018**, *30*, 2305–2317. [CrossRef]
38. Binh, H.T.T.; Hanh, N.T.; Nghia, N.D.; Dey, N. Metaheuristics for maximization of obstacles constrained area coverage in heterogeneous wireless sensor networks. *Appl. Soft Comput.* **2020**, *86*, 105939. [CrossRef]
39. Li, Q.; Liu, N. Monitoring area coverage optimization algorithm based on nodes perceptual mathematical model in wireless sensor networks. *Comput. Commun.* **2020**, *155*, 227–234. [CrossRef]
40. Kashi, S.S. Area coverage of heterogeneous wireless sensor networks in support of Internet of Things demands. *Computing* **2019**, *101*, 363–385. [CrossRef]
41. Miao, Z.; Yuan, X.; Zhou, F.; Qiu, X.; Song, Y.; Chen, K. Grey wolf optimizer with an enhanced hierarchy and its application to the wireless sensor network coverage optimization problem. *Appl. Soft Comput.* **2020**, *96*, 106602. [CrossRef]
42. Wang, F.Y.; Pedrycz, W.; Herrera, F.; Su, S.F. Fuzzy Logic and Artificial Intelligence: A Special Issue on Emerging Techniques and Their Applications. *IEEE Trans. Fuzzy Syst.* **2020**, *28*, 3063–3064. [CrossRef]
43. Vilela, M.; Oluyemi, G.; Petrovski, A. A fuzzy inference system applied to value of information assessment for oil and gas industry. *Decis. Making Appl. Manag. Eng.* **2019**, *2*, 1–18. [CrossRef]
44. Nguyen, P.L.; La, V.Q.; Nguyen, A.D.; Nguyen, T.H.; Nguyen, K. An On-Demand Charging for Connected Target Coverage in WRSNs Using Fuzzy Logic and Q-Learning. *Sensors* **2021**, *21*, 5520. [CrossRef]
45. Bayrakdar, M.E. Enhancing sensor network sustainability with fuzzy logic based node placement approach for agricultural monitoring. *Comput. Electron. Agric.* **2020**, *174*, 105461. [CrossRef]
46. Peng, W.; Li, C.; Zhang, G.; Yi, J. Interval type-2 fuzzy logic based transmission power allocation strategy for lifetime maximization of WSNs. *Eng. Appl. Artif. Intell.* **2020**, *87*, 103269. [CrossRef]
47. Baradaran, A.A.; Navi, K. HQCA-WSN: High-quality clustering algorithm and optimal cluster head selection using fuzzy logic in wireless sensor networks. *Fuzzy Sets Syst.* **2020**, *389*, 114–144. [CrossRef]
48. Wang, B.; Lim, H.B.; Ma, D. A coverage-aware clustering protocol for wireless sensor networks. *Comput. Netw.* **2012**, *56*, 1599–1611. [CrossRef]

*mathematics*

MDPI

*Article*

# Fuzzy Bit-Plane-Dependence Region Competition

**Siukai Choy *, Tszching Ng, Carisa Yu and Benson Lam**

Department of Mathematics, Statistics and Insurance, The Hang Seng University of Hong Kong, Hong Kong 999077, China; tcng@hsu.edu.hk (T.N.); carisayu@hsu.edu.hk (C.Y.); bensonlam@hsu.edu.hk (B.L.)
* Correspondence: skchoy@hsu.edu.hk; Tel.: +852-3963-5113

**Abstract:** This paper presents a novel variational model based on fuzzy region competition and statistical image variation modeling for image segmentation. In the energy functional of the proposed model, each region is characterized by the pixel-level color feature and region-level spatial/frequency information extracted from various image domains, which are modeled by the windowed bit-plane-dependence probability models. To efficiently minimize the energy functional, we apply an alternating minimization procedure with the use of Chambolle's fast duality projection algorithm, where the closed-form solutions of the energy functional are obtained. Our method gives soft segmentation result via the fuzzy membership function, and moreover, the use of multi-domain statistical region characterization provides additional information that can enhance the segmentation accuracy. Experimental results indicate that the proposed method has a superior performance and outperforms the current state-of-the-art superpixel-based and deep-learning-based approaches.

**Keywords:** bit-plane; fuzzy region competition; image segmentation

**Citation:** Choy, S.; Ng, T.; Yu, C.; Lam, B. Fuzzy Bit-Plane-Dependence Region Competition. *Mathematics* **2021**, *9*, 2392. https://doi.org/10.3390/math9192392

Academic Editor: Michael Voskoglou

Received: 2 September 2021
Accepted: 22 September 2021
Published: 26 September 2021



## 1. Introduction

Image segmentation, which aims to partition an image into homogeneous regions [1–3], is one of the most challenging problems in computer vision and has various applications, such as pattern recognition and medical imaging. Among the existing approaches, variational methods have been extensively investigated and the best-known approach is the classical active contour model [4–6], which adopts a boundary function to evolve the curve on the object boundary. Nevertheless, this approach is sensitive to noise, and thus, an unsatisfactory segmentation result may be obtained for a noisy image. In order to obtain a smooth segmentation from a noisy image, Tong et al. [7] proposed a multi-scale approach to suppress various types of noises by minimizing a boundary threshold surface function. Although these methods work well for some natural images, they largely consider edge information without involving other essential image features, and hence, fail to segment images with complex texture structures. As well as boundary-based methods, region-based approaches are also popular methodologies that make use of both the boundary and region information. The most influential approach is the variational model proposed by Mumford and Shah [8], which estimates an image by the piecewise smooth functions with regular boundaries. Chan and Vese [9] studied a particular case of the Mumford-Shah model using the piecewise constant functions and applied their model to a two-phase image segmentation problem. They proposed a curve evolution technique with a level set [10] formulation to minimize the energy functional. The Chan-Vese model was then extended to vector-valued [11] and multiphase [12] cases. However, experimental results indicate that the piecewise constant functions can only be applied to simple images with homogeneous structures and fail to segment images with complex texture patterns. In [13], the authors proposed a non-convex and convex coupling variational segmentation model based on the total generalized $p$-variation regularizer and Mumford-Shah model to preserve the boundary and detect the structure in the image. Region competition [1] is another widely used variational image segmentation method that penalizes the boundary length and the

Bayes error in each image region is characterized by a probability distribution. Based on the classical region competition model, a novel clustering-based region competition approach [14] was proposed for image segmentation. A non-parametric approach using information theory and curve evolution [15] was also studied, with remarkable success.

The aforementioned approaches adopt binary segmentation that gives hard results. Nevertheless, hard-labeling may not be the optimal scheme because natural images usually have a small dynamic range or limited spatial resolution, which blurs the distinction between image regions, leading to the degradation of boundary identification. The fuzzy segmentation method [16–21], which applies a membership function valued between zero and one to measure the association degree of each pixel to all regions, is an alternative approach that has been frequently used in data mining, medical images [22–24], and so on. The major advantage of a fuzzy approach is that the optimization problem is convex with respect to the membership function. As a result, the model is not sensitive to initialization and the global minimum may be found explicitly. In [2], Li et al. applied a piecewise constant fuzzy region competition model for multiphase image segmentation. The energy functional was solved using the alternating minimization procedure in which the closed-form solutions were obtained. Experimental results for typical gray-scale and color images have shown satisfactory results. A variational multiphase image segmentation model with the fuzzy membership functions and L1-norm fidelity was proposed in [25]. An alternating direction method of multipliers was adopted to solve the energy functional. Experiments demonstrate that this approach is robust to impulse noise and thus provides satisfactory results. As with the Chan-Vese model, however, the segmentation accuracy of the above methods will be lower for complex images because the piecewise constant functions are not suffice in characterizing indispensable image region information. Recently, a robust active contour segmentation by a fractional-order differential method and fuzzy statistical information of boundaries was proposed for vascular image segmentation [26]. Luo et al. [27] developed an unsupervised multi-region method based on fuzzy active contour model for segmenting SAR images. Compared with the level set-based framework, this method is computationally much more efficient and robust to strong noise. A level set model using an optimized fuzzy region clustering technique [28] was also presented for biomedical MRI and CT scan image segmentation. Their proposed algorithm is capable of identifying weak boundaries and can segment the desired components of an image. In [29], the authors proposed an improved fuzzy region competition-based framework via the hierarchical strategy so that the minimization problem is always convex during the iterative calculation. Their method was applied to noisy SAR images, with satisfactory segmentation results.

Although most variational region-based segmentation approaches perform satisfactorily for some natural and textural images, they consider only simple features from a particular image domain as region characterization, and thus, may not perform well for images with sophisticated texture patterns. In such a case, high-level features from various image domains are critical to deal with complex images. In [30], the authors used a geodesic active contour in conjunction with the Gabor features to segment texture images. A vectorial piecewise constant Mumford-Shah model [31] was adopted for the Gabor filtered images, producing a satisfactory performance. Moreover, a level set formulation with a structure tensor and nonlinear diffusion [32] was employed for unsupervised texture segmentation. A new large-scale image segmentation method that combines fuzzy region competition and the Gaussian mixture model [33] was also proposed. Experimental results indicate that this approach has a superior performance on remote sensing images. In addition to the image features mentioned above, the distribution of image variation is one of the most important and useful features which has been widely used in various areas with satisfactory results. Nevertheless, the distribution should not be directly used because the high dimensionality leads to extremely high computational cost for real-time applications. Hence, there are compelling reasons to develop a more powerful representation to replace the distribution while preserving its important properties. Recently, many effective and efficient statistical methods have been proposed to model the distributions. Essentially, the choice of a parametric family of models depends on the applications and the model itself should be mathematically and statistically tractable. For instance, Do and Vetterli [34] proposed the use of a generalized Gaussian density (GGD) to model wavelet subband histograms and successfully applied GGD to texture retrieval. A characteristic GGD based on Kullback-Leibler divergence [35] and the generalized Gamma density [36] were proposed and applied to supervised texture classification with promising results. While these models usually work well for most distributions of image variation, they always assume the distributions have a specific structure (such as symmetry, monotone and periodicity) and cannot model fluctuating distributions. To remedy this shortcoming, the bit-plane-based probability models [19,37,38] were proposed to characterize image variations that do not need to have specific structures. Thus, incorporating these models to characterize image regions into the energy functional would help to enhance the segmentation of texture images and deal with challenging segmentation problem.

*Motivation and Contribution*

Variational image segmentation methodology is well-established in the literature and fuzzy region competition is by far one of the most popular approaches. Traditional fuzzy region competition models consider simple boundary and region features extracted in a specific image domain, but they are unable to capture essential image information, and thus, hard to segment images with low color contrast and complex textured patterns. In addition, an appropriate and sophisticated probability distribution should be adopted to correctly characterize the image region in order to enhance the segmentation accuracy. Nevertheless, a simple probability distribution (e.g., Gaussian distribution) is typically employed in order to obtain a closed-form solution of the energy functional so that a time-consuming numerical algorithm is avoided to estimate the parameters of the probability distribution. Motivated by the above issues and recent research on statistical image variation modeling, we propose a novel variational approach that can tackle the limitations of existing algorithms. The contributions of this paper are summarized below.

- We propose a novel variational model that integrates the pixel-level color feature and region-level spatial/frequency information into the fuzzy region competition for image segmentation. Specifically, we propose using the windowed bit-plane-dependence probability models to characterize spatial/frequency region information extracted from various image domains to improve the segmentation accuracy;
- A fuzzy bit-plane-dependence region competition algorithm is developed based on the alternating minimization procedure with the Chambolle's fast duality projection algorithm. In addition, the closed-form solutions for model parameters and fuzzy membership function are obtained and no numerical algorithm is necessary for parameter estimation, thus making the proposed algorithm much faster.

This paper is organized as follows. Section 2 introduces the bit-plane-based probability models for image region characterization. In Section 3, we present the fuzzy bit-plane-dependence region competition model. Section 4 presents the optimization procedure and the overall implementation. Experimental results are shown in Sections 5 and 6 concludes the paper.

## 2. Bit-Plane-Dependence Probability Model

The modeling of image variation by a parametric family of statistical distributions plays an important role in many applications. Many studies reveal that using a robust parametric model to represent image variation leads to satisfactory texture classification and retrieval performance. In this section, we present the bit-plane-dependence probability model and use it as a region characterization for our proposed segmentation model as presented in Section 3.

Pi et al. [37] first proposed using the product of Bernoulli distributions (PBD) to model the distributions of image variation. The idea is summarized as follows: given a collection of coefficients of image variation, each coefficient $Y$ is quantized into a nonnegative integer, which is then transformed into the following $m$ binary bit-planes:

$$Y = \sum_{i=0}^{m-1} 2^i Y_i, \tag{1}$$

where $Y_i \in \{0,1\}$ is a Bernoulli random variable representing the $i$th binary bit of the quantized coefficient. Based on (1), the joint probability distribution of the quantized coefficients is

$$P(Y = y) = P(Y_0 = y_0, Y_1 = y_1, \ldots, Y_{m-1} = y_{m-1}), y = 0,\ 1, \ldots,\ 2^m - 1, \tag{2}$$

where $\{y_0, y_1, \ldots, y_{m-1}\}$ is a binary representation of $y$. Let$p_i = P(Y_i = 1), i = 0, 1, \ldots,$ $m-1$, and assume that $Y_i : i = 0, 1, \ldots,\ m-1$ are statistically independent, then (2) can be written as PBD, as follows:

$$P^{\mathrm{PBD}}(Y = y) = \prod_{i=0}^{m-1} P(Y_i = y_i) = \prod_{i=0}^{m-1} p_i^{y_i} (1 - p_i)^{1-y_i}. \tag{3}$$

The major advantage of PBD is that it performs excellently in modeling wavelet subbands and provides a satisfactory performance in fitting low-degree fluctuating histograms [38]. Experimental results [37,38] also show that PBD performs better than GGD [34] in supervised texture retrieval. Furthermore, compared with most existing model parameter estimation methods, the bit-plane probabilities $p_i$ can be efficiently extracted via the counting of 1-bit occurrence for each bit-plane.

Note that the PBD model (3) assumes all bit-planes are independent, but such an assumption may not be appropriate because dependencies may exist between bit-planes. This shortcoming can be alleviated by incorporating conditional probabilities between successive bit-planes into (2):

$$P(Y = y) = P(Y_0 = y_0) \prod_{i=1}^{m-1} P(Y_i = y_i | Y_{i-1} = y_{i-1}), y = 0,\ 1, \ldots,\ 2^m - 1.$$

Let $\lambda_i = P(Y_i = 1 | Y_{i-1} = 1), i = 1, 2, \ldots, m-1$, and assume successive bit-plane dependence. Then, we obtain the following bit-plane-dependence probability model (BDPM):

$$\begin{aligned} P^{\mathrm{BDPM}}(Y = y) &= p_0^{y_0} (1 - p_0)^{1-y_0} \prod_{i=1}^{m-1} \lambda_i^{y_{i-1} y_i} (1 - \lambda_i)^{y_{i-1}(1-y_i)} \\ &\times \left( \tfrac{p_i - \lambda_i p_{i-1}}{1 - p_{i-1}} \right)^{(1-y_{i-1}) y_i} \left( 1 - \tfrac{p_i - \lambda_i p_{i-1}}{1 - p_{i-1}} \right)^{(1-y_{i-1})(1-y_i)} \end{aligned} \tag{4}$$

where $\max(0, 1 - (1 - p_i)/p_{i-1}) \le \lambda_i \le \min(p_i/p_{i-1}, 1)$ such that the conditional probabilities are between zero and one. Note that (4) reduces to (3) when $\lambda_i = p_i, i = 1, \ldots,\ m-1$. The major advantages of (4) are threefold [19]. Firstly, the maximum likelihood estimators of model parameters are joint sufficient statistics, which capture all possible information about the model parameters that is in the data. Secondly, compared with the current image variation models which assume that the distributions have specific structures such as symmetry, monotone, and periodicity, BDPM provides a universal parametric representation that can be used to model random distributions without enforcing any specific restrictions on the distributions. Thirdly, experiments show that BDPM outperforms PBD in terms of image variation modeling.

## 3. Fuzzy Bit-Plane-Dependence Region Competition Model

Having introduced the bit-plane-dependence probability model, we present, in this section, the fuzzy bit-plane-dependence region competition model. We start by formulating the segmentation problem as follows: let $I$ be an image with image domain $\Omega$, the goal of segmentation is to partition $\Omega$ into $N$ regions $\{\Omega_j : j = 1, 2, \ldots, N\}$ by a suitable measure such that $\Omega_i \cap \Omega_j = \varnothing$, $i \neq j$, and $\Omega = \Omega_i \cup \cdots \cup \Omega_N \cup \Gamma$ with $\Gamma$ representing the boundaries of all regions.

Various successful fuzzy region competition approaches in the literature are generally based on the optimization of an energy functional consisting of both the boundary and region information. The general form of energy functional for segmenting $I$ into $N$ phases can be represented as:

$$E(\delta, U) = \sum_{j=1}^{N} \int_{\Omega} |\nabla u_j| dx - \alpha \sum_{j=1}^{N} \int_{\Omega} u_j \log P_j(I|\delta_j) dx \tag{5}$$

with constraints

$$\text{(i)} \sum_{j=1}^{N} u_j = 1, \ \text{(ii)} \ 0 \leq u_j \leq 1, j = 1, 2, \ldots, N, \tag{6}$$

where $\delta = \{\delta_j : j = 1, 2, \ldots, N\}$ is a set of parameters for the regions $\{\Omega_j : j = 1, 2, \ldots, N\}$, $U = \left\{u_j : u_j \in BV_{[0,1]}(\Omega),\ j = 1, 2, \ldots, N\right\}$ with $BV_{[0,1]}(\Omega)$ is a space of the functions of the bounded variations taking their values between zero and one, $P_j(I|\delta_j)$ is a probability distribution of region $\Omega_j$ characterized by the parameter $\delta_j$, and $\alpha$ is a positive constant that balances the two energy terms. In (5), the first term is a total variation that measures the lengths of boundaries for all of the image regions in a fuzzy manner whereas the second term is the sum of the cost for coding the intensity of every pixel inside each region according to a probability distribution $P_j(I|\delta_j)$.

Most existing fuzzy region competition models consider only simple image features extracted from a particular image domain, but these features may not capture essential region information, especially for images with low color contrast and complex textured structures. Hence, it is expected that the overall segmentation results would improve if the effective texture features extracted from different image domains could be adopted in conjunction with color for region characterization. As mentioned in Section 2, we propose using the bit-plane-dependence probability model to characterize local region information in various image domains and incorporating (4) into the energy functional (5).

*The Proposed Model*

Let $I^0$ be a color image and $I^1$ be the associated gray-scale image. We assume that the spatial image components of $I^1$ in a particular region $\Omega_j$ are independent and identically distributed (i.i.d.) samples generated by a family of probability distribution $P_j^1\left(I^1|\phi_j^1\right)$, where $\phi_j^1$ is the parameter of the distribution $P_j^1$. To utilize the region information extracted from other image domains, we let $\{\Psi_q : q = 2, 3, \ldots, Q\}$ be a collection of image transform operators which transform $I^1$ into a series of transformed images $\{I^q : q = 2, 3, \ldots, Q\}$ in the associated image domains, i.e., $I^q = \Psi_q(I^1)$. In the same region $\Omega_j$, we further assume that the region components of the respective image domain are i.i.d. samples generated by a family of probability distribution $P_j^q\left(I^q|\phi_j^q\right)$, where $\phi_j^q$ is the parameter of the distribution $P_j^q$. To integrate the model (4) into the energy functional (5), we use BDPM for all probability distributions $\left\{P_j^q : j = 1, 2, \ldots, N; q = 1, 2, \ldots, Q\right\}$. That is,

$$\begin{aligned} P_j^q(I^q|\phi_j^q) = & \left(p_{0j}^q\right)^{y_0^q} (1 - p_{0j}^q)^{1-y_0^q} \prod_{i=1}^{m-1} \left(\lambda_{ij}^q\right)^{y_{i-1}^q y_i^q} (1 - \lambda_{ij}^q)^{y_{i-1}^q (1-y_i^q)} \\ & \times \left(\frac{p_{ij}^q - \lambda_{ij}^q p_{i-1j}^q}{1 - p_{i-1j}^q}\right)^{(1-y_{i-1}^q) y_i^q} \left(1 - \frac{p_{ij}^q - \lambda_{ij}^q p_{i-1j}^q}{1 - p_{i-1j}^q}\right)^{(1-y_{i-1}^q)(1-y_i^q)} \end{aligned} \tag{7}$$

where $\phi_j^q = \left\{ \left( p_{0j}^q, p_{ij}^q, \lambda_{ij}^q \right) : i = 1,2,\ldots,m-1 \right\}$. In addition, the CIELAB color feature with the $L_2$-norm as a dissimilarity measurement is incorporated into (5) to capture pixel-level information. The CIELAB color space is adopted because it is perceptually uniform with respect to human color vision and performs well in various applications. Then, we obtain the following fuzzy bit-plane-dependence region competition energy functional:

$$E(\phi, C, U) = \sum_{j=1}^{N} \int_\Omega |\nabla u_j| dx + \alpha_0 \sum_{j=1}^{N} \int_\Omega u_j \left( I^0 - c_j \right)^2 dx - \sum_{q=1}^{Q} \alpha_q \sum_{j=1}^{N} \int_\Omega u_j \log P_j^q \left( I^q | \phi_j^q \right) dx \tag{8}$$

subject to the constraints (6), where $\phi = \left\{ \phi_j^q : j = 1,2,\ldots,N; q = 1,2,\ldots Q \right\}$ is a set of parameters for the probability distributions $\left\{ P_j^q : j = 1,2,\ldots,N; q = 1,2,\ldots,Q \right\}$, $C = \left\{ c_j : j = 1,2,\ldots,N \right\}$ is a set of CIELAB color parameters, $U = \left\{ u_j : j = 1,2,\ldots,N \right\}$ is a fuzzy membership function, and $\left\{ \alpha_q : q = 0,1,2,\ldots,Q \right\}$ are fixed parameters.

Note that the major drawback of (8) is that the misclassification of an image pixel would occur because of the noise or statistical fluctuation of data in various image domains, as only a single sample is taken from each probability distribution. To overcome this shortcoming, we propose incorporating the neighboring information around each pixel into (8). Let $W_x^M$ be an $M \times M$ window centered at pixel x. For each image domain, the probability distribution $P_j^q \left( I^q | \phi_j^q \right)$ is replaced by $\left( \prod_{W_x^M} P_j^q \left( I^q | \phi_j^q \right) \right)^{1/M^2}$, which is the geometric mean of BDPM over $W_x^M$. In fact, $\log P_j^q \left( I^q | \phi_j^q \right)$ is replaced by $(1/M^2) \sum_{W_x^M} \log P_j^q \left( I^q | \phi_j^q \right)$, which is the average of log-likelihood functions over $W_x^M$. Hence, we can rewrite the energy functional (8), as follows:

$$\begin{aligned} E(\phi, C, U) = & \sum_{j=1}^{N} \int_\Omega |\nabla u_j| dx + \alpha_0 \sum_{j=1}^{N} \int_\Omega u_j (I^0 - c_j)^2 dx \\ & - \sum_{q=1}^{Q} \alpha_q \sum_{j=1}^{N} \int_\Omega u_j \left( \log \left( \prod_{W_x^M} P_j^q \left( I^q | \phi_j^q \right) \right)^{1/M^2} \right) dx \end{aligned} \tag{9}$$

We remark that the CIELAB color characterizes pixel-level information whereas the windowed BDPM model captures region-level information. In addition, the energy functional (9) not only provides local region information in the spatial domain, as in the original and existing region competition models, but also provides local region information extracted from other image domains (i.e., when $q = 2,3,\ldots,Q$), which is expected to improve the overall segmentation performance.

## 4. The Optimization Procedure

The minimization of (9) with the BDPM model (7) and the constraints of (6) form a class of constrained nonlinear optimization problems whose solutions are unknown. Various methodologies can be used to minimize the energy functional, such as curve evolution via the level-set formulation or alternating minimization method. In this paper, we shall use the alternating minimization procedure and make use of the fast duality projection algorithm of Chambolle [39]. Note that the data fidelity and regularization terms in the energy functional are coupled, thus we introduce a collection of auxiliary variables $V = \left\{ v_j : j = 1,2,\ldots,N \right\}$ to decouple these two terms. Specifically, we shall approximate (9) by replacing $u_j$ with $v_j$ in the regularization term and adding convex terms that force $u_j$ and $v_j$ to be sufficiently close:

$$\begin{aligned} E(\phi, C, U, V) = & \sum_{j=1}^{N} \int_\Omega |\nabla v_j| dx + \frac{1}{2\theta} \sum_{j=1}^{N} \int_\Omega (v_j - u_j)^2 dx \\ & + \alpha_0 \sum_{j=1}^{N} \int_\Omega u_j (I^0 - c_j)^2 dx - \sum_{q=1}^{Q} \alpha_q \sum_{j=1}^{N} \int_\Omega u_j \left( \log \left( \prod_{W_x^M} P_j^q \left( I^q | \phi_j^q \right) \right)^{1/M^2} \right) dx \end{aligned} \tag{10}$$

where $\theta$ is a small positive constant such that $u_j$ is sufficiently close to $v_j$ with respect to the $L_2$-norm. In what follows, the alternating minimization procedure is adopted to perform the optimization of (10).

### 4.1. CIELAB Color Parameter

Fixing $\phi$, $U$ and $V$, we compute $C = \{c_j : j = 1, 2, \ldots, N\}$ by setting

$$\frac{\partial E_{\phi,U,V}(C)}{\partial c_j} = \int_\Omega u_j \left( I^0 - c_j \right) dx = 0$$

It is straight forward to demonstrate that

$$\hat{c}_j = \frac{\int_\Omega u_j I^0 dx}{\int_\Omega u_j dx}, j = 1, 2, \ldots, N, \tag{11}$$

which is simply the CIELAB color weighted by the fuzzy membership function.

### 4.2. Windowed BDPM Parameter

Fixing $C, U, V,$ we solve $\phi = \left\{ \phi_j^q : j = 1, 2, \ldots, N; q = 1, 2, \ldots Q \right\}$ with $\phi_j^q = \left\{ \left( p_{0j}^q, p_{ij}^q, \lambda_{ij}^q \right) : i = 1, 2, \ldots, m-1 \right\}$ by minimizing

$$E_{C,U,V}(\phi) = \sum_{q=1}^{Q} \alpha_q \sum_{j=1}^{N} \int_\Omega u_j \left( \log \left( \prod_{W_x^M} P_j^q \left( I^q | \phi_j^q \right) \right)^{1/M^2} \right) dx. \tag{12}$$

Taking the partial derivatives of (12) with respect to $p_{ij}^q$ and $\lambda_{ij}^q$ followed by setting them to zero leads to

$$\hat{p}_{i,j}^q = \frac{\int_\Omega u_j \left( \frac{1}{M^2} \int_{W_x^M} y_i^q dz \right) dx}{\int_\Omega u_j dx}, i = 0, 1, \ldots, m-1; j = 1, 2, \ldots, N; q = 1, 2, \ldots, Q, \tag{13}$$

$$\hat{\lambda}_{i,j}^q = \frac{\int_\Omega u_j \left( \int_{W_x^M} y_{i-1}^q y_i^q dz \right) dx}{\int_\Omega u_j \left( \int_{W_x^M} y_{i-1}^q dz \right) dx}, i = 1, 2, \ldots, m-1; j = 1, 2, \ldots, N; q = 1, 2, \ldots, Q. \tag{14}$$

In (13) and (14), the estimators are the weighted local sample mean of 1-bit occurrence, and the weighted local average of 1-bit occurrence in successive bit-planes, respectively, within a window for each region in a particular image domain. It is important to remark that the windowed BDPM parameter has a closed-form solution, which implies that it can be obtained efficiently via only the bit-plane extraction. Note that when $M = 1$, the neighboring information is neglected and only pixel-level bit-plane information is captured, whereas the region-level bit-plane information is extracted through the windowed BDPM when $M > 1$.

### 4.3. Total Variation Minimization

Fixing $\phi$, $C$ and $U$, we compute $V$ by minimizing

$$E_{\phi,C,U}(V) = \int_\Omega |\nabla v_j| dx + \frac{1}{2\theta} \int_\Omega \left( v_j - u_j \right)^2 dx$$

which can be solved efficiently using the Chambolle's fast duality projection algorithm [39]. Then, the solution is given by

$$\hat{v}_j = u_j - \theta \operatorname{div} k_j, \tag{15}$$

where div is the divergence operator. The vector $k_j$ can be computed using a fixed-point algorithm:

$$k_j^{n+1} = \frac{k_j^n + \tau\nabla(\text{div}\, k_j^n - u_j/\theta)}{1+\tau\left|\nabla(\text{div}\, k_j^n - u_j/\theta)\right|}$$

with initial value $k_j^0 = 0$ and $0 < \tau \leq 1/8$ to ensure the convergence of the algorithm [39].

### 4.4. Fuzzy Membership Function

Fixing $\phi$, $C$ and $V$, we solve $U$ by minimizing

$$\begin{aligned} E_{\phi,C,V}(U) = &\tfrac{1}{2\theta}\sum_{j=1}^{N}\int_\Omega (v_j - u_j)^2 dx + \alpha_0 \sum_{j=1}^{N}\int_\Omega u_j (I^0 - c_j)^2 dx \\ &- \sum_{q=1}^{Q}\alpha_q \sum_{j=1}^{N}\int_\Omega u_j \left(\log\left(\prod_{W_x^M} P_j^q\left(I^q|\phi_j^q\right)\right)^{1/M^2}\right)dx \end{aligned}$$

subject to

$$\text{(i)} \sum_{j=1}^{N} u_j = 1,\ \text{(ii)}\ 0 \leq u_j \leq 1, j = 1,2,\ldots,N.$$

Equivalently, we can minimize the energy

$$\widetilde{E}_{\phi,C,V}(U) = \frac{1}{2\theta}\int_\Omega \sum_{j=1}^{N}(H_j - u_j)^2 dx + K,$$

subject to the same constraints (i) and (ii), where

$$H_j = v_j - \alpha_0\theta\left(I^0 - c_j\right)^2 + \theta\sum_{q=1}^{Q}\alpha_q\left(\log\left(\prod_{W_x^M} P_j^q\left(I^q|\phi_j^q\right)\right)^{1/M^2}\right)$$

and

$$K = -\frac{1}{2\theta}\sum_{j=1}^{N}\int_\Omega H_j^2 dx$$

Note that both constraints (i) and (ii) apply to membership function independently for each point $x \in \Omega$. Hence the minimizer $\hat{U}$ of $\widetilde{E}_{\phi,C,V}$ is also the pointwise minimizer of the function $f(U) = \sum_{j=1}^{N}(H_j - u_j)^2$ subject to the same constraints. That is, for each point $x \in \Omega$, $\hat{U}(x)$ is the solution to the problem

$$\min_U \sum_{j=1}^{N}(H_j(x) - u_j(x))^2,$$

subject to

$$\text{(i)} \sum_{j=1}^{N} u_j(x) = 1,\ \text{(ii)}\ 0 \leq u_j(x) \leq 1, j = 1,2,\ldots,N.$$

The above minimization problem is exactly the problem of computing the Euclidean projection of the vector $H(x) = [H_1(x),\cdots,H_N(x)]$ on the probability simplex $\Delta^N$. According to [40], the projection $z$ of a vector $y \in R^N$ onto $\Delta^N$ can be expressed as $z_i = \max\{y_i + \lambda, 0\}$, where $i = 1,2,\ldots,N$, and $\lambda$ is the Lagrange multiplier chosen such that the constraint $\sum_{i=1}^{N} z_i = 1$ holds. An algorithm to compute $\lambda$, with $y = H(x)$, consists of the following steps. Firstly, we reorder the components $\{H_j(x) : 1 \leq j \leq N\}$ into $H_{(1)}(x) \geq H_{(2)}(x) \geq \cdots \geq H_{(N)}(x)$, and find the integer $\rho(x)$ such that

$$\rho(x) = \max\left\{ j : H_j(x) + \frac{1}{j}\left(1 - \sum_{i=1}^{j} H_i(x)\right) > 0 \right\}$$

Then, the Lagrange multiplier $\lambda(x)$ can be computed as

$$\lambda(x) = \frac{1}{\rho(x)}\left(1 - \sum_{i=1}^{\rho(x)} H_{(i)}(x)\right)$$

Finally, the minimizer $\hat{U}$ of $\widetilde{E}_{\phi,C,V}$, which is also the projection of $H(x)$ on $\Delta^N$ for each $x \in \Omega$, is given by

$$\hat{u}_j = \max\{H_j + \lambda, 0\},\ j = 1, 2, \ldots, N. \tag{16}$$

### 4.5. The Overall Implementation

The optimization of (9) is performed by the alternating minimization between $\phi$, $C$ and $U$. The fuzzy bit-plane-dependence region competition algorithm (Algorithm 1) is summarized below. The overall implementation of the proposed method is shown in Figure 1.

**Algorithm 1** Fuzzy Bit-plane-dependence Region Competition Algorithm

**Input**: Input image $I$, number of regions $N$, number of bit-planes $m$, number of image domains $Q$, regularization parameters $\alpha_q$, $q = 0, 1, \ldots, Q$, size of window $M$, parameters of Chambolle's fast duality projection algorithm $\theta$ and $\tau$, initial fuzzy membership function $U^0$ and parameter of termination criterion $\varepsilon$.
**Output**: Optimal fuzzy membership function $\hat{U}^{opt}$

Step 1: Compute the color and windowed BDPM parameters ($C$ and $\phi$) using (11), (13) and (14), respectively.

Step 2: Compute the auxiliary variable and fuzzy membership function ($V$ and $U$) using (15) and (16), respectively.

Step 3: Repeat Step 1 and Step 2 till termination. The termination criterion is $\left|U^{new} - U^{old}\right|_{\infty} < \varepsilon$, where $\varepsilon$ is a small positive constant.

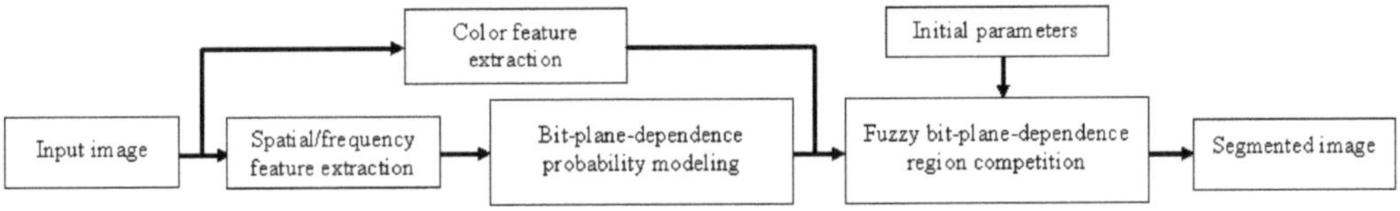


**Figure 1.** The overall implementation of the proposed method.

In order to visualize the segmentation results and compare our method with the existing approaches, as reported in the following section, the defuzzification process is performed as follows. Given the optimal fuzzy membership function, $\hat{U}^{opt} = \left\{\hat{u}_j^{opt} : j = 1, 2, \ldots, N\right\}$, obtained from the algorithm above, the final segmentation result is constructed by assigning each pixel a label $j^*$ where $j^* = \underset{j}{\operatorname{argmax}} \hat{u}_j^{opt}$.

## 5. Experiments

### 5.1. Experimental Setting

The proposed method is applied to real-world natural images. Unless otherwise specified, we fix the parameters, which achieve the best results, in all the following experiments: $m = 8$, $\theta = 1.0$, $\tau = 0.125$, $M = 25$, $\alpha_0 \in [0.0001, 0.005]$, $\alpha_q = 50\alpha_0$, $q = 1, 2, \ldots, Q$, and $\varepsilon = 10^{-2}$. To characterize local region information in various image domains using the windowed BDPM model, a collection of transformed images $\{I^q : q = 2, 3, \ldots, Q\}$ should be generated. In this paper, we use 3-level wavelet transform (i.e., $Q = 10$) followed by the Hilbert transform to construct the transformed images. We simply report results of 3-level wavelet transform since our segmentation results reveal that 3-level decomposition is good enough to capture essential wavelet information and usually performs better than the others. Note that when 4-level decomposition is used, the subband information at the highest level is redundant and does not enhance the segmentation performance. To obtain the transformed images, we first index each wavelet subband $q = \{2, 3, \ldots, 10\} = \{(l, \theta) : l = 1, 2, 3; \theta = (H, V, D)\}$, where $l$ denotes the level of wavelet decomposition and $\theta$ is the direction with $H$, $V$ and $D$ representing horizontal, vertical, and diagonal directions, respectively. Evaluation of all possible wavelet transforms, and filter banks is beyond the scope of this paper; thus, we focus on undecimated wavelet transform (UWT) with Symlets filter bank. Dissimilar to the traditional discrete wavelet transform in which downsampling is performed in each decomposition level, UWT is used so that the filtered image is not subsampled, and therefore, each subband is the same size as the original image. It is important to remark that the UWT coefficients may exhibit a wide spectrum of sinusoidal oscillation, which affects the image variation modeling performance, leading to the degradation of segmentation accuracy. Thus, we narrow down the spectrum of sinusoidal oscillation by applying the Hilbert transform [41] to the UWT coefficients and consider their magnitude to obtain the transformed image. Mathematically, let $C_{(l,b)}$ be the UWT coefficients of the corresponding $q$th subband and $H(C_{(l,b)})$ be the Hilbert transform of $C_{(l,b)}$. Then the transformed image is given by Figure 2

$$I^q = 255 \times \frac{\left|H(C_{(l,b)})\right| - \min\left|H(C_{(l,b)})\right|}{\max\left|H(C_{(l,b)})\right| - \min\left|H(C_{(l,b)})\right|}.$$

To quantify the effectiveness of the proposed method, we use three measures, namely: segmentation covering [42], F-measure [43] and Jaccard index [44]. The segmentation covering (SC) measures the overlap of regions of the final segmentation and the regions of the ground truth, F-measure (F) is defined as a harmonic mean of precision and recall, while Jaccard index (JI) measures the intersection over the union of the labelled segments.

### 5.2. Comparative Segmentation Results

We compare the proposed fuzzy bit-plane-dependence region competition (FBRC) algorithm with several state-of-the-art variational-based, superpixel-based and deep-learning-based approaches, namely: fuzzy region competition with Gaussian mixture model (FRCGMM) [33], L1 fuzzy segmentation (L1FS) [25], piecewise constant fuzzy region competition (PCFRC) [2], superpixel-based fast fuzzy c-means clustering (SFFCM) [45], automatic fuzzy clustering framework (AFCF) [46], backpropagation (BP) [47] and differentiable feature clustering (DFC) [48] algorithms using the well-known Microsoft research in Cambridge dataset [49], Berkeley segmentation dataset 500 [50], Weizmann segmentation evaluation (WSE) database [51] and PH2 database [52]. In the implementation of the above algorithms, we have tried different combinations of parameters to obtain the best possible performance.

Figure 2 displays the comparative segmentation results. In this experiment, we shall simply assess their performance based on visual satisfaction. The following are some discussions about the algorithms and main points observed from the figures.

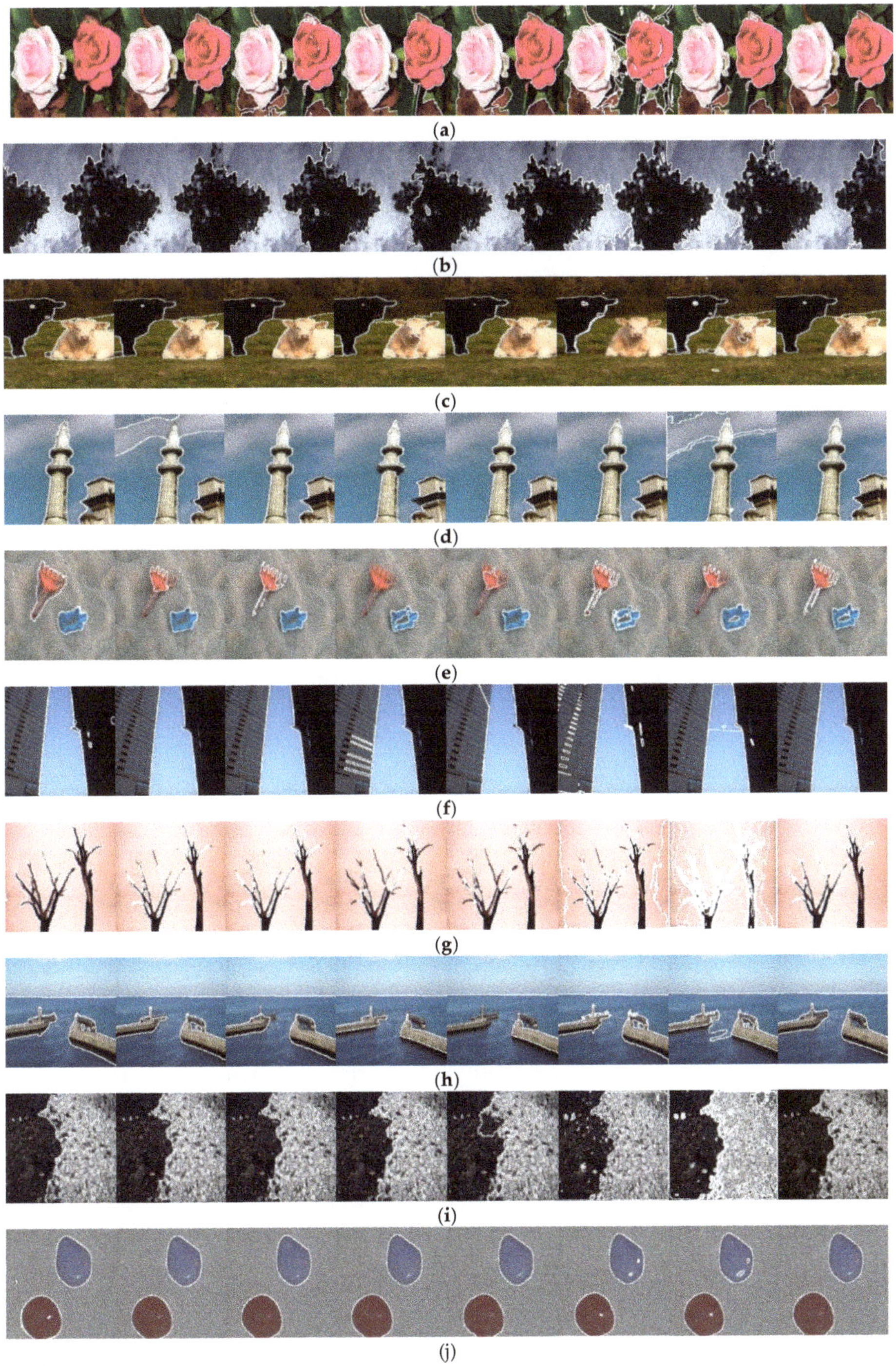


**Figure 2.** Comparative segmentation results for various algorithms. (**a**–**j**) are images from [49–52]. The 1st to the 8th columns are the results for FRCGMM, L1FS, PCFRC, SFFCM, AFCF, BP, DFC and FBRC, respectively.

(1) The segmentation results of the proposed method for all images are visually satisfying whereas the rest gives unsatisfactory performance for some images. Specifically, the variational-based FRCGMM, L1FS and PCFRC and superpixel-based SFFCM and AFCF perform similarly while the deep-learning-based BP and DFC provide undesirable results. The success of FBRC is mainly due to the fact that it adopts the CIELAB color feature to capture pixel-level information and the windowed BDPM model to characterize region-level information while the rest employs only pixel-level information in a particular image domain. In addition, the proposed method incorporates additional information from various image domains to further enhance the segmentation accuracy;

(2) The proposed method usually adheres well to object boundaries for all images, but other approaches give approximated object boundaries for some cases, see, for instance, the segmented boundaries of Figure 2d by FRCGMM, Figure 2b by SFFCM, and Figure 2h by DFC. Essentially, the unsatisfactory boundary adherence of the cases reveals the insufficiency of feature representation adopted by these methods. Note that the proposed method uses the windowed BDPM to characterize local region information and the window may straddle multiple objects in the image, and thus, the quality of the neighboring information in the window will degrade. Nevertheless, the use of windowed BDPM to capture region information from multi-domain provides additional information so that our proposed method can still capture the object boundaries well;

(3) The proposed method performs better than the other algorithms in terms of mis-segmentation of object parts. For instance, L1FS mis-segments the "Sky" in Figure 2d, AFCF mis-segments the "Rake" in Figure 2e, and BP mis-segments the "Cow" in Figure 2c. Similar examples can also be found in other images. The results clearly indicate that the use of windowed BDPM model to characterize texture patterns is shown to be effective in most cases, see, for instance, the "Tree" in Figure 2b.

Figure 3 shows the comparative segmentation results with the provided ground truths, which are obtained by asking human subjects to manually segment the images into various object parts for all of the algorithms. As can be seen, the segmentation results of Figure 3 for FBRC are visually satisfying and the proposed method outperforms other algorithms for all images. As previously mentioned, this is mainly because most algorithms use a single feature in a particular image domain to characterize image regions, but our method adopts both the color and multi-domain windowed BDPM model to capture essential pixel and region levels information. In addition, we also remark that the proposed method adopts BDPM to capture texture information, and thus, our algorithm can segment images with low color contrast and complex textured patterns. Table 1 reports the average quantitative measures for all the algorithms using the WSE database. As far as the segmentation accuracy is concerned, we observe that the variational-based and superpixel-based algorithms perform similarly, and FBRC outperforms the recently developed deep-learning-based algorithms. Lastly, it is important to emphasize that the proposed method generally performs better than all other algorithms in the sense that it achieves the best measures in SC, JI and F.

To provide an additional justification of our approach, we shall compare the proposed method with the aforementioned approaches using the PH2 database, which consists of 200 dermoscopic images of melanocytic lesions. Table 2 shows the corresponding quantitative results. As with the results of the WSE database, both variational-based and superpixel-based methods have similar performance, and FBRC performs better than the deep-learning-based algorithms. Compared with the current state-of-the-art methodologies, the results clearly reveal the superior performance of the proposed method.

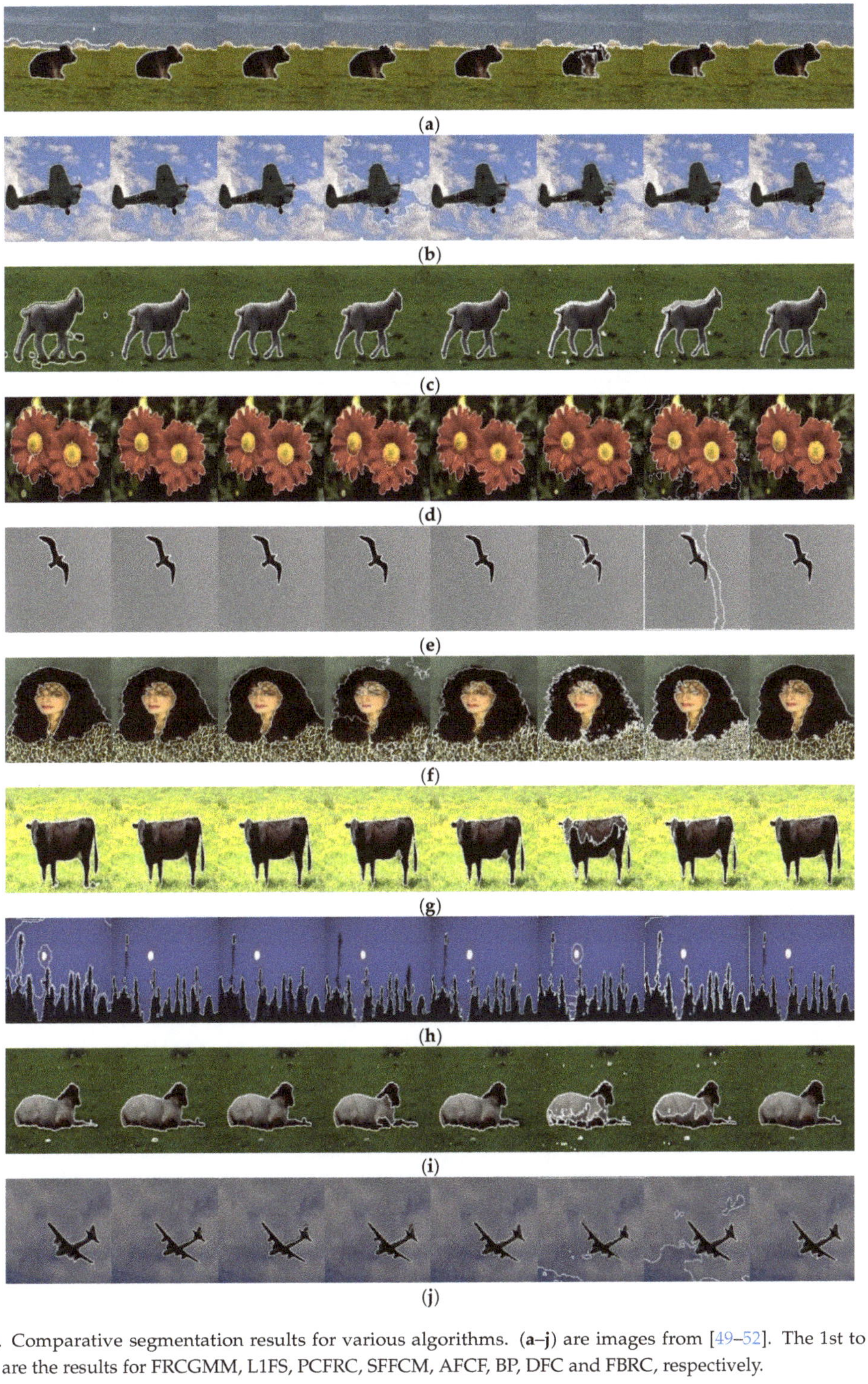


**Figure 3.** Comparative segmentation results for various algorithms. (**a**–**j**) are images from [49–52]. The 1st to the 8th columns are the results for FRCGMM, L1FS, PCFRC, SFFCM, AFCF, BP, DFC and FBRC, respectively.

**Table 1.** Quantitative comparisons of various approaches for WSE database. The best results are highlighted in bold.

| Methods | SC | JI | F | Time (s) |
|---|---|---|---|---|
| FRCGMM | 0.799 | 0.666 | 0.765 | 45.282 |
| L1FS | 0.758 | 0.644 | 0.748 | 72.296 |
| PCFRC | 0.821 | 0.687 | 0.773 | 39.619 |
| SFFCM | 0.798 | 0.671 | 0.766 | 0.815 |
| AFCF | 0.801 | 0.657 | 0.751 | **0.673** |
| BP | 0.726 | 0.408 | 0.496 | 97.358 |
| DFC | 0.640 | 0.420 | 0.528 | 79.903 |
| FBRC | **0.829** | **0.701** | **0.788** | 31.473 |

**Table 2.** Quantitative comparisons of various approaches for PH2 database. The best results are highlighted in bold.

| Methods | SC | JI | F | Time (s) |
|---|---|---|---|---|
| FRCGMM | 0.765 | 0.674 | 0.778 | 35.431 |
| L1FS | 0.814 | 0.712 | 0.800 | 35.912 |
| PCFRC | 0.807 | 0.665 | 0.753 | 26.769 |
| SFFCM | 0.723 | 0.659 | 0.773 | **4.561** |
| AFCF | 0.690 | 0.591 | 0.711 | 4.609 |
| BP | 0.805 | 0.471 | 0.543 | 285.990 |
| DFC | 0.626 | 0.285 | 0.373 | 195.900 |
| FBRC | **0.821** | **0.739** | **0.827** | 25.783 |

### 5.3. Parameter Sensitivity

In this subsection, we analyze the sensitivity of parameters to the segmentation performance. In the Chambolle's fast duality projection algorithm, we set $\theta = 1.0$ and $\tau = 0.125$. Our experiments show that changing the values of $\theta$ and $\tau$ will not affect the segmentation results unless the values of $\theta$ and $\tau$ are sufficiently large. In fact, the algorithm of Chambolle may not converge if $\tau > 0.125$ [39]. To update the windowed BDPM parameter during the optimization process, the window of size $M = 25$ is used. Here, we study the effect of window size to the segmentation accuracy by comparing the performance for different values of $M$. Figure 4 displays some visual examples when $M$ = 1, 25, 50 and 75, and Table 3 reports the average quantitative measures using different window sizes for the WSE database. While the segmentation results are generally satisfactory, we notice that the performance is inferior when the window size is sufficiently small/large, see, for instance, Figure 4a when $M = 1$ and Figure 4b when $M = 75$. This phenomenon can be understood as follows: the larger the window size, the smaller the segmentation error because larger window provides more statistical information for image variation modeling. Nevertheless, when the window is sufficiently large, the segmentation error increases since the window may straddle multiple image regions, and thus, the information extracted from the windows centered at the pixels near the region boundaries could be inaccurate. On the other hand, when the window size is small, the quality of image variation modeling will degrade which would increase the segmentation error. When $M = 1$, the neighboring information is neglected, and the promising segmentation results may not be achieved since only a single sample is taken from the probability distribution. As evident in our experiments, setting the window of size $M = 25$ is suffice for achieving satisfactory segmentation results. It is important to remark that in the case when the neighboring information is neglected (then (9) reduces to (8)), the use of the BDPM model for region characterization from various image domains can provide additional information to discriminate regions with similar spatial statistics, which in turn improves the segmentation performance. Lastly, we shall investigate the effectiveness of the BDPM model in the proposed energy functional by comparing the segmentation performance between $\alpha_q = 0$ and $\alpha_q > 0$ for $q \geq 1$. When $\alpha_q = 0$, the BDPM model in the energy functional is neglected while it is adopted when

$\alpha_q > 0$. Figure 5 displays some visual examples. As can be seen, the results for $\alpha_q > 0$ performs better than that for $\alpha_q = 0$, see, for instance, the "neck of goat" in Figure 5a, the "tail of the plane" in Figure 5c and the "hair of lady" in Figure 5d. Table 4 reports the average quantitative performance for the effectiveness of BDPM to the segmentation performance for the WSE database. We observe that the three measures, namely, SC, JI and F, for $\alpha_q > 0$ performs better than the cases when $\alpha_q = 0$. These results qualitatively and quantitatively justify that the use of BDPM model for region characterization from multi-domain can improve the segmentation performance.

(a)

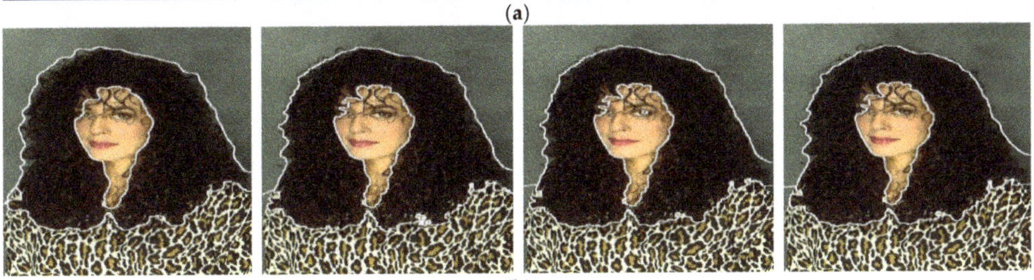

(b)

**Figure 4.** Effectiveness of window size to the segmentation results. (**a**,**b**) are images from [49,50]. The 1st to the 4th columns are the results for $M$ = 1, $M$ = 25, $M$ = 50 and $M$ = 75, respectively.

**Table 3.** Quantitative comparisons using different window sizes for WSE database. The best results are highlighted in bold.

| M | SC | JI | F |
|---|---|---|---|
| 1 | **0.829** | 0.692 | 0.779 |
| 25 | **0.829** | **0.701** | **0.788** |
| 50 | 0.828 | 0.689 | 0.777 |
| 75 | 0.827 | 0.688 | 0.776 |

### 5.4. Computational Cost

All of the experiments have been implemented on the Intel Core i7-6700HQ laptop. Tables 1 and 2 list the average computation times of all methods for WSE and PH2 databases, respectively. Briefly speaking, the superpixel-based methods are the fastest since they simply perform standard fuzzy c-means clustering on the superpixels while the deep-learning-based algorithms have high computational cost because they require optimizing complex convolutional neural networks. FRCGMM and LIFS are slower than PCFRC. This may be explained by the fact that FRCGMM performs highly precise fitting of data with Gaussian mixture model, and that L1FS introduces two sets of auxiliary variables and requires solving a collection of sub-problems based on the alternating direction methods of multipliers. The computation time for FBRC is slightly shorter than PCFRC. Both methods adopt the alternating minimization procedure and apply the Chambolle's fast duality projection algorithm to solve the total variation minimization problem to speed up the segmentation process.

**Figure 5.** Effectiveness of BDPM to the segmentation results. (**a–d**) are images from [49,50]. First row: $\alpha_q = 0, q \geq 1$. Second row: $\alpha_q > 0, q \geq 1$.

**Table 4.** Quantitative comparisons for the effectiveness of BDPM to the segmentation performance for WSE database. The best results are highlighted in bold.

| | SC | JI | F |
|---|---|---|---|
| $\alpha_q = 0,\ q \geq 1$ | 0.818 | 0.695 | 0.780 |
| $\alpha_q > 0,\ q \geq 1.$ | **0.829** | **0.701** | **0.788** |

## 6. Conclusions

In this paper, we have presented a novel multiphase image segmentation model based on fuzzy region competition and statistical image variation modeling. In the proposed energy functional, each region is characterized by the color and spatial/frequency information modeled by the windowed bit-plane-dependence probability models in various image domains, and is represented by the fuzzy membership function. We have employed the alternating minimization procedure in conjunction with the Chambolle's fast duality projection algorithm to minimize the energy functional, where its closed-form solutions are obtained. Comparative experiments have demonstrated the effectiveness of our proposed method.

While the proposed method provides satisfactory segmentation performance, we shall study the following as future work. Firstly, a few parameters in the algorithm need to be manually selected in order to achieve promising results. Nevertheless, our experiments reveal that selecting a value for each parameter in a certain range is good enough to provide similar performance. In fact, some parameters have significant impact to the segmentation accuracy. Specifically, an automatic parameter selection scheme for $\alpha_q, q \geq 0$ is necessary so that these parameters can be adaptively adjusted during the optimization procedure, which may improve the segmentation results. Secondly, we use the wavelet and Hilbert transforms to construct the transformed images in all our experiments. However, various image domains are available in the literature and can be adopted in our case. Thus, the selection of image domains and their advantages for image segmentation (or in a specific application domains) should be investigated.

**Author Contributions:** Conceptualization, S.C. and T.N.; methodology, S.C., T.N., C.Y. and B.L.; software, T.N.; validation, T.N.; formal analysis, T.N.; investigation, S.C., T.N., C.Y. and B.L.; data curation, T.N.; writing—original draft preparation, S.C.; visualization, T.N. All authors have read and agreed to the published version of the manuscript.

**Funding:** The work described in this paper was partially supported by the grant from the Research Grants Council of the Hong Kong Special Administration Region (Project Reference No. UGC/FDS14/P01/17).

**Institutional Review Board Statement:** Not applicable.

**Informed Consent Statement:** Not applicable.

**Data Availability Statement:** Publicly available datasets were analyzed in this study. These data can be found here: https://www.microsoft.com/en-us/download/details.aspx?id=52644; https://www2.eecs.berkeley.edu/Research/Projects/CS/vision/bsds/; https://www.wisdom.weizmann.ac.il/~vision/Seg_Evaluation_DB/dl.html; https://www.fc.up.pt/addi/ph2%20database.html. (accessed on 25 September 2021).

**Acknowledgments:** This work is supported by the Big Data Intelligence Centre of The Hang Seng University of Hong Kong.

**Conflicts of Interest:** The authors declare no conflict of interest.

## References

1. Zhu, S.C.; Yuille, A. Region competition: Unifying snake/balloon, region growing and Bayes/MDL/energy for multi-band image segmentation. *IEEE Trans. Pattern Anal. Mach. Intell.* **1996**, *18*, 884–900.
2. Li, F.; Ng, M.K.; Zeng, T.Y.; Shen, C. A multiphase image segmentation method based on fuzzy region competition. *SIAM J. Imaging Sci.* **2010**, *3*, 277–299. [CrossRef]
3. Zhao, Y.; Zhu, S.-C.; Luo, S. $CO_3$ for ultra-fast and accurate interactive segmentation. In Proceedings of the 18th ACM International Conference on Multimedia, Firenze, Italy, 25–29 October 2010; pp. 93–102.
4. Caselles, V.; Catte, F.; Coll, T.; Dibos, F. A geometric model for active contours in image processing. *Numer. Math.* **1993**, *66*, 1–31. [CrossRef]
5. Caselles, V.; Kimmel, R.; Sapiro, G. Geodesic active contours. *Int. J. Comput. Vis.* **1997**, *22*, 61–79. [CrossRef]
6. Kass, M.; Witkin, A.; Terzopoulos, D. Snakes: Active contour models. *Int. J. Comput. Vis.* **1988**, *1*, 321–331. [CrossRef]
7. Tong, C.S.; Zhang, Y.; Zheng, N. Variational image binarization and its multi-scale realizations. *J. Math. Imaging Vis.* **2005**, *23*, 185–198. [CrossRef]
8. Mumford, D.; Shah, J. Optimal approximations by piecewise smooth functions and associated variational problems. *Commun. Pure Appl. Math.* **1989**, *42*, 577–685. [CrossRef]
9. Chan, T.; Vese, L. Active contours without edges. *IEEE Trans. Image Process.* **2001**, *10*, 266–277. [CrossRef]
10. Osher, S.; Sethian, J.A. Fronts propagating with curvature-dependent speed: Algorithms based on Hamilton-Jacobi formulation. *J. Comput. Phys.* **1988**, *79*, 12–49. [CrossRef]
11. Chan, T.; Sandberg, B.; Vese, L. Active contours without edges for vector-valued images. *J. Visual Commun. Image Represent.* **2000**, *11*, 130–141. [CrossRef]
12. Vese, L.; Chan, T. A multiphase level set framework for image segmentation using the Mumford and Shah model. *Int. J. Comput. Vis.* **2002**, *50*, 271–293. [CrossRef]
13. Wu, T.; Shao, J. Non-convex and convex coupling image segmentation via TGpV regularization and thresholding. *Adv. Appl. Math. Mech.* **2020**, *12*, 849–878.
14. Tang, M.; Ma, S. General scheme of region competition based on scale space. *IEEE Trans. Pattern Anal. Mach. Intell.* **2001**, *13*, 1366–1378. [CrossRef]
15. Kim, J.; Fisher, J.; Yezzi, A.; Cetin, M.; Willsky, A. A nonparametric statistical method for image segmentation using information theory and curve evolution. *IEEE Trans. Image Process.* **2005**, *14*, 1486–1502.
16. Mory, B.; Ardon, R.; Thiran, J.-P. Variational segmentation using fuzzy region competition and local non-parametric probability density functions. In Proceedings of the 2007 IEEE 11th International Conference on Computer Vision, Rio de Janeiro, Brazil, 14–21 October 2007.
17. Mory, B.; Ardon, R. Fuzzy region competition: A convex two-phase segmentation framework. In Proceedings of the International Conference on Scale Space and Variational Methods in Computer Vision, Ischia, Italy, 30 May–2 June 2007.
18. Ni, K.; Bresson, X.; Chan, T.; Esedoglu, S. Local histogram-based segmentation using the Wasserstein distance. *Int. J. Comput. Vis.* **2009**, *84*, 97–111. [CrossRef]
19. Choy, S.K.; Yuen, K.; Yu, C. Fuzzy bit-plane-dependence image segmentation. *Signal. Process.* **2019**, *154*, 30–44. [CrossRef]
20. Zhang, X.; Pan, W.; Wu, Z.; Chen, J.; Mao, Y.; Wu, R. Robust image segmentation using fuzzy c-means clustering with spatial information based on total generalized variation. *IEEE Access* **2020**, *8*, 95681–95697. [CrossRef]

21. Choy, S.K.; Ng, T.C.; Yu, C. Unsupervised fuzzy model-based image segmentation. *Signal Process.* **2020**, *171*, 107483. [CrossRef]
22. Pham, D.; Prince, J. Adaptive fuzzy segmentation of magnetic resonance images. *IEEE Trans. Med. Imaging* **1999**, *18*, 737–752. [CrossRef] [PubMed]
23. Ahmed, M.; Yamany, S.; Mohamed, N.; Farag, A.; Moriarty, T. A modified fuzzy c- means algorithm for bias field estimation and segmentation of MRI data. *IEEE Trans. Med. Imaging* **2002**, *21*, 193–199. [CrossRef] [PubMed]
24. Zhang, Z.; Song, J. An adaptive fuzzy level set model with local spatial information for medical image segmentation and bias correction. *IEEE Access* **2019**, *7*, 27322–27338. [CrossRef]
25. Li, F.; Osher, S.; Qin, J.; Yan, M. A multiphase image segmentation based on fuzzy membership functions and L1-norm fidelity. *J. Sci. Comput.* **2016**, *69*, 82–106. [CrossRef]
26. Lv, H.; Wang, Z.; Fu, S.; Zhang, C.; Zhai, L.; Liu, X. A robust active contour segmentation based on fractional-order differentiation and fuzzy energy. *IEEE Access* **2017**, *5*, 7753–7761. [CrossRef]
27. Luo, S.; Sarabandi, K.; Tong, L.; Guo, S. Unsupervised multiregion partitioning of fully polarimetric SAR images with advanced fuzzy active contours. *IEEE Geosci. Remote Sens.* **2020**, *58*, 1475–1486. [CrossRef]
28. Ramudu, K.; Babu, T.R. Level set evolution of biomedical MRI and CT scan images using optimized fuzzy region clustering. *Comput. Methods Biomech. Biomed. Eng. Imaging Vis.* **2019**, *7*, 96–107. [CrossRef]
29. Luo, S.; Sarabandi, K.; Tong, L.; Guo, S. An improved fuzzy region competition-based framework for the multiphase segmentation of SAR images. *IEEE Geosci. Remote Sens.* **2020**, *58*, 2457–2470. [CrossRef]
30. Sagiv, C.; Sochen, N.; Zeevi, Y. Integrated active contours for texture segmentation. *IEEE Trans. Image Process.* **2006**, *15*, 1633–1646.
31. Sandberg, B.; Chan, T.; Vese, L. A Level-Set and Gabor-Based Active Contour Algorithm for Segmenting Textured Images. Available online: http://citeseerx.ist.psu.edu/viewdoc/download?doi=10.1.1.7.3145&rep=rep1&type=pdf (accessed on 24 May 2021).
32. Rousson, M.; Brox, T.; Deriche, R. Active unsupervised texture segmentation on a diffusion-based feature Space. In Proceedings of the 2003 IEEE Computer Society Conference on Computer Vision and Pattern Recognition, Madison, WI, USA, 18–20 June 2003.
33. Yin, S.; Zhang, Y.; Karim, S. Large scale remote sensing image segmentation based on fuzzy region competition and Gaussian mixture model. *IEEE Access* **2018**, *6*, 26069–26080. [CrossRef]
34. Do, M.N.; Vetterli, M. Wavelet-based texture retrieval using generalized Gaussian density and Kullback-Leibler distance. *IEEE Trans. Image Process.* **2002**, *11*, 146–158. [CrossRef]
35. Choy, S.K.; Tong, C.S. Supervised texture classification using characteristic generalized Gaussian density. *J. Math. Imaging Vis.* **2007**, *29*, 35–47. [CrossRef]
36. Choy, S.K.; Tong, C.S. Statistical wavelet subband characterization based on generalized Gamma density and its application in texture retrieval. *IEEE Trans. Image Process.* **2010**, *19*, 281–289. [CrossRef]
37. Pi, M.; Tong, C.S.; Choy, S.K.; Zhang, H. A fast and effective model for wavelet subband histograms and its application in texture image retrieval. *IEEE Trans. Image Process.* **2006**, *15*, 3078–3088. [CrossRef] [PubMed]
38. Choy, S.K.; Tong, C.S. Statistical properties of bit-plane probability model and its application in supervised texture classification. *IEEE Trans. Image Process.* **2008**, *17*, 1399–1405. [CrossRef] [PubMed]
39. Chambolle, A. An algorithm for total variation minimization and applications. *J. Math. Imaging Vis.* **2004**, *20*, 89–97.
40. Wang, W.; Carreira-Perpinan, M.A. Projection onto the probability simplex: An efficient algorithm with a simple proof, and an application. *arXiv* **2013**, arXiv:1309.1541v1.
41. Bulow, T.; Sommer, G. A novel approach to the 2D analytic signal. Computer Analysis of Images and Patterns, Lecture Notes in Computer Science. In Proceedings of the International Conference on Computer Analysis of Images and Patterns, Ljubljana, Slovenia, 1–3 September 1999.
42. Arbelaez, P.; Maire, M.; Fowlkes, C.; Malik, J. From contours to regions: An empirical evaluation. In Proceedings of the 2009 IEEE Conference on Computer Vision and Pattern Recognition, Miami, FL, USA, 20–25 June 2009.
43. Van Rijsbergen, C.J. *Information Retrieval*; Butterworths: London, UK, 1979.
44. Jaccard, P. Nouvelles recherches sur la distribution florale. *Bull. Soc. Vaud. Sci. Nat.* **1908**, *44*, 223–270.
45. Lei, T.; Jia, X.; Zhang, Y.; Liu, S.; Meng, H.; Nandi, A.K. Superpixel-based fast fuzzy c- means clustering for color image segmentation. *IEEE Trans. Fuzzy Syst.* **2019**, *27*, 1753–1766. [CrossRef]
46. Lei, T.; Liu, P.; Jia, X.; Zhang, X.; Meng, H.; Nandi, A.K. Automatic fuzzy clustering framework for image segmentation. *IEEE Trans. Fuzzy Syst.* **2020**, *28*, 2078–2092. [CrossRef]
47. Kanezaki, A. Unsupervised image segmentation by backpropagation. In Proceedings of the ICASSP, Calgary, AB, Canada, 15–20 April 2018.
48. Kim, W.; Kanezaki, A.; Tanaka, M. Unsupervised learning of image segmentation based on differentiable feature clustering. *IEEE Trans. Image Process.* **2020**, *28*, 8055–8068. [CrossRef]
49. Shotton, J.; Winn, J.; Rother, C.; Criminisi, A. TextonBoost for image understanding: Multi-class object recognition and segmentation by jointly modeling texture, layout, and context. *Int. J. Comput. Vis.* **2009**, *81*, 2–23. [CrossRef]
50. Arbelaez, P.; Maire, M.; Fowlkes, C.; Malik, J. Contour detection hierarchical image segmentation. *IEEE Trans. Pattern Anal. Mach. Intell.* **2011**, *33*, 898–916. [CrossRef] [PubMed]

51. Alpert, S.; Galun, M.; Basri, R.; Brandt, A. Image segmentation by probabilistic bottom-up aggregation and cue integration. In Proceedings of the 2007 IEEE Computer Society Conference on Computer Vision and Pattern Recognition, Minneapolis, MN, USA, 17–22 June 2007.
52. Mendonça, T.; Ferreira, P.M.; Marques, J.; Marcal, A.R.S.; Rozeira, J. PH2—A dermoscopic image database for research and benchmarking. In Proceedings of the 2013 35th Annual International Conference of the IEEE Engineering in Medicine and Biology Society (EMBC), Osaka, Japan, 3–7 July 2013.

mathematics

MDPI

*Article*

# GPS Data Correction Based on Fuzzy Logic for Tracking Land Vehicles

**Pedro J. Correa-Caicedo [1], Horacio Rostro-González [2], Martin A. Rodriguez-Licea [1,3], Óscar Octavio Gutiérrez-Frías [4], Carlos Alonso Herrera-Ramírez [5], Iris I. Méndez-Gurrola [6], Miroslava Cano-Lara [7] and Alejandro I. Barranco-Gutiérrez [1,3,*]**

1 Autotrónica, Tecnológico Nacional de Mexico en Celaya, Celaya 38010, Mexico; D1803025@itcelaya.edu.mx (P.J.C.-C.); martin.rodriguez@itcelaya.edu.mx (M.A.R.-L.)
2 Departamento de Electrónica, DICIS, Universidad de Guanajuato, Salamanca 36885, Mexico; hrostrog@ugto.mx
3 Cátedras-CONACyT, Av. Insurgentes Sur 1582, Col. Crédito Constructor, Ciudad de Mexico 03940, Mexico
4 SEPI, UPIITA, Instituto Politécnico Nacional, Ciudad de Mexico 07340, Mexico; ogutierrezf@ipn.mx
5 Departamento de Ingeniería Robótica, Universidad Politécnica de Guanajuato, Guanajuato 38496, Mexico; aherrera@upgto.edu.mx
6 Departamento de Diseño, Universidad Autónoma de Ciudad Juárez, Cd. Juárez, Chihuahua 32310, Mexico; iris.mendez@uacj.mx
7 Departamento de Ingeniería Mecatrónica, Tecnológico Nacional de Mexico, ITS de Irapuato, Guanajuato 36821, Mexico; miroslava.cl@irapuato.tecnm.mx
* Correspondence: israel.barranco@itcelaya.edu.mx

**Citation:** Correa-Caicedo, P.J.; Rostro-González, H.; Rodriguez-Licea, M.A.; Gutiérrez-Frías, Ó.O.; Herrera-Ramírez, C.A.; Méndez-Gurrola, I.I.; Cano-Lara, M.; Barranco-Gutiérrez, A.I. GPS Data Correction Based on Fuzzy Logic for Tracking Land Vehicles. *Mathematics* **2021**, *9*, 2818. https://doi.org/10.3390/math9212818

Academic Editor: Michael Voskoglou

Received: 23 September 2021
Accepted: 4 November 2021
Published: 6 November 2021

**Publisher's Note:** MDPI stays neutral with regard to jurisdictional claims in published maps and institutional affiliations.



**Abstract:** GPS sensors are widely used to know a vehicle's location and to track its route. Although GPS sensor technology is advancing, they present systematic failures depending on the environmental conditions to which they are subjected. To tackle this problem, we propose an intelligent system based on fuzzy logic, which takes the information from the sensors and correct the vehicle's absolute position according to its latitude and longitude. This correction is performed by two fuzzy systems, one to correct the latitude and the other to correct the longitude, which are trained using the MATLAB ANFIS tool. The positioning correction system is trained and tested with two different datasets. One of them collected with a Pmod GPS sensor and the other a public dataset, which was taken from routes in Brazil. To compare our proposal, an unscented Kalman filter (UKF) was implemented. The main finding is that the proposed fuzzy systems achieve a performance of 69.2% higher than the UKF. Furthermore, fuzzy systems are suitable to implement in an embedded system such as the Raspberry Pi 4. Another finding is that the logical operations facilitate the creation of non-linear functions because of the 'if else' structure. Finally, the existence justification of each fuzzy system section is easy to understand.

**Keywords:** localization; fuzzy systems; unscented Kalman filter; adaptive neuro-fuzzy inference system (ANFIS); GPS; autonomous navigation

## 1. Introduction

The absolute location of a ground vehicle is the starting point for any autonomous movement and it is of vital importance to reduce the error in the accuracy of GPS receivers to ensure the safety of passengers. The main objective of this work is to obtain an intelligent system capable of improving the accuracy in the estimation of the absolute position of a land vehicle without relying on high-cost sensors or hardware with high computational power, as a first step to develop a low-cost autonomous electric navigation car.

On the other hand, the reduction of the triangulation error to calculate the location of the GPS receiver is the most outstanding contribution of this work, since the average accuracy of the estimated location is increased from 3 m to 30 cm. However, it also contributes from the electronic point of view, since simple logical operations, addition, and division, are used to implement the fuzzy system in a small embedded system such as the Raspberry Pi 3 in a simple way. Compared to Kalman filters, it is not necessary to know the nature of the noise. Moreover, because the fuzzy system has a structure that converts numerical values to logical rules and vice versa, the knowledge base can be easily understood, which is in contrast to neural networks [1].

The proposal of the present work consists of implementing a pair of fuzzy systems that have the direct responsibility of correcting the latitude and longitude coordinate coming from the GPS sensor, avoiding complex mathematical operations, and obtaining a complete location system embedded in an electric car. Contrasting with what is found in the state of the art where it is more common to find fuzzy logic as a tool of artificial intelligence complementary to more classical techniques in the subject of location and tracking of land vehicles such as the Kalman filter. For example, in [2], the unscented Kalman filter (UKF) is combined with the unscented H-infinity (UH) filter in order to reduce the accuracy error when tracking the position of a ground vehicle as it travels along a defined route. This system uses fuzzy logic to automatically weight whether the UKF or the UH will act at a given instant along that route, presenting an error reduction of approximately 5.6% in the estimation, with respect to that of the pure UKF, improving the accuracy of the GPS receiver.

In [3], the design of a fuzzy system that adaptively modifies the extended Kalman filter (EKF) noisy covariances by fusing data from GPS, IMU, an odometer (at each wheel) and the mathematical model of the vehicle is shown. In this work, an improvement (on average) in the accuracy of the absolute position of the vehicle of about 49% is shown, making the response of the proposed algorithm superior to that of the original Kalman filter. Similarly, in [4] there is a four-wheeled robot where the EKF is used to fuse data from a GPS, IMU, odometers on the wheels, and additionally a camera on the front of the robot; a fuzzy system is designed to modify the noisy covariances of the EKF. The main objective of this proposal is to strengthen the accuracy in the estimation of the trajectory to be followed by the robot, achieving an average accuracy improvement of 80.6% with respect to the EKF correction. On the other hand, [5] seeks to improve the movement of a two-wheeled robot in environments with many obstacles. This is done by using measurements from a GPS sensor and an adaptive neuro-fuzzy inference system (ANFIS) as control techniques; obtaining a system capable of evading obstacles and estimating the best route for the robot to travel.

In parallel, other artificial intelligence techniques are also currently being applied to improve the response of the Kalman filter. As in [6] where they propose the use of a recurrent neural network (RNN) to adaptively modify the input values of a network real-time kinematic (NRTK) that fuses data from a GPS and an IMU and the kinematic model of the car in real time. This is done in order to improve the tracking of the trajectory of a car with an embedded sensor system, reducing the location accuracy error to 67.71% on average. In [7], the authors use the variation of the Kalman filter, the cubature Kalman filter (CKF), to adaptively modify the noisy covariances creating the strong tracking cubature Kalman filter. The algorithm proposed in this work manages to improve the position estimation of a vehicle with GPS and IMU sensors coupled, obtaining an average error reduction of 56% with respect to the original version of the CFK when traveling along a route. On the other hand, in [8] a classification algorithm is developed that combines a convolutional neural network (CNN) mathematical model of different types of vehicles and data coming from a GPS sensor to analyze the trajectory travelled by the sensor to determine what type of vehicle is making the journey. The authors report a classification accuracy of over 74%.

Again in [9], the authors present a fuzzy logic system capable of determining the position of a moving robot in a shaded indoor environment (such as a tunnel or a covered car park). Using GPS data and analyzing the chromaticity and frequency-component ratio of the LED lights installed in the ceiling and compared to a navigation potential system. The fuzzy system achieves, in the best case, an advantage of up to 89%. Similarly, in [10], a combination of fuzzy logic and optimal control theory is proposed to control the motors of a racing car and achieve its displacement along a specific route without a driver. This is done by taking advantage of the data provided by a GPS sensor, calculating the vehicle's yaw angle and using the mathematical model of the car. In this work, the authors achieve a 30% improvement in the accuracy of vehicle trajectory tracking. In [11], a GPS sensor is used as a reference and an inertial measurement unit (IMU) delivers data to an inertial navigation system (INS) to reconstruct a trajectory. The INS by itself has a significant error and to reduce it an ANFIS is used which has as inputs the IMU data and the error between the INS and the GPS and as output delivers a corrected estimate of the INS. The authors manage to reduce the INS error by up to 9.83%.

In [12], a GPS receiver delivers data to an extended Kalman filter (EKF) to track the position of a car as it travels along a defined route. The EKF alone is not good at estimating the position of the vehicle when the GPS receives poor signals from the satellites. The authors propose a fuzzy system that adaptively adjusts the internal parameters of the Kalman filter, such as the noisy covariances, to improve its estimates when the GPS has a weak signal. The authors manage to improve vehicle tracking in adverse conditions for the GPS sensor by up to 70%. In [13], by exploiting the fusion of data from an INS and a GNSS sensor attached to a vehicle, the authors present a new fuzzy strong-tracking curbature Kalman filter (FSTCKF) algorithm to improve the CKF response using a fuzzy logic system and reduce the vehicle trajectory estimation error by 72.3%.

On the other hand, in [14], an algorithm is proposed that joins model free adaptive control (MFAC) and particle swarm optimization (PSO) techniques to improve the position tracking of unmanned ground vehicles. For this, they have a GPS, a sensor to measure the angle of rotation of the wheel (which are fused by the mathematical model of the car) and an INS. The authors propose a control algorithm that estimates the heading angle (or direction that the vehicle should have in an instant of time) obtaining a high precision in both the estimation of the angle and the tracking of the vehicle's path. In contrast, in [15], the authors use ultra-wideband (UWB) technology to improve the localization and tracking accuracy of unmanned ground vehicles (UGV). Three UWB base stations are used as a cluster in a 2D space for localization. Here, by collecting data from multiple tests, they developed an algorithm composed of PSO techniques and genetic algorithms (GA) to implement multiple groups of UWB base stations. The authors report UGV position estimation accuracies between 20 cm and 60 cm. Finally, in [16], they have a GPS sensor and an IMU as input to an extended Kalman filter with an adaptation mechanism to remove noise coming from the IMU and guarantee a better INS response. The authors also develop a deep learning framework with multiple short to long term memory modules (multi-LSTM) to predict the vehicle position increment based on the Gaussian mixture model (GMM) and the Kullback–Leibler (KL) distance. They then combine both algorithms to optimize the estimation of a vehicle's position achieving an error reduction of up to 93.9%.

In Section 2, the experiments performed are presented; in Section 3, it is shown how the absolute position correction fuzzy system was designed; in Section 4, the design to implement the UKF filter to compare its response with the proposed fuzzy system is exposed; in Section 5, the results are shown with their discussion and finally in Section 6, the conclusions are presented.

## 2. Materials and Methods

For the experimental development of this work we have a data acquisition system (see Figure 1), which contains the Pmod GPS sensor [17] that receives signals from the GPS satellite system of the United States of America. There is also a Sense HAT [18] nine-axis inertial measurement unit to measure the vehicle's steering angle for use by the Kalman filter. The data from these sensors is acquired and recorded by a Raspberry Pi 3 using the Python language. The module is coupled to an electric trolley with which several routes were travelled (see Figure 2).

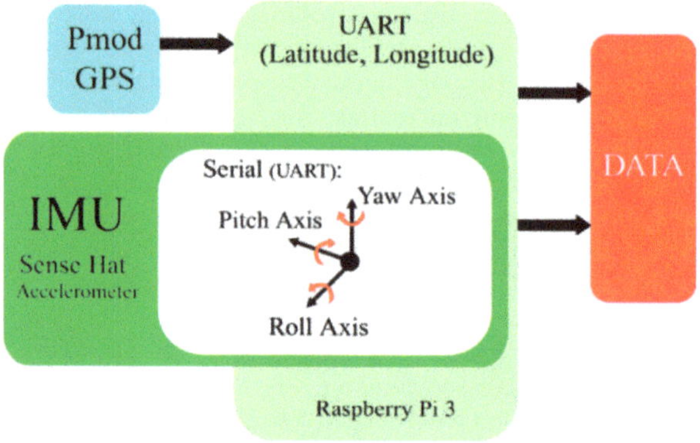


**Figure 1.** Acquisition data system.

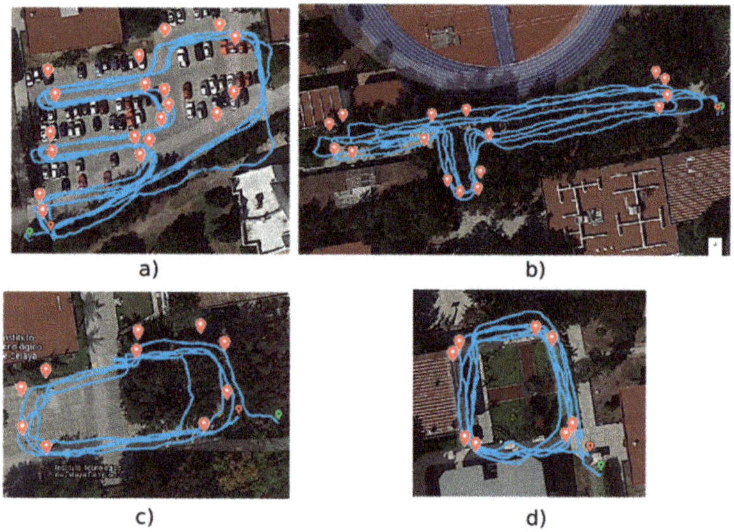


**Figure 2.** Test routes: (**a**) route 1, (**b**) route 2, (**c**) route 3, (**d**) route 4.

The collected data were processed by the MATLAB tool anfisedit (adaptive neuro-fuzzy inference system) for training and testing the proposed fuzzy algorithms. In the same way, the behavior of the fuzzy systems in the presence of unknown data was evaluated with the help of the evalfis toolbox. The design and implementation process of the proposed fuzzy systems is described below.

### 2.1. *The Data Acquisition System*

In Figure 1, we show the modular data acquisition system implemented in this work. The system consists of a GPS Pmod sensor that is used to obtain latitude and longitude coordinates of the current position and a shield Sense HAT for Raspberry to measure the current inclination on the three Pich, Roll, and Yaw axes through its accelerometer. All the register data is stored in CSV format files for post processing on a PC.

To test our system, we traced four routes, which are shown in Figure 2. These routes were traveled four times in order to generate enough data for the training and validation of the fuzzy system.

The red markers in Figure 2 correspond to initial and final points from which the lines that circumscribe the reference are constructed and the blue lines represent the path of the data acquisition module along each route. Parameters such as distance traveled, duration, and velocity are presented in Table 1.

**Table 1.** Relevant data of the acquisition stage.

| Route | Distance (m) | Time (s) | Velocity (m/s) |
|---|---|---|---|
| (a) 1 | 282.45736 | 1020 | 0.276918 |
| (b) 2 | 282.9798 | 840 | 0.336880 |
| (c) 3 | 151.8607 | 480 | 0.316376 |
| (d) 4 | 104.3988 | 420 | 0.248568 |

From the latitude and longitude data provided by the GPS sensor, we can estimate the distance traveled by means of the Haversines equation [19] as

$$\mathrm{d} = 2 \cdot r \cdot \sin^{-1}(M) \tag{1}$$

with $r = 6371$ km (radius or the earth) and $M = \sqrt{\sin^2\left(\frac{\varphi_2 - \varphi_1}{2}\right) + \cos\varphi_1 \cdot \cos\varphi_2 \cdot \sin^2\left(\frac{\lambda_2 - \lambda_1}{2}\right)}$. Here, $\varphi$ are the latitudes and $\lambda$ the longitudes obtained from the sensors.

## 2.2. Approximation Data

On the approximation data, the fuzzy system performs a correction from the GPS data (latitude and longitude). To do this, there is a training stage where, the system indicates the size, proportion, form, or nature of the mentioned correction. In this stage, reference points were established on each route (see red markers on each route of Figure 2) and straight lines were drawn between point and point calculating their equations (see Figure 3).

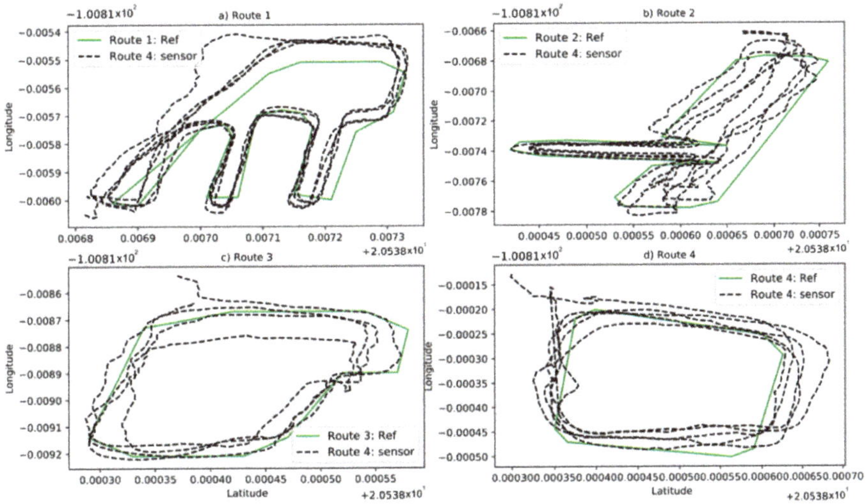


**Figure 3.** Sensor data and reference, (**a**) route 1, (**b**) route 2, (**c**) route 3, (**d**) route 4.

In Figure 3, a green line represents the reference of each route and the black dashed line represents the data captured by the GPS sensor. Equation (1) is used to calculate the distance between the coordinates given by the GPS sensor and the midpoints of the straight lines that make up the routes (Equations (2) and (3)).

$$\varphi_{\mathrm{m}} = \frac{\varphi_1 + \varphi_2}{2} \tag{2}$$

$$\lambda_m = \frac{\lambda_1 + \lambda_2}{2} \tag{3}$$

with $\varphi$ and $\lambda$ for latitude and longitude respectively.

In Figure 4, it can be observed how the system performs a correction on route 1 from a coordinate point (black point) given by the GPS sensor. The distance of the sensor data to each midpoint of the lines that make up the path of the route is calculated. From the calculated distances (blue lines in Figure 4), we select the smallest one to determine the line of reference to which the sensor data should be corrected or approximated.

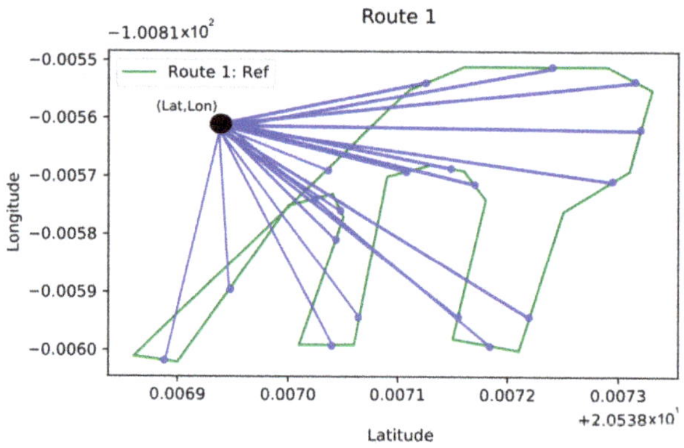


**Figure 4.** Distance's estimation from a point to the line.

Once the minimum distance has been calculated, the data who belongs to the line of reference is evaluated. From this evaluation, the approximation of the GPS sensor data is achieved as it is shown in Figure 5.

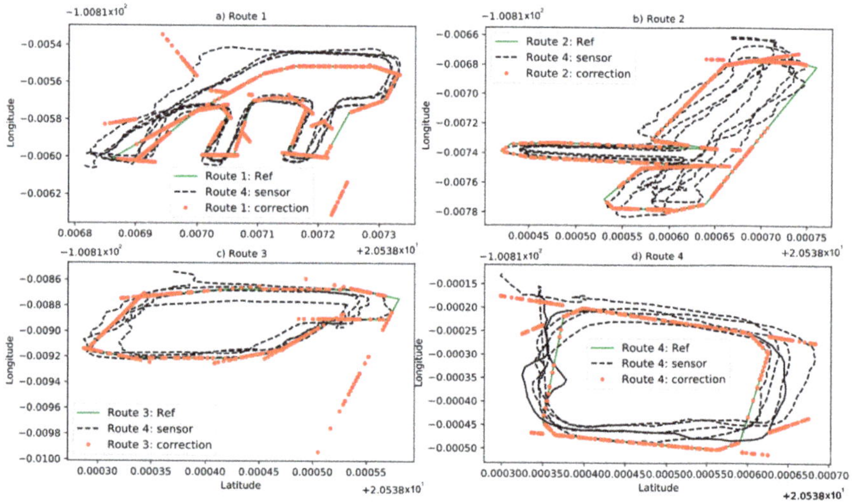


**Figure 5.** Data correction, (**a**) route 1, (**b**) route 2, (**c**) route 3, (**d**) route 4.

The red dots in Figure 5, represent the approximation of the sensor data to the reference and the black dashed line represents the GPS sensor data and the green straight lines represent the reference of each route. Once the corrected coordinate points are obtained, they were stored in matrices for training and validation of the fuzzy systems, which will automatically correct new incoming sensor data. It should be noted that this post-processing stage of the data was done offline using a desktop computer with the characteristics specified Section 2.

This strategy for establishing the fuzzy sets resembles the way a human being would intuitively calculate the distance of his current position with respect to a specific street; the issue of establishing the linguistic variables and their intuitive nature is discussed more extensively in [20,21].

Before using these corrected coordinates (red dots in Figure 5) in the training stage, it is necessary to apply a data cleaning technique such as removing the outliers. The criterion used was the distance between the reference and the corrected latitude and longitude data: when the distance is greater than 3 m then the point is considered an outlier and is removed from the data set to be used for training. It is important to note that the raw data coming directly from the GPS sensor was used in the testing stage.

### 2.3. Fuzzy System Design

In this work, we use the ANFIS toolbox [22], which allows us to generate a MISO (multiple input, single output) fuzzy inference system based on the Takagi Sugeno method [23]. With this toolbox, the fuzzy system can simultaneously perform a correction from two inputs, latitude and longitude. In this regard, we generated two fuzzy systems one for latitude correction and the other one for longitude correction. Both fuzzy systems receive the same information from the sensor. The data used for training and validation is shown in Table 2. This is the data collected with the sensor for each route. This is illustrated in Figure 6, where 6a and 6b correspond to the training setup of the two fuzzy systems. Figure 6c represents the system on the testing stage.

**Table 2.** Datasets for the fuzzy systems.

| Route | Training Data | Validation Data | Total |
|---|---|---|---|
| 1 | 751 | 250 | 1001 |
| 2 | 645 | 215 | 860 |
| 3 | 356 | 118 | 474 |
| 4 | 412 | 102 | 514 |

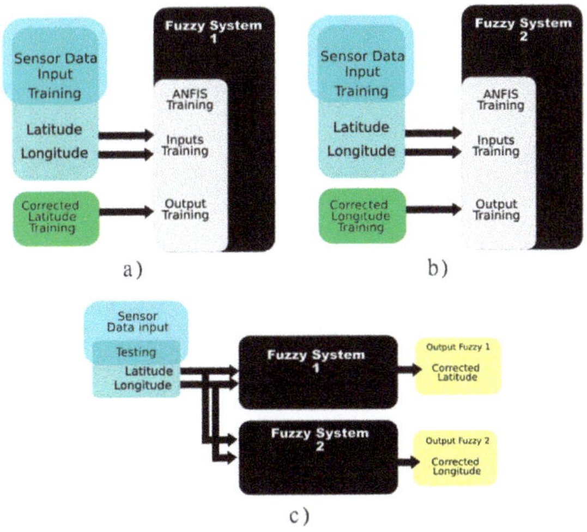


**Figure 6.** Fuzzy system design, (**a**) Fuzzy system 1 (training): Latitude; (**b**) Fuzzy system 2 (training): Longitude; (**c**) Testing both fuzzy systems.

From the training we found that the fuzzy systems for latitude and longitude correction were designed with 5 and 3 gaussian membership functions of type two [24], respectively, it is 25 and 9 fuzzy rules for each. For both systems, linear type membership functions were defined at the output. The results of the training stage for both fuzzy systems are shown in Table 3.

**Table 3.** ANIFS training output.

| Fuzzy System | MF Input Lat | MF Input Lon | MF Output | Fuzzy Rules | RMSE (Train) |
|---|---|---|---|---|---|
| Latitude | 5 gaussian type 2 | 5 gaussian type 2 | linear | 25 | $4.29 \times 10^{-7}$ |
| Longitude | 3 gaussian type 2 | 3 gaussian type 2 | linear | 9 | $1.1 \times 10^{-4}$ |

The selection of the membership functions was carried out by means of an optimization process that consisted of varying both, the number of functions for each input and their type (triangular, trapezoidal, Gaussian, and Gaussian type two). From this, we observed the effect at the output for the different configurations and that with the best performance on each fuzzy system is presented in Table 3.

To choose an adequate number on the membership functions that guarantees best compromise between a low error and a minimum number of membership functions, a tuning was performed on each fuzzy system. Multiple tests were launched varying the number of membership functions for each entry in both fuzzy systems, results are presented in Table 3.

After training, MATLAB's evalfis tool [25] was used to evaluate them with the test data. From the evaluation of both fuzzy systems, two vectors were obtained with the corrected latitude and longitude outputs.

Figure 7 graphically shows the output of each system for the testing data. Figure 7a,b shows the operating range of the fuzzy system correcting latitude and longitude respectively; having as input the GPS sensor data. To compare our results, we implemented the unscented Kalman filter (UKF) and results are presented below.

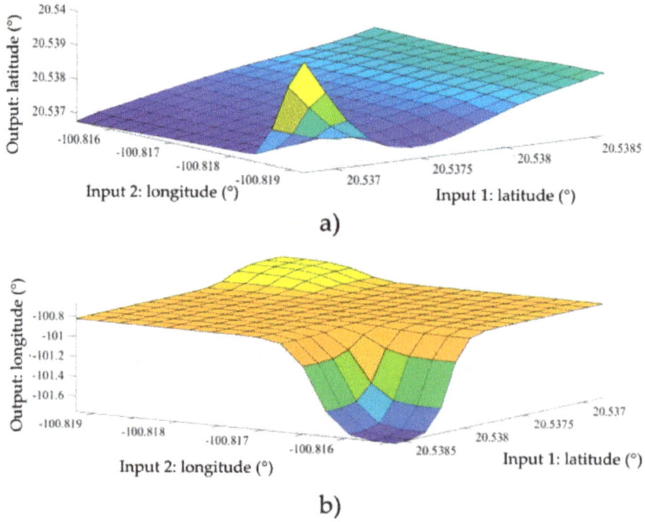


**Figure 7.** Fuzzy systems testing, (**a**) Fuzzy system 1 (testing): Latitude; (**b**) Fuzzy system 2 (testing): Longitude.

### 2.4. Kinematic Model of Car and Tuning of UKF

The UKF takes the data from the inertial measurement unit (IMU) that measures the rotation angle of the front vehicle wheels and the GPS sensor, which estimates the vehicle position located in the center of the axis of the rear wheels as shown in Figure 8.

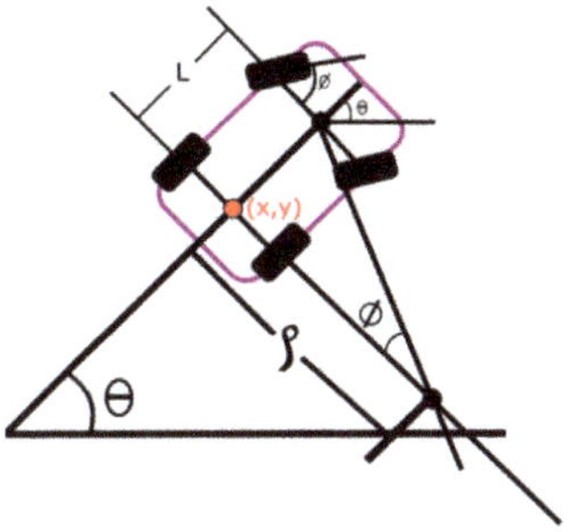


**Figure 8.** Vector diagram of the car model.

The land vehicle model is linearized as follows:

$$\dot{\varphi} = \varphi + s * dt * \cos(\phi) \tag{4}$$

$$\dot{\lambda} = \lambda + s * dt * \sin(\phi) \tag{5}$$

$$\dot{\phi} = \phi + dt\phi \tag{6}$$

$$\dot{s} = s \tag{7}$$

where $s$ is the vehicle speed (measured by the GPS); $\phi$ the steering angle; $\varphi$ and $\lambda$ correspond to latitude and longitude respectively (also given by the GPS). Analyzing the vehicle model in the state space we have the equation

$$\dot{X} = F * X + B * u \tag{8}$$

$$\begin{bmatrix} \dot{\varphi} \\ \dot{\lambda} \\ \dot{\varnothing} \\ \dot{s} \end{bmatrix} = \begin{bmatrix} 1 & 0 & 0 & 0 \\ 0 & 1 & 0 & 0 \\ 0 & 0 & 1 & 0 \\ 0 & 0 & 0 & 0 \end{bmatrix} * \begin{bmatrix} \varphi \\ \lambda \\ \varnothing \\ s \end{bmatrix} + \begin{bmatrix} \sin(\phi)dt & 0 \\ \cos(\phi)dt & 0 \\ 0 & dt \\ 1 & 0 \end{bmatrix} * \begin{bmatrix} s \\ \varnothing \end{bmatrix} \tag{9}$$

where $X$ is the vector states used by the UKF and $u$ the vector of inputs from the sensors and those used by the UKF.

Table 4 shows a synthesis of the optimization process of the UKF to find the values of the noisy covariances that would help to improve the filter response without distorting its output. This process consisted of varying the values of the main diagonals of the Q (process noisy covariance) and R (measurement noisy covariance) matrices of the UKF filter [26] and observing its effect at the filter's. Here, 10 tests were performed and the one with the best results is shown in row 6 of Table 4.

Equations (10) and (11), show the values of the R and Q covariance matrices for tuning the UKF, highlighting, those that delivered the best correction response of the sensor data.

$$Q = \begin{bmatrix} 0.001 & 0 & 0 & 0 \\ 0 & 0.001 & 0 & 0 \\ 0 & 0 & \mathrm{rad}(350) & 0 \\ 0 & 0 & 0 & 0.001 \end{bmatrix}^3 \tag{10}$$

$$R = \begin{bmatrix} 0.025 & 0 \\ 0 & -0.025 \end{bmatrix}^3 \tag{11}$$

**Table 4.** Tuning of the covariances Q and R of UKF.

| # | Q | R |
|---|---|---|
| 1 | $([0.1,\ 0.1,\ \mathrm{rad}(350),\ 0.1]) \times 10^2$ | $([0.1, -0.1])2$ |
| 2 | $([0.1,\ 0.1,\ \mathrm{rad}(350),\ 0.1]) \times 10^3$ | $([0.1, -0.1]) \times 10^3$ |
| 3 | $([0.1,\ 0.1,\ \mathrm{rad}(350),\ 0.1]) \times 10^3$ | $([0.05, -0.05]) \times 10^3$ |
| 4 | $([0.001,\ 0.001,\ \mathrm{rad}(350),\ 0.001]) \times 10^3$ | $([0.025, -0.025]) \times 10^3$ |
| 5 | $([0.0001,\ 0.0001,\ \mathrm{rad}(350),\ 0.0001]) \times 10^3$ | $([0.025, -0.025]) \times 10^3$ |
| **6** | $\mathbf{([0.001,\ 0.001,\ rad(350),\ 0.001]) \times 10^3}$ | $\mathbf{([0.025, -0.025]) \times 10^3}$ |
| 7 | $([0.001,\ 0.001,\ \mathrm{rad}(350),\ 0.001]) \times 10^3$ | $([0.025, -0.025]) \times 10^3$ |
| 8 | $([0.001,\ 0.001,\ \mathrm{rad}(350),\ 0.001]) \times 10^4$ | $([0.025, -0.025]) \times 10^4$ |
| 9 | $([0.001,\ 0.001,\ \mathrm{rad}(350),\ 0.001]) \times 10^5$ | $([0.025, -0.025]) \times 10^5$ |
| 10 | $([0.001,\ 0.001,\ \mathrm{rad}(350),\ 0.001]) \times 10^6$ | $([0.025, -0.025]) \times 10^6$ |

The final response of the UKF is obtained and shown in Figure 9, where the correction made by the Kalman filter is observed. The difference of this correction with respect to the reference is also observed. For this, the same data of the fuzzy system was used (Table 2).

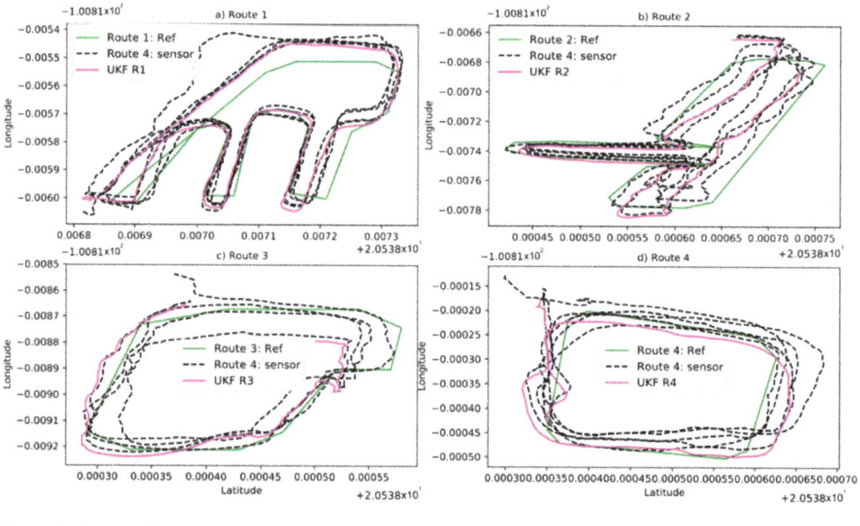


**Figure 9.** Sensor data vs. UKF response. (**a**) route 1, (**b**) route 2, (**c**) route 3, (**d**) route 4.

Figure 9 shows the reference in green, the dashed black line represents the GPS sensor data and the purple line corresponds to the data correction produced by the Kalman filter.

Additionally, the UKF has a scaling parameter kappa ($\kappa$) whose value is 3-L (where L is the length of the variable to be analyzed, i.e., 2); Beta ($\beta$) that incorporates a priori knowledge of the variable to analyze, in this case it is assumed that the variables have a gaussian distribution being then, $\beta = 2$. Finally, alpha ($\alpha$) is a parameter that indicates the propagation through the mean of the variable to be analyzed and it varies between 1 and $1 \times 10^{-4}$, in our case we set this value to 0.01. The selection of these parameters is based on the recommendations made in [27] and a tuning process to find the most optimal value. The following section shows, graphically and numerically, the results obtained in both the fuzzy system and those of the UKF, also a comparison of the two systems is presented.

## 3. Results

### *3.1. Analysis of Results with Our Own Dataset*

To facilitate the description of results, we abbreviate fuzzy position correction as FPC. The comparison between the UKF response (purple) and our method (blue) is graphically depicted for each route in Figure 10. In such figure both results are also contrasted with the reference (green). These results are further quantified numerically by means of the RMSE and presented in Table 5. From the RMSE results observed in Table 5, it is evident that the proposed fuzzy system improves the absolute vehicle location accuracy by 26% for route 1, 69.2% for route 2, 40% for route 3, and 7% for route 4, compared to the UKF response.

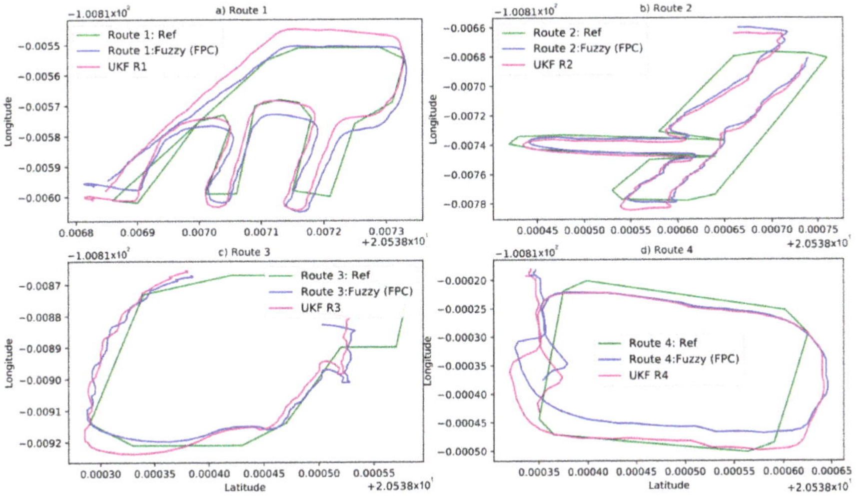


**Figure 10.** Reference (green) vs. FPC response (blue) vs. UKF (magenta). (**a**) route 1, (**b**) route 2, (**c**) route 3, (**d**) route 4.

**Table 5.** RMSE results of the UKF and fuzzy system (FPC).

| Route | UKF: RMSE (m) | Fuzzy (FPC): RMSE (m) |
|---|---|---|
| 1 | $1.989 \times 10^{-4}$ | $1.490 \times 10^{-4}$ |
| 2 | $7.539 \times 10^{-4}$ | $2.289 \times 10^{-4}$ |
| 3 | $4.865 \times 10^{-4}$ | $2.926 \times 10^{-4}$ |
| 4 | $2.698 \times 10^{-4}$ | $2.510 \times 10^{-4}$ |

Figure 11 shows the error (in meters) between the UKF output and the reference (purple), as well as the output of the fuzzy systems and the reference (blue graph). This graph shows that, for some sections of each trajectory, the error of the fuzzy systems is smaller than that observed in the UKF, in others the opposite is true or they are similar. This shows that the designed fuzzy systems have a consistent response and offer a competitive alternative to the UKF.

It is important to mention that even if the response is similar in most of the cases, the UKF performs a fusion of data from four inputs (angle of rotation of the front wheels, vehicle speed, latitude, and longitude) to be able to deliver an estimate of the position of the vehicle; while the FPC only needs two inputs, those of the GPS (latitude, longitude), to deliver a better estimate.

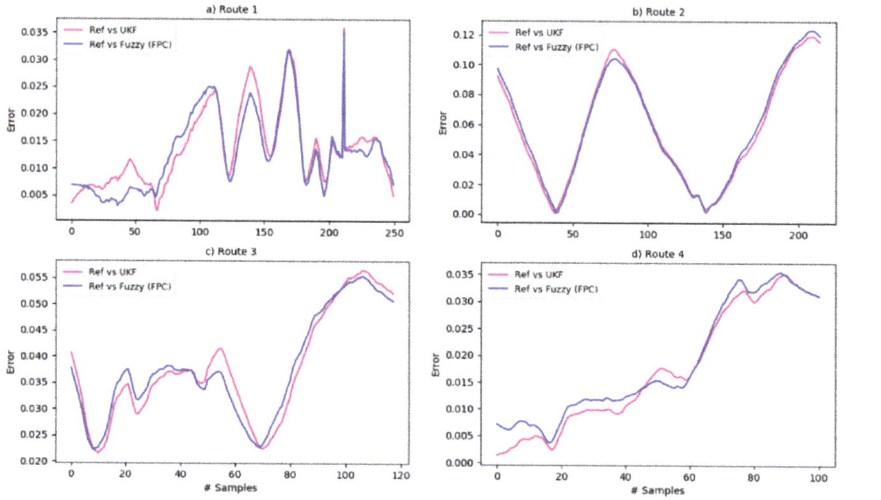


**Figure 11.** Error: reference vs. fuzzy systems response vs. UKF. (**a**) route 1, (**b**) route 2, (**c**) route 3, (**d**) route 4.

Also, the UKF filter needs parameters tuning to obtain the optimal R and Q covariance values for a more accurate estimate, in addition to the behavior of the random variables processed by this algorithm setting the values of $\kappa$, $\beta$, and $\alpha$. In contrast, the proposed FPC system is not dependent on any parameters since it only needs the latitude and longitude data given by the GPS to operate. Table 6 reports the statistical tests of media and variance that serve as a comparison of the performance of the UKF and the proposed fuzzy FPC system. For this calculation, the equation 1 of the haversines is used to find the distance of each point of the output of the fuzzy system FPC and the UKF respect to the reference in each route.

**Table 6.** Statistical performance tests (mean and variance).

| | **UKF** | |
|---|---|---|
| **Route** | Mean (m) | Variance $(m^2)$ |
| 1 | $1.366 \times 10^{-2}$ | $4.764 \times 10^{-5}$ |
| 2 | $5.744 \times 10^{-2}$ | $1.297 \times 10^{-3}$ |
| 3 | $3.755 \times 10^{-2}$ | $1.039 \times 10^{-4}$ |
| 4 | $1.736 \times 10^{-2}$ | $1.233 \times 10^{-4}$ |
| | **FPC (Fuzzy system)** | |
| **Route** | Mean (m) | Variance $(m^2)$ |
| 1 | $1.300 \times 10^{-2}$ | $4.983 \times 10^{-5}$ |
| 2 | $5.829 \times 10^{-2}$ | $1.315 \times 10^{-3}$ |
| 3 | $3.766 \times 10^{-2}$ | $9.634 \times 10^{-5}$ |
| 4 | $1.852 \times 10^{-2}$ | $1.114 \times 10^{-4}$ |

The variance represents the degree of dispersion of the data of a variable with respect to its mean (in the case of a Gaussian distribution). From Table 6, it is observed that in the variance calculation test the error variable of the FPC fuzzy system is slightly greater for the first two routes respect to the variance of the UKF. From this result, it can be inferred that—as expected—the UKF has more advantage to correct certain data than the fuzzy system and vice versa.

### 3.2. *Analysis of Results with Public Dataset*

In order to validate the robustness of our method, the public GPS trajectories data set [28,29] containing about 163 routes or trajectories travelled by car on the streets of Brazil and recorded with the Android application "Go! Track" was used. This database is perfectly adapted to the design needs of the proposed fuzzy systems and gives the possibility to test its performance with data that were not taken by the acquisition system shown in Section 2.1 and under poorly controlled conditions.

For the test, two random paths were chosen from the dataset and one of them was used to retrain the designed fuzzy systems (see Figure 12). This retraining is necessary due to the fact that the coefficients of the Gaussian functions must fit the new data and the fuzzy systems can perform their task.

**Figure 12.** Route 1: data training, Brazil dataset.

Subsequently, the second route (see Figure 13) was used to validate the performance of the fuzzy systems under these new conditions. This data was not used in the training.

**Figure 13.** Route 2: data testing, Brazil dataset.

Finally, in Figure 14 the response of the proposed fuzzy systems to the new data can be seen. The green graph represents the reference of the route, the black dashed line contains the input data coming from the sensor (in this case, the data collected by the Go!Track app), the red dots are the data calculated with the strategy seen in Section 2.2 and finally the blue dots contain the output of the fuzzy systems.

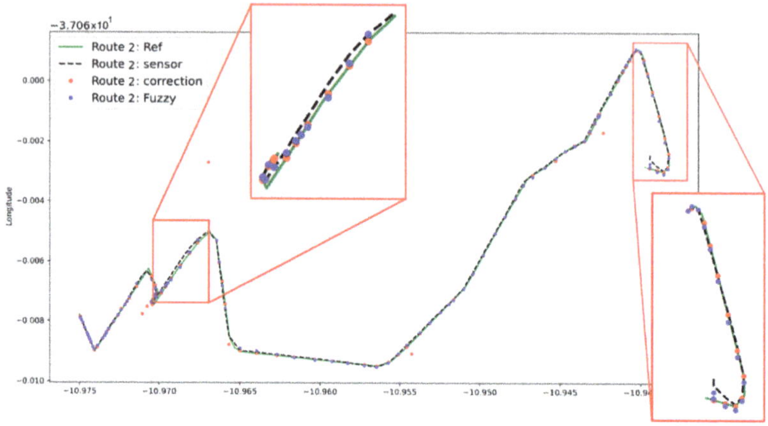


**Figure 14.** Route 2: Fuzzy systems output.

The purpose of the fuzzy systems is to get the data represented by the dashed black line as close as possible to the reference (green plot), in other words, the closer the blue are to the red dots, the better their performance will be. The red boxes in Figure 14 highlight two segments of the route where the correction made by the fuzzy systems is most noticeable.

Figure 15 shows the error (in meters), between the sensor measurements and the reference (green graph); as well as the error between the output of the fuzzy systems and the reference (in red). From this image, it can be seen that—for most of the data—there is a reduction of the error when the proposed fuzzy systems are in action.

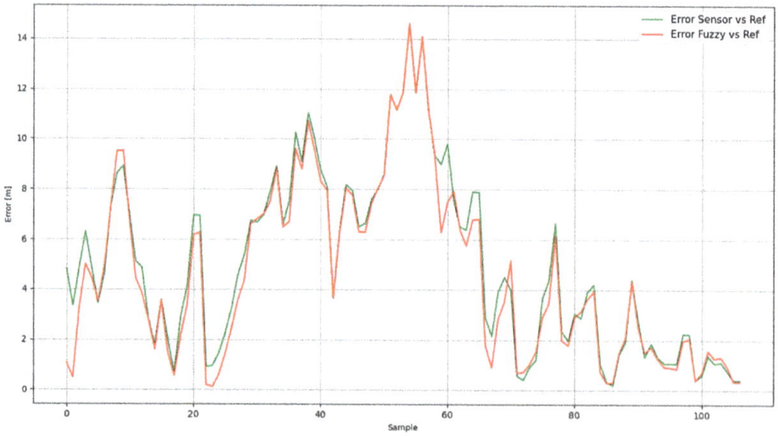


**Figure 15.** Error: reference vs. sensor (green) and reference vs. fuzzy systems response (red).

Table 7 shows how the RMSE of the fuzzy system outputs is lower than the error of the sensors compared to the reference.

**Table 7.** RMSE reference vs. sensor and fuzzy system (FPC).

| RMSE Sensor vs. Ref (m) | RMSE: Fuzzy (FPC) vs. Ref (m) |
|---|---|
| $5.51 \times 10^{-4}$ | $5.250 \times 10^{-4}$ |

## 4. Discussion

According to the results, the Kalman filter manages to reduce errors with decent performance but needs—as input—data to the covariance matrix that implicitly contains information on noise parameters. On the other hand, the fuzzy system managed to reduce the error in a better way without knowing the type of noise of the system because it was trained in the data region, making it easier and cheaper to implement with respect to works found in the state of the art. The main disadvantage is that, in order to better exploit the performance of the systems, retraining needs to be deployed in order to adjust the parameters of the membership functions when they are tested in geographical areas that are far away from the original data. The main limitation of the proposed fuzzy systems is that: if the error in the GPS measurements is too large, the correction of the GPS measurements will no longer be as effective.

An own data set was collected to take advantage of the data acquisition system (implemented and described in Section 2.1) since the characteristics of the sensors are known, such as the sampling period and the precision of each one, facilitating the post-processing calculations and the use of the information in different applications. Similarly, as the central limit theorem states, the more data that can be collected on a phenomenon, the more the distribution function that describes it will approximate the normal function and most of the data will be clustered around the mean. As shown in Table 8, the RMSE of both data sets is similar, being lower for the eigendata. Comparing these values with the information in Table 6, it can be said that they are around the mean of the latitude and longitude variables.

**Table 8.** RMSE: reference vs. output fuzzy system (FPC).

| Dataset | RMSE: Fuzzy (FPC) vs. Ref (m) |
|---|---|
| Own | $2.510 \times 10^{-4}$ |
| Brazil [28,29] | $5.250 \times 10^{-4}$ |

In Table 9, a numerical comparison between the accuracy (concerning the Kalman filter response) of the developed algorithm (FPC) and the reported in references [2,3,26] is presented.

**Table 9.** Maximum accuracy comparison over Kalman filter.

| Algorithm | Maximum Accuracy over Kalman Filter (%) |
|---|---|
| FPC | 69.2 |
| AFUKHF [2] | 56.14 |
| FI-AKF [3] | 58.48 |
| Cons.T2FKF [26] | 67.53 |

As shown in Table 9, the proposed algorithm has a maximum accuracy, concerning the Kalman Filter, higher than that reported in the papers compared. Although, this accuracy is reduced depending on the route being evaluated (as mentioned above).

## 5. Conclusions

The proposed FPC fuzzy system delivers competitive GPS data correction with the UKF response which is less dependent on tuning parameters, making it as easy (in terms of processing cost) to use and implement on mobile platforms. The proposed fuzzy system (FPC) emulates the way in which a human being describes the shape of a route through lines, so the calculation of these lines is used to approximate the sensor data to the reference.

The response of the fuzzy systems developed in this article improves the accuracy by up to 69.2% to determine the absolute position of a ground vehicle with respect to the classical techniques in this subject such as the UKF. Being highly competitive with techniques developed in the works presented in [2,3,26] (see Table 9). In addition, our method is less dependent on parameters and sensors, since it only uses GPS data and the reference for design.

Despite improving the response of the UKF, the proposed fuzzy system is limited to the region of the GPS map for which it was trained; that is, if the inputs are extremely different from the data the system was trained in, the FPC prediction will have a large errors. To solve this, it is necessary to collect a greater amount of data covering a wider region of the map to retrain the FPC system and expand its scope. Despite this, something similar happens with the UKF because the covariances R and Q must be re-tuned when the data changes dramatically.

The proposed fuzzy systems were tested on a public dataset [28,29], having a favorable performance under poorly controlled conditions both in the way of acquiring the data and in the geographical area where they were collected. As shown in Figure 14, Figure 15, and Table 7.

One of the points of improvement (in future work) for the proposed fuzzy systems is to achieve generalization of their response. This issue can be approached from two different points of view. The first one can be the collection and processing of the largest number of routes travelled with the GPS sensor to make a more complete training of the systems; the second one is to implement fuzzy systems whose training is online, that is, that the fuzzy systems are trained as the data from the GPS sensor arrives when a route is travelled.

## 6. Recommendations

In order to successfully reproduce this work, the data must be compiled in a CSV file whose first and second column must be the latitude and longitude data respectively coming from the GPS sensor. In a third and fourth column should be the latitude and longitude data corrected using the technique explained in Section 2.2. To achieve the data correction seen in Section 2.2, it is necessary to plot each new route in Google maps to extract the latitude and longitude points of each corner of the routes and obtain the line equations between each pair of corners.

One of the limitations of the proposed systems is generalization, as re-training is necessary when testing in geographical areas far away from the original data. This is necessary to readjust the parameters of the membership functions to the new data. The combination of MATLAB's ANFIS and GENFIS tools facilitates the task of deploying multiple training of fuzzy systems and accelerates the design process.

**Author Contributions:** Conceptualization, P.J.C.-C., A.I.B.-G., and H.R.-G.; Methodology, C.A.H.-R., A.I.B.-G., Ó.O.G.-F., M.C.-L., and H.R.-G.; Software, P.J.C.-C. and M.C.-L.; Validation, P.J.C.-C., Ó.O.G.-F., and M.A.R.-L.; Formal analysis, P.J.C.-C., A.I.B.-G., and H.R.-G.; Investigation, P.J.C.-C., C.A.H.-R., A.I.B.-G., and H.R.-G.; Resources, H.R.-G. and A.I.B.-G.; Writing—original draft preparation, P.J.C.-C., A.I.B.-G., and H.R.-G.; Writing—review and editing, A.I.B.-G., M.C.-L., and H.R.-G.; Visualization, P.J.C.-C., I.I.M.-G., and M.A.R.-L.; Supervision, A.I.B.-G. and H.R.-G.; Project administration, A.I.B.-G. All authors have read and agreed to the published version of the manuscript.

**Funding:** This research was funded by [Consejo Nacional de Ciencia y Tecnología] [Cátedras CONACyT y Becas Nacionales CONACyT], [National Technological Institute of Mexico] [TecNM en Celaya] and [Universidad de Guanajuato] [Unidad Salamanca].

**Institutional Review Board Statement:** Not applicable.

**Informed Consent Statement:** Not applicable.

**Acknowledgments:** The authors acknowledge the support provided by the TecNM and CONACyT.

**Conflicts of Interest:** The authors declare no conflict of interest.

## References


1. Fatima, B.; Amine, C.M.; Bekr, A. A Neuro-Fuzzy Inference Model for Breast Cancer Recognition. *Int. J. Comput. Sci. Inf. Technol.* **2012**, *4*, 163–173. [CrossRef]
2. Tehrani, M.; Nariman-Zadeh, N.; Masoumnezhad, M. Adaptive Fuzzy Hybrid Unscented/H-Infinity Filter for State Estimation of Nonlinear Dynamics Problems. *Trans. Inst. Meas. Control* **2019**, *41*, 1676–1685. [CrossRef]
3. Woo, R.; Yang, E.-J.; Seo, D.-W. A Fuzzy-Innovation-Based Adaptive Kalman Filter for Enhanced Vehicle Positioning in Dense Urban Environments. *Sensors* **2019**, *19*, 1142. [CrossRef]
4. Zhu, J.; Tang, Y.; Shao, X.; Xie, Y. Multisensor Fusion Using Fuzzy Inference System for a Visual-IMU-Wheel Odometry. *IEEE Trans. Instrum. Meas.* **2021**, *70*, 2505216. [CrossRef]
5. Gharajeh, M.S.; Jond, H.B. Hybrid Global Positioning System-Adaptive Neuro-Fuzzy Inference System based autonomous mobile robot navigation. *Robot. Auton. Syst.* **2020**, *134*, 103669. [CrossRef]
6. Kim, H.-U.; Bae, T.-S. Deep Learning-Based GNSS Network-Based Real-Time Kinematic Improvement for Autonomous Ground Vehicle Navigation. *J. Sens.* **2019**, *2019*, 3737265. [CrossRef]
7. Shen, C.; Zhang, Y.; Guo, X.; Chen, X.; Cao, H.; Tang, J.; Li, J.; Liu, J. Seamless GPS/Inertial Navigation System Based on Self-Learning Square-Root Cubature Kalman Filter. *IEEE Trans. Ind. Electron.* **2021**, *68*, 499–508. [CrossRef]
8. Dabiri, S.; Marković, N.; Heaslip, K.; Reddy, C.K. A deep convolutional neural network based approach for vehicle classification using large-scale GPS trajectory data. *Transp. Res. Part C Emerg. Technol.* **2020**, *116*, 102644. [CrossRef]
9. Jeong, J.-H.; Park, K. Numerical Analysis of 2-D Positioned, Indoor, Fuzzy-Logic, Autonomous Navigation System Based on Chromaticity and Frequency-Component Analysis of LED Light. *Sensors* **2021**, *21*, 4345. [CrossRef] [PubMed]
10. Li, G.; Zhang, S.; Liu, L.; Zhang, X.; Yin, Y. Trajectory Tracking Control in Real-Time of Dual-Motor-Driven Driverless Racing Car Based on Optimal Control Theory and Fuzzy Logic Method. *Complexity* **2021**, *2021*, 5549776. [CrossRef]
11. Duan, Y.; Li, H.; Wu, S.; Zhang, K. INS Error Estimation Based on an ANFIS and Its Application in Complex and Covert Surroundings. *ISPRS Int. J. Geo-Inf.* **2021**, *10*, 388. [CrossRef]
12. Farhad, M.A.; Mosavi, M.R.; Abedi, A.A. Fully Adaptive Smart Vector tracking of Weak GPS Signals. *Arab. J. Sci. Eng.* **2021**, *46*, 1383–1393. [CrossRef]
13. Chang, Y.; Wang, Y.; Shen, Y.; Ji, C. A new fuzzy strong tracking cubature Kalman filter for INS/GNSS. *GPS Solut.* **2021**, *25*, 120. [CrossRef]
14. Jiang, Y.; Xu, X.; Zhang, L. Heading tracking of 6WID/4WIS unmanned ground vehicles with variable wheelbase based on model free adaptive control. *Mech. Syst. Signal Process.* **2021**, *159*, 107715. [CrossRef]
15. Wu, Y.; Ding, S.; Ding, Y.; Li, M. UWB Base Station Cluster Localization for Unmanned Ground Vehicle Guidance. *Math. Probl. Eng.* **2021**, *2021*, 6639574. [CrossRef]
16. Liu, J.; Guo, G. Vehicle Localization During GPS Outages with Extended Kalman Filter and Deep Learning. *IEEE Trans. Instrum. Meas.* **2021**, *70*, 7503410. [CrossRef]
17. *Pmod GPS Reference Manual*; Digilent Inc.: Pullman, WA, USA. Available online: https://reference.digilentinc.com/reference/pmod/pmodgps/reference-manual (accessed on 23 September 2021).
18. Raspberry, Documentation, Hardware, Sense Hat. "Shaun the Sheep" and "Farmageddon" Elements Are © 2019 Aardman and Studiocanal SAS. Available online: https://www.raspberrypi.org/documentation/hardware/sense-hat/ (accessed on 23 September 2021).
19. Sofwan, A.; Soetrisno, Y.A.A.; Ramadhani, N.P.; Rahmayani, A.; Handoyo, E.; Arfan, M. Vehicle Distance Measurement Tuning using Haversine and Micro-Segmentation. In Proceedings of the 2019 International Seminar on Intelligent Technology and Its Applications (ISITIA), Surabaya, Indonesia, 28–29 August 2019; pp. 239–243. [CrossRef]
20. Bakbak, D.; Uluça, V. Multicriteria decision-making method using the cosine vector similarity measure under intuitionistic trapezoidal fuzzy multi-numbers in architecture. In Proceedings of the 6th International Multidisciplinary Studies Congress (Multicongress' 19), Gaziantep, Turkey, 1 August 2019.
21. Uluçay, V.; Deli, I.; Şahin, M. Trapezoidal fuzzy multi-number and its application to multi-criteria decision-making problems. *Neural Comput. Appl.* **2018**, *30*, 1469–1478. [CrossRef]
22. ANFIS: Adaptive Neuro Fuzzy Inference System. The Math-Works, Inc.: USA 1994–2018. Available online: https://www.mathworks.com/help/fuzzy/anfis.html (accessed on 23 September 2021).
23. Kukolj, D. Design of adaptive Takagi–Sugeno–Kang fuzzy models. *Appl. Soft Comput.* **2002**, *2*, 89–103. [CrossRef]
24. Bergsten, P.; Palm, R.; Driankov, D. Observers for Takagi-Sugeno fuzzy systems. *IEEE Trans. Syst. Man Cybern. Part B (Cybern.)* **2002**, *32*, 114–121. [CrossRef]
25. evalfis: Evaluate Fuzzy Inference System. The Math-Works, Inc.: USA 1994–2018. Available online: https://www.mathworks.com/help/fuzzy/evalfis.html (accessed on 23 September 2021).
26. Rafatnia, S.; Nourmohammadi, H.; Keighobadi, J. Fuzzy-adaptive constrained data fusion algorithm for indirect centralized integrated SINS/GNSS navigation system. *GPS Solut.* **2019**, *23*, 62. [CrossRef]

27. Jeffrey, S.J.; Uhlmann, K. New extension of the Kalman filter to nonlinear systems. In Proceedings of the Signal Processing, Sensor Fusion, and Target Recognition, Orlando, FL, USA, 21–25 April 1997; Volume 3068, pp. 182–193.
28. Cruz, M.O.; Macedo, H.; Guimaraes, A. Grouping Similar Trajectories for Carpooling Purposes. In Proceedings of the 2015 Brazilian Conference on Intelligent Systems (BRACIS), Natal, Brazil, 4–7 November 2015; pp. 234–239.
29. Dua, D.; Graff, C. UCI Machine Learning Repository. University of California, School of Information and Computer Science: Irvine, CA, USA; Available online: http://archive.ics.uci.edu/ml (accessed on 3 November 2021).

mathematics

Article

# Fuzzy Logical Algebra and Study of the Effectiveness of Medications for COVID-19

**Shuker Khalil [1,*], Ahmed Hassan [1], Haya Alaskar [2], Wasiq Khan [3] and Abir Hussain [3,4]**

1 Department of Mathematics, College of Science, University of Basrah, Basrah 61004, Iraq; ahmed.naji@uobasrah.edu.iq
2 Department of Computer Science, College of Computer Engineering and Sciences, Prince Sattam bin Abdulaziz University, Alkharj 11942, Saudi Arabia; h.alaskar@psau.edu.sa
3 Computer Science Department, Liverpool John Moores University, Liverpool L3 3AF, UK; W.Khan@ljmu.ac.uk (W.K.); A.Hussain@ljmu.ac.uk or abir.hussain@sharjah.ac.ae (A.H.)
4 Electrical Engineering Department, Faculty of Engineering, University of Sharjah, Sharjah P.O. Box 27272, United Arab Emirates
* Correspondence: shuker.khalil@uobasrah.edu.iq

**Abstract:** A fuzzy logical algebra has diverse applications in various domains such as engineering, economics, environment, medicine, and so on. However, the existing techniques in algebra do not apply to delta-algebra. Therefore, the purpose of this paper was to investigate new types of cubic soft algebras and study their applications, the representation of cubic soft sets with $\delta$-algebras, and new types of cubic soft algebras, such as cubic soft $\delta$-subalgebra based on the parameter $\lambda$ ($\lambda$-$CS\delta$-$SA$) and cubic soft $\delta$-subalgebra ($CS\delta$-$SA$) over $\eta$. This study explains why the P-union is not really a soft cubic $\delta$-subalgebra of two soft cubic $\delta$-subalgebras. We also reveal that any R/P-cubic soft subsets of ($CS\delta$-$SA$) is not necessarily ($CS\delta$-$SA$). Furthermore, we present the required conditions to prove that the R-union of two members is ($CS\delta$-$SA$) if each one of them is ($CS\delta$-$SA$). To illustrate our assumptions, the proposed ($CS\delta$-$SA$) is applied to study the effectiveness of medications for COVID-19 using the python program.

**Keywords:** fuzzy soft sets; COVID-19; python program; logical algebra; cubic sets; P/R-union; $\delta$-algebra

**Citation:** Khalil, S.; Hassan, A.; Alaskar, H.; Khan, W.; Hussain, A. Fuzzy Logical Algebra and Study of the Effectiveness of Medications for COVID-19. *Mathematics* **2021**, *9*, 2838. https://doi.org/10.3390/math9222838

Academic Editor: Michael Voskoglou

Received: 22 September 2021
Accepted: 3 November 2021
Published: 9 November 2021



## 1. Introduction

Artificial Intelligence (AI) and logical algebra are studied in different non-classical sets like soft sets [1], fuzzy sets [2], and others, to solve various problems in our life. For example, in 2021, nano-sets have been used to study COVID-19 [3]. COVID-19 has also been studied by Arfan and others [4]. Zhong et al. [5] showed that the majority of inhabitants with an above-average socioeconomic status, particularly females, expressed optimism about COVID-19. A variety of AI and logic applications have been introduced in diverse domains including the medical field [6,7]. The concept of fuzzy set (FS) was introduced by Zadeh [8] in 1965 and has been then successfully applied in different domains [9,10]. The connotation of fuzzy algebra determined by G. Xi [9] is called fuzzy $BCK$-algebra. Several applications of fuzzy $BCK$-algebras were discussed by Y. B. Jun [10].

In [11], some concepts of fuzzy algebras such as fuzzy $\rho$-subalgebra ($F\rho$-$SA$), fuzzy $\rho$-ideal ($F\rho$-$I$), and fuzzy $\overline{\rho}$-ideal ($F\overline{\rho}$-$I$) were introduced. The mathematical idea of soft sets is a fresh notion studied by D. Molodtsov [12]. This theory has been applied in various fields, as fuzzy sets theory [13]. The notion of fuzzy soft algebra was introduced by Jun and others [14], who called it fuzzy soft $BCK$-algebra.

The connotations of interval-valued fuzzy sets (IVFS) were investigated as an extension of FS [15]. Similar to BCK, IVFS has been applied to various domains and subgroups [2]. Moreover, the general ideas of algebraic fuzzy systems (AFS) are enriched by introducing the notion of fuzzy subsets. Jun et al. [16] presented some operations such as P/R-union and P/R-intersection on cubic sets. They described several different ways to find the solutions for intricate problems in engineering, economics, and environment.

While conventional methods have been successfully applied in diverse domains, these methods do not handle uncertainties. Sometimes traditional methods in logical algebra are not sufficient to solve some problems or to obtain good results because different uncertainties models are necessary for those problems. The majority of system algebras are not commutative for any non-fixed pair of their members. Therefore, some algebra structures that are commutative for any non-fixed pair of their members, such as $\rho$-algebra [11] and $\delta$-algebra [17], have been proposed. In this work, we used $\delta$-algebra to consider new types of cubic soft algebras, such as ($\lambda$-$CS\delta$-$SA$) and ($CS\delta$-$SA$). These classes in $\delta$-algebra are different from any other class, since any pair $\omega \neq v \in \eta - \{f\}$ in algebra $(\eta,, f)$, they satisfy the condition $(v(v\omega))(\omega v) = f$. We also proved that P-union is not really a soft cubic subalgebra of two soft cubic $\delta$-subalgebras. We revealed that for any R/P-cubic soft subset of ($CS\delta$-$SA$), it is not necessarily true to be ($CS\delta$-$SA$). Furthermore, we present the required conditions to prove that the R-union of two members is ($CS\delta$-$SA$) if each one of them is ($CS\delta$-$SA$). To illustrate our notations, the applied ($CS\delta$-$SA$) to study the effectiveness of medications for COVID-19.

## 2. Preliminary

In this section, we will present some definitions that are necessary for our work.

**Definition 1.** ([17]) *We denote $(\eta,, f)$ as $\delta$-algebra (briefly, ($\delta$-A)) if $f \in$, and the following assumptions are fulfilled:*

(i) $vv = f$
(ii) $fv = f$
(iii) $v\omega = f$ *and* $\omega v = f \rightarrow v = \omega$, *for all* $\omega, v \in \eta$.
(iv) *For all* $\omega \neq v \in \eta - \{f\} \rightarrow v\omega = \omega v \neq f$.
(v) *For all* $\omega \neq v \in \eta - \{f\} \rightarrow (v(v\omega))(\omega v) = f$.

**Definition 2.** ([8]) *Let $\eta \neq \varnothing$. A mapping $\psi : \eta \rightarrow [0,1]$ is called fuzzy set (FS) of $\eta$. We denote the family of all (FSs) in $\eta$ by $B^\eta$. Let $\leq$ be a relation on $B^\eta$ specified by:*

$$(\psi \leq \psi', \forall \psi, \psi' \in B^\eta) \Leftrightarrow (\psi(v) \leq \psi'(v), \forall v \in \eta) \tag{1}$$

*Let ($\vee$) and ($\wedge$) be operations on $B^\eta$, specified by:*

$$(\psi \vee \psi')(v) = \max\{\psi(v), \psi'(v)\},$$

$$(\psi \wedge \psi')(v) = \min\{\psi(v), \psi'(v)\}, \forall v \in \eta \tag{2}$$

*For each $\psi \in B^\eta$, we denote its complement as $\psi^c$, specified by*

$$\psi^c(v) = 1 - \psi(v), \forall v \in \eta \tag{3}$$

*Let $\{\psi_\lambda | \lambda \in \Delta\}$ be a collection of (FSs), where $\Delta$ is an index set. Therefore, ($\vee$) and ($\wedge$) are specified by:*

$$(\underset{\lambda\in\Delta}{\vee}\psi)(v) = \sup\{\psi_\lambda(v) | \lambda \in \Delta\}, \tag{4}$$

$$(\underset{\lambda\in\Delta}{\wedge}\psi)(v) = \inf\{\psi_\lambda(v) | \lambda \in \Delta\}, \forall v \in \eta$$

**Definition 3.** ([18]) *Let $Z = [\theta^-, \theta^+]$ be a closed subinterval of $B = [0,1]$; $Z$ is said to be an interval number (IN), where $0 \leq \theta^- \leq \theta^+ \leq 1$. The family of all interval numbers (INs) is symbolized by $[B]$.*

Some operations on $[B]$ like $r$ min (refined minimum), $r$ max (refined maximum), "$\tilde{\geq}$", "$\tilde{\leq}$" and "=", are specified by:

$$r\min\{Z, Z'\} = [\min\{\theta^-, \theta'^-\}, \min\{\theta^+, \theta'^+\}]$$

$$r\max\{Z, Z'\} = [\max\{\theta^-, \theta'^-\}, \max\{\theta^+, \theta'^+\}] \tag{5}$$

$Z\tilde{\geq}Z' \Leftrightarrow \theta^- \geq \theta'^-$ and $\theta^+ \geq \theta'^+$, Moreover, $Z = Z' \Leftrightarrow \theta^- = \theta'^-, \theta^+ = \theta'^+$, if $\underset{\lambda\in\Delta}{\psi} \in \{[B]/\lambda \in \Delta\}$, is a collection of INs. Then,

$$r\inf_{\lambda\in\Delta} Z_\lambda = [\inf_{\lambda\in\Delta}\theta_\lambda^-, \inf_{\lambda\in\Delta}\theta_\lambda^+],$$

$$r\sup_{\lambda\in\Delta} Z_\lambda = [\sup_{\lambda\in\Delta}\theta_\lambda^-, \sup_{\lambda\in\Delta}\theta_\lambda^+] \tag{6}$$

We refer to the complement of any $Z \in [B]$ by $Z^c$, where

$$Z^c = [1 - \theta^+, 1 - \theta^-] \tag{7}$$

Let $\varnothing \neq \eta$. Then, $\zeta : \eta \to [B]$ is called an interval-valued fuzzy set (IVFS) in $\eta$. We refer to the family of all interval-valued fuzzy sets (IVFSs) in $\eta$ by $[B]^\eta$. On the other side, if $\xi \in [B]^\eta$ and $v \in \eta$, we refer to the degree of membership of $v$ to $\eta$ by $\xi(v) = [\xi^-(v), \xi^+(v)]$ or $\xi = [\xi^-, \xi^+]$, where $\xi^- : \eta \to B$ is the lower fuzzy set (LFS), and $\xi^+ : \eta \to B$ is the upper fuzzy set (UFS) in $\eta$. The definitions of the symbols "$\subseteq$" and "=" on any $\xi, \xi' \in [B]^\eta$ can be given as follows:

$$\xi \subseteq \xi' \Leftrightarrow \xi(v)\tilde{\leq}\xi'(v), \forall v \in \eta$$

$$\xi = \xi' \Leftrightarrow \xi(v) = \xi'(v), \forall v \in \eta \tag{8}$$

We refer to the complement of any $\xi \in [B]^\eta$ by $\xi^c$, where $\xi^c(v) = \xi(v)^c$, $\forall v \in \eta$. That means

$$\xi^c(v) = [1 - \xi^+(v), 1 - \xi^-(v)]\forall v \in \eta \tag{9}$$

If $\{\xi_\lambda \in [B]^\eta | \lambda \in \Delta\}$ is a family of (IVFSs), then "$\cup$ " and "$\cap$ " are defined in $[B]^\eta$ as follows:

$$(\cup_{\lambda\in\Delta}\xi_\lambda)(v) = r\sup_{\lambda\in\Delta}\xi_\lambda(v), \forall v \in \eta,$$

$$(\cap_{\lambda\in\Delta}\xi_\lambda)(v) = r\inf_{\lambda\in\Delta}\xi_\lambda(v), \forall v \in \eta. \tag{10}$$

**Definition 4.** ([12]) *Let $\eta$ be a universal set, with parameter set $\Delta$; $(\varepsilon, \sigma)$ is said to be a soft set (over $\eta$), where $\varepsilon : \sigma \to P(\eta)$, and $P(\eta)$ is the power set of $\eta$ with $\sigma \subseteq \Delta$.*

**Definition 5.** ([16]) *We define a cubic set $\Phi$ (CS) in $\eta$ by*

$$\Phi = \{\langle v, \xi(v), \psi(v)\rangle / v \in \eta\} \tag{11}$$

*We can also write it as $\Phi = \langle \xi, \psi \rangle$, where $\xi$ is IVFS, and $\psi$ is FS.*

**Definition 6.** ([16]) *Let $\Phi = \langle \xi, \psi \rangle$ and $\Phi' = \langle \xi', \psi' \rangle$ be a pair of cubic sets (CSs) in $\eta$. We define "$\subseteq_P$", "$\subseteq_R$", and "=" by the following:*

(i) *(P-order) $\Phi \subseteq_P \Phi' \Leftrightarrow \xi \subseteq \xi'$ and $\psi \leq \psi'$.*
(ii) *(R-order) $\Phi \subseteq_R \Phi' \Leftrightarrow \xi \subseteq \xi'$ and $\psi \geq \psi'$.*
(iii) *(Equality) $\Phi = \Phi' \Leftrightarrow \xi = \xi'$ and $\psi = \psi'$.*

**Definition 7.** ([16]) *Let $\{\Phi_\lambda = \{\langle v, \xi_\lambda(v), \psi_\lambda(v)\rangle / v \in \eta\}\}_{\lambda\in\Delta}$ be a collection of (CSs) in $\eta$. The symbol "$\cup_P$" (resp., "$\cap_P$", "$\cup_R$" and "$\cap_R$") is said to be (P-union) (resp., P-intersection, R-union, and R-intersection) and is obtained as follows:*

(1) $\cup_{p,\lambda\in\Delta}\Phi_\alpha = \{\langle v, \underset{\lambda\in\Delta}{\cup}\xi_\lambda(v), \underset{\lambda\in\Delta}{\vee}\psi_\lambda(v)\rangle / v \in \eta\}$,

(2) $\cap_{p,\lambda\in\Delta}\Phi_\lambda = \{\langle v, \underset{\lambda\in\Delta}{\cap}\xi_\lambda(v), \underset{\lambda\in\Delta}{\wedge}\psi\lambda(v)\rangle / v \in \eta\}$,

(3) $\cup_{R,\lambda\in\Delta}\Phi_\alpha = \{\langle v, \underset{\lambda\in\Delta}{\cup}\xi_\lambda(v), \underset{\lambda\in\Delta}{\vee}\psi_\lambda(v)\rangle / v \in \eta\}$,

(4) $\cap_{R,\lambda\in\Delta}\Phi_\lambda = \{\langle v, \underset{\lambda\in\Delta}{\cap}\xi_\lambda(v), \underset{\lambda\subset\Delta}{\wedge}\psi\lambda(v)\rangle / v \in \eta\}$,

**Remark 1.** ([19])

*The complement of* $\Phi = \langle \xi, \psi \rangle$ *is defined as:*

$$\Phi^c = \{\langle v, \xi(v)^c, \psi^c(v)\rangle / v \in \eta\} \tag{12}$$

$$(\Phi^c)^c = \Phi \tag{13}$$

*If* $\{\Phi_\lambda = \{\langle v, \xi_\lambda(v), \psi_\alpha(v)\rangle / v \in \eta\}\}_{\lambda\in\Delta}$ *is a collection of (CSs) in* $\eta$, *then we have the followng;*

$$(\cup_{p,\lambda\in\Delta}\Phi_\lambda)^c = \cup_{p,\lambda\in\Delta}(\Phi_\lambda)^c,\ (\cap_{p,\lambda\in\Delta}\Phi\lambda)^c = \cap_{p,\lambda\in\Delta}(\Phi_\lambda)^c,\ (\cup_{R,\lambda\in\Delta}\Phi_\lambda)^c = \cap_{R,\lambda\in\Delta}(\Phi_\lambda)^c \\ \text{and } (\cap_{R,\lambda\in\Delta}\Phi_\lambda)^c = \cup_{R,\lambda\in\Delta}(\Phi_\lambda)^c \tag{14}$$

*Therefore, a (CS)* $\Phi = \{\langle v, \xi_\Phi(v), \psi_\Phi(v)\rangle / v \in \eta\}$ *is denoted by* $\Phi = \langle \xi_\Phi, \psi_\Phi \rangle$. *The family of all (CSs) in* $\eta$ *is referred to as* $\int^\eta$.

**Definition 8.** ([19]) *Let* $\eta$ *be a universal set with the parameter set* $\Delta$; $(\Omega, \Re)$ *is said to be a cubic soft set (CSS) over* $\eta$, *where* $\Re \subseteq \Delta$, *and* $\Omega : \Re \to \int^\eta$ *is a mapping. We write* $(\Omega, \Re)$ *as:*

$$(\Omega, \Re) = \{\Omega(\lambda)/\lambda \in \Re\}, \text{ where } \Omega(\lambda) = \left\langle \xi_{\Omega(\lambda)}, \psi_{\Omega(\lambda)} \right\rangle. \tag{15}$$

*The set of all cubic soft sets (CSSs) is symbolized by* ${}_\Delta\int^\eta$.

**Definition 9.** ([19]) *Let* $(\Omega, \Re)$, $(\Omega', \Re') \in_\Delta \int^\eta$. *The R-union of* $(\Omega, \Re)$ *and* $(\Omega', \Re')$ *is a (CSS)* $(D, W)$ *symbolized by* $(D, W) = (\Omega, \Re)\, \overline{\cup}_R (\Omega', \Re')$, *where* $W = \Re \cup \Re'$ *and*

$$(\lambda) = \begin{cases} \Omega(\lambda), if \lambda \in \Re \backslash \Re' \\ \Omega'(\lambda), if \lambda \in \Re' \backslash \Re \\ \Omega(\lambda) \cup_R \Omega'(\lambda), if \lambda \in \Re \cap \Re' \end{cases}, \forall \lambda \in W \tag{16}$$

**Definition 10.** ([19]) *Let* $(\Omega, \Re)$, $(\Omega', \Re') \in_\Delta \int^\eta$. *The p-union of* $(\Omega, \Re)$ *and* $(\Omega', \Re')$ *is a (CSS)* $(D, W)$ *symbolized by* $(D, W) = (\Omega, \Re) \overline{\cup}_P (\Omega', \Re')$, *where* $W = \Re \cup \Re'$ *and*

$$(\lambda) = \begin{cases} \Omega(\lambda), if \lambda \in \Re \backslash \Re' \\ \Omega'(\lambda), if \lambda \in \Re' \backslash \Re \\ \Omega(\lambda) \cup_P \Omega'(\lambda), if \lambda \in \Re \cap \Re' \end{cases}, \forall \lambda \in W \tag{17}$$

**Definition 11.** ([19]) *Let* $(\Omega, \Re)$, $(\Omega', \Re') \in_\Delta \int^\eta$. *The p-intersection of* $(\Omega, \Re)$ *and* $(\Omega', \Re')$ *is a (CSS)* $(D, W)$ *symbolized by* $(D, W) = (\Omega, \Re) \overline{\cap}_P (\Omega', \Re')$, *where* $W = \Re \cup \Re'$ *and*

$$D(\lambda) = \begin{cases} \Omega(\lambda), if \lambda \in \Re \backslash \Re' \\ \Omega'(\lambda), if \lambda \in \Re' \backslash \Re \\ \Omega(\lambda) \cap_P \Omega'(\lambda), if \lambda \in \Re \cap \Re' \end{cases}, \forall \lambda \in W \tag{18}$$

**Definition 12.** ([19]) *Let* $(\Omega, \Re)$, $(\Omega', \Re') \in_\Delta \int^\eta$. *We say* $(\Omega, \Re)$ *is an R-cubic soft subset of* $(\Omega', \Re')$ *if*

$$\Re \subseteq \Re',\ \Omega(\lambda) \subseteq_R \Omega'(\lambda),\ \forall \lambda \in \Re. \tag{19}$$

**Definition 13.** ([19]) *Let* $(\Omega, \Re)$, $(\Omega', \Re') \in_\Delta \int^\eta$. *We say* $(\Omega, \Re)$ *is a P-cubic soft subset of* $(\Omega', \Re')$ *if*

$$\Re \subseteq \Re',\ \Omega(\lambda) \subseteq_P \Omega'(\lambda),\ \forall\lambda \in \Re. \tag{20}$$

**Example 1.** *Let the set of students under consideration be* $\eta = \{a_1, a_2, a_3\}$. *Let E = {pleasing personality* $(e_1)$*; conduct* $(e_2)$*; good result* $(e_3)$*; sincerity* $(e_4)$*} be the set of parameters used to choose the best student. Suppose that the soft set* $(F, A)$ *describing Mr. X's opinion about the best student in an academic year is defined by*

$$A = \{e_1, e_2\}, F(e_1) = \{a_1\},\ F(e_2) = \{a_1, a_2, a_3\}$$

The description of Mr. *X*'s opinion is explained see Figure 1.

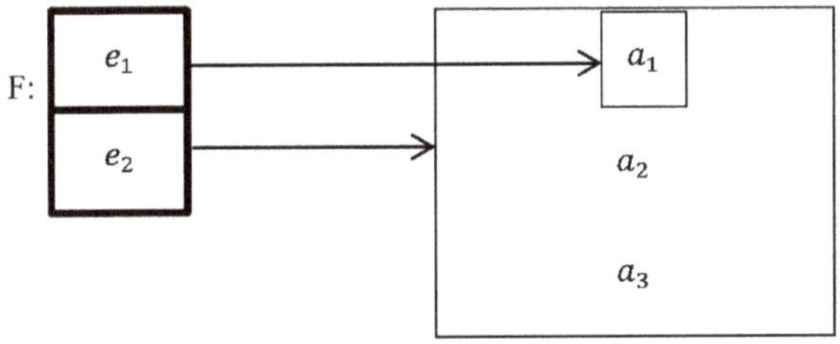


**Figure 1.** The description of Mr. *X*'s opinion by $(F, A)$.

However, if we define $(\Omega, A) = \{\{\langle[0.5,\ 0.7],\ 0.8\rangle,\ \langle[0.3,\ 0.5],\ 0.3\rangle,\ \langle[0.4,\ 0.6],\ 0.7\rangle\},\ \{\langle[0.4,\ 0.5],\ 0.8\rangle,\ \langle[0.3,\ 0.4],\ 0.8\rangle,\ \langle[0.2,\ 0.5],\ 0.6\rangle\}\}$, then $(\Omega, A)$ is a cubic soft set over $\eta = \{a_1, a_2,\ a_3\}$, dependent on (FS) to describe the best student by the rates of some activities $A = \{e_1, e_2\}$ of *E*; each rate ranges between 0 and 1 and approaches 0 when an activity is low, while it approaches 1 when an activity is high).

## 3. Cubic Soft $\delta$-Subalgebras in $\delta$-Algebras and Its Application for COVID-19

In this section, we will consider several new forms of cubic soft algebras and see how they can be used to study the effectiveness of medications for COVID-19.

**Definition 14.** *Let* $(\Omega, \Re)$ *be (CSS) over* $\eta$; $(\eta, , f)$ *is* $(\delta\text{-}A)$, *if there exists a parameter* $\lambda \in \Im$ *that satisfies the following:*

$$\xi_{\Omega(\lambda)}(v \circ \omega) \tilde{\succeq} r\min\{\xi_{\Omega(\lambda)}(v), \xi_{\Omega(\lambda)}(\omega)\} \forall v, \omega \in \eta \tag{21}$$

$$\psi_{\Omega(\lambda)}(v \circ \omega) \tilde{\preceq} r\max\{\psi_{\Omega(\lambda)}(v), \psi_{\Omega(\lambda)}(\omega)\} \forall v, \omega \in \eta \tag{22}$$

$(\Omega, \Re)$ *is said to be a cubic soft* $\delta$*-subalgebra over* $\eta$ *based on a parameter* $\lambda$ *(briefly,* $(\lambda\text{-CS}\delta\text{-SA})$ *over* $\eta$*) and is called a cubic soft* $\delta$*-subalgebra (CS*$\delta$*-SA) over* $\eta$, *if it is an* $(\lambda\text{-CS}\delta\text{-SA})$ *over* $\eta, \forall\lambda \in \Re$.

**Theorem 1.** *If* $(\Omega, \Re)$, $(\Omega', \Re') \in_\Delta \int^\eta$ *with* $\Re$ *and* $\Re'$ *are disjoint, then their P-union is a (CS*$\delta$*-SA) over* $\eta$.

**Proof.** From Definition (10), we have $(D, W) = (\Omega, \Re)\overline{\cup}_P(\Omega', \Re')$, where $W = \Re \cup \Re'$ and

$$D(\lambda) = \begin{cases} \Omega(\lambda), if \lambda \in \Re \backslash \Re' \\ \Omega'(\lambda), if \lambda \in \Re' \backslash \Re \\ \Omega(\lambda) \cup_P \Omega'(\lambda), if \lambda \in \Re \cap \Re' \end{cases},\ \forall\lambda \in W \tag{23}$$

Therefore, either $\lambda \in \Re \backslash \Re'$ or $\lambda \in \Re' \backslash \Re, \forall \lambda \in W$ (since $\Re \cap \Re' = \varphi$). If $\lambda \in \Re \backslash \Re'$, then $D(\lambda) = \Omega(\lambda)$ is a $CS\delta$-subalgebra over $\eta$. In addition, if $\lambda \in \Re' \backslash \Re$, then $D(\lambda) = \Omega'(\lambda)$ is a ($CS\delta$-$SA$) over $\eta$. So, $(D, W) = (\Omega, \Re)\ \bar{\cup}_P(\Omega', \Re')$ is a ($CS\delta$-$SA$) over $\eta$. □

**Remark 2.** *The above theorem is not true in general when $\Re$ and $\Re'$ are not disjoint.*

**Example 2.** *Let $\eta = \{f, \upsilon, \omega, \sigma, \tau\}$ be a universal set of some medications for (COVID-19), as follows $f$ = Chloroquine, $\upsilon$ = Arbidol, $\omega$ = Tamiflu, $\sigma$ = Kaletra, $\tau$ = Remdesivir. These medications were chosen because they have been tried and discussed by researchers, for example, Chloroquine in [20], Arbidol in [21], Tamiflu in [22], Kaletra in [23], and Remdesivir in [24]. We used virtual reality to introduce a mathematical method where the composition of the members forms an algebraic system; we determined how to find the cubic soft set over $\eta$, when it is dependent on (FS) to describe the best medication in the basis of its activity evaluated by rates, with each rate confined between 0 and 1. If a rate appr2oaches 0, then activity is low, whereas if the rate is closer to 1, the activity is high. Suppose that for any two members in $\eta$, their composition under operation is defined by the python program as follows:*

```
from numpy import array
X = ['f','v','w','σ','τ']
i = 0
lst = array (range (25), dtype = str). reshape (5,5)
for a in X:
    j = 0
    for b in X:
        # print (a, '        ', b)
        if ((a == 'f') or (a == b) :
            m = 'f'
        elif ((b = 'f')):
            m = a
        elif ((a! = 'f') and (b! = 'f') ):
            m = 'v'
        lst [i,j] = m
        j = j + 1
    I = I + 1
print(lst)
```

Using this program, let us consider Figure 2, where rows are placed in a table.

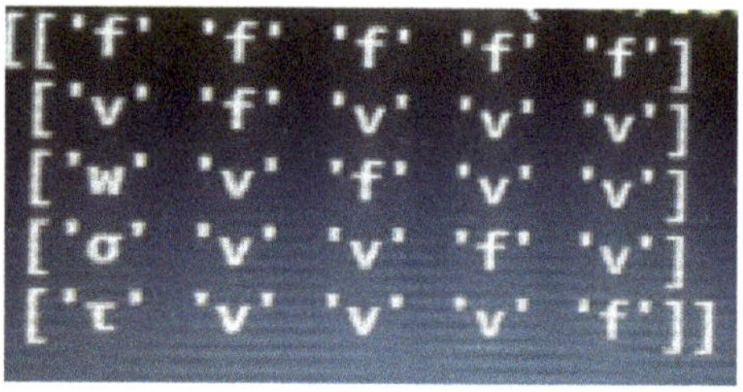


**Figure 2.** Composition $xy$, for any $x, y$ of a universal set of medications.

This algorithm makes the members distributive for any set $\eta = \{r_1, r_2, \ldots, r_n\}$ that has $n$ members inside a matrix $M = \begin{pmatrix} m_{11} & \cdots & m_{1n} \\ \vdots & \ddots & \vdots \\ m_{n1} & \cdots & m_{nn} \end{pmatrix}$ of degree $(n \times n)$, where $m_{ij} = r_i r_j = r_k \in \eta$ for some $(1 \leq k \leq n)$ and all $(1 \leq i, j \leq n)$. By this matrix, our table can have the structure of $\delta$-algebra.

Therefore, the binary operation is described in a Table 1.

**Table 1.** ($\eta$,o,$f$) is a $\delta$-algebra.

| $\tau$ | $\sigma$ | $\omega$ | $\upsilon$ | $f$ | |
|---|---|---|---|---|---|
| $f$ | $f$ | $f$ | $f$ | $f$ | $f$ |
| $\upsilon$ | $\upsilon$ | $\upsilon$ | $f$ | $\upsilon$ | $\upsilon$ |
| $\upsilon$ | $\upsilon$ | $f$ | $\upsilon$ | $\omega$ | $\omega$ |
| $\upsilon$ | $f$ | $\upsilon$ | $\upsilon$ | $\sigma$ | $\sigma$ |
| $f$ | $\upsilon$ | $\upsilon$ | $\upsilon$ | $\tau$ | $\tau$ |

Then, $(\eta, , f)$ is a $\delta$-algebra. Figure 3 explains that the member $f$ does not change and retains more than 50% of its properties if $f$ is entered from pipe 1, and any member $h$ in $\eta$ is entered from pipe 2.

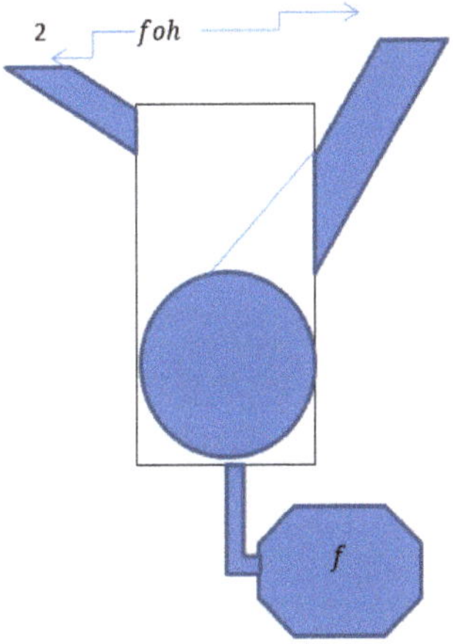


**Figure 3.** The composition $f\upsilon$ explains when $f$ is entered from pipe 1.

Moreover, the same engineering device in Figure 4 explains that $f$ will lose more than 50% of its properties if it is entered from pipe 2 and any member $h$ in $\eta$ is entered from pipe 1; the member $f$ will chang and get the same properties of the member $h$. In $\delta$-algebra, the member $f$ is called the fixed member.

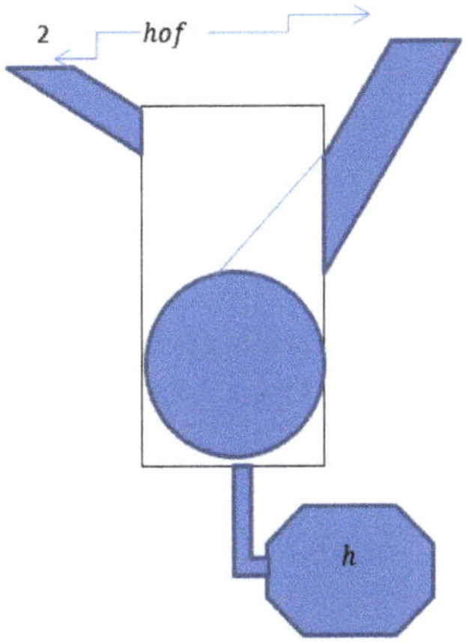


**Figure 4.** The composition $\upsilon f$ explains when $f$ is entered from pipe 2.

Now, let $\Delta = \{$"body temperature" $(\lambda_1)$, "cough with chest congestion" $(\lambda_2)$, "body ache" $(\lambda_3)$, "cough with no chest congestion" $(\lambda_4)$, "breathing trouble", $(\lambda_5)\}$ be a parameter set. Here, $\Delta$ give us the effectiveness for these medications that help somebody want to select one of them based on his opinion of what he prefers of these attributives. Take $\Re = \{\lambda_1, \lambda_3, \lambda_5\}$ and $\Re' = \{\lambda_1, \lambda_2, \lambda_3, \lambda_4\}$, then from Tables 2 and 3, we consider that $(\Omega, \Re)$ and $(\Omega', \Re')$ are $CS\delta$-subalgebras over $\eta$.

**Table 2.** $(\Omega, \Re)$ is $(CS\delta\text{-}SA)$.

| | $\lambda_1$ | $\lambda_3$ | $\lambda_5$ |
|---|---|---|---|
| $f$ | $\langle[0.6, 0.8], 0.2\rangle$ | $\langle[0.5, 0.6], 0.1\rangle$ | $\langle[0.5, 0.8], 0.5\rangle$ |
| $v$ | $\langle[0.6, 0.7], 0.5\rangle$ | $\langle[0.4, 0.6], 0.4\rangle$ | $\langle[0.5, 0.8], 0.7\rangle$ |
| $\omega$ | $\langle[0.5, 0.7], 0.8\rangle$ | $\langle[0.4, 0.5], 0.8\rangle$ | $\langle[0.5, 0.7], 0.9\rangle$ |
| $\sigma$ | $\langle[0.4, 0.6], 0.7\rangle$ | $\langle[0.2, 0.5], 0.6\rangle$ | $\langle[0.2, 0.4], 0.6\rangle$ |
| $\tau$ | $\langle[0.3, 0.5], 0.3\rangle$ | $\langle[0.3, 0.4], 0.8\rangle$ | $\langle[0.5, 0.7], 0.5\rangle$ |

**Table 3.** $(\Omega', \Re')$ is $(CS\delta\text{-}SA)$.

| | $\lambda_1$ | $\lambda_2$ | $\lambda_3$ | $\lambda_4$ |
|---|---|---|---|---|
| $f$ | $\langle[0.4, 0.7], 0.4\rangle$ | $\langle[0.6, 0.9], 0.6\rangle$ | $\langle[0.5, 0.6], 0.1\rangle$ | $\langle[0.4, 0.5], 0.3\rangle$ |
| $v$ | $\langle[0.4, 0.6], 0.6\rangle$ | $\langle[0.4, 0.8], 0.8\rangle$ | $\langle[0.4, 0.5], 0.3\rangle$ | $\langle[0.4, 0.5], 0.5\rangle$ |
| $\omega$ | $\langle[0.4, 0.6], 0.8\rangle$ | $\langle[0.6, 0.8], 0.7\rangle$ | $\langle[0.4, 0.5], 0.6\rangle$ | $\langle[0.3, 0.4], 0.4\rangle$ |
| $\sigma$ | $\langle[0.1, 0.3], 0.5\rangle$ | $\langle[0.3, 0.5], 0.7\rangle$ | $\langle[0.3, 0.5], 0.8\rangle$ | $\langle[0.1, 0.4], 0.8\rangle$ |
| $\tau$ | $\langle[0.4, 0.7], 0.4\rangle$ | $\langle[0.5, 0.8], 0.6\rangle$ | $\langle[0.2, 0.3], 0.8\rangle$ | $\langle[0.2, 0.3], 0.3\rangle$ |

Here, $\Re$ and $\Re'$ are not disjoint. The $R$-union $(D, W) = (\Omega, \Re)\overline{\cup}_p(\Omega', \Re')$ is given in Table 4.

**Table 4.** $(D, W)$ is (CSS).

| | $\lambda_1$ | $\lambda_2$ | $\lambda_3$ | $\lambda_4$ | $\lambda_5$ |
|---|---|---|---|---|---|
| $f$ | $\langle[0.6, 0.7], 0.4\rangle$ | $\langle[0.6, 0.9], 0.6\rangle$ | $\langle[0.5, 0.6], 0.1\rangle$ | $\langle[0.4, 0.5], 0.3\rangle$ | $\langle[0.5, 0.8], 0.5\rangle$ |
| $v$ | $\langle[0.6, 0.7], 0.6\rangle$ | $\langle[0.4, 0.8], 0.8\rangle$ | $\langle[0.4, 0.6], 0.4\rangle$ | $\langle[0.1, 0.3], 0.5\rangle$ | $\langle[0.3, 0.8], 0.7\rangle$ |
| $\omega$ | $\langle[0.5, 0.7], 0.8\rangle$ | $\langle[0.6, 0.8], 0.7\rangle$ | $\langle[0.4, 0.5], 0.8\rangle$ | $\langle[0.3, 0.4], 0.4\rangle$ | $\langle[0.5, 0.7], 0.9\rangle$ |
| $\sigma$ | $\langle[0.4, 0.6], 0.7\rangle$ | $\langle[0.3, 0.5], 0.7\rangle$ | $\langle[0.3, 0.5], 0.8\rangle$ | $\langle[0.1, 0.4], 0.8\rangle$ | $\langle[0.2, 0.4], 0.6\rangle$ |
| $\tau$ | $\langle[0.4, 0.7], 0.4\rangle$ | $\langle[0.5, 0.8], 0.6\rangle$ | $\langle[0.3, 0.4], 0.8\rangle$ | $\langle[0.2, 0.3], 0.3\rangle$ | $\langle[0.5, 0.7], 0.5\rangle$ |

We have

$$\xi_{D(\lambda_4)}(\omega\tau) = \xi_{D(\lambda_4)}(v) = [0.1,\ 0.3],\ [0.2,\ 0.3] = r\min\{[0.3, 0.4],\ [0.2, 0.3]\} = r\min\{\xi_{D(\lambda_4)}(\omega),\ \xi_{D(\lambda_4)}(\tau)\} \tag{24}$$

and/or

$$\psi_{D(\lambda_4)}(\omega\tau) = \psi_{D(\lambda_4)}(v) = 0.5\ >\ 0.3 = \max\{0.4,\ 0.3\} = \max\{\psi_{D(\lambda_4)}(\omega),\ \psi_{D(\lambda_4)}(\tau)\} \tag{25}$$

**Remark 3.**

(1) *For any R-cubic soft subset of (CSδ-SA), it is not necessary that each one is (CSδ-SA).*
(2) *For any P-cubic soft subset of (CSδ-SA), it is not necessary that each one is (CSδ-SA) too.*

**Example 3.** *In Example 2, let* $\eta = \{f, v, \omega, \sigma, \tau\}$ *and* $(\Omega', \Re')$ *be an R-cubic soft subset of* $(\Omega, \Re)$ *as shown in Table 5.*

**Table 5.** $(\Omega', \Re')$ R-cubic soft subset of $(\Omega, \Re)$.

| | $\lambda_1$ | $\lambda_5$ |
|---|---|---|
| $f$ | $\langle[0.3, 0.5], 0.8\rangle$ | $\langle[0.5, 0.8], 0.5\rangle$ |
| $v$ | $\langle[0.3, 0.6], 0.6\rangle$ | $\langle[0.3, 0.8], 0.7\rangle$ |
| $\omega$ | $\langle[0.4, 0.5], 0.8\rangle$ | $\langle[0.5, 0.7], 0.9\rangle$ |
| $\sigma$ | $\langle[0.3, 0.4], 0.8\rangle$ | $\langle[0.2, 0.4], 0.6\rangle$ |
| $\tau$ | $\langle[0.2, 0.4], 0.5\rangle$ | $\langle[0.5, 0.7], 0.5\rangle$ |

*Then, we have*

$\xi_{D(\lambda_1)}(\sigma\omega) = \xi_{D(\lambda_1)}(v) = [0.2, 0.3] \leq [0.3, 0.4] = r \min \{[0.3, 0.4], [0.4, 0.5]\} = r \min \{\xi_{D(\lambda_1)}(\sigma), \xi_{D(\lambda_1)}(\omega)\}$. $(\Omega', \Re')$ *is not a (CSδ-SA) over* $\eta$.

*Here, we consider that it is not necessary that any P-cubic soft subset of (CSδ-SA) is (CSδ-SA) too.*

**Example 4.** *In Example 2, let* $\eta = \{f, v, \omega, \sigma, \tau\}$ *and* $(\Omega\prime, \Re')$ *be a P-cubic soft subset of* $(\Omega, \Re)$, *as defined in Table 6:*

**Table 6.** $(\Omega', \Re')$ P-cubic soft subset of $(\Omega, \Re)$.

| | $\lambda_1$ | $\lambda_5$ |
|---|---|---|
| $f$ | $\langle[0.3, 0.5], 0.1\rangle$ | $\langle[0.5, 0.8], 0.5\rangle$ |
| $v$ | $\langle[0.2, 0.3], 0.4\rangle$ | $\langle[0.3, 0.8], 0.7\rangle$ |
| $\omega$ | $\langle[0.4, 0.5], 0.7\rangle$ | $\langle[0.5, 0.7], 0.9\rangle$ |
| $\sigma$ | $\langle[0.3, 0.4], 0.6\rangle$ | $\langle[0.2, 0.4], 0.6\rangle$ |
| $\tau$ | $\langle[0.2, 0.4], 0.2\rangle$ | $\langle[0.5, 0.7], 0.5\rangle$ |

$\xi_{D(\lambda_1)}(\sigma\omega) = \xi_{D(\lambda_1)}(v) = [0.2, 0.3] \precsim [0.3, 0.4] = r \min \{[0.3, 0.4], [0.4, 0.5]\} = r \min \{\xi_{D(\lambda_1)}(\sigma), \xi_{D(\lambda_1)}(\omega)\}$. $(\Omega', \Re')$ *is not a (CSδ-SA) over* $\eta$. *Here, we consider that for any R-cubic soft subset of (CSδ-SA), it is not necessary to be (CSδ-SA) too.*

**Proposition 1.** *Let* $(\Omega, \Re) \in_\Delta \int^\eta$ *with* $(\eta, , f)$ *is (δ-A) and* $\lambda \in \Delta$. *Then,* $\xi_{\Omega(\lambda)}(f) \succsim \xi_{\Omega(\lambda)}(v)$ *and* $\psi_{\Omega(\lambda)}(f) \precsim \psi_{\Omega(\lambda)}(v)$, $\forall v \in \eta$, *if* $(\Omega, \Re)$ *is (λ-CSδ-SA) over* $\eta$.

**Proof.** $\forall v \in \eta$, we consider that:

$\xi_{\Omega(\lambda)}(f) = \xi_{\Omega(\lambda)}(vv) \succsim r \min \{\xi_{\Omega(\lambda)}(v), \xi_{\Omega(\lambda)}(v)\} = r \min\{[\xi_{\Omega(\lambda)}(v)^-, \xi_{\Omega(\lambda)}(v)^+], [\xi_{\Omega(\lambda)}(v)^-, \xi_{\Omega(\lambda)}(v)^+]\} = [\xi_{\Omega(\lambda)}(v)^-, \xi_{\Omega(\lambda)}(v)^+] = \xi_{\Omega(\lambda)}(v)$ and $\psi_{\Omega(\lambda)}(f) = \psi_{\Omega(\lambda)}(vv) \precsim \max \{\psi_{\Omega(\lambda)}(v), \psi_{\Omega(\lambda)}(v)\} = \psi_{\Omega(\lambda)}(v)$. □

**Theorem 2.** *Assume* $(\Omega, \Re) \in_\Delta \int^\eta$ *is (λ-CSδ-SA) over* $\eta$ *with* $(\eta, , f)$ *is (δ-A). Then,* $\xi_{\Omega(\lambda)}(v_n) = [1, 1]$ *and* $\psi_{\Omega(\lambda)}(v_n) = 0$, *if* $\langle v_n \rangle$ *is a sequence in* $\eta$ *with* $\lim_{n\to\infty} \xi_{\Omega(\lambda)}(v_n) = [1, 1]$ *and* $\lim_{n\to\infty} \psi_{\Omega(\lambda)}(v_n) = 0$.

**Proof.** Since $\xi_{\Omega(\lambda)}(f) \succsim \xi_{\Omega(\lambda)}(v)$, $\psi_{\Omega(\lambda)}(f) \precsim \psi_{\Omega(\lambda)}(v)$, $\forall v \in \eta$, we have

$$\xi_{\Omega(\lambda)}(f) \succsim \xi_{\Omega(\lambda)}(v_n), \forall n \in N,$$

$$\psi_{\Omega(\lambda)}(f) \precsim \psi_{\Omega(\lambda)}(v), \forall n \in N. \tag{26}$$

However, $[1, 1] \succsim \xi_{\Omega(\lambda)}(f) \succsim \lim_{n\to\infty} \xi_{\Omega(\lambda)}(v_n) = [1, 1]$. Also, $0 \precsim \lim_{n\to\infty} \psi_{\Omega(\lambda)}(v_n) \precsim \lim_{n\to\infty} \psi_{\Omega(\lambda)}(v_n) = 0$. Therefore $\xi_{\Omega(\lambda)}(v_n) = [1, 1]$ and $\psi_{\Omega(\lambda)}(v_n) = 0$. □

**Theorem 3.** *If each of* $(\Omega, \Re), (\Omega\prime, \Re') \in_\Delta \int^\eta$ *is a (CSδ-SA), then their R-intersection is also (CSδ-SA).*

**Proof.** Let $(\Omega, \Re)$ and $(\Omega', \Re')$ are $(CS\delta\text{-}SA)$ and $(D, W) = (\Omega, \Re)\overline{\sqcap}_P(\Omega', \Re')$, where $W = \Re \cup \Re'$ and

$$D(\lambda) = \begin{cases} \Omega(\lambda), if \lambda \in \Re \backslash \Re' \\ \Omega'(\lambda), if \lambda \in \Re' \backslash \Re \\ \Omega(\lambda) \cap_R \Omega'(\lambda), if \lambda \in \Re \cap \Re' \end{cases}, \forall \lambda \in W \tag{27}$$

Now, $\forall \lambda \in W$, we consider three states: (i) $\lambda \in \Re / \Re'$, (ii) $\lambda \in \Re' / \Re$, (iii) $\lambda \in \Re \cap \Re'$. In state (i), we obtain;

$$\begin{aligned} \xi_{D(\lambda)}(v \circ \omega) &= \xi_{\Omega(\lambda)}(v \circ \omega) \widetilde{\geq} r\min\{\xi_{\Omega(\lambda)}(v), \xi_{\Omega(\lambda)}(\omega)\} = r\min\{\xi_{D(\lambda)}(v), \xi_{D(\lambda)}(\omega)\}, \\ \psi_{D(\lambda)}(v \circ \omega) &= \psi_{\Omega(\lambda)}(v \circ \omega) \widetilde{\leq} \max\{\psi_{\Omega(\lambda)}(v), \psi_{\Omega(\lambda)}(\omega)\} = \max\{\psi_{D(\lambda)}(v), \psi_{D(\lambda)}(\omega)\}, \end{aligned} \tag{28}$$

In state (ii), we obtain;

$$\begin{aligned} \xi_{D(\lambda)}(v \circ \omega) &= \xi_{\Omega'(\lambda)}(v \circ \omega) \widetilde{\geq} r\min\{\xi_{\Omega'(\lambda)}(v), \xi_{\Omega(\lambda)}(\omega)\} = r\min\{\xi_{D(\lambda)}(v), \xi_{D(\lambda)}(\omega)\}, \\ \psi_{D(\lambda)}(v \circ \omega) &= \psi_{\Omega'(\lambda)}(v \circ \omega) \widetilde{\leq} \max\{\psi_{\Omega'(\lambda)}(v), \psi_{\Omega'(\lambda)}(\omega)\} = \max\{\psi_{D(\lambda)}(v), \psi_{D(\lambda)}(\omega)\}, \end{aligned} \tag{29}$$

In state (iii), we obtain;

$$\begin{aligned} &\xi_{D(\lambda)}(v \circ \omega) = (\xi_{\Omega(j)} \overline{\sqcap}_R \xi_{\Omega'(\lambda)})(v \circ \omega) = r\min\{\xi_{\Omega(\lambda)}(v \circ \omega), \xi_{\Omega'(\lambda)}(v \circ \omega)\} \\ &\widetilde{\geq} r\min\{r\min\{\xi_{\Omega(\lambda)}(v), \xi_{\Omega(\lambda)}(\omega)\}, r\min\{\xi_{\Omega'(\lambda)}(v), \xi_{\Omega'(\lambda)}(\omega)\}\} \\ &= r\min\{r\min\{\xi_{\Omega(\lambda)}(v), \xi_{\Omega'(\lambda)}(v)\}, r\min\{\xi_{\Omega(\lambda)}(v), \xi_{\Omega'(\lambda)}(\omega)\}\} \\ &= r\min\{(\xi_{\Omega(\lambda)} \overline{\sqcap}_R \xi_{\Omega'(\lambda)})(v), (\xi_{\Omega(\lambda)} \overline{\sqcap}_R \xi_{\Omega'(\lambda)})(\omega)\} = r\min\{\xi_{D(\lambda)}(v), \xi_{D(\lambda)}(\omega)\}. \end{aligned} \tag{30}$$

Also,

$$\begin{aligned} &\psi_{D(\lambda)}(v \circ \omega) = \left(\psi_{\Omega(j)} \overline{\sqcap}_R \psi_{\Omega'(\lambda)}\right)(v \circ \omega) = r\min\{\psi_{\Omega(\lambda)}(v \circ \omega), \psi_{\Omega'(\lambda)}(v \circ \omega)\} \\ &\widetilde{\leq} \max\{\max\{\psi_{\Omega(\lambda)}(v), \psi_{\Omega(\lambda)}(\omega)\}, \max\{\psi_{\Omega'(\lambda)}(v), \psi_{\Omega'(\lambda)}(\omega)\}\} \\ &= \max n\{\max\{\psi_{\Omega(\lambda)}(v), \psi_{\Omega'(\lambda)}(v)\}, \max\{\psi_{\Omega(\lambda)}(v), \psi_{\Omega'(\lambda)}(\omega)\}\} \\ &= \max\{\left(\psi_{\Omega(\lambda)} \overline{\sqcap}_R \psi_{\Omega'(\lambda)}\right)(v), \left(\psi_{\Omega(\lambda)} \overline{\sqcap}_R \psi_{\Omega'(\lambda)}\right)(\omega)\} = \max\{\psi_{D(\lambda)}(v), \psi_{D(\lambda)}(\omega)\}. \end{aligned} \tag{31}$$

Hence $(D, W) = (\Omega, \Re)\overline{\sqcap}_R(\Omega', \Re')$ is a ($CS\delta$-$SA$) over $\eta$. □

**Corollary 1.** *If* $\Re = \{(\Omega\prime, \Re')_\lambda \in_\Delta \int^{\eta} | \lambda \in \Delta\}$ *is a family of cubic soft* δ*-subalgebras over* η*, then the R-intersection* $\overline{\sqcap}_R\{(\Omega\prime, \Re')_\lambda\}_{\lambda \in \Re'}$ *is a (CS*δ*-SA) over* η.

**Proof.** From Definition (7) and Theorem (3), the proof is straightforward. □

## 4. Comparative Study

In 2021 [8], a technique used nano-sets to study medications suitable for COVID-19 depending on the lower approximation, upper approximation, and boundary region for nano-topological space (NTS). However, a parameter set was not used, which means this work discussed the rate of health recovery for patients in general, without any other detail. Therefore, in our work, we used cubic soft $\delta$-algebras and parameters such as $\Delta = \{$"body temperature" ($\lambda_1$), "cough with chest congestion" ($\lambda_2$), "body ache" ($\lambda_3$), "cough with no chest congestion" ($\lambda_4$), "breathing trouble" ($\lambda_5$)} and hence we introduced more factors related to patients to study the activity of medications.

## 5. Conclusions

We showed that is not necessarily any R/P-cubic soft subset of ($CS\delta$-$SA$) is ($CS\delta$-$SA$). That means the P-union is not really a soft cubic $\delta$-subalgebra of two soft cubic

$\delta$-subalgebras. We further provide the necessary criteria to demonstrate that the R-union of two members is $(CS\delta\text{-}SA)$ if each of them is $(CS\delta\text{-}SA)$. To demonstrate our notations, we use the used $(CS\delta\text{-}SA)$ to investigate the efficacy of medicines for COVID-19. In the future, more engineering device applications may express the composition of two or more members in engineering devices as a P/R-union, specifying the member that will be considered from the composition of known members. Moreover, there is a recent development in soft set theory, i.e., the idea of T-Bipolar soft set, as explained by Tahir [25]. Therefore, we can increase the application of T-Bipolar soft sets using new classes of operations.

**Author Contributions:** Conceptualization, S.K., A.H. (Ahmed Hassan), H.A., W.K. and A.H. (Abir Hussain). These authors contributed equally to this work. All authors have read and agreed to the published version of the manuscript.

**Funding:** This project was supported by the Deanship of Scientific Research At Prince Sattam Bin Abdulaziz University (Project No 2020/01/1174).

**Institutional Review Board Statement:** Not applicable.

**Informed Consent Statement:** Not applicable.

**Data Availability Statement:** Not applicable.

**Acknowledgments:** The authors thank the reviewers for their useful comments, which led to the improvement of the content of the paper.

**Conflicts of Interest:** The authors declare no conflict of interest.

## References

1. Maji, P.; Roy, A.; Biswas, R. An application of soft sets in a decision making problem. *Comput. Math. Appl.* **2002**, *44*, 1077–1083. [CrossRef]
2. Biswas, R. Rosenfeld's fuzzy subgroups with interval-valued membership functions. *Fuzzy Sets Syst.* **1994**, *63*, 87–90. [CrossRef]
3. Khalil, S.M.; Abbas, N.M.A. New Technical Using Nano in Medical Field to Determine Medications that are Suitable Activities for COVID-19. In *Data Intelligence and Cognitive Informatics. Algorithms for Intelligent Systems*; Springer: Singapore, 2021; pp. 917–921. [CrossRef]
4. Arfan, M.; Alrabaiah, H.; Rahman, M.U.; Sun, Y.-L.; Hashim, A.S.; Pansera, B.A.; Ahmadian, A.; Salahshour, S. Investigation of fractal-fractional order model of COVID-19 in Pakistan under Atangana-Baleanu Caputo (ABC) derivative. *Results Phys.* **2021**, *24*, 104046. [CrossRef]
5. Zhong, B.; Luo, W.; Li, H.; Zhang, Q.; Liu, X.; Li, W.; Li, Y. Knowledge, attitudes, and practices towards COVID-19 among chinese residents during the rapid rise period of the COVID-19 Outbreak: A quick online cross-sectional survey. *Int. J. Biol. Sci.* **2020**, *16*, 1745–1752. [CrossRef]
6. Khalil, S.M. Decision making using algebraic operations on soft effect matrix as new category of similarity measures and study their application in medical diagnosis problems. *J. Intell. Fuzzy Syst.* **2019**, *37*, 1865–1877. [CrossRef]
7. Khalil, S.M. Decision making using new category of similarity measures and study their applications in medical diagnosis problems. *Afr. Mat.* **2021**, *32*, 865–878. [CrossRef]
8. Zadeh, A.L. Fuzzy sets. *Inf. Control* **1965**, *8*, 338–353. [CrossRef]
9. Xi, O.G. Fuzzy algebras. *Math. Jpn.* **1991**, *36*, 935–942.
10. Muhiuddin, G.; Song, S.Z.; Kim, H.S.; Jun, Y.B. Characterizations of fuzzy subalgebras in BCK/BCI-algebras. *Appl. Math. Sci.* **2015**, *9*, 7187–7196. [CrossRef]
11. Khalil, S.M.; Hameed, F. Applications of fuzzy ρ-ideals in ρ-algebras. *Soft Comput.* **2020**, *24*, 13997–14004. [CrossRef]
12. Molodtsov, D. Soft set theory—First results. *Comput. Math. Appl.* **1999**, *37*, 19–31. [CrossRef]
13. Khalil, S.M.; Hameed, F. An algorithm for generating permutation algebras using soft spaces. *J. Taibah Univ. Sci.* **2018**, *12*, 299–308. [CrossRef]
14. Jun, Y.B.; Lee, K.J.; Park, C.H. Fuzzy soft set theory applied to BCK/BCI-algebras. *Comput. Math. Appl.* **2010**, *59*, 3180–3192. [CrossRef]
15. Zadeh, L.A. The concept of a linguistic variable and its application to approximate reasoning—I. *Inf. Sci.* **1975**, *8*, 199–249. [CrossRef]
16. Jun, Y.B.; Kim, C.S.; Yang, K.O. Cubic sets. *Ann. Fuzzy Math. Inf.* **2012**, *4*, 83–98.
17. Khalil, S.M.; Hassan, A.N. The Characterizations of δ-Algebras with Their Ideals. *J. Physics: Conf. Ser.* **2021**, *1999*, 012108. [CrossRef]
18. Gorzalczany, M.B. A method of inference in approximate reasoning based on interval-valued fuzzy sets. *Fuzzy Sets Syst.* **1987**, *21*, 1–17. [CrossRef]

19. Muhiuddin, G.; Al-roqi, A.M. Cubic soft sets with applications in BCK/BCI-algebras. *Ann. Fuzzy Math. Inf.* **2014**, *8*, 291–304.
20. Saghir, S.A.; AlGabri, A.N.; Alagawany, M.M.; Attia, A.Y.; Alyileili, S.R.; Elnesr, S.S.; Shafi, E.M.; Al-Shargi, O.Y.; Al-Balagi, N.; Alwajeeh, A.S.; et al. Chloroquine and Hydroxychloroquine for the Prevention and Treatment of COVID-19: A Fiction, Hope or Hype? An Updated Review. *Ther. Clin. Risk Manag.* **2021**, *17*, 371–387. [CrossRef]
21. Nojomi, M.; Yassin, Z.; Keyvani, H.; Makiani, M.J.; Roham, M.; Laali, A.; Dehghan, N.; Navaei, M.; Ranjbar, M. Effect of Arbidol (Umifenovir) on COVID-19: A randomized controlled trial. *BMC Infect. Dis.* **2020**, *20*, 954. [CrossRef]
22. Godlee, F. Covid-19: The lost lessons of Tamiflu. *BMJ* **2020**, *371*, m4701. [CrossRef]
23. Kalantari, S.; Fard, S.R.; Maleki, D.; Taher, M.T.; Yassin, Z.; Alimohamadi, Y.; Minaeian, S. Comparing the effectiveness of Atazanavir/Ritonavir/Dolutegravir/Hydroxychloroquine and Lopinavir/Ritonavir/Hydroxychloroquine treatment regimens in COVID-19 patients. *J. Med. Virol.* **2021**, *93*, 6557–6565. [CrossRef]
24. Beigel, J.H.; Tomashek, K.M.; Dodd, L.E.; Mehta, A.K.; Zingman, B.S.; Kalil, A.C.; Hohmann, E.; Chu, H.Y.; Luetkemeyer, A.; Kline, S.; et al. Remdesivir for the Treatment of Covid-19—Final Report. *N. Engl. J. Med.* **2020**, *383*, 1813–1826. [CrossRef]
25. Mahmood, T. A Novel Approach towards Bipolar Soft Sets and Their Applications. *J. Math.* **2020**, *2020*, 1–11. [CrossRef]

mathematics MDPI

*Article*

# Computing the Number of Failures for Fuzzy Weibull Hazard Function

**Hennie Husniah [1,*] and Asep K. Supriatna [2]**

1 Department of Industrial Engineering, Langlangbuana University, Bandung 40261, Indonesia
2 Department of Mathematics, Padjadjaran University, Jatinangor 45363, Indonesia; a.k.supriatna@unpad.ac.id
* Correspondence: h.husniah@unla.ac.id

**Abstract:** The number of failures plays an important factor in the study of maintenance strategy of a manufacturing system. In the real situation, this number is often affected by some uncertainties. Many of the uncertainties fall into the possibilistic uncertainty, which are different from the probabilistic uncertainty. This uncertainty is commonly modeled by applying the fuzzy theoretical framework. This paper aims to compute the number of failures for a system which has Weibull failure distribution with a fuzzy shape parameter. In this case two different approaches are used to calculate the number. In the first approach, the fuzziness membership of the shape parameter propagates to the number of failures so that they have exactly the same values of the membership. While in the second approach, the membership is computed through the $\alpha$-cut or $\alpha$-level of the shape parameter approach in the computation of the formula for the number of failures. Without loss of generality, we use the Triangular Fuzzy Number (*TFN*) for the Weibull shape parameter. We show that both methods have succeeded in computing the number of failures for the system under investigation. Both methods show that when we consider the function of the number of failures as a function of time then the uncertainty (the fuzziness) of the resulting number of failures becomes larger and larger as the time increases. By using the first method, the resulting number of failures has a *TFN* form. Meanwhile, the resulting number of failures from the second method does not necessarily have a *TFN* form, but a *TFN-like* form. Some comparisons between these two methods are presented using the Generalized Mean Value Defuzzification (*GMVD*) method. The results show that for certain weighting factor of the *GMVD*, the cores of these fuzzy numbers of failures are identical.

**Keywords:** Weibull hazard function; number of failures; *TFN*; $\alpha$-cut; defuzzification

**Citation:** Husniah, H.; Supriatna, A.K. Computing the Number of Failures for Fuzzy Weibull Hazard Function. *Mathematics* **2021**, *9*, 2858. https://doi.org/10.3390/math9222858

Academic Editor: Michael Voskoglou

Received: 30 September 2021
Accepted: 5 November 2021
Published: 10 November 2021



## 1. Introduction

Uncertainty is present in almost all decision problems, including in the field of reliability and maintenance. This is due to unknown future events and imprecision as well as human subjectivity in a decision process [1]. There are some important factors that significantly affect the decision-making in any field. In the field of reliability and maintenance, the number of failures plays important roles in the study of maintenance strategy of a manufacturing system. In the real situation, this number is often affected by some uncertainties. Many of the uncertainties fall into the possibilistic uncertainty, which is different from the probabilistic uncertainty. In many cases, at least one of the parameters or variables of the decision function has fuzzy value, instead of crisp value. This uncertainty is commonly modeled by applying fuzzy theoretical framework, e.g., the variable and parameter have fuzzy values and the calculation is done using extension principle approach [2].

As an important factor, the number of failures is essential to obtain, and subsequently is used as a base for further decision processes in reliability and maintenance analysis. As an example, this "number" is used in the calculation to design optimal maintenance strategies which are directed to minimize the number of failures while also minimizing the costs of operation [3–5]. For this reason, the knowledge on how to compute or predict the number of failures becomes vital. Considering the occurrence of uncertainty and imprecision—together with complexity of the system under investigation, failure data are often difficult to obtain. In this case, the theory of fuzzy sets has been widely used to provide a framework to deal with these uncertainty and imprecision [6]. Among the important questions needed to be addressed related to the number of failures of a system having a possibilistic uncertainty is, first, how to compute this number for a given possibility distribution with fuzzy parameters. Nowadays, some calculator for fuzzy numbers are readily available [2]. Second, it is also important to know how the degree of uncertainty of the parameters propagates to the resulting failure numbers. This is commonly known as the propagation of fuzziness, which is defined as "the way in which the amount of imprecision in the model's inputs affects the changes in the model's output" [7], (p. 163). Technically the propagation of uncertainty happens through mathematical operations involved in the model and in the computation. Knowing the method to calculate the number and its degree of uncertainty, will significantly improve the quality of the decision being sought (see also [8,9] for similar cases in other area). In general, fuzziness propagation in complex engineering systems may constitute a significant challenge [10].

The aims of the paper are two-fold, namely, to calculate the number of failures for a system which has Weibull failure distribution with a fuzzy shape parameter and to understand how the fuzziness of this shape parameter propagates to the resulting number of failures. These two objectives constitute the importance and contributions of the work presented in this paper. In addition, in this paper we look for the number of failures and two different approaches are used to calculate this number. In the first approach, the fuzziness membership of the shape parameter propagates to the number of failures so that they have exactly the same values of the membership. While in the second approach, the membership is computed through the $\alpha$-cut or $\alpha$-level of the shape parameter.

*Literature Review*

As it is explained earlier, the motivation of the paper is due the importance of finding the number of failures in the field of maintenance strategy. Some examples of such importance can be seen in [11–16] from various perspectives. It is often found that most of the problems in maintenance engineering are finding optimal strategies that minimize the cost of operation to manipulate the system as well as minimize the number of failures of the system (e.g., [17]). In many cases, the number of failures is represented in its distribution function. Several type of distribution functions are commonly used to model the failures of an industrial equipment, among others is the Weibull distribution function together with its hazard function [18,19]. This distribution function could appear either in two-parameters model or in three-parameters model [20,21]. Hence, the Weibull distribution function plays vital roles in areas of research related to maintenance strategy in which understanding a system, predicting the outcome of a system, and prescribing an optimal intervention to obtain the best performance of a system are being sought. In fact, the spectrum of the area applications of the Weibull distribution is quite broad from engineering, social sciences, to biological and health problems.

Apart from the abundant usage of the Weibull distribution in many areas of research, especially in maintenance strategy, most of the analysis only consider the crisp form of data, i.e., ignoring the presence of possibilistic uncertainty which might be often found in many real phenomena. For example, in maintenance engineering, most maintenance models in literature mainly consider certain or crisp condition, e.g., [22,23]. However, as mentioned earlier, these kinds of models do not seem to fit in the real condition. Readers may find a brief review of the importance of the possibilistic uncertainty in [24]. In reliability and maintenance problems, uncertainty may affect the models, the nonhomogeneous Poisson process (*NHPP*), and the Weibull generalized renewal process parameters [25,26], and the probability distribution parameters [8], and it is important to know how this uncertainty propagates through the models which likely affect the insight and prediction from the models [27].

There are several approaches to model the possibilistic uncertainty, one of them is by applying the fuzzy number theory, as suggested by Zadeh [28,29] and his followers. The popularity of fuzzy number theory in reliability and maintenance literatures is now getting higher [30] resulting in new modeling approach in many aspects, like maintenance risk-based inspection interval optimization with fuzzy failure interaction for two-component repairable system [31] and many others. The authors in [32] are among the few authors who consider fuzzy Weibull distribution in their works. They consider the Weibull distribution function as a fuzzy function and use it for analyzing the behavior of an industrial system stochastically by utilizing vague, imprecise, and uncertain data, which in turn result in the reliability indices (such as hazard function, maintainability, etc.) of time of time varying failure rate instead of the constant failure rate for the system.

In general, the author in [33] (pp. 152–157) shows several methods on how to implement a fuzzy function in addressing problems with possibilistic uncertainty. The methods can be classified into three different ways depending to which aspect of the crisp function the fuzzy concept was applied, namely (i) crisp function with fuzzy constraint, (ii) crisp function which propagates the fuzziness of independent variable to dependent variable, and (iii) function that is itself fuzzy. However, in this paper we will only look for the number of failures by using the first and the second approaches above. The fuzziness of the shape parameter is assumed to propagate to the number of failures with the same form of fuzzy number membership in the first approach, as found in [34,35]. While in the second approach, the concept of $\alpha$-cut or $\alpha$-level of the fuzziness of the shape parameter is used in the computation to calculate the number of failures, as found in [36]. An example of the methodology on how to compare fuzzy numbers, such as those resulting from different approaches of fuzzy function concepts above can be seen in [37].

In this paper we re-visit the model in [34,35] by giving some more detail analysis and results discussed in those papers. The authors in [34] discussed the Weibull hazard function by assuming a fuzzy shape parameter, which conceptually can be used to compute the number of failures without actually showing the resulting number of failures (either in crisp number form or fuzzy number form). They show how to compute the fuzzy number of failures of Weibull hazard function in [35] by assuming a fuzzy shape parameter in the Weibull hazard function via the second approach in [33], (p. 154), i.e., by considering the Weibull function as a crisp function which propagates the fuzziness of independent variable to dependent variable. In this paper we use different approaches by considering the fuzziness of the shape parameter in the computation of the number of failures directly, through the concept of $\alpha$-cut or $\alpha$-level [33] (p. 130) and [38], (pp. 7–16). Further we discuss the generalized mean value defuzzification (*GMVD*) and use it to compare the resulting fuzzy number of failures from different approaches of computation. The proposed defuzzification method (*GMVD*) is able to find a crisp number which is close to the core of the triangular fuzzy number (*TFN*).

We organize the presentation of the paper as follows. Section 2 presents briefly some basic methods that are utilized in the preceding sections, namely, the Weibull distribution function, fuzzy number and its membership function, $\alpha$-cut of a fuzzy number, defuzzification process with Generalized Mean Value Defuzzification (*GMVD*), and the number of failures for Weibull hazard function with fuzzy parameter. Section 3 gives the main results together with numerical examples to show the visual illustration of the main results. This includes the comparisons from two different methods, i.e., the results from the method considering propagation of the fuzziness of independent variable to dependent variable and the results from the $\alpha$-cut method. Section 4 presents the discussions of the results and it is finally followed by concluding remarks and further direction of research in Section 5.

## 2. Materials and Methods

The object being investigated in this paper is the Weibull distribution function as a mathematical model describing the deterioration of life cycle of an industrial system or an equipment. This deterioration or failure data are commonly modeled by the Weibull distribution function such as found in [39]. The reason of popularity of the Weibull function is its flexibility, so that it can be regarded as the generalization of exponential and Rayleigh distribution functions, which are also commonly used in reliability and maintenance studies [40]. The Weibull distribution is a continuous probability distribution function having the form:

$$f(t) = \begin{cases} \frac{\beta}{\theta}\left(\frac{t}{\theta}\right)^{(\beta-1)} \exp\left[-\left(\frac{t}{\theta}\right)^{\beta}\right], & x > 0,\ \theta > 0,\ \beta > 0, \\ 0, & \text{otherwise.} \end{cases} \tag{1}$$

where $\theta$ is the scale parameter and $\beta$ is the shape parameter. The first mathematician who described it in detail is Waloddi Weibull in 1951. The Weibull distribution has a flexibility to model various lifetime data by changing the value of the shape parameter, e.g., if $\beta = 1$ the Weibull distribution is reduced to an exponential distribution and if $\beta = 2$ the Weibull distribution is identical to Rayleigh distribution [40]. Throughout the paper we will assume the scale parameter $\theta = 1$ for some reasons. For example, this choice is sufficient in our context of maintenance modeling if we assume that the average of first failure of the equipment/system under investigation happens within one unit of time—say one month or one year, because of its warranty and good quality control. The authors in [41] give an example with $\theta = 1$ in their simulation.

Using this Weibull distribution function we can calculate some reliability indices, such as hazard function, number of failures, mean time between failures, preventive maintenance time, and replacement time. The standard methods on the calculation of these indices, both for standard and complex systems, can be found among others in [42,43]. Details theory and applications of the Weibull distribution function can be found in [44,45]. In the Section 2.1 we present some concepts of fuzzy theoretical framework which are used in the subsequent method and analysis, namely, fuzzy number and its membership function, $\alpha$-cut of a fuzzy number, defuzzification process with Generalized Mean Value Defuzzification.

### 2.1. Fuzzy Number and Its Membership Function

As an introduction to the section that follows we define several concepts of fuzzy number theory that will be used later on. A fuzzy number can be regarded as an extension of a real number in the sense that it has a membership function other than binary to represent uncertainty. Binary membership gives a crips value for the membership, i.e., either a member or not a member. Fuzzy number gives a wide spectrum of membership from zero (definitely not a member of a set S) to one (definitely a member of a set S). Technically, a fuzzy number $\widetilde{A}$ refers to a connected set of possible values, where each possible value of $\widetilde{A}$, say $a$, has its own membership value in the interval [0,1]. This value that measures the degree of possibility for $a$ to be a member of $\widetilde{A}$ is called the membership function, usually written as $\mu : a \in A \to x \in [0,1]$. This fuzzy number is commonly written with the symbol $\widetilde{A} = (A, \mu(A))$ or alternatively $\widetilde{A} = \{(x, \mu_{\widetilde{A}}(x)) | x \in X\}$ representing the underlying connected set $A$ with the membership function $\mu(A)$. In this regards, the fuzzy number is viewed as a pair of mathematical objects comprising of a set together with its grade or membership function. The fuzzy number is purportedly designed to represent the possibilistic uncertainty and to quantify the unclear and inaccuracies of the abundance of information.

The membership of a fuzzy number can be determined by several functional approaches, which can be classified into the linear and the non-linear functional forms. Among the most popular functional form of fuzzy number are the Triangular Fuzzy Number (TFN) which is often written as *(a;b;c)* and the Trapezoidal Fuzzy Number (TrFN) which is often written as *(a;b;c;d)*. The functional forms or the membership functions of these fuzzy numbers are given in Equations (2) and (3), which are graphically shown in Figures 1 and 2. Note that for the TrFN in Equation (3), the membership function within the intervals [*a*,*b*] and [*c*,*d*] are given by increasing and decreasing linear curves respectively. This concept is generalized by the LR-Flat Fuzzy Number which is then used as a new method for solving fuzzy transportation problems [2,46,47].

- The membership function of a triangular fuzzy number (TFN):

$$\mu_{\tilde{A}}(x) = \begin{cases} 0\,, x \le a \\ \frac{x-a}{b-a}\,, a \le x \le b \\ \frac{x-c}{b-c}\,, b \le x \le c \\ 0\,, x \ge c. \end{cases} \tag{2}$$

- The membership function of a trapezoidal fuzzy number (TrFN):

$$\mu_{\tilde{A}}(x) = \begin{cases} 0\,, x \le a \\ \frac{x-a}{b-a}\,, a \le x \le b \\ 1\,, b \le x \le c \\ \frac{x-d}{c-d}\,, c \le x \le d \\ 0\,, x \ge d. \end{cases} \tag{3}$$

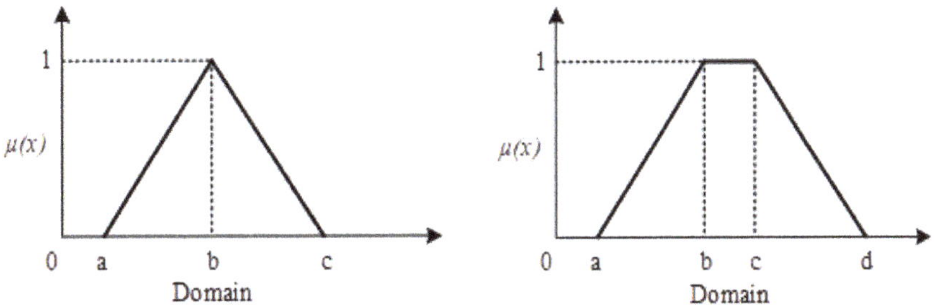


**Figure 1.** Graphical representation of a triangular fuzzy number *(a;b;c)*—**left** figure, and a trapezoidal fuzzy number *(a;b;c;d)*—**right** figure.

In Equation (2), $a$, $b$, and $c$ are real numbers satisfying $a < b < c$ which constitute the *TFN* core and support components. In this case $b$ is called the core of the fuzzy number and the sets $[a,b)$ and $(b,c]$ are called the support of the fuzzy number. Similarly, for TrFN, in Equation (3) the core of the fuzzy number is given by $[b,c]$ and the support is given by the set $[a,b)$ and $(c,d]$. Other forms of fuzzy numbers are piecewise quadratic fuzzy number [48], pentagonal fuzzy number [49], Bell shaped fuzzy number [50], parabolic trapezoidal fuzzy number [51], new bell shaped fuzzy number [52], and many others. A good reference on how some new methods and techniques are developed to advance fuzzy numbers concepts for modern analytics can be found in [46]. However, for simplicity, to emphasize the methodological aspect all examples in this paper assume the triangular fuzzy numbers (TFN). In the next section we briefly describe the α-cut of a triangular fuzzy numbers (α-cut, α-level cut, α-level set or sometimes simply is called a cut).

### 2.2. The α-Cut of a Fuzzy Number

Each fuzzy number is associated with its α-cut. This α-cut sometimes is also called the α-level set. It is technically defined as the set of objects in the associated fuzzy set which have the membership with the values which are at least α. This actually can be seen as a crisp set representation of a fuzzy number. Following this definition, it can be shown that the α-cut of the triangular fuzzy number (1) is given by:

$$\widetilde{A}_\alpha = [a_1^\alpha, a_2^\alpha] = [(b-a)\alpha + a, (b-c)\alpha + c] \tag{4}$$

for all $\alpha \in [0,1]$.

### 2.3. Generalized Mean Value Defuzzification

For some reasons, the information regarding the best representation of a crisp number for a fuzzy number is needed. In this case, defuzzification of the fuzzy number is done. It is a mathematical calculation which converts the fuzzy number into a single crisp value with respect to a fuzzy set. Some defuzzification formulas are available in literature, such as basic defuzzification distributions, center of area, center of gravity, fuzzy mean, last of maxima, weighted fuzzy mean, etc., [53–55]. In this paper we will use the generalized mean value defuzzification method (*GMVD*) which is defined as

$$N(\widetilde{A}) = \frac{a + nb + c}{n + 2}, \tag{5}$$

where $\widetilde{A} = (a; b; c)$ is a *TFN* and $n$ can be regarded as the weight of the core of the fuzzy number. The larger the weight of the core, the closer the resulting crisp number from the GMVD to the core of the fuzzy number. The properties of this GMVD will be discussed later on and used in the comparation of the resulting number of failures.

## 3. Results

### 3.1. Number of Failures for Weibull Hazard Function with Fuzzy Parameter

As explained in the previous section we consider the one-parameter Weibull distribution function, since this choice is sufficient in our context of maintenance modeling if we assume that the average of first failure of the equipment/system under investigation happens within one unit of time—say one month or one year—because of its warranty and good quality control. By considering this assumption ($\theta = 1$) and fuzzy parameter $\widetilde{\beta}$ the number of failure is computed using the first method, in which the calculation of the fuzzy number is done point-wise (will be defined later), and we only need the crisp function for the computation. From Equation (1) we have the following one-parameter Weibull cumulative distribution, $g$, and its hazard function, $h$:

$$g(t) = 1 - e^{-t^{\beta}}, \tag{6}$$

and

$$h(t) = \beta t^{\beta - 1}, \tag{7}$$

so that the number of failures is given by

$$N(t) = t^{\beta}. \tag{8}$$

The parameter $\widetilde{\beta}$ is the fuzzy number of the shape parameter of the Weibull function. We will treat the fuzziness of the shape parameter in two different approaches: (i) Crisp function which propagates the fuzziness of independent variable to dependent variable and, in which the computation is done point-wise; (ii) crisp function with fuzzy constraint through the level-set computation.

The First Method (Point-wise Method): Let $\widetilde{\beta}$ be a *TFN* which is identified by three crisp numbers $a$, $b$, and $c$, i.e., $\widetilde{\beta} = (a; b; c)$ satisfying Equation (2). We compute the number of failures point-wise, i.e., by substituting these crisp numbers one at a time to obtain the crisp output, say $a'$, $b'$, and $c'$. By assuming the same fuzzy measure propagates to the output, we will have $\mu(a') = \mu(a)$, $\mu(b') = \mu(b)$, and $\mu(c') = \mu(c)$, which give a *TFN* fuzzy output $(a'; b'; c')$ for the function $g(t)$, $h(t)$, and $N(t)$ [34].

The Second Method (α-Cut Method): In the second approach, the fuzzy number $\widetilde{\beta}$ is identified as an α-cut satisfying Equation (4). As it is explained in [34], the fuzzy number of the shape parameter is approximated by a sequence of interval associated with the number α in [0,1]. This sequence consists of crisp numbers in the interval indicating the support of the fuzzy number for every α in [0, 1). If α is one then the supports converge to/become the core of the fuzzy number. The calculation to determine the number of failures is done at the end points of the interval. In this case, the stack of the end points of the intervals need not to be a *TFN*, which in many cases forms a *TFN-like* form (see numerical examples for the details).

To facilitate comparison between the results from the two methods, we use the *GMVD* defined in Equation (5). This *GMVD* has the properties as described in Theorem 1.

**Theorem 1.** *Let a TFN is given by (a;b;c), then the generalized mean value defuzzification (GMVD) defined by Equation (5) has the following properties:*

1. *For a symmetrical case, i.e.,* $b - a = c - b = \Delta$ *then* $N(\widetilde{A}) = b$
2. *For an asymmetrical case, i.e.,* $b - a = \Delta_a \neq c - b = \Delta_c$ *then*
   a. $N(\widetilde{A}) > b$ *if* $\Delta_a < \Delta_c$
   b. $N(\widetilde{A}) < b$ *if* $\Delta_a > \Delta_c$
3. If $n \to \infty$ then $N(\widetilde{A}) = b$ regardless the value of $p$ and $q$.

**Proof of Theorem 1:**

1. Case 1: symmetrical TFN, i.e., $b - a = c - b = \Delta$ then

$$\begin{aligned} N(\widetilde{A}) &= \tfrac{a+nb+c}{n+2} = \tfrac{a+nb+(a+2\Delta)}{n+2} = \tfrac{2a+nb+2\Delta}{n+2} \\ &= \tfrac{2(a+\Delta)+nb}{n+2} = \tfrac{2b+nb}{n+2} = \tfrac{(2+n)b}{n+2} = b. \end{aligned}$$

   Hence, $N(\widetilde{A}) = b$.

2. Case 2: non-symmetrical TFN, i.e., $b - a = \Delta_a \neq c - b = \Delta_c$ then
   a. if $\Delta_a < \Delta_c$ then

$$N(\widetilde{A}) = \tfrac{a+nb+c}{n+2} = \tfrac{a+nb+(a+\Delta_a+\Delta_c)}{n+2} > \tfrac{a+nb+(a+2\Delta_a)}{n+2} = \tfrac{2a+nb+2\Delta_a}{n+2}$$

   Hence, $N(\widetilde{A}) > b$.

   b. if $\Delta_a > \Delta_c$ then

$$N(\widetilde{A}) = \tfrac{a+nb+c}{n+2} = \tfrac{a+nb+(a+\Delta_a+\Delta_c)}{n+2} < \tfrac{a+nb+(a+2\Delta_a)}{n+2} = \tfrac{2a+nb+2\Delta_a}{n+2}$$

   Hence, $N(\widetilde{A}) < b$.

3. If $n \to \infty$ then $\lim_{n\to\infty} N(\widetilde{A}) = \lim_{n\to\infty} \tfrac{a+nb+c}{n+2} = b.$ □

As shown by the theorem, the *GMVD* above has a special characteristic, i.e., it is able to find a crisp number which is close to the core of the triangular fuzzy number (*TFN*). As examples, first consider the symmetrical *TFN* in Figure 2(left), i.e.,$\widetilde{\beta} = (p = 1.25;$ $q = 1.55;\ s = 1.85)$. It has *GMVD* = 1.55 for $n = 1$ and *GMVD* = 1.55 for $n = 1000$. Since it is symmetrical, the values of *GMVD* are the same as the core of the *TFN* for all $n$. However, for the non-symmetrical *TFN*, such as skewed left *TFN*$\widetilde{\beta} = (p = 2.50;\ q = 2.75;\ s = 2.80)$ in Figure 2(right), it has *GMVD* = 2.6833 for $n = 1$ and *GMVD* = 2.74980 for $n = 1000$. In this case, the larger is $n$ the closer it is to the core of the *TFN*, i.e., 2.75. We will use this method of defuzzification for comparing the fuzzy output from two different methods in this paper.

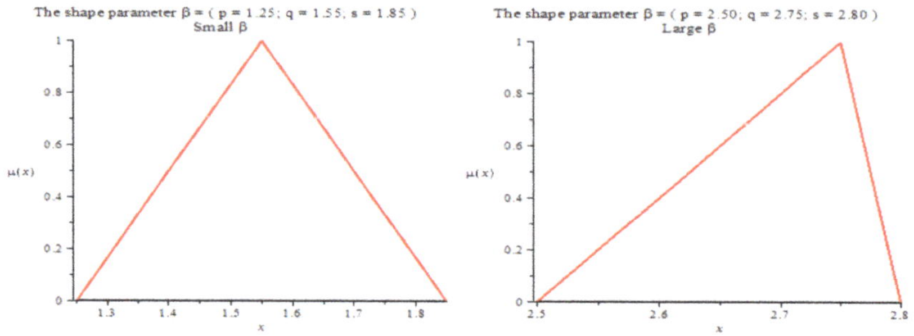


**Figure 2.** On the **left** figure is shown the relatively small shape parameter $\widetilde{\beta} = (p = 1.25;\ q = 1.55;\ s = 1.85)$ and on the **right** figure is shown the relatively large shape parameter $\widetilde{\beta} = (p = 2.50;\ q = 2.75;\ s := 2.80)$. The vertical axis is the fuzzy membership μ of the shape parameter's TFN. The first shape parameter is a symmetrical TFN and the second shape parameter is a nonsymmetrical TFN. These TFNs are used to calculate their respective number of failures in the subsequent figures.

Next we look at the fuzzy number of failures generated by the Weibull distribution via the α-cut method. Let us recall the α-cut of the triangular fuzzy number $\widetilde{A} = (a; b; c)$ is given by $\widetilde{A}_\alpha = [a_1^\alpha, a_2^\alpha] = [(b-a)\alpha + a, (b-c)\alpha + c]$ then the shape parameter, the Weibull cumulative distribution, the Weibul hazard function, and the number of failures are, respectively, given in the form of α-cut as follows. The shape parameter will have the form

$$\beta_\alpha = [x_1 + x_3^\alpha, x_2 - x_3^\alpha], \tag{9}$$

for some $x_1,\ x_2,\ x_3 \in$ R.By considering the α-cut in Equation (9) and substituting it into Equations (6) and (7) using the fuzzy arithmetic give rise to the cumulative distribution

$$g(t)_\alpha = [1 - \exp(-t^{y_1 + y_3\alpha}), 1 - \exp(-t^{y_2 - y_3\alpha})], \tag{10}$$

for some $y_1,\ y_2,\ y_3 \in$ R and the hazard function

$$h(t)_\alpha = [(z_1 + z_3\alpha)t^{z_4 + z_6\alpha}, (z_2 - z_3\alpha)t^{z_5 - z_6\alpha}], \tag{11}$$

for some $z_1,\ z_2,\ z_3,\ z_4,\ z_5,\ z_6 \in$ R. So that by integrating both sides of Equation (11) we end up with the number of failures, which is given by

$$N(t)_\alpha = [t^{u_1 + u_3\alpha}, t^{u_2 - u_3\alpha}] \tag{12}$$

for some $u_1,\ u_2,\ u_3 \in$ R.

The following theorem shows that as time goes, the GMVD of the number of failures increases and the support of the number of failures becomes wider. This means that the degree of uncertainty becomes larger.

**Theorem 2.** *For $\Delta t > 0$ let $N(t)_\alpha$ and $N(t+\Delta t)_\alpha$ be the fuzzy number of failures at time t and $t + \Delta t$, respectively, then:*

1. $N(t)_\alpha = (t^{p_\alpha},\ t^{s_\alpha})$ and $N(t+\Delta t)_\alpha = ((t+\Delta t)^{p_\alpha},\ (t+\Delta t)^{s_\alpha})$,
2. $GMVD(N(t+\Delta t)_\alpha) \geq GMVD(N(t)_\alpha)$ *for all* $t \in R^+$,
3. $((t+\Delta t)^{p_\alpha} - (t+\Delta t)^{s_\alpha}) - (t^{p_\alpha} - t^{s_\alpha}) \geq 0$ *for all* $t \in Z^+$.

**Proof of Theorem 2:**

1. It is clear.
2. It can be proved by using Theorem 1.

3. Note that for every $\alpha \in [0,1]$, the interval in Equation (12) has the form $(t^{p_\alpha}, t^{s_\alpha})$ for some $p_\alpha, s_\alpha \in R$. Without loss of generality, we will drop the index $\alpha$, so that to prove the theorem we need $\left((t+\Delta t)^p - (t+\Delta t)^s\right) - (t^p - t^s) \geq 0$.

Consider the following binomial rule,
$(x+\Delta x)^n = \sum\limits_{k=0}^{n} \frac{n!}{(n-k)!k!} \Delta x^{n-k} x^k$. Then we have

$$\begin{aligned}(x+\Delta x)^n &= \sum_{k=0}^{n-1} \frac{(n-1)!}{((n-1)-k)!k!} \Delta x^{(n-1)-k} x^k + \frac{n!}{(n-k)!k!} \Delta x^{n-k} x^k \\ &= \sum_{k=0}^{n-1} \frac{(n-1)!}{((n-1)-k)!k!} \Delta x^{(n-1)-k} x^k + x^n.\end{aligned}$$

Using this rule then for $p, s \in Z^+$ we have

$$(t+\Delta t)^p = \sum_{k=0}^{p-1} \frac{(p-1)!}{((p-1)-k)!k!} \Delta t^{(p-1)-k} y^k + t^p$$

$$(t+\Delta t)^s = \sum_{k=0}^{s-1} \frac{(s-1)!}{((s-1)-k)!k!} \Delta t^{(s-1)-k} y^k + t^s$$

A little algebraic manipulation gives

$$\begin{aligned}\left((t+\Delta t)^p - (t+\Delta t)^s\right) - (t^p - t^s) &= \sum_{k=0}^{p-1} \frac{(p-1)!}{((p-1)-k)!k!} \Delta t^{(p-1)-k} t^k - \sum_{k=0}^{s-1} \frac{(s-1)!}{((s-1)-k)!k!} \Delta t^{(s-1)-k} t^k, \\ &= \sum_{k=s}^{p-1} \frac{(p-1)!}{((p-1)-k)!k!} \Delta t^{(p-1)-k} t^k \geq 0,\end{aligned}$$

Which shows that $\left((t+\Delta t)^p - (t+\Delta t)^s\right) - (t^p - t^s) \geq 0$ for all $t \in Z^+$. Note that the theorem can be extended to any case of $p, s \in R^+$. One can prove this using the Newton's generalized Binomial theorem [56,57] in the form of infinite series rather than an infinite sum such as in the above case of $t \in Z^+$. □

### 3.2. Numerical Examples

To obtain better insight regarding the results presented in the previous section we illustrate the concept above by using two different values for the shape parameters, the relatively small value $\widetilde{\beta} = (p = 1.25;\ q = 1.55;\ s = 1.85)$ and the relatively large value $\widetilde{\beta} = (p = 2.50;\ q = 2.75;\ s := 2.80)$. Here $p$, $q$, and $s$ are the TFN components which constitute the TFN defined just the same as $a$, $b$, and $c$ in Equation (2). The graphs of these TFNs are shown in Figure 2. For the first method, the number of failures for the shape parameters in Figure 2 at t = 10 is presented in Figure 3 while Figure 4 (top figures) shows the number of failures for t in [0,100] with 10 steps size. Figure 4 (bottom figures) shows the nonlinearity of the failure numbers as a function of t. Similarly, for the second method, the number of failures for the shape parameters in Figure 2 at t = 10 is presented in Figure 5 while Figure 6 shows the number of failures for t in [0,100] with all steps of time. For the finer step size, i.e., 100 steps size, the graph of the number of failures from the second method is presented in Figure 7. Clearly the number of failures in Figure 3 are in triangular forms since the first method assumes that the fuzziness of the shape parameter propagates to the number of failures with the same form of fuzzy number membership, while the number of failures in Figure 5 does not have a triangular form since the fuzziness uncertainty is considered and affects the functional calculation of the number of failures through the $\alpha$-cut arithmetic. Figure 8 gives the comparisons between these two relatively different shapes. Further, if we plot the numbers of failures over time (see bottom figures in Figure 4), then the curves are non-linear and seem to be "exponentially" increase as expected in the theory. The bottom graphs in Figure 4 actually show the numbers of failures over time for the end points and core of the shape parameter TFNs. To be exact these figures show the graphs of Weibull's numbers of failures bands, which analytically is given by Equation (8) and comparable to Equations (10) and (14) for the α-cat, hence it has a power curve. This is consistent with the curve for Weibull's number of failures with crisp parameters [58]. This is also true for the second method (the α-cut approach), but we do not show the graphs here.

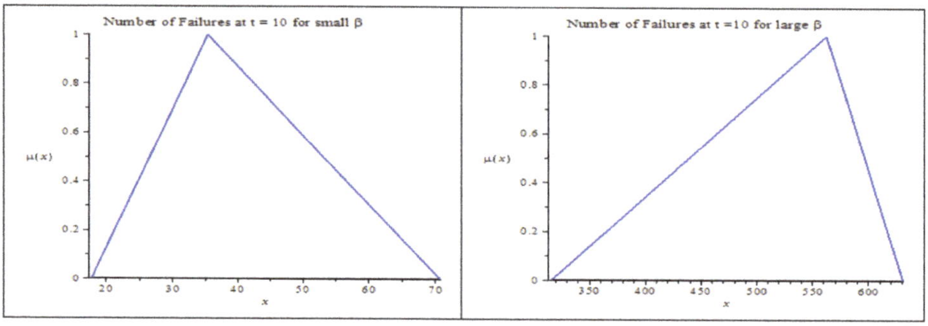


**Figure 3.** The **left** figure is the number of failures for the shape parameter $\widetilde{\beta} = (p = 1.25;\ q = 1.55;\ s = 1.85)$ at t = 10—see left figure in Figure 1. The **right** figure is the number of failures for the shape parameter $\widetilde{\beta} = (p = 2.50;\ q = 2.75;\ s = 2.80)$ at t = 10—see right figure in Figure 2. Note that the vertical axis indicates the fuzzy membership μ.

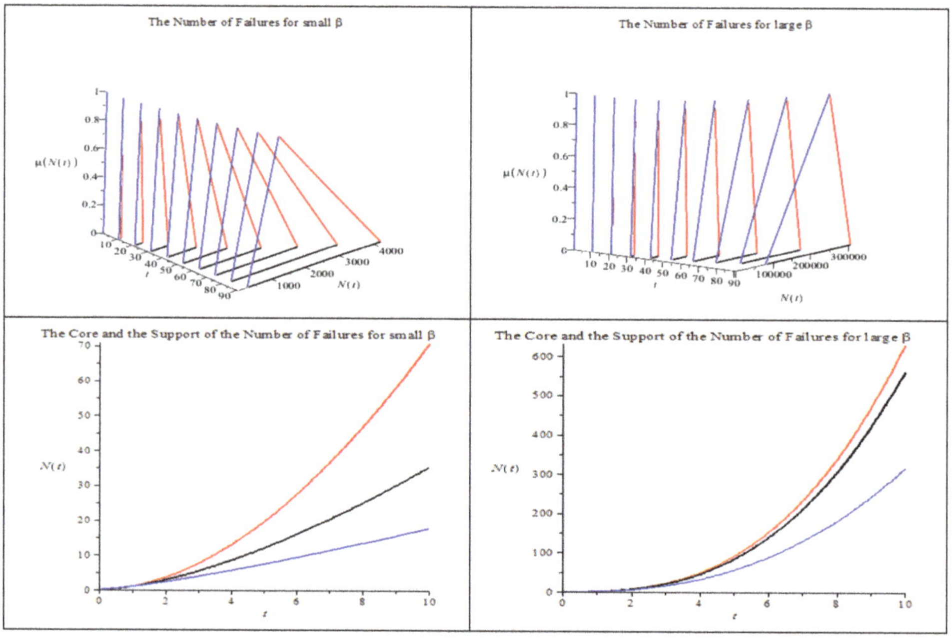


**Figure 4.** The description is as in Figure 3 above but with t = 0 to t = 100 and step size of t is 10. The left axis is time, the right axis is the number of failures, and the vertical axis is the fuzzy membership degree of the number of failures (above). The figures in the bottom show the core (black), the lower bound (blue), and the upper bound (red) for the resulting number of failures with small shape parameter (**left**) and large shape parameter (**right**).

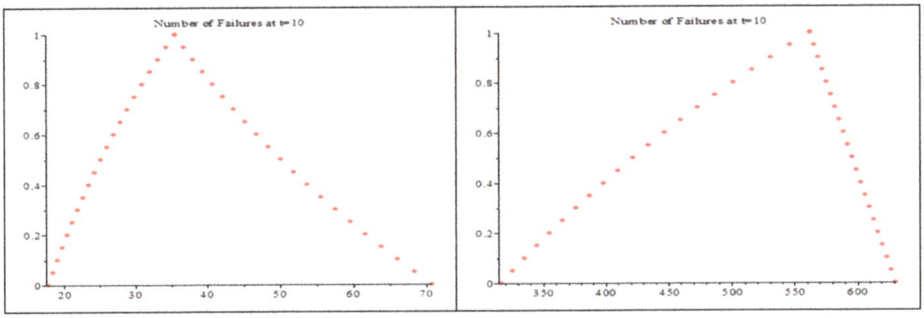


**Figure 5.** The **left** figure is the number of failures for the shape parameter $\beta = (p = 1.25; q = 1.55; s = 1.85)$ at t = 10. The **right** figure is the number of failures for the shape parameter $\beta = (p = 2.50; q = 2.75; s = 2.80)$ at t = 10. Both figures are generated by the second method with 20 levels of $\alpha$, i.e., $\alpha_0 = 0$ as the base to $\alpha_{21} = 1$ as the peak.

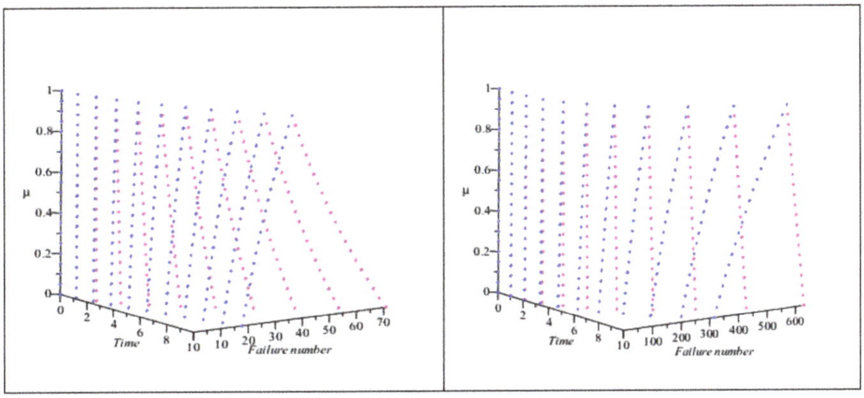


**Figure 6.** The description is as in Figure 5 above but with complete steps form t = 0 to t = 10. The **left** axis is time, the **right** axis is the number of failures, and the vertical axis is the fuzzy membership degree of the number of failures.

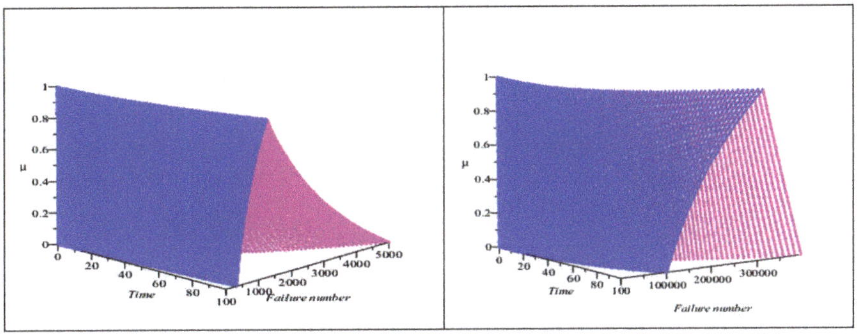


**Figure 7.** The plots of the number of failures for the shape parameter $\beta = (p = 1.25; q = 1.55; s = 1.85)$ and $\beta = (p = 0.9; q = 1.0; s = 1.5)$ from the second method against time from t = 0 to t = 100 as in Figure 6 but with a finer step size of t (other parameters are the same as in Figures 5 and 6).

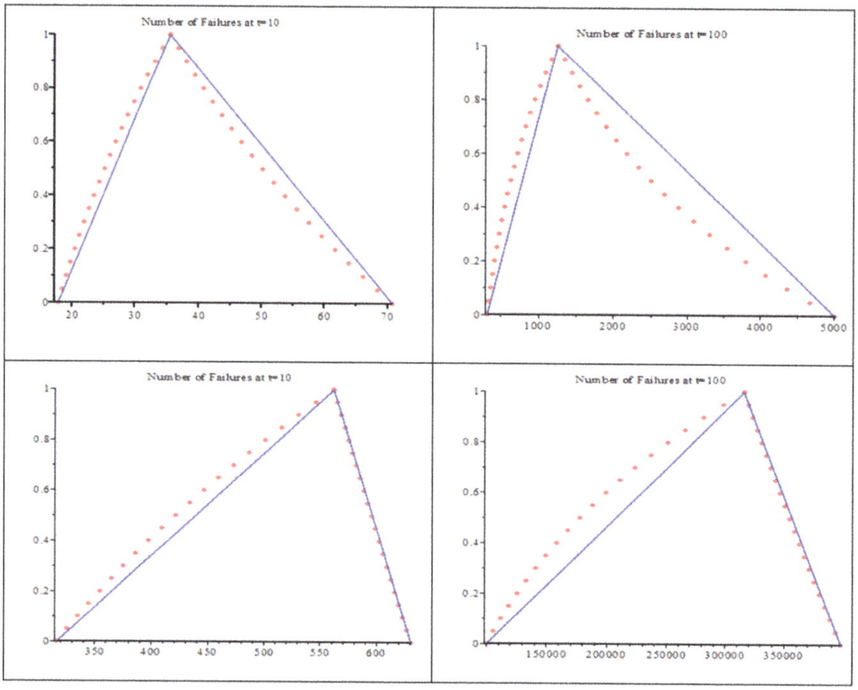


**Figure 8.** The **top** and **bottom** figures are plots of the number of failures for $\beta = (p = 1.25;\ q = 1.55;\ s = 1.85)$ and $\beta = (p = 2.50;\ q = 2.75;\ s = 2.80)$, respectively, with the left hand side is for t = 10 and the right hand side is for t = 100.

The figures show that for both values of fuzzy shape parameters $\widetilde{\beta}$, the relatively small value $\widetilde{\beta} = (p = 1.25;\ q = 1.55;\ s = 1.85)$ and the relatively large value $\widetilde{\beta} = (p = 2.50;\ q = 2.75;\ s = 2.80)$, the length of the fuzziness of the resulting number of failures get bigger as the time t increases. This means the increase of the possibilistic uncertainty of the number of failures. This phenomenon also appears in the $\alpha$-cut method as is shown in the next section.

### 3.3. Results from the $\alpha$-Cut Method

The following results are plotted from the calculation of the number of failures using the $\alpha$-cut method. Recall the $\alpha$-cut of the triangular fuzzy number $\widetilde{A} = (a; b; c)$ is given by $\widetilde{A}_\alpha = [a_1^\alpha, a_2^\alpha] = [(b-a)\alpha + a, (b-c)\alpha + c]$ hence for the fuzzy shape parameter $\widetilde{\beta} = (p = 1.25;\ q = 1.55;\ s = 1.85)$ we obtain its $\alpha$-cut is

$$\beta_\alpha = [1.25 + 0.30\alpha, 1.85 - 0.30\alpha], \tag{13}$$

as the fuzzy number of the shape parameter. By considering the $\alpha$-cut in Equation (7) and substituting it into Equations (5) and (6) using the fuzzy arithmetic give rise to the cumulative distribution

$$g(t)_\alpha = [1 - \exp(-t^{1.25+0.30\alpha}), 1 - \exp(-t^{1.85-0.30\alpha})], \tag{14}$$

and the hazard function

$$h(t)_\alpha = [(1.25 + 0.30\alpha)t^{0.25+0.30\alpha}, (1.85 - 0.30\alpha)t^{0.85-0.30\alpha}], \tag{15}$$

So that by integrating both sides of Equation (9) we end up with the number of failures, which is given by

$$N(t)_\alpha = [t^{1.25+0.30\alpha}, t^{1.85-0.30\alpha}]. \tag{16}$$

When we use the $\alpha$-cut method, we will have a triangular-like fuzzy number which is comparable (not necessarily the same) to the triangular fuzzy number (*p;q;r*) defined by:

$$p = \min N(t)_{\alpha=0} = t^{5/4}, \tag{17}$$

$$q = N(t)_{\alpha=1} = t^{31/20}, \tag{18}$$

$$r = \min N(t)_{\alpha=0} = t^{37/20}, \tag{19}$$

We enumerate the fuzzy number of failures in Table 1 based on the calculation of these formulas for t = 0 to t = 10.

**Table 1.** Number of failures comparisons for $\beta = (p = 1.25;\ q = 1.55;\ s = 1.85)$. Note that for the $\alpha$ -cut method we use $\alpha$ = 0 to obtain the support (*a,c*) and $\alpha$ = 1 to find the core *b* of the resulting fuzzy number so that we have an analogous *TFN* (*a;b;c*).

| Time t | Crisp Method | Fuzzy Propagation Method | | Fuzzy $\alpha$-Cut Method | |
|---|---|---|---|---|---|
| | | TFN (p;q;s) | Defuzzification (p + 4q + s)/6 | TFN-like (p;q;s) | Defuzzification (p + 4q + s)/6 |
| 0 | 0 | 0 | 0 | $p$ = 0<br>$q$ = 0<br>$s$ = 0 | 0 |
| 1 | 1 | 1 | 1 | $p$ = 1<br>$q$ = 1<br>$s$ = 1 | 1 |
| 2 | 2.949350275 | $p$ = 2.378414230<br>$q$ = 2.928171392<br>$s$ = 3.605001850 | 2.949350275 | $p$ = 2.378414230<br>$q$ = 2.928171392<br>$s$ = 3.605001850 | 2.949350275 |
| 3 | 5.589852442 | $p$ = 3.948222039<br>$q$ = 5.489565165<br>$s$ = 7.632631956 | 5.589852442 | $p$ = 3.948222039<br>$q$ = 5.489565165<br>$s$ = 7.632631956 | 5.589852442 |
| 4 | 8.824940564 | $p$ = 5.656854248<br>$q$ = 8.574187700<br>$s$ = 12.99603834 | 8.824940564 | $p$ = 5.656854248<br>$q$ = 8.574187700<br>$s$ = 12.99603834 | 8.824940564 |
| 5 | 12.59725950 | $p$ = 7.476743905<br>$q$ = 12.11723434<br>$s$ = 19.63787576 | 12.59725950 | $p$ = 7.476743905<br>$q$ = 12.11723434<br>$s$ = 19.63787576 | 12.59725950 |
| 6 | 16.86728508 | $p$ = 9.390507480<br>$q$ = 16.07438767<br>$s$ = 27.51565232 | 16.86728508 | $p$ = 9.390507480<br>$q$ = 16.07438767<br>$s$ = 27.51565232 | 16.86728508 |
| 7 | 21.60548840 | $p$ = 11.38603593<br>$q$ = 20.41277093<br>$s$ = 36.59581083 | 21.60548840 | $p$ = 11.38603593<br>$q$ = 20.41277093<br>$s$ = 36.59581083 | 21.60548840 |
| 8 | 26.78864158 | $p$ = 13.45434265<br>$q$ = 25.10669114<br>$s$ = 46.85074227 | 26.78864158 | $p$ = 13.45434265<br>$q$ = 25.10669114<br>$s$ = 46.85074227 | 26.78864158 |
| 9 | 32.39780510 | $p$ = 15.58845727<br>$q$ = 30.13532570<br>$s$ = 58.25707056 | 32.39780510 | $p$ = 15.58845727<br>$q$ = 30.13532570<br>$s$ = 58.25707056 | 32.39780510 |
| 10 | 38.41712138 | $p$ = 17.78279410<br>$q$ = 35.48133892<br>$s$ = 70.79457844 | 38.41712138 | $p$ = 17.78279410<br>$q$ = 35.48133892<br>$s$ = 70.79457844 | 38.41712138 |

Table 1 also gives the counterpart of the fuzzy number of failure calculated by the first method. Note that in Table 1, *TFN* is a triangle fuzzy number, while FN is not necessarily a triangle fuzzy number. However, they both have the same core and the same support but the shapes are different (see Figure 8).

Further, to compare the resulting fuzzy number of failures among the methods, we defuzzified them using the generalized mean value defuzzification (GMVD) which is defined by (4) with n = 4. The comparison shows that the defuzzified numbers both from the first method and the second method are exactly the same to the results from the crisp method. Table 2 shows that if n is getting larger, then, the defuzzified number gets closer to the core of the fuzzy number, e.g., for t = 10, with n = 1,000,000 the defuzzified number is 35.4813565346595 which approaches the core of its fuzzy number, i.e., $q$ = 35.48133892. This agrees with Theorem 1. We plot the resulting number of failures for t = 10 in Figure 5 and for t = 0 to t = 10 in Figure 6. The same procedure is done for the relatively large value of the shape parameter $\widetilde{\beta} = (p = 2.50;\ q = 2.75;\ s = 2.80)$ but the details are not presented here. The plots are presented in the righthand side of Figures 5–7.

**Table 2.** The illustration of Theorem 1 of the *GMVD* for non-symmetrical fuzzy number in Figure 5 (left). The fuzzy number is (17.782794100; 35.481338920; 70.794578440).

| n | GMVD | n | GMVD |
|---|---|---|---|
| 0 | 44,28868627 | 6 | 37,68317576 |
| 1 | 41,35290382 | 7 | 37,43852722 |
| 2 | 39,88501260 | 8 | 37,24280839 |
| 3 | 39,00427786 | 9 | 37,08267480 |
| 4 | 38,41712137 | 10 | 36,94923015 |
| 5 | 37,99772388 | 10,000,000 | 35,48135653 |

The time-series plots of the Cumulative Distribution Function, the Hazard Function, and the Number of Failures are presented in Figure 9. The shape parameter on the upper-left of Figure 9 is $\beta = (p = 1.25;\ q = 1.55;\ s = 1.85)$ and on the upper-right of Figure 9 is $\beta = (p = 2.50;\ q = 2.75;\ s = 2.80)$. The figure shows the plots for a short period of time, up to t = 1.5.

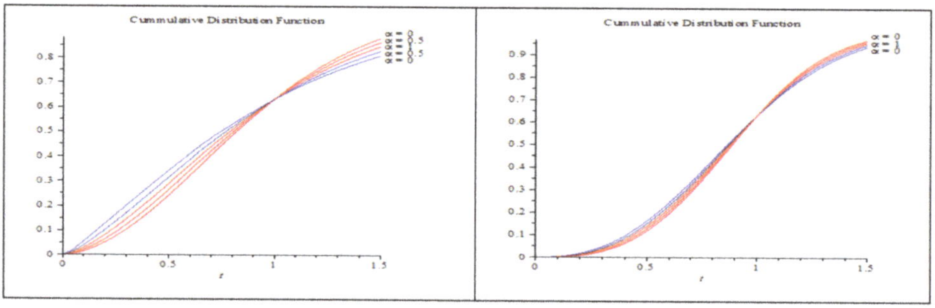


**Figure 9.** *Cont.*

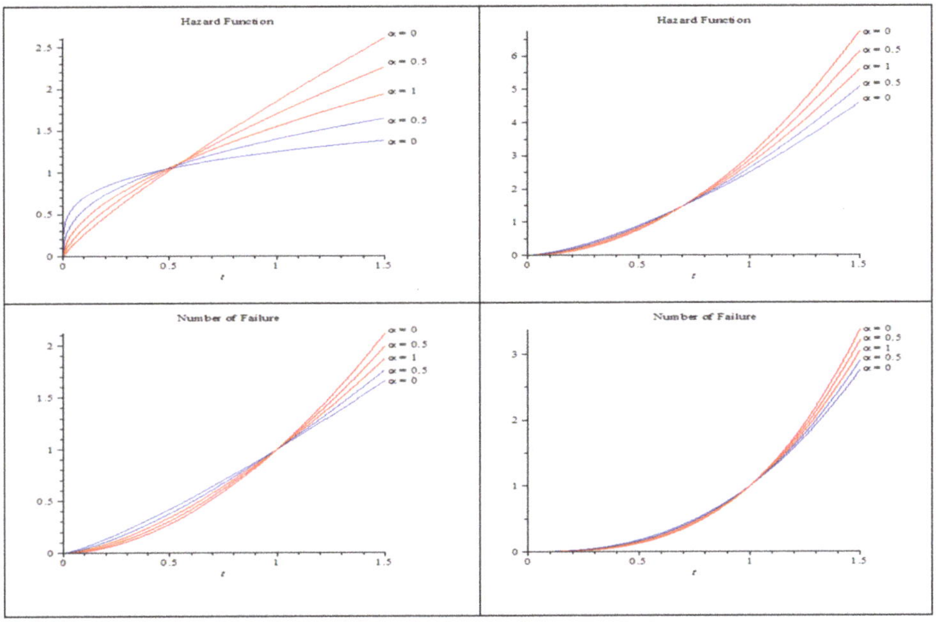


**Figure 9.** The time-series plots of the Cumulative Distribution Function, the Hazard Function, and the Number of Failures. The shape parameter on **left** figure is $\beta = (p = 1.25;\ q = 1.55;\ s = 1.85)$ and on the **right** figure is $\beta = (p = 2.50;\ q = 2.75;\ s = 2.80)$.

## 4. Discussions

The analytical results in Theorems 1 to 3 are illustrated by numerical examples to gain visual understanding regarding the analytical finding above by using $\widetilde{\beta} = (p = 1.25;\ q = 1.55;\ s = 1.85)$ and $\widetilde{\beta} = (p = 2.50;\ q = 2.75;\ s := 2.80)$ reflecting a relatively small and a relatively large shape parameter, respectively. Here $p$, $q$, and $s$ are the *TFN* components which constitute the *TFN* defined just the same as $a$, $b$, and $c$ in Equation (1). See Figure 2 for the graphs of these TFNs and Figure 3 for the resulting number of failures at t = 10 from the first method and Figure 5 (for the second method). While Figure 4 (top figures) shows the number of failures for t in [0,100] for the first method and Figure 6 for the second method with 10 steps size, (for the finer step size, i.e., 100 steps size see Figure 7). Clearly the number of failures in Figure 3 are in triangular forms due to the assumption in the first method in which the fuzziness of the shape parameter propagates with the same form of fuzzy number membership to the number of failures, while the number of failures in Figure 5 does not have a triangular form since the fuzziness uncertainty is considered and affecting the functional calculation of the number of failures through the α-cut arithmetic. Figure 8 gives the comparisons between these two relatively different shapes. The time-series plots of the cumulative distribution function, the hazard function, and the number of failures are presented in Figure 9. All curves are familiar in shape as it conform to their crisp parameter of Weibull distribution, but here they form twisted-cumulative band, -hazard band, and -number of failures band instead of single curve, respectively.

Furthermore, if we plot the numbers of failures over time (see bottom figures in Figure 4), then the curves are non-linear and seem to "exponentially" increase as expected in the theory. The bottom graphs in Figure 4 actually show the numbers of failures over time for the end points and core of the shape parameter TFNs. To be exact these figures show the graphs of Weibull's numbers of failures bands, which analytically is given by Equations (12) and (16), hence it has a power curve shape which conforms to the known curve for Weibull's number of failures with crisp parameters [58]. This is also true for the second method (the α-cut approach), but we do not show the graphs here.

When considering a Weibull distribution with fuzzy shape parameter to calculate the fuzzy number of failures, usually in such imprecise situations, extension principle approach is often used as one choice of calculation though it could lead to a complex form. Here we have proposed a simple method (the first method) to calculate the number of failures, by assuming that the fuzziness of the shape parameter propagates to the number of failures with the same form of fuzzy number membership, and also proposed an alternative method (the second method) which is the calculation done using the $\alpha$-cut method. This method could be extended to the Weibull distribution with more parameters to enlarge the applicability to other area [59].

## 5. Conclusions

In this paper we have discussed the Weibull hazard function by assuming a fuzzy shape parameter to calculate the fuzzy number of failures. Here we have proposed a simple method (the first method) to calculate the number of failures, by assuming that the fuzziness of the shape parameter propagates to the number of failures with the same form of fuzzy number membership, and also proposed an alternative method (the second method) which is the calculation done using the $\alpha$-cut method.

We have shown that both methods have succeeded in computing the number of failures for the system under investigation. Both methods show that when we consider the function of the number of failures as a function of time then the uncertainty (the fuzziness) of the resulting number of failures becomes larger and larger as the time increases. This indicates the propagation of uncertainty in the shape parameter into the resulting number of failures, in which for large values of $t$, a small value of uncertainty in the shape parameter will produce a large support to the fuzzy number of failures. In practical implication, one should be aware of these properties when using the resulting number of failures as a base for the further process of decision-making.

In this paper we have used a *TFN* for the shape parameter and by using the first method, the resulting number of failures has a *TFN* form. Meanwhile, the resulting number of failures from the second method does not necessarily have a *TFN* form, but a *TFN*-like form. Some comparisons between these two methods are presented using the Generalized Mean Value Defuzzification (*GMVD*) method. The results show that for certain weighting factor of the *GMVD*, the cores of these fuzzy numbers of failures are identical. We did the comparation between the two methods after we use the *GMVD* which produces crisp number of failures. This can be regarded as a shortcoming of the study since once we defuzzify the resulting number of failures we lose the information of the uncertainty. Further study can be done by considering the comparation with a method that preserves the uncertainty.

The *TFN* form and value of the shape parameter used in the Weibull distribution function was taken for granted. For the practical applications this would be not easy. The true form of the fuzzy number should be correctly decided from the available real data and the value should be estimated from the same data. These issues are among the limitations of the methods presented here and could also lead to future direction of research. Other concern is that here we only consider one parameter which has fuzzy value. In realty all of the Weibull parameters could also have imprecise measure or uncertainty. This also will lead to important future venue of research (currently four-parameter Weibull distribution has already around in crisp value application ref). Here we only consider one-parameter Weibull distribution by assuming the scale parameter is assumed to be one. This is sufficient in our context of maintenance modeling if we assume that the average of first failure of the equipment/system under investigation happens within one unit of time. However, in general case this may not be true, so we need to extend the analysis into Weibull distribution having arbitrary values of the scale parameters. Further studies can also be done for different approaches with different forms of fuzzy numbers, different uses of defuzzification methods, and explore the applications of the theory in different related field, such as the number of failures in biological processes (e.g., failure in protecting healthy status (susceptibility) for people who are infected by COVID-19 disease), which currently we are working on.

**Author Contributions:** H.H.: conceptualization, investigation, project administration, resources, data curation, validation, writing—original draft preparation; A.K.S.: methodology and software, formal analysis, visualization, supervision, writing—review and editing, funding acquisition. All authors have read and agreed to the published version of the manuscript.

**Funding:** This research and the APC were funded by the Ministry of Research, Technology, and Higher Education of the Republic of Indonesia, through the scheme of "Penelitian Hibah Riset dan Teknologi/Badan Riset dan Inovasi Nasional", with grant number 1207/UN6.3.1/PT.00/202.

**Institutional Review Board Statement:** Not applicable.

**Informed Consent Statement:** Not applicable.

**Data Availability Statement:** Not applicable.

**Acknowledgments:** We thank the anonymous referees who have read the earlier version of the manuscript and raised many constructive comments that helped to improve the content and the presentation of the paper.

**Conflicts of Interest:** The authors declare no conflict of interest.

## References

1. Esogbue, A.O.; Hearnes, W.E. On replacement models via a fuzzy set theoretic framework. *IEEE Trans. Syst. Man Cybern. Part C Appl. Rev.* **1998**, *28*, 549–560. [CrossRef]
2. Parchami, A. Calculator for fuzzy numbers. *Complex. Intell. Syst.* **2019**, *5*, 331–342. [CrossRef]
3. Husniah, H.; Supriatna, A.K.; Iskandar, B.P. Lease contract with servicing strategy model for used product considering crisp and fuzzy usage rate. *Int. J. Artif. Intell.* **2018**, *18*, 177–192.
4. Husniah, H.; Pasaribu, U.S.; Iskandar, B.P. Multi-period lease contract for remanufactured products. *Alex. Eng. J.* **2020**, *60*, 2279–2289. [CrossRef]
5. Husniah, H.; Pasaribu, U.S.; Wangsaputra, R.; Iskandar, B.P. Condition-based maintenance policy for a leased reman product. *Heliyon* **2021**, *7*, e06494. [CrossRef] [PubMed]
6. Verma, A.K. The use of fuzzy numbers in reliability calculations. *IETE Tech. Rev.* **2001**, *18*, 27–31. [CrossRef]
7. Glöckner, I. *Fuzzy Quantifiers: A Computational Theory*; Springer: Berlin/Heidelberg, Germany, 2006.
8. Venkatesh, A.; Elango, S. A mathematical model for the effect of TRH using fuzzy reliability analysis. *Glob. J. Pure Appl. Math.* **2017**, *13*, 5673–5686.
9. Venkatesh, A.; Subramani, G.; Elango, S. A mathematical model for the effect of gastrin in humans using fuzzy Weibull distribution. *Int. J. Pure Appl. Math.* **2017**, *117*, 155–164.
10. Adhikari, S.; Khodaparast, H.H. A spectral approach for fuzzy uncertainty propagation in finite element analysis. *Fuzzy Sets Syst.* **2014**, *243*, 1–24. [CrossRef]
11. Khalaf, A.; Djouani, K.; Hamam, Y.; Alayli, Y. Failure-cost mathematical model for medical equipment maintenance. In Proceedings of the Fourth International Conference on Advances in Biomedical Engineering (ICABME), Beirut, Lebanon, 19–21 October 2017; pp. 1–4. [CrossRef]
12. Li, G.; Li, Y.; Zhang, X.; Hou, C.; He, J.; Xu, B.; Chen, J. Development of a preventive maintenance strategy for an automatic production line based on group maintenance method. *Appl. Sci.* **2018**, *8*, 1781. [CrossRef]
13. Lee, J.; Kim, B.; Ahn, S. Maintenance optimization for repairable deteriorating systems under imperfect preventive maintenance. *Mathematics* **2019**, *7*, 716. [CrossRef]
14. Husniah, H.; Herdiani, L.; Kusmaya, K.; Supriatna, A.K. Fuzzy usage pattern in customizing public transport fleet and its maintenance options. *J. Phys. Conf. Ser.* **2018**, *1013*, 012186. [CrossRef]
15. Mohammed, A.; Ghaithan, A.; Al-Saleh, M.; Al-Ofi, K. Reliability-based preventive maintenance strategy of truck unloading systems. *Appl. Sci.* **2020**, *10*, 6957. [CrossRef]
16. Nordal, H.; El-Thalji, I. Assessing the technical specifications of predictive maintenance: A case study of centrifugal compressor. *Appl. Sci.* **2021**, *11*, 1527. [CrossRef]
17. Husniah, H.; Supriatna, A.K.; Iskandar, B.P. Improving service contract management with availability and negotiation. In *Interdisciplinary Behavior and Social Sciences, Proceedings of the 3rd International Congress on Interdisciplinary Behavior and Social Science 2014 (ICIBSoS 2014), Bali, Indonesia, 1–2 November 2014*; Gaol, L., Ed.; CRC Press-Taylor and Francis Group: London, UK, 2015; pp. 409–413.
18. Wisniewski, R. Using Weibull Analysis to Guide Preventative Maintenance Strategy. *Def. Syst. Inf. Anal. Cent.* **2014**, *2*. Available online: https://dsiac.org/articles/using-weibull-analysis-to-guide-preventative-maintenance-strategy/ (accessed on 2 September 2021).

19. Pascale, E.; Freneaux, T.; Sista, R.; Sannino, P.; Marmo, P.; Bouillaut, L. Application of the Weibull distribution for the optimization of maintenance policies of an electronic railway signaling system. In Proceedings of the ESREL 2017 European Safety and Reliability Conference, Portoroz, Slovenia, 18–22 June 2017. Available online: https://hal.archives-ouvertes.fr/hal-01521640/file/doc00026876.pdf (accessed on 2 September 2021).
20. Hong, J. Modified Weibull Distributions in Reliability Engineering. Ph.D. Thesis, National University of Singapore, Singapore, 2010. Available online: http://scholarbank.nus.edu.sg/handle/10635/17099 (accessed on 2 September 2021).
21. Baloui Jamkhaneh, E. Analyzing system reliability using fuzzy weibull lifetime distribution. *Int. J. Appl. Oper. Res.* **2014**, *4*, 81–90.
22. Husniah, H.; Supriatna, A.K. Optimal number of fishing fleet for a sustainable fishery industry with a generalized logistic production function. In Proceedings of the 2015 International Conference on Industrial Engineering and Systems Management (IESM), Seville, Spain, 21–23 October 2015. [CrossRef]
23. Husniah, H.; Pasaribu, U.S.; Supriatna, A.K.; Iskandar, B.P. Optimal number of fleet maintenance contract with policy limit cost. In Proceedings of the 4th International Conference on Control, Decision and Information Technologies (CoDIT), Bandung, Indonesia, 5–7 April 2017. [CrossRef]
24. Zio, E.; Pedroni, N. Possibilistic methods for uncertainty treatment applied to maintenance policy assessment. In *Industrial Safety Cahiers*; Foundation for an Industrial Safety Culture: Toulouse, France, 2014; no. 2014-07. Available online: https://www.foncsi.org/en/publications/collections/industrial-safety-cahiers/possibilistic-methods-uncertainty-maintenance-policy/CSI-uncertainty-maintenance.pdf (accessed on 2 September 2021).
25. Basile, O.; Dehombreux, P.; Riane, P. Identification of reliability models for non repairable and repairable systems with small samples. In *Faculte Polytechnique de Mons Research Report*; Arles: Mons, Belgium, 2004; Available online: http://citeseerx.ist.psu.edu/viewdoc/download?doi=10.1.1.595.8268&rep=rep1&type=pdf (accessed on 2 September 2021).
26. Basile, O.; Dehombreux, P.; Riane, P. Evaluation of the uncertainty affecting reliability models. *J. Qual. Maint. Eng.* **2007**, *13*, 137–151. [CrossRef]
27. Baraldi, P.; Compare, M.; Zio, E. Uncertainty treatment in expert information systems for maintenance policy assessment. *Appl. Soft Comput.* **2014**, *22*, 297–310. [CrossRef]
28. Zadeh, L. The concept of a linguistic variable and its application to approximate reasoning–I. *Inf. Sci.* **1975**, *8*, 199–249. [CrossRef]
29. Zadeh, L. Fuzzy sets as a basis for a theory of possibility. *Fuzzy Sets Syst.* **1999**, *100*, 9–34. [CrossRef]
30. Rotshtein, A.; Katielnikov, D.; Pustylnik, L. Reliability modeling and optimization using fuzzy logic and chaos theory. *Int. J. Qual. Stat. Reliab.* **2012**, *2012*, 847416. [CrossRef]
31. Rezaei, E.; Imani, D.M. A new modeling of maintenance risk based inspection interval optimization with fuzzy failure interaction for two-component repairable system. *Indian J. Nat. Sci.* **2015**, *6*, 9003–9017.
32. Garg, H.; Sharma, S.P.; Rani, M. Weibull fuzzy probability distribution for analysing the behaviour of pulping unit in a paper industry. *Int. J. Ind. Syst. Eng.* **2013**, *14*, 395–413. [CrossRef]
33. Lee, K.H. *First Course on Fuzzy Theory and Applications*; Springer: Berlin/Heidelberg, Germany, 2005.
34. Husniah, H.; Widjajani, W.; Rohmana, R.; Supriatna, A.K. Number of failures for weibull hazard function with a fuzzy shape parameter. *J. Phys. Conf. Ser.* **2019**, *1280*, 022034. [CrossRef]
35. Husniah, H.; Supriatna, A.K. Application of fuzzy theory in determining the number of failures for Weibull hazard function. In Proceedings of the ICOCSIM, Lombok, Indonesia, 21 March 2019.
36. Sharma, R.K.; Sharma, P. System failure behavior and maintenance decision making using, RCA, FMEA and FM. *J. Qual. Maint. Eng.* **2010**, *16*, 64–88. [CrossRef]
37. Rahmani, A.; Lotfi, F.H.; Rostamy-Malkhalifeh, M.; Allahviranloo, T. A new method for defuzzification and ranking of fuzzy numbers based on the statistical beta distribution. *Adv. Fuzzy Syst.* **2016**, *2016*, 1–8. [CrossRef]
38. Buckley, J.J.; Eslami, E.; Feuring, T. *Fuzzy Mathematics in Economics and Engineering*; Springer: Berlin/Heidelberg, Germany, 2002.
39. Lai, C.D.; Murthy, D.N.; Xie, M. Weibull distributions and their applications. In *Springer Handbook of Engineering Statistics*; Pham, H., Ed.; Springer: New York, NY, USA, 2006; pp. 63–78.
40. Kumar, P.; Singh, S.B. Fuzzy system reliability using intuitionistic fuzzy Weibull lifetime distribution. *Int. J. Reliab. Appl.* **2015**, *16*, 15–26.
41. Iskandar, B.P.; Jack, N.; Murthy, D.N.P. Two new servicing strategies for products sold with warranty. *Asia Pac. J. Oper. Res.* **2012**, *29*, 1240022. [CrossRef]
42. Nakagawa, T. *Maintenance Theory of Reliability*; Springer-Verlag: London, UK, 2005.
43. Kobbacy, K.A.H.; Murthy, D.N.P. *Complex System Maintenance Handbook*; Springer Nature: Cham, Switzerland, 2008.
44. Rinne, H. *The Weibull Distribution A Handbook*, 1st ed.; Chapman and Hall/CRC: New York, NY, USA, 2008.
45. McCool, J.I. *Using the Weibull Distribution: Reliability, Modeling, and Inference*; John Wiley & Sons: Hoboken, NJ, USA, 2012. [CrossRef]
46. Ebrahimnejad, A.; Verdegay, J.L. *Fuzzy Sets-Based Methods and Techniques for Modern Analytics*; Springer International Publishing: Cham, Switzerland, 2018. [CrossRef]
47. Ebrahimnejad, A. New method for solving Fuzzy transportation problems with LR flat fuzzy numbers. *Inf. Sci.* **2016**, *357*, 108–124. [CrossRef]
48. Jain, S. Close interval approximation of piecewise quadratic fuzzy numbers for fuzzy fractional program. *Iran. J. Oper. Res.* **2010**, *2*, 77–88.

49. Panda, A.; Pal, M. A study on pentagonal fuzzy number and its corresponding matrices. *Pac. Sci. Rev. B. Humanit. Soc. Sci.* **2015**, *1*, 131–139. [CrossRef]
50. Maturo, F.; Fortuna, F. Bell-shaped fuzzy numbers associated with the normal curve. In *Topics on Methodological and Applied Statistical Inference*; Di Battista, T., Moreno, E., Racugno, W., Eds.; Springer Nature: Cham, Switzerland, 2016; pp. 131–144. [CrossRef]
51. Thangavelu, K.; Uthra, G.; Shunmugapriya, S. A new approach on the membership functions of fuzzy numbers. *Int. J. Pure Appl. Math.* **2017**, *114*, 145–152.
52. Bagheri, N.; Hashemin, S.S. A new bell shape fuzzy number. *Int. J. Math. Trends Technol.* **2018**, *54*, 377–382. [CrossRef]
53. van Leekwijck, W.; Kerre, E.E. Defuzzification: Criteria and classification. *Fuzzy Sets Syst.* **1999**, *108*, 159–178. [CrossRef]
54. Madau, D.P.; Feldkamp, L.A. Influence value defuzzification method. In Proceedings of the IEEE 5th International Fuzzy Systems, New Orleans, LA, USA, 11 September 1996; pp. 1819–1824. [CrossRef]
55. Jager, B.; Verbruggen, H.B.; Bruijn, P.M. The role of defuzzification methods in the application of fuzzy control. *IFAC Proc. Umes* **1992**, *25*, 75–80. [CrossRef]
56. Available online: https://en.wikibooks.org/wiki/Advanced_Calculus/Newton%27s_general_binomial_theorem (accessed on 2 September 2021).
57. Koh, Y.; Ree, S. The Origin of Newton's Generalized Binomial Theorem. *J. Hist. Math.* **2014**, *27*, 127–138. [CrossRef]
58. Scheideggera, A.; Scholtena, L.; Maurera, M.; Reichert, P. Extension of pipe failure models to consider the absence of data from replaced pipes. *Water Res.* **2013**, *47*, 3696–3705. [CrossRef] [PubMed]
59. Izadparast, H.A.; Niedzwecki, J.M. Four-parameter Weibull probability distribution model for weakly non-linear random variables. *Probabilistic Eng. Mech.* **2013**, *32*, 31–38. [CrossRef]

**mathematics**

MDPI

*Article*

# On the Search for a Measure to Compare Interval-Valued Fuzzy Sets

**Susana Díaz-Vázquez *,†, Emilio Torres-Manzanera †, Irene Díaz † and Susana Montes †**

Department of Statistics and O. R. and Department of Computer Sciences, University of Oviedo, 33007 Oviedo, Spain; torres@uniovi.es (E.T.-M.); sirene@uniovi.es (I.D.); montes@uniovi.es (S.M.)

* Correspondence: diazsusana@uniovi.es; Tel.: +34-985-10-33-80

† These authors contributed equally to this work.

**Abstract:** Multiple definitions have been put forward in the literature to measure the differences between two interval-valued fuzzy sets. However, in most cases, the outcome is just a real value, although an interval could be more appropriate in this environment. This is the starting point of this contribution. Thus, we revisit the axioms that a measure of the difference between two interval-valued fuzzy sets should satisfy, paying special attention to the condition of monotonicity in the sense that the closer the intervals are, the smaller the measure of difference between them is. Its formalisation leads to very different concepts: distances, divergences and dissimilarities. We have proven that distances and divergences lead to contradictory properties for this kind of sets. Therefore, we conclude that dissimilarities are the only appropriate measures to measure the difference between two interval-valued fuzzy sets when the outcome is an interval.

**Keywords:** interval-valued fuzzy set; interval order; difference; distance; divergence; dissimilarity

**Citation:** Díaz-Vázquez, S.; Torres-Manzanera, E.; Díaz, I.; Montes, S. On the Search for a Measure to Compare Interval-Valued Fuzzy Sets. *Mathematics* **2021**, *9*, 3157. https://doi.org/10.3390/math9243157

Academic Editor: Michael Voskoglou

Received: 29 October 2021
Accepted: 1 December 2021
Published: 7 December 2021



## 1. Introduction

It us usually understood that knowledge of comparisons of objects, opinions, etc. are incomplete. A widely accepted theory (and methodology) to cope with imprecision is fuzzy sets theory, where elements are not necessarily in a set or out of it, but rather intermediate degrees of membership are allowed. In this context, the classical ways to contrast sets do not apply, and several measures for comparing fuzzy sets have been introduced and can be found in the literature. An in-depth study was carried out by Bouchon-Meunier et al. in 1996 [1]. After this, many other measures have been proposed. Some of them are constructive definitions, i.e., specific formulae (see, among many others, Refs. [2–5]) and others are based on axiomatic definitions (see, for example, Refs. [6–8]).

The presence of imprecision in real-life situations has been a challenge even from a theoretical point of view. In order to cope with this handicap, different extensions of fuzzy sets have been proposed. Interval-valued fuzzy sets (IVFSs) are one of the most successful and challenging extensions. This generalization was introduced independently and almost simultaneously by Zadeh [9], Grattan-Guiness [10], Jahn [11], and Sambuc [12]. Interval-valued fuzzy sets are a useful tool. They are used to model situations where the "classical" fuzzy sets are not appropriate. This occurs in the case when an objective procedure to determine crisp membership degrees is not available. IVFSs show high potential in practical applications. They were used in medical diagnosis in thyrodian pathology (see Sambuc [12]), in approximate reasoning (see, for instance, the contributions of Bustince [13] and Gozalczany [14]) and Cornelis et al. [15] and Turksen [16] applied this theory in logic.

Due to its potential utility, different notions and tools connected to this extension must be studied. In particular, our interest is focused on the measures of comparison of two interval-valued fuzzy sets, which have been studied in the last years. Some of them are based on comparing the degree of similarity between them (see, e.g., [17–20]). However, it is also possible to consider a dual approach, based on measuring the difference (see, e.g., [21]). Another previous study related to this topic can be obtained from the related concept of intuitionistic fuzzy sets. It was introduced by Atanassov [22].

Closely connected to IVFSs is the theory of intuitionistic fuzzy sets, introduced by Atanassov [22] about a decade after IVFSs were defined. Despite they are semantically different, it is widely known that intuitionistic and interval-valued fuzzy sets are equipollent (see, for instance, [23,24]); that is, there is a bijective function that maps one onto the other. Measures to compare intuitionistic fuzzy sets have already been introduced (see, for example, [25,26]). These proposals could provide us with an initial idea on the way to compare two interval-valued fuzzy sets. However, they cannot be directly used, as was shown in [27–29].

The previously introduced measures provide a unique real value as the result of the comparison. However, this is not a desirable result. If we are dealing with interval-valued fuzzy sets from an epistemic point of view, even the absolute similarity between incomplete descriptions does not guarantee the absolute similarity of the described elements. In order to cope with this situation, it could be more appropriate to formalize the idea of similarity using a range of values. However, this perspective is not the usual one. To the best of our knowledge, the literature where we can find this approach is rather limited [30–33]. These papers can be considered as the starting point of our research [34]. Thus, our main purpose is to study the different approaches considered in the literature that measure the degree of difference between two interval-valued fuzzy sets by means of an interval, in order to preserve the uncertainty that we have about the description of the involved sets. In this paper, we will consider the different approaches, compare them and conclude which ones are the best axioms in order to characterise a measure of the difference between two interval-valued fuzzy sets.

More precisely, we will focus on distances, divergences, and dissimilarities and study how sound these definitions are. We provide examples that show that distances lead to counterintuitive situations and that the axioms involved in the definition of an interval-valued divergence are conflicting. Therefore, we consider dissimilarities as the only reasonable way to compare IVFSs among the three considered. As a consequence, we finally compare the different proposals given in the literature for this concept.

The contribution is organised as follows. In Section 2, basic concepts and results are introduced, and the notation used in the subsequent sections is fixed. Section 3 is devoted to studying the possible definitions of a measure of how different two interval-valued fuzzy sets can be. Section 4 closes the contribution with some conclusions. We also put forward some questions that remain open in this section.

## 2. Basic Concepts

In this section, we recall some basic notions and properties that are important to understand the following section of this contribution. We begin with the classical theory of fuzzy sets.

Let $X$ denote the universe of discourse. A fuzzy set in $X$ is a mapping $A : X \to [0,1]$ where $A(x)$ stands for the degree to which element $x$ belongs to the subset $A$ of $X$. We will denote $FS(X)$ the family of all the fuzzy sets defined on the universe $X$.

An interval-valued fuzzy subset (IVFS for short) of $X$ is a mapping $A : X \to L([0,1])$ such that $A(x) = [\underline{A}(x), \overline{A}(x)]$, where $L([0,1])$ denotes the family of closed intervals included in the unit interval $[0,1]$. It is therefore easy to check that an interval-valued fuzzy set $A$ is characterized by two mappings, $\underline{A}$ and $\overline{A}$, from $X$ into $[0,1]$ such that $\underline{A}(x) \leq \overline{A}(x), \forall x \in X$. These functions provide the lower and upper bounds, respectively, of the associated intervals. Observe that if $\underline{A}(x) = \overline{A}(x), \forall x \in X$, then $A$ is a classical fuzzy set. The abbreviation $IVFS(X)$ stands for set of all the interval-valued fuzzy sets in $X$.

For IVFSs, we can consider the epistemic or the ontic interpretation. In our study, the former is chosen. Thus, we assume that there is one actual, real-valued membership degree of an element inside the membership interval of possible membership degrees.

**Example 1.** *Consider the IVFS drawn in Figure 1. The IVFS assigns to element x the interval* $[0.45, 0.75]$.

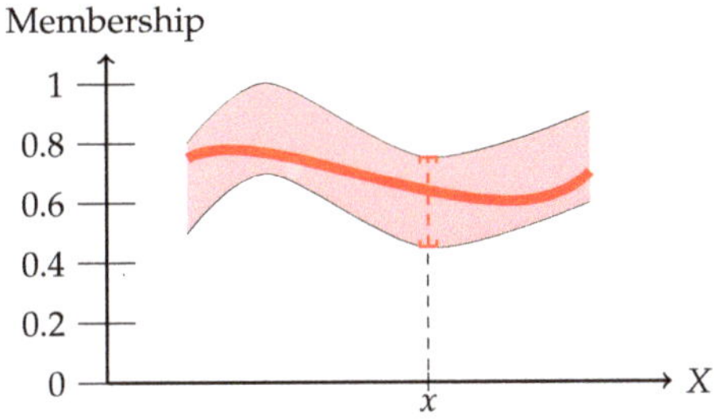


**Figure 1.** Idea of IVFS.

*This means that the real membership degree for x may be* 0.65, *but we are not sure about it and we can only say that it is between* 0.45 *and* 0.75.

As we explained in detail at the Introduction, we define a measure to compare two IVFSs such that the value of this comparison is again an interval. In order to do this, some operations and previous concepts have to be fixed.

### 2.1. Inclusion

The inclusion for IVFSs is directly connected to an order relation between intervals. In [35], we can find a summary of the main interval orders.

**Definition 1.** *([35]) Let* $a = [\underline{a}, \overline{a}]$ *and* $b = [\underline{b}, \overline{b}]$ *be two intervals in* $L([0,1])$. *Then a is smaller than or equal to b for the following orders between intervals if:*

- *Interval dominance [36]:* $a \preceq_{ID} b$ *if* $\overline{a} \leq \underline{b}$.
- *Lattice order [37]:* $a \preceq_{Lo} b$ *if* $\underline{a} \leq \underline{b}$ *and* $\overline{a} \leq \overline{b}$, *which is induced by the usual partial order in* $\mathbb{R}^2$.
- *Lexicographical order of type 1 [38]:* $a \preceq_{Lex1} b$ *if* $\underline{a} < \underline{b}$ *or* ($\underline{a} = \underline{b}$ *and* $\overline{a} \leq \overline{b}$).
- *Lexicographical order of type 2 [38]:* $a \preceq_{Lex2} b$ *if* $\overline{a} < \overline{b}$ *or* ($\overline{a} = \overline{b}$ *and* $\underline{a} \leq \underline{b}$).
- *The Xu and Yager order [39]:* $a \preceq_{XY} b$ *if* $\underline{a} + \overline{a} < \underline{b} + \overline{b}$ *or* ($\underline{a} + \overline{a} = \underline{b} + \overline{b}$ *and* $\overline{a} - \underline{a} \leq \overline{b} - \underline{b}$).
- *Maximin order [40,41]:* $a \preceq_{Mm} b$ *if* $\underline{a} \leq \underline{b}$.
- *Maximax order [42]:* $a \preceq_{MM} b$ *if* $\overline{a} \leq \overline{b}$.
- *Hurwicz order [43]:* $a \preceq_{H(\alpha)} b$ *if* $\alpha \cdot \underline{a} + (1-\alpha) \cdot \overline{a} \leq \alpha \cdot \underline{b} + (1-\alpha) \cdot \overline{b}$ *with* $\alpha \in [0,1]$.
- *Weak order [44]:* $a \preceq_{wo} b$ *if* $\underline{a} \leq \overline{b}$.

Given an order $\preceq_o$, the equality between intervals can be defined as follows: $a =_o b$ if and only if $a \preceq_o b$ and $b \preceq_o a$.

Most of the previously recalled orders are connected. First of all, it is well known that if one interval $a$ is lower than or equal to another interval $b$ w.r.t. interval dominance, $a$ is also lower than or equal to $b$ w.r.t. the lattice order. Interval dominance is also a stronger relation than the lexicographical order of type 1, which implies the maximax order which, in turn, implies the weak order. Figure 2 summarizes these and other similar connections.

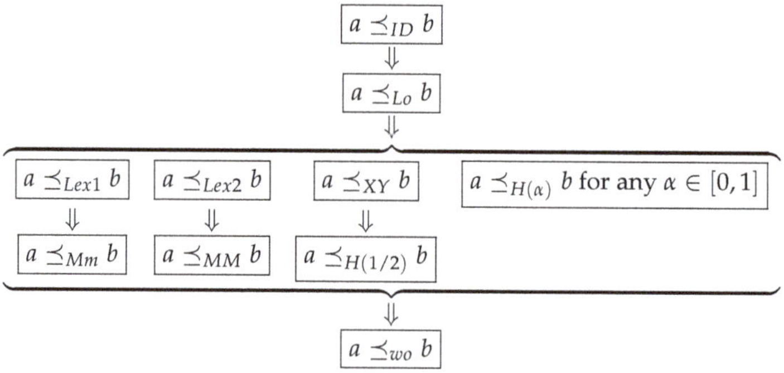


**Figure 2.** Relationships among the different relations.

Observe that $ID$ is the strongest relation in the sense that if two intervals are connected by it, then they are connected by any of the other relations previously recalled.

Apart from that, it is important to notice that, although all of them are called orders, they are not really orders, in the mathematical sense, in all the cases, as we can see in Table 1. Thus, only the lattice order, the lexicographical orders and the Xu-Yager order are really orders and the first one is not a total order.

**Table 1.** Some properties of the considered relations on $L([0,1])$.

| | Reflexive | Antisymmetric | Transitive | Total | Preorder | Order |
|---|---|---|---|---|---|---|
| $ID$ | ✗ | ✓ | ✓ | ✗ | ✗ | ✗ |
| $Lo$ | ✓ | ✓ | ✓ | ✗ | ✓ | ✓ |
| $Lex_1$ | ✓ | ✓ | ✓ | ✓ | ✓ | ✓ |
| $Lex_2$ | ✓ | ✓ | ✓ | ✓ | ✓ | ✓ |
| $XY$ | ✓ | ✓ | ✓ | ✓ | ✓ | ✓ |
| $Mm$ | ✓ | ✗ | ✓ | ✓ | ✓ | ✗ |
| $MM$ | ✓ | ✗ | ✓ | ✓ | ✓ | ✗ |
| $H(\alpha)$ | ✓ | ✗ | ✓ | ✓ | ✓ | ✗ |
| $wo$ | ✓ | ✗ | ✗ | ✓ | ✗ | ✗ |

Regarding total orders in $L([0,1])$, we consider the so-called admissible orders, whose definition we now recall.

**Definition 2.** *([38]) An admissible order on $L([0,1])$ is a total order $\preceq_{to}$ that refines the lattice order; that is, for every $a, b \in L([0,1])$, if $a \preceq_{Lo} b$ then $a \preceq_{to} b$.*

An interesting feature of admissible orders is that they can be built using aggregation functions, as stated in the following result. Recall that an aggregation function is a increasing function $\mathcal{A} : [0,1]^n \to [0,1]$ with $\mathcal{A}(0,\ldots,0) = 0$ and $\mathcal{A}(1,\ldots,1) = 1$ (see [45]).

Observe that there is an easy bijection between the sets $L([0,1])$ and $K([0,1]) = \{(u,v) \in [0,1]^2 \mid u \leq v\}$. It assigns to each interval $[\underline{a}, \overline{a}]$ the point in $\mathbb{R}^2$ whose coordinates are the extreme values of the interval, i.e., $(\underline{a}, \overline{a})$ (see [38]). Therefore, aggregation functions can be used to summarize the information provided by an interval. This idea is beneath the following method provided by Bustince et al. to build admissible orders.

**Proposition 1.** *([38]) Let $\mathcal{A}$ and $\mathcal{B} : [0,1]^2 \to [0,1]$ be continuous aggregation functions, verifying that for all $(u,v), (w,z) \in K([0,1])$, the equalities $\mathcal{A}(u,v) = \mathcal{A}(w,z)$ and $\mathcal{B}(u,v) = \mathcal{B}(w,z)$ can only hold if $(u,v) = (w,z)$. Define the relation $\preceq_{\mathcal{A},\mathcal{B}}$ on $L([0,1])$ by:*

$$a \preceq_{\mathcal{A},\mathcal{B}} b \text{ if } \mathcal{A}(\underline{a}, \overline{a}) < \mathcal{A}(\underline{b}, \overline{b}) \text{ or } (\mathcal{A}(\underline{a}, \overline{a}) = \mathcal{A}(\underline{b}, \overline{b}) \text{ and } \mathcal{B}(\underline{a}, \overline{a}) \leq \mathcal{B}(\underline{b}, \overline{b})).$$

*Then $\preceq_{\mathcal{A},\mathcal{B}}$ is an admissible order on $L([0,1])$.*

The weighted mean provides a particular way to obtain admissible orders on $L([0,1])$. The definition is as follows (see [46]):

$$K_\alpha(u,v) = (1-\alpha)\cdot u + \alpha \cdot v s. \text{ with } \alpha \in [0,1].$$

This operator can be interpreted as the $\alpha$-quantile of a probability distribution uniformly distributed on the interval $[u,v]$. Applying Proposition 1 to the aggregation operators $K_\alpha$ and $K_\beta$ with $\alpha \neq \beta$, the admissible order $\preceq_{K_\alpha,K_\beta}$ is obtained. For the sake of simplicity, it is denoted $\preceq_{\alpha,\beta}$.

Particular cases of admissible orders obtained by the weighted mean are the lexicographical orders of type one and two and the Xu and Yager order. Note that $\preceq_{Lex1}\equiv\preceq_{0,1}$, $\preceq_{Lex2}\equiv\preceq_{1,0}$ and $\preceq_{XY}\equiv\preceq_{1/2,\beta}$ for $\beta$ any value in $(1/2,1]$ (see [38]).

Any order $\preceq_o$ defined over $L([0,1])$ induces an order over $IVFS(X)$ that is the content relation derived from this order ($\subseteq_o$). The following result formalized what said above and is straightforward to prove it.

**Proposition 2.** *Let $\preceq_o$ be an interval order in $L([0,1])$ and $A$ and $B$ in $IVFS(X)$. Then $\subseteq_o$ defined as*

$$A \subseteq_o B \text{ iff } A(x) \preceq_o B(x), \forall x \in X.$$

*is a partial order in $IVFS(X)$.*

**Example 2.** *If we consider the IVFSs A, B, and C represented in Figure 3, it is clear that $A, B \subseteq_{ID} C$ and therefore they are included in C with respect to any of the orders recalled in Definition 1. We also have that $A \subseteq_{Lo} B$ but $A \not\subseteq_{ID} B$. Thus, A is included in B for any considered order except for the interval dominance. Finally, we can say that neither B nor C are included in A for any order.*

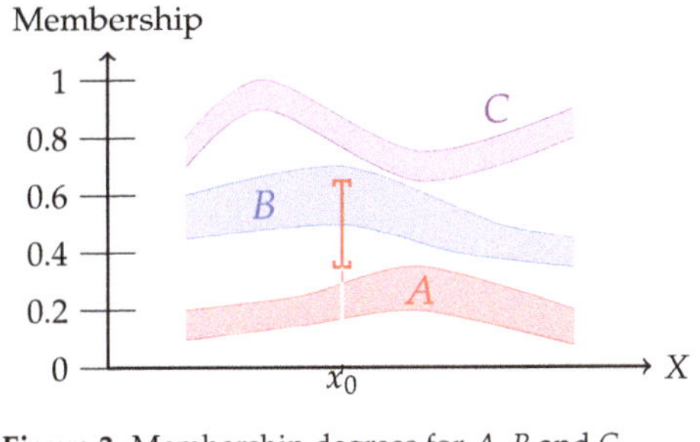


**Figure 3.** Membership degrees for $A$, $B$ and $C$.

*On the other hand, $\subseteq_o$ is not a total order in general. Consider for instance the lattice order $\subseteq_{Lo}$ and the IVFSs given in Figure 3, A and B are incomparable. In fact, we can obtain incomparable IVFSs even in the case we are considering a total order.*

### *2.2. Embedding*

Another important partial order on $IVFS(X)$ could be defined as follows.

**Definition 3.** *Let $\subseteq$ be the usual inclusion between intervals and A and B in $IVFS(X)$. It is said that A is embedded in B, and it is denoted as $A \sqsubseteq B$ if and only if $A(x) \subseteq B(x), \forall x \in X$.*

The following example shows the idea behind this definition.

**Example 3.** *If we consider the IVFSs A and B represented in Figure 4, we have that A is embedded in B, since $A(x) \subseteq B(x), \forall x \in X$.*

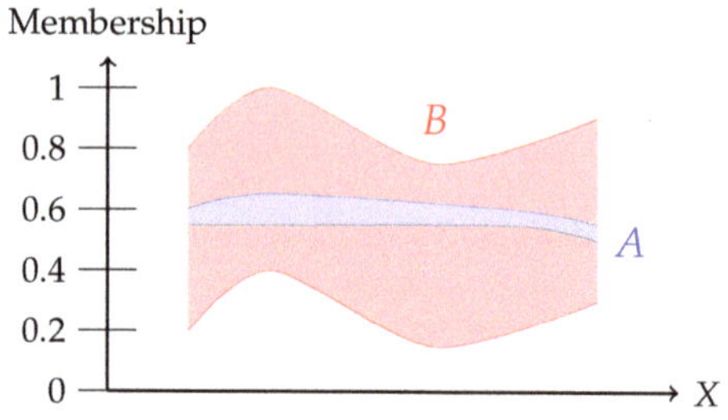


**Figure 4.** $A$ is embedded in $B$.

Nor is it a total order, as the following example shows.

**Example 4.** *Consider the two IVFSs drawn in Figure 5.*

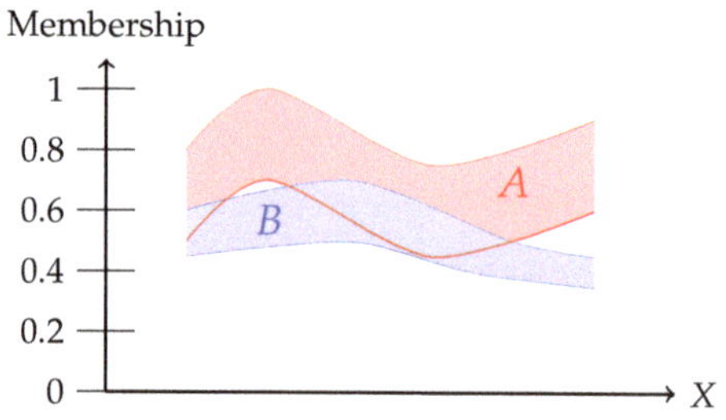


**Figure 5.** Not embedded IVFSs.

*It is clear that $A$ is not embedded in $B$ and $B$ is not embedded in $A$.*

### 2.3. Intersection

There are different proposals to formalize the notion of intersection in the literature. We will base our definition on the idea that the intersection of two sets is the greatest set contained in both departing sets. Since this definition is based on contents, we will obtain a different definition of intersection for each order we consider in $IVFS(X)$ as explained in [35,47].

**Definition 4.** *Let $A$, $B$ be two interval-valued fuzzy sets in $X$ and let $\preceq_o$ be an order relation between intervals in $L([0,1])$. We define the o-intersection of $A$ and $B$, and we denote it by $A \cap_o B$ as the greatest interval-valued fuzzy set such that $A \cap_o B \subseteq_o A$ and $A \cap_o B \subseteq_o B$.*

For any two interval orders $\preceq_{o_1}$ and $\preceq_{o_2}$ in $L([0,1])$ such that $a \preceq_{o_1} b$ implies that $a \preceq_{o_2} b, \forall a, b \in L([0,1])$, we have that $A \cap_{o_1} B \subseteq_{o_2} A \cap_{o_2} B$ for any $A, B \in IVFS(X)$.

Considering the connection among the orders in Definition 1, we next discuss the definition of intersection obtained for each of them. If possible, we describe general behaviours.

**Proposition 3.** *([35]) Let $A$, $B$ be two sets in $IVFS(X)$. Then, for any $x \in X$, we have that:*

- *Interval dominance:* $A \cap_{ID} B(x) = [\min\{\underline{A(x)}, \underline{B(x)}\}, \min\{\underline{A(x)}, \underline{B(x)}\}]$.
- *Lattice order:* $A \cap_{Lo} B(x) = [\min\{\underline{A(x)}, \underline{B(x)}\}, \min\{\overline{A(x)}, \overline{B(x)}\}]$.
- *Lexicographical order of type 1:* $A \cap_{Lex1} B(x) = \begin{cases} A(x) & \text{if } A(x) \preceq_{Lex1} B(x) \\ B(x) & \text{if } B(x) \preceq_{Lex1} A(x) \end{cases}$
- *Lexicographical order of type 2:* $A \cap_{Lex2} B(x) = \begin{cases} A(x) & \text{if } A(x) \preceq_{Lex2} B(x) \\ B(x) & \text{if } B(x) \preceq_{Lex2} A(x) \end{cases}$
- *Xu and Yager order:* $A \cap_{XY} B(x) = \begin{cases} A(x) & \text{if } A(x) \preceq_{XY} B(x) \\ B(x) & \text{if } B(x) \preceq_{XY} A(x) \end{cases}$

- *Maximim order:* $A \cap_{Mm} B(x) = [\min\{\underline{A(x)}, \underline{B(x)}\}, v]$ *for* $v$ *any number in the interval* $[\min\{\underline{A(x)}, \underline{B(x)}\}, 1]$.
- *Maximax order:* $A \cap_{MM} B(x) = [u, \min\{\overline{A(x)}, \overline{B(x)}\}]$ *for* $u$ *any number in the interval* $[0, \min\{\overline{A(x)}, \overline{B(x)}\}]$.
- *Hurwicz order:* $A \cap_{H(\alpha)} B(x) = \left[u, \frac{k-\alpha \cdot u}{1-\alpha}\right]$ *for* $k = \min\{\alpha \cdot \underline{A(x)} + (1-\alpha) \cdot \overline{A(x)}, \alpha \cdot \underline{B(x)} + (1-\alpha) \cdot \overline{B(x)}\}$ *and* $u$ *any value in the interval* $\left[\max\{0, \frac{k-(1-\alpha)}{\alpha}\}, k\right]$.
- *Weak order:* $A \cap_{wo} B(x) = [u, v]$ *for* $u$ *any value in the interval* $[0, \min\{\overline{A(x)}, \overline{B(x)}\}]$ *and* $v$ *any value in the interval* $[\min\{\overline{A(x)}, \overline{B(x)} 1]$.

Lexicographical orders and the Xu and Yager order are particular cases of admissible orders, and the associated intersections are obtained as a consequence of the following result.

**Corollary 1.** *Let* $A$ *and* $B \in FS(X)$ *and denote* $A'$ *and* $B'$ *as the previous fuzzy sets written in terms of IVFSs:* $A'(x) = [A(x), A(x)]$ *and* $B'(x) = [B(x), B(x)]$ *for every* $x \in X$. *Let* $\preceq_0$ *be the interval dominance, the lattice order, the lexicographical order of types 1 and 2, or the Xu and Yager order. Then* $A' \cap_0 B' = (A \cap B)'$, *where* $\cap$ *denotes the classical intersection of fuzzy sets based on the minimum.*

**Proof.** Fix $x \in X$. Denote $A(x) = a$ and $B(x) = b$, then $A'(x) = [a, a]$ and $B'(x) = [b, b]$.

On the one hand it holds that $(A \cap B)(x) = \min(A(x), B(x))$. Therefore, $(A \cap B)'(x) = [\min(a, b), \min(a, b)]$.

On the other hand, $\underline{A'(x)} = \overline{A'(x)} = a$ and $\underline{B'(x)} = \overline{B'(x)} = b$ and it follows from Proposition 3 that $A' \cap_0 B'(x) = [\min(a, b), \min(a, b)]$. □

**Proposition 4.** *([35]) Let* $\mathcal{A}$ *and* $\mathcal{B} : [0,1]^2 \to [0,1]$ *be two continuous aggregation functions such that* $\forall (u, v), (u', v') \in K([0,1])$, $\mathcal{A}(u, v) = \mathcal{A}(u', v')$ *and* $\mathcal{B}(u, v) = \mathcal{B}(u', v')$ *hold simultaneously if and only if* $(u, v) = (u', v')$. *Let* $\preceq_{\mathcal{A},\mathcal{B}}$ *be the admissible order on* $L([0,1])$ *induced by these aggregation functions. For all* $A, B \in IVFS(X)$, *the* $\mathcal{A}, \mathcal{B}$*-intersection of* $A$ *and* $B$ *is the interval-valued fuzzy set defined by:*

$$A \cap_{\mathcal{A},\mathcal{B}} B(x) = \begin{cases} A(x) & \text{if } A(x) \preceq_{\mathcal{A},\mathcal{B}} B(x) \\ B(x) & \text{if } B(x) \preceq_{\mathcal{A},\mathcal{B}} A(x) \end{cases}$$

Taking into account Proposition 3, we can see that in some cases the intersection is not uniquely defined for the four last relations. Moreover, for the first one, we have that the intersection of two IVFSs is just a fuzzy set. This is summarized in Table 2.

**Table 2.** Uniqueness of the intersection of IVFSs.

| Interval Order | Is the Intersection Unique? | Is the Intersection an IVFS? |
|---|---|---|
| Interval dominance | ✓ | ✗ |
| Lattice order | ✓ | ✓ |
| Lex. order type 1 | ✓ | ✓ |
| Lex. order type 2 | ✓ | ✓ |
| Xu and Yager order | ✓ | ✓ |
| Maximim order | ✗ | |
| Maximax order | ✗ | |
| Hurwicz order | ✗ | |
| Weak order | ✗ | |

The following examples can help to clarify the previous remarks.

**Example 5.** *Let us consider the case* $X = \{x\}$ *and the interval-valued fuzzy sets A and B defined by* $A(x) = [0.4, 0.8]$ *and* $B(x) = [0.2, 0.9]$. *Then, the intersection for the four last orders is given in Table 3 and shown in Figure 6.*

**Table 3.** No uniqueness of the intersection of IVFSs for some orders.

| $A \cap_{MM} B(x)$ | $A \cap_{Mm} B(x)$ | $A \cap_{H(1/2)} B(x)$ | $A \cap_{wo} B(x)$ |
|---|---|---|---|
| $[u, 0.8]$ | $[0.2, v]$ | $[u, 1.1 - u]$ | $[u, v]$ |
| $u \in [0, 0.8]$ | $v \in [0.2, 1]$ | $u \in [0.1, 0.55]$ | $u \in [0, 0.8]$<br>$v \in [0.8, 1]$ |

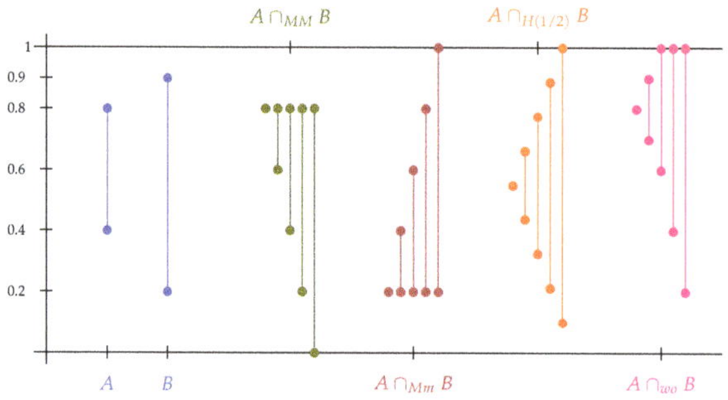


**Figure 6.** Intersection for different orders.

*If we consider the orders that lead to a unique set as intersection, we obtain an interval uniquely defined, as we can see in Table 4. A graphical representation is shown in Figure 7.*

**Table 4.** Uniqueness of the intersection of IVFSs for some orders.

| $A \cap_{ID} B$ | $A \cap_{Lo} B$ | $A \cap_{Lex1} B$ | $A \cap_{Lex2} B$ | $A \cap_{XY} B$ |
|---|---|---|---|---|
| 0.2 | $[0.2, 0.8]$ | $[0.2, 0.9]$ | $[0.4, 0.8]$ | $[0.2, 0.9]$ |

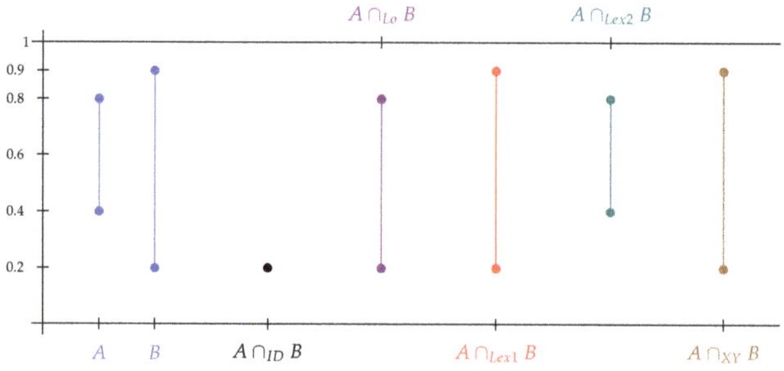


**Figure 7.** Intersection w.r.t. $ID$, $Lo$, $Lex1$, $Lex2$ and $XY$.

*It is clear that the intersection is just a fuzzy set for the case of the interval dominance.*

*In this case the lexicographical order of type 1 and the Xu and Yager order provide the same intersection, but, of course, this does not hold in general. For example, if we consider C an IVFS such that* $C(x) = [0.4, 0.5]$, *we have that* $B \preceq_{Lex1} C$ *and* $C \preceq_{XY} B$ *and therefore* $B \cap_{Lex1} C = B \neq B \cap_{XY} C = C$.

*This example also emphasises that the intersection depends on the considered order, which is logical from the considered definition.*

### 2.4. Union

In this subsection, we reproduce for the union the discussion included in the previous one concerning intersection.

We assume that the union of two sets is the smallest set that contains both sets. Then we have a different definition of union for every order we consider in $L([0,1])$.

**Definition 5.** *Let $A, B \in IVFS(X)$ and let $\preceq_o$ be an order in $L([0,1])$. The o-union of A and B, denoted $A \cup_o B$, is the smallest interval-valued fuzzy set such that $A \subseteq_o A \cup_o B$ and $B \subseteq_o A \cup_o B$.*

Thus, for the orders where the intersection is unique, we have that:

**Proposition 5.** *([35]) Let A, B be two sets in $IVFS(X)$. Then, for any $x \in X$, we have that:*

- *Interval dominance:* $A \cup_{ID} B(x) = [\max\{\overline{A(x)}, \overline{B(x)}\}, \max\{\overline{A(x)}, \overline{B(x)}\}]$.
- *Lattice order:* $A \cup_{Lo} B(x) = [\max\{\underline{A(x)}, \underline{B(x)}\}, \max\{\overline{A(x)}, \overline{B(x)}\}]$.
- *Lexicographical order of type 1:* $A \cup_{Lex1} B(x) = \begin{cases} B(x) & \text{if } A(x) \preceq_{Lex1} B(x) \\ A(x) & \text{if } B(x) \preceq_{Lex1} A(x) \end{cases}$
- *Lexicographical order of type 2:* $A \cup_{Lex2} B(x) = \begin{cases} B(x) & \text{if } A(x) \preceq_{Lex2} B(x) \\ A(x) & \text{if } B(x) \preceq_{Lex2} A(x) \end{cases}$
- *Xu and Yager order:* $A \cup_{XY} B(x) = \begin{cases} B(x) & \text{if } A(x) \preceq_{XY} B(x) \\ A(x) & \text{if } B(x) \preceq_{XY} A(x) \end{cases}$

We can prove again that the considered definition preserves the classical definition of union for the particular case of fuzzy sets.

**Corollary 2.** *Let $A, B \in FS(X)$ and denote $A'$ and $B'$ the previous fuzzy sets written in terms of IVFSs: $A'(x) = [A(x), A(x)]$ and $B'(x) = [B(x), B(x)]$ for every $x \in X$. Let $\preceq_0$ be the interval dominance, the lattice order, the lexicographical order of types 1 and 2 or the Xu and Yager order. Then $A' \cup_0 B' = (A \cup B)'$, where $\cup$ denotes the classical union of fuzzy sets based on the maximum.*

**Proof.** Fix $x \in X$. Denote $A(x) = a$ and $B(x) = b$, then $A'(x) = [a,a]$ and $B'(x) = [b,b]$.

On the one hand, it holds that $(A \cup B)(x) = \max(A(x), B(x))$. Therefore, $(A \cup B)'(x) = [\max(a,b), \max(a,b)]$.

On the other hand, $\underline{A'(x)} = \overline{A'(x)} = a$ and $\underline{B'(x)} = \overline{B'(x)} = b$, and it follows from Proposition 5 that $A' \cup_0 B'(x) = [\max(a,b), \max(a,b)]$. □

The lexicographical orders and the Xu and Yager order are particular cases of admissible order, and the union can also be obtained as a consequence of the following general result.

**Proposition 6.** *([35]) Let $\mathcal{A}, \mathcal{B} : [0,1]^2 \to [0,1]$ be two continuous aggregation functions, such that $\forall (u,v), (u',v') \in K([0,1])$, $\mathcal{A}(u,v) = \mathcal{A}(u',v')$ and $\mathcal{B}(u,v) = \mathcal{B}(u',v')$ hold simultaneously if and only if $(u,v) = (u',v')$. Let $\preceq_{\mathcal{A},\mathcal{B}}$ be the admissible order on $L([0,1])$ induced by them. For any $A, B \in IVFS(X)$, the $\mathcal{A},\mathcal{B}$-union of A and B is the IVFS defined by:*

$$A \cup_{\mathcal{A},\mathcal{B}} B(x) = \begin{cases} B(x) & \text{if } A(x) \preceq_{\mathcal{A},\mathcal{B}} B(x) \\ A(x) & \text{if } B(x) \preceq_{\mathcal{A},\mathcal{B}} A(x) \end{cases}$$

**Example 6.** *Let the universe $X = \{x\}$ and let $A, B, C \in IVFS(X)$ such that $A(x) = [0.4, 0.8]$, $B(x) = [0.2, 0.6]$ and $C(x) = [0.3, 0.9]$.*

- *The ID-union of A and B is the IVFS $A \cup_{ID} B(x) = [0.8, 0.8]$ and the ID-union of A and C is the IVFS $A \cup_{ID} C(x) = [0.9, 0.9]$. Figure 8 provides a graphical representation.*

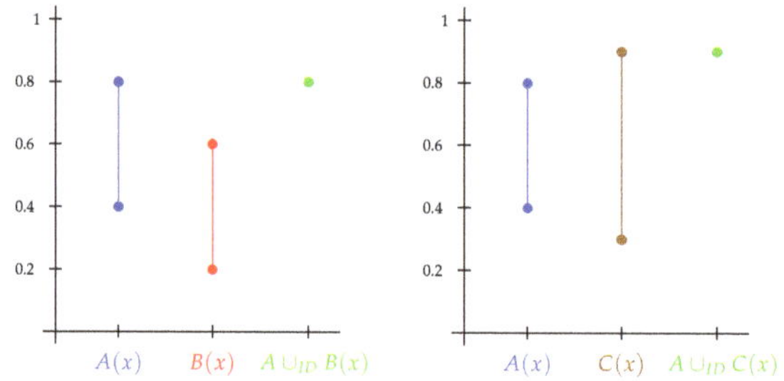


**Figure 8.** $ID$-union.

*It is clear that* $A \cap_{ID} B \neq A$ *and* $A \cap_{ID} B \neq B$.

- *The Lo-union of A and B is the IVFS* $A \cup_{Lo} B(x) = [0.2, 0.6]$ *and the Lo-union of A and C is the IVFS* $A \cup_{Lo} C(x) = [0.3, 0.8]$.
  *As we can see in Figure 9,* $A \cup_{Lo} B = B$, *but* $A \cup_{Lo} C \neq A$ *and* $A \cup_{ID} C \neq C$.

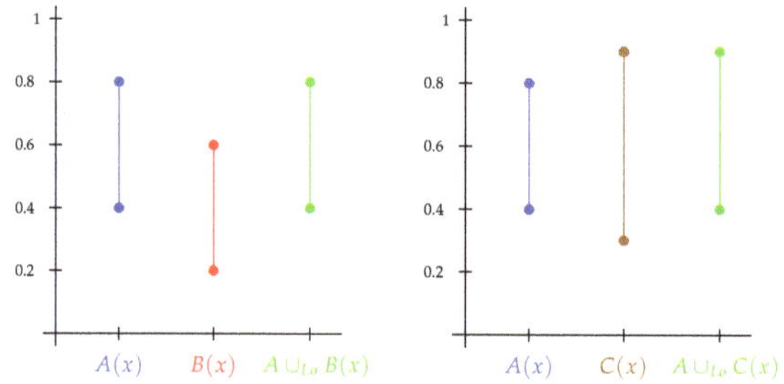


**Figure 9.** $Lo$-union.

- *The* $Lex1$*-union of A and B is the IVFS* $A \cup_{Lex1} B(x) = [0.4, 0.8]$ *and the* $Lex1$*-union of A and C is the IVFS* $A \cup_{Lex1} C(x) = [0.4, 0.8]$. *Thus, in this case,* $A \cup_{Lex1} B = A \cup_{Lex1} C = A$.
- *The* $Lex2$*-union of A and B is the IVFS* $A \cup_{Lex2} B(x) = [0.4, 0.8]$. *and the* $Lex2$*-union of A and C is the IVFS* $A \cup_{Lex2} C(x) = [0.3, 0.9]$. *Thus, in this case,* $A \cup_{Lex2} B = A$ *and* $A \cup_{Lex2} C = C$.
- *The XY-union of A and B is the IVFS* $A \cup_{XY} B(x) = [0.4, 0.8]$, *and the XY-union of A and C is the IVFS* $A \cup_{XY} C(x) = [0.3, 0.9]$. *Thus, again* $A \cup_{XY} B = A$ *and* $A \cup_{XY} C = C$ *and the union obtained for* $Lex2$ *and for XY are the same.*
  *However, this is not true in general, since* $Lex2$ *compares the right endpoint of intervals and XY the sum of both endpoints. For instance, if we consider* $D(x) = [0.2, 0.9]$, *the XY-union of A and D is the IVFS* $A \cup_{XY} D(x) = [0.4, 0.8]$, *but their* $Lex2$*-union is* $A \cup_{Lex2} D(x) = [0.2, 0.9]$, *as we can see in Figure 10.*

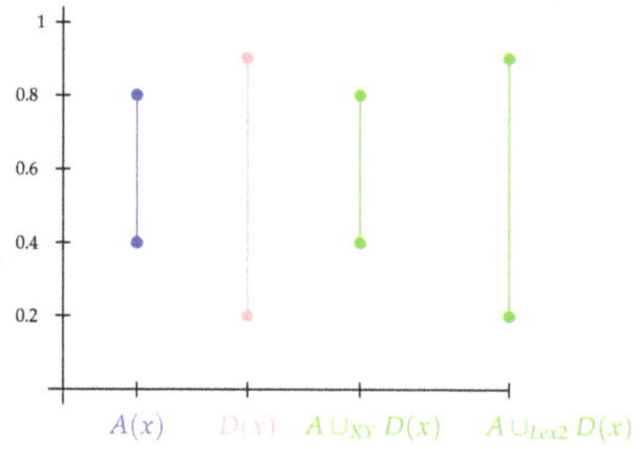


**Figure 10.** $Lex2$-union is different from $XY$-union.

Once we have introduced the basic concepts about different operations between IVFSs, we can start to think about the necessary requirements of a measure to be an appropriate way to quantify the difference between two IVFSs.

## 3. How to Compare Two Interval-Valued Fuzzy Sets?

As we described in detail at the Introduction, most of the measures of comparison between IVFSs found in the literature provide a unique number as final outcome. Such a simplification necessarily means a loss of information. In order to keep the idea underlying IVFSs, the result of the comparison should not be an isolated value. This section contains a discussion on the definition of measure of comparison between IVFSs. We consider the axioms that should be included in the definition.

There are some natural requirements that underlie the idea of difference between two interval-valued fuzzy sets:

REQ1 Non-negativity;
REQ2 Symmetry;
REQ3 It becomes zero when the two sets are "equal";
REQ4 It takes into account the uncertainty associated to the width of the intervals;
REQ5 It decreases when the sets are closer.

Requirements REQ1, REQ2, and REQ3 are the usual ones for comparing any set, in particular fuzzy sets. Requirement REQ4 gives expression to the idea that the width of the interval is important. Requirement REQ5 describes the idea of proximity, and, as will later be shown, it will be the characteristic axiom.

Let us study them in detail one by one.

### *3.1. Non-Negativity*

Initially, the degree of difference between two IVFSs $A$ and $B$ is a closed interval in $\mathbb{R}$, that is, $D(A,B) \in L(\mathbb{R})$.

It seems natural to require that $D(A,B)$ is "non-negative". This is required as follows:

$$\underline{D(A,B)} \geq 0$$

and therefore the codomain of $D$ is not $L(\mathbb{R})$ in general, but $L([0,\infty))$.

We can relate this requirement to the different orders among intervals as follows:

**Proposition 7.** *Let $D$ be a map from $IVFS(X) \times IVFS(X)$ into $L(\mathbb{R})$ and consider the orders recalled in subsection. For the statements*

i) $\underline{D(A,B)} \geq 0$
ii) $[0,0] \preceq_{ID} D(A,B)$
iii) $[0,0] \preceq_{Lo} D(A,B)$
iv) $[0,0] \preceq_{Lex1} D(A,B)$
v) $[0,0] \preceq_{Lex2} D(A,B)$
vi) $[0,0] \preceq_{XY} D(A,B)$
vii) $[0,0] \preceq_{Mm} D(A,B)$
viii) $[0,0] \preceq_{MM} D(A,B)$
ix) $[0,0] \preceq_{H(\alpha)} D(A,B)$
x) $[0,0] \preceq_{wo} D(A,B)$
xi) $[0,0] \preceq_{AB} D(A,B)$
xii) $[0,0] \preceq_{to} D(A,B)$

*we have that*

$$i) \Leftrightarrow ii) \Leftrightarrow iii) \Leftrightarrow iv) \Leftrightarrow vii)$$

*and $i)$ implies $v)$, $vi)$, $viii)$, $ix)$, $x)$, $xi)$, and $xii)$, but the converse is not true in general.*

**Proof.** Since $0 \leq \underline{D(A,B)}$ implies that $[0,0] \preceq_{ID} D(A,B)$, by the relationship among the orders, we have the implication from $i)$ to any other statement. For the last two cases we have used that $[0,0] \preceq_{Lo} D(A,B)$ implies $[0,0] \preceq_{to} D(A,B)$ and therefore, in particular, $[0,0] \preceq_{\mathcal{AB}} D(A,B)$.

On the other hand, if $[0,0] \preceq_{Mm} D(A,B)$, then $0 \leq \underline{D(A,B)}$. Again taking into account the relationship among the orders, we have $vii) \Rightarrow i)$ and therefore also $ii), iii)$ and $iv)$ implies $i)$.

However, we have that $[0,0] \preceq_{Lex2} [-0.1,0.2]$, $[0,0] \preceq_{XY} [-0.1,0.2]$, $[0,0] \preceq_{MM} [-0.1,0.2]$, $[0,0] \preceq_{H(\alpha)} [-0.1,b]$ for any $b \geq \frac{0.1\alpha}{1-\alpha}$ and $[0,0] \preceq_{wo} [-0.1,0.2]$, but $0 \not\leq -0.1$, so the converse implication is not fulfilled for these orders.

Since the lexicographical order of type 2 is an example of an $\mathcal{AB}$-admissible order, the converse implication is not fulfilled for this particular case of admissible order and, in general, for admissible orders. □

This proposition is represented in Figure 11.

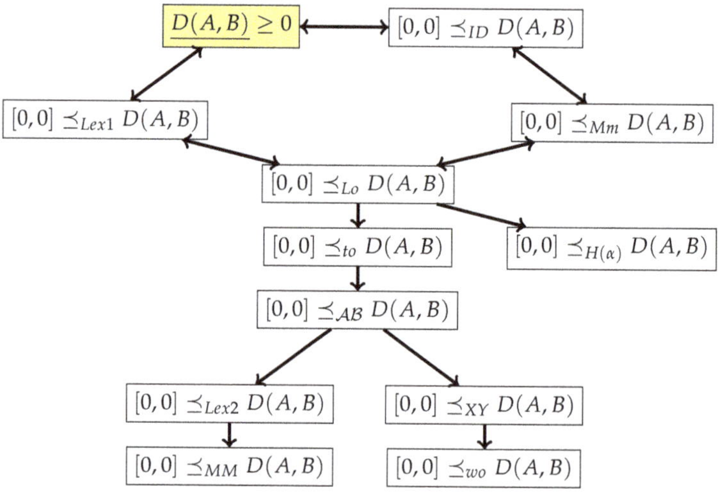


**Figure 11.** Non-negativity for different orders.

Thus, the first axiom for a measure of difference could be described as follows, depending on the order considered:

A1 $[0,0] \preceq_o D(A,B)$

On the other hand, if we suppose that the measure is upper bounded, then we can normalize it and work in the same spaces where the IVFSs are defined, that is,

$$D(A,B) \in L(\mathbb{R}) \overset{\text{Axiom 1}}{\Rightarrow} D(A,B) \in L([0,\infty)) \overset{\text{Upper bound}}{\Rightarrow} D(A,B) \in L([0,1]))$$

We will therefore assume that every measure of the difference, $D$, will have $L([0,1])$ as codomain:

$$\begin{array}{rccc} D: & IVFS(X) \times IVFS(X) & \longrightarrow & L([0,1]) \\ & (A,B) & \rightsquigarrow & [\underline{D(A,B)}, \overline{D(A,B)}] \end{array}$$

### 3.2. Symmetry

Taking into account the previous comments, the logical way to formalize symmetry is:

A2 $D(A,B) =_o D(B,A)$

Thus, this axiom depends on the considered order and so the measure of difference. If the relation is antisymmetric, it is clear that this requirement means that both intervals are exactly the same. Thus, this happens for any real order (reflexive, antisymmetri,c and transitive), but this is not true for any relation considered in Definition 1.

**Proposition 8.** *Let $D$ be a map from $IVFS(X) \times IVFS(X)$ into $L([0,1])$. For the statements*

i) $\underline{D(A,B)} = \underline{D(B,A)}$ *and* $\overline{D(A,B)} = \overline{D(B,A)}$
ii) $D(A,B) =_{ID} D(B,A)$
iii) $D(A,B) =_{Lo} D(B,A)$
iv) $D(A,B) =_{Lex1} D(B,A)$
v) $D(A,B) =_{Lex2} D(B,A)$
vi) $D(A,B) =_{XY} D(B,A)$
vii) $D(A,B) =_{Mm} D(B,A)$
viii) $D(A,B) =_{MM} D(B,A)$
ix) $D(A,B) =_{H(\alpha)} D(B,A)$
x) $D(A,B) =_{wo} D(B,A)$
xi) $D(A,B) =_{\mathcal{AB}} D(B,A)$

*we have that*

$$i) \Leftrightarrow iii) \Leftrightarrow iv) \Leftrightarrow v) \Leftrightarrow vi) \Leftrightarrow xi)$$

*and they imply $vii)$, $viii)$, $ix)$, and $x)$, but the converse is not true in general. Moreover, $ii)$ implies $i)$, but the converse is not true.*

**Proof.** The equivalences are clear by antisymmetry and reflexivity of the involved orders (see Table 1).

For the maximax order, we have that $[0.2, 0.6] =_{MM} [0.3, 0.6]$. Thus, $viii) \not\Rightarrow i)$. Since $viii) \Rightarrow x)$, we also have proven that $x) \not\Rightarrow i)$.

We also have that $[0.2, 0.5] =_{Mm} [0.2, 0.6]$ and so $vii) \not\Rightarrow i)$.

Furthermore, $[0.2, 0.6] =_{H(1/2)} [0.3, 0.5]$ and then $ix) \not\Rightarrow i)$.

Finally, $ii) \Rightarrow i)$ follows from the antisymmetry of interval dominance. Furthermore, $i) \not\Rightarrow ii)$ follows from the fact that interval dominance is not reflexive. □

This proposition is represented in Figure 12.

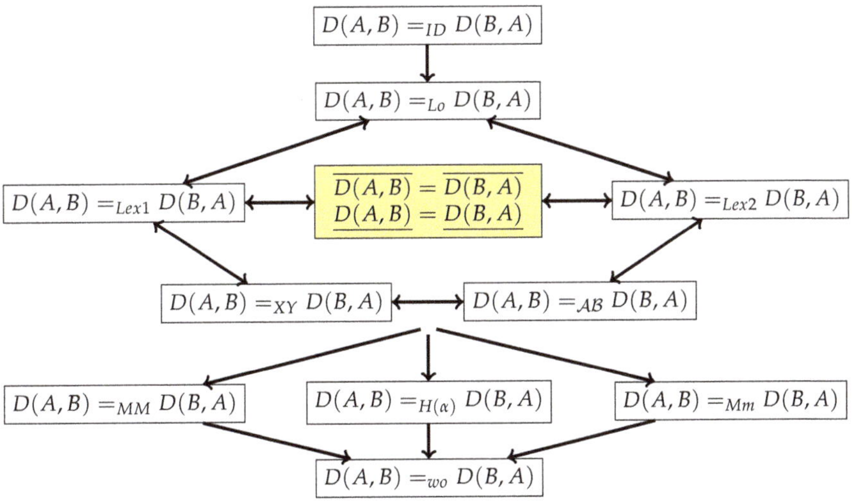


**Figure 12.** Symmetry for different orders.

The fact that the equality given by the interval dominance is stronger that Condition i) in the previous proposition should not be undervalued. If we study in depth Condition ii), we find the following lemma.

**Lemma 1.** *Let $D$ be a map from $IVFS(X) \times IVFS(X)$ into $L([0,1])$. Then $D$ is symmetric with respect to the interval dominance if and only if its image is a number in $[0,1]$; that is, if and only if $D(A,B)$ is a unique value (not an interval) for any $A, B \in IVFS(X)$.*

**Proof.** Take $A, B$ any two $IVFS(X)$ and call $D(A,B) = [\underline{d}, \overline{d}]$ and $D(B,A) = [\underline{d'}, \overline{d'}]$. In order for $D(A,B) =_{ID} D(B,A)$, it should hold both $D(A,B) \leq_{ID} D(B,A)$ and $D(B,A) \leq_{ID} D(A,B)$.

Now $D(A,B) \leq_{ID} D(B,A)$ holds if and only if $\overline{d} \leq \underline{d'}$ and $D(B,A) \leq_{ID} D(A,B)$ holds if and only if $\overline{d'} \leq \underline{d}$.

So $\overline{d} \leq \underline{d'} \leq \overline{d'} \leq \underline{d}$. Then, necessarily, $\overline{d} = \underline{d'} = \overline{d'} = \underline{d}$ and $D(A,B)$ becomes a number for any pair of IVFSs, $A$ and $B$, considered. □

Thus, if interval dominance is the interval order chosen the measure of difference between any two IVFSs has to be a unique value. However, this is counterintuitive as we have explained above: the measure that quantifies how different two IVFSs are should be an interval. This is again an argument to consider orders in $L([0,1])$ and not any relation in Definition 1.

### 3.3. Zero Difference

Another condition that is assumed to be logical when measuring differences is that the difference should be zero only when the two sets compared are the same. The original idea would be that

$$D(A,B) =_0 [0,0] \qquad \text{if and only if} \qquad A = B\,, \text{ for } A, B \in IVFS(X)\,,$$

where the equality between IVFSs is the classical equality between sets: $A(x) = B(x)$ for all $x \in X$. However, according to the epistemic interpretation, two elements with the same interval membership need not necessarily have the same (unknown) actual real-valued membership degree, as we can see with the following example.

**Example 7.** *If we consider the IVFSs $A$ and $B$ represented in Figure 13, where the known membership degree is represented as well as the (unknown) real membership function, we have that*

$$A(x) = B(x), \forall x \in X \text{ but } A \neq B$$

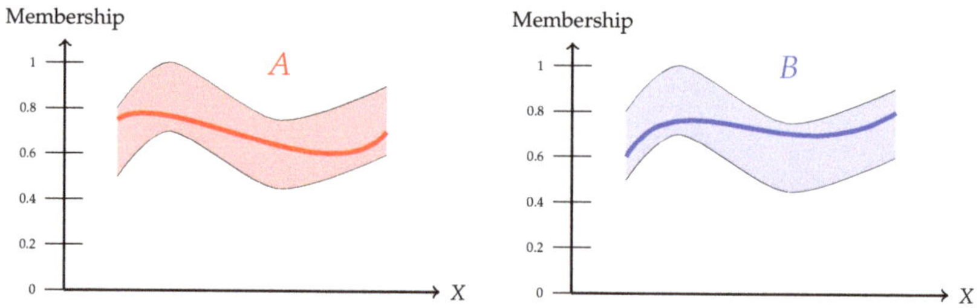


**Figure 13.** Comparing the real value of the sets.

Thus, under the epistemic viewpoint, two IVFSs are only considered to be truly equal if they necessarily take the same value, i.e., if they are the same fuzzy set. So the difference between two IVFSs has to be zero if and only if both are fuzzy sets and they are equal. The axiom can be written as follows:

A3 $\quad D(A,B) =_o [0,0]$ iff $A, B \in FS(X)$ and $A = B$.

The equality above depends on the order considered between IVFSs. Next, we study for which of the orders considered in Definition 1 the previous equality actually means $D(A,B) = [0,0]$.

**Proposition 9.** *Let $D$ be a map from $IVFS(X) \times IVFS(X)$ into $L([0,1])$, and consider the orders recalled in Section 2.1. For the statements*

i) $\underline{D(A,B)} = \overline{D(A,B)} = 0$
ii) $D(A,B) =_{ID} [0,0]$
iii) $D(A,B) =_{Lo} [0,0]$
iv) $D(A,B) =_{Lex1} [0,0]$
v) $D(A,B) =_{Lex2} [0,0]$
vi) $D(A,B) =_{XY} [0,0]$
vii) $D(A,B) =_{Mm} [0,0]$
viii) $D(A,B) =_{MM} [0,0]$
ix) $D(A,B) =_{H(\alpha)} [0,0]$
x) $D(A,B) =_{wo} [0,0]$
xi) $D(A,B) =_{AB} [0,0]$

*we have that*

$$i) \Leftrightarrow ii) \Leftrightarrow iii) \Leftrightarrow iv) \Leftrightarrow v) \Leftrightarrow vi) \Leftrightarrow viii) \Leftrightarrow ix) \Leftrightarrow xi)$$

*and they imply vii) , and x) but the converse is not true in general.*

**Proof.** By simplicity, we denote $D(A,B)$ by $a = [\underline{a}, \overline{a}]$.

By antisymmetry, it is clear that

$$i) \Leftrightarrow ii) \Leftrightarrow iii) \Leftrightarrow iv) \Leftrightarrow v) \Leftrightarrow vi) \Leftrightarrow xi)$$

From Proposition 8 we know that $\underline{a} = \overline{a} = 0$ implies that $[\underline{a}, \overline{a}] =_{Mm} [0,0]$, $[\underline{a}, \overline{a}] =_{MM} [0,0]$, $[\underline{a}, \overline{a}] =_{H(\alpha)} [0,0]$, and $[\underline{a}, \overline{a}] =_{wo} [0,0]$. Conversely, it is trivial to prove that $[\underline{a}, \overline{a}] =_{MM} [0,0]$ is only fulfilled if both numbers are zero. Moreover, if $[\underline{a}, \overline{a}] =_{H(\alpha)} [0,0]$, we obtain that $\alpha\underline{a} + (1-\alpha)\overline{a} = 0$, and this is equivalent to saying that $\underline{a} = \overline{a} = 0$. So the equivalence is also obtained for the maximax and the Hurwicz orders.

However, $[0,0] =_{Mm} [0,0.2]$ and $[0,0] =_{wo} [0,0.2]$, and therefore the reciprocal is not fulfilled for these orders. □

The above proposition is summarized in Figure 14.

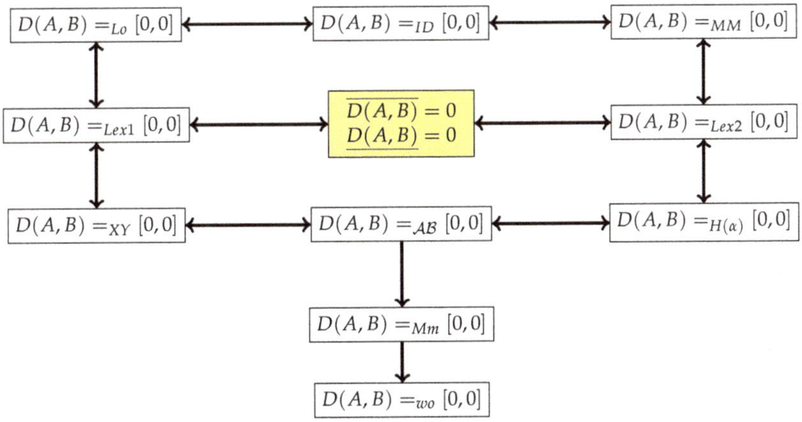


**Figure 14.** Zero difference for different orders.

### 3.4. The Importance of the Widths of the Intervals

The previous axioms are just direct translations from the ones considered in the context of fuzzy sets, and they will be the same even in the case the measure of difference is just a number. However, now we have to take into account the widths of the intervals. The next requirement is considered in order to deal properly with this uncertainty.

First of all, we will consider the following example for understanding the idea we are trying to formalise.

**Example 8.** *Let A, B, and C be the IVFSs represented in Figure 15.*

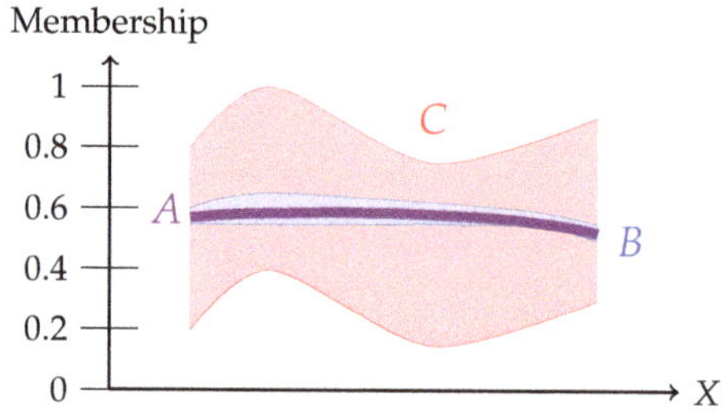


**Figure 15.** Related IVFSs with different widths.

*It is clear that B is embedded in C, which is denoted by* $B \sqsubseteq C$*, since*

$$B(x) \subseteq C(x), \forall x \in X$$

*As a consequence, for any third IVFS, A, the uncertainty when comparing A and C must be greater than the uncertainty when comparing A and B. Thus, for instance, in Figure 15 we are almost sure that A and B are very similar and the difference should be something similar to* $D(A,B) \approx [0, 0.1]$*, but when we compare A to C, we find that they could be equal but they could also be very different. A reasonable value could be* $D(A,C) \approx [0, 0.7]$.

Thus, bigger uncertainty of the IVFS $C$ with respect to $B$ should mean bigger uncertainty in the measure of difference between $C$ and a third IVFS $A$ than between $B$ and $A$. This implies that $D(A,C)$ is a more imprecise interval than $D(A,B)$, which is equivalent to saying that

$$D(A,B) \subseteq D(A,C)$$

In general, this requirement can be formalized as follows:

A4 If $B \sqsubseteq C$, then $D(A,B) \subseteq D(A,C)$

Here no order between intervals is involved, just the classical content between intervals, and therefore, no study about the behaviour of the different interval orders is required.

**Corollary 3.** *Let* $D : IVFS(X) \times IVFS(X) \to L([0,1])$ *satisfying Axioms A2, A3, and A4. If A and B are two IVFSs satisfying that* $A(x) \cap B(x) \neq \emptyset$ *for every* $x \in X$*, then it holds that* $\underline{D(A,B)} = 0$.

**Proof.** Assume that $\alpha_x \in A(x) \cap B(x)$. Now take $C$ the IVFS $C(x) = [\alpha_x, \alpha_x]$ for every $x \in X$; that is, $C$ is a fuzzy set. According to Axiom A3, $D(C,C) = [0,0]$. On the other hand, $C \sqsubseteq A$ and $C \sqsubseteq B$; therefore, applying Axiom A4 twice and the symmetry (Axiom A2), we have that $0 = \underline{D(C,C)} \geq \underline{D(A,C)} \geq \underline{D(A,B)}$. □

Moreover, this axiom ensures that the imprecision about the difference between any two interval-valued fuzzy sets is greater than or equal to the one between the two furthest apart (fuzzy) sets in $A$ and $B$, as we can see from the following corollary.

**Corollary 4.** *Let $D : IVFS(X) \times IVFS(X) \to L([0,1])$ satisfying Axioms A2 and A4. Let $A$ and $B$ be any two IVFSs defined as $A(x) = [\underline{A(x)}, \overline{A(x)}]$ and $B(x) = [\underline{B(x)}, \overline{B(x)}]$ for any $x \in X$. If we consider the fuzzy set $\overline{A}$ and $\underline{B}$ defined as $\overline{A}(x) = \overline{A(x)}$ and $\underline{B}(x) = \underline{B(x)}$ for any $x \in X$, we have that $D(\overline{A}, \underline{B}) \subseteq D(A, B)$.*

**Proof.** It is clear that $\overline{A} \sqsubseteq A$ and $\underline{B} \sqsubseteq B$. Then, $D(\overline{A}, \underline{B}) \subseteq D(\overline{A}, B) = D(B, \overline{A}) \subseteq D(B, A) = D(A, B)$, by applying twice Axioms A2 and A4. □

### 3.5. Proximity

It is clear that every definition of the measure of the comparison between two IVFSs should satisfy the four properties REQ1–REQ4 and, from the previous subsection, they could be immediately rewritten as:

A1. $[0,0] \preceq_o D(A,B)$.
A2. $D(A,B) =_o D(B,A)$.
A3. $D(A,B) =_o [0,0]$ iff $A, B \in FS(X)$ and $A = B$.
A4. If $B \sqsubseteq C$, then $D(A,B) \subseteq D(A,C)$.

However, they should also fulfil the fifth natural requirement:

REQ5 For closer IVFs, the difference measure has to be smaller.

The four previous conditions are commonly accepted in the literature in the sense that most authors formalise them in the same way. However, for this fifth condition, multiple (quite different) alternatives have been proposed, leading to different definitions such us the notion of distance, divergence, or dissimilarity. We next revisit the three definitions and discuss about their convenience to model differences among IVFSs quantified by means of intervals.

#### 3.5.1. Distances

In the definition of distance, Requirement REQ5 is formalized by means of the well-known triangular inequality:

DIST.A5 Triangular inequality: $D(A,B) \preceq_o D(A,C) + D(C,B)$.

which is here adapted to the case of IVFSs and orders in $L([0,1])$.

However, this could be a little difficult to justify if we consider that the interval which represents the membership function is just an imprecise information, as we can see with the following example.

**Example 9.** *Let us consider a referential $X$ and $A(x) = [0, 0.2]$, $B(x) = [0.8, 1]$ and $C = [0.1, 0.9]$ for any $x \in X$.*

*These sets are graphically represented in Figure 16.*

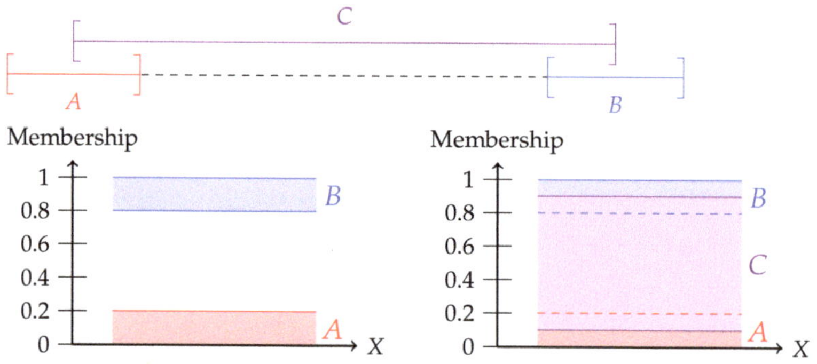


**Figure 16.** Distance between different IVFSs.

*Then $D(A,B)$ seems to be greater than 0, since they have never the same membership function. However, $A(x)$ and $C(x)$ could have the same value, and, from Corollary 3, we have that $D(A,C) = [0,\alpha]$. The same happens for $B$ and $C$, since $B(x) \cap C(x) \neq \emptyset, \forall x \in X$. Thus, $D(C,B) = [0,\beta]$ and $D(A,C) + D(C,B) = [0,\gamma]$, and it is not greater than or equal to $D(A,B)$ for the lattice order or the lexicographical order type 1.*

**Remark 1.** *About distances we have yet another problem apart from the previous counterintuitive example we considered for the triangular inequality. This is that if we deal with fuzzy sets, the distance is a number. If we deal with IVFSs, the distance should be an interval. In both cases, we can define the sum. However, what happens if we consider lattice-valued fuzzy sets, for instance, if the membership function assumes values that are colours? In that case, the definition of the sum is not so immediate. However, if we just consider an order, as we do for dissimilarities and divergences, we can deal with this concept in a more general environment.*

3.5.2. Divergences

Trying to avoid the previous problems, the fifth axiom should not be based on a triangular inequality, since we are not trying to measure a distance, but the difference between two sets, which is not exactly the same in general. Now we are not studying if they are "close" or "far", but if they are similar in the sense of the description of the set.

In this sense, the fifth requirement expresses the idea that the more similar the sets are, the lower the measure of difference between them. For fuzzy sets this condition can be formalised as follows:

$$D(A \cap C, B \cap C) \leq D(A,B) \text{ and } D(A \cup C, B \cup C) \leq D(A,B)$$

and the result is the notion of divergence between fuzzy sets. Montes et al. [8] showed that this is a good option to compare fuzzy sets. Then, it is natural to think of translating this property into the context of IVFSs and that it could perform well in this context too. Consider that the value of the divergence is now an interval and taking into account any order in $L([0,1])$, Axiom 5 could be as follows:

DIV.A5 $\quad D(A \cap_o C, B \cap_o C) \preceq_o D(A,B)$ and $D(A \cup_o C, B \cup_o C) \preceq_o D(A,B)$.

It is again based on the interval order chosen, but if we consider a total order, we are requiring these conditions for any $A, B, C \in IVFS(X)$. For the particular case of the lattice order, we can obtain some nice properties that follow from this condition.

**Proposition 10.** *Let $D : IVFS(X) \times IVFS(X) \to L([0,1])$ satisfy Axiom DIV.A5. Then, $\forall A, B \in IVFS(X)$*

1. $D(A \cap_{Lo} B, B) \preceq_{Lo} D(A, A \cup_{Lo} B)$.
2. $D(A \cap_{Lo} B, B) \preceq_{Lo} D(A,B)$.
3. $D(A \cap_{Lo} B, B) \preceq_{Lo} D(A \cap_{Lo} B, A \cup_{Lo} B)$.

4. $D(B, A \cup_{Lo} B) \preceq_{Lo} D(A \cap_{Lo} B, A \cup_{Lo} B)$.

**Proof.** 1. Call $E = A$, $F = A \cup_{Lo} B$ and $G = B$ and apply the first part of Axiom DIV.A5:

$$D(E \cap_{Lo} G, F \cap_{Lo} G) \preceq_{Lo} D(E, F),$$

since $F \cap_{Lo} G = (A \cup_{Lo} B) \cap_{Lo} B = B$, the inequality follows.

2. It Follows from the first part of Axiom DIV.A5 taking $C = B$.
3. Call $E = A \cap_{Lo} B$, $F = A \cup_{Lo} B$ and $G = B$. Applying the first condition in Axiom DIV.A5:

$$D(E \cap_{Lo} G, F \cap_{Lo} G) \preceq_{Lo} D(E, F),$$

since $F \cap_{Lo} G = (A \cup_{Lo} B) \cap_{Lo} B = B$, the inequality follows.

4. It follows from applying the second condition in Axiom DIV.A5 to the sets $E = A \cap_{Lo} B$ and $F = A \cup_{Lo} B$ and $G = B$.

□

In general, for any order $\preceq_o$, we obtain the following definition of divergence in $IVFS(X)$.

**Definition 6.** *A mapping* $D : IVFS(X) \times IVFS(X) \to L([0,1])$ *satisfying*

*A1.* $[0,0] \preceq_o D(A,B)$
*A2.* $D(A,B) =_o D(B,A)$
*A3.* $D(A,B) =_o [0,0]$ *iff* $A, B \in FS(X)$ *and* $A = B$
*A4.* *If* $B \sqsubseteq C$*, then* $D(A,B) \subseteq D(A,C)$
*DIV.A5* $D(A \cap_o C, B \cap_o C) \preceq_o D(A,B)$ *and* $D(A \cup_o C, B \cup_o C) \preceq_o D(A,B)$.

*is a divergence between IVFSs.*

For the particular case of the lattice order or the interval dominance, we can obtain divergences between fuzzy sets from divergences between IVFSs as follows.

**Proposition 11.** *Let* $\preceq_0$ *be the lattice order or the interval dominance and let* $\mathcal{A}$ *be an aggregation function.*
*Let D be a divergence measure in* $IVFS(X)$*. Then the map* $D|_{FS(X)} : FS(X) \times FS(X) \to FS(X)$*, defined as*

$$D|_{FS(X)}(A,B) = \mathcal{A}(\underline{D(A',B')}, \overline{D(A',B')})$$

*with* $A'(x) = [A(x), A(x)]$ *and* $B'(x) = [B(x), B(x)]$ *for any* $x \in X$ *is a divergence measure in* $FS(X)$.

**Proof.** We have to check that $D|_{FS(X)}$ satisfies the three conditions of the definition of divergence between fuzzy sets.

1. Symmetry of $D|_{FS(X)}$ follows from symmetry of $D$.
2. Since $D(A', A') = [0,0]$ for every $A \in FS(X)$, also $\mathcal{A}(\underline{D(A',A')}, \overline{D(A',A')}) = \mathcal{A}(0,0) = 0$.
3. Let us first prove that $D|_{FS(X)}(A \cap C, B \cap C) \leq D|_{FS(X)}(A,B)$ for any $C \in FS(X)$. By definition, $D|_{FS(X)}(A,B) = \mathcal{A}(\underline{D(A',B')}, \overline{D(A',B')})$ and

$$D|_{FS(X)}(A \cap C, B \cap C) = \mathcal{A}(\underline{D((A \cap C)', (B \cap C)')}, \overline{D((A \cap C)', (B \cap C)')}).$$

According to Corollary 1, $A' \cap_0 C' = (A \cap C)' = [\min(a,c), \min(a,c)]$ and $B' \cap_0 C' = (B \cap C)' = [\min(b,c), \min(b,c)]$. Then $D((A \cap C)', (B \cap C)') = D(A' \cap_0 C', B' \cap_0 C') \preceq_0 D(A', B')$, where the inequality follows from Axiom DIV.A5. For the interval dominance order this implies that $\underline{D(A' \cap_0 C', B' \cap_0 C')} \leq \underline{D(A',B')}$ and $\overline{D(A' \cap_0 C', B' \cap_0 C')} \leq \overline{D(A',B')}$ and the proof follows from the monotonicity of $\mathcal{A}$.

The proof for the union is totally analogous.

Therefore, $D|_{FS(X)}$ is a divergence between fuzzy sets. □

The previous results seems to strengthen the idea of divergence. However, for most of the interval orders recalled in Section 2.1, Axiom DIV.A5 is incompatible with the other axioms.

For Axiom A3, we obtain the following lemma, which could be considered as a stronger version of this axiom.

**Lemma 2.** *For every mapping $D : IVFS(X) \times IVFS(X) \to L([0,1])$ satisfying Axioms A3 and DIV.A5 for one of the following interval orders: lattice order, lexicographic order of type 1 or type 2 or Xu and Yager, it holds that*

$$D(A, A) = [0, 0]$$

*for every $A \in IVFS(X)$.*

**Proof.** Let $A$ be any element in $IVFS(X)$ and let $B$ be the element in $IVFS(X)$ defined as:

$$B(x) = \left[\sup_{x \in X} \overline{A(x)}, \sup_{x \in X} \overline{A(x)}\right]$$

for any $x \in X$.

According to Proposition 3, using the lattice order, any of the lexicographic orders or Xu and Yager order, we get that $A \cap_o B = A$.

Then, for a measure of difference that satisfies Axiom DIV.A5, it holds that

$$D(A, A) = D(A \cap_o B, A \cap_o B) \preceq_O D(B, B)\,.$$

According to Axiom A3, $D(B, B) = [0, 0]$ for any $B$ being a fuzzy set. So we get $D(A, A) \preceq_o [0, 0]$. However, for the interval orders considered above (lattice order, lexicographic orders and Xu and Yager order), the only possibility then is $D(A, A) = [0, 0]$. □

Even if we consider IVFSs from an ontic point of view and we relax Axiom A3, that is, even if we admit $D(A, A) =_o [0, 0]$ for any $A$ as a reasonable property, Axiom A4 forces the difference between any set and its subsets to be zero:

**Corollary 5.** *For any $D : IVFS(X) \times IVFS(X) \to L([0,1])$ satisfying Axioms A2, A3, A4, and DIV.A5 for one of the following interval orders: lattice order, lexicographic order of type 1 or type 2 or Xu and Yager, it holds that:*

$$D(A, B) = [0, 0] \text{ for any IVFSs such that } A \sqsubseteq B\,.$$

**Proof.** To prove this, it suffices to apply Axioms A2 and A4: $D(A, B) \subseteq D(B, B)$. However, as proven in Lemma 2, $D(B, B) = [0, 0]$ and therefore $D(A, B) = [0, 0]$. □

Furthermore, this implies that the difference between any two IVFSs is zero, as we will see now.

**Corollary 6.** *For any $D : IVFS(X) \times IVFS(X) \to L([0,1])$ satisfying Axioms A2, A3, A4, and DIV.A5 for one of the interval orders lattice order, lexicographic order of type 1 or type 2, or Xu and Yager, it holds that:*

$$D(A, B) = [0, 0] \text{ for any } A, B \in IVFS(X).$$

**Proof.** Take $A, B$, and any IVFSs. Since $A \sqsubseteq O_1$, where $O_1(x) = [0, 1], \forall x \in X$, by Axioms A2 and A4, it holds that $D(A, B) \subseteq D(O_1, B)$. However, also $B \sqsubseteq O_1$, then

$D(O_1, B) = [0,0]$ as proven above. Therefore, $D(A, B) \subseteq [0,0]$. Equivalently, $D(A, B) = [0,0]$. □

Thus, if Axiom DIV.A5 is kept and we consider the most common interval orders, including lattice order, a contradiction between Axiom DIV.A5 and the other axioms in the definition of divergence arrives. Even if we admit a weaker version of Axiom 3, the combination of this relaxed version of Axiom 3, Axiom 2, Axiom 4, and Axiom DIV.A5 makes the constant function that assigns to every pair of IVFSs the value $[0,0]$, the only possible measure of difference between IVFSs.

Therefore, the combination of Axioms 2, 3, 4, and DIV.A5 forces the use of interval dominance to compare the intervals. However, interval dominance is not an order, and due to the lack of reflexivity, it also leads to the constant function if we combine it with Axiom 2, as proven in Lemma 1.

By all theses studies, we can conclude that the use of divergences is not appropriate for the case of IVFSs.

#### 3.5.3. Dissimilarities

We have seen that the notion of distance, in particular the triangular inequality, is not appropriate to capture the idea of difference between two IVFSs. However, we find intuitive a property of the type "the closer the sets, the smaller the difference". We have seen that the attempt to formalize "closer" by intersections and unions of IVFSs, that is, by generalizing divergencies to IVFSs leads to incompatibilities among axioms. Then, an alternative way to express the closeness of IVFSs must be considered. Dissimilarities use interval orders to capture the proximity notion: given an interval order and three IVFSs $A, B$, and $C$, $A$ is supposed to be closer to $B$ than to $C$ if $A \subseteq_o B \subseteq_o C$, and since $A$ is closer to $B$ than to $C$ and, on the contrary, $C$ is closer to $B$ than to $A$, the corresponding dissimilarities should be ordered in accordance with this idea of proximity.

A5 If $A \subseteq_o B \subseteq_o C$, then $D(A, B) \preceq_o D(A, C)$ and $D(B, C) \preceq_o D(A, C)$.

With this condition, the definition of dissimilarity between IVFSs would look as follows:

**Definition 7.** *Let $\preceq_o$ be any of the orders recalled in Section 2.1. A mapping $D : IVFS(X) \times IVFS(X) \to L([0,1])$ satisfying*

*A1.* $[0,0] \preceq_o D(A, B)$
*A2.* $D(A, B) =_o D(B, A)$
*A3.* $D(A, B) =_o [0,0]$ *iff* $A, B \in FS(X)$ *and* $A = B$
*A4.* *If* $B \sqsubseteq C$, *then* $D(A, B) \subseteq D(A, C)$
*A5.* *If* $A \subseteq_o B \subseteq_o C$, *then* $D(A, B) \preceq_o D(A, C)$ *and* $D(B, C) \preceq_o D(A, C)$

*is a dissimilarity between IVFSs.*

**Example 10.** • *The map*

$$D_0(A, B) = \begin{cases} [0,0] & \text{if } A, B \in FS(X), A = B, \\ [0,1] & \text{otherwise.} \end{cases}$$

*is a dissimilarity w.r.t. the lattice order since for any $A, B, C \in IVFS(X)$ we have that:*

*A1.* $[0,0] \preceq_{Lo} D_0(A, B)$.
*By definition $0 \leq \underline{D_0(A, B)}$ and $0 \leq \overline{D_0(A, B)}$ for every $A, B \in IVFS(x)$.*

*A2.* $D_0(A, B) =_{Lo} D_0(B, A)$.
*Symmetry also follows immediately from the definition.*

*A3.* $D_0(A, B) =_{Lo} [0,0]$ *iff* $A, B \in FS(X)$ *and* $A = B$.
*As proven in Proposition 8, $D_0(A, B) =_{Lo} [0,0]$ if and only if $D_0(A, B) = [0,0]$. (Remember that this is not always the case. For instance, if we set the Mm-order, the equality $D_0(A, B) =_{Mm} [0,0]$ holds for any $A, B \in IVFS(X)$).*

A4. *If $B \sqsubseteq C$, then $D_0(A,B) \subseteq D_0(A,C)$.*
*If $D_0(A,B)$ takes the value $[0,0]$, it is trivial.*
*If $D_0(A,B)$ takes the value $[0,1]$, this means that either $A$ is not a fuzzy set, or $B$ is not a fuzzy set or both of them are fuzzy sets but they are not equal. In the first case, $D_0(A,C)$ is also $[0,1]$. In the second case, since $B \sqsubseteq C$, $C$ is not a fuzzy set and therefore $D_0(A,C)$ also coincides with $[0,1]$. In the third case, since $B$ is a fuzzy set different from $A$ and $B \sqsubseteq C$, we have that either*

- *$C$ is the same fuzzy set as $B$ and then $A$ and $C$ are two different fuzzy sets and $D_0(A,C)$ is $[0,1]$.*
- *Or $C$ is a proper IVFS containing $B$. Since $C$ is not a fuzzy set, then $D_0(A,C)$ is $[0,1]$.*

A5. *If $A \subseteq_{Lo} B \subseteq_{Lo} C$, then $D_0(A,B) \preceq_{Lo} D_0(A,C)$ and $D_0(B,C) \preceq_{Lo} D_0(A,C)$.*
*If $D_0(A,C)$ is $[0,1]$ the proof is trivial.*
*If $D_0(A,C)$ is $[0,0]$, then $A$ and $C$ are the same fuzzy set. From $A \subseteq_{Lo} B \subseteq_{Lo} C$ we have that then $B$ is the same fuzzy set and the proof is concluded.*

*As a direct consequence of Propositions 7, 8 and 9 $D_0$ also fulfils Axioms A1, A2, A3 and A4 for any $\mathcal{AB}$-order (recall that Axiom A4 does not depend on the order considered). Moreover, Axiom A5 is also fulfilled for any $\mathcal{AB}$-order, by taking into account that $[0,0] \preceq_{\mathcal{AB}} [0,1]$ by the monotonicity of the aggregation functions, and then we could provide a proof similar to the previous one.*
*Thus, $D_0$ is an Lo-dissimilarity and an $\mathcal{AB}$-dissimilarity, and it is called the trivial dissimilarity.*

- *For $X$ a finite set, the dissimilarity induced by a numerical distance:*

$$D_1(A,B) = \frac{1}{|X|}\sum_{x\in X}\left[\inf_{a\in A(x),b\in B(x)} |a-b|, \sup_{a\in A(x),b\in B(x)} |a-b|\right]$$

*is a dissimilarity with respect to the lattice order.*
*Axiom A1: Follows from the fact that $|a-b| \geq 0$ for any two values $a$ and $b \in \mathbb{R}$.*
*Axiom A2: Follows from the symmetry of the absolute value of the difference: $|a-b| = |b-a|$ for any two values $a$ and $b \in \mathbb{R}$.*
*Axiom A3: $D_1(A,B) = [0,0]$ if and only if*

$$\left[\inf_{a\in A(x),b\in B(x)} |a-b|, \sup_{a\in A(x),b\in B(x)} |a-b|\right] = [0,0]$$

*for all $x \in X$. For each $x \in X$, this happens if and only if $|a-b| = 0$ for all $a \in A(x), b \in B(x)$; therefore, if and only if $A(x) = B(x)$ and equal to just one value. If this happens for all $x \in X$, then it is equivalent to $A$ and $B$ being the same fuzzy set.*
*Axiom A4: Assume $B \sqsubseteq C$. We have to prove that $D_1(A,B) \subseteq D_1(A,C)$. It is sufficient to prove that for every $x \in X$ it holds that*

$$\left[\inf_{a\in A(x),b\in B(x)} |a-b|, \sup_{a\in A(x),b\in B(x)} |a-b|\right] \leq \left[\inf_{a\in A(x),c\in C(x)} |a-c|, \sup_{a\in A(x),c\in C(x)} |a-c|\right].$$

*Equivalently, we will prove that*

(I) $\inf_{a\in A(x),c\in C(x)} |a-c| \leq \inf_{a\in A(x),b\in B(x)} |a-b|$.

(II) $\sup_{a\in A(x),b\in B(x)} |a-b| \leq \sup_{a\in A(x),c\in C(x)} |a-c|$.

*Call $A(x) = [\underline{a},\overline{a}]$, $B(x) = [\underline{b},\overline{b}]$ and $C(x) = [\underline{c},\overline{c}]$. Since $B \sqsubseteq C$, it holds that $[\underline{b},\overline{b}] \subseteq [\underline{c},\overline{c}]$. Equivalently, $\underline{c} \leq \underline{b} \leq \overline{b} \leq \overline{c}$.*

(I) *To prove that $\inf_{a\in A(x),c\in C(x)} |a-c| \leq \inf_{a\in A(x),b\in B(x)} |a-b|$, we distinguish three cases:*

- $\overline{a} < \underline{c}$ (then $[\underline{a}, \overline{a}] \cap [\underline{c}, \overline{c}] = \emptyset$).
  In this case
$$\inf_{a\in A(x), c\in C(x)} |a-c| = |\overline{a}-\underline{c}| \leq |\overline{a}-\underline{b}| = \inf_{a\in A(x), b\in B(x)} |a-b|.$$
- $[\underline{a}, \overline{a}] \cap [\underline{c}, \overline{c}] \neq \emptyset$
  In this case
$$\inf_{a\in A(x), c\in C(x)} |a-c| = 0 \leq \inf_{a\in A(x), b\in B(x)} |a-b|.$$
- $\overline{c} < \underline{a}$ (then $[\underline{a}, \overline{a}] \cap [\underline{c}, \overline{c}] = \emptyset$).
  In this case,
$$\inf_{a\in A(x), c\in C(x)} |a-c| = |\overline{c}-\underline{a}| \leq |\overline{b}-\underline{a}| = \inf_{a\in A(x), b\in B(x)} |a-b|.$$

*In any case, (I) follows.*

*In order to prove (II), let us note the following: for any closed intervals* $D = [\underline{d}, \overline{d}]$ *and* $E = [\underline{e}, \overline{e}]$ *in* $\mathbb{R}$ *it holds that*
$$\sup_{d\in D, e\in E} |d-e| = \max\{|\underline{d}-\overline{e}|, |\overline{d}-\underline{e}|\}.$$

*The equality* $|\underline{d}-\overline{e}| = |\overline{d}-\underline{e}|$ *can only hold if* $D = E$. *If this is not the case,* $\max\{|\overline{d}-\underline{e}|, |\overline{e}-\underline{d}|\} = |\underline{d}-\overline{e}| > |\overline{d}-\underline{e}|$ *implies* $\underline{d} < \overline{e}$ *(otherwise* $\overline{d} \geq \underline{d} \geq \overline{e} \geq \underline{e}$ *and* $|\underline{d}-\overline{e}| \leq |\overline{d}-\underline{e}|$. *A contradiction).*

(II) *The proof of* $\sup_{a\in A(x), b\in B(x)} |a-b| \leq \sup_{a\in A(x), c\in C(x)} |a-c|$ *follows from the previous remark.*

- *If* $[\underline{a}, \overline{a}] = [\underline{b}, \overline{b}]$, *then* $[\underline{a}, \overline{a}] \subseteq [\underline{c}, \overline{c}]$ *and*
$$\sup_{a\in A(x), b\in B(x)} |a-b| = |\overline{b}-\underline{b}| \leq \max\{|\overline{b}-\underline{c}|, |\overline{c}-\underline{b}|\} \leq \max\{|\overline{a}-\underline{c}|, |\overline{c}-\underline{a}|\} = \sup_{a\in A(x), c\in C(x)} |a-c|.$$

*Otherwise,*

- *If* $\sup_{a\in A(x), b\in B(x)} |a-b| = |\underline{a}-\overline{b}|$ *then* $\underline{a} < \overline{b} \leq \overline{c}$ *so that*
$$\sup_{a\in A(x), b\in B(x)} |a-b| = |\underline{a}-\overline{b}| \leq |\underline{a}-\overline{c}| \leq \sup_{a\in A(x), c\in C(x)} |a-c|.$$
- *Analogously, if* $\sup_{a\in A(x), b\in B(x)} |a-b| = |\overline{a}-\underline{b}|$ *then* $\underline{c} \leq \underline{b} < \overline{a}$ *so that*
$$\sup_{a\in A(x), b\in B(x)} |a-b| = |\overline{a}-\underline{b}| \leq |\overline{a}-underlinec| \leq \sup_{a\in A(x), c\in C(x)} |a-c|.$$

*Axiom A5: Assume* $A \subseteq_{Lo} B \subseteq_{Lo} C$. *Observe that*
$$D_1(A,B) = \left[\frac{1}{|X|}\sum_{x\in X} \inf_{a\in A(x), b\in B(x)} |a-b|, \frac{1}{|X|}\sum_{x\in X} \sup_{a\in A(x), b\in B(x)} |a-b|\right].$$

*Then, in order to prove that* $D_1(A,B) \preceq_{Lo} D_1(A,C)$, *it suffices to prove that for every* $x \in X$,
$$\inf_{a\in A(x), b\in B(x)} |a-b| \leq \inf_{a\in A(x), c\in C(x)} |a-c| \quad \text{and} \quad \sup_{a\in A(x), b\in B(x)} |a-b| \leq \sup_{a\in A(x), c\in C(x)} |a-c|.$$

*Fix an element* $x \in X$ *and call* $A(x) = [\underline{a}, \overline{a}], B(x) = [\underline{b}, \overline{b}]$ *and* $C(x) = [\underline{c}, \overline{c}]$. *Since* $A \subseteq_{Lo} B \subseteq_{Lo} C$, $\underline{a} \leq \overline{b} \leq \overline{c}$, *so that*

$$\sup_{a \in A(x), b \in B(x)} |a-b| = \overline{b} - \underline{a} \leq \overline{c} - \underline{a} = \sup_{a \in A(x), c \in C(x)} |a-c|.$$

*We now prove* $\inf_{a \in A(x), b \in B(x)} |a-b| \leq \inf_{a \in A(x), c \in C(x)} |a-c|$.

- *if* $\overline{a} \leq \underline{b}$, *then* $\inf_{a \in A(x), b \in B(x)} |a-b| = \underline{b} - \overline{a} \leq \underline{c} - \overline{a} = \inf_{a \in A(x), c \in C(x)} |a-c|$.
- *If* $\overline{a} > \underline{b}$, *then* $\inf_{a \in A(x), b \in B(x)} |a-b| = 0 \leq \inf_{a \in A(x), c \in C(x)} |a-c|$.

*Therefore, in any case,*

$$D_1(A,B) = \frac{1}{|X|} \sum_{x \in X} \left[ \inf_{a \in A(x), b \in B(x)} |a-b|, \sup_{a \in A(x), b \in B(x)} |a-b| \right] \preceq_{Lo}$$

$$\frac{1}{|X|} \sum_{x \in X} \left[ \inf_{a \in A(x), c \in C(x)} |a-c|, \sup_{a \in A(x), c \in C(x)} |a-c| \right] = D_1(A,C).$$

- *For* $X$, *a non-finite set, the previous function may not be a dissimilarity.* *Take* $X = [0,1]$ *and*

$$\begin{aligned} D_1(A,B) &= \frac{1}{|X|} \int_{x \in X} \left[ \inf_{a \in A(x), b \in B(x)} |a-b|, \sup_{a \in A(x), b \in B(x)} |a-b| \right] \\ &= \int_0^1 \left[ \inf_{a \in A(x), b \in B(x)} |a-b|, \sup_{a \in A(x), b \in B(x)} |a-b| \right] \end{aligned}$$

  *Take* $A(x) = [0,0]$ *for* $x \in X$ *and* $B(x) = [0,1]$ *for* $x = \frac{1}{n}$ *and* $B(x) = 0$ *elsewhere. Then,* $\sup_{a \in A(x), b \in B(x)} |a-b| = 1$ *for* $x \in \{\frac{1}{n} | n \in \mathbb{N}\}$ *and* $\sup_{a \in A(x), b \in B(x)} |a-b| = 0$, *elsewhere.*
  *Since* $\sup_{a \in A(x), b \in B(x)} |a-b| = 0$ *almost everywhere,* $\int_{x \in X} \sup_{a \in A(x), b \in B(x)} |a-b| = 0$ *and* $D_1(A,B) = [0,0]$ *despite they are not the same fuzzy set. We have then proven that* $D_1$ *does not satisfy Axiom A3.*
- *Let* $\mathcal{A}$ *and* $\mathcal{B}$ *be two continuous aggregation functions. The dissimilarity induced by a numerical distance:*

$$D_1(A,B) = \frac{1}{|X|} \sum_{x \in X} \left[ \inf_{a \in A(x), b \in B(x)} |a-b|, \sup_{a \in A(x), b \in B(x)} |a-b| \right]$$

  *is NOT necessarily a dissimilarity with respect to the admissible order* $\preceq_{\mathcal{A},\mathcal{B}}$.
  *Take as an example the aggregation functions* $\mathcal{A} = \min$ *and* $\mathcal{B} = \max$. *Consider the universe* $X = \{x\}$ *and the IVFSs* $A(x) = [0.2, 0.8]$, $B(x) = [0.3, 0.6]$ *and* $C(x) = [0.45, 0.55]$. *Then clearly* $A \subseteq_{\mathcal{A},\mathcal{B}} B \subseteq_{\mathcal{A},\mathcal{B}} C$ *but*

$$D_1(A,B) = \left[ \inf_{a \in A(x), b \in B(x)} |a-b|, \sup_{a \in A(x), b \in B(x)} |a-b| \right] = [0, 0.5] \not\preceq_{\mathcal{A},\mathcal{B}}$$

$$[0, 0.35] = \left[ \inf_{a \in A(x), c \in C(x)} |a-c|, \sup_{a \in A(x), c \in C(x)} |a-c| \right] = D_1(A,C).$$

Axiom A5 is a generalization of the condition found in Torres-Manzanera et al. [32]:

TOR.A5 If $A \subseteq_{Lo} B \subseteq_{Lo} C$, then $D(A,B) \preceq_{Lo} D(A,C)$ and $D(B,C) \preceq_{Lo} D(A,C)$.

This is Axiom A5 for the particular case of the lattice order.
Takáč et al. [31] provided a similar condition but only for intervals with the same width.

TAK.A4 If $A \sqsubseteq_{Lo} B \sqsubseteq_{Lo} C$ and $w(A(x)) = w(B(x)) = w(C(x))$ for all $x \in X$, then $D(A,B) \preceq_{Lo} D(A,C)$ and $D(B,C) \preceq_{Lo} D(A,C)$,

where for any $[a,b] \subseteq [0,1]$, $w([a,b])$ is the width of the interval, that is, $w([a,b]) = b - a$.

Despite its similarity to our Axiom A5, we have called it here TAK.A4, since it is the forth axiom in the definition of dissimilarity considered in [31]. These authors do not include any condition similar to Axiom A4 in their definition. For the sake of completeness, we next recall the definition given by Takáč et al.:

**Definition 8.** *[31] Let $\preceq_{Lo}$ be the lattice order. A mapping $D : IVFS(X) \times IVFS(X) \to L([0,1])$ is a dissimilarity measure in $IVFS(X)$ if it satisfies:*

*TAK.A1* $D(A,B) = D(B,A)$;
*TAK.A2* $D(A,B) =_{Lo} [0,0]$ *if and only if* $A = B$ *and* $A, B \in FS(X)$;
*TAK.A3* $D(A,B) =_{Lo} [1,1]$ *if and only if* $A(x), B(x) = 0,0], [1,1]$ *for all* $x \in X$;
*TAK.A4* *If* $A \sqsubseteq_{Lo} A' \sqsubseteq_{Lo} B' \sqsubseteq_{Lo} B$ *and* $w(A(x)) = w(A'(x)) = w(B'(x)) = w(B(x))$ *for all* $x \in X$, *then* $D(A,B) \preceq_{Lo} D(A',B')$.

This definition is clearly less restrictive than Definition 7. Condition TAK.A4 is less restrictive than A5. It neither implies Axiom A4 as we prove next.

**Proposition 12.** *Consider the lattice order.*

- *Axiom A5 implies Condition TAK.A4.*
- *Condition TAK.A4 does not imply Axiom A4, even in the case Conditions TAK.A1, TAK.A2, and TAK.A3 are fulfilled.*
- *Condition TAK.A4 does not imply Axiom A5, even in the case Conditions TAK.A1, TAK.A2, and TAK.A3 are fulfilled.*

**Proof.**
- Condition TAK.A4 is a particular case of Axiom A5, so the implication is immediate.
- Let us now see that Axiom TAK.A4 does not imply Axiom A4. Take $X = \{x\}$. Then the function

$$D(A,B) = \begin{cases} [1,1] & \text{if } \{A(x), B(x)\} = \{[1,1],[0,0]\} \\ [0, w(A)] & \text{if } A(x) = B(x) \\ [0.2, 1] & \text{otherwise.} \end{cases}$$

is a dissimilarity measure in the sense of Takáč et al. In fact, conditions TAK.A1, TAK.A2 and TAK.A3 are satisfied by the definition of $D$. Condition TAK.A4 also holds for the lattice order: we will prove that if $A \sqsubseteq_{Lo} B \sqsubseteq_{Lo} C$ and $w(A(x)) = w(B(x)) = w(C(x))$, then $D(A,B) \preceq_{Lo} D(A,C)$ (the case $D(B,C) \preceq_{Lo} D(A,C)$ being analogous). If $D(A,C) = [1,1]$, then the condition holds trivially. Now assume $D(A,C) \neq [1,1]$; then $A \neq [0,0]$ or $C \neq [1,1]$. If $A = C$, then also $A = B = C$, and the inequality also holds trivially.
If $A \neq C$, then $D(A,C) = [0.2,1]$. If $A = B$, then $D(A,B) = [0, w(A)] \preceq_{Lo} [0.2,1]$ whatever $w(A)$ is. Furthermore, if $A \neq B$, then $D(A,B) = [0.2,1] = D(A,C)$ and the inequality also holds.
However, this function does not satisfy A4. Consider $B(x) = [0.3, 0.4]$ and $C(x) = [0.2, 0.5]$; we have that $B \sqsubseteq C$ and

$$D(B,B) = [0, 0.1] \not\sqsubseteq D(B,C) = [0.2, 1]\,.$$

- Take $X = \{x\}$ and the function $D : IVFS(X) \times IVFS(X) \to L([0,1])$ defined as:

$$D(A,B) = \begin{cases} [0,0] & \text{if } A = B \in FS(X) \\ [1,1] & \text{if } \{A(x), B(x)\} = \{[0,0],[1,1]\} \\ [0.2,0.2] & \text{if } w(A(x)) = w(B(x)), A \neq B \\ [0.4,0.4] & \text{if } w(A(x)) \neq w(B(x)) \end{cases}$$

It is straightforward to check that $D$ satisfies Definition 8 for a dissimilarity. However, it does not satisfy Axiom A5: consider $A = [0.2, 0.3]$, $B = [0.4, 0.6]$ and $C = [0.7, 0.8]$. Then $D(A,B) = [0.4, 0.4] \not\preceq_{Lo} [0.2, 0.2] = D(A,C)$.

□

Condition TAK.A4 is weaker than Condition TOR.A5, even if we also impose the other four axioms we have discussed above, i.e.,

$$A1 + A2 + A3 + A4 + TAK.A4 \not\Rightarrow A5$$

If we take the lattice order as the interval order, even if we combine the previous axioms with Condition TAK.A3, Axiom TOR.A5 is not guaranteed:

$$\left.\begin{array}{l} A1 \\ A2 \\ A3 \\ A4 \\ TAK.A3 \\ TAK.A4 \end{array}\right\} \not\Rightarrow A5$$

as the following example shows.

**Example 11.** *Take* $X = \{x\}$ *and* $D : IVFS(X) \times IVFS(X) \to L([0,1])$ *defined as*

$$D(A,B) = \begin{cases} [0,0] & \text{if } A = B \in FS(X), \\ [1,1] & \text{if } \{A,B\} = \{[0,0],[1,1]\}, \\ [0,1] & \text{if } A = [0,\alpha] \text{ and } B = [\beta,1] \text{ or } B = [0,\alpha] \text{ and } A = [\beta,1] \\ & \text{but } \{A,B\} \neq \{[0,0],[1,1]\}, \\ [0,0.3] & \text{if } 0 \notin A \text{ or } 1 \notin B \text{ (and the opposite: } 0 \notin B \text{ or } 1 \notin A) \\ & \text{and } \max(w(A(x)), w(B(x))) \leq 0.1 \text{ and if} \\ & \{A,B\} \in FS(x), \text{ then } A \neq B \\ [0,0.4] & \text{if } 0 \notin A \text{ or } 1 \notin B \text{ (and the opposite: } 0 \notin B \text{ or } 1 \notin A) \\ & \text{and } \max(w(A(x)), w(B(x))) > 0.1 \end{cases}$$

*It is easy to check that D satisfies conditions A1, A2, A3, A4, and TAK.A3 and TAK.A4. However, it does not satisfy Axiom A5 for the lattice order. It suffices to take* $A = [0.1, 0.2]$, $B = [0.3, 0.6]$ *and* $C = [0.7, 0.8]$. *It holds that* $A \subseteq_{Lo} B \subseteq_{Lo} C$ *but* $D(A,B) = [0, 0.4] \not\preceq_{Lo} [0, 0.3] = D(A,C)$.

Dissimilarities are a frequent tool to compare two sets. However, they are based on a partial order. Thus, in our case, one of the main properties only applies for some of the elements in $IVFS(X)$. This is an important drawback. This also happens for fuzzy sets, where the same problem arises. For IVFSs, we have considered that

$$A \subseteq_o B \Leftrightarrow A(x) \preceq_o B(x), \forall x \in X$$

It is clearly not unique since it depends on the interval order $\preceq_o$ considered to compare IVFSs. However, in all the cases, even for total orders between intervals, we cannot obtain a total order for the family of IVFSs even if the order does not hold just for one point as the following example shows:

**Example 12.** *Let us take* $A(x) \preceq_o B(x), \forall x \in X - \{x_0\}$ *and* $B(x_0) \prec_o A(x_0)$*; that is, A contained in B for all the elements of the universe except for one. An example of A and B in this situation is represented in Figure 17.*

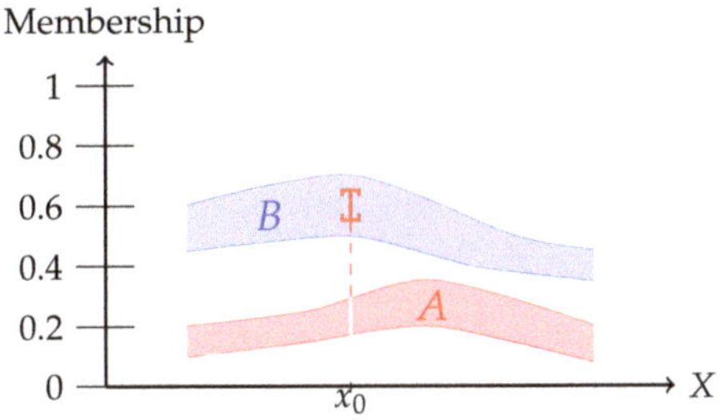


**Figure 17.** $A$ and $B$ are not comparable due to a single element $x_0$.

*Even if the cardinality of X is infinite, one point is enough to state that A and B are incomparable and then Axiom A5 is not applicable.*

*We have that* $A(x) \preceq_{Lo} B(x), \forall x \in X - \{x_0\}$ *but* $A(x_o)$ *and* $B(x_o)$ *are incomparable w.r.t.* $\preceq_{Lo}$ *for instance.*

The previous example shows that although Axiom A5 is without any doubt a desirable property, it is may be too weak in the sense that it only applies to a few number of IVFSs. The departing condition, $A \subseteq_o B \subseteq_o C$ (partial order) is maybe too restrictive and should be relaxed in order to apply conditions $D(A,B) \preceq_o D(A,C)$ and $D(B,C) \preceq_o D(A,C)$ to more triplets $A, B, C$.

Yet, although Axiom A5 has its own drawbacks, it does not lead to counterintuitive situations. We have provided examples that show that this is the case for the fifth axioms associated with distances and divergences, but we have not found any example that leads to a contradiction with the notion of dissimilarity given in Definition 7. Since the characteristic axiom, Axiom A5, is based on a partial order, it is probably not a "definitive Axiom 5", but to the best of our knowledge, it is the best way to formalize the idea of "the closer, the less different" and therefore, the best way to compare two IVFSs would be a measure that satisfies Axioms A1 to A5; that is, the measure provided in Definition 7.

## 4. Concluding Remarks

In this contribution, we have recalled the basic conditions that a function should satisfy in order to formalise the differences between IVFSs. We have seen that interval orders appear naturally in the formalisation of these axioms. Furthermore, since the definitions depend on the interval order, they do not have an associated definitive expression but a different one for each interval order considered.

We have also seen that the fifth logical requirement is the most problematic one to be formalised, and we have discussed the suitability of the most popular proposals: distances, divergences, and dissimilarities. We have shown that distances and divergences lead to unnatural situations, and therefore, they are not appropriate to formalise the differences between IVFSs. However, Axiom A5, the one considered in the definition of dissimilarity, does not lead to counterintuitive situations and therefore is the most appropriate among the three definitions studied in detail. Thus, our main conclusion is that dissimilarities are the only appropriate way to compare two IVFSs by means of an interval. Graphically, this is represented in Figure 18.

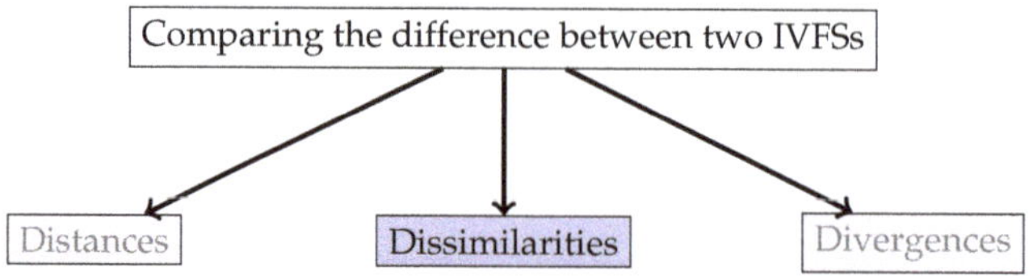


**Figure 18.** Suitable way to compare IVFSs.

Thus, our final recommendation after this study on different possible approaches to compare IVFSs is to consider dissimilarity measures assuming values in $L([0,1])$ where a partial order (lattice order) or a total order (lexicographical orders, Xu-Yager order or, in general, admissible orders) should be considered.

Apart from that, we have compared our proposal for the definition of dissimilarity for $IVFS(X)$ assuming values in $L([0,1])$ with the two other approaches that we have found in the literature.

The drawback of Axiom A5 is the departing point for a future work: it is necessary to find an axiom by collecting the ideas discussed in Example 12, that is, not only for the very restricted content relation in $IVFS(X)$. In a more applied future work, we would like to study the behaviour of this definition in the comparison of two colour images.

**Author Contributions:** Conceptualization, E.T.-M. and S.M.; Formal analysis, S.D.-V., I.D. and S.M.; Funding acquisition, I.D. and S.M.; Investigation, S.D.-V., E.T.-M., I.D. and S.M.; Resources, S.M.; Supervision, I.D. and S.M.; Writing – original draft, S.M.; Writing – review & editing, S.D.-V. and E.T.-M. All authors have read and agreed to the published version of the manuscript.

**Funding:** This research was funded by the Spanish Ministry of Science and Technology under Projects PGC2018-098623-B-I00 (Susana Díaz, Emilio Torres-Manzanera and Susana Montes) and TIN-2017-87600-P (Irene Díaz).

**Institutional Review Board Statement:** Not applicable.

**Informed Consent Statement:** Not applicable.

**Acknowledgments:** The authors acknowledge financial support by the Spanish Ministry of Science and Technology under Projects PGC2018-098623-B-I00 (Susana Díaz, Emilio Torres-Manzanera and Susana Montes) and TIN-2017-87600-P (Irene Díaz).

**Conflicts of Interest:** The authors declare no conflict of interest.

## References

1. Bouchon-Meunier, B.; Rifqi, M.; Bothorel, S. Towards general measures of comparison of objects. *Fuzzy Sets Syst.* **1996**, *84*, 143–153. [CrossRef]
2. Anthony, M.; Hammer, P.L. A boolean measure of similarity. *Discret. Appl. Math.* **2006**, *154*, 2242–2246. [CrossRef]
3. Valverde, L.; Ovchinnikov, S. Representations of T-similarity relations. *Fuzzy Sets Syst.* **2008**, *159*, 211–220. [CrossRef]
4. Wilbik, A.; Keller, J.M. A Fuzzy Measure Similarity Between Sets of Linguistic Summaries. *IEEE Trans. Fuzzy Syst.* **2013**, *21*, 183–189. [CrossRef]
5. Zhang, C.; Fu, H. Similarity measures on three kinds of fuzzy sets. *Pattern Recognit. Lett.* **2006**, *27*, 1307–1317. [CrossRef]
6. Couso, I.; Montes, S. An axiomatic definition of fuzzy divergence measures. *Int. J. Uncertain. Fuzziness Knowl.-Based Syst.* **2008**, *16*, 1–17. [CrossRef]
7. Kobza, V.; Janis, V.; Montes, S. Generalizated local divergence measures. *J. Intell. Fuzzy Syst.* **2017**, *33*, 337–350. [CrossRef]
8. Montes, S.; Couso, I.; Gil, P.; Bertoluzza, C. Divergence measure between fuzzy sets. *Int. J. Approx. Reason.* **2002**, *30*, 91–105. [CrossRef]
9. Zadeh, L. The concept of a linguistic variable and its application to approximate reasoning-I. *Inf. Sci.* **1975**, *8*, 199–249. [CrossRef]
10. Grattan-Guinness, I. Fuzzy Membership Mapped onto Intervals and Many-Valued Quantities. *Math. Log. Q.* **1976**, *22*, 149–160. [CrossRef]
11. Jahn, K. Intervall-wertige Mengen. *Math. Nach.* **1975**, *68*, 115–132. [CrossRef]
12. Sambuc, R. Fonctions and Floues: Application a l'aide au Diagnostic en Pathologie Thyroidienne. Ph.D. Thesis, Faculté de Médecine de Marseille, Marseille, France, 1975.
13. Bustince, H.; Burillo, P. Mathematical analysis of interval-valued fuzzy relations: Application to approximate reasoning. *Fuzzy Sets Syst.* **2000**, *113*, 205–219. [CrossRef]

14. Gorzałczany, M. A method of inference in approximate reasoning based on interval-valued fuzzy sets. *Fuzzy Sets Syst.* **1987**, *21*, 1–17. [CrossRef]
15. Cornelis, C.; Deschrijver, G.; Kerre, E. Implication in intuitionistic fuzzy and interval-valued fuzzy set theory: Construction, classification, application. *Int. J. Approx. Reason.* **2004**, *35*, 55–95. [CrossRef]
16. Turksen, I.; Zhong, Z. An approximate analogical reasoning schema based on similarity measures and interval-valued fuzzy sets. *Fuzzy Sets Syst.* **1990**, *34*, 323–346. [CrossRef]
17. Arefi, M.; Taheri, S. Weighted similarity measure on interval-valued fuzzy sets and its application to pattern recognition. *Iran. J. Fuzzy Syst.* **2014**, *11*, 67–79.
18. Deng, G.; Song, L.; Jiang, Y.; Fu, J. Monotonic Similarity Measures of Interval-Valued Fuzzy Sets and Their Applications. *Int. J. Uncertain. Fuzziness Knowl.-Based Syst.* **2017**, *25*, 515–544. [CrossRef]
19. Pękala, B.; Dyczkowski, K.; Grzegorzewski, P.; Bentkowska, U. Inclusion and similarity measures for interval-valued fuzzy sets based on aggregation and uncertainty assessment. *Inf. Sci.* **2021**, *547*, 1182–1200. [CrossRef]
20. Wu, C.; Luo, P.; Li, Y.; Ren, X. A New Similarity Measure of Interval-Valued Intuitionistic Fuzzy Sets Considering Its Hesitancy Degree and Applications in Expert Systems. *Math. Probl. Eng.* **2014**, *2014*, 359214. [CrossRef]
21. Zhang, H.; Zhang, W.; Mei, C. Entropy of interval-valued fuzzy sets based on distance and its relationship with similarity measure. *Knowl.-Based Syst.* **2009**, *22*, 449–454. [CrossRef]
22. Atanassov, K. Intuitionistic fuzzy sets. *Fuzzy Sets Syst.* **1986**, *20*, 87–96. [CrossRef]
23. Atanassov, K.; Gargov, G. Interval valued intuitionistic fuzzy sets. *Fuzzy Sets Syst.* **1989**, *31*, 343–349. [CrossRef]
24. Deschrijver, G.; Kerre, E. On the relationship between some extensions of fuzzy set theory. *Fuzzy Sets Syst.* **2003**, *133*, 227–235. [CrossRef]
25. Montes, I.; Pal, N.R.; Janis, V.; Montes, S. Divergence measures for intuitionistic fuzzy sets. *IEEE Trans. Fuzzy Syst.* **2015**, *23*, 444–456. [CrossRef]
26. Montes, I.; Janiš, V.; Pal, N.R.; Montes, S. Local divergences for Atanassov intuitionistic fuzzy sets. *IEEE Trans. Fuzzy Syst.* **2016**, *24*, 360–373. [CrossRef]
27. Chen, T.Y. A note on distances between intuitionistic fuzzy sets and/or interval-valued fuzzy sets based on the Hausdorff metric. *Fuzzy Sets Syst.* **2007**, *158*, 2523–2525. [CrossRef]
28. Szmidt, E.; Kacprzyk, J. Intuitionistic fuzzy sets—Two and three term representations in the context of a Hausdorff distance. *Acta Univ. Matthiae Belii Ser. Math.* **2011**, *19*, 53–62.
29. Szmidt, E.; Kacprzyk, J. A Perspective on Differences between Atanassov's Intuitionistic Fuzzy Sets and Interval-Valued Fuzzy Sets. In *Fuzzy Sets, Rough Sets, Multisets and Clustering*; Studies in Computational Intelligence; Torra, V., Dahlbom, A., Narukawa, Y., Eds.; Springer: Berlin/Heidelberg, Germany, 2017; Volume 671, pp. 221–237. [CrossRef]
30. Bustince, H.; Marco-Detchart, C.; Fernandez, J.; Wagner, C.; Garibaldi, J.; Takáč, Z. Similarity between interval-valued fuzzy sets taking into account the width of the intervals and admissible orders. *Fuzzy Sets Syst.* **2020**, *390*, 23–47. [CrossRef]
31. Takáč, Z.; Bustince, H.; Pintor, J.; Marco-Detchart, C.; Couso, I. Width-Based Interval-Valued Distances and Fuzzy Entropies. *IEEE Access* **2019**, *7*, 14044–14057. [CrossRef]
32. Torres-Manzanera, E.; Kral, P.; Janis, V.; Montes, S. Uncertainty-Aware Dissimilarity Measures for Interval-Valued Fuzzy Sets. *Int. J. Uncertain. Fuzziness Knowl.-Based Syst.* **2020**, *28*, 757–768. [CrossRef]
33. Żywica, P.; Stachowiak, A. Uncertainty-aware similarity measures-properties and construction method. In Proceedings of the 11th Conference of the European Society for Fuzzy Logic and Technology (EUSFLAT 2019), Prague, Czech Republic, 9–13 September 2019; pp. 512–519. [CrossRef]
34. Díaz, S.; Díaz, I.; Montes, S. An Interval-Valued Divergence for Interval-Valued Fuzzy Sets. In *Information Processing and Management of Uncertainty in Knowledge-Based Systems*; Lesot, M.J., Vieira, S., Reformat, M.Z., Carvalho, J.P., Wilbik, A., Bouchon-Meunier, B., Yager, R.R., Eds.; Springer International Publishing: Cham, Switzerland, 2020; pp. 241–249.
35. Huidobro, P.; Alonso, P.; Janiš, V.; Montes, S. Convexity and level sets for interval-valued fuzzy sets. *Fuzzy Optim. Decis. Mak.* **2021**, in press.
36. Fishburn, P. *Interval Ordenings*; Wiley: New York, NY, USA, 1987.
37. Goguen, J.A. L-fuzzy sets. *J. Math. Anal. Appl.* **1967**, *18*, 145–174. [CrossRef]
38. Bustince, H.; Fernandez, J.; Kolesárová, A.; Mesiar, R. Generation of linear orders for intervals by means of aggregation functions. *Fuzzy Sets Syst.* **2013**, *220*, 69–77. [CrossRef]
39. Xu, Z.; Yager, R.R. Some geometric aggregation operators based on intuitionistic fuzzy sets. *Int. J. Gen. Syst.* **2006**, *35*, 417–433. [CrossRef]
40. Sniedovich, M. Wald's maximin model: A treasure in disguise! *J. Risk Financ.* **2008**, *9*, 287–291. [CrossRef]
41. Wald, A. Statistical decision functions which minimize the maximum risk. *Ann. Math.* **1945**, *46*, 265–280. [CrossRef]
42. Satia, J.; Lave, R. Markovian decision processes with uncertain transition probabilities. *Oper. Res.* **1973**, *21*, 728–740. [CrossRef]
43. Hurwicz, L. A class of criteria for decision-making under ignorance. *Cowles Com. Discuss. Pap. Stat.* **1951**, *370*, 1–16.
44. Bogart, K.P.; Bonin, J.; Mitas, J. Interval orders based on weak orders. *Discret. Appl. Math.* **1995**, *60*, 93–98. [CrossRef]
45. Mesiar, R.; Komorníková, M. Aggregation Functions on Bounded Posets. In *35 Years of Fuzzy Set Theory. Studies in Fuzziness and Soft Computing*; Cornelis, C., Deschrijver, G., Nachtegael, M., Schockaert, S., Shi, Y., Eds.; Springer: Berlin/Heidelberg, Germany, 2010; Volume 261, pp. 3–17. [CrossRef]

46. Bustince, H.; Calvo, T.; De Baets, B.; Fodor, J.; Mesiar, R.; Montero, J.; Paternain, D.; Pradera, A. A class of aggregation functions encompassing two-dimensional OWA operators. *Inf. Sci.* **2010**, *180*, 1977–1989. [CrossRef]
47. Huidobro, P.; Alonso, P.; Janiš, V.; Montes, S. Orders Preserving Convexity Under Intersections for Interval-Valued Fuzzy Sets. In Proceedings of the International Conference on Information Processing and Management of Uncertainty in Knowledge-Based Systems, Lisbon, Portugal, 15–19 June 2020; Springer: Cham, Switzerland, 2020; pp. 493–505.

*mathematics*

MDPI

*Article*

# New MCDM Algorithms with Linear Diophantine Fuzzy Soft TOPSIS, VIKOR and Aggregation Operators

**Ibtesam Alshammari [1,*], Mani Parimala [2], Cenap Ozel [3,*], Muhammad Riaz [4] and Rania Kammoun [1]**

1 Department of Mathematics, Faculty of Science, University of Hafr Al Batin, Hafar Al-Batin 31991, Saudi Arabia
2 Department of Mathematics, Bannari Amman Institute of Technology, Sathyamangalam 638401, India
3 Department of Mathematics, King Abdulaziz University, Jeddah 21589, Saudi Arabia
4 Department of Mathematics, University of the Punjab, Lahore 54590, Pakistan
* Correspondence: iealshamri@uhb.edu.sa (I.A.); cozel@kau.edu.sa (C.O.)

**Abstract:** In this paper, we focus on several ideas associated with linear Diophantine fuzzy soft sets (LDFSSs) along with its algebraic structure. We provide operations on LDFSSs and their specific features, elaborating them with real-world examples and statistical depictions to construct an inflow of linguistic variables based on linear Diophantine fuzzy soft (LDFSS) information. We offer a study of LDFSSs to the multi-criteria decision-making (MCDM) process of university determination, together with new algorithms and flowcharts. We construct LDFSS-TOPSIS, LDFSS-VIKOR and the LDFSS-AO techniques as robust extensions of TOPSIS (a technique for order preferences through the ideal solution), VIKOR (Vlse Kriterijumska Optimizacija Kompromisno Resenje) and AO (aggregation operator). We use the LDFSS-TOPSIS, LDFSS-VIKOR and LDFSS-AO techniques to solve a real-world agricultural problem. Moreover, we present a small-sized robotic agri-farming to support the proposed technique. A comparison analysis is also performed to examine the symmetry of optimal decision and to analyze the efficiency of the suggested algorithms.

**Keywords:** linear Diophantine fuzzy soft sets; MCDM; linear Diophantine fuzzy soft topological spaces; symmetry; LDFSS-TOPSIS; LDFSS-VIKOR; LDFSS-AO

**MSC:** 03E72; 94D05; 90B50

**Citation:** Alshammari, I.; Parimala, M.; Ozel, C.; Riaz, M.; Kammoun, R. New MCDM Algorithms with Linear Diophantine Fuzzy Soft TOPSIS, VIKOR and Aggregation Operators. *Mathematics* **2022**, *10*, 3080. https://doi.org/10.3390/math10173080

Academic Editor: Michael Voskoglou

Received: 30 July 2022
Accepted: 19 August 2022
Published: 26 August 2022



## 1. Introduction

Many real-world problems have uncertainties, inconsistent information and data are not crisp. Zadeh [1] established the theory known as fuzzy set (FS) to deal with imprecise data. Many generalizations of fuzzy sets can be found which are developed to handle real world problems. Soft sets (SS) are one such extension which are introduced by Molodtsov [2]. This theory can handle uncertain information in a parametric way. Sabir and Naz [3] initiated the concept of soft topological space which presents the parametrized (precomputed) set values of topologies in the primary universe. In addition, Aygunoglu et al. [4] extended soft topological space to fuzzy set theory as fuzzy soft set topology in 2014.

The intuitionistic fuzzy set (IFS) concept was developed by Atanassov [5] in 1986. Like FS theory, IFS can also handle imprecise information with each element in the set having both satisfaction and dis-satisfaction grade values, provided that the addition of these two values should not exceed one. Maji et al. [6] initiated the notion of intuitionistic fuzzy soft sets (IFSSs) by incorporating IFS and SS. Bayramov and Gunduz [7] developed intuitionistic fuzzy soft topological spaces. In their work, they have investigated the properties of continuous mapping. Picture fuzzy set (PFS), [8] introduced by Coung et al. in 2014, is an amplification of Atanassov's IFS theory and Zadeh's FS theory. Picture fuzzy set and its application in decision making [9] is developed to explain when we have the three different answers (yes, avoid, no). Yager [10,11] initiated the concept of Pythagorean fuzzy set (PyFS) and it is introduced to overcome a circumstance when the sum of satisfaction and dis-satisfaction grades exceeds unity. q-rung orthopair fuzzy [12,13] set (q-ROFS) is an extension of PyFS, IFS whose sum of q-power of satisfaction and dis-satisfaction grade values are less than unity. q-rung orthopair picture fuzzy (q-ROPFS) [14] set is an extension of IFS whose sum of q-power of truth, abstinence and false grade values are less than unity. Riaz and Hashmi [15] unravelled the notion of linear Diophantine fuzzy set (LDFS) which is an amplification of fuzzy, intuitionistic fuzzy and picture fuzzy sets provided the addition of $\alpha(x)T(x)$ and $\beta(x)F(x)$ should not exceed unity, where $\alpha, \beta$ are the reference parameters and $T(x), F(x)$ are the true and false membership grades.

Forging decisions is an essential element of our day to day lives. A highly renowned graphic designer, James Victor, was asked by an interviewer what prompted him to be so versatile. He just stated, "I make decisions." Every day, we make millions of micro-choices, from how to communicate with someone, what to focus our energy on, how to respond to an email, what to consume to meet our health needs. One may easily state that becoming a better and faster decision-maker is the quickest way to increase one's productivity levels. Every individual, whether a layperson or a politician, an employer or an employee, a teacher or a student, a mature man or a child, takes hundreds and thousands, if not millions, of decisions in his or her everyday existence. When a newborn is hungry and unable to communicate, she/he determines to uproar in order to attract the concentration of her/his caregiver and to demonstrate that her/his belly is unfilled through body motions.

We are frequently duped by our tumults into making significant judgments in life, only to have regret afterwards. Assume we are faced with a difficult decision that will have a huge influence on our lives. Every time we believe we've made a decision, the other choice pulls us back. We return to where we began: it's a tie. Should we construct ever-more-detailed lists of advantages and disadvantages and seek advice from increasingly more reliable sources? Should we trust our instincts? Another critical difficulty is deciding how to decide. Mathematics, in addition to its numerous applications, assists us in making scientific judgments. Many researchers in [16–20] presented diverse decision making (DM) techniques utilizing the LDFSs with their applications.

MCDM is designed to make a optimum decision by a single person or group with the help of ranking. The application of MCDM can be seen when shortlisting people for interview, selecting new gadgets, machines, etc. The idea of TOPSIS is that the selected alternant should have a minimum distance positive ideal solution (PIS) and far from negative ideal solution (NIS). The TOPSIS method is used in MCDM because it can choose the optimum alternative among a group of alternants based on MCDM. The VIKOR method is proposed to deal with MCDM. This technique is used to choose an optimum alternative among a group of alternatives by ranking them in the presence of conflicting criteria. Like TOPSIS and VIKOR, aggregation operator is used in MCDM and the main aim of the aggregation operator in MCDM is to aggregate the set of inputs to a single number.

Many authors such as Biswas and Sarkar [21], Boran et al. [22], Kumar and Garg [23], Xu and Zhang [24], Xu [25], Hashmi et al. [26], Eraslan and Karaaslan [27], Peng and Yuan [28], Liu et al. [29], and Garg and Arora [30] applied the concept of VIKOR, TOPSIS and aggregation operator methods for DM problems with the extension of FSs and systems in different disciplines such as graph theory, operations research, etc. Khalid Naeem et al. [31] developed the notion of Pythagorean m-polar fuzzy topological space with the TOPSIS approach. Recently, Gul & Aydogdu [32] introduced and studied TOPSIS in an LDF environment.

Mathematics, in addition to its numerous applications, assists us in making scientific judgments. In this paper, we present an LDFSS decision-making application. Assume we have an aggregate LDFSS; therefore, we must select the optimal alternate form of this set. Using the following approach, we may use an MCDM based on LDFSSs.

The objective of the paper is given below:

(i) In IFS, each element has satisfaction and dis-satisfaction grades. Each element in LDFS has three grades namely, satisfaction, dissatisfaction and refusal with reference parameters provided the sum of product of grades with reference parameters does not exceed unity. Few theories such as IFS, PFS, q-ROFS fail to meet their own conditions in few cases.
(ii) Our goal is to initiate the concept of LDFSS to fill the research gap. In addition, we introduce a notion of linear Diophantine fuzzy soft topological space (LDFSTS) whose members in this LDFSTS are LDFSS.
(iii) LDFSSs, which are the inference of LDFSs and FSSs, are a more valuable medium in DM situations since they are dealing with two parametrized families of LDFS. TOPSIS, VIKOR, and AO techniques are also useful for decision-making challenges. In this work, we created three approaches in the Linear Diophantine fuzzy soft environment by integrating the modelling benefits of LDF flexible sets with the advantages of TOPSIS, VIKOR, and AO methods.
(iv) LDFSS-TOPSIS, LDFSS-VIKOR and the LDFSS-aggregation operators method are designed to apply the proposed notion in MCDM. A real life problem is considered and applied these proposed algorithm.

The structure of the manuscript is as follows: fundamental definitions are bestowed in Section 2. The definition of LDFSTS, neighbourhood, interior, closure, frontier and base are introduced and the properties of LDFSTS are studied in Section 3. We explained the importance of the targeted method for MCDM based on LDFSSs via LDFSS-TOPSIS, LDFSS-VIKOR, LDFSS-AO methods with numerical real life examples in Sections 4–6 respectively. The suggested MCDM approaches are exemplified by numerical examples in the previous sections and are supported by comparative analysis with various current techniques in Section 7. Section 8 detailed this lucubration work with a definite conclusion.

## 2. Preliminaries

We review and give some fundamental definitions of the LDFSs in this section.

**Definition 1** ([15]). *An LDFS $\mathfrak{L}_\eth$ is an element on the non-void reference or connecting set $\mathfrak{Q}$ that composes:*

$$\mathfrak{L}_\eth = \{(\xi, \langle \mathfrak{t}_\eth(\xi), \mathfrak{f}_\eth(\xi)\rangle, \langle \alpha_\eth(\xi), \beta_\eth(\xi)\rangle) : \xi \in \mathfrak{Q}\}$$

*where, $\mathfrak{t}_\eth(\xi), \mathfrak{f}_\eth(\xi)$, are the satisfaction grade and dis-satisfaction grade, and $\alpha(\xi), \beta(\xi) \in [0,1]$ are the connecting parameters, respectively. These grades gratify the condition $0 \le \alpha_\eth(\xi)\mathfrak{t}_\eth(\xi) + \beta_\eth(\xi)\mathfrak{f}_\eth(\xi) \le 1$ for all $\xi \in \mathfrak{Q}$ and with $0 \le \alpha(\xi) + \beta(\xi) \le 1$. Comparison parameters aid classifying a specific system. By traversing the tangible meaning of these parameters, we might classify the system. They increase the amount of space available in LDFS for grades and remove restrictions. The rejection (refusal) grade is defined as follows: $\gamma_\eth(\xi)\mathfrak{r}_\eth = (\xi) = 1 - (\alpha_\eth(\xi)\mathfrak{t}_\eth(\xi) + \beta_\eth(\xi)\mathfrak{f}_\eth(\xi))$, where $\gamma_\eth(\xi)$ is the rejection connecting parameter. Linear Diophantine fuzzy number (LDFN) is outlined as $\mathfrak{L}_\eth = (\langle \mathfrak{t}_\eth, \mathfrak{f}_\eth\rangle, \langle \alpha_\eth, \beta_\eth\rangle)$ and with $0 \le \alpha + \beta \le 1$, $0 \le \alpha_\eth \mathfrak{t}_\eth + \beta_\eth \mathfrak{f}_\eth \le 1$.*

**Definition 2** ([15]). *An LDFS on $\mathfrak{Q}$ is called a*

*(i) void LDFS, if $\mathfrak{L}_\eth^0 = \{\xi, (\langle 0,1\rangle, \langle 0,1\rangle) : \xi \in \mathfrak{Q}\}$.*
*(ii) absolute LDFS, if $\mathfrak{L}_\eth^1 = \{\xi, (\langle 1,0\rangle, \langle 1,0\rangle) : \xi \in \mathfrak{Q}\}$.*

**Definition 3** ([15]). *Let $\mathfrak{L}_\eth = (\langle \mathfrak{t}_\eth, \mathfrak{f}_\eth\rangle, \langle \alpha_\eth, \beta_\eth\rangle)$ be an LDFN, then*

1. *the score function (SF) is displayed by $S_{(\mathfrak{L}_\eth)}$ and is depicted as*

$$S_{(\mathfrak{L}_\eth)} = \frac{1}{2}[(\mathfrak{t}_\eth - \mathfrak{f}_\eth) + (\alpha_\eth - \beta_\eth)]$$

*where $S : \mathfrak{L}_\eth(\mathfrak{Q}) \longrightarrow [-1,1]$*

2. *the accuracy function (AF) is displayed by* $A_{(\mathfrak{L}_{\mathfrak{d}})}$ *and is depicted as*

$$A_{(\mathfrak{L}_{\mathfrak{d}})} = \frac{1}{2}[\frac{(\mathfrak{t}_{\mathfrak{d}} + \mathfrak{f}_{\mathfrak{d}})}{2} + (\alpha_{\mathfrak{d}} + \beta_{\mathfrak{d}})]$$

*where* $A : \mathfrak{L}_{\mathfrak{d}}(\Omega) \longrightarrow [0,1]$
*where* $\mathfrak{L}_{\mathfrak{d}}(\Omega)$ *is the foregathering of every LDFNs on* $\Omega$

**Definition 4** ([15]). *Two LDFNs* $\mathfrak{L}_{\mathfrak{d}_1}$ *and* $\mathfrak{L}_{\mathfrak{d}_2}$ *can be comparable using SF and AF. It is defined as follows:*

*(i)* $\mathfrak{L}_{\mathfrak{d}_1} > \mathfrak{L}_{\mathfrak{d}_2}$ *if* $S(\mathfrak{L}_{\mathfrak{d}_1}) > S(\mathfrak{L}_{\mathfrak{d}_2})$
*(ii)* $\mathfrak{L}_{\mathfrak{d}_1} < \mathfrak{L}_{\mathfrak{d}_2}$ *if* $S(\mathfrak{L}_{\mathfrak{d}_1}) < S(\mathfrak{L}_{\mathfrak{d}_2})$
*(iii)* *If* $S(\mathfrak{L}_{\mathfrak{d}_1}) = S(\mathfrak{L}_{\mathfrak{d}_2})$, *then*
  *(a)* $\mathfrak{L}_{\mathfrak{d}_1} > \mathfrak{L}_{\mathfrak{d}_2}$ *if* $A(\mathfrak{L}_{\mathfrak{d}_1}) > A(\mathfrak{L}_{\mathfrak{d}_2})$
  *(b)* $\mathfrak{L}_{\mathfrak{d}_1} < \mathfrak{L}_{\mathfrak{d}_2}$ *if* $A(\mathfrak{L}_{\mathfrak{d}_1}) < A(\mathfrak{L}_{\mathfrak{d}_2})$
  *(c)* $\mathfrak{L}_{\mathfrak{d}_1} = \mathfrak{L}_{\mathfrak{d}_2}$ *if* $A(\mathfrak{L}_{\mathfrak{d}_1}) = A(\mathfrak{L}_{\mathfrak{d}_2})$

**Definition 5** ([15]). *Let* $\mathfrak{L}_{\mathfrak{d}_i} = (\langle \mathfrak{t}_{\mathfrak{d}_i}, \mathfrak{f}_{\mathfrak{d}_i} \rangle, \langle \alpha_{\mathfrak{L}_i}, \beta_{\mathfrak{L}_i} \rangle)$ *for* $i \in \Delta$ *be a convene of LDFNs on* $\Omega$ *and* $\mathfrak{X} > 0$ *then*

*(i)* $\mathfrak{L}^{c}_{\mathfrak{d}_1} = (\langle \mathfrak{f}_{\mathfrak{d}_1}, \mathfrak{t}_{\mathfrak{D}_1} \rangle, \langle \beta_{\mathfrak{L}_1}, \alpha_{\mathfrak{L}_1} \rangle)$
*(ii)* $\mathfrak{L}_{\mathfrak{d}_1} = \mathfrak{L}_{\mathfrak{d}_2} \Leftrightarrow \mathfrak{t}_{\mathfrak{d}_1} = \mathfrak{t}_{\mathfrak{d}_2}, \mathfrak{f}_{\mathfrak{d}_1} = \mathfrak{f}_{\mathfrak{d}_2}, \alpha_{\mathfrak{L}_1} = \alpha_{\mathfrak{L}_2}, \beta_{\mathfrak{L}_1} = \beta_{\mathfrak{L}_2}$
*(iii)* $\mathfrak{L}_{\mathfrak{d}_1} \subseteq \mathfrak{L}_{\mathfrak{d}_2} \Leftrightarrow \mathfrak{t}_{\mathfrak{d}_1} \leq \mathfrak{t}_{\mathfrak{d}_2}, \mathfrak{f}_{\mathfrak{d}_1} \geq \mathfrak{f}_{\mathfrak{d}_2}, \alpha_{\mathfrak{L}_1} \leq \alpha_{\mathfrak{L}_2}, \beta_{\mathfrak{L}_1} \geq \beta_{\mathfrak{L}_2}$
*(iv)* $\mathfrak{L}_{\mathfrak{d}_1} \oplus \mathfrak{L}_{\mathfrak{d}_2} = (\langle \mathfrak{t}_{\mathfrak{d}_1} + \mathfrak{t}_{\mathfrak{d}_2} - \mathfrak{t}_{\mathfrak{d}_1}\mathfrak{t}_{\mathfrak{d}_2}, \mathfrak{f}_{\mathfrak{d}_1}\mathfrak{f}_{\mathfrak{d}_2} \rangle, \langle \alpha_{\mathfrak{L}_1} + \alpha_{\mathfrak{L}_2} - \alpha_{\mathfrak{L}_1}\alpha_{\mathfrak{L}_2}, \beta_{\mathfrak{L}_1}\beta_{\mathfrak{L}_2} \rangle)$
*(v)* $\mathfrak{L}_{\mathfrak{d}_1} \otimes \mathfrak{L}_{\mathfrak{d}_2} = (\langle \mathfrak{t}_{\mathfrak{d}_1}\mathfrak{t}_{\mathfrak{d}_2}, \mathfrak{f}_{\mathfrak{d}_1} + \mathfrak{f}_{\mathfrak{d}_2} - \mathfrak{f}_{\mathfrak{d}_1}\mathfrak{f}_{\mathfrak{d}_2} \rangle, \langle \alpha_{\mathfrak{L}_1}\alpha_{\mathfrak{L}_2}, \beta_{\mathfrak{L}_1} + \beta_{\mathfrak{L}_2} - \beta_{\mathfrak{L}_1}\beta_{\mathfrak{L}_2} \rangle)$
*(vi)* $\mathfrak{L}_{\mathfrak{d}_1} \cup \mathfrak{L}_{\mathfrak{d}_2} = (\langle \mathfrak{t}_{\mathfrak{d}_1} \vee \mathfrak{t}_{\mathfrak{d}_2}, \mathfrak{f}_{\mathfrak{d}_1} \wedge \mathfrak{f}_{\mathfrak{d}_2} \rangle, \langle \alpha_{\mathfrak{L}_1} \vee \alpha_{\mathfrak{L}_2}, \beta_{\mathfrak{L}_1} \wedge \beta_{\mathfrak{L}_2} \rangle)$
*(vii)* $\mathfrak{L}_{\mathfrak{d}_1} \cap \mathfrak{L}_{\mathfrak{d}_2} = (\langle \mathfrak{t}_{\mathfrak{d}_1} \wedge \mathfrak{t}_{\mathfrak{d}_2}, \mathfrak{f}_{\mathfrak{d}_1} \vee \mathfrak{f}_{\mathfrak{d}_2} \rangle, \langle \alpha_{\mathfrak{L}_1} \wedge \alpha_{\mathfrak{L}_2}, \beta_{\mathfrak{L}_1} \vee \beta_{\mathfrak{L}_2} \rangle)$
*(viii)* $\mathfrak{X}\mathfrak{L}_{\mathfrak{d}_1} = (\langle (1 - (1 - \mathfrak{t}_{\mathfrak{d}_1})^{\mathfrak{X}}), \mathfrak{f}^{\mathfrak{X}}_{\mathfrak{d}_1} \rangle, \langle (1 - (1 - {}_{\mathfrak{L}_1})^{\mathfrak{X}}), {}^{\mathfrak{X}}_{\mathfrak{L}_1} \rangle)$
*(ix)* $\mathfrak{L}^{\mathfrak{X}}_{\mathfrak{d}_1} = (\langle \mathfrak{t}^{\mathfrak{X}}_{\mathfrak{d}_1}, (1 - (1 - \mathfrak{f}_{\mathfrak{d}_1})^{\mathfrak{X}}) \rangle, \langle {}^{\mathfrak{X}}_{\mathfrak{L}_1}, (1 - (1 - {}_{\mathfrak{L}_1})^{\mathfrak{X}} \rangle)$

**Example 1.** *Let* $\mathfrak{L}_{\mathfrak{d}_1} = (\langle 0.87, 0.63 \rangle, \langle 0.56, 0.21 \rangle)$ *and* $\mathfrak{L}_{\mathfrak{d}_2} = (\langle 0.76, 0.69 \rangle, \langle 0.41, 0.33 \rangle)$ *be two LDFNs, then*

*(i)* $\mathfrak{L}^{c}_{\mathfrak{d}_1} = (\langle 0.63, 0.87 \rangle, \langle 0.21, 0.56 \rangle)$
*(ii)* $\mathfrak{L}_{\mathfrak{d}_2} \subseteq \mathfrak{L}_{\mathfrak{d}_1}$ *by the Definition 9 (iii)*
*(iii)* $\mathfrak{L}_{\mathfrak{d}_1} \oplus \mathfrak{L}_{\mathfrak{d}_2} = (\langle 0.9688, 0.4347 \rangle, \langle 0.7404, 0.0693 \rangle)$
*(iv)* $\mathfrak{L}_{\mathfrak{d}_1} \otimes \mathfrak{L}_{\mathfrak{d}_2} = (\langle 0.6612, 0.8853 \rangle, \langle 0.2296, 0.4707 \rangle)$
*(v)* $\mathfrak{L}_{\mathfrak{d}_1} \cup \mathfrak{L}_{\mathfrak{d}_2} = (\langle 0.87, 0.63 \rangle, \langle 0.56, 0.21 \rangle) = \mathfrak{L}_{\mathfrak{d}_1}$
*(vi)* $\mathfrak{L}_{\mathfrak{d}_1} \cap \mathfrak{L}_{\mathfrak{d}_2} = (\langle 0.76, 0.69 \rangle, \langle 0.41, 0.33 \rangle) = \mathfrak{L}_{\mathfrak{d}_2}$

*If* $\mathfrak{X} = 0.1$, *then we have the following*
*(vii)* $\mathfrak{X}\mathfrak{L}_{\mathfrak{d}_1} = (\langle 0.1846, 0.9548 \rangle, \langle 0.0788, 0.8555 \rangle)$
*(viii)* $\mathfrak{L}^{\mathfrak{X}}_{\mathfrak{d}_1} = (\langle 0.9862, 0.0946 \rangle, \langle 0.9437, 0.02330 \rangle)$

**Definition 6** ([15]). *The euclidean distance within the two LDFSs* $\mathfrak{L}_{\mathfrak{d}_1}$ *and* $\mathfrak{L}_{\mathfrak{d}_2}$ *is determined as* $\mathfrak{d}(\mathfrak{L}_{\mathfrak{d}_1}, \mathfrak{L}_{\mathfrak{d}_2}) = \frac{1}{2}\sqrt{\{(\mathfrak{t}_{\mathfrak{d}_1} - \mathfrak{t}_{\mathfrak{d}_2})^2 + (\mathfrak{f}_{\mathfrak{d}_1} - \mathfrak{f}_{\mathfrak{d}_2})^2 + ({}_{\mathfrak{d}_1} - {}_{\mathfrak{d}_2})^2 + ({}_{\mathfrak{d}_1} - {}_{\mathfrak{d}_2})^2\}}$.

**Definition 7** ([2]). *Let* $\mathfrak{E}$ *be the set of attributes and* $\mathfrak{X}$ *be a crisp set. The soft set will be outlined as* $(\psi, \mathfrak{A}) = \{(\mathfrak{e}, \psi(\mathfrak{e})) : \mathfrak{e} \in \mathfrak{A}, \psi(\mathfrak{e}) \in \mathfrak{P}(\mathfrak{X})\}$, *where* $\mathfrak{A} \subseteq \mathfrak{E}$ *and* $\psi : \mathfrak{A} \rightarrow \mathfrak{P}(\mathfrak{X})$ *is the set-valued function.* $\psi_{\mathfrak{A}}$ *is the shortest method of writing the couplet* $(\psi, \mathfrak{A})$.

**Definition 8** ([33]). *Let* $\mathfrak{E}$ *be the set of parameters and* $\mathfrak{X}$ *be the universal set. If we suppose that* $\mathfrak{A} \subseteq \mathfrak{E}$ *and* $LDF^{\mathfrak{X}}$ *signifies the assembly of all linear Diophantine fuzzy subsets over* $\mathfrak{X}$ *and* $\kappa : \mathfrak{A} \rightarrow LDF^{\mathfrak{X}}$ *is a mapping. An LDFSS on* $\mathfrak{X}$ *is denoted by* $(\kappa, \mathfrak{A})$ *or* $\kappa_{\mathfrak{A}}$ *and outlined by* $(\kappa, \mathfrak{A}) = \{\mathfrak{e}, (\zeta, \langle \mathfrak{t}_{\kappa_{\mathfrak{A}}}(\zeta), \mathfrak{f}_{\kappa_{\mathfrak{A}}}(\zeta) \rangle, \langle \alpha_{\kappa_{\mathfrak{A}}}(\zeta), \beta_{\kappa_{\mathfrak{A}}}(\zeta) \rangle) : \mathfrak{e} \in \mathfrak{A}, \zeta \in \mathfrak{X}\}$.

*where* $t_{\kappa_{\mathfrak{A}}}, f_{\kappa_{\mathfrak{A}}}, \alpha_{\kappa_{\mathfrak{A}}}, \beta_{\kappa_{\mathfrak{A}}} : \mathfrak{X} \to [0,1]$ *delineates functions called satisfaction function, dis-satisfaction function, satisfaction parameter function, dis-satisfaction parameter function, respectively. Specifically,* $t_{\kappa_{\mathfrak{A}}}(\zeta)$ *denotes the satisfaction grade,* $f_{\kappa_{\mathfrak{A}}}(\zeta)$ *represents the dis-satisfaction grade,* $\alpha_{\kappa_{\mathfrak{A}}}(\zeta)$ *denotes the parameter of the satisfaction grade,* $\beta_{\kappa_{\mathfrak{A}}}(\zeta)$ *represents the parameter of the dis-satisfaction grade of the alternative* $\zeta \in \mathfrak{X}$ *to the set* $(\kappa, \mathfrak{A})$ *having the following constraints:*

- $0 \leq \alpha_{\kappa_{\mathfrak{A}}}(\zeta)t_{\kappa_{\mathfrak{A}}}(\zeta) + \beta_{\kappa_{\mathfrak{A}}}(\zeta)f_{\kappa_{\mathfrak{A}}}(\zeta) \leq 1$ *for all* $\zeta \in \mathfrak{X}$
- $0 \leq \alpha_{\kappa_{\mathfrak{A}}}(\zeta) + \beta_{\kappa_{\mathfrak{A}}}(\zeta) \leq 1$

For each attribute $\mathfrak{e}$, the value $\kappa(\mathfrak{e})$ evinces $\kappa(\mathfrak{e})$-approximate point.

The multitude of all LDFSS over $\mathfrak{X}$ taken from $\mathfrak{E}$ is defined as LDFS class and is represented as LDFS$(\mathfrak{X}, \mathfrak{E})$.

Let us consider $t_{ij} = t_{\kappa_{\mathfrak{A}}}(\mathfrak{e}_j)(\zeta_i)$, $f_{ij} = f_{\kappa_{\mathfrak{A}}}(\mathfrak{e}_j)(\zeta_i)$, $\alpha_{ij} = \alpha_{\kappa_{\mathfrak{A}}}(\mathfrak{e}_j)(\zeta_i)$ and $\beta_{ij} = \beta_{\kappa_{\mathfrak{A}}}(\mathfrak{e}_j)(\zeta_i)$ where i run from from one to m and j run from one to n. Thus the LDFSS $\kappa_{\mathfrak{A}}$ may be written in tabular form as cited in Table 1.

**Table 1.** Tabular array of LDFSS $\kappa_{\mathfrak{A}}$.

| $\kappa_{\mathfrak{A}}$ | $\mathfrak{e}_1$ | $\mathfrak{e}_2$ | $\cdots$ | $\mathfrak{e}_n$ |
|---|---|---|---|---|
| $\rho_1$ | $(\langle t_{11}, f_{11}\rangle, \langle \alpha_{11}, \beta_{11}\rangle)$ | $(\langle t_{12}, f_{12}\rangle, \langle \alpha_{12}, \beta_{12}\rangle)$ | $\cdots$ | $(\langle t_{1n}, f_{1n}\rangle, \langle \alpha_{1n}, \beta_{1n}\rangle)$ |
| $\rho_2$ | $(\langle t_{21}, f_{21}\rangle, \langle \alpha_{21}, \beta_{21}\rangle)$ | $(\langle t_{22}, f_{22}\rangle, \langle \alpha_{22}, \beta_{22}\rangle)$ | $\cdots$ | $(\langle t_{2n}, f_{2n}\rangle, \langle \alpha_{2n}, \beta_{2n}\rangle)$ |
| $\vdots$ | $\vdots$ | $\vdots$ | $\ddots$ | $\vdots$ |
| $\rho_m$ | $(\langle t_{m1}, f_{m1}\rangle, \langle \alpha_{m1}, \beta_{m1}\rangle)$ | $(\langle t_{m2}, f_{m2}\rangle, \langle \alpha_{m2}, \beta_{m2}\rangle)$ | $\cdots$ | $(\langle t_{mn}, f_{mn}\rangle, \langle \alpha_{mn}, \beta_{mn}\rangle)$ |

The corresponding matrix form is

$$(\kappa, \mathfrak{A}) = [\langle t_{ij}, f_{ij}\rangle, \langle \alpha_{ij}, \beta_{ij}\rangle]_{m \times n} =$$
$$\begin{pmatrix} (\langle t_{11}, f_{11}\rangle, \langle \alpha_{11}, \beta_{11}\rangle) & (\langle t_{12}, f_{12}\rangle, \langle \alpha_{12}, \beta_{12}\rangle) & \cdots & (\langle t_{1n}, f_{1n}\rangle, \langle \alpha_{1n}, \beta_{1n}\rangle) \\ (\langle t_{21}, f_{21}\rangle, \langle \alpha_{21}, \beta_{21}\rangle) & (\langle t_{22}, f_{22}\rangle, \langle \alpha_{22}, \beta_{22}\rangle) & \cdots & (\langle t_{2n}, f_{2n}\rangle, \langle \alpha_{2n}, \beta_{2n}\rangle) \\ \vdots & \vdots & \ddots & \vdots \\ (\langle t_{m1}, f_{m1}\rangle, \langle \alpha_{m1}, \beta_{m1}\rangle) & (\langle t_{m2}, f_{m2}\rangle, \langle \alpha_{m2}, \beta_{m2}\rangle) & \cdots & (\langle t_{mn}, f_{mn}\rangle, \langle \alpha_{mn}, \beta_{mn}\rangle) \end{pmatrix}$$

The matrix displayed above is said to be linear Diophantine fuzzy soft matrix (LDFSM).

**Definition 9** ([33]). *Let* $(\kappa_1, \mathfrak{A}_1)$ *and* $(\kappa_2, \mathfrak{A}_2)$ *be a convene of LDFSSs on* $\mathfrak{X}$*, then*

*(i)* $\kappa^c_{\mathfrak{A}_1} = (\langle f_{\kappa_1}, t_{\kappa_1}\rangle, \langle \beta_{\kappa_1}, \alpha_{\kappa_1}\rangle)$

*(ii)* $\kappa_{\mathfrak{A}_1} \widetilde{\subseteq} \kappa_{\mathfrak{A}_1}$*, if* $\mathfrak{A}_1 \subseteq \mathfrak{A}_2$ *and* $\kappa_1(\mathfrak{e}) \subseteq \kappa_2(\mathfrak{e})$*, for all* $\mathfrak{e} \in \mathfrak{A}_1$.

*(iii)* $\kappa_{\mathfrak{A}} = \kappa_{\mathfrak{A}_1} \widetilde{\cup} \kappa_{\mathfrak{A}_1}$*, if* $\mathfrak{A}_1 \cup \mathfrak{A}_2$ *and* $\kappa_1(\mathfrak{e}) \cup \kappa_2(\mathfrak{e})$*, for all* $\mathfrak{e} \in \mathfrak{A}$.

*(iv)* $\kappa_{\mathfrak{A}} = \kappa_{\mathfrak{A}_1} \widetilde{\cap} \kappa_{\mathfrak{A}_1} \neq \phi$*, if* $\mathfrak{A}_1 \cap \mathfrak{A}_2$ *and* $\kappa_1(\mathfrak{e}) \cap \kappa_2(\mathfrak{e})$*, for all* $\mathfrak{e} \in \mathfrak{A}$.

**Definition 10** ([33]). *If* $\tau$ *is a collection of linear Diophantine fuzzy subsets of a non-void set* $\mathfrak{X}$ *and if*

*(i)* $1_{\mathfrak{X}}, 0_{\mathfrak{X}} \in \tau$

*(ii)* $\mathfrak{A}_1 \cap \mathfrak{A}_2 \in \tau$*, for any* $\mathfrak{A}_1, \mathfrak{A}_2 \in \tau$

*(iii)* $\cup_i \mathfrak{A}_i \in \tau$ *where* $i \in \Delta$*, for any* $\mathfrak{A}_i \in \tau$

*then the couplet* $(\mathfrak{X}, \tau)$ *is known as an LDFTS, where* $\tau$ *is known as an LDFTS on* $\mathfrak{X}$.

## 3. Linear Diophantine Fuzzy Soft Topological Spaces

The concept of LDFSTS is constituted and to a greater extent we explored its peculiarities.

Let $\widetilde{\mathfrak{X}}$ be the inception of the universal set and $LDF(\widetilde{\mathfrak{X}}, \widetilde{\mathfrak{E}})$ represents the kindred of LDFSs on $\widetilde{\mathfrak{X}}$.

**Definition 11.** *An LDFSS* $(\widetilde{\mathfrak{F}}, \widetilde{\mathfrak{E}})$ *aloft* $\widetilde{\mathfrak{X}}$ *is known as*

- *an absolute LDFSS* ($\widetilde{1}$), *if and only if for every* $\xi \in \widetilde{\mathfrak{E}}$, $(\widetilde{\mathfrak{F}}, \widetilde{\mathfrak{E}})(\xi) = (\langle \tilde{1}, \tilde{0} \rangle, \langle \tilde{1}, \tilde{0} \rangle)$
- *an empty LDFSS* ($\widetilde{0}$), *if and only if for every* $\xi \in \widetilde{\mathfrak{E}}$, $(\widetilde{\mathfrak{F}}, \widetilde{\mathfrak{E}})(\xi) = (\langle \tilde{0}, \tilde{1} \rangle, \langle \tilde{0}, \tilde{1} \rangle)$

*where* $\tilde{0}, \tilde{1}, \tilde{0}, \tilde{1}$ *are the value of the grade of satisfaction, grade of dis-satisfaction, the parameter of the satisfaction grade and the parameter of the dis-satisfaction grade, respectively of the absolute and empty LDFSSs over* $\widetilde{\mathfrak{X}}$.

**Definition 12.** *Let* $\widetilde{\mathcal{T}} \subset LDF(\widetilde{\mathfrak{X}}, \widetilde{\mathfrak{E}})$, *then* $\widetilde{\mathcal{T}}$ *on* $\widetilde{\mathfrak{X}}$ *is said to be an LDFSTS, if the following constraints hold good*

- $\widetilde{0}, \widetilde{1} \in \widetilde{\mathcal{T}}$
- $\cap_{i=1}^{n} \widetilde{\mathfrak{L}}_i \in \widetilde{\mathcal{T}} \ \forall \ \widetilde{\mathfrak{L}}_i \in \widetilde{\mathcal{T}}$
- $\cup_{i=1}^{\infty} \widetilde{\mathfrak{L}}_i \in \widetilde{\mathcal{T}} \ \forall \ \widetilde{\mathfrak{L}}_i \in \widetilde{\mathcal{T}}$

*The triple* $(\widetilde{\mathfrak{X}}, \widetilde{\mathcal{T}}, \widetilde{\mathfrak{E}})$ *over* $\widetilde{\mathfrak{X}}$ *is called an LDFSTS. The objects of* $\widetilde{\mathcal{T}}$ *are known as linear Diophantine fuzzy soft open sets (LDFSOS) and their complements are said to be linear Diophantine fuzzy soft closed sets (LDFSCS).*

**Definition 13.** *Let* $\widetilde{\mathcal{T}_1}$ *and* $\widetilde{\mathcal{T}_2}$ *be any two LDFSTS. If for every* $\widetilde{\mathcal{L}}_1 \in \widetilde{\mathcal{T}_1}$ *is in* $\widetilde{\mathcal{T}_2}$, *then* $\widetilde{\mathcal{T}_1}$ *is linear Diophantine fuzzy soft coarser (weaker) than* $\widetilde{\mathcal{T}_2}$ *or* $\widetilde{\mathcal{T}_2}$ *is linear Diophantine fuzzy soft finer than* $\widetilde{\mathcal{T}_1}$.

**Example 2.** *Let* $\widetilde{\mathfrak{X}} = \{\xi_1, \xi_2, \xi_3\}$ *be the reference set (distinct models of bikes) and* $\widetilde{\mathfrak{E}} = \{\zeta_1, \zeta_2, \zeta_3, \zeta_4\}$ *be the attributes or parameters set, where* $\zeta_1$*=affordable,* $\zeta_2$*=caliber,* $\zeta_3$*=comfort,* $\zeta_4$*=recovery service. Let* $\widetilde{\mathfrak{A}} = \{\zeta_1, \zeta_2\} \subset \widetilde{\mathfrak{E}}$ *and* $\widetilde{\mathfrak{B}} = \{\zeta_2\} \subset \widetilde{\mathfrak{E}}$. *Then we contemplate two LDFSS* $(\widetilde{\mathfrak{F}}, \widetilde{\mathfrak{A}})$ *and* $(\widetilde{\mathfrak{G}}, \widetilde{\mathfrak{B}})$ *are given by:*
$(\widetilde{\mathfrak{F}}, \widetilde{\mathfrak{A}}) = \{(\zeta_1, \widetilde{\mathfrak{F}}(\zeta_1)), (\zeta_2, \widetilde{\mathfrak{F}}(\zeta_2))\}$, *and* $(\widetilde{\mathfrak{G}}, \widetilde{\mathfrak{B}}) = \{(\zeta_2, \widetilde{\mathfrak{G}}(\zeta_2))\}$, *where*
$\widetilde{\mathfrak{F}}(\zeta_1) = \{\xi_1 = (\langle 0.7, 0.4 \rangle, \langle 0.4, 0.2 \rangle), \xi_2 = (\langle 0.7, 0.5 \rangle, \langle 0.4, 0.2 \rangle), \xi_3 = (\langle 0.8, 0.3 \rangle, \langle 0.5, 0.2 \rangle)\}$
$\widetilde{\mathfrak{F}}(\zeta_2) = \{\xi_1 = (\langle 0.4, 0.6 \rangle, \langle 0.2, 0.5 \rangle), \xi_2 = (\langle 0.6, 0.7 \rangle, \langle 0.4, 0.3 \rangle), \xi_3 = (\langle 0.6, 0.4 \rangle, \langle 0.6, 0.3 \rangle)\}$
$\widetilde{\mathfrak{G}}(\zeta_2) = \{\xi_1 = (\langle 0.7, 0.5 \rangle, \langle 0.3, 0.5 \rangle), \xi_2 = (\langle 0.4, 0.5 \rangle, \langle 0.2, 0.5 \rangle), \xi_3 = (\langle 0.7, 0.3 \rangle, \langle 0.2, 0.5 \rangle)\}$
*Here,*

1. $\widetilde{\mathcal{T}} = \{(\widetilde{\mathfrak{F}}, \widetilde{\mathfrak{A}}), (\widetilde{\mathfrak{G}}, \widetilde{\mathfrak{B}}), \widetilde{0}, \widetilde{1}\}$ *is a LDFSTS.*
2. $\widetilde{\mathcal{T}_1} = \{(\widetilde{\mathfrak{F}}, \widetilde{\mathfrak{A}}), \widetilde{0}, \widetilde{1}\}$ *and* $\widetilde{\mathcal{T}_2} = \{(\widetilde{\mathfrak{F}}, \widetilde{\mathfrak{A}}), (\widetilde{\mathfrak{G}}, \widetilde{\mathfrak{B}}), \widetilde{0}, \widetilde{1}\}$ *are two LDFSTSs. It is obvious that* $\widetilde{\mathcal{T}_1} \subseteq \widetilde{\mathcal{T}_2}$. *Thus,* $\widetilde{\mathcal{T}_2}$ *is said to be LDFSS-finer than* $\widetilde{\mathcal{T}_1}$ *and* $\widetilde{\mathcal{T}_1}$ *is said to be LDFS-coarser* $\widetilde{\mathcal{T}_2}$.

**Theorem 1.** *If* $\widetilde{\mathcal{T}_1} \cap \widetilde{\mathcal{T}_2} = \{\widetilde{\mathfrak{L}} \in LDFSSs(\widetilde{\mathfrak{X}}, \widetilde{\mathfrak{E}}) : \widetilde{\mathfrak{L}} \in \widetilde{\mathcal{T}_1} \cap \widetilde{\mathcal{T}_2}\}$, *where* $(\widetilde{\mathfrak{X}}, \widetilde{\mathcal{T}_1}, \widetilde{\mathfrak{E}})$ *and* $(\widetilde{\mathfrak{X}}, \widetilde{\mathcal{T}_2}, \widetilde{\mathfrak{E}})$ *are two LDFSTSs over* $(\widetilde{\mathfrak{X}}, \widetilde{\mathfrak{E}})$, *then* $\widetilde{\mathcal{T}_1} \cap \widetilde{\mathcal{T}_2}$ *is also an LDFSTS on* $(\widetilde{\mathfrak{X}}, \widetilde{\mathfrak{E}})$.

**Proof.** (i) It is obvious that $\widetilde{1}, \widetilde{0} \in \widetilde{\mathcal{T}_1}, \widetilde{\mathcal{T}_2}$
(ii) Let $\widetilde{\mathfrak{L}_1}, \widetilde{\mathfrak{L}_2} \in \widetilde{\mathcal{T}_1} \cap \widetilde{\mathcal{T}_2}$. This implies that $\widetilde{\mathfrak{L}_1}, \widetilde{\mathfrak{L}_2} \in \widetilde{\mathcal{T}_1}$ and $\widetilde{\mathfrak{L}_1}, \widetilde{\mathfrak{L}_2} \in \widetilde{\mathcal{T}_2}$, this implies that $\widetilde{\mathfrak{L}_1} \cap \widetilde{\mathfrak{L}_2} \in \widetilde{\mathcal{T}_1}$ and $\widetilde{\mathfrak{L}_1} \cap \widetilde{\mathfrak{L}_2} \in \widetilde{\mathcal{T}_2}$, this implies that $\widetilde{\mathfrak{L}_1} \cap \widetilde{\mathfrak{L}_2} \in \widetilde{\mathcal{T}_1} \cap \widetilde{\mathcal{T}_2}$.
(iii) Let $\{\widetilde{\mathfrak{L}}_i : i \in \Gamma\} \in \widetilde{\mathcal{T}_1} \cap \widetilde{\mathcal{T}_2}$. This implies that $\{\widetilde{\mathfrak{L}}_i\} \in \widetilde{\mathcal{T}_1}$ and $\{\widetilde{\mathfrak{L}}_i\} \in \widetilde{\mathcal{T}_2}$, this implies that $\cup_i \widetilde{\mathfrak{L}}_i \in \widetilde{\mathcal{T}_1}$ and $\cup_i \widetilde{\mathfrak{L}}_i \in \widetilde{\mathcal{T}_2}$, this implies that $\cup_i \widetilde{\mathfrak{L}}_i \in \widetilde{\mathcal{T}_1} \cap \widetilde{\mathcal{T}_2}$.
Therefore, $\widetilde{\mathcal{T}_1} \cap \widetilde{\mathcal{T}_2}$ is an LDFSTS on $(\widetilde{\mathfrak{X}}, \widetilde{\mathfrak{E}})$. □

**Remark 1.** *The union of two LDFSTSs might not be such.*

*Let the reference set be* $\widetilde{\mathfrak{X}} = \{\xi_1, \xi_2, \xi_3\}$ *and the attribute set be* $\widetilde{\mathfrak{E}} = \{\zeta_1, \zeta_2, \zeta_3, \zeta_4, \zeta_5\}$. *Let* $\widetilde{\mathfrak{A}} = \{\zeta_1, \zeta_2, \zeta_3\} \subset \widetilde{\mathfrak{E}}$ *and* $\widetilde{\mathfrak{B}} = \{\zeta_3, \zeta_4, \zeta_5\} \subset \widetilde{\mathfrak{E}}$. *Now let us take two LDFSSs* $(\widetilde{\mathfrak{F}}, \widetilde{\mathfrak{A}})$ *and* $(\widetilde{\mathfrak{G}}, \widetilde{\mathfrak{B}})$ *such that:*

$(\widetilde{\mathfrak{F}}, \widetilde{\mathfrak{A}}) = \{(\zeta_1, \widetilde{\mathfrak{F}}(\zeta_1)), (\zeta_2, \widetilde{\mathfrak{F}}(\zeta_2)), (\zeta_3, \widetilde{\mathfrak{F}}(\zeta_3))\}$, *and* $(\widetilde{\mathfrak{G}}, \widetilde{\mathfrak{B}}) = \{(\zeta_3, \widetilde{\mathfrak{G}}(\zeta_3)), (\zeta_4, \widetilde{\mathfrak{F}}(\zeta_4)), (\zeta_5, \widetilde{\mathfrak{F}}(\zeta_5))\}$, *where*
$\widetilde{\mathfrak{F}}(\zeta_1) = \{\xi_1 = (\langle 0.6, 0.6 \rangle, \langle 0.3, 0.4 \rangle), \xi_2 = (\langle 0.6, 0.7 \rangle, \langle 0.4, 0.3 \rangle), \xi_3 = (\langle 0.4, 0.4 \rangle, \langle 0.2, 0.3 \rangle)\}$
$\widetilde{\mathfrak{F}}(\zeta_2) = \{\xi_1 = (\langle 0.7, 0.5 \rangle, \langle 0.4, 0.2 \rangle), \xi_2 = (\langle 0.5, 0.4 \rangle, \langle 0.3, 0.5 \rangle), \xi_3 = (\langle 0.2, 0.3 \rangle, \langle 0.3, 0.2 \rangle)\}$
$\widetilde{\mathfrak{F}}(\zeta_3) = \{\xi_1 = (\langle 0.5, 0.3 \rangle, \langle 0.3, 0.3 \rangle), \xi_2 = (\langle 0.7, 0.5 \rangle, \langle 0.4, 0.1 \rangle), \xi_3 = (\langle 0.4, 0.3 \rangle, \langle 0.3, 0.1 \rangle)\}$,
$\widetilde{\mathfrak{G}}(\zeta_3) = \{\xi_1 = (\langle 0.3, 0.4 \rangle, \langle 0.6, 0.5 \rangle), \xi_2 = (\langle 0.7, 0.4 \rangle, \langle 0.4, 0.7 \rangle), \xi_3 = (\langle 0.7, 0.5 \rangle, \langle 0.4, 0.3 \rangle)\}$
$\widetilde{\mathfrak{G}}(\zeta_4) = \{\xi_1 = (\langle 0.7, 0.6 \rangle, \langle 0.3, 0.1 \rangle), \xi_2 = (\langle 0.8, 0.3 \rangle, \langle 0.5, 0.4 \rangle), \xi_3 = (\langle 0.5, 0.4 \rangle, \langle 0.2, 0.4 \rangle)\}$
$\widetilde{\mathfrak{G}}(\zeta_5) = \{\xi_1 = (\langle 0.8, 0.4 \rangle, \langle 0.6, 0.3 \rangle), \xi_2 = (\langle 0.6, 0.5 \rangle, \langle 0.3, 0.7 \rangle), \xi_3 = (\langle 0.9, 0.4 \rangle, \langle 0.3, 0.1 \rangle)\}$.

*Then, the two LDFSTSs over $\widetilde{\mathfrak{X}}$ are $\widetilde{\mathcal{T}_1} = \{\widetilde{1}, \widetilde{0}, (\widetilde{\mathfrak{F}}, \widetilde{\mathfrak{A}})\}$ and $\widetilde{\mathcal{T}_2} = \{\widetilde{1}, \widetilde{0}, (\widetilde{\mathfrak{G}}, \widetilde{\mathfrak{B}})\}$. The opposite hand, since $(\widetilde{\mathfrak{F}}, \widetilde{\mathfrak{A}}), (\widetilde{\mathfrak{G}}, \widetilde{\mathfrak{B}}) \in \widetilde{\mathcal{T}_1} \cup \widetilde{\mathcal{T}_2}$. However, $(\widetilde{\mathfrak{F}}, \widetilde{\mathfrak{A}}) \cup (\widetilde{\mathfrak{G}}, \widetilde{\mathfrak{B}}) \notin \widetilde{\mathcal{T}_1} \cup \widetilde{\mathcal{T}_2}$, $(\widetilde{\mathfrak{F}}, \widetilde{\mathfrak{A}}) \cap (\widetilde{\mathfrak{G}}, \widetilde{\mathfrak{B}}) \notin \widetilde{\mathcal{T}_1} \cup \widetilde{\mathcal{T}_2}$. Thus, $\widetilde{\mathcal{T}_1} \cup \widetilde{\mathcal{T}_2}$ is not an LDFSTS on $\widetilde{\mathfrak{X}}$. But $\widetilde{\mathcal{T}_1} \cap \widetilde{\mathcal{T}_2}$ is an LDFSS on $\widetilde{\mathfrak{X}}$.*

**Definition 14.** *Let $\widetilde{\mathfrak{L}}_1, \widetilde{\mathfrak{L}}_2 \in LDFSS(\widetilde{\mathfrak{X}}, \widetilde{\mathfrak{E}})$ and $\widetilde{\mathcal{T}}$ be an LDFSTS on $(\widetilde{\mathfrak{X}}, \widetilde{\mathfrak{E}})$. Then $\widetilde{\mathfrak{L}}_2$ is called a neighbourhood (nbd) of $\widetilde{\mathfrak{L}}_1$, if $\exists$ an LDFSOS $\widetilde{\gamma}$ (i.e., $\widetilde{\gamma} \in \widetilde{\mathcal{T}}$) $\ni \widetilde{\mathfrak{L}}_1 \subset \widetilde{\gamma} \subset \widetilde{\mathfrak{L}}_1$.*

**Theorem 2.** *A LDFSS $\widetilde{\gamma} \in LDFSSs(\widetilde{\mathfrak{X}}, \widetilde{\mathfrak{E}})$ is an LDFSOS if and only if $\widetilde{\gamma}$ is a nbd of each LDFSS $\widetilde{\mathfrak{L}}_1 \subset \widetilde{\gamma}$.*

**Proof.** Let $\widetilde{\mathfrak{L}}_1$ be an LDFSSs in $\widetilde{\gamma}$, where $\widetilde{\gamma}$ is an LDFSOS. As we have $\widetilde{\mathfrak{L}}_1 \subset \widetilde{\gamma} \subset \widetilde{\gamma} \implies \widetilde{\gamma}$ is a nbd of $\widetilde{\mathfrak{L}}_1$. Thereupon, if we suppose $\widetilde{\gamma}$ is an nbd for all LDFSS $\subseteq \widetilde{\gamma}$. Since $\widetilde{\gamma} \subset \widetilde{\gamma}$, $\exists$ an LDFSOS $\widetilde{\mathfrak{L}}_2 \ni \widetilde{\gamma} \subset \widetilde{\mathfrak{L}}_2 \subset \widetilde{\gamma}$. Thus, $\widetilde{\gamma}$ is open and $\widetilde{\gamma} = \widetilde{\mathfrak{L}}_2$. □

**Theorem 3.** *Let $\widetilde{\gamma} \in (\widetilde{\mathfrak{X}}, \widetilde{\mathfrak{E}})$ and $(\widetilde{\mathfrak{X}}, \widetilde{\mathcal{T}_1}, \widetilde{\mathfrak{E}})$ be an LDFSTS. $\widetilde{\gamma}$ is said to be the nbd system or nbd filter of $\widetilde{\gamma}$, the set of all nbds, upto topology $\widetilde{\mathcal{T}_1}$ (in short, $LDFSSnbd(\widetilde{\gamma})$).*

**Theorem 4.** *Let the nbd filter of the LDFSS $\widetilde{\gamma}$ be $LDFSSnbd(\widetilde{\gamma})$. Then,*

1. *finite intersections of the members of $LDFSSnbd(\widetilde{\gamma}) \in LDFSSnbd(\widetilde{\gamma})$.*
2. *each LDFSS containing a member of $LDFSSnbd(\widetilde{\gamma}) \in LDFSSnbd(\widetilde{\gamma})$.*

**Proof.**

1. Let $\widetilde{\mathfrak{L}}_1, \widetilde{\mathfrak{L}}_2 \in LDFSSnbd(\widetilde{\gamma})$. Then $\exists \widetilde{\mathfrak{L}_1'}, \widetilde{\mathfrak{L}_2'} \in \widetilde{\mathcal{T}} \ni \widetilde{\gamma} \subset \widetilde{\mathfrak{L}_1'} \subset \widetilde{\mathfrak{L}}_1$ and $\widetilde{\gamma} \subset \widetilde{\mathfrak{L}_2'} \subset \widetilde{\mathfrak{L}}_2$. Since, $\widetilde{\mathfrak{L}_1'} \cap \widetilde{\mathfrak{L}_2'} \in \widetilde{\mathcal{T}}$, we have, $\widetilde{\gamma} \subset \widetilde{\mathfrak{L}_1'} \cap \widetilde{\mathfrak{L}_2'} \subset \widetilde{\mathfrak{L}}_1 \cap \widetilde{\mathfrak{L}}_2$. Thus, $\widetilde{\mathfrak{L}}_1 \cap \widetilde{\mathfrak{L}}_2 \in LDFSSnbd(\widetilde{\gamma})$.
2. If $\widetilde{\mathfrak{L}}_1 \in LDFSSnbd(\widetilde{\gamma})$ and $\widetilde{\mathfrak{L}}_2$ be an LDFSS containing $\widetilde{\mathfrak{L}}_1$, then $\exists \widetilde{\mathfrak{L}_1'} \in \widetilde{\mathcal{T}} \ni \widetilde{\gamma} \subset \widetilde{\mathfrak{L}_1'} \subset \widetilde{\mathfrak{L}}_1 \subset \widetilde{\mathfrak{L}}_2$. This proves that $\widetilde{\mathfrak{L}}_2 \in LDFSSnbd(\widetilde{\gamma})$

□

**Definition 15.** *Let $\widetilde{\mathfrak{L}} \in LDFSS(\widetilde{\mathfrak{X}}, \widetilde{\mathfrak{E}})$ be an arbitrary LDFSS and let $(\widetilde{\mathfrak{X}}, \widetilde{\mathcal{T}}, \widetilde{\mathfrak{E}})$ be an LDFSTS over $(\widetilde{\mathfrak{X}}, \widetilde{\mathfrak{E}})$. Then the interior and closure of $\widetilde{\mathfrak{L}}$ are defined as follows:*

1. $\widetilde{\mathfrak{L}}^{\mathfrak{LDFS}o} = \cup\{\widetilde{\mathfrak{G}} : \widetilde{\mathfrak{G}}$ *is LDFSO and* $\widetilde{\mathfrak{G}} \subseteq \widetilde{\mathfrak{L}}\}$,
2. $\widetilde{\mathfrak{L}}^{\mathfrak{LDFS}-} = \cap\{\widetilde{\mathfrak{G}} : \widetilde{\mathfrak{G}}$ *is LDFSC and* $\widetilde{\mathfrak{G}} \supseteq \widetilde{\mathfrak{L}}\}$.

**Remark 2.** *For any LDFSS $\widetilde{\mathfrak{L}}$ in $(\widetilde{\mathfrak{X}}, \widetilde{\mathcal{T}}, \widetilde{\mathfrak{E}})$, we have*

1. $[\widetilde{\mathfrak{L}}^c]^{\mathfrak{LDFS}-} = [\widetilde{\mathfrak{L}}^{\mathfrak{LDFS}o}]^c$.
2. $[\widetilde{\mathfrak{L}}^c]^{\mathfrak{LDFS}o} = [\widetilde{\mathfrak{L}}^{\mathfrak{LDFS}-}]^c$.
3. $\widetilde{\mathfrak{L}}$ *is an LDFSCS if and only if* $\widetilde{\mathfrak{L}}^{\mathfrak{LDFS}-} = \widetilde{\mathfrak{L}}$.
4. $\widetilde{\mathfrak{L}}$ *is an LDFSOS if and only if* $\widetilde{\mathfrak{L}}^{\mathfrak{LDFS}o} = \widetilde{\mathfrak{L}}$.
5. $\widetilde{\mathfrak{L}}^{LDFS-}$ *is an LDFSCS in* $(\widetilde{\mathfrak{X}}, \widetilde{\mathfrak{E}})$.
6. $\widetilde{\mathfrak{L}}^{\mathfrak{LDFS}o}$ *is an LDFSOS in* $(\widetilde{\mathfrak{X}}, \widetilde{\mathfrak{E}})$.

**Theorem 5.** *Let $(\widetilde{\mathfrak{X}}, \widetilde{\mathcal{T}}, \widetilde{\mathfrak{E}})$ be an LDFSTS with respect to $(\widetilde{\mathfrak{X}}, \widetilde{\mathfrak{E}})$. Let $\widetilde{\mathfrak{L}}_1$ and $\widetilde{\mathfrak{L}}_2$ be linear Diophantine fuzzy soft subsets of $(\widetilde{\mathfrak{X}}, \widetilde{\mathfrak{E}})$. Then the following holds:*

1. $\widetilde{\mathfrak{L}} \subseteq \widetilde{\mathfrak{L}}^{\mathfrak{LDFS}-}$.
2. $\widetilde{\mathfrak{L}}$ *is an LDFSCS if and only if* $\widetilde{\mathfrak{L}}^{\mathfrak{LDFS}-} = \widetilde{\mathfrak{L}}$.
3. $\widetilde{0}^{\mathfrak{LDFS}-} = \widetilde{0}$ *and* $\widetilde{1}^{\mathfrak{LDFS}-} = \widetilde{1}$.
4. $\widetilde{\mathfrak{L}}_1 \subseteq \widetilde{\mathfrak{L}}_2 \Rightarrow \widetilde{\mathfrak{L}}_1^{\mathfrak{LDFS}-} \subseteq \widetilde{\mathfrak{L}}_2^{\mathfrak{LDFS}-}$.
5. $(\widetilde{\mathfrak{L}}_1 \cup \widetilde{\mathfrak{L}}_2)^{\mathfrak{LDFS}-} = \widetilde{\mathfrak{L}}_1^{\mathfrak{LDFS}-} \cup \widetilde{\mathfrak{L}}_2^{\mathfrak{LDFS}-}$.
6. $(\widetilde{\mathfrak{L}}_1 \cap \widetilde{\mathfrak{L}}_2)^{\mathfrak{LDFS}-} = \widetilde{\mathfrak{L}}_1^{\mathfrak{LDFS}-} \cap \widetilde{\mathfrak{L}}_2^{\mathfrak{LDFS}-}$.
7. $(\widetilde{\mathfrak{L}}^{\mathfrak{LDFS}-})^{\mathfrak{LDFS}-} = \widetilde{\mathfrak{L}}^{\mathfrak{LDFS}-}$.

**Proof.**

1. From Definition 3.5 (ii), $\widetilde{\mathfrak{L}} \subseteq \widetilde{\mathfrak{L}}^{\mathfrak{LDFS}-}$
2. If $\widetilde{\mathfrak{L}}$ is a linear Diophantine fuzzy soft closed set (LDFSCS), then $\widetilde{\mathfrak{L}}$ is the tiniest LDFSCS carrying oneself and therefore $\widetilde{\mathfrak{L}}^{\mathfrak{LDFS}-} = \widetilde{\mathfrak{L}}$. In the reverse way, if $\widetilde{\mathfrak{L}}^{\mathfrak{LDFS}-} = \widetilde{\mathfrak{L}}$, then $\widetilde{\mathfrak{L}}$ is the tiniest LDFSCS containing itself and therefore $\widetilde{\mathfrak{L}}$ is an LDFSCS.
3. Since $\widetilde{0}$ and $\widetilde{1}$ are LDFSCSs in $(\widetilde{\mathfrak{X}}, \widetilde{\mathcal{T}}, \widetilde{\mathfrak{E}})$, $\widetilde{0}^{\mathfrak{LDFS}-} = \widetilde{0}$ and $\widetilde{1}^{\mathfrak{LDFS}-} = \widetilde{1}$.
4. If LDFSS $\widetilde{\mathfrak{L}}_1$ is a subset of LDFSS $\widetilde{\mathfrak{L}}_2$, since LDFSS $\widetilde{\mathfrak{L}}_2$ is a subset of $\widetilde{\mathfrak{L}}_2^{\mathfrak{LDFS}-}$, then LDFSS $\widetilde{\mathfrak{L}}_1$ is a subset of $\widetilde{\mathfrak{L}}_2^{\mathfrak{LDFS}-}$. That is, $\widetilde{\mathfrak{L}}_2^{\mathfrak{LDFS}-}$ is an LDFSCS containing $\widetilde{\mathfrak{L}}_1$. However, $\widetilde{\mathfrak{L}}_1^{\mathfrak{LDFS}-}$ is the littlest LDFSCS containing $\widetilde{\mathfrak{L}}_1$. Therefore, $\widetilde{\mathfrak{L}}_1^{\mathfrak{LDFS}-} \subseteq \widetilde{\mathfrak{L}}_2^{\mathfrak{LDFS}-}$
5. Since the union of two LDFSSs $\widetilde{\mathfrak{L}}_1$ and $\widetilde{\mathfrak{L}}_2$ contains the LDFSS $\widetilde{\mathfrak{L}}_1$ and the union of two LDFSSs $\widetilde{\mathfrak{L}}_1$ and $\widetilde{\mathfrak{L}}_2$ contains the LDFSS $\widetilde{\mathfrak{L}}_2$, $(\widetilde{\mathfrak{L}}_1 \cup \widetilde{\mathfrak{L}}_2)^{\mathfrak{LDFS}-} \supseteq \widetilde{\mathfrak{L}}_1^{\mathfrak{LDFS}-}$. Then the closure of the union of two LDFSSs $\widetilde{\mathfrak{L}}_1$ and $\widetilde{\mathfrak{L}}_2$ contains the closure of LDFSS $\widetilde{\mathfrak{L}}_1$ and the closure of the union of two LDFSSs $\widetilde{\mathfrak{L}}_1$ and $\widetilde{\mathfrak{L}}_2$ contains the closure of LDFSS $\widetilde{\mathfrak{L}}_2$. Hence, the union of closure of LDFSSs $\widetilde{\mathfrak{L}}_1^{\mathfrak{LDFS}-}$, $\widetilde{\mathfrak{L}}_2^{\mathfrak{LDFS}-}$ is a subset of closure of the union of $(\widetilde{\mathfrak{L}}_1^{\mathfrak{LDFS}-}, \widetilde{\mathfrak{L}}_2)^{\mathfrak{LDFS}-}$. By the fact that $\widetilde{\mathfrak{L}}_1 \cup \widetilde{\mathfrak{L}}_2 \subseteq \widetilde{\mathfrak{L}}_1^{\mathfrak{LDFS}-} \cup \widetilde{\mathfrak{L}}_2^{\mathfrak{LDFS}-}$, and since $(\widetilde{\mathfrak{L}}_1 \cup \widetilde{\mathfrak{L}}_2)^{\mathfrak{LDFS}-}$ is the littlest LDFSCS containing $\widetilde{\mathfrak{L}}_1 \cup \widetilde{\mathfrak{L}}_2$, so $(\widetilde{\mathfrak{L}}_1 \cup \widetilde{\mathfrak{L}}_2)^{\mathfrak{LDFS}-} \subseteq \widetilde{\mathfrak{L}}_1^{\mathfrak{LDFS}-} \cup \widetilde{\mathfrak{L}}_2^{\mathfrak{LDFS}-}$. Thus, $(\widetilde{\mathfrak{L}}_1 \cup \widetilde{\mathfrak{L}}_2)^{\mathfrak{LDFS}-} = \widetilde{\mathfrak{L}}_1^{\mathfrak{LDFS}-} \cup \widetilde{\mathfrak{L}}_2^{\mathfrak{LDFS}-}$.
6. Since $\widetilde{\mathfrak{L}}_1 \cap \widetilde{\mathfrak{L}}_2 \subseteq \widetilde{\mathfrak{L}}_1$ and $\widetilde{\mathfrak{L}}_1 \cap \widetilde{\mathfrak{L}}_2 \subseteq \widetilde{\mathfrak{L}}_2$, $(\widetilde{\mathfrak{L}}_1 \cap \widetilde{\mathfrak{L}}_2)^{\mathfrak{LDFS}-} \subseteq \widetilde{\mathfrak{L}}_1^{\mathfrak{LDFS}-} \cap \widetilde{\mathfrak{L}}_2^{\mathfrak{LDFS}-}$.
7. Since $\widetilde{\mathfrak{L}}^{\mathfrak{LDFS}-}$ is a LDFSCS, then $(\widetilde{\mathfrak{L}}^{\mathfrak{LDFS}-})^{\mathfrak{LDFS}-} = \widetilde{\mathfrak{L}}^{\mathfrak{LDFS}-}$.

□

**Theorem 6.** *$(\widetilde{\mathfrak{X}}, \widetilde{\mathcal{T}}, \widetilde{\mathfrak{E}})$ be a LDFSTS over $(\widetilde{\mathfrak{X}}, \widetilde{\mathfrak{E}})$. Let $\widetilde{\mathfrak{L}}$ be a linear Diophantine fuzzy soft subset of $(\widetilde{\mathfrak{X}}, \widetilde{\mathfrak{E}})$. Then*

1. $\widetilde{1} - \widetilde{\mathfrak{L}}^{\mathfrak{LDFS}\circ} = (\widetilde{1} - \widetilde{\mathfrak{L}})^{\mathfrak{LDFS}-}$.
2. $\widetilde{1} - \widetilde{\mathfrak{L}}^{\mathfrak{LDFS}-} = (\widetilde{1} - \widetilde{\mathfrak{L}})^{\mathfrak{LDFS}\circ}$.

**Theorem 7.** *Let $(\widetilde{\mathfrak{X}}, \widetilde{\mathcal{T}}, \widetilde{\mathfrak{E}})$ be an LDFSTS in relation to $(\widetilde{\mathfrak{X}}, \widetilde{\mathfrak{E}})$. Let $\widetilde{\mathfrak{L}}_1$ and $\widetilde{\mathfrak{L}}_2$ be linear Diophantine fuzzy soft subsets of $(\widetilde{\mathfrak{X}}, \widetilde{\mathfrak{E}})$. Then the following claims are true:*

1. *$\widetilde{\widetilde{\mathfrak{L}}}$ is an LDFSOS open if and only if $\widetilde{\mathfrak{L}}^{\mathfrak{LDFS}\circ} = \widetilde{\mathfrak{L}}$.*
2. *$\widetilde{0}^{\mathfrak{LDFS}\circ} = \widetilde{0}$ and $\widetilde{1}^{\mathfrak{LDFS}\circ} = \widetilde{1}$.*
3. *$\widetilde{\mathfrak{L}}_1 \subseteq \widetilde{\mathfrak{L}}_2 \Rightarrow \widetilde{\mathfrak{L}}_1^{\mathfrak{LDFS}\circ} \subseteq \widetilde{\mathfrak{L}}_2^{\mathfrak{LDFS}\circ}$.*
4. *$(\widetilde{\mathfrak{L}}_1 \cup \widetilde{\mathfrak{L}}_2)^{\mathfrak{LDFS}\circ} = \widetilde{\mathfrak{L}}_1^{\mathfrak{LDFS}\circ} \cup \widetilde{\mathfrak{L}}_2^{\mathfrak{LDFS}\circ}$.*
5. *$(\widetilde{\mathfrak{L}}_1 \cap \widetilde{\mathfrak{L}}_2)^{\mathfrak{LDFS}\circ} = \widetilde{\mathfrak{L}}_1^{\mathfrak{LDFS}\circ} \cap \widetilde{\mathfrak{L}}_2^{\mathfrak{LDFS}\circ}$.*
6. *$(\widetilde{\mathfrak{L}}^{\mathfrak{LDFS}\circ})^{\mathfrak{LDFS}\circ} = \widetilde{\mathfrak{L}}^{\mathfrak{LDFS}\circ}$.*

**Proof.**

1. $\widetilde{\mathfrak{L}}$ is an LDFSOS if and only if $\widetilde{1} - \widetilde{\mathfrak{L}}$ is an LDFSCS, if and only if $(\widetilde{1} - \widetilde{\mathfrak{L}})^{\mathfrak{LDFS}-} = \widetilde{1} - \widetilde{\mathfrak{L}}$, if and only if $\widetilde{1} - (\widetilde{1} - \widetilde{\mathfrak{L}})^{\mathfrak{LDFS}-} = \widetilde{\mathfrak{L}}$ if and only if $\widetilde{\mathfrak{L}}^{\mathfrak{LDFS}\circ} = \widetilde{\mathfrak{L}}$.
2. As $\widetilde{0}$ and $\widetilde{1}$ are LDFSOSs in $(\widetilde{\mathfrak{X}}, \widetilde{\mathcal{T}}, \widetilde{\mathfrak{E}})$, $\widetilde{0}^{\mathfrak{LDFS}\circ} = \widetilde{0}$ and $\widetilde{1}^{\mathfrak{LDFS}\circ} = \widetilde{1}$.
3. If $\widetilde{\mathfrak{L}}_1 \subseteq \widetilde{\mathfrak{L}}_2$, since $\widetilde{\mathfrak{L}}_2 \supseteq \widetilde{\mathfrak{L}}_2^{\mathfrak{LDFS}\circ}$, then $\widetilde{\mathfrak{L}}_1 \supseteq \widetilde{\mathfrak{L}}_2^{\mathfrak{LDFS}\circ}$. That is, $\widetilde{\mathfrak{L}}_2^{\mathfrak{LDFS}\circ}$ is an LDFSOS containing $\widetilde{\mathfrak{L}}_1$. However, $\widetilde{\mathfrak{L}}_1^{\mathfrak{LDFS}\circ}$ is the largest LDFSOS contained in $\widetilde{\mathfrak{L}}_1$. Therefore, $\widetilde{\mathfrak{L}}_1^{\mathfrak{LDFS}\circ} \subseteq \widetilde{\mathfrak{L}}_2^{\mathfrak{LDFS}\circ}$
4. Since $\widetilde{\mathfrak{L}}_1 \subseteq \widetilde{\mathfrak{L}}_1 \cup \widetilde{\mathfrak{L}}_2$ and $\widetilde{\mathfrak{L}}_2 \subseteq \widetilde{\mathfrak{L}}_1 \cup \widetilde{\mathfrak{L}}_2$, $\widetilde{\mathfrak{L}}_1^{\mathfrak{LDFS}\circ} \subseteq (\widetilde{\mathfrak{L}}_1 \cup \widetilde{\mathfrak{L}}_2)^{\mathfrak{LDFS}\circ}$ and $\widetilde{\mathfrak{L}}_2^{\mathfrak{LDFS}\circ} \subseteq (\widetilde{\mathfrak{L}}_1 \cup \widetilde{\mathfrak{L}}_2)^{\mathfrak{LDFS}\circ}$. Therefore, $\widetilde{\mathfrak{L}}_1^{\mathfrak{LDFS}\circ} \cup \widetilde{\mathfrak{L}}_2^{\mathfrak{LDFS}\circ} \subseteq (\widetilde{\mathfrak{L}}_1 \cup \widetilde{\mathfrak{L}}_2)^{\mathfrak{LDFS}\circ}$. By the fact that $\widetilde{\mathfrak{L}}_1 \cup \widetilde{\mathfrak{L}}_2 \subseteq \widetilde{\mathfrak{L}}_1^{\mathfrak{LDFS}\circ} \cup \widetilde{\mathfrak{L}}_2^{\mathfrak{LDFS}\circ}$, and since $(\widetilde{\mathfrak{L}}_1 \cup \widetilde{\mathfrak{L}}_2)^{\mathfrak{LDFS}\circ}$ is the largest LDFSOS containing $\widetilde{\mathfrak{L}}_1 \cup \widetilde{\mathfrak{L}}_2$, so $(\widetilde{\mathfrak{L}}_1 \cup \widetilde{\mathfrak{L}}_2)^{\mathfrak{LDFS}\circ} \subseteq \widetilde{\mathfrak{L}}_1^{\mathfrak{LDFS}\circ} \cup \widetilde{\mathfrak{L}}_2^{\mathfrak{LDFS}\circ}$. Thus, $(\widetilde{\mathfrak{L}}_1 \cup \widetilde{\mathfrak{L}}_2)^{\mathfrak{LDFS}\circ} = \widetilde{\mathfrak{L}}_1^{\mathfrak{LDFS}\circ} \cup \widetilde{\mathfrak{L}}_2^{\mathfrak{LDFS}\circ}$.
5. Since $\widetilde{\mathfrak{L}}_1 \cap \widetilde{\mathfrak{L}}_2 \subseteq \widetilde{\mathfrak{L}}_1$ and $\widetilde{\mathfrak{L}}_1 \cap \widetilde{\mathfrak{L}}_2 \subseteq \widetilde{\mathfrak{L}}_2$, $(\widetilde{\mathfrak{L}}_1 \cap \widetilde{\mathfrak{L}}_2)^{\mathfrak{LDFS}\circ} \subseteq \widetilde{\mathfrak{L}}_1^{\mathfrak{LDFS}\circ} \cap \widetilde{\mathfrak{L}}_2^{\mathfrak{LDFS}\circ}$.
6. Since $\widetilde{\mathfrak{L}}^{\mathfrak{LDFS}\circ}$ is an LDFSOS, then $(\widetilde{\mathfrak{L}}^{\mathfrak{LDFS}\circ})^{\mathfrak{LDFS}\circ} = \widetilde{\mathfrak{L}}^{\mathfrak{LDFS}\circ}$.

□

**Definition 16.** *Let* $\widetilde{\mathfrak{L}} \in LDFSSs(\widetilde{\mathfrak{X}}, \widetilde{\mathfrak{E}})$ *and* $(\widetilde{\mathfrak{X}}, \widetilde{\mathcal{T}}, \widetilde{\mathfrak{E}})$ *be a LDFSTS over* $(\widetilde{\mathfrak{X}}, \widetilde{\mathfrak{E}})$*. Then LDFS frontier of* $\widetilde{\mathfrak{L}}$ *is represented by* $LDFSB(\widetilde{\mathfrak{L}})$ *and is outlined as* $LDFSB(\widetilde{\mathfrak{L}}) = \widetilde{\mathfrak{L}}^{\mathfrak{LDFS}-} \cap (\widetilde{\mathfrak{L}}^c)^{\mathfrak{LDFS}-}$.

**Theorem 8.** *Let* $(\widetilde{\mathfrak{X}}, \widetilde{\mathcal{T}}, \widetilde{\mathfrak{E}})$ *be an LDFSTS over* $(\widetilde{\mathfrak{X}}, \widetilde{\mathfrak{E}})$ *and* $\widetilde{\mathfrak{L}} \in LDFSSs(\widetilde{\mathfrak{X}}, \widetilde{\mathfrak{E}})$*. Then,*

1. $\widetilde{\mathfrak{L}}^{\mathfrak{LDFS}\circ} \cap LDFSB(\widetilde{\mathfrak{L}}) = \widetilde{0}$
2. $\widetilde{\mathfrak{L}}^{\mathfrak{LDFS}-} = \widetilde{\mathfrak{L}}^{\mathfrak{LDFS}\circ} \cup LDFSB(\widetilde{\mathfrak{L}})$
3. $LDFSB(\widetilde{\mathfrak{L}}) = \widetilde{0}$ *if and only if* $\widetilde{\mathfrak{L}}$ *is both open and closed.*
4. $LDFSB(\widetilde{\mathfrak{L}}) = \widetilde{\mathfrak{L}}^{\mathfrak{LDFS}-} \cap (\widetilde{\mathfrak{L}}^{\mathfrak{LDFS}\circ})^c = \widetilde{0}$

**Proof.**

1. $\widetilde{\mathfrak{L}}^{\mathfrak{LDFS}\circ} \cap LDFSB(\widetilde{\mathfrak{L}}) = \widetilde{\mathfrak{L}}^{\mathfrak{LDFS}\circ} \cap (\widetilde{\mathfrak{L}}^{\mathfrak{LDFS}-} \cap (\widetilde{\mathfrak{L}}^c)^{\mathfrak{LDFS}-}) = \widetilde{\mathfrak{L}}^{\mathfrak{LDFS}\circ} \cap (\widetilde{\mathfrak{L}}^{\mathfrak{LDFS}-} \cap (\widetilde{\mathfrak{L}}^{\mathfrak{LDFS}\circ})^c) = \widetilde{\mathfrak{L}}^{\mathfrak{LDFS}\circ} \cap (\widetilde{\mathfrak{L}}^{\mathfrak{LDFS}\circ})^c \cap \widetilde{\mathfrak{L}}^{\mathfrak{LDFS}-} = \widetilde{0} \cap \widetilde{\mathfrak{L}}^{\mathfrak{LDFS}-} = \widetilde{0}$.
2. $\widetilde{\mathfrak{L}}^{\mathfrak{LDFS}\circ} \cup LDFSB(\widetilde{\mathfrak{L}}) = \widetilde{\mathfrak{L}}^{\mathfrak{LDFS}\circ} \cup (\widetilde{\mathfrak{L}}^{\mathfrak{LDFS}-} \cap (\widetilde{\mathfrak{L}}^c)^{\mathfrak{LDFS}-}) = \widetilde{\mathfrak{L}}^{\mathfrak{LDFS}\circ} \cup (\widetilde{\mathfrak{L}}^{\mathfrak{LDFS}-} \cap (\widetilde{\mathfrak{L}}^{\mathfrak{LDFS}\circ})^c) = (\widetilde{\mathfrak{L}}^{\mathfrak{LDFS}\circ} \cup \widetilde{\mathfrak{L}}^{\mathfrak{LDFS}-}) \cap (\widetilde{\mathfrak{L}}^{\mathfrak{LDFS}\circ} \cup (\widetilde{\mathfrak{L}}^{\mathfrak{LDFS}\circ})^c) = (\widetilde{\mathfrak{L}}^{\mathfrak{LDFS}\circ} \cup \widetilde{\mathfrak{L}}^{\mathfrak{LDFS}-}) \cap \widetilde{1} = (\widetilde{\mathfrak{L}}^{\mathfrak{LDFS}\circ} \cup \widetilde{\mathfrak{L}}^{\mathfrak{LDFS}-}) = \widetilde{\mathfrak{L}}^{\mathfrak{LDFS}-}$. Since $\widetilde{\mathfrak{L}}^{\mathfrak{LDFS}\circ} \subset \widetilde{\mathfrak{L}} \subset \widetilde{\mathfrak{L}}^{\mathfrak{LDFS}-}$.
3. $LDFSB(\widetilde{\mathfrak{L}}) = \widetilde{\mathfrak{L}}^{\mathfrak{LDFS}-} \cap (\widetilde{\mathfrak{L}}^c)^{\mathfrak{LDFS}-} = \widetilde{0} \Rightarrow \widetilde{\mathfrak{L}}^{\mathfrak{LDFS}-} \cap (\widetilde{\mathfrak{L}}^{\mathfrak{LDFS}\circ})^c = \widetilde{0} \Rightarrow \widetilde{\mathfrak{L}}^{\mathfrak{LDFS}-} \cap ((\widetilde{\mathfrak{L}}^{\mathfrak{LDFS}\circ})^c)^c = \widetilde{0} \Rightarrow \widetilde{\mathfrak{L}}^{\mathfrak{LDFS}-} \cap \widetilde{\mathfrak{L}}^{\mathfrak{LDFS}\circ} = \widetilde{0} \Rightarrow \widetilde{\mathfrak{L}}^{\mathfrak{LDFS}-} \subset \widetilde{\mathfrak{L}}^{\mathfrak{LDFS}\circ}$ i.e., $\widetilde{\mathfrak{L}} \subset \widetilde{\mathfrak{L}}^{\mathfrak{LDFS}-} \subset \widetilde{\mathfrak{L}}^{\mathfrak{LDFS}\circ} \Rightarrow \widetilde{\mathfrak{L}} \subset \widetilde{\mathfrak{L}}^{\mathfrak{LDFS}\circ}$.
   In addition, we know that $\widetilde{\mathfrak{L}}^{\mathfrak{LDFS}\circ} \subset \widetilde{\mathfrak{L}}$. Thus $\widetilde{\mathfrak{L}}^{\mathfrak{LDFS}\circ} = \widetilde{\mathfrak{L}}$. This shows that $\widetilde{\mathfrak{L}}$ is open.
   Furthermore, $\widetilde{\mathfrak{L}}^{\mathfrak{LDFS}-} \subset \widetilde{\mathfrak{L}}^{\mathfrak{LDFS}\circ} \subset \widetilde{\mathfrak{L}} \Rightarrow \widetilde{\mathfrak{L}}^{\mathfrak{LDFS}-} \subset \widetilde{\mathfrak{L}}$. Moreover, we know that $\widetilde{\mathfrak{L}} \subset \widetilde{\mathfrak{L}}^{\mathfrak{LDFS}-}$. Thus $\widetilde{\mathfrak{L}}^{\mathfrak{LDFS}-} = \widetilde{\mathfrak{L}}$. This shows that $\widetilde{\mathfrak{L}}$ is closed.
   Conversely, if $\widetilde{\mathfrak{L}}$ is open and closed, then $\widetilde{\mathfrak{L}}^{\mathfrak{LDFS}\circ} = \widetilde{\mathfrak{L}}$ and $\widetilde{\mathfrak{L}}^{\mathfrak{LDFS}-} = \widetilde{\mathfrak{L}}$. Now, $LDFSB(\widetilde{\mathfrak{L}}) = \widetilde{\mathfrak{L}}^{\mathfrak{LDFS}-} \cap (\widetilde{\mathfrak{L}}^c)^{\mathfrak{LDFS}-} = \widetilde{\mathfrak{L}}^{\mathfrak{LDFS}-} \cap (\widetilde{\mathfrak{L}}^{\mathfrak{LDFS}\circ})^c = \widetilde{\mathfrak{L}}^{\mathfrak{LDFS}-} \cap \widetilde{\mathfrak{L}}^c = \widetilde{0}$.
4. $LDFSB(\widetilde{\mathfrak{L}}) = \widetilde{\mathfrak{L}}^{\mathfrak{LDFS}-} \cap (\widetilde{\mathfrak{L}}^c)^{\mathfrak{LDFS}-} = \widetilde{\mathfrak{L}}^{\mathfrak{LDFS}-} \cap (\widetilde{\mathfrak{L}}^{\mathfrak{LDFS}\circ})^c$

□

**Definition 17.** *Let* $(\widetilde{\mathfrak{X}}, \widetilde{\mathcal{T}}, \widetilde{\mathfrak{E}})$ *be an LDFSTS over* $(\widetilde{\mathfrak{X}}, \widetilde{\mathfrak{E}})$*. The accumulation* $\widetilde{\mathfrak{B}} \subset \widetilde{\mathcal{T}}$ *is known as a base for* $\widetilde{\mathcal{T}}$*. If* $\forall \widetilde{\mathscr{A}} \in \widetilde{\mathcal{T}}$ *can be written as the supercilious union of some objects of LDFSS* $\widetilde{\mathfrak{B}}$*, then* $\widetilde{\mathfrak{B}}$ *is called as a linear Diophantine fuzzy soft basis (LDFSB) for the LDFST* $\widetilde{\mathcal{T}}$*. Linear Diophantine fuzzy basic open sets are the elements of* $\widetilde{\mathfrak{B}}$*.*

**Theorem 9.** *Let* $(\widetilde{\mathfrak{X}}, \widetilde{\mathcal{T}}, \widetilde{\mathfrak{E}})$ *be an LDFSTS over* $(\widetilde{\mathfrak{X}}, \widetilde{\mathfrak{E}})$ *and* $\widetilde{\mathfrak{B}}$ *an LDFSB for* $\widetilde{\mathcal{T}}$*. Then,* $\widetilde{\mathfrak{T}}$ *is the set of linear Diophantine fuzzy soft unions of* $\widetilde{\mathfrak{B}}$ *components.*

**Proof.** The evidence is unambiguous. □

**Theorem 10.** *Let the two LDFSTS over* $(\widetilde{\mathfrak{X}}, \widetilde{\mathfrak{E}})$ *be* $(\widetilde{\mathfrak{X}}, \widetilde{\mathcal{T}}_1, \widetilde{\mathfrak{E}})$ *and* $(\widetilde{\mathfrak{X}}, \widetilde{\mathcal{T}}_2, \widetilde{\mathfrak{E}})$*. Moreover, let* $\widetilde{\mathfrak{B}}_1$ *be an LDFSB for* $\widetilde{\mathcal{T}}_1$ *and* $\widetilde{\mathfrak{B}}_2$ *be an LDFSB for* $\widetilde{\mathcal{T}}_2$*. If* $\widetilde{\mathfrak{B}}_1 \subset \widetilde{\mathfrak{B}}_2$*, then* $\widetilde{\mathcal{T}}_1 \subset \widetilde{\mathcal{T}}_2$*.*

**Proof.** The proof is straightforward. □

## 4. MCDM via LDFSS-TOPSIS Approach

TOPSIS is used to select the best choice from a set of venture options. The reasonable compromise is the option that is nearest to the PIS but farthest from the NIS. In this part, we will look at how LDFSSs may be used in MCDM with TOPSIS. Primarily, we will expand TOPSIS to LDFSSs, and then we will look at a stock exchange investing problem. TOPSIS is one of the most powerful strategies available in the literature for dealing with such issues. Every approach has advantages and limitations depending on the nature of the problem at hand.

We start by discussing the targeted approach procedure by procedure. The suggested LDFSS TOPSIS is a generalization of Eraslan and Karaaslan's [27] fuzzy soft TOPSIS.

---

Step 7: The normalized euclidean distance (NED) of each attribute and its LDFSSV-PIS can be defined as:

$$\eth_{\mathfrak{E}}^{\mathfrak{N}+} = \frac{1}{4n}\sum_{j=1}^{q}[({}^{i}t_{ij} - {}^{i}t_{j}^{+})^2 + ({}^{i}f_{ij} - {}^{i}f_{j}^{+})^2 + ({}^{i}\alpha_{ij} - {}^{i}\alpha_{j}^{+})^2 + ({}^{i}\beta_{ij} - {}^{i}\beta_{j}^{+})^2]$$

The normalized euclidean distance (NED) of each alternative and its LDFSSV-NIS can be defined as:

$$\eth_{\mathfrak{E}}^{\mathfrak{N}-} = \frac{1}{4n}\sum_{j=1}^{q}[({}^{i}t_{ij} - {}^{i}t_{j}^{-})^2 + ({}^{i}f_{ij} - {}^{i}f_{j}^{-})^2 + ({}^{i}\alpha_{ij} - {}^{i}\alpha_{j}^{-})^2 + ({}^{i}\beta_{ij} - {}^{i}\beta_{j}^{-})^2]$$

Step 8: Compute the LDFSS relative closeness with the formula:

$$\mathfrak{C}_{j}^{+} = \frac{\eth_{\mathfrak{E}}^{\mathfrak{N}-}}{\eth_{\mathfrak{E}}^{\mathfrak{N}+} + \eth_{\mathfrak{E}}^{\mathfrak{N}-}}$$

Step 9: Finally, the alternate ranking order is found. The best attribute is the one with the greatest revised coefficient value.

---

The proposed LDFSS-TOPSIS is portrayed as a flow chart in Figure 1.

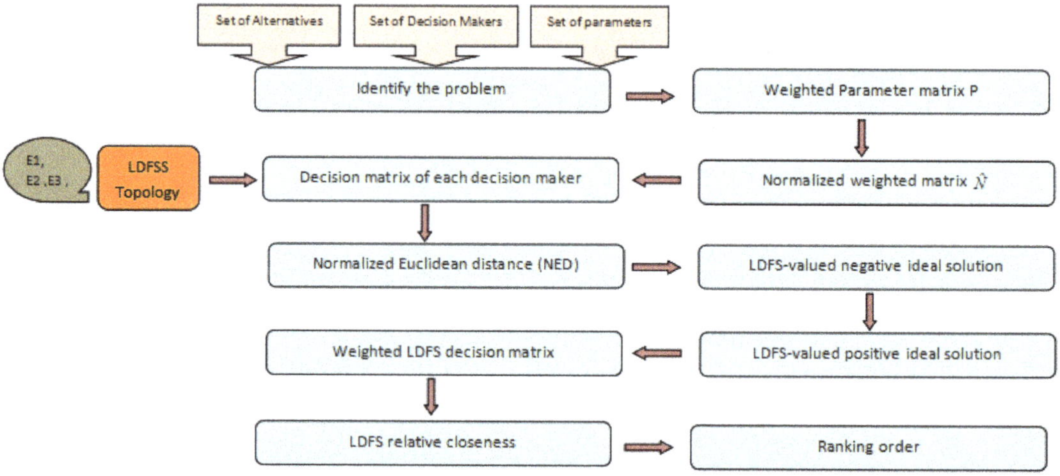


**Figure 1.** Procedural steps of Algorithm 1.

**Algorithm 1:** LDFSS-TOPSIS.

Step 1: Identify the issue: $\mathfrak{E} = \{\mathfrak{e}_i\}$ is the set of decision makers/experts, the assemblage of alternatives/attributes is $\mathfrak{A} = \{\mathfrak{a}_j\}$ and $\mathfrak{C} = \{\mathfrak{c}_{\mathfrak{k}}\}$ is the family of parameters/criteria, where $i, j, \mathfrak{k} \in N$ and $i = \{1, 2, 3, \ldots, \mathfrak{p}\}, j = \{1, 2, 3, \ldots, \mathfrak{q}\}, \mathfrak{k} = \{1, 2, 3, \ldots, \mathfrak{r}\}$.

Step 2: If $w_{ij}$ denotes the weight allocated by $\mathfrak{E}_{\mathfrak{k}}$ to $\mathfrak{C}_j$ keeping in view the linguistic variables (LVs) Table 2, build a weighted criteria matrix

$$\mathcal{P} = [w_{ij}]_{\mathfrak{p}\times\mathfrak{q}} = \begin{pmatrix} w_{11} & w_{12} & \cdots & w_{1\mathfrak{q}} \\ w_{21} & w_{22} & \cdots & w_{2\mathfrak{q}} \\ \vdots & \vdots & \ddots & \vdots \\ w_{\mathfrak{p}1} & w_{\mathfrak{p}2} & \cdots & w_{\mathfrak{p}\mathfrak{q}} \end{pmatrix}.$$

Step 3: Normalize the weighted parameter matrix $\mathcal{P}$ that was created in Step 2 above. There is no need to split the criteria as cost and benefits. As a result, we apply the normalized approach described below to convert the cost criteria to the benefit parameter. The normalized values are represented as a matrix indicated by

$$\widehat{\mathfrak{N}} = [\widehat{\mathfrak{n}}_{ij}]_{\mathfrak{p}\times\mathfrak{q}} = \begin{pmatrix} \widehat{\mathfrak{n}}_{11} & \widehat{\mathfrak{n}}_{12} & \cdots & \widehat{\mathfrak{n}}_{1\mathfrak{q}} \\ \widehat{\mathfrak{n}}_{21} & \widehat{\mathfrak{n}}_{22} & \cdots & \widehat{\mathfrak{n}}_{2\mathfrak{q}} \\ \vdots & \vdots & \ddots & \vdots \\ \widehat{\mathfrak{n}}_{\mathfrak{p}1} & \widehat{\mathfrak{n}}_{\mathfrak{p}2} & \cdots & \widehat{\mathfrak{n}}_{\mathfrak{p}\mathfrak{q}} \end{pmatrix}, \text{ where } \widehat{\mathfrak{n}}_{ij} = \frac{w_{ij}}{\sqrt{\sum_{i=1}^{\mathfrak{p}} w_{ij}^2}} \text{ and acquire the}$$

weight vector $\mathfrak{W} = (\eta_j : j = 1, 2, \ldots, \mathfrak{q})$, where $\eta_j = \frac{\sum_{i=1}^{\mathfrak{q}} \widehat{\mathfrak{n}}_{ij}}{\mathfrak{n}\sum_{\mathfrak{k}=1}^{\mathfrak{m}} \widehat{\mathfrak{n}}_{i\mathfrak{k}}}$

$\omega_{\mathfrak{k}} = \frac{1-\sqrt{[(1-({}^{\mathfrak{k}}\mathfrak{t}(\xi)^2+{}^{\mathfrak{k}}\mathfrak{f}(\xi))^2)+(1-({}^{\mathfrak{k}}\alpha(\xi)^2+({}^{\mathfrak{k}}\beta(\xi))^2)]/2}}{\sum_{\mathfrak{k}=1}^{\mathfrak{r}}[1-\sqrt{[(1-({}^{\mathfrak{k}}\mathfrak{t}(\xi)^2+{}^{\mathfrak{k}}\mathfrak{f}(\xi)^2))+(1-({}^{\mathfrak{k}}\alpha(\xi)^2+{}^{\mathfrak{k}}\beta(\xi)^2)]/2}]}$ where $\mathfrak{k} = 1, 2, 3, \ldots, \mathfrak{r}$ and $\sum_{\mathfrak{k}=1}^{\mathfrak{r}} \omega_{\mathfrak{k}} = 1$,

Step 4: Construct the LSFS-decision matrix, where $\mathfrak{a}_{ij}$ is a LDFSS element, for the ith decision maker makes LDFSS topology for each i. The decision matrix is

represented as $\mathfrak{D}_i = [a_{ij}]_{\mathfrak{p}\times\mathfrak{q}} = \begin{pmatrix} a_{11} & a_{12} & \cdots & a_{1\mathfrak{q}} \\ a_{21} & a_{22} & \cdots & a_{2\mathfrak{q}} \\ \vdots & \vdots & \ddots & \vdots \\ a_{\mathfrak{p}1} & a_{\mathfrak{p}2} & \cdots & a_{\mathfrak{p}\mathfrak{q}} \end{pmatrix}$

where $a_{\mathfrak{r}\mathfrak{q}}$ is a LDFSS-element, for $\mathfrak{k}$ expert/decision maker so that $\mathcal{D}$ makes LDFSS-topology for each i. Then bring out the aggregated matrix $\mathfrak{A} = \frac{\mathfrak{L}_1+\mathfrak{L}_2+\ldots+\mathfrak{L}_n}{n} = [\mathfrak{z}_{\mathfrak{k}j}]_{\mathfrak{r}\times\mathfrak{q}}$.

Step 5: Acquire the weighted LDFSS decision matrix $\mathfrak{J} = [\check{\mathfrak{z}}_{j\mathfrak{k}}]_{\mathfrak{l}\times\mathfrak{q}} = \begin{pmatrix} \check{\mathfrak{z}}_{11} & \check{\mathfrak{z}}_{12} & \cdots & \check{\mathfrak{z}}_{1\mathfrak{q}} \\ \check{\mathfrak{z}}_{21} & \check{\mathfrak{z}}_{22} & \cdots & \check{\mathfrak{z}}_{2\mathfrak{q}} \\ \vdots & \vdots & \ddots & \vdots \\ \check{\mathfrak{z}}_{\mathfrak{p}1} & \check{\mathfrak{z}}_{\mathfrak{p}2} & \cdots & \check{\mathfrak{z}}_{\mathfrak{p}\mathfrak{q}} \end{pmatrix}$,

where $\check{\mathfrak{z}}_{\mathfrak{k}} = \mathfrak{w}_{\mathfrak{k}} \times \dot{\mathfrak{z}}_{j\mathfrak{k}}$

$$\begin{aligned} \check{\mathfrak{z}}_{\mathfrak{k}} &= LDFWG(\mathfrak{z}_{ij}{}^1, \mathfrak{z}_{ij}{}^2, \ldots, \mathfrak{z}_{ij}^{\mathfrak{k}}) \\ &= \xi_1\mathfrak{z}_{ij}{}^1 \otimes \xi_2\mathfrak{z}_{ij}{}^2 \otimes \cdots \otimes \xi_{\mathfrak{k}}\mathfrak{z}_{ij}^{\mathfrak{k}} \\ &= (\langle \Pi_{\mathfrak{k}=1}^{\mathfrak{r}}(\mathfrak{t}_{ij}{}^{\mathfrak{k}})^{\xi_{\mathfrak{k}}}, 1 - \Pi_{\mathfrak{k}=1}^{\mathfrak{r}}(1-\mathfrak{f}_{ij}{}^{\mathfrak{k}})^{\xi_{\mathfrak{k}}}\rangle, \\ &\langle \Pi_{\mathfrak{k}=1}^{\mathfrak{r}}(\alpha_{ij}{}^{\mathfrak{k}})^{\xi_{\mathfrak{k}}}, 1 - \Pi_{\mathfrak{k}=1}^{\mathfrak{r}}(1-\beta_{ij}{}^{\mathfrak{k}})^{\xi_{\mathfrak{k}}}\rangle). \end{aligned}$$

Step 6: Locate LDFSS-valued PIS (LDFSSV-PIS) and LDFSS-valued NIS (LDFSSV-NIS), employing in order

$$\mathfrak{s}_j^+ = \{\ddot{\rho}_1^+, \ddot{\rho}_2^+, \ldots, \ddot{\rho}_{\mathfrak{q}}^+\} = \{\langle \vee^i \mathfrak{t}_{ij}, \wedge^i \mathfrak{f}_{ij}\rangle, \langle \vee^i \alpha_{ij}, \wedge^i \beta_{ij}\rangle\}$$

$$\mathfrak{s}_j^- = \{\ddot{\rho}_1^-, \ddot{\rho}_2^-, \ldots, \ddot{\rho}_{\mathfrak{q}}^-\} = \{\langle \wedge^i \mathfrak{t}_{ij}, \vee^i \mathfrak{f}_{ij}\rangle, \langle \wedge^i \alpha_{ij}, \vee^i \beta_{ij}\rangle\}$$

where, $\wedge$ represents LDFSS intersection and $\vee$ represents LDFSS union and.

**Table 2.** Lingual phrases for importance weights of criteria.

| Linguistic Variables | Fuzzy Weights |
|---|---|
| Less crop production (LCP) | 0.10 |
| Ordinary crop production (OCP) | 0.30 |
| Good crop production (GCP) | 0.50 |
| More crop production (MCP) | 0.70 |
| Exceptional crop production (ECP) | 0.90 |

### *4.1. Numerical Example: MCDM for Robotic Agri-Farming*

This section outlines MCDM, which is used to rank alternatives from high to low relevance. In MCDM, DMs must choose the best option from a set of appropriate attributes in a specific scenario. Although there are several aggregation approaches, we suggest extensions of TOPSIS, VIKOR, and aggregation operators to LDFSSs and topologies for MCDM in this context. As an example, the application we are describing here is connected to farming. Alternatives are compared against the chosen criteria to get the best response. As a result, we may conclude that MCDM is a collection of options, various criteria, and subsequent comparability. With the aid of MCDM, we must select those choices that are ideal in every manner.

#### 4.1.1. An Empirical Case Study

Farming is the practice of cultivating food and rearing livestock. Farming includes raising animals and cultivating crops, both of which provide humans with food and raw resources. Farming originated nearly millions of years ago, but we do not know when or where it started. Farming is a way of life, not simply a profession. This also lends credence to modern civilisation, and without it, our survival on Earth would be impossible. Agriculture was once described as "the most beneficial, most valuable, and most honorable occupation of men" by former American President George Washington. Actually, we are all farmers since we all like gardening, whether at home or at fields. We cultivate plants in little mud pots at home, but we are free to grow crops, plants, or trees in the field. This passion of horticulture must be a lifelong habit, whether you are young or elderly. We now are dismantling our homelands and reducing cultivable areas in the name of industrialization, reinforcement, and habitation communities. Food costs will skyrocket as a result of the land destruction process, and we will have to pay considerably more for our daily food requirements. Agriculture is the science and practice of raising plants and livestock. Overall, there are about ten types of farming practiced across the world such as arable farming, commercial farming, extensive farming, fish farming, intense farming, mixed farming, nomadic farming, pastoral farming, poultry farming, sedentary farming, and subsistence farming.

People require more food to survive as the world's population grows rapidly. Because of the strong demand for food, farmers are under pressure to increase crop production. To address this dilemma, farmers must focus on increasing crop output through the use of agricultural robots. The employment of robots in agriculture is an example of creativity that goes beyond innovation. Agriculture is run like an industry, and it is on its way to becoming a high-tech enterprise in the future. Farmers' agricultural capacities are rising at a rapid pace as technology advances. Robotics and automation technologies are now increasing manufacturing yields. Agriculture robotic uses include harvesting, weeding, trimming, sowing, spraying, sorting, and packing etc. Agriculture robots are also referred to as "agri-bots" or "agri-robots." Agribots will play an important part in agriculture in the future. We are just examining one application here, the usage of robots in horticulture. Horticulture is the cultivation of comfort plants, material plants, food plants, and beautiful plants. A next generation robot called "Terra Sentia" (the smallest robot with a width of 12.5 inches and a height of 12.5 inches and a weight of 30 pounds) appears like a lawn mower and navigates a field by producing laser pulses to scan it. It is used to find the plant health and size, plant counting, portrait of the field, stem diameter, and fruit producing plants. This robot has been demonstrated to be useful in a variety of areas, including almond farms, apple orchards, citrus crops, wheat, maize, soybean, tomatoes, cotton, strawberries, sorghum, and vineyards.

We are investigating the effectiveness of farming robots. The characteristics of robotic agri-farming are listed below.

(i) Accuracy and perfection in placement: Plant placement is critical in the field. The precision will result in excellence. Automation of nursing operations completes grafting, propagation, and spacing.
(ii) Automating manual chores: Farmers enhance their productivity by spending little time on duties and more time on amelioration by adopting automation.
(iii) Completion of a difficult work: Scientists, technicians, researchers, and farmers are all in agreement that the utilization of automation will accomplish the difficult duty in a easy and simple manner.
(iv) High quality production: Quality goods are influenced by certain farming aspects such as (soil, time of ripeness, climate, fertilizer etc). Cereal yield is affected by maturity level and degree of dryness (barley, oats, wheat, rice etc.)
(v) Lowering production costs: There is an innovative method for reducing production costs in agriculture by employing robots. We must handle some uncontrolled aspects that reduce profit margins, such as weather stipulations, acquiring various brands of seeds, and employing an adequate amount of pesticides.
(vi) Minimizing necessity physical labour: Because labour costs are substantially higher in agriculture, i.e., (paying to manual labor and skilled workers).
(vii) Persistent function to complete a task: To perform an agreeable role, the farm must be operated using artificial intelligence (automate the entire agricultural process from sowing to harvesting).

4.1.2. Problem Description

Exemplification: A farmer running a large agriculture farm; it may be an expensive endeavor, but he wants to gain a lot of money from it. He comes from a farming family and inherited the skills and enthusiasm for comprehensive sustainable agri-farming. He aspires to live a happy life and provide outstanding education for his children. He wants to update his vision using robots in order to fulfill his thoughts, ambitions, and worries by decreasing available resources and making this career a high-tech vocation. To turn it into a profitable business, the farmer delegated this responsibility to his sons in order to reach a consensus conclusion based upon that technically controlled method.

We apply Algorithm 1 (LDF-TOPSIS) in this example as follows:

Step 1: Let $\mathfrak{E} = \{\mathfrak{e}_i : i = 1,2,3,4\}$ be the family of experts, $\mathfrak{A} = \{\mathfrak{a}_j : j = 1,2,3,\ldots,5\}$ the set of alternatives for robotic agri-farming under study and we determine the possible set of qualities or criterion for robotic agri-farming $\mathfrak{C} = \{\mathfrak{c}_\mathfrak{k} : \mathfrak{k} = 1,2,\ldots,7\}$, where, $\mathfrak{c}_1$ = Accuracy and perfection in placement, $\mathfrak{c}_2$ = Automating manual chores, $\mathfrak{c}_3$ = Completion of a difficult work, $\mathfrak{c}_4$ = High quality production, $\mathfrak{c}_5$ = Lowering production costs, $\mathfrak{c}_6$ = Minimizing necessary physical labour, and $\mathfrak{c}_7$ = Persistent function to complete a task.

Step 2: The board of family specialists generates linear Diophantine fuzzy soft information as a weighted parameter matrix, shown in Table 2, by reviewing the track record of the list of agri-farming robots and their performance.

$$\mathcal{P} = [w_{ij}]_{4\times 7} = \begin{pmatrix} ECP & GCP & MCP & LCP & LCP & OCP & GCP \\ MCP & GCP & ECP & OCP & GCP & ECP & LCP \\ GCP & MCP & OCP & ECP & LCP & MCP & ECP \\ ECP & MCP & ECP & MCP & OCP & GCP & LCP \end{pmatrix}$$

$$= \begin{pmatrix} 0.9 & 0.5 & 0.7 & 0.1 & 0.1 & 0.3 & 0.5 \\ 0.7 & 0.5 & 0.9 & 0.3 & 0.5 & 0.9 & 0.1 \\ 0.5 & 0.7 & 0.3 & 0.9 & 0.1 & 0.7 & 0.9 \\ 0.9 & 0.7 & 0.9 & 0.7 & 0.3 & 0.5 & 0.1 \end{pmatrix}.$$

where $w_{ij}$ is the weight provided by the experts $\mathfrak{e}_i$ (row-wise) to each quality or criterion $\mathfrak{c}_j$ (column-wise).

Step 3: The normalized weighted matrix is

$$\widehat{\mathfrak{N}} = [\widehat{\mathfrak{n}}_{ij}]_{4\times 7} = \begin{pmatrix} 0.5859 & 0.4110 & 0.4719 & 0.0845 & 0.1667 & 0.2343 & 0.4811 \\ 0.4557 & 0.4110 & 0.6068 & 0.2535 & 0.8333 & 0.7028 & 0.0962 \\ 0.3255 & 0.5754 & 0.2023 & 0.7606 & 0.1667 & 0.5466 & 0.8660 \\ 0.5859 & 0.5754 & 0.6068 & 0.5916 & 0.5000 & 0.3904 & 0.0962 \end{pmatrix}$$

Hence the weight vectors are $\omega = (0.16\ 0.21\ 0.17\ 0.11\ 0.12\ 0.10\ 0.13)$

Step 4: Taking into account the historical track record of the agri-bots, the LDFSS decision matrix $\mathfrak{D}$ of each specialist is provided, with choices indicated row-wise and parameters expressed column-wise. $\mathfrak{D} = \frac{\mathfrak{L}_1+\mathfrak{L}_2+\mathfrak{L}_3+\mathfrak{L}_4}{4} = [\dot{\mathfrak{z}}_{\mathfrak{k}j}]_{5\times 7}$
The aggregated decision matrix is now stated as

$$\begin{pmatrix}
(\langle 0.91,0.18\rangle,\langle 0.62,0.12\rangle) & (\langle 0.90,0.17\rangle,\langle 0.36,0.64\rangle) & (\langle 0.49,0.56\rangle,\langle 0.55,0.26\rangle) & (\langle 0.73,0.28\rangle,\langle 0.62,0.19\rangle) & (\langle 0.94,0.28\rangle,\langle 0.76,0.23\rangle) & (\langle 0.55,0.44\rangle,\langle 0.27,0.32\rangle) & (\langle 0.65,0.62\rangle,\langle 0.29,0.34\rangle) \\
(\langle 0.57,0.52\rangle,\langle 0.22,0.31\rangle) & (\langle 0.95,0.31\rangle,\langle 0.88,0.11\rangle) & (\langle 0.52,0.38\rangle,\langle 0.40,0.36\rangle) & (\langle 0.61,0.37\rangle,\langle 0.52,0.22\rangle) & (\langle 0.56,0.76\rangle,\langle 0.67,0.28\rangle) & (\langle 0.67,0.55\rangle,\langle 0.25,0.36\rangle) & (\langle 0.92,0.12\rangle,\langle 0.74,0.26\rangle) \\
(\langle 0.69,0.41\rangle,\langle 0.28,0.41\rangle) & (\langle 0.56,0.66\rangle,\langle 0.10,0.70\rangle) & (\langle 0.63,0.27\rangle,\langle 0.49,0.16\rangle) & (\langle 0.35,0.70\rangle,\langle 0.30,0.50\rangle) & (\langle 0.87,0.41\rangle,\langle 0.81,0.17\rangle) & (\langle 0.89,0.15\rangle,\langle 0.56,0.36\rangle) & (\langle 0.74,0.27\rangle,\langle 0.55,0.31\rangle) \\
(\langle 0.71,0.46\rangle,\langle 0.26,0.38\rangle) & (\langle 0.58,0.49\rangle,\langle 0.47,0.32\rangle) & (\langle 0.56,0.76\rangle,\langle 0.58,0.39\rangle) & (\langle 0.50,0.45\rangle,\langle 0.45,0.35\rangle) & (\langle 0.97,0.32\rangle,\langle 0.67,0.25\rangle) & (\langle 0.83,0.29\rangle,\langle 0.33,0.61\rangle) & (\langle 0.83,0.29\rangle,\langle 0.23,0.67\rangle) \\
(\langle 0.87,0.37\rangle,\langle 0.24,0.45\rangle) & (\langle 0.63,0.49\rangle,\langle 0.27,0.46\rangle) & (\langle 0.66,0.69\rangle,\langle 0.36,0.35\rangle) & (\langle 0.50,0.55\rangle,\langle 0.50,0.40\rangle) & (\langle 0.83,0.29\rangle,\langle 0.23,0.67\rangle) & (\langle 0.87,0.41\rangle,\langle 0.91,0.02\rangle) & (\langle 0.36,0.16\rangle,\langle 0.37,0.22\rangle)
\end{pmatrix}$$

Step 5: The weighted LDFSS decision matrix is $\mathfrak{B} = [\breve{\mathfrak{z}}_{\mathfrak{k}j}]_{\mathfrak{r}\times\mathfrak{q}} = \mathfrak{w}_j \times \dot{\mathfrak{z}}_{\mathfrak{k}j}$

$$\begin{pmatrix}
(\langle 0.320,0.967\rangle,\langle 0.143,0.712\rangle) & (\langle 0.383,0.689\rangle,\langle 0.089,0.911\rangle) & (\langle 0.108,0.906\rangle,\langle 0.127,0.795\rangle) & (\langle 0.134,0.869\rangle,\langle 0.101,0.833\rangle) & (\langle 0.287,0.858\rangle,\langle 0.157,0.838\rangle) & (\langle 0.077,0.921\rangle,\langle 0.031,0.038\rangle) & (\langle 0.128,0.940\rangle,\langle 0.044,0.869\rangle) \\
(\langle 0.126,0.901\rangle,\langle 0.039,0.829\rangle) & (\langle 0.467,0.782\rangle,\langle 0.359,0.629\rangle) & (\langle 0.117,0.848\rangle,\langle 0.083,0.841\rangle) & (\langle 0.098,0.896\rangle,\langle 0.078,0.847\rangle) & (\langle 0.094,0.968\rangle,\langle 0.125,0.858\rangle) & (\langle 0.105,0.942\rangle,\langle 0.028,0.044\rangle) & (\langle 0.280,0.759\rangle,\langle 0.161,0.839\rangle) \\
(\langle 0.171,0.867\rangle,\langle 0.051,0.867\rangle) & (\langle 0.158,0.916\rangle,\langle 0.022,0.928\rangle) & (\langle 0.156,0.800\rangle,\langle 0.108,0.732\rangle) & (\langle 0.046,0.962\rangle,\langle 0.038,0.927\rangle) & (\langle 0.217,0.899\rangle,\langle 0.181,0.808\rangle) & (\langle 0.198,0.827\rangle,\langle 0.079,0.044\rangle) & (\langle 0.161,0.843\rangle,\langle 0.099,0.859\rangle) \\
(\langle 0.180,0.883\rangle,\langle 0.047,0.857\rangle) & (\langle 0.167,0.861\rangle,\langle 0.125,0.787\rangle) & (\langle 0.130,0.954\rangle,\langle 0.137,0.852\rangle) & (\langle 0.073,0.916\rangle,\langle 0.064,0.891\rangle) & (\langle 0.343,0.872\rangle,\langle 0.125,0.847\rangle) & (\langle 0.162,0.884\rangle,\langle 0.039,0.090\rangle) & (\langle 0.206,0.851\rangle,\langle 0.033,0.949\rangle) \\
(\langle 0.279,0.853\rangle,\langle 0.043,0.880\rangle) & (\langle 0.188,0.861\rangle,\langle 0.064,0.850\rangle) & (\langle 0.168,0.939\rangle,\langle 0.073,0.837\rangle) & (\langle 0.073,0.936\rangle,\langle 0.073,0.904\rangle) & (\langle 0.192,0.862\rangle,\langle 0.031,0.953\rangle) & (\langle 0.185,0.915\rangle,\langle 0.214,0.002\rangle) & (\langle 0.056,0.788\rangle,\langle 0.058,0.821\rangle)
\end{pmatrix}$$

Step 6: Find a positive ideal solution (LDFSSV-PIS) with an LDFSS value, as well as the LDFSS-valued negative ideal solution (LDFSSV-NIS) using in order and are listed, respectively, as

LDFSSV-PIS= $\mathfrak{s}_j^+ = \{\ddot{\rho}_1^+, \ddot{\rho}_2^+, \ldots, \ddot{\rho}_q^+\} =$
$\{(\langle 0.320, 0.853\rangle, \langle 0.143, 0.712\rangle), (\langle 0.467, 0.689\rangle, \langle 0.359, 0.629\rangle), (\langle 0.168, 0.800\rangle, \langle 0.137, 0.732\rangle),$
$(\langle 0.134, 0.869\rangle, \langle 0.101, 0.833\rangle), (\langle 0.343, 0.858\rangle, \langle 0.181, 0.808\rangle), (\langle 0.198, 0.827\rangle, \langle 0.214, 0.002\rangle),$
$(\langle 0.280, 0.759\rangle, \langle 0.161, 0.821\rangle)\}$

LDFSSV-NIS= $\mathfrak{s}_j^- = \{\ddot{\rho}_1^-, \ddot{\rho}_2^-, \ldots, \ddot{\rho}_q^-\} =$
$\{(\langle 0.126, 0.967\rangle, \langle 0.039, 0.880\rangle), (\langle 0.158, 0.916\rangle, \langle 0.022, 0.928\rangle), (\langle 0.108, 0.954\rangle, \langle 0.073, 0.852\rangle),$
$(\langle 0.046, 0.962\rangle, \langle 0.038, 0.927\rangle), (\langle 0.094, 0.968\rangle, \langle 0.031, 0.953\rangle), (\langle 0.077, 0.942\rangle, \langle 0.028, 0.090\rangle),$
$(\langle 0.056, 0.940\rangle, \langle 0.033, 0.949\rangle)\}$

Step 7: We determine the Table 3 LDFSS relative PIS and NIS for the calculated aggregated weighted.

**Table 3.** Distance Measure of Each Alternative.

| Alternatives $\mathfrak{a}_j$ | $\mathfrak{d}_{\mathfrak{E}}^{\mathfrak{N}+}$ | $\mathfrak{d}_{\mathfrak{E}}^{\mathfrak{N}-}$ |
|---|---|---|
| $\mathfrak{a}_1$ | 0.0116 | 0.0112 |
| $\mathfrak{a}_2$ | 0.0083 | 0.0172 |
| $\mathfrak{a}_3$ | 0.0178 | 0.0065 |
| $\mathfrak{a}_4$ | 0.0141 | 0.0066 |
| $\mathfrak{a}_5$ | 0.0167 | 0.0061 |

Step 8: Table 4 shows the proximity coefficients calculated via LDFSS-Euclidean distances of each alternative from LDFSSV-PIS and LDFSSV-NIS:

**Table 4.** LDF Closseness Coefficient of Each Alternative.

| Alternatives $\mathfrak{a}_j$ | $\mathfrak{C}_j^+$ | Rank |
|---|---|---|
| $\mathfrak{a}_1$ | 0.49083 | 2 |
| $\mathfrak{a}_2$ | 0.67360 | 1 |
| $\mathfrak{a}_3$ | 0.26764 | 4 |
| $\mathfrak{a}_4$ | 0.32023 | 3 |
| $\mathfrak{a}_5$ | 0.26758 | 5 |

Step 9: The priority order of the robots as seen in Table 4 is $\mathfrak{a}_2 > \mathfrak{a}_1 > \mathfrak{a}_4 > \mathfrak{a}_3 > \mathfrak{a}_5$: thus, $\mathfrak{a}_2$ is the best robot for the concerned problem of agriculture.

## 5. MCDM Using LDFSS VIKOR Method

VIKOR (Vlse Kriterijumska Optimizacija Kompromisno Resenje) is a Serbian direct reference to various efficiency and compromise parameters. Serafim Opricovic developed it to alleviate decision-making problems with contrasting and non-commensurable (different units) demands, assuming that compromise is suitable for conflict management, the decision-maker appears to have a workable alternative that is the closest to the ideal, and the alternatives are analysed using all indicators. VIKOR rates the options and determines the workable compromise that is closest to the ideal.

We will start by demonstrating the proposed approach step by step:

We begin by breaking down the proposed approach piece by piece. We omit the very first six stages since they are the same as in Algorithm 1 for the LDFSS TOPSIS technique. The remaining stages are as follows:

Figure 2 depicts a flow chart of the planned LDFSS-VIKOR (Algorithm 2).

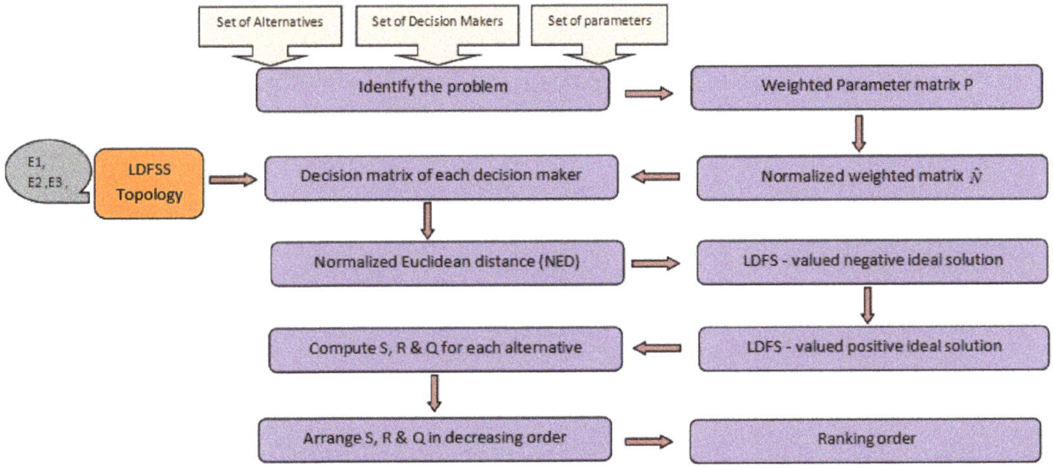


**Figure 2.** Procedural steps of Algorithm 2.

**Algorithm 2:** LDFSS-VIKOR.

Step 1 to 6: See Algorithm 1

Step 7: Generate the VIKOR method's core characteristics for each alternative, namely the group utility value $\mathfrak{S}_j$, individual regret value $\mathfrak{R}_j$, and compromise value $\mathfrak{Q}_j$, using

$$\mathfrak{S}_j = \sum_{\mathfrak{k}=1}^{\mathfrak{r}} \mathfrak{W}_{\mathfrak{k}} \left( \frac{d(\ddot{\rho}_{\mathfrak{k}}^{+}, \ddot{\rho}_{j\mathfrak{k}})}{d(\ddot{\rho}_{\mathfrak{k}}^{+}, \ddot{\rho}_{\mathfrak{k}}^{-})} \right)$$

$$\mathfrak{R}_j = \max_{\mathfrak{k}=1}^{\mathfrak{r}} \mathfrak{W}_{\mathfrak{k}} \left( \frac{d(\ddot{\rho}_{\mathfrak{k}}^{+}, \ddot{\rho}_{j\mathfrak{k}})}{d(\ddot{\rho}_{\mathfrak{k}}^{+}, \ddot{\rho}_{\mathfrak{k}}^{-})} \right)$$

$$\mathfrak{Q}_j = \kappa \left( \frac{\mathfrak{S}_j - \mathfrak{S}^{-}}{\mathfrak{S}^{+} - \mathfrak{S}^{-}} \right) + (1-\kappa) \left( \frac{\mathfrak{R}_j - \mathfrak{R}^{-}}{\mathfrak{R}^{+} - \mathfrak{R}^{-}} \right)$$

where $\mathfrak{S}^{+} = max_j \mathfrak{S}_j$, $\mathfrak{S}^{-} = min_j \mathfrak{S}_j$, $\mathfrak{R}^{+} = max_j \mathfrak{R}_j$, $\mathfrak{R}^{-} = min_j \mathfrak{R}_j$. The real value $\kappa$ is referred to as the decision mechanism coefficient. The purpose of the coefficient $\kappa$ is that if the compromise option is to be chosen by majority vote, we use $\kappa > 0.5$; for concurrence, we use $\kappa = 0.5$; and $\kappa < 0.5$ symbolises veto. The weight of the $\mathfrak{k}$ criteria is represented by $\mathfrak{W}_{\mathfrak{k}}$, which reflects its relative relevance.

Step 8: Sort the options and come up with a reasonable solution. Organize $\mathfrak{S}_i$, $\mathfrak{R}_i$, and $\mathfrak{Q}_i$ in ascending order to create three rating lists, $\mathfrak{S}_{[.]}$, $\mathfrak{R}_{[.]}$, and $\mathfrak{Q}_{[.]}$. The alternative $\ddot{\rho}_\eta$ will be designated the compromise solution if it ranks first in $\mathfrak{Q}_{[.]}$ (with the least value) and concurrently meets the accompanying main specifications:

C1 Acceptable advantage:
If $\ddot{\rho}_\eta$ and $\ddot{\rho}_\zeta$ represent top two alternatives in $\mathfrak{Q}_j$, then

$$\mathfrak{Q}(\ddot{\rho}_\eta) - \mathfrak{Q}(\ddot{\rho}_\zeta) \geq \frac{1}{n-1}$$

where $n$ is the number of parameters.

C2 Acceptable stability:
The alternative $\ddot{\rho}_\eta$ should be best ranked by $\mathfrak{S}_j$ and/or $\mathfrak{R}_j$.

If the aforementioned two requirements are not satisfied simultaneously, there are several compromise solutions:

(i) If only criterion [C1] is met, then both possibilities $\ddot{\rho}_\eta$ and $\ddot{\rho}_\zeta$ are the compromise solutions.

(ii) If condition [C1] is not met, the options $\ddot{\rho}_\eta, \ddot{\rho}_\zeta, \ldots, \ddot{\rho}_\gamma$ would be the acceptable compromise solutions, where $\ddot{\rho}_\gamma$ may be calculated via

$$\mathfrak{Q}(\ddot{\rho}_\zeta) - \mathfrak{Q}(\ddot{\rho}_\gamma) \geq \frac{1}{n-1}$$

for the maximum.

*Example*

We re-solve Example Section 4.1.2 using the VIKOR approach and the strategy described in Algorithm 2. The first six stages are identical to those in Example Section 4.1.2. So we will start with step 7.

Step 1 to 6: Refer Algorithm 1

Step 7: By taking $\kappa = 0.5$, we determine the important components of the VIKOR approach for each choice, namely the group utility value $\mathfrak{S}_i$, the individual regret value

$\mathfrak{R}_i$, and the conciliation value $\mathfrak{Q}_i$, using the following formulas the values are calculated and displayed in Table 5 and Figure 3:

$$\mathfrak{S}_j = \sum_{\mathfrak{k}=1}^{\mathfrak{r}} \mathfrak{W}_{\mathfrak{k}} \left( \frac{d(\ddot{\rho}_{\mathfrak{k}}^{+}, \ddot{\rho}_{j\mathfrak{k}})}{d(\ddot{\rho}_{\mathfrak{k}}^{+}, \ddot{\rho}_{\mathfrak{k}}^{-})} \right)$$

$$\mathfrak{R}_j = \max_{\mathfrak{k}=1}^{\mathfrak{r}} \mathfrak{W}_{\mathfrak{k}} \left( \frac{d(\ddot{\rho}_{\mathfrak{k}}^{+}, \ddot{\rho}_{j\mathfrak{k}})}{d(\ddot{\rho}_{\mathfrak{k}}^{+}, \ddot{\rho}_{\mathfrak{k}}^{-})} \right)$$

$$\mathfrak{Q}_j = \kappa \left( \frac{\mathfrak{S}_j - \mathfrak{S}^{-}}{\mathfrak{S}^{+} - \mathfrak{S}^{-}} \right) + (1-\kappa) \left( \frac{\mathfrak{R}_j - \mathfrak{R}^{-}}{\mathfrak{R}^{+} - \mathfrak{R}^{-}} \right)$$

**Table 5.** The values of $\mathfrak{S}_j$, $\mathfrak{R}_j$ and $\mathfrak{Q}_j$ of Each Alternative.

| **Alternatives $\mathfrak{a}_j$** | $\mathfrak{S}_j$ | $\mathfrak{R}_j$ | $\mathfrak{Q}_j$ |
|---|---|---|---|
| $\mathfrak{a}_1$ | 0.6708 | 0.1416 | 0.1898 |
| $\mathfrak{a}_2$ | 0.6456 | 0.1356 | 0.0000 |
| $\mathfrak{a}_3$ | 0.8424 | 0.2100 | 0.8888 |
| $\mathfrak{a}_4$ | 0.8471 | 0.1586 | 0.5529 |
| $\mathfrak{a}_5$ | 0.8986 | 0.1749 | 0.7644 |

Step 8: The following are the options in order of preference:
By $\mathfrak{S}_i : \mathfrak{a}_2 \prec \mathfrak{a}_1 \prec \mathfrak{a}_3 \prec \mathfrak{a}_4 \prec \mathfrak{a}_5$
By $\mathfrak{R}_i : \mathfrak{a}_2 \prec \mathfrak{a}_1 \prec \mathfrak{a}_4 \prec \mathfrak{a}_5 \prec \mathfrak{a}_3$
By $\mathfrak{Q}_i : \mathfrak{a}_2 \prec \mathfrak{a}_1 \prec \mathfrak{a}_4 \prec \mathfrak{a}_5 \prec \mathfrak{a}_3$
We have $\mathfrak{Q}\{(\mathfrak{a}_1) - (\mathfrak{a}_2)\} = 0.1898 - 0.0000 = 0.189 \geq \frac{1}{6}$, condition C1 is met. As a result, we conclude that $\mathfrak{a}_2$ is an acceptable advantage solution. Therefore, $\mathfrak{a}_2$ is the best robot for the concerned problem of agriculture.

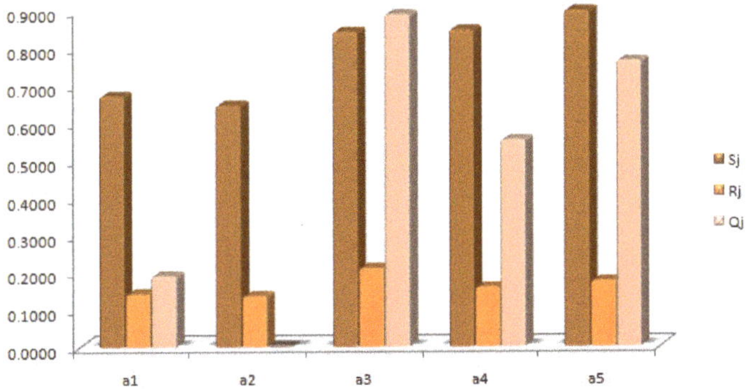


**Figure 3.** Bar chart of rankings.

## 6. Multiple Criteria Decision Making Using LDFSS-AO Method

To begin, we generalize the LDFSS aggregation operators to meet our case. The very first five phases are identical to those in Algorithm 1. As a consequence, we bypass them and proceed to step 6.

The proposed LDFSS-VIKOR is represented as a flow chart in the Figure 4.

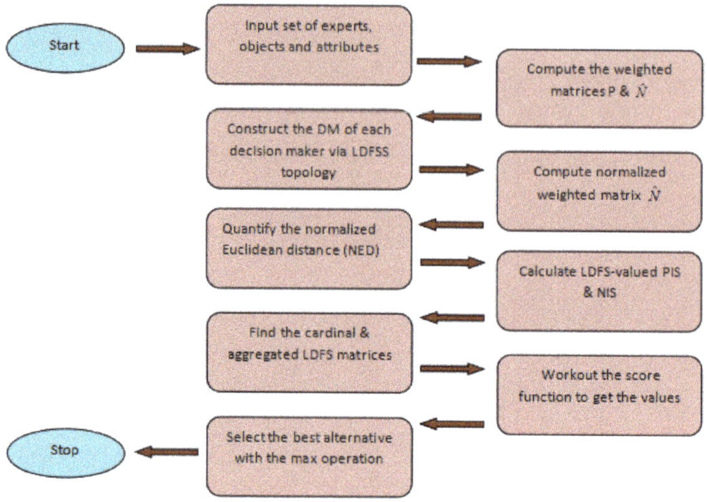


**Figure 4.** Procedural steps of Algorithm 3.

*Example*

We repeat Example Section 4.1.2 using the extended LDFSS aggregation operators as described in Algorithm 3.

---

**Algorithm 3:** LDFSS-aggregation operator(LDFSS-AO).

---

Step 1 to 5: Refer Algorithm 1

Step 6: Compute the cardinal matrix

$$\mathfrak{M}_{\mathfrak{C}(\mathfrak{B})} = \left[ \frac{1}{p} \sum_{i=1}^{p} a_{pq} : j = 1, 2, \ldots, q \right]_{p \times q}$$

Step 7: Calculate the aggregated LDFSS matrix $\mathfrak{M}^*$ using $\mathfrak{M}^* = \frac{\mathfrak{B} \times \mathfrak{M}^{\mathfrak{T}}_{\mathfrak{C}(\mathfrak{B})}}{|\mathfrak{E}|}$.

Step 8: The score function values are calculated with the formula $S(\mathfrak{L}_\mathfrak{d}) = \frac{1}{2}[(\mathfrak{t}_\mathfrak{d} - \mathfrak{f}_\mathfrak{d}) + (\alpha_\mathfrak{d} - \beta_\mathfrak{d})]$. The best option is the one with the largest $S(\mathfrak{L}_\mathfrak{d})$ value.

---

Step 6: The cardinal matrix

$$\mathfrak{M}_{\mathfrak{C}(\mathfrak{B})} = \left[ \frac{1}{5} \sum_{i=1}^{5} a_{ij} : j = 1, 2, \ldots, 7 \right]_{5 \times 7}$$

$$\begin{aligned}\mathfrak{M}_{\mathfrak{C}(\mathfrak{J})} = [&(\langle 0.215, 0.894 \rangle, \langle 0.065, 0.829 \rangle), (\langle 0.273, 0.822 \rangle, \langle 0.132, 0.821 \rangle),\\ &(\langle 0.136, 0.890 \rangle, \langle 0.106, 0.811 \rangle), (\langle 0.085, 0.916 \rangle, \langle 0.071, 0.880 \rangle),\\ &(\langle 0.227, 0.892 \rangle, \langle 0.124, 0.861 \rangle), (\langle 0.145, 0.898 \rangle, \langle 0.078, 0.043 \rangle),\\ &(\langle 0.166, 0.836 \rangle, \langle 0.079, 0.868 \rangle)]\end{aligned}$$

Step 7: Gauge the aggregated LDFSS matrix $\mathfrak{M}^*$ with the formula $\mathfrak{M}^* = \frac{\mathfrak{B} \times \mathfrak{M}^{\mathfrak{T}}_{\mathfrak{C}(\mathfrak{B})}}{|\mathfrak{C}|}$.

$$= \begin{pmatrix} (\langle 0.0424, 0.9838\rangle, \langle 0.0096, 0.8451\rangle) \\ (\langle 0.0374, 0.9823\rangle, \langle 0.0135, 0.8429\rangle) \\ (\langle 0.0299, 0.9845\rangle, \langle 0.0081, 0.8493\rangle) \\ (\langle 0.0348, 0.9858\rangle, \langle 0.0085, 0.8568\rangle) \\ (\langle 0.0314, 0.9842\rangle, \langle 0.0070, 0.8465\rangle) \end{pmatrix}$$

Step 8: The score function for the alternatives found in step 7 is calculated using the formula $S(\mathfrak{L}_{\mathfrak{d}}) = \frac{1}{2}[(\mathfrak{t}_{\mathfrak{d}} - \mathfrak{f}_{\mathfrak{d}}) + (\alpha_{\mathfrak{d}} - \beta_{\mathfrak{d}})]$.
$S(\mathfrak{a}_1) = -0.8401, S(\mathfrak{a}_2) = -0.8369, S(\mathfrak{a}_3) = -0.8448, S(\mathfrak{a}_4) = -0.8523, S(\mathfrak{a}_5) = -0.8420$ . Thus, the archetypal of the robots is $\mathfrak{a}_2 \succ \mathfrak{a}_1 \succ \mathfrak{a}_5 \succ \mathfrak{a}_3 \succ \mathfrak{a}_4$. The optimal choice is the one with the greatest score function value. i.e., $S(\mathfrak{a}_2)$.

## 7. Comparison and Advantages

### 7.1. Three Techniques Are Compared: Commentary

Figure 5 depicts the agri-robot ranks obtained using the TOPSIS, VIKOR, and generalised LDFSS aggregation operator techniques. To make the comparison possible, we used the values $1 - \mathfrak{Q}$ instead of $\mathfrak{Q}$ in VIKOR. In addition, to render the columns representing score values legible, we normalized the scores by multiplying them by 1000. TOPSIS is the first series on the left, VIKOR is the second, and scaled score values are the third.

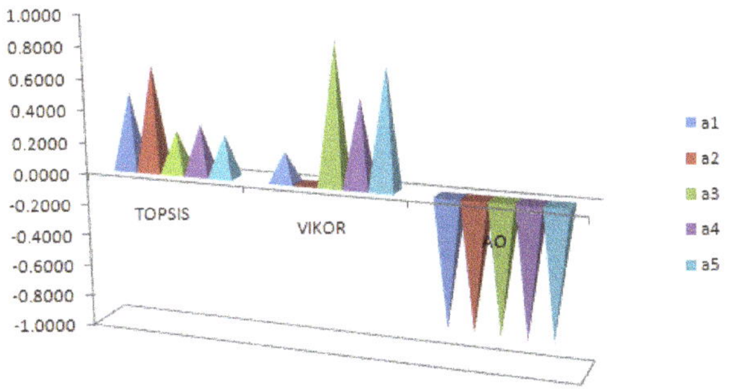


**Figure 5.** LDFSSS-TOPSIS, VIKOR, and generalized AO approaches were used to compare rankings.

We can see that the best option for all three tactics is the same, which is $\mathfrak{a}2$. TOPSIS simply has one check: the optimal solution must be closest to the positive ideal solution and the furthest away from the negative ideal solution. VIKOR has a number of checkpoints. For example, we choose $\mathfrak{Q}_j$, $\mathfrak{R}_j$, and $\mathfrak{S}_j$ values to ensure appropriate advantage and stability. As a result, if a poor solution passes one check, it will be rejected at the next. VIKOR offers a variety of compromise choices.

TOPSIS uses the grade metric, which takes into account distances between PIS and NIS. Without consideration for their virtual importance, the predicted distances are simply added. The distance may naturally represent some equilibrium between overall and individual happiness, but in VIKOR, it does so in a different way. In VIKOR, the weight $\kappa$ is quite well. Both methods establish a ranking grade. The top-ranked answer obtained by VIKOR is nearly perfect. Nonetheless, TOPSIS's top-ranked choice takes priority in the ranking table. This does not imply that it is always close to the ultimate solution. Apart from ranking, VIKOR offers a compromise alternative with an improvement (advantage) level.

In comparison to the other two ways, the method of generalized LDFSS aggregation operators is easier to handle and gives greater computational ease. Based on this debate, we may infer that the VIKOR model outperforms TOPSIS and produces more dependable results. However, in terms of computing convenience, the approach of generalized PFS aggregation operators is preferred. How much precision we want depends on the problem under consideration. We select the procedure based on the amount of precision necessary.

### 7.2. *Analysis of Comparisons and the Superiority of Suggested Work*

We see that using any of the three algorithms in this article yields the same best answer. Furthermore, the techniques provided in this article are simple to use and produce clear results. Table 6 shows a comparison of final ranks with several known techniques.

**Table 6.** The proposed approaches are compared to certain existing procedures.

| Methodology | The Best Option |
|---|---|
| Prioritized weighted AOs (Liu et al. [29]) | $\alpha_2$ |
| IF AOs (Xu [25]) | $\alpha_2$ |
| Generalized IF soft power AOs (Garg and Arora [30]) | $\alpha_2$ |
| Pythagorean fuzzy AOs (Peng and Yuan [28]) | $\alpha_2$ |
| Algorithms 1–3 (Proposed) | $\alpha_2$ |

Furthermore, in this section, we compared and analyzed the existing soft topological space under different environments with the defined notion. Each FST, IFST, PyFST, SFST, LDFT and LDFST is superior to the other but also has its own in-build limitation given in Table 7.

**Table 7.** Comparison of different fuzzy soft extensions.

| Set | Advantages | Limitations |
|---|---|---|
| FST [4] | It can handle imprecise parametrized element | It cannot handle dis-satisfaction grade values of parametrized element |
| IFST [7] | It can handle both satisfaction and dis-satisfaction grade of parametrized element | This theory could not support for some cases when sum of satisfaction and dis-satisfaction grade of parametrized element exceeds unity. This concepts failed to address grades such as abstinence |
| PyFST [34] | This notion can support when satisfaction and dis-satisfaction grade of parametrized element exceeds 1 | It has inherent limitations like sum of square of satisfaction and dis-satisfaction grade of parametrized element exceeds 1. This concepts failed to address grades like abstinence |
| SFST [35] | This concept can handle each parametrized elements positive, neural and negative membership grade | It is not developed with reference parameters. It cannot handle when the sum of squares of parametrized elements positive, neural and negative membership grade exceeds 1. |
| LDFST (Proposed) | This concept is initiated to deal the parametrized elements with reference parameter | We cannot use for some case which do not have reference parameters. |

## 8. Conclusions

We proposed the concept of linear Diophantine fuzzy soft set topological spaces and analyzed their features. We also suggested three strategies for modeling uncertainties in the MCDM problem from agri robot selection using LDFSSs: LDFSS-TOPSIS, LDFSS-VIKOR, and the extended LDFSS-AO approach. The suggested algorithms have been successfully used to rate various robots. A brief but detailed description of the various types of robots, as well as their job efficiency, was provided. We used statistical graphics to help us understand the final ranks. A comparison of three ranks, as well as a good argument for the more viable technique, was also discussed. With the help of a statistical chart, we compared the final gradings provided by the three models. The suggested model has enormous theoretical and application potential, and it may be conveniently utilized in different hybrid architectures of fuzzy sets with little modifications. The notion may be utilized to deal with uncertainty successfully in a variety of real-world situations, including artificial intelligence, business, chemical engineering, coding theory, electoral system, energy management, environment management, forecasting, game theory, image processing, logistics, machine learning, manufacturing, marketing, medical diagnosis, pattern recognition, recruitment, robotics, and trade analysis problems.

**Author Contributions:** All authors contributed equally to this paper. The individual responsibilities and contributions of all authors can be described as follows: the idea of this whole paper was put forward by M.P. M.R., I.A. and C.O. completed the preparatory work of the paper. M.R., I.A. and R.K. analyzed the existing work. The revision and submission of this paper were completed by C.O. and M.P. All authors read and agreed to the published version of the manuscript.

**Funding:** This research received no external funding.

**Institutional Review Board Statement:** Not applicable.

**Informed Consent Statement:** Not applicable.

**Data Availability Statement:** Not applicable.

**Acknowledgments:** The authors extent their appreciation to the Deanship of scientific Research, University of Hafer Al batin for funding this work through the research group project No. 0050-1443-S.

**Conflicts of Interest:** The authors declare no conflict of interest.

## References

1. Zadeh, L.A. Fuzzy sets. *Inf. Control* **1965**, *8*, 338–353. [CrossRef]
2. Molodtsov, D. Soft Set Theory-First Results. *Comput. Math. Appl.* **1999**, *37*, 19–31. [CrossRef]
3. Shabir, M.; Naz, M. On Soft Topological Spaces. *Comput. Math. Appl.* **2011**, *61*, 1786–1799. [CrossRef]
4. Aygunoglu, A.; Cetkin, V.; Aygun, H. An Introduction to Fuzzy Soft Topological Spaces. *Hacet. J. Math. Stat.* **2014**, *43*, 197–208.
5. Atanassov, K.T. Intuitionistic fuzzy sets. *Fuzzy Sets Syst.* **1986**, *20*, 87–96. [CrossRef]
6. Maji, P.K.; Biswas, R.; Roy, A.R. Intuitionistic Fuzzy Soft Sets. *J. Fuzzy Math.* **2001**, *9*, 677–691.
7. Bayramov, S.; Gunduz, G. On intuitionistic fuzzy soft topological spaces. *Int. J. Pure Appl. Math.* **2014**, *5*, 66–79.
8. Cuong, B.C. Picture fuzzy sets. *J. Comput. Sci. Cybern.* **2014**, *30*, 409–420.
9. Wang, L.; Zhang, H.Y.; Wang, J.Q.; Wu, G.F. Picture fuzzy multi-criteria group decision-making method to hotel building energy efficiency retrofit project selection. *RAIRO-Oper. Res.* **2020**, *54*, 211–229. [CrossRef]
10. Yager, R.R.; Abbasov, A.M. Pythagorean membership grades, complex numbers, and decision making. *Int. J. Intell. Syst.* **2013**, *28*, 436–452. [CrossRef]
11. Yager, R.R. Pythagorean membership grades in multi-criteria decision making. *IEEE Trans. Fuzzy Syst.* **2013**, *22*, 958–965. [CrossRef]
12. Ali, M.I. Another view on q-rung orthopair fuzzy sets. *Int. J. Intell. Syst.* **2018**, *33*, 2139–2153. [CrossRef]
13. Akram, M. Multi-criteria decision-making methods based on q-rung picture fuzzy information. *J. Intell. Fuzzy Syst.* **2021**, *40*, 10017–10042. [CrossRef]
14. Pinar, A.; Boran, F.E. A novel distance measure on q-rung picture fuzzy sets and its application to decision making and classification problems. *Artif. Intell. Rev.* **2022**, *55*, 1317–1350. [CrossRef]
15. Riaz, M.; Hashmi, M.R. Linear Diophantine fuzzy set and its applications towards multi-attribute decision-making problems. *J. Intell. Fuzzy Syst.* **2019**, *37*, 5417–5439. [CrossRef]
16. Ayub, S.; Shabir, M.; Riaz, M.; Aslam, M.; Chinram, R. Linear Diophantine fuzzy relations and their algebraic properties with decision making. *Symmetry* **2021**, *13*, 945. [CrossRef]
17. Iampan, A.; Garcia, G.S.; Riaz, M.; Athar Farid, H.M.; Chinram, R. Linear Diophantine fuzzy Einstein aggregation operators for multi-criteria decision-making problems. *J. Math.* **2021**, *2021*, 5548033. [CrossRef]
18. Parimala, M.; Jafari, S.; Riaz, M.; Aslam, M. Applying the Dijkstra algorithm to solve a linear Diophantine fuzzy environment. *Symmetry* **2021**, *13*, 1616. [CrossRef]
19. Riaz, M.; Farid, H.M.A.; Aslam, M.; Pamucar, D.; Bozanic, D. Novel approach for third-party reverse logistic provider selection process under linear Diophantine fuzzy prioritized aggregation operators. *Symmetry* **2021**, *13*, 1152. [CrossRef]
20. Riaz, M.; Farid, H.M.A.; Wang, W.; Pamucar, D. Interval-Valued Linear Diophantine Fuzzy Frank Aggregation Operators with Multi-Criteria Decision-Making. *Mathematics* **2022**, *10*, 1811. [CrossRef]
21. Biswas, A.; Sarkar, B. Pythagorean fuzzy TOPSIS for multi-criteria group decision-making with unknown weight information through entropy measure. *Int. J. Intell. Syst.* **2019**, *34*, 1108–1128. [CrossRef]
22. Boran, F.E.; Genc, S.; Kurt, M.; Akay, D. A multi-criteria intuitionistic fuzzy group decision making for supplier selection with TOPSIS method. *Expert Syst. Appl.* **2009**, *36*, 11363–11368. [CrossRef]
23. Kumar, K.; Garg, H. TOPSIS method based on the connection number of set pair analysis under interval-valued intuitionistic fuzzy set environment. *Comput. Appl. Math.* **2018**, *37*, 1319–1329. [CrossRef]
24. Xu, Z.; Zhang, X. Hesitant fuzzy multi-attribute decision making based on TOPSIS with incomplete weight information. *Knowl.-Based Syst.* **2013**, *52*, 53–64. [CrossRef]
25. Xu, Z. Intuitionistic fuzzy aggregation operators. *IEEE Trans. Fuzzy Syst.* **2007**, *15*, 1179–1187.
26. Hashmi, M.R.; Tehrim, S.T.; Riaz, M.; Pamucar, D.; Cirovic, G. Spherical Linear Diophantine Fuzzy Soft Rough Sets with Multi-Criteria Decision Making. *Axioms* **2021**, *10*, 185. [CrossRef]

27. Eraslan, S.; Karaaslan, F. A group decision making method based on TOPSIS under fuzzy soft environment. *J. New Theory* **2015**, *3*, 30–40.
28. Peng, X.D.; Yuan, H.Y. Fundamental properties of Pythagorean fuzzy aggregation operators. *Fundam. Inform.* **2016**, *147*, 415–446. [CrossRef]
29. Liu, P.; Akram, M.; Sattar, A. Extensions of prioritized weighted aggregation operators for decision making under complex q-rung orthopair fuzzy information. *J. Intell. Fuzzy Syst.* **2020**, *39*, 7469–7493. [CrossRef]
30. Garg, H.; Arora, R. Generalized intuitionistic fuzzy soft power aggregation operator based on t-norm and their application in multicriteria decision-making. *Int. J. Intell. Syst.* **2019**, *34*, 215–246. [CrossRef]
31. Naeem, K.; Riaz, M.; Peng, X.; Afzal, D. Pythagorean m-polar fuzzy topology with TOPSIS approach in exploring most effectual method for curing from COVID-19. *Int. J. Biomath.* **2020**, *13*, 2050075. [CrossRef]
32. Gül, S.; Aydoğdu, A. Novel distance and entropy definitions for linear Diophantine fuzzy sets and an extension of TOPSIS (LDF-TOPSIS). *Expert Syst.* **2022**. [CrossRef]
33. Riaz, M.; Hashmi, M.R.; Kalsoom, H.; Pamucar, D.; Chu, Y.M. Linear Diophantine fuzzy soft rough sets for the selection of sustainable material handling equipment. *Symmetry* **2020**, *12*, 1215. [CrossRef]
34. Riaz, M.; Naeem, K.; Aslam, M.; Afzal, D.; Almahdi, F.A.A.; Jamal, S.S. Multi-criteria group decision making with Pythagorean fuzzy soft topology. *J. Intell. Fuzzy Syst.* **2020**, *39*, 6703–6720. [CrossRef]
35. Garg, H.; Perveen P.A., F.; John, S.J.; Perez-Dominguez, L. Spherical Fuzzy Soft Topology and Its Application in Group Decision-Making Problems. *Math. Probl. Eng.* **2022**, *2022*, 1007133. [CrossRef]

**mathematics**

MDPI

*Article*

# Construction of Fuzzy Numbers via Cumulative Distribution Function

**Georgios Souliotis [1], Yousif Alanazi [2] and Basil Papadopoulos [1,*]**

[1] Department of Civil Engineering Section of Mathematics and Informatics, Democritus University of Thrace, 67100 Kimeria, Greece
[2] Department of Mathematics, College of Science, Kuwait University, Kuwait City 13060, Kuwait; yousif.alanazi@ku.edu.kw
* Correspondence: papadob@civil.duth.gr

**Abstract:** The first person to introduce possibility theory was Lotfi A. Zadeh, in 1977. It was, of course, of no coincidence that he directly combined it with the theory of fuzzy sets. Later, several researchers dealt with the mathematical foundations of the theory of possibilities. They introduced possibility distribution as a concept, and they directly combined it with fuzzy numbers. A fuzzy number corresponds to a possibility distribution and vice versa. This correspondence gave a key advantage to possibility theory over probability theory. This advantage is the facility of operations. However, there is also a basic: problem how is a possibility distribution generated? In this paper, we introduce a method of constructing a possibility distribution via a cumulative probability function. The advantage of this method is the simplicity of construction, which is nothing more than the construction of a fuzzy triangular or trapezoidal number via a cumulative probability function. This construction introduces a way to determine a fuzzy number without relying on the experience or intuition of the researcher. We should, of course, emphasize that this specific construction is within the framework of a theoretical model. We do not apply it to specific data. We also considered that the theoretical construction model should be presented through the theory of possibilities, thus avoiding the theory of probabilities.

**Keywords:** fuzzy numbers; possibility measure; necessity measure; cumulative distribution function; possibility distributions

**MSC:** 28E10; 03E72; 94D05

**Citation:** Souliotis, G.; Alanazi, Y.; Papadopoulos, B. Construction of Fuzzy Numbers via Cumulative Distribution Function. *Mathematics* **2022**, *10*, 3350. https://doi.org/10.3390/math10183350

Academic Editor: Michael Voskoglou

Received: 2 August 2022
Accepted: 13 September 2022
Published: 15 September 2022



## 1. Introduction

The possibility theory initiated by Zadeh in [1] is a generalization of probability theory. Many authors had a hand in the development of possibility theory, especially Dubois and Prade [2]. It has been successfully applied in decision-making problems in conditions of uncertainty [3], in fuzzy cooperative games [4], fuzzy neural networks [5], etc. An important role in the development of possibility theory was played by the concept of fuzzy numbers. In general, fuzzy numbers represent an important class of possibility measure. The main reasons why fuzzy numbers make a very good instrument both for theoretical approaches and applications are as follows: Fuzzy numbers generalize real numbers, and by Zadeh's extension principle [6], the operations of fuzzy numbers are extensions of the operations of real numbers [6]. Moreover, the operations with fuzzy numbers have good arithmetical properties [2]. The link that connects the two concepts of fuzzy numbers and possibility is the possibility distribution of an event. This possibility distribution is most often expressed by a fuzzy number. This fuzzy number plays a role in corresponding to the probability distribution. In other words, it works in a similar way, but instead of probabilities, it uses the concept of possibility. The above procedure has been used quite effectively in risk theory [7]. The main disadvantage of this procedure is the choice of the fuzzy number. This disadvantage is usually covered by the researcher's experience. In this work, we construct the fuzzy number with the help of a cumulative distribution function. That is, from basic data, we produce the cumulative distribution function and then transform it into a fuzzy number, which we can use as a possibility distribution. The process of transformation is simple and produces triangular or trapezoidal fuzzy numbers retaining all the properties of these numbers.

This paper is organized as follows: In Section 2, we present fundamental concepts regarding the formulation of fuzzy numbers and possibility distribution. In Section 3, we show the construction of fuzzy numbers through the cumulative distribution function, and we also give several examples of its operation. General comments and concluding remarks are set out in Sections 4 and 5.

## 2. Definitions and Basic Properties

In this section, we present the most basic concepts concepts used in this paper and their definitions and properties drawn from the relevant literature, starting with fuzzy numbers. It should also be noted that the definitions and properties of fuzzy numbers have been drawn from the book by G. Klir and B. Yuan, titled *Fuzzy sets and fuzzy logic* [6].

### *2.1. Fuzzy Numbers*

**Definition 1** (See [6,7]). *A fuzzy subset of X is a function* $A : X \to [0,1]$. *For* $x \in X$*, the real number* $A(x)$ *from the interval* $[0,1]$ *is called the degree of membership of x in A and represents the degree of truth of the statement "x belongs to A".*

We demote by $\mathcal{F}(X) = [0,1]^X$ the family of fuzzy subsets of X. Let us give an example.

**Example 1.** *Let us consider the statement "the real numbers close to 5". This statement is represented by a fuzzy set. For this purpose, we define the function* $A : \mathbb{R} \to [0,1]$ *with the form:*

$$A(x) = \frac{1}{1 + (x-5)^2}, x \in \mathbb{R}.$$

*where A is a fuzzy subset of* $\mathbb{R}$ *and* $A(x)$ *represents the degree to which the real number x is "close to 5". For the graph of the membership function* $A(x)$*, see Figure 1.*

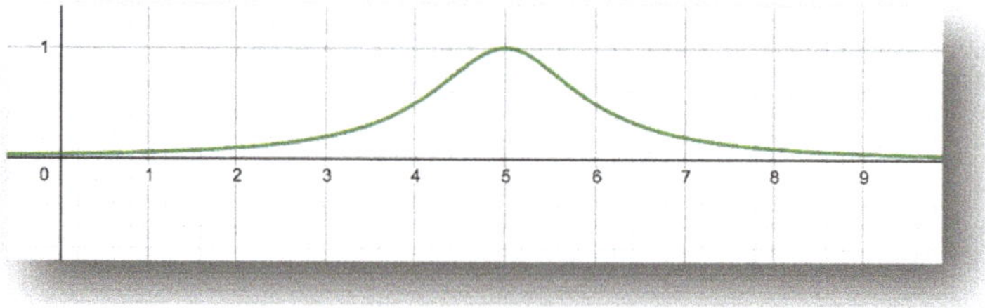


**Figure 1.** Membership function graph $A(x)$.

As we have seen, a fuzzy set is essentially a function $A : X \to [0,1]$. If, in addition, $X \subseteq \mathbb{R}$, then it is possible to have the graph of the fuzzy set as we saw in Example 1. The fuzzy sets for which $X \subseteq \mathbb{R}$ applies are, in essence, the fuzzy numbers we will define below.

**Definition 2** (See [6]). *A subset A of* $\mathbb{R}$ *is called a fuzzy number if the following conditions are fulfilled:*

a. *The function* $A : \mathbb{R} \to [0,1]$ *is continuous;*
b. *A is normal, i.e., there exists* $x \in \mathbb{R}$ *such that* $A(x) = 1$*;*
c. *A is fuzzy convex;*
d. $sup(A)$ *is a bounded subset of* $\mathbb{R}$*.*

We will denote by $\mathcal{F}$ the set of fuzzy numbers.

**Remark 1.** *We recall that support of A is the crisp subset of* $\mathbb{R}$ *defined by* $sup(A) = \{x \in \mathbb{R} | A(x) > 0\}$.

Usually, the triangular and trapezoidal shapes of membership functions shown in Figure 2 most often represent fuzzy numbers. Other shapes may be preferable in some applications.

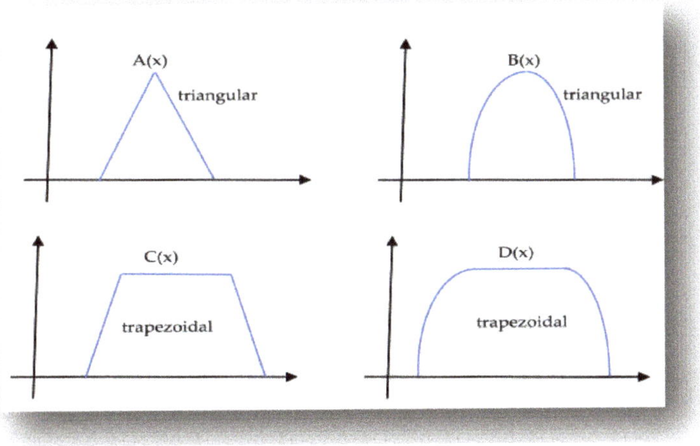


**Figure 2.** Basic types of fuzzy numbers.

The following theorem shows that membership functions of fuzzy numbers may be, in general, piece-defined functions.

**Theorem 1** *(For proof, see Theorem 4.1 in [8]). Let* $A \in \mathcal{F}(\mathbb{R})$*. Then, A is a fuzzy number if and only if there exists a closed interval* $[a, b] \neq \varnothing$ *such that*

$$A(x) = \begin{cases} 1 & for \quad x \in [a,b] \\ l(x) & for \quad x \in (-\infty, a) \\ r(x) & for \quad x \in (b, +\infty), \end{cases} \tag{1}$$

*where l is a function from* $(-\infty, a)$ *to* $[0,1]$ *that is monotonic increasing, continuous from the right, and such that* $l(x) = 0$ *for* $x \in (-\infty, \Omega_1)$*, r is a function* $(b, +\infty)$ *to* $[0,1]$ *that is monotonic degreasing, continuous from the left that* $r(x) = 0$ *for* $x \in (\Omega_2, +\infty)$.

So, the construction of a fuzzy number should satisfy the conditions of Theorem 1.

### 2.2. *Cumulative Distribution Function and Possibility Distribution*

In this paragraph, we will give the definitions of the cumulative distribution function or simple distribution function and the main properties of possibility measure. It should also be noted that the definitions and properties have been drawn from [9–11].

**Definition 3.** *Let X be a random variable with respect to the probability space* $(\Omega, K, P)$*. The cumulative distribution function or simple distribution function of X is the function* $F_X : \mathbb{R} \longrightarrow \mathbb{R}$ *defined by* $F_X(x) = P(X < x)$ *for any* $x \in \mathbb{R}$.

**Remark 2.** *A distribution function is a function F with domain* $[-\infty, +\infty]$ *such that:*

*a.* *F is monotonic increasing;*
*b.* $F(-\infty) = 0$ *and* $F(+\infty) = 1$*;*

c. *If the random variable is discrete, the cumulative distribution function will be discontinuous, and the discontinuity points will correspond to the values of the random variable that have a positive probability.*

**Definition 4.** *Let $\Omega$ be a nonempty set and $\mathcal{P}(\Omega)$ its powerset. Then,*

a. *the elements of $\mathcal{P}(\Omega)$ will be called events;*
b. *a possibility measure on $\Omega$ is a function $\Pi : \mathcal{P}(\Omega) \longrightarrow [0,1]$ such that the following conditions are verified:*
   *($Pos_1$) $\Pi(\varnothing) = 0$ and $\Pi(\Omega) = 1$*
   *($Pos_2$) $\Pi\left(\bigcup_{i\in I} A_i\right) = \sup_{i\in I}\Pi(A_i)$, for any family $\{A_i\}_{i\in I}$ of subsets of $\Omega$.*

**Proposition 1** *(For proof, see [7]). Let $\Pi$ be a possibility measure on $\Omega$. For any $A_1, A_2 \in \mathcal{P}(\Omega)$, if $A_1 \subseteq A_2$, then $\Pi(A_1) \subseteq \Pi(A_2)$.*

**Definition 5.** *A possibility distribution on $\Omega$ is a function $\mu : \Omega \longrightarrow [0,1]$ such that $sup\, \mu(x) = 1$; $\mu$ is said to be normalized if $\mu(x) = 1$ for some $x \in \Omega$.*

Next, we will see how close these two concepts are. Additionally, we should emphasize that the distribution function of probability has nothing to do with the probability distribution. They are completely different concepts. Their differences have been highlighted in [1,2,11]. In the paper, we will not emphasize these differences, and neither will we develop a philosophical view of these concepts. However, the conceptual framework of the possibility distribution function should be made clear. The possibility distribution does not refer to the random variable of the population and, therefore, has nothing to do with the probability. The possibility distribution refers to a fuzzy variable and measures the degree of possibility of a value of the variable belonging to a set.

**Definition 6.** *Let $\Pi$ be a possibility measure on $\Omega$ and $\mu : \Omega \longrightarrow [0,1]$ a possibility distribution. Then, we define the functions:*

a. *$\mu_\Pi : \Omega \longrightarrow [0,1]$ such that $\mu_\Pi(x) = \Pi(\{x\})$ for any $x \in \Omega$;*
b. *$Pos_\mu : \Omega \longrightarrow [0,1]$ such that*

$$Pos_\mu(A) = \sup_{x\in A}\mu(x), \tag{2}$$

*for any $A \in \mathcal{P}(\Omega)$.*

According to the functions we defined in Definition 5, we have the results of the following proposition:

**Proposition 2** *(For proof, see Proposition 3.2.7 in [9]).*

a. *$\mu_\Pi$ is a possibility distribution on $\Omega$;*
b. *$Pos_\mu$ is a possibility measure on $\Omega$;*
c. *$\mu_{Pos_\mu} = \mu$, and $Pos_{\mu_\Pi} = \Pi$.*

*Next, we will define the fuzzy variable. For this, we should assume that $\Omega = \mathbb{R}$.*

**Definition 7.** *A fuzzy variable is an arbitrary function $\zeta : \mathbb{R} \longrightarrow \mathbb{R}$. If is a fuzzy variable, $x_0 \in \mathbb{R}$ and $C \subseteq \mathbb{R}$, then we will define the following concepts: $\zeta \in C = \{x \in \mathbb{R} | \zeta(x) \in C\}$, $\{\zeta = x_0\} = \{x \in \mathbb{R} | \zeta(x) = x_0\}$, $\{\zeta \le x_0\} = \{x \in \mathbb{R} | \zeta(x) \le x_0\}$, etc. Furthermore, we will say that a possibility distribution $\mu : \mathbb{R} \longrightarrow [0,1]$ is associated with the fuzzy variable $\zeta$ if*

$$\mu(x) = Pos_\mu(\zeta = x), \tag{3}$$

*for any* $x \in \mathbb{R}$.

**Proposition 3** *(For Proof, see Proposition 3.2.9 [7]). Let* $\zeta$ *be a fuzzy variable with possibility distribution* $\mu$*. For any* $A \subseteq \mathbb{R}$ *we have:*

$$Pos_{\mu}(\zeta \in A) = \sup_{x \in A} \mu(x) \tag{4}$$

*So, according to Equation (4), we have the following corresponding equations. Let* $\zeta$ *be a fuzzy variable with possibility distribution* $\mu$*. For any* $x_0,\ x_1 \in \mathbb{R}$ *the following applies:*

$$Pos_{\mu}(\zeta \leq x_0) = \sup_{x \leq x_0} \mu(x), \tag{5}$$

$$Pos_{\mu}(\zeta < x_0) = \sup_{x < x_0} \mu(x), \tag{6}$$

$$Pos_{\mu}(\zeta \geq x_0) = \sup_{x \geq x_0} \mu(x), \tag{7}$$

$$Pos_{\mu}(\zeta > x_0) = \sup_{x > x_0} \mu(x), \tag{8}$$

$$Pos_{\mu}(x_0 < \zeta < x_1) = \sup_{x_0 < x < x_1} \mu(x), \tag{9}$$

With the above equations, we are now able to connect the two basic concepts that we presented above—fuzzy numbers and the possibility distribution [2,7,12]. This connection will be best seen with two examples. The first example is with a triangular number, and the second example is with a trapezoidal number.

**Example 2.** *Let* $A \in \mathcal{F}(\mathbb{R})$ *be a triangular number with form:*

$$A(x) = \begin{cases} l(x), & for\ x \in [a,b] \\ r(x), & for\ x \in [b,c] \\ 0 & otherwise, \end{cases} \tag{10}$$

*where* $l$ *is a function from* $[a,b]$ *to* $[0,1]$ *that is monotonic increasing,* $r$ *is a function from* $[b,c]$ *to* $[0,1]$ *that is monotonic decreasing, and* $l(a) = r(c) = 0$ *and* $l(b) = r(b) = 1$*. Furthermore, let* $\zeta$ *be a fuzzy variable such that the triangular fuzzy number* $A$ *of Equation (10) is the possibility distribution associated with* $\zeta$*. We denote by* $Pos_A$ *the possibility measure associated with* $A$*. For any* $x_0 \in \mathbb{R}$ *we have*

$$Pos_A(\zeta \leq x_0) = \sup_{x \leq x_0} A(x) = \begin{cases} 0 & if\ x_0 \leq a \\ A(x_0) & if\ a \leq x_0 \leq b \\ 1 & if\ \ x_0 \geq b, \end{cases} \tag{11}$$

$$Pos_A(\zeta \geq x_0) = \sup_{x \geq x_0} A(x) = \begin{cases} 1 & if\ x_0 \leq a \\ A(\ x_0) & if\ b \leq x_0 \leq c \\ 0 & if\ \ x_0 \geq c, \end{cases} \tag{12}$$

**Example 3.** *Let* $B \in \mathcal{F}(\mathbb{R})$ *be a trapezoidal number with the form:*

$$B(x) = \begin{cases} l(x), & for\ \ x \in [a,b] \\ 1 & for\ \ x \in [b,c] \\ r(x), & for\ \ x \in [c,d] \\ 0 & otherwise, \end{cases} \tag{13}$$

*where $l$ is a function from $[a, b]$ to $[0, 1]$ that is monotonic increasing, $r$ is a function from $[c, d]$ to $[0, 1]$ that is monotonic decreasing, and $l(a) = r(d) = 0$ and $l(b) = r(c) = 1$. Furthermore, let $\zeta$ be a fuzzy variable such that the triangular fuzzy number $B$ of Equation (13) is the possibility distribution associated with $\zeta$. We denote by $Pos_B$ the possibility measure associated with $B$. For any $x_0 \in \mathbb{R}$ we have*

$$Pos_B(\zeta \le x_0) = \sup_{x \le x_0} B(x) = \begin{cases} 0 & if\ x_0 \le a \\ B(x_0) & if\ a \le x_0 \le b \\ 1 & if\ \ x_0 \ge b, \end{cases} \tag{14}$$

$$Pos_B(\zeta \ge x_0) = \sup_{x \ge x_0} B(x) = \begin{cases} 1 & if\ x_0 \le c \\ B(x_0) & if\ c \le x_0 \le d \\ 0 & if\ \ x_0 \ge c, \end{cases} \tag{15}$$

## 3. Results

As we know, probability theory and possibility theory try to express randomness and fuzziness, respectively. Both randomness and fuzziness, despite their diversity, in essence, attempt to "capture" uncertainty, so a collaboration between random variables (probability theory) and fuzzy numbers (possibility theory) in practice is very useful [12–14]. However, for this cooperation, the best representative of fuzziness is the fuzzy number. For the most part, real-world uncertainty problems contain fuzziness and randomness together. A characteristic example of the coexistence of randomness and fuzziness was given by Zadeh in [14]. Nevertheless, the question of how a fuzzy number is determined remains. By what mechanism will we assign a degree of possibility (degree of truth) to our data? Is the experience of researchers enough? The answers are not easily found. However, some efforts gave results [11,13,15,16]. Following these efforts, we propose a way to convert the cumulative distribution function to a fuzzy number. Specifically, from research data, we construct the cumulative distribution function and then convert it into a fuzzy number. This fuzzy number also serves as the distribution of the possibility of this research. Below, we give the conversion form of a given cumulative distribution function to a fuzzy number as well as some examples of this conversion using possibility theory.

### 3.1. Construction of a Fuzzy Number via Cumulative Distribution Function

According to Definition 3, suppose we have a cumulative distribution function $F_X : \mathbb{R} \longrightarrow \mathbb{R}$ defined by $F_X(x) = P(X < x)$ for any $x \in \mathbb{R}$. In addition, $F_X$ is continuous and nondecreasing, so the following proposition applies:

**Proposition 4.** *If $F_X : \mathbb{R} \longrightarrow \mathbb{R}$ is a cumulative distribution function, then the function given by the form*

$$A(x) = \begin{cases} \frac{F_X(x)}{F_X(a)} & if\ x \le a \\ \frac{1-F_X(x)}{1-F_X(a)} & if\ x \ge a \end{cases}, \quad x, a \in \mathbb{R}, \tag{16}$$

*is a triangular fuzzy number.*

**Proof of Proposition 4.**

1. For $x < a$, the function $A(x)$ is increasing since $F_X$ is increasing (from Definition 3 and $F_X(a) > 0$), and for $x > a$, the function $A(x)$ is decreasing since $1 - F_X$ is decreasing;
2. $A(x)$ is a continuous function since $F_X$ is continuous for $x \in (-\infty, a) \cup (a, +\infty)$ and $\lim_{x \to a^-} A(x) = \lim_{x \to a^+} A(x) = A(a) = 1$;
3. $A(a) = \frac{F_X(a)}{F_X(a)} = \frac{1-F_X(a)}{1-F_X(a)} = 1$.

Therefore, the conditions of Theorem 1 are satisfied. Hence, the function $A(x)$ is a fuzzy number and triangular as in Equation (10). □

**Remark 3.** *The choice of the real number $a \in \mathbb{R}$ can be a measure of location. In other words, it can be the average median mode, etc. A typical example of converting a cumulative distribution function into a fuzzy triangular number is a uniform distribution. The cumulative distribution function of the continuous uniform distribution is*

$$F(x) = \begin{cases} 0 & for\ x < a \\ \frac{x-a}{b-a} & for\ a \le x \le b \\ 1 & for\ x > b. \end{cases} \quad (17)$$

*The above function has average $\mu = (a+b)/2$ and variance $s^2 = (b-a)^2/12$. With the help of Equation (16), we want to create a triangular fuzzy number "**close to $\mu$**", meaning we will obtain the fuzzy number with the membership function $A(x)$*

$$A(x) = \begin{cases} 2F(x) & if\ x \le \mu \\ 2(1-F(x)) & if\ x \ge \mu \end{cases}, \quad x \in \mathbb{R}, \quad (18)$$

This conversion is shown in Figure 3.

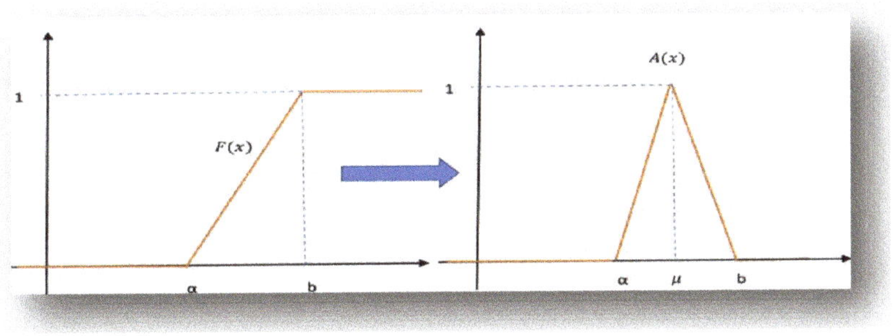


**Figure 3.** Conversion from *F(x)* to *A(x)*.

In a similar way, we can construct a trapezoidal fuzzy number with a variant of Proposition 4. In this case, we determine two points at which we will break the cumulative distribution function. So, we have the following proposition:

**Proposition 5.** *If $F_X : \mathbb{R} \longrightarrow \mathbb{R}$ is a cumulative distribution function, then the functions given by the form*

$$B(x) = \begin{cases} \frac{F_X(x)}{F_X(c)} & if\ x \le c \\ 1 & if\ c \le x \le r, \\ \frac{1-F_X(x)}{1-F_X(r)} & if\ x \ge r \end{cases} \quad (19)$$

*is a trapezoidal fuzzy number.*

**Proof of Proposition 5.** The proof is like the proof in Proposition 4. □

**Remark 4.** *If, in the example of Remark 3, instead of triangular, we wanted to construct trapezoidal fuzzy number $c,\ r \in [a,b]$, then according to Equation (19) we would have the following graph of the trapezoidal fuzzy number, Figure 4.*

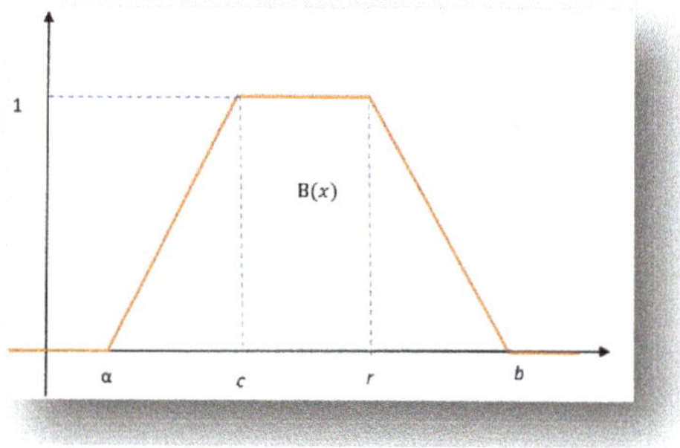


**Figure 4.** The trapezoidal fuzzy number created via the cumulative uniform distribution function $F(x)$.

### *3.2. A Simple Paradigm in the Theory of Possibility of Fuzzy Numbers Created by Cumulative Distribution Function*

Let us look at the paradigm below linking the construction of Proposition 4 to the theory of possibilities and suppose the following:

**Paradigm 1.** *The duration in minutes of telephone conversations follows a distribution with a cumulative function*

$$F(x) = \begin{cases} 1 - e^{-\frac{x}{5}} & , \quad x > 0 \\ 0 & , \quad x \leq 0' \end{cases} \tag{20}$$

*When a subscriber was asked how long a call is, the answer was* ***about 1 min****. The questions that arise are:*

a. *How possible is it for the subscriber's call to be longer than 5 min?*
b. *How possible is it to be between 3 min and 5 min?*

**Proof of Paradigm 1.** It is difficult for probability theory alone to give an answer since we have a fuzzy "***about 1 min***" variable, but we can use the cumulative distribution function, see Equation (16). According to Proposition 4, we have the fuzzy triangular number we need to measure the possibilities. So, we create the fuzzy number "***about 1 min***" from the Equation (16) with $a = 1$, and we have

$$A(x) = \begin{cases} \frac{F(x)}{F(1)} & , \quad x \leq 1 \\ \frac{1-F(x)}{1-F(1)} & , \quad x \geq 1 \end{cases} \quad or \quad A(x) = \begin{cases} 0 & , \quad x \leq 0 \\ \frac{1-e^{-\frac{x}{5}}}{1-e^{-\frac{1}{5}}} & , \quad 0 \leq x \leq 1 \\ \frac{e^{-\frac{x}{5}}}{e^{-\frac{1}{5}}} & , \quad x > 1 \end{cases} \tag{21}$$

where $A(x)$ is the membership function of the fuzzy number "***about 1 min***" and graph, Figure 5.

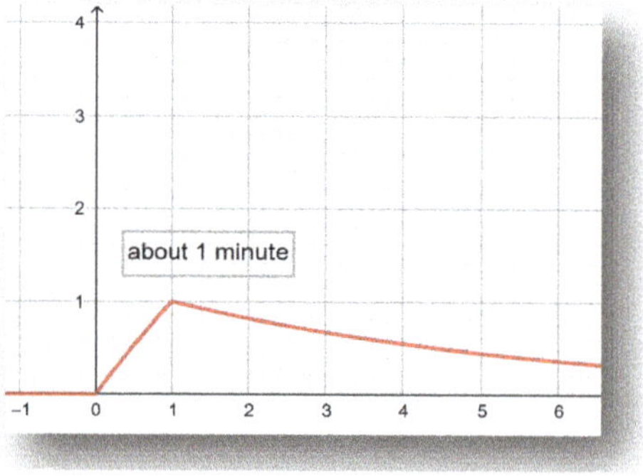


**Figure 5.** The fuzzy number "***about 1 min***" according to *F(x)*.

This fuzzy number $A(x)$ will play the role of possibility distribution according to Proposition 3 and Example 2. For question (a.), from Equation (15), we have

$$Pos_A(X \geq 5) = \sup_{x \geq 5} A(x) = A(5)\frac{e^{-\frac{5}{5}}}{e^{-\frac{1}{5}}} = e^{-\frac{4}{5}}$$

while for question (b.), according to Equation (9) we have

$$Pos_A(3 < \zeta < 5) = \sup_{3<x<5} A(x) = A(3) = \frac{e^{-\frac{3}{5}}}{e^{-\frac{1}{5}}} = e^{-\frac{2}{5}}$$

□

## 4. Discussion

It becomes obvious that the construction of the fuzzy triangular number via a cumulative distribution function is a simple process; it does not have difficult calculations, and it is applied in a very simple way. It is understood through the last paradigm that fuzziness, as Zadeh defined it, has much to offer to the theory of possibilities. The main advantage of this construction is that it minimizes the arbitrary choice of the fuzzy number, which will then play the role of possibility distribution. In future research, we will extend the theoretical results to the expected average and variance by minimizing our reference to probability theory. It should also be understood that our goal is to use the primary concept of statistics free from the concept of probability. How is this achieved? We use the tool of descriptive statistics. This is free from probability as a measure of uncertainty. Hereafter we define the possibility distribution and, consequently, the concept of the fuzzy number. In many works that use fuzzy numbers [17–19], their construction is based on intuitive or empirical data [20,21]. Therefore, in addition to the simplicity, the construction we propose would also have the following advantage: from the collection of project data (for example, a questionnaire), we could obtain the cumulative distribution function, and then, through the construction, propose to extract the fuzzy number, essentially turning the experience into a countable quantity and then a fuzzy number.

## 5. Conclusions

Throughout history, one of the main goals of science was to measure and consequently compare quantities. Since the middle of the last century, it became evident that some sizes are unquantifiable. Spoken languages have adapted to this fact, and we have been able to discuss and understand concepts such as medium, good, very good, etc. These concepts have become conceptual constants innate in our logic. Similarly, the future fuzzy numbers will be an important tool in scientific endeavors. We believe this paper gives a sound basis for constructing fuzzy numbers by linking them to research data. The construction we propose is a step towards determining the fuzzy numbers not based only on the intuition or experience of the researchers but through a construction method based on research data. Because the method we presented in this work has a clear theoretical background, we will be able to orient our future studies to research data and make our results comparable with other research studies.

**Author Contributions:** G.S. and Y.A. conceptualized and designed the study. G.S. and Y.A. wrote the manuscript. G.S., Y.A. and B.P. revised the manuscript. Y.A. and B.P. attributed the final approval of the version to be submitted. All authors have read and agreed to the published version of the manuscript.

**Funding:** This research received no external funding.

**Conflicts of Interest:** The authors declare no conflict of interest.

## References


1. Goguen, J.A. L. A. Zadeh. Fuzzy sets. *Information and control*, vol. 8 (1965), pp. 338–353.—L. A. Zadeh. Similarity relations and fuzzy orderings. *Information sciences*, vol. 3 (1971), pp. 177–200. *J. Symb. Log.* **1973**, *38*, 656–657. [CrossRef]
2. Dubois, D.; Prade, H. Possibility theory. In *Encyclopedia of Complexity and Systems Science*; Meyers, R.A., Ed.; Springer: New York, NY, USA, 2009; pp. 6927–6939. [CrossRef]
3. Carlsson, C.; Fullér, R. *Fuzzy Reasoning in Decision Making and Optimization*; Physica: Heidelberg, Germany, 2001; Volume 82.
4. Mareš, M. Fuzzy shapley value. In *Fuzzy Cooperative Games: Cooperation with Vague Expectations*; Physica-Verlag HD: Heidelberg, Germany, 2001; pp. 89–93. [CrossRef]
5. Fullér, R. Artificial neural networks. In *Introduction to Neuro-Fuzzy Systems*; Physica-Verlag HD: Heidelberg, Germany, 2000; pp. 133–170. [CrossRef]
6. Klir, G.; Yuan, B. *Fuzzy Sets and Fuzzy Logic*; Prentice Hall: Hoboken, NJ, USA, 1995; Volume 4.
7. Georgescu, I. *Possibility Theory and the Risk*; Springer: Berlin/Heidelberg, Germany, 2012; Volume 274. [CrossRef]
8. Park, K. *Fundamentals of Probability and Stochastic Processes with Applications to Communications*; Springer: Cham, Switzerland, 2018. [CrossRef]
9. Carlsson, C.; Fullér, R. On possibilistic mean value and variance of fuzzy numbers. *Fuzzy Sets Syst.* **2001**, *122*, 315–326. [CrossRef]
10. Nelsen, R.B. *An Introduction to Copulas*; Springer Science & Business Media: Berlin/Heidelberg, Germany, 2007.
11. Sugeno, M. Fuzzy measures and fuzzy integrals—A survey. In *Readings in Fuzzy Sets for Intelligent Systems*; Elsevier: Amsterdam, The Netherlands, 1993; pp. 251–257.
12. Zadeh, L.A. Fuzzy sets as a basis for a theory of possibility. *Fuzzy Sets Syst.* **1978**, *1*, 3–28. [CrossRef]
13. Sfiris, D.S.; Papadopoulos, B.K. Fuzzy estimators in expert systems. *Appl. Math. Sci.* **2012**, *6*, 1695–1718.
14. Yager, R.R.; Zadeh, L.A. *An Introduction to Fuzzy Logic Applications in Intelligent Systems*; Springer Science & Business Media: Berlin/Heidelberg, Germany, 2012; Volume 165.
15. Mylonas, N.; Papadopoulos, B. Unbiased Fuzzy Estimators in Fuzzy Hypothesis Testing. *Algorithms* **2021**, *14*, 185. [CrossRef]
16. Murofushi, T.; Sugeno, M. Fuzzy measures and fuzzy integrals. *Fuzzy Meas. Integrals Theory Appl.* **2000**, *2000*, 3–41.
17. Hatefi, S.M.; Tamošaitienė, J. An integrated fuzzy DEMATEL-fuzzy ANP model for evaluating construction projects by considering interrelationships among risk factors. *J. Civ. Eng. Manag.* **2019**, *25*, 114–131. [CrossRef]
18. Marín, L.G.; Cruz, N.; Sáez, D.; Sumner, M.; Núñez, A. Prediction interval methodology based on fuzzy numbers and its extension to fuzzy systems and neural networks. *Expert Syst. Appl.* **2019**, *119*, 128–141. [CrossRef]
19. Peddi, P. Defuzzification method for ranking fuzzy numbers based on centroids and maximizing and minimizing set. *Decis. Sci. Lett.* **2019**, *8*, 411–428. [CrossRef]
20. Li, M.; Wang, H.; Wang, D.; Shao, Z.; He, S. Risk assessment of gas explosion in coal mines based on fuzzy AHP and bayesian network. *Process Saf. Environ. Prot.* **2020**, *135*, 207–218. [CrossRef]
21. Seiti, H.; Hafezalkotob, A.; Martínez, L. R-numbers, a new risk modeling associated with fuzzy numbers and its application to decision making. *Inf. Sci.* **2019**, *483*, 206–231. [CrossRef]

mathematics

MDPI

*Review*

# Fuzziness, Indeterminacy and Soft Sets: Frontiers and Perspectives

**Michael Gr. Voskoglou**

Department of Applied Mathematics, Graduate Technological Educational Institute of Western Greece, 22334 Patras, Greece; mvoskoglou@gmail.com or voskoglou@teiwest.gr

**Abstract:** The present paper comes across the main steps that were laid from Zadeh's fuzziness and Atanassov's intuitionistic fuzzy sets to Smarandache's indeterminacy and to Molodstov's soft sets. Two hybrid methods for assessment and decision making, respectively, under fuzzy conditions are also presented using suitable examples that use soft sets and real intervals as tools. The decision making method improves on an earlier method of Maji et al. Further, it is described how the concept of topological space, the most general category of mathematical spaces, can be extended to fuzzy structures and how to generalize the fundamental mathematical concepts of limit, continuity compactness and Hausdorff space within such kinds of structures. In particular, fuzzy and soft topological spaces are defined and examples are given to illustrate these generalizations.

**Keywords:** fuzzy set (FS); fuzzy logic (FL); intuitionistic FS (IFS); indeterminacy; neutrosophic set (NS); soft set (SS); decision making (DM); fuzzy topological space (FTS); soft topological space (STS)

**MSC:** O3E72

**Citation:** Voskoglou, M.G. Fuzziness, Indeterminacy and Soft Sets: Frontiers and Perspectives. *Mathematics* **2022**, *10*, 3909. https://doi.org/10.3390/math10203909

Academic Editors: Salvatore Sessa and Gia Sirbiladze

Received: 28 July 2022
Accepted: 18 October 2022
Published: 21 October 2022



## 1. Introduction

### 1.1. Multi-Valued LOGICS

The development of human science and civilization owes a lot to Aristotle's (384–322 BC) *bivalent logic (BL)*, which was at the center of human reasoning for more than two thousand years. BL is based on the "Principle of the Excluded Middle", according to which each proposition is either true or false.

Opposite views also appeared early in human history, however, supporting the existence of a third area between true and false, where these two notions can exist together; e.g., by Buddha Siddhartha Gautama (India, around 500 BC), by Plato (427–377 BC), and more recently by the philosophers Hegel, Marx, Engels, etc. Integrated propositions of multi-valued logics appeared, however, only during the early 1900s by Lukasiewicz, Tarski, and others. According to the "Principle of Valence", formulated by Lukasiewicz, propositions are not only either true or false, but they can have an intermediate truth-value.

### 1.2. Literature Review

Zadeh introduced, in 1965, the concept of *fuzzy set (FS)* [1] and with the help of this developed the infinite in the unit interval [0, 1] *fuzzy logic* [2] with the purpose of dealing with partial truths. FL, where truth values are modelled by numbers in the unit interval, satisfies the Lukasiewicz's "Principle of Valence". It was only in a second moment that FS theory and FL were used to embrace *uncertainty* modelling [3,4]. This happened when membership functions were reinterpreted as possibility distributions. *Possibility theory* is an uncertainty theory devoted to the handling of incomplete information [5]. Zadeh articulated the relationship between possibility and probability, noticing that what is probable must preliminarily be possible [3].

The uncertainty that exists in everyday life and science is connected to inadequate information about the corresponding case. A reduction, therefore, of the existing uncertainty (via new evidence) means the addition of an equal piece of information. This is why the methods of measuring information (Hartley's formula, Shannon's entropy, etc.) are also used for measuring uncertainty and vice versa; e.g., see ([6], Chapter 5).

*Probability* theory used to be, for a long period, the unique way to deal with problems connected to uncertainty. Probability, however, is suitable only for tackling cases of uncertainty that are due to *randomness* [7]. However, randomness characterizes events with known outcomes that cannot be predicted in advance, e.g., games of chance. Starting from Zadeh's FS, however, various generalizations of FSs and other related theories have been proposed enabling, among others, a more effective management of all types of existing uncertainty. These generalizations and theories include *type-n FS*, $n \geq 2$ [8], *interval-valued FS* [9], *intuitionistic FS (IFS)* [10], *hesitant FS* [11], *Pythagorean FS* [12], *neutrosophic set* [13], *complex FS* [14], *grey system* [15], *rough set* [16], *soft set (SS)* [17], *picture FS* [18], etc. A brief description of all the previous generalizations and theories, the catalogue of which does not end here, can be found in [19].

Fuzzy mathematics have found many and important practical applications (e.g., see [6,20–24], etc.), but also have interesting connections with branches of pure mathematics, such as Algebra, Geometry, Topology, etc. (e.g., see [25,26], etc.).

### 1.3. Organization of the Paper

The paper at hand reviews the process that was laid from Zadeh's fuzziness and Atanassov's IFS to Smarandache's indeterminacy and to Molodstov's soft set. It also presents, using suitable examples, two hybrid methods for *assessment* and *decision making (DM)* under fuzzy conditions using SS and real intervals as tools, and describes how one can extend in a natural way the fundamental notion of *topological space (TS)* to fuzzy structures and can generalize the fundamental mathematical concepts of limit, continuity compactness, etc. within such kinds of structures. More explicitly, Section 2 contains the basics about FSs and FL needed for this work. In Section 3, the concepts of IFS and NS are defined. The concept of SS is presented in Section 4, where basic operations on SSs are also defined. The hybrid assessment and DM methods are developed in Section 5 and the notion of TS is extended to fuzzy structures in Section 6. The last section, Section 7, contains the article's final conclusion and some suggestions for future research.

## 2. Fuzzy Sets and Fuzzy Logic

This section contains the basic information about FSs and FL needed for the understanding of the rest of the paper.

### 2.1. Fuzzy Sets and Systems

Zadeh defined the concept of FS as follows [1]:

**Definition 1.** *Let U be the universe, then a FS F in U is of the form*

$$F = \{(x, m(x)) : x \in U\} \tag{1}$$

*In (1) m: U → [0, 1] is the membership function of F and m(x) is called the membership degree of x in F. The closer m(x) to 1, the better x satisfies the property of F.*

A crisp subset F of U is a FS in U with membership function such that m(x) = 1 if x belongs to F and 0 otherwise.

FSs successfully tackle the uncertainty due to *vagueness*, which is created when one is unable to distinguish between two properties, such as "a good player" and "a mediocre player". A serious disadvantage of FSs, however, is that there is not any exact rule for properly defining their membership function. The methods used for this are usually statistical, intuitive or empirical. Moreover, the definition of the membership function is not unique depending on the "signals" that each person receives from the environment. For example, defining the FS of "old people", one could consider as old all those aged more than 50 years and for another one, all those aged more than 60 years. As a result, the first person will assign membership degree 1 to all people aged between 50 and 60 years, whereas the second will assign membership degrees less than 1. Analogous differences will appear, therefore, to the membership degrees of all the other people. Consequently, the only restriction for the definition of the membership function is that it must be compatible with common sense; otherwise, the resulting FS does not give a creditable description of the corresponding real case. This could happen, for instance, if in the previous example, people aged less than 20 years possessed membership degrees $\geq 0.5$.

**Definition 2.** *The universal FS $F_U$ and the empty FS $F_\emptyset$ in the universe U are defined as the FSs on U with membership functions m(x) = 1 and m(x) = 0 respectively, for all x in U.*

**Definition 3.** *If K and L are FSs in U with membership functions $m_K$ and $m_L$ respectively, then K is called a fuzzy subset of L if $m_K(x) \leq m_L(x)$, for all x in U. We write then $K \subseteq L$. If $m_K(x) < m_L(x)$, for all x in U, then K is said to be a proper fuzzy subset of L and we write $K \subset L$.*

**Definition 4.** *If K and L are FSs in U with membership functions $m_K$ and $m_L$ respectively, then:*

- *The union K∪L is said to be the FS in U with membership function $m_{K \cup L}(x) = max\,\{m_K(x), m_L\,(x)\}$, for each x in U.*
- *The intersection K∩L is said to be the FS in U with membership function $m_{\,K \cap L}\,(x) = min\,\{m_K(x), m_L\,(x)\}$, for each x in U.*
- *The complement of K is the FS K* in U with membership function $m^*(x) = 1 - m(x)$, for all x in U.*

If K and L are crisp subsets of U, then all of the previous definitions reduce to the ordinary definitions for crisp sets.

Zadeh realized that FSs correspond to words (adjectives or adverbs) of the natural language [27]; e.g., the word "clever" corresponds to the FS of clever people, since how clever everyone is, is a matter of degree. A synthesis of FSs related to each other is said to be a *fuzzy system,* which mimics the way of human reasoning. For example, a fuzzy system can control the function of an air-conditioner, or can send signals for purchasing shares, etc. [21].

### 2.2. Probabilistic vs. Fuzzy Logic—Bayesian Reasoning

Many of the traditional supporters of the classical BL claimed that, since BL works effectively in science and computing and explains the phenomena of the real world, except perhaps those that happen in the boundaries, there is no reason to introduce the unstable principles of a multi-valued logic. FL, however, aims exactly at clearing the happenings in the boundaries! Look, for example, at Figure 1 [28] representing the FS T of "tall people". People with a height less than 1.50 m possess a membership degree 0 in T. The membership degrees increase for heights greater than 1.50 m, taking the value 1 for heights as being equal to or greater than 1.80 m. Therefore, the "fuzzy part" of the graph—which is represented, for simplicity, in Figure 1 by the straight line segment AC—but its exact form depends upon the definition of the membership function—lies in the area of the rectangle ABCD formed by the OX axis, its parallel passing through point E and the two perpendicular to the OX lines at points A and B.

BL, on the contrary, considers a boundary (e.g., 1.8 m) above which people are tall and below which they are short. Thus, an individual with a height of 1.805 m is considered to be tall, whereas another with a height of 1.795 m is considered to be short!

In conclusion, FL generalizes and completes the traditional BL fitting better, not only to our everyday life situations, but also to the scientific way of thinking. More details about FL can be found in Section 2 of [28].

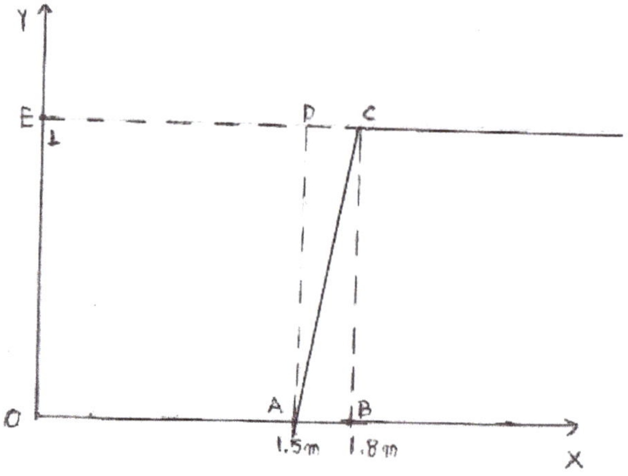


**Figure 1.** Graph of the FS of "tall people".

E. Jaynes argued that probability theory is a generalization of BL, reducing it in cases where something is either absolutely true or absolutely false [29]. A considerable number of scientists, such as D. Mumford, famous for his contributions to Algebraic Geometry [30], supported his ideas. Nevertheless, as we have already seen in our Introduction, probability, due to its bivalent texture, effectively tackles the uncertainty due to randomness. Therefore, Jaynes' probabilistic logic is subordinate to FL.

*Bayesian Reasoning*, however, connects BL and FL [31]. In fact, the *Bayes' rule* expressed by Equation (2) below, calculates the *conditional probability* P(A/B) with the help of P(B/A), of the *prior probability* P(A) and the *posterior probability* P(B)

$$\mathrm{P(A/B)} = \frac{\mathrm{P(B/A)P(A)}}{\mathrm{P(B)}} \tag{2}$$

The value of P(A) is fixed before the experiment, whereas the value of P(B) is obtained from the experiment's data. Frequently, however, the value of P(A) is not standard. In such cases, different values of the conditional probability P(A/B) are obtained for all the possible values of P(A). Consequently, Bayes' rule tackles the existing, due to the imprecision of the value of the prior probability, uncertainty in a way analogous to FL ([32], Section 5).

Bayesian reasoning is very important in everyday life situations and for the whole science too. Recent researches have shown that most of the mechanisms under which the human brain works are Bayesian [33]. Thus, Bayesian reasoning is a very useful tool for *Artificial Intelligence (AI)*, which mimics human behavior. The physicist and Nobel prize winner John Mather has already expressed his uneasiness about the possibility that the Bayesian machines could become too smart in future, making humans look useless [34]! Consequently, Sir Harold Jeffreys (1891–1989) has successfully characterized the Bayesian rule as the "Pythagorean Theorem of Probability Theory" [35].

## 3. Intuitionistic Fuzzy Sets and Neutrosophic Sets

K. Atanassov, Professor of Mathematics at the Bulgarian Academy of Sciences added, in 1986, to Zadeh's membership degree the degree of *non-membership* and introduced the concept of IFS as follows [10]:

**Definition 5.** *An IFS A in the universe U is defined as the set of the ordered triples*

$$\mathrm{A} = \{(\mathrm{x}, \mathrm{m(x)}, \mathrm{n(x)}) : \mathrm{x} \in \mathrm{U},\ 0 \le \mathrm{m(x)} + \mathrm{n(x)} \le 1\} \tag{3}$$

*In Equation (3) m: U →[0, 1] is the membership function and n: U →[0, 1] is the non-membership function.*

We can write m(x) + n(x) + h(x) = 1, where h(x) is the *hesitation* or *uncertainty degree* of x. If h(x) = 0, then the IFS becomes a FS. The name intuitionistic was given because an IFS has an inherent intuitionistic idea by incorporating the degree of hesitation.

For example, if A is the IFS of the good students of a class and (x, 0.7, 0.2) ∈ A, then x is characterized as a good student by 70% of the teachers of the class, and as not good by 20% of them; whereas, there is hesitation by 10% of the teachers to characterize him or her as either a good or not good student. Most concepts and operations about FSs can be extended to IFSs, which successfully simulate the existing imprecision in human thinking [36].

F. Smarandache, Professor of the New Mexico University, defined, in 1995, the concept of NS as follows [13]:

**Definition 6.** *A single valued NS (SVNS) A in the universe U has the form*

$$A = \{(x, T(x), I(x), F(x)) : x \in U,\ T(x), I(x), F(x) \in [0,1],\ 0 \le T(x) + I(x) + F(x) \le 3\} \quad (4)$$

*In Equation (4) T(x), I(x), F(x) are the degrees of truth (or membership), indeterminacy (or neutrality) and falsity (or non-membership) of x in A respectively, called the neutrosophic components of x. For simplicity, we write A < T, I, F>.*

The word "neutrosophy" is a synthesis of the word "neutral" and the Greek word "sophia" (wisdom) and means "the knowledge of neutral thought".

For example, let U be the set of employees of a company and let A be the SVNS of the working hardly employees. Then, each employee x is characterized by a neutrosophic triplet (t, i, f) with respect to A, with t, i, f in [0, 1]. For example, x(0.7, 0.1, 0.4) ∈ A means that the manager of the company is 70% sure that x works hard, but at the same time he or she has 10% doubt about it and a 40% belief that x is not working hard. In particular, x(0, 1, 0) ∈ A means that the manager does not know absolutely nothing about x's affiliation with A.

Indeterminacy is defined, in general, as being everything that exists between the opposites of truth and falsity [37]. In an IFS, it is I(x) = 1 − T(x) − F(x), i.e., the indeterminacy is equal with the hesitancy. In an FS, it is I(x) = 0 and F(x) = 1 − T(x) and in a crisp set it is T(x) = 1 (or 0) and F(x) = 0 (or 1). Consequently, crisp sets, FSs and IFSs are special cases of SVNSs.

If T(x) + I(x) + F(x) < 1, then it leaves room for incomplete information about x, when it is equal to 1, it leaves room for complete information, and when it is > 1 it leaves room for *paraconsistent* (i.e., contradiction tolerant) information about x. A SVNS may contain simultaneous elements, leaving room for all of the previous types of information.

If T(x) + I(x) + F(x) < 1, ∀ x ∈ U, then the corresponding SVNS is called a *picture FS (PiFS)* [18]. In this case, 1 − T(x) − I(x) − F(x) is the degree of *refusal membership* of x in A. The PiFSs are successfully tackling cases related to human opinions involving answers of types yes, abstain, no and a refusal to participate, such as in the voting process.

The difference between the *general definition of an NS* and the already given definition of an SVNS is that, in the former case, T(x), I(x) and F(x) may take values in the non-standard unit interval ]−0, 1+[, which includes values <0 or >1. For example, a banker with full-time work, 35 h per week, one upon his or her work could belong by $\frac{35}{35} = 1$ to the bank (full-time) or by $\frac{20}{35} < 1$ (part-time) or by $\frac{40}{35} > 1$ (over-time). Assume further that an employee caused damage that is balanced with his salary. Then, if the cost is equal to $\frac{40}{35}$ of his weekly salary, the employee belongs, this week, to the bank by $-\frac{5}{35} < 0$.

Most concepts and operations of FSs and IFSs are extended to NSs [38], which, apart from vagueness, tackle adequately the uncertainty due to *ambiguity* and *inconsistency*. Ambiguity takes place when the available information can be interpreted in several ways. This could happen, for example, among the jurymen of a trial. Inconsistency appears when two or more pieces of information cannot be true at the same time. As a result, the obtainable in this case information is conflicted or undetermined. For example, "The probability for being windy tomorrow is 90%, but this does not mean that the probability of not having strong winds is 10%, because they might be hidden meteorological conditions".

For the same reason as for the membership function of an FS there is a difficulty to properly define the neutrosophic components of the elements of the universe in an NS. The same happens in the case of all generalizations of FSs involving membership degrees (e.g., IFSs, etc.). This caused, in 1975, the introduction of the interval-valued FS (IVFS) defined by mapping the universe U to the set of closed intervals in [0, 1] [9]. Other related to FSs theories were also developed, in which the definition of a membership function is either not necessary (grey systems and numbers [15]), or it is passed over, either by using a pair of sets that give the lower and upper approximations of the original crisp set (rough sets [16]), or by introducing a suitable set of parameters (SSs [17]).

## 4. Soft Sets

### 4.1. The Concept of Soft Set

In 1999, D. Molodstov, Professor of the Russian Academy of Sciences, introduced the notion of the *soft set (SS)* as a means for tackling uncertainty, in terms of a suitable set of parameters, in the following way [17]:

**Definition 7.** *Let E be a set of parameters, let A be a subset of E, and let f be a map from A into the power set P(U) of the universe U. Then the SS (f, A) in U has the form*

$$(f, A) = \{(e, f(e)) : e \in A\} \tag{5}$$

In other words, an SS can be considered as a parametrized family of subsets of U. The name "soft" is due to the fact that the form of (f, A) depends on the parameters of A. For each $e \in A$, its image f(e) in P(U) is called the value set of e in (f, A), while f is called the approximation function of (f, A).

For example, let $U = \{C_1, C_2, C_3\}$ be a set of cars and let $E = \{e_1, e_2, e_3\}$ be the set of the parameters $e_1$ = cheap, $e_2$ = hybrid (petrol and electric power), and $e_3$ = expensive. Let us further assume that $C_1$, $C_2$ are cheap, $C_3$ is expensive, and $C_2$, $C_3$ are the hybrid cars. Then, a map $f: E \to P(U)$ is defined by $f(e_1) = \{C_1, C_2\}$, $f(e_2) = \{C_2, C_3\}$ and $f(e_3) = \{C_3\}$. Therefore, the SS (f, E) in U is the set of the ordered pairs $(f, E) = \{(e_1, \{C_1, C_2\}), (e_2, \{C_2, C_3\}, (e_3, \{C_3\}\}$. The SS (f, E) can be represented by the graph of Figure 2.

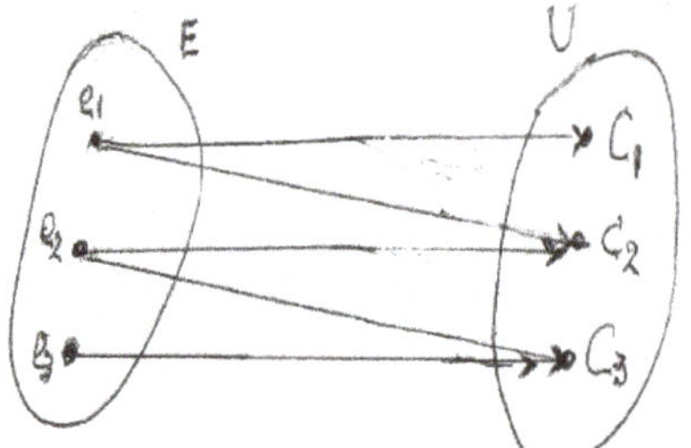


**Figure 2.** Graphical representation of the SS (f, E).

On comparing the graphs of Figures 1 and 2, one can see that an FS is represented by a simple graph, whereas a bipartite graph [39] is needed for the representation of an SS.

Maji et al. [40] introduced a *tabular representation* of SSs in the form of a binary matrix in order to be stored easily in a computer's memory. For example, the tabular representation of the soft set (f, E) is given in Table 1.

**Table 1.** Tabular representation of the SS (f, E).

| | $e_1$ | $e_2$ | $e_3$ |
|---|---|---|---|
| $C_1$ | 1 | 0 | 0 |
| $C_2$ | 1 | 1 | 0 |
| $C_3$ | 0 | 1 | 1 |

An FS in U with the membership function y = m(x) is an SS in U of the form (f, [0, 1]), where

$f(\alpha) = \{x \in U: m(x) \geq \alpha\}$ is the corresponding *a-cut* of the FS, for each $\alpha$ in [0, 1]. Consequently, the concept of SS is a generalization of the concept of FS.

An important advantage of SSs is that, by using the parameters, they pass through the already mentioned difficulty of properly defining membership functions.

### 4.2. Operations on Soft Sets

**Definition 8.** *The absolute SS $A_U$ is the SS (f, A) in which f(e) = U,$\forall$ e$\in$ A, and the null soft set $A_\emptyset$ is the SS (f, A) in which f(e) =$\emptyset$,$\forall$ e$\in$A.*

**Definition 9.** *If (f, A) and (g, B) are SSs in U, (f, A) is a soft subset of (g, B), if $A \subseteq B$ and $f(e) \subseteq g(e)$, $\forall$ e $\in$ A. We write then $(f, A) \subseteq (g, B)$. If $A \subset B$, then (f, A) is called a proper soft subset of B and we write $(f, A) \subset (g, B)$.*

**Definition 10.** *Let (f, A) and (g, B) be SSs in U. Then:*

- *The union $(f, A) \cup (g, B)$ is the SS $(h, A\cup B)$ in U, with h(e) = f(e) if e$\in$ A-B, h(e) = g(e) if e$\in$ B-A and $h(e) = f(e)\cup g(e)$ if e$\in$ $A\cap B$.*
- *The intersection $(f, A) \cap (g, B)$ is the soft set $(h, A\cap B)$ in U, with $h(e) = f(e)\cap g(e)$,$\forall$ e$\in$ $A\cap B$.*
- *The complement $(f, A)^C$ of the soft SS (f, A) in U, is defined to be the SS (f*, A) in U, in which the function f* is defined by f*(e) = U−f(e),$\forall$ e$\in$ A.*

For general facts on soft sets, we refer to [41].

**Example 1.** *Let $U = \{H_1, H_2, H_3\}$, $E = \{e_1, e_2, e_3\}$ and $A = \{e_1, e_2\}$. Consider the SS*
*$S = (f, A) = \{(e_1, \{H_1, H_2\}), (e_2, \{H_2, H_3\})\}$ of U. Then the soft subsets of S are the following:*
*$S_1 = \{(e_1, \{H_1\})\}$, $S_2 = \{(e_1, \{H_2\})\}$, $S_3 = \{(e_1, \{H_1, H_2\})\}$,*
*$S_4 = \{(e_2, \{H_2\})\}$, $S_5 = \{(e_2, \{H_3\})\}$, $S_6 = \{(e_2, \{H_2, H_3\})\}$,*
*$S_7 = \{(e_1, \{H_1\}, (e_2, \{H_2\})\}$, $S_8 = \{(e_1, \{H_1\}, (e_2, \{H_3\})\}$,*
*$S_9 = \{(e_1, \{H_2\}, (e_2, \{H_2\})\}$, $S_{10} = \{(e_1, \{H_2\}, (e_2, \{H_3\})\}$,*
*$S_{11} = \{(e_1, \{H_1, H_2\}, (e_2, \{H_2\})\}$, $S_{12} = \{(e_1, \{H_1, H_2\}, (e_2, \{H_3\})\}$,*
*$S_{13} = \{(e_1, \{H_1\}, (e_2, \{H_2, H_3\})\}$, $S_{14} = \{(e_1, \{H_2\}, (e_2, \{H_2, H_3\})\}$,*
*S, $A_\emptyset = \{(e_1,\emptyset), (e_2,\emptyset)\}$. It is also easy to check that $(f, A)^C = \{(e_1, \{H_3\}), (e_2, \{H_1\})\}$.*

## 5. Hybrid Assessment and Decision Making Methods under Fuzzy Conditions

Each of the various theories that have been proposed for tackling existing real world uncertainty [19] is more suitable for certain types of uncertainty. Frequently, however, a combination of two or more of these theories gives better results. To support this argument, we present here two hybrid methods for assessment [42] and decision making [43] respectively under fuzzy conditions using SSs and closed real intervals as tools

### 5.1. Using Closed Real Intervals for Handling Approximate Data

An important perspective of the closed intervals of real numbers is their use for handling approximate data. In fact, a numerical interval I = [x, y], with x, y real numbers, x < y, is actually representing a real number with a known range, whose exact value is unknown. When no other information is given about this number, it looks logical to consider, as its representative approximation, the real value

$$V(I) = \frac{x+y}{2} \tag{6}$$

The closer x to y, the better V(I) approximates the corresponding real number.

Moore et al. introduced in 1995 [44] the basic arithmetic operations on closed real intervals.

In particular, and according to the interests of the present article, if $I_1 = [x_1, y_1]$ and $I_2 = [x_2, y_2]$ are closed intervals, then their *sum* $I_1 + I_2$ is the closed interval

$$I_1 + I_2 = [x_1 + x_2, y_1 + y_2] \tag{7}$$

Also, if k is a positive number then the *scalar product* $kI_1$ is the closed interval

$$kI_1 = [kx_1, ky_1] \tag{8}$$

When the closed real intervals are used for handling approximate data, are also referred to as *grey numbers (GNs)*. A GN [x, y], however, may also be connected with a *whitenization function*

f: [x, y] → [0, 1], such that, ∀ a ∈ [x, y], the closer f(a) to 1, the better the approximates of the unknown number represented by [x, y] ([22], Section 6.1).

We close this subsection about closed real intervals with the following definition, which will be used in the assessment method that follows.

**Definition 11.** *Let $I_1, I_2, \ldots, I_k$ be a finite number of closed real intervals and assume that $I_i$ appears $n_i$ times in an application, i = 1, 2, . . . ., k. Set $n = n_1 + n_2 + \ldots + n_k$. Then the mean value of all these intervals is defined to be the closed real interval*

$$I = \frac{1}{n}\left(n_1 I_1 + n_2 I_2 + \ldots . n_k I_k\right) \tag{9}$$

### 5.2. The Assessment Method

Assessment is one of the most important components of all human and machine activities, helping to determine possible mistakes and to improve performance with respect to a certain activity.

The assessment processes are realized by using either numerical or linguistic (qualitative) grades, such as excellent, good, moderate, etc. Traditional assessment methods are applied in the former case, which give accurate results, the most standard among them being the calculation of the mean value of the numerical scores.

Frequently, however, the use of numerical scores is either not possible (e.g., in the case of approximate data) or not desirable (e.g., when more elasticity is required for the assessment). In such cases, assessment methods based on principles of FL are usually applied. A great part of the present author's earlier researches were focused on developing such kinds of methods, most of which are reviewed in detail in [22]. It seems, however, that proper combinations of the previous methodologies could give better results (e.g., see [42]). The assessment method developed by the present author in [42] will be illustrated here with the help of the following example.

**Example 2.** *Let $U = \{p_1, p_2, \ldots, p_{19}, p_{20}\}$ be the set of the players in a football team. Assume that the first 3 of them are excellent players, the next 7 very good players, the following 5 good players, the next 3 mediocre players, and the last 2 new players have no satisfactory performance yet. It is asked: (1) to make a parametric assessment of the team's quality, and (2) to estimate the mean potential of the team.*

*Solution*: (1) Consider the linguistic grades A = excellent, B = very good, C = good, D = mediocre, and F = not satisfactory, set E = {A, B, C, D, F} and define a map f: E → P(U) by f(A) = {$p_1$, $p_2$, $p_3$}, f(B) = {$p_4$, $p_5$, … ,$p_{10}$}, f(C) = {$p_{11}$, $p_{12}$, … , $p_{15}$}, f(D) = {$p_{16}$, $p_{17}$, $p_{18}$}, and f(F) = {$p_{19}$, $p_{20}$}. Then the required parametric assessment of the team's quality can be represented by the soft set

$$(f, E) = \{(A, f(A)), (B, f(B)), (C, f(C)), (D, f(D)), (F, f(F))\}$$

(2) Assign to each parameter (linguistic grade) of E a closed real interval, denoted for simplicity by the same letter, as follows: A = [85, 100], B = [75, 84], C = [60, 74], D = [50, 59], F = [0, 49]. Then by (9), the mean potential of the football team can be approximated by the real interval

$$M = \frac{1}{20}(3A + 7B + 5C + 3D + 2F)$$

Applying Equations (7) and (8) and making the corresponding calculations one finds that

$M = \frac{1}{20}[1230, 1533] = [61.5, 76.65]$. Thus, Equation (5) gives that V(M) = 69.075, which shows that the mean potential of the football team is good (C).

**Remark 1.** *The choice of the intervals in case 2 of the previous example corresponds to generally accepted standards for translating the linguistic grades A, B, C, D, F in the numerical scale 0 –100. By no means, however, should this choice be considered as being unique, since it depends on the special beliefs of the user. For example, one could as well choose A = [80, 100], B = [70, 79], C = [60, 69], D = [50, 59], F = [0, 49], etc.*

**Remark 2.** *One could equivalently use triangular fuzzy numbers (TFNs) instead of closed real intervals in the previous example [22].*

### *5.3. The Decision Making Method*

Maji et al. [40] developed a parametric DM method using SSs as tools. In an earlier work [42], we have improved their method by adding closed real intervals (GNs) to the tools. Here, we illustrate our improved method with the following example.

**Example 3.** *A candidate buyer, who believes that the ideal house to buy should be cheap, beautiful, wooden and in the country, has to choose among six houses $H_1$, $H_2$, $H_3$, $H_4$, $H_5$ and $H_6$, which are for sale. Assume further that $H_1$, $H_2$, $H_6$ are the beautiful houses, $H_2$, $H_3$, $H_5$, $H_6$ are in the country, $H_3$, $H_5$ are wooden and $H_4$ is the unique cheap house. Which is the best choice for the candidate buyer?*

*Solution:* First we solve this DM problem following the method of Maji et al. [40]. For this, consider U = {$H_1$, $H_2$, $H_3$, $H_4$, $H_5$, $H_6$} as the set of the discourse and let E = {$e_1$, $e_2$, $e_3$, $e_4$} be the set of the parameters $e_1$ = beautiful, $e_2$ = in the country, $e_3$ = wooden and $e_4$ = cheap. Then a map f: E → P(U) is defined by f($e_1$) = { $H_1$, $H_2$, $H_6$}, f($e_2$) = { $H_2$, $H_3$, $H_5$, $H_6$}, f($e_3$) = { $H_3$, $H_5$}, f($e_4$) = { $H_4$}, which gives rise to the SS (f, E) = {($e_1$, f($e_1$)), ($e_2$, f($e_2$)), ($e_3$, f($e_3$)), ($e_4$, f($e_4$))}.

One can write the previous SS in its tabular form as it is shown in Table 2.

Then, the *choice value* of each house is calculated by adding the binary elements of the row of Table 1 in which it belongs. The houses $H_1$ and $H_4$ have, therefore, choice value 1 and all the others have choice value 2. Consequently, the candidate buyer must choose one of the houses $H_2$, $H_3$, $H_5$ or $H_6$.

The previous decision, however, is obviously not so helpful. This gives us a hint to revise the previous DM method of Maji et al. In fact, observe that, in contrast to $e_2$ and $e_3$, the parameters $e_1$ and $e_4$ in the present problem do not have a bivalent texture. This means that it is closer to reality to characterize them using the qualitative grades A, B, C, D and F of Example 1, than by the binary elements 0, 1.

**Table 2.** Tabular representation of the SS (f, E).

| | $e_1$ | $e_2$ | $e_3$ | $e_4$ |
|---|---|---|---|---|
| $H_1$ | 1 | 0 | 0 | 0 |
| $H_2$ | 1 | 1 | 0 | 0 |
| $H_3$ | 0 | 1 | 1 | 0 |
| $H_4$ | 0 | 0 | 0 | 1 |
| $H_5$ | 0 | 1 | 1 | 0 |
| $H_6$ | 1 | 1 | 0 | 0 |

Assume, therefore, that the candidate buyer, after carefully studying all of the existing information about the six houses for sale, decided to use the following Table 3 instead of Table 2 to make the right decision.

**Table 3.** Revised tabular representation of the SS (f, E).

| | $e_1$ | $e_2$ | $e_3$ | $e_4$ |
|---|---|---|---|---|
| $H_1$ | A | 0 | 0 | C |
| $H_2$ | A | 1 | 0 | F |
| $H_3$ | C | 1 | 1 | C |
| $H_4$ | D | 0 | 0 | A |
| $H_5$ | D | 1 | 1 | C |
| $H_6$ | A | 1 | 0 | D |

From Table 3, one calculates the choice value $C_i$ of the house Hi, i = 1, 2, 3, 4, 5, 6 as follows:

$C_1 = V(A + C)$, or by (6) $C_1 = V([0.85 + 0.6, 1 + 0.74])$ and finally by (5) $C_1 = \frac{1.45+1.74}{2} = 1.595$. Similarly, $C_2 = 1 + V(A + F) = 1 + \frac{0.85+1.49}{2} = 2.17$, $C_3 = 2 + V(C + C) = 3.34$, $C_4 = V(D + A) = 1.47$, $C_5 = 2 + V(D + C) = 3.215$, and $C_6 = 1 + V(A + D) = 2.47$. The right decision is, therefore, to buy house $H_3$.

**Remark 3.** *One could, as in Example 2, use TFNs instead of closed real intervals [45] in this DM problem.*

**Remark 4.** *The novelty of our hybrid DM method, with respect to the DM method of Maji et al. [40], is that, by using closed real intervals instead of the binary elements 0, 1 in the tabular matrix of the corresponding SS in cases where some (or all) of the parameters are not of bivalent texture, we succeed in making a better decision.*

### *5.4. Weighted Decision Making*

When the goals put by the decision-maker are not of the same importance, weight coefficients must be assigned to each parameter to make the proper decision. Assume, for instance, that in the previous example the candidate buyer assigned the weight coefficients 0.9 to $e_1$, 0.7 to $e_2$, 0.6 to $e_3$ and 0.5 to $e_4$. Then, the weighted choice values of the houses in Example 3 are calculated as follows:

$C_1 = V(0.9A + 0.5C)$, or by (5), (6) and (7) $C_1 = V([1.65, 1.27]) = 1.46$. Similarly, $C_2 = 0.7 + V(0.9A + 0.5F) = 0.7 + V([0.765,1.145]) = 1.655$, $C_3 = 0.7 + 0.6 + V(0.9C + 0.5C) = 1.3 + V([0.84,1.036]) = 2.238$, $C_4 = V(0.9D + 0.5A) = V([0.875,1.031]) = 0.953$, $C_5 = 0.7 + 0.6 + V(0.9D + 0.5C) = 1.3 + V([0.75, 0.901]) = 2.1255$, $C_6 = 0.7 + V(0.9A + 0.5D) = 0.7 + V([1.015, 1.195]) = 1.805$. Consequently, the right decision is, again, to buy house $H_3$.

## 6. Topological Spaces in Fuzzy Structures

TSs is the most general category of mathematical spaces, in which fundamental mathematical notions are defined [46]. In this section, we describe how the concept of TS is extended to fuzzy structures.

### 6.1. Fuzzy Topological Spaces

**Definition 12 ([25]).** *A fuzzy topology (FT) T on a non-empty set U is a family of FSs in U such that:*

- *The universal and the empty FSs belong to T;*
- *The intersection of any two elements of T and the union of an arbitrary number (finite or infinite) of elements of T also belong to T.*

Trivial examples of FTs are the *discrete FT* $\{F_\emptyset, F_U\}$ and the *non-discrete FT* of all FSs in U. Another example is the set of all *constant FSs* in U, i.e., all FSs in U with a membership function defined by m(x) = c, for some c in [0, 1], and all x in U.

The elements of an FT T on U are referred to as *fuzzy open sets* in U and their complements are referred to as *fuzzy closed sets* in U. The pair (U, T) is called a *fuzzy topological space (FTS)* on U.

Next, it is described how the fundamental notions of *limit, continuity, compactness, and Hausdorff TS* can be extended to FTSs [25].

**Definition 13.** *Given two FSs A and B of the FTS (U, T), B is called a neighborhood of A, if there exists an open FS O such that $A \subseteq O \subset B$.*

**Definition 14.** *A sequence $\{A_n\}$ of FSs of (U, T) converges to the FS A of (U, T), if there exists a positive integer m, such that for each integer $n \geq m$ and each neighborhood B of A we have that $A_n \subset B$. Then A is said to be the limit of $\{A_n\}$.*

**Lemma 1.** *(Zadeh's extension principle.) Let X and Y be two non-empty crisp sets and let f: $X \to Y$ be a function. Then f is extended to a function F mapping FSs in X to FSs in Y.*

**Proof.** Let A be an FS in X with a membership function $m_A$. Then, its image F(A) is an FS B in Y with a membership function $m_B$, which is defined as follows: Given y in Y, consider the set $f^{-1}(y) = \{x \in X: f(x) = y\}$. If $f^{-1}(y) = \emptyset$, then $m_B(y) = 0$, and if $f^{-1}(y) \neq \emptyset$, then $m_B(y) = \max \{m_A(x): x \in f^{-1}(y)\}$. Conversely, the inverse image $F^{-1}(B)$ is the FS A in X with a membership function $m_A(x) = m_B(f(x))$, for each $x \in X$. □

**Definition 15.** *Let (X, T) and (Y, S) be two FTSs and let f: $X \to Y$ be a function. Then f is extended to a function F mapping FSs in X to FSs in Y. Then f is said to be a fuzzily continuous function, if, and only if, the inverse image of each open FS in Y through F is an open FS in X.*

**Definition 16.** *A family $A = \{A_i, i \in I\}$ of FSs of an FTS (U, T) is said to be a cover of U, if $U = \bigcup_{i \in I} A_i$. If the elements of A are open FSs, then A is said to be an open cover of U. A subset of A, which is also a cover of U, is called a sub-cover of A. The FTS (U, T) is said to be compact, if every open cover of U contains a sub-cover with many finite elements.*

**Definition 17.** *An FTS (U, T) is said to be:*

1. *A $T_1$-FTS, if, and only if, for each pair of elements $u_1$, $u_2$ of U, $u_1 \neq u_2$, there exist at least two open FSs $O_1$ and $O_2$ such that $u_1 \in O_1$, $u_2 \notin O_1$ and $u_2 \in O_2$, $u_1 \notin O_2$.*
2. *A $T_2$-FTS (or a separable or Hausdorff FTS), if, and only if, for each pair of elements $u_1$, $u_2$ of U, $u_1 \neq u_2$, there exist at least two open FSs $O_1$ and $O_2$ such that $u_1 \in O_1$, $u_2 \in O_2$ and $O_1 \cap O_2 = \emptyset_F$.*

Obviously a $T_2$-FTS is always a $T_1$-FTS.

### 6.2. Soft Topological Spaces

Observe that the concept of FTS (Definition 12) is obtained from the classical definition of TS [45] by replacing the statement "a family of subsets of U" by the statement "a family of FSs in U". In an analogous way, one can obtain the concepts of *intuitionistic FTS (IFTS)* [26], of *neutrosophic TS (NTS)* [47], of *soft TS (STS)* [48], etc. In particular, an STS is defined as follows:

**Definition 18.** *A soft topology T on a non-empty set U is a family of SSs in U with respect to a set of parameters E such that:*

- *The absolute and S null soft sets $E_U$ and $E_\emptyset$ belong to T;*
- *The intersection of any two elements of T and the union of an arbitrary number (finite or infinite) of elements of T also belong to T.*

The elements of an ST T on U are said to be *open SS* and their complements are said to be *closed SS*. The triple (U, T, E) is said to be an STS on U.

Trivial examples of STs are the *discrete ST* $\{E_\emptyset, E_U\}$ and the *non-discrete ST* of all SSs in U. Reconsider also Example 1. It is straightforward to check then that $T = \{E_U, E_\emptyset, S, S_2, S_9, S_{11}\}$ is ST on U.

The concepts of limit, continuity, compactness, and Hausdorff TS are extended to STs in a way analogous to FTSs [49,50]. In fact, Definitions 13, 14, 16 and 17 are easily turned to corresponding definitions of STSs by replacing the expression "fuzzy sets" with the expression "soft sets". For the concept of continuity, we need the following Lemma ([49], definition 3.12):

**Lemma 2.** *Let (U, T, A), (V, S, B) be STSs and let u: U → V, p: A → B be given maps. Then a map $f_{pu}$ is defined with respect to u and p mapping the soft sets of T to soft sets of S.*

**Proof.** If (F, A) is a soft set of T, then its image $f_{pu}((F, A))$ is a soft set of S defined by

$f_{pu}((F, A)) = (f_{pu}(F), p(A))$, where, $\forall\, y \in B$ is $f_{pu}(F)(y) = \bigcup_{x \in p^{-1}(y) \cap A} u(F(x))$ if $p^{-1}(y) \cap A \neq \emptyset$ and $f_{pu}(F)(y) = \emptyset$ otherwise. □

Conversely, if (G, B) is a soft set of S, then its inverse image $f_{pu}^{-1}((G, B))$ is a soft set of T defined by $f_{pu}^{-1}((G, B)) = (f_{pu}^{-1}(G), p^{-1}(B))$, where $\forall\, x \in A$ is

$$f_{pu}^{-1}(G)(x) = u^{-1}(G(p(x))).$$

**Definition 19.** *Let (U, T, A), (V, S, B) be STSs and let u: U → V, p: A → B be given maps. Then the map $f_{pu}$, defined by Lemma 2, is said to be soft pu-continuous, if, and only if, the inverse image of each open soft set in Y through $f_{pu}$ is an open soft set in X.*

## 7. Discussion and Conclusions

Three were the goals of the present review paper:

1. We came across the main steps that were laid from Zadeh's FS and Atanassov's IFS to Smarandache's NS and to Molodstov's SS.
2. We presented, using suitable examples, two recently developed by us hybrid methods for assessment and DM, respectively, using SSs and closed real intervals (GNs) as tools.
3. We described how one can extend the concept of TS to fuzzy structures and how we can define limits, continuity, compactness and Hausdorff spaces on those structures. In particular, FTSs and STSs were defined, and characteristic examples were presented.

For reasons of completeness, however, we ought to note that, despite the fact that IFSs and SSs have already found many and important applications, there exist reports in the literature disputing the significance of these concepts, and in extension, of the notions of

IFSTS and STs, considering them as redundant, representing an unnecessarily complicated way, a standard fixed-basis set theory and topology [51–54]. In the Abstract of [52], for example, one reads: "In particular, a soft set on X with a set E of parameters actually can be regarded as a 2E-fuzzy set or a crisp subset of E × X [the correct is E × P(X)]. This shows that the concept of (fuzzy) soft set is redundant". I completely disagree with this way of thinking. Adopting it, one could claim that, since an FS A in X is a subset of the Cartesian product X × m(X), where m is the membership function of A, the concept of FS is redundant!

Among probability, FSs and the other related generalizations and theories [19], there is not an ideal model for effectively tackling all the existing types of real world uncertainty. Each one of these theories is more suitable for dealing with special types of uncertainty, e.g., probability for randomness, FSs for vagueness, IFSs for imprecision in human thinking, NSs for ambiguity and inconsistency, etc. All these theories together, however, provide an adequate framework for managing the uncertainty.

Even more, it seems that proper combinations of the previous theories give frequently better results, not only for tackling the existing uncertainty, but also for assessment purposes [42], for DM under fuzzy conditions [43], and possibly for various other human and machine activities. This is, therefore, a promising area for future research.

As we have mentioned in our Introduction, the concept of the ordinary FS, otherwise termed as type-1 FS, was generalized to the type-2 FS and further to type-n FS, $n \geq 2$, so that more uncertainty can be handled and connected to the membership function [8]. The membership function of a type-2 FS is three-dimensional, its third dimension being the value of the membership function at each point of its two-dimensional domain, which is called the footprint of uncertainty (FOU). The FOU is completely determined by its two bounding functions, a lower membership function and an upper membership function, both of which are type-1 FSs. When no uncertainty exists about the membership function, then a type-2 FS reduces to a type-1 FS, in a way analogous to probability reducing to determinism when unpredictability vanishes. However, when Zadeh proposed the type-2 FS in 1975 [8], the time was not right for researchers to drop what they were doing with type-1 FS and focus on type-2 FS. This changed in the late 1990s as a result of Prof. Jerry Mendel's works on type-2 FS and logic [55]. Since then, more and more researchers around the world are writing articles about type-2 FS and systems, while some important applications of type-3 FS and logic were also reported recently, e.g., [56,57]. This is, therefore, another promising area for future research.

**Funding:** This research received no external funding.

**Acknowledgments:** The author wishes to thank the two reviewers of the paper for their useful remarks and the suggested literature.

**Conflicts of Interest:** The author declares no conflict of interest.

## References

1. Zadeh, L.A. Fuzzy Sets. *Inf. Control* **1965**, *8*, 338–353. [CrossRef]
2. Zadeh, L.A. Outline of a new approach to the analysis of complex systems and decision processes. *IEEE Trans. Syst. Man Cybern.* **1973**, *3*, 28–44. [CrossRef]
3. Zadeh, L.A. Fuzzy Sets as a basis for a theory of possibility. *Fuzzy Sets Syst.* **1978**, *1*, 3–28. [CrossRef]
4. Dubois, D.; Prade, H. Possibility theory, probability theory and multiple-valued logics: A clarification. *Ann. Math. Artif. Intell.* **2001**, *32*, 35–66. [CrossRef]
5. Dubois, D.; Prade, H. Possibility theory and its applications: A retrospective and prospective view. In *Decision Theory and Multi-Agent Planning*; Della Riccia, G., Dubois, D., Kruse, R., Lenz, H.J., Eds.; CISM International Centre for Mechanical Sciences (Courses and Lectures); Springer: Vienna, Austria, 2006; Volume 482.
6. Klir, G.J.; Folger, T.A. *Fuzzy sets, Uncertainty and Information*; Prentice-Hall: London, UK, 1988.
7. Kosko, B. Fuzziness Vs. *Probability. Int. J. Gen. Syst.* **1990**, *17*, 211–240. [CrossRef]
8. Zadeh, L.A. The Concept of a Linguistic Variable and its Application to Approximate Reasoning. *Inf. Sci.* **1975**, *8*, 199–249. [CrossRef]

9. Dubois, D.; Prade, H. Interval-Valued Fuzzy Sets, Possibility Theory and Imprecise Probability. *Proc. EUSFLAT-LFA* **2005**, *1*, 314–319.
10. Atanassov, K.T. Intuitionistic Fuzzy Sets. *Fuzzy Sets Syst.* **1986**, *20*, 87–96. [CrossRef]
11. Torra, V.; Narukawa, Y. On hesitant fuzzy sets and decision. In Proceedings of the 18th IEEE International Conference on Fuzzy Systems, Jeju, Korea, 20–24 August 2009; Volume 544, pp. 1378–1382.
12. Yager, R.R. Pythagorean fuzzy subsets. In Proceedings of the Joint IFSA World Congress and NAFIPS Annual Meeting, Edmonton, AB, Canada, 24–28 June 2013; pp. 57–61.
13. Smarandache, F. *Neutrosophy/Neutrosophic Probability, Set, and Logic*; ProQuest: Ann Arbor, MI, USA, 1998.
14. Ramot, D.; Milo, R.; Friedman, M.; Kandel, A. Complex fuzzy sets. *IEEE Trans. Fuzzy Syst.* **2002**, *10*, 171–186. [CrossRef]
15. Deng, J. Control Problems of Grey Systems. *Syst. Control Lett.* **1982**, *1*, 288–294.
16. Pawlak, Z. *Rough Sets: Aspects of Reasoning about Data*; Kluer Academic Publishers: Dordrecht, The Netherlands, 1991.
17. Molodtsov, D. Soft set theory—First results. *Comput. Math. Appl.* **1999**, *37*, 19–31. [CrossRef]
18. Cuong, B.C. Picture Fuzzy Sets. *J. Comput. Sci. Cybern* **2014**, *30*, 409–420.
19. Voskoglou, M.G. Generalizations of Fuzzy Sets and Related Theories. In *An Essential Guide to Fuzzy Systems*; Voskoglou, M., Ed.; Nova Science Publishers: Hauppauge, NY, USA, 2019; pp. 345–352.
20. Voskoglou, M.G. *Finite Markov Chain and Fuzzy Logic Assessment Models: Emerging Research and Opportunities*; Createspace.com–Amazon: Columbia, SC, USA, 2017.
21. Voskoglou, M.G. Fuzzy Control Systems. *WSEAS Trans. Syst.* **2020**, *19*, 295–300. [CrossRef]
22. Voskoglou, M.G. Methods for Assessing Human-Machine Performance under Fuzzy Conditions. *Mathematics* **2019**, *7*, 230. [CrossRef]
23. Tripathy, B.K.; Arun, K.R. Soft Sets and Its Applications. In *Handbook of Research on Generalized and Hybrid Set Structures and Applications for Soft Computing*; Jacob, J.S., Ed.; IGI Global: Hersey, PA, USA, 2016; pp. 65–85.
24. Kharal, A.; Ahmad, B. Mappings on soft classes. *New Math. Nat. Comput.* **2011**, *7*, 471–481. [CrossRef]
25. Chang, S.L. Fuzzy topological spaces. *J. Math. Anal. Appl.* **1968**, *24*, 182–190. [CrossRef]
26. Luplanlez, F.G. On Intuitionistic Fuzzy Topological Spaces. *Kybernetes* **2006**, *35*, 743–747.
27. Zadeh, L.A. Fuzzy logic = computing with words. *IEEE Trans. Fuzzy Syst.* **1996**, *4*, 103–111. [CrossRef]
28. Voskoglou, M.G. Managing the Uncertainty: From Probability to Fuzziness, Neutrosophy and Soft Sets. *Trans. Fuzzy Sets Syst.* **2022**, *1*, 46–58. [CrossRef]
29. Jaynes, E.T. *Probability Theory: The Logic of Science*; 8th Printing; Cambridge University Press: Cambridge, UK, 2011.
30. Mumford, D. The Dawning of the Age of Stochasticity. In *Mathematics: Frontiers and Perspectives*; Amoid, V., Atiyah, M., Laxand, P., Mazur, B., Eds.; AMS: Providence, RI, USA, 2000; pp. 197–218.
31. Voskoglou, M.G. The Importance of Bayesian Reasoning in Every Day Life and Science. *Int. J. Educ. Dev. Soc. Technol.* **2020**, *8*, 24–33.
32. Gentili, P.L. Establishing a New Link between Fuzzy Logic, Neuroscience, and Quantum Mechanics through Bayesian Probability: Perspectives in Artificial Intelligence and Unconventional Computing. *Molecules* **2021**, *26*, 5987. [CrossRef]
33. Bertsch McGrayne, S. *The Theory That Would Not Die*; Yale University Press: New Haven, CT, USA; London, UK, 2012.
34. What Do You Think about Machines That Think? 2015. Available online: http://edge.org/response-detail/26871 (accessed on 24 March 2022).
35. Jeffreys, H. *Scientific Inference*, 3rd ed.; Cambridge University Press: Cambridge, UK, 1973.
36. Atanassov, K.T. *Intuitionistic Fuzzy Sets*; Physica-Verlag: Heidelberg, Germany, 1999.
37. Smarandache, F. Indeterminacy in Neutrosophic Theories and their Applications. *Int. J. Neutrosophic Sci.* **2021**, *15*, 89–97. [CrossRef]
38. Wang, H.; Smarandanche, F.; Zhang, Y.; Sunderraman, R. Single Valued Neutrosophic Sets. *Rev. Air Force Acad.* **2010**, *1*, 10–14.
39. Farid, F.; Saeed, M.; Ali, M. Representation of Soft Set and its Operations by Bipartite Graph. *Sci. Inq. Rev.* **2019**, *3*, 30–42. [CrossRef]
40. Maji, P.K.; Roy, A.R.; Biswas, R. An Application of Soft Sets in a Decision Making Problem. *Comput. Math. Appl.* **2002**, *44*, 1077–1083. [CrossRef]
41. Maji, P.K.; Biswas, R.; Ray, A.R. Soft Set Theory. *Comput. Math. Appl.* **2003**, *45*, 555–562. [CrossRef]
42. Voskoglou, M.G.; Broumi, S. A Hybrid Method for the Assessment of Analogical Reasoning Skills. *J. Fuzzy Ext. Appl.* **2022**, *3*, 152–157.
43. Voskoglou, M.G. A Combined Use of Softs Sets and Grey Numbers in Decision Making. *J. Comput. Cogn. Eng.* **2022**, in press. [CrossRef]
44. Moore, R.A.; Kearfort, R.B.; Clood, M.G. *Introduction to Interval Analysis*, 2nd ed.; SIAM: Philadelphia, PA, USA, 1995.
45. Voskoglou, M.G. A Hybrid Model for Decision Making Utilizing TFNs and Soft Sets as Tools. *Equations* **2022**, *2*, 65–69. [CrossRef]
46. Willard, S. *General Topology*; Dover Publ. Inc.: Mineola, NY, USA, 2004.
47. Salama, A.A.; Alblowi, S.A. Neutrosophic Sets and Neutrosophic Topological Spaces. *IOSR J. Math.* **2013**, *3*, 31–35. [CrossRef]
48. Shabir, M.; Naz, M. On Soft Topological Spaces. *Comput. Math. Appl.* **2011**, *61*, 1786–1799. [CrossRef]
49. Zorlutuna, I.; Akdag, M.; Min, W.K.; Amaca, S. Remarks on Soft Topological Spaces. *Ann. Fuzzy Math. Inform.* **2011**, *3*, 171–185.
50. Georgiou, D.N.; Megaritis, A.C.; Petropoulos, V.I. On Soft Topological Spaces. *Appl. Math. Inf. Sci.* **2013**, *7*, 1889–1901. [CrossRef]

51. Garcia, J.; Rodabaugh, S.E. Order-theoretic, topological, categorical redundancies of interval-valued sets, grey sets, vague sets, interval-valued "intuitionistic" sets, "intuitionistic" fuzzy sets and topologies. *Fuzzy Sets Syst.* **2005**, *156*, 445–484. [CrossRef]
52. Shi, F.G.; Fan, C.Z. Fuzzy soft sets as L-fuzzy sets. *J. Intell. Fuzzy Syst.* **2019**, *37*, 5061–5066. [CrossRef]
53. Shi, F.G.; Pang, B. Redundancy of fuzzy soft topological spaces. *J. Intell. Fuzzy Syst.* **2014**, *27*, 1757–1760. [CrossRef]
54. Shi, F.G.; Pang, B. A note on soft topological spaces. *Iran. J. Fuzzy Syst.* **2015**, *12*, 149–155.
55. Mendel, J.M. *Uncertain Rule-Based Fuzzy Logic Systems: Introduction and New Directions*; Prentice-Hall: Upper-Saddle River, NJ, USA, 2001.
56. Mohammadzadeh, A.; Sabzalian, M.H.; Zhang, W. An interval type-3 fuzzy system and a new online fractional-order learning algorithm: Theory and practice. *IEEE Trans. Fuzzy Syst.* **2020**, *28*, 1940–1950. [CrossRef]
57. Cao, Y.; Raise, A.; Mohammadzadeh, A.; Rathinasamy, S.; Band, S.S.; Mosavi, A. Deep learned recurrent type-3 fuzzy system: Application for renewable energy modeling/prediction. *Energy Rep.* **2021**, *7*, 8115–8127. [CrossRef]

*mathematics*

MDPI

*Article*

# Some Certain Fuzzy Aumann Integral Inequalities for Generalized Convexity via Fuzzy Number Valued Mappings

**Muhammad Bilal Khan [1], Hakeem A. Othman [2], Michael Gr. Voskoglou [3,*], Lazim Abdullah [4,*] and Alia M. Alzubaidi [2]**

1 Department of Mathematics, COMSATS University Islamabad, Islamabad 44000, Pakistan
2 Department of Mathematics, AL-Qunfudhah University College, Umm Al-Qura University, Makkah 24382, Saudi Arabia
3 Mathematical Sciences, Graduate TEI of Western Greece, 26334 Patras, Greece
4 Management Science Research Group, Faculty of Ocean Engineering Technology and Informatics, Universiti Malaysia Terengganu, Kuala Nerus 21030, Terengganu, Malaysia
* Correspondence: mvoskoglou@gmail.com (M.G.V.); lazim_m@umt.edu.my (L.A.)

**Abstract:** The topic of convex and nonconvex mapping has many applications in engineering and applied mathematics. The Aumann and fuzzy Aumann integrals are the most significant interval and fuzzy operators that allow the classical theory of integrals to be generalized. This paper considers the well-known fuzzy Hermite–Hadamard (HH) type and associated inequalities. With the help of fuzzy Aumann integrals and the newly introduced fuzzy number valued up and down convexity ($\mathcal{UD}$-convexity), we increase this mileage even further. Additionally, with the help of definitions of lower $\mathcal{UD}$-concave (lower $\mathcal{UD}$-concave) and upper $\mathcal{UD}$-convex (concave) fuzzy number valued mappings ($\mathcal{FNVM}$s), we have gathered a sizable collection of both well-known and new extraordinary cases that act as applications of the main conclusions. We also offer a few examples of fuzzy number valued $\mathcal{UD}$-convexity to further demonstrate the validity of the fuzzy inclusion relations presented in this study.

**Keywords:** fuzzy number valued mapping; fuzzy Aumann integral; up and down convex fuzzy number valued mapping; Hermite–Hadamard inequality; Hermite–Hadamard–Fejér inequality

**MSC:** 26A33; 26A51; 26D10

**Citation:** Khan, M.B.; Othman, H.A.; Voskoglou, M.G.; Abdullah, L.; Alzubaidi, A.M. Some Certain Fuzzy Aumann Integral Inequalities for Generalized Convexity via Fuzzy Number Valued Mappings. *Mathematics* **2023**, *11*, 550. https://doi.org/10.3390/math11030550

Academic Editor: Salvatore Sessa

Received: 9 December 2022
Revised: 30 December 2022
Accepted: 13 January 2023
Published: 19 January 2023



## 1. Introduction

Many fields make use of the convexity of functions such as game theory, variational science, mathematical programming theory, economics, and optimal control theory. Convex analysis, a brand-new mathematics branch, started taking shape in the 1960s. Many writers have employed related concepts of convexity during the past 20 years and generalized other inequalities, including h-convex functions (see References [1–10]), log convex functions (see References [11–19], and coordinated convex functions (see References [20,21]). Convexity is a fundamental term in optimization theory applied in operations research, economics, control theory, decision-making, and management. Several writers have expanded and generalized integral inequalities using various convex functions; see Refs. [22,23]. For more information, see [24–33] and references therein.

Calculating mistakes in a numerical analysis has always been difficult. The interval analysis has received a lot of attention as a novel method for resolving uncertainty issues because of its capacity to reduce calculation errors and make calculations meaningless. Set-valued analysis, a set-centric approach to mathematics and topology, includes interval analysis. It deals with interval variables rather than point variables, and the computation results are expressed as intervals; therefore, it removes mistakes that lead to incorrect conclusions. Moore [34] first adapted an interval analysis to automatic error analysis to deal with data uncertainty in 1966. The work garnered a lot of attention from academics and led to an improvement in calculation performance. They are helpful in many applications because of their capacity to be expressed as uncertain variables, including computer graphics [35], automatic error analysis [36], decision analysis [37], etc. There are numerous great applications and results for readers interested in interval analysis in other branches of mathematics; see References [38–53].

On the other hand, a generalized convexity mapping has the potential to solve a wide range of issues in both a nonlinear and pure analysis. Recently, well-known inequalities such as Jensen, Simpson, Opial, Ostrowski, Bullen, and the famous Hermite–Hadamard that are extended in the setting of interval-valued functions ($\mathcal{IVM}$) have been constructed using a variety of related classes of convexity. Chalco-Cano [54] established interval-based inequalities for the Ostrowski type using a derivative of the Hukuhara type. Opial-type inequalities for $\mathcal{IVM}$s were developed by Costa in [55]. The Minkowski inequalities for $\mathcal{IVM}$s were one of the inequalities suggested by Beckenbach and Roman-Flores [56]. According to the literature assessment, the majority of authors used an inclusion connection, similarly to in 2018, to evaluate inequality. These inequalities were created by Zhao et al. [57] for the harmonic h-convex $\mathcal{IVM}$s and the h-convex $\mathcal{IVM}$s. The authors who came after used both harmonical $(h_1, h_2)$-convex functions and $(h_1, h_2)$-convex functions to create these inequalities; for more information, see Refs. [58–75].

Using the radius and interval midpoint, Bhunia and his co-author defined the center-radius order in 2014; see Ref. [76]. The following findings for the cr-h-convex, harmonically cr-h-convex, and cr-h-GL functions were developed in 2022 by Wei Liu and his co-authors; see References [77–88]. Our examination of the literature showed that inclusion and fuzzy inclusion relations are the main sources of the majority of these discrepancies. The fundamental benefit of the up and down fuzzy relation for up and down functions is that the inequality term generated by employing these conceptions is more exact, and the argument's validity can be supported by intriguing examples of illustrated theorems. For further study related to interval-valued functions and fuzzy mappings, see [89–111].

This study provides an introduced class of convexity based on the fuzzy inclusion order and is known as $\mathcal{UD}$-convex $\mathcal{FNVM}$s, and is inspired by Refs. [56,57]. We create new H.H. inequalities with the aid of these innovative ideas, and eventually, the Jensen inequality is developed. The study includes a variety of examples to help bolster the results reached.

The article is formatted as follows, in order: Section 2 gives some background information. Section 3 each provide an overview of the primary conclusions. A succinct conclusion is explored in Section 4.

## 2. Preliminaries

We recall a few definitions, which can be found in the literature and that will be relevant in the follow-up.

Let us consider that $\mathbb{X}_o$ is the space of all closed and bounded intervals of $\mathbb{R}$, and that $\mathcal{S} \in \mathbb{X}_o$ is given by

$$\mathcal{S} = [\mathcal{S}_*,\ \mathcal{S}^*] = \{\mathfrak{w} \in \mathbb{R} |\ \mathcal{S}_* \leq \mathfrak{w} \leq \mathcal{S}^*,\ \mathcal{S}_*,\ \mathcal{S}^* \in \mathbb{R}\}, \tag{1}$$

If $\mathcal{S}_* = \mathcal{S}^*$, then $\mathcal{S}$ is degenerate. In the follow-up, all intervals are considered non-degenerate. If $\mathcal{S}_* \geq 0$, then $\mathcal{S}$ is positive. We denote by $\mathbb{X}_o^+ = \{[\mathcal{S}_*,\ \mathcal{S}^*] : [\mathcal{S}_*,\ \mathcal{S}^*] \in \mathbb{X}_o$ and $\mathcal{S}_* \geq 0\}$ the set of all positive intervals.

Let $\varpi \in \mathbb{R}$ and $\varpi \cdot \mathcal{S}$ be given by

$$\varpi \cdot \mathcal{S} = \begin{cases} [\varpi\mathcal{S}_*,\ \varpi\mathcal{S}^*] \text{ if } \varpi > 0, \\ \{0\} \quad \text{ iff } \varpi = 0, \\ [\varpi\mathcal{S}^*, \varpi\mathcal{S}_*] \text{ if } \varpi < 0. \end{cases} \tag{2}$$

We consider the Minkowski sum, $\mathcal{S}+\mathcal{O}$, product, $\mathcal{S}\times\mathcal{O}$, and difference, $\mathcal{O}-\mathcal{S}$, for $\mathcal{S},\mathcal{O}\in\mathbb{X}_o$, as

$$[\mathcal{O}_*,\ \mathcal{O}^*]+[\mathcal{S}_*,\ \mathcal{S}^*]=[\mathcal{O}_*+\mathcal{S}_*,\ \ \mathcal{O}^*+\mathcal{S}^*], \tag{3}$$

$$[\mathcal{O}_*,\ \mathcal{O}^*]\times[\mathcal{S}_*,\ \mathcal{S}^*]=[\min\{\mathcal{O}_*\mathcal{S}_*,\ \mathcal{O}^*\mathcal{S}_*,\ \mathcal{O}_*\mathcal{S}^*,\ \mathcal{O}^*\mathcal{S}^*\},\ \max\{\mathcal{O}_*\mathcal{S}_*,\ \mathcal{O}^*\mathcal{S}_*,\ \mathcal{O}_*\mathcal{S}^*,\ \mathcal{O}^*\mathcal{S}^*\}] \tag{4}$$

$$[\mathcal{O}_*,\ \mathcal{O}^*]-[\mathcal{S}_*,\ \mathcal{S}^*]=[\mathcal{O}_*-\mathcal{S}^*,\ \ \mathcal{O}^*-\mathcal{S}_*]. \tag{5}$$

**Remark 1.**

(i) *For given $[\mathcal{O}_*,\ \mathcal{O}^*],\ [\mathcal{S}_*,\ \mathcal{S}^*]\in\mathbb{R}_I$, the relation " $\supseteq_I$ ", defined on $\mathbb{R}_I$ by*

$$[\mathcal{S}_*,\ \mathcal{S}^*]\supseteq_I[\mathcal{O}_*,\ \mathcal{O}^*]\text{ if and only if }\mathcal{S}_*\le\mathcal{O}_*,\ \ \mathcal{O}^*\le\mathcal{S}^*, \tag{6}$$

*for all $[\mathcal{O}_*,\ \mathcal{O}^*],\ [\mathcal{S}_*,\ \mathcal{S}^*]\in\mathbb{R}_I$, is a partial interval inclusion relation. Moreover, $[\mathcal{S}_*,\ \mathcal{S}^*]\supseteq_I[\mathcal{O}_*,\ \mathcal{O}^*]$ coincides with $[\mathcal{S}_*,\ \mathcal{S}^*]\supseteq[\mathcal{O}_*,\ \mathcal{O}^*]$ on $\mathbb{R}_I$. The relation " $\supseteq_I$ " is of UD order [105].*

(ii) *For given $[\mathcal{O}_*,\ \mathcal{O}^*],\ [\mathcal{S}_*,\ \mathcal{S}^*]\in\mathbb{R}_I$, the relation " $\le_I$ ", defined on $\mathbb{R}_I$ by $[\mathcal{O}_*,\ \mathcal{O}^*]\le_I[\mathcal{S}_*,\ \mathcal{S}^*]$ if and only if $\mathcal{O}_*\le\mathcal{S}_*,\ \mathcal{O}^*\le\mathcal{S}^*$ or $\mathcal{O}_*\le\mathcal{S}_*,\ \mathcal{O}^*<\mathcal{S}^*$, is a partial interval order relation. Plus, we have $[\mathcal{O}_*,\ \mathcal{O}^*]\le_I[\mathcal{S}_*,\ \mathcal{S}^*]$ that coincides with $[\mathcal{O}_*,\ \mathcal{O}^*]\le[\mathcal{S}_*,\ \mathcal{S}^*]$ on $\mathbb{R}_I$. The relation " $\le_I$ " is of the left and right (LR) type [104,105].*

*Given the intervals $[\mathcal{O}_*,\ \mathcal{O}^*],\ [\mathcal{S}_*,\ \mathcal{S}^*]\in\mathbb{X}_o$, their Hausdorff–Pompeiu distance is*

$$d_H([\mathcal{O}_*,\ \mathcal{O}^*],\ [\mathcal{S}_*,\ \mathcal{S}^*])=max\{|\mathcal{O}_*-\mathcal{S}_*|,\ |\mathcal{O}^*-\mathcal{S}^*|\}. \tag{7}$$

*We have $(\mathbb{X}_o,d_H)$ that is a complete metric space [94,102,103].*

**Definition 1** ([93,94]). *A fuzzy subset L of $\mathbb{R}$ is a mapping $\widetilde{\mathcal{S}}:\mathbb{R}\to[0,1]$, a denoted membership mapping of L. We adopt the symbol  to represent the set of all fuzzy subsets of $\mathbb{R}$.*

Let us consider $\widetilde{\mathcal{S}}\in$ . If the following properties hold, then $\widetilde{\mathcal{S}}$ is a fuzzy number:

(1) $\widetilde{\mathcal{S}}$ is normal if there exists $\mathfrak{w}\in\mathbb{R}$ and $\widetilde{\mathcal{S}}(\mathfrak{w})=1$;

(2) $\widetilde{\mathcal{S}}$ is upper semi-continuous on $\mathbb{R}$ if for a $\mathfrak{w}\in\mathbb{R}$ there exists $\varepsilon>0$ and $\delta>0$ yielding $\widetilde{\mathcal{S}}(\mathfrak{w})-\widetilde{\mathcal{S}}(y)<\varepsilon$ for all $y\in\mathbb{R}$ with $|\mathfrak{w}-y|<\delta$;

(3) $\widetilde{\mathcal{S}}$ is a fuzzy convex, meaning that $\widetilde{\mathcal{S}}((1-\varpi)\mathfrak{w}+\varpi y)\ge\min\left(\widetilde{\mathcal{S}}(\mathfrak{w}),\ \widetilde{\mathcal{S}}(y)\right)$, for all $\mathfrak{w},y\in\mathbb{R}$, and $\varpi\in[0,\ 1]$;

(4) $\widetilde{\mathcal{S}}$ is compactly supported, which means that $\mathrm{cl}\left\{\mathfrak{w}\in\mathbb{R}\middle|\ \widetilde{\mathcal{S}}(\mathfrak{w})\right\rangle 0\Big\}$ is compact.

The symbol $_o$ will be adopted to designate the set of all fuzzy numbers of $\mathbb{R}$.

**Definition 2.** ([93,94]). *For $\widetilde{\mathcal{S}}\in{}_o$, the $\vartheta$-level, or $\vartheta$-cut, sets of $\widetilde{\mathcal{S}}$ are $\left[\widetilde{\mathcal{S}}\right]^{\vartheta}=\left\{\mathfrak{w}\in\mathbb{R}\middle|\ \widetilde{\mathcal{S}}(\mathfrak{w})\right\rangle\vartheta\Big\}$ for all $\vartheta\in[0,\ 1]$, and $\left[\widetilde{\mathcal{S}}\right]^{0}=\left\{\mathfrak{w}\in\mathbb{R}\middle|\ \widetilde{\mathcal{S}}(\mathfrak{w})\right\rangle 0\Big\}$.*

**Proposition 1.** ([96]). *Let $\widetilde{\mathcal{S}},\widetilde{\mathcal{O}}\in{}_o$. The relation " $\le_{\mathbb{F}}$ ", defined on $_o$ by*

$$\widetilde{\mathcal{S}}\le_{\mathbb{F}}\widetilde{\mathcal{O}}\text{ when and only when }\left[\widetilde{\mathcal{S}}\right]^{\vartheta}\le_I\left[\widetilde{\mathcal{O}}\right]^{\vartheta},\text{ for every }\vartheta\in[0,\ 1], \tag{8}$$

*is a LR order relation.*

**Proposition 2.** ([79]). *Let $\widetilde{\mathcal{S}},\widetilde{\mathcal{O}}\in{}_o$. The relation " $\supseteq_{\mathbb{F}}$ ", defined on $_o$ by*

$$\widetilde{\mathcal{S}}\supseteq_{\mathbb{F}}\widetilde{\mathcal{O}}\text{ when and only when }\left[\widetilde{\mathcal{S}}\right]^{\vartheta}\supseteq_I\left[\widetilde{\mathcal{O}}\right]^{\vartheta},\text{ for every }\vartheta\in[0,\ 1], \tag{9}$$

*is an UD order relation.*

*If* $\widetilde{\mathcal{S}}, \widetilde{\mathcal{O}} \in {}_o$ *and* $\mathfrak{s} \in \mathbb{R}$, *then, for every* $\mathfrak{s} \in [0,\ 1]$,

$$\left[\widetilde{\mathcal{S}} \oplus \widetilde{\mathcal{O}}\right]^{\mathfrak{s}} = \left[\widetilde{\mathcal{S}}\right]^{\mathfrak{s}} + \left[\widetilde{\mathcal{O}}\right]^{\mathfrak{s}}, \tag{10}$$

$$\left[\widetilde{\mathcal{S}} \otimes \widetilde{\mathcal{O}}\right]^{\mathfrak{s}} = \left[\widetilde{\mathcal{S}}\right]^{\mathfrak{s}} \times \left[\widetilde{\mathcal{O}}\right]^{\mathfrak{s}}, \tag{11}$$

$$\left[\varpi \odot \widetilde{\mathcal{S}}\right]^{\mathfrak{s}} = \mathfrak{s}.\left[\widetilde{\mathcal{S}}\right]^{\mathfrak{s}} \tag{12}$$

*result from Equations (4)–(6), respectively.*

**Theorem 1** ([94]). *For* $\widetilde{\mathcal{S}},\ \widetilde{\mathcal{O}} \in {}_o$, *the supremum metric*

$$d_\infty\left(\widetilde{\mathcal{S}},\ \widetilde{\mathcal{O}}\right) = \sup_{0 \le \mathfrak{s} \le 1} d_H\left(\left[\widetilde{\mathcal{S}}\right]^{\mathfrak{s}},\ \left[\widetilde{\mathcal{O}}\right]^{\mathfrak{s}}\right) \tag{13}$$

*is a complete metric space, where H stands for the Hausdorff metric on a space of intervals.*

**Theorem 2** ([94,95]). *If* $\mathcal{H} : [\mathfrak{b}, z] \subset \mathbb{R} \to \mathbb{X}_o$ *is an* $\mathcal{IVM}$ *satisfying* $\mathcal{H}(\mathfrak{w}) = [\mathcal{H}_*(\mathfrak{w}),\ \mathcal{H}^*(\mathfrak{w})]$, *then* $\mathcal{H}$ *is Aumann integrable (IA-integrable) over* $[\mathfrak{b}, z]$ *when and only when* $\mathcal{H}_*(\mathfrak{w})$ *and* $\mathcal{H}^*(\mathfrak{w})$ *are integrable over* $[\mathfrak{b}, z]$, *meaning*

$$(IA)\int_{\mathfrak{b}}^{z} \mathcal{H}(\mathfrak{w})d\mathfrak{w} = \left[\int_{\mathfrak{b}}^{z} \mathcal{H}_*(\mathfrak{w})d\mathfrak{w},\ \int_{\mathfrak{b}}^{z} \mathcal{H}^*(\mathfrak{w})d\mathfrak{w}\right] \tag{14}$$

**Definition 3** ([104]). *Let* $\widetilde{\mathcal{H}} : \mathbb{I} \subset \mathbb{R} \to {}_o$ *be a* $\mathcal{FNVM}$. *The family of* $\mathcal{IVM}$*s, for every* $\mathfrak{s} \in [0,\ 1]$, *is* $\mathcal{H}_{\mathfrak{s}} : \mathbb{I} \subset \mathbb{R} \to \mathbb{X}_o$ *satisfying* $\mathcal{H}_{\mathfrak{s}}(\mathfrak{w}) = [\mathcal{H}_*(\mathfrak{w}, \mathfrak{s}),\ \mathcal{H}^*(\mathfrak{w}, \mathfrak{s})]$ *for every* $\mathfrak{w} \in \mathbb{I}$. *For every* $\mathfrak{s} \in [0,\ 1]$, *the lower and upper mappings of* $\mathcal{H}_{\mathfrak{s}}$ *are the endpoint real-valued mappings* $\mathcal{H}_*(\cdot, \mathfrak{s}),\ \mathcal{H}^*(\cdot, \mathfrak{s}) : \mathbb{I} \to \mathbb{R}$.

**Definition 4** ([104]). *Let* $\widetilde{\mathcal{H}} : \mathbb{I} \subset \mathbb{R} \to {}_o$ *be a* $\mathcal{FNVM}$. *Then,* $\widetilde{\mathcal{H}}(\mathfrak{w})$ *is continuous at* $\mathfrak{w} \in \mathbb{I}$, *if for every* $\mathfrak{s} \in [0,\ 1]$, $\mathcal{H}_{\mathfrak{s}}(\mathfrak{w})$ *is continuous when and only when* $\mathcal{H}_*(\mathfrak{w}, \mathfrak{s})$ *and* $\mathcal{H}^*(\mathfrak{w}, \mathfrak{s})$ *are continuous at* $\mathfrak{w} \in \mathbb{I}$.

**Definition 5** ([95]). *Let* $\widetilde{\mathcal{H}} : [\mathfrak{b},\ z] \subset \mathbb{R} \to {}_o$ *be a* $\mathcal{FNVM}$. *The fuzzy Aumann integral (FA-integral) of* $\widetilde{\mathcal{H}}$ *over* $[\mathfrak{b},\ z]$ *is*

$$\left[(FA)\int_{\mathfrak{b}}^{z} \widetilde{\mathcal{H}}(\mathfrak{w})d\mathfrak{w}\right]^{\mathfrak{s}} = (IA)\int_{\mathfrak{b}}^{z} \mathcal{H}_{\mathfrak{s}}(\mathfrak{w})d\mathfrak{w} = \left\{\int_{\mathfrak{b}}^{z} \mathcal{H}(\mathfrak{w}, \mathfrak{s})d\mathfrak{w} : \mathcal{H}(\mathfrak{w}, \mathfrak{s}) \in S(\mathcal{H}_{\mathfrak{s}})\right\}, \tag{15}$$

*where* $S(\mathcal{H}_{\mathfrak{s}}) = \{\mathcal{H}(., \mathfrak{s}) \to \mathbb{R} : \mathcal{H}(., \mathfrak{s})$ *is integrable, and* $\mathcal{H}(\mathfrak{w}, \mathfrak{s}) \in \mathcal{H}_{\mathfrak{s}}(\mathfrak{w})\}$, *for every* $\mathfrak{s} \in [0,\ 1]$. *Moreover,* $\widetilde{\mathcal{H}}$ *is* $(FA)$*-integrable over* $[\mathfrak{b},\ z]$ *if* $(FA)\int_{\mathfrak{b}}^{z} \widetilde{\mathcal{H}}(\mathfrak{w})d\mathfrak{w} \in {}_o$.

**Theorem 3** [96]. *Let* $\widetilde{\mathcal{H}} : [\mathfrak{b},\ z] \subset \mathbb{R} \to {}_o$ *be a* $\mathcal{FNVM}$, *whose* $\mathfrak{s}$*-levels define the family of* $\mathcal{IVM}$*s* $\mathcal{H}_{\mathfrak{s}} : [\mathfrak{b},\ z] \subset \mathbb{R} \to \mathbb{X}_o$ *satisfying* $\mathcal{H}_{\mathfrak{s}}(\mathfrak{w}) = [\mathcal{H}_*(\mathfrak{w}, \mathfrak{s}),\ \mathcal{H}^*(\mathfrak{w}, \mathfrak{s})]$ *for every* $\mathfrak{w} \in [\mathfrak{b},\ z]$ *and* $\mathfrak{s} \in [0,\ 1]$. $\widetilde{\mathcal{H}}$ *is* $(FA)$*-integrable over* $[\mathfrak{b},\ z]$ *when and only when* $\mathcal{H}_*(\mathfrak{w}, \mathfrak{s})$ *and* $\mathcal{H}^*(\mathfrak{w}, \mathfrak{s})$ *are integrable over* $[\mathfrak{b},\ z]$. *Moreover, if* $\widetilde{\mathcal{H}}$ *is* $(FA)$*-integrable over* $[\mathfrak{b},\ z]$, *then we have*

$$\left[(FA)\int_{\mathfrak{b}}^{z} \widetilde{\mathcal{H}}(\mathfrak{w})d\mathfrak{w}\right]^{\mathfrak{s}} = \left[\int_{\mathfrak{b}}^{z} \mathcal{H}_*(\mathfrak{w}, \mathfrak{s})d\mathfrak{w},\ \int_{\mathfrak{b}}^{z} \mathcal{H}^*(\mathfrak{w}, \mathfrak{s})d\mathfrak{w}\right] = (IA)\int_{\mathfrak{b}}^{z} \mathcal{H}_{\mathfrak{s}}(\mathfrak{w})d\mathfrak{w} \tag{16}$$

*for every* $\mathfrak{s} \in [0,\ 1]$.

*Breckner discussed the coming emerging idea of interval-valued convexity in [97].*

*An I·V·M $\mathcal{H} : \mathbb{I} = [\mathfrak{b},\ z] \to \mathcal{X}_o$ is called convex I·V·M if*

$$\mathcal{H}(\varpi\mathfrak{w} + (1-\varpi)s) \supseteq \varpi\mathcal{H}(\mathfrak{w}) + (1-\varpi)\mathcal{H}(s), \tag{17}$$

*for all $\mathfrak{w},\ y \in [\mathfrak{b},\ z]$, $\varpi \in [0,\ 1]$, where $\mathcal{X}_o$ is the collection of real-valued intervals. If (17) is reversed, then $\mathcal{H}$ is called concave.*

**Definition 6** ([89]). *The $\mathcal{FNVM}$ $\widetilde{\mathcal{H}} : [\mathfrak{b},\ z] \to_0$ is called convex $\mathcal{FNVM}$ on $[\mathfrak{b},\ z]$ if*

$$\widetilde{\mathcal{H}}(\varpi\mathfrak{w} + (1-\varpi)s\ ) \leq_{\mathbb{F}} \varpi \odot \widetilde{\mathcal{H}}(\mathfrak{w}) \oplus (1-\varpi) \odot \widetilde{\mathcal{H}}(s), \tag{18}$$

*for all $\mathfrak{w},\ s \in [\mathfrak{b},\ z]$, $\varpi \in [0,\ 1]$, where $\widetilde{\mathcal{H}}(\mathfrak{w}) \geq_{\mathbb{F}} \tilde{0}$ for all $\mathfrak{w} \in [\mathfrak{b},\ z]$. If (18) is reversed, then $\widetilde{\mathcal{H}}$ is called concave $\mathcal{FNVM}$ on $[\mathfrak{b},\ z]$. $\widetilde{\mathcal{H}}$ is affine if and only if it is both convex and concave $\mathcal{FNVM}$.*

**Definition 7** ([105]). *The $\mathcal{FNVM}$ $\widetilde{\mathcal{H}} : [\mathfrak{b},\ z] \to_0$ is called $\mathcal{UD}$-convex $\mathcal{FNVM}$ on $[\mathfrak{b},\ z]$ if*

$$\widetilde{\mathcal{H}}(\varpi\mathfrak{w} + (1-\varpi)s) \supseteq_{\mathbb{F}} \varpi \odot \widetilde{\mathcal{H}}(\mathfrak{w}) \oplus (1-\varpi) \odot \widetilde{\mathcal{H}}(s), \tag{19}$$

*for all $\mathfrak{w},\ s \in [\mathfrak{b},\ z]$, $\varpi \in [0,\ 1]$, where $\widetilde{\mathcal{H}}(\mathfrak{w}) \geq_{\mathbb{F}} \tilde{0}$ for all $\mathfrak{w} \in [\mathfrak{b},\ z]$. If (19) is reversed then, $\widetilde{\mathcal{H}}$ is called $\mathcal{UD}$-concave $\mathcal{FNVM}$ on $[\mathfrak{b},\ z]$. $\widetilde{\mathcal{H}}$ is $\mathcal{UD}$-affine $\mathcal{FNVM}$ if and only if it is both $\mathcal{UD}$-convex and $\mathcal{UD}$-concave $\mathcal{FNVM}$.*

**Theorem 4** ([105]). *Let $\widetilde{\mathcal{H}} : [\mathfrak{b}, z] \to_0$ be a $\mathcal{FNVM}$, whose $\mathfrak{e}$-cuts define the family of inteval-valued mappings $\mathcal{H}_{\mathfrak{e}} : [\mathfrak{b}, z] \to \mathcal{X}_o^+ \subset \mathcal{X}_o$ are given by*

$$\mathcal{H}_{\mathfrak{e}}(\mathfrak{w}) = [\mathcal{H}_*(\mathfrak{w}, \mathfrak{e}),\ \mathcal{H}^*(\mathfrak{w}, \mathfrak{e})], \tag{20}$$

*for all $\mathfrak{w} \in [\mathfrak{b}, z]$ and for all $\mathfrak{e} \in [0,\ 1]$. Then, $\widetilde{\mathcal{H}}$ is $\mathcal{UD}$-convex $\mathcal{FNVM}$ on $[\mathfrak{b}, z]$, if and only if, for all $\mathfrak{e} \in [0,\ 1]$, $\mathcal{H}_*(\mathfrak{w},\ \mathfrak{e})$ is a convex mapping and $\mathcal{H}^*(\mathfrak{w},\ \mathfrak{e})$ is a concave mapping.*

**Remark 2.** *If $\mathcal{H}_*(\mathfrak{w}, \mathfrak{e}) \neq \mathcal{H}^*(\mathfrak{w}, \mathfrak{e})$ and $\mathfrak{e}\ =\ 1$, then we obtain the inequality (17).*

If $\mathcal{H}_*(\mathfrak{w}, \mathfrak{e}) = \mathcal{H}^*(\mathfrak{w}, \mathfrak{e})$ and $\mathfrak{e}\ =\ 1$, then we obtain the classical definition of convex mappings.

Now we have obtained some new definitions from the literature which will be helpful to investigate some classical and new results as special cases of main results.

**Definition 8.** ([79]). *Let $\widetilde{\mathcal{H}} : [\mathfrak{b}, z] \to_0$ be a $\mathcal{FNVM}$, whose $\mathfrak{e}$-cuts define the family of $\mathcal{IVM}$s $\mathcal{H}_{\mathfrak{e}} : [\mathfrak{b}, z] \to \mathcal{X}_o^+ \subset \mathcal{X}_o$ are given by*

$$\mathcal{H}_{\mathfrak{e}}(\mathfrak{w}) = [\mathcal{H}_*(\mathfrak{w}, \mathfrak{e}),\ \mathcal{H}^*(\mathfrak{w}, \mathfrak{e})], \tag{21}$$

*for all $\mathfrak{w} \in [\mathfrak{b}, z]$ and for all $\mathfrak{e} \in [0,\ 1]$. Then, $\widetilde{\mathcal{H}}$ is lower $\mathcal{UD}$-convex (concave) $\mathcal{FNVM}$ on $[\mathfrak{b}, z]$, if and only if, for all $\mathfrak{e} \in [0,\ 1]$, $\mathcal{H}_*(\mathfrak{w},\ \mathfrak{e})$ is a convex (concave) mapping and $\mathcal{H}^*(\mathfrak{w},\ \mathfrak{e})$ is an affine mapping.*

**Definition 9.** ([79]). *Let $\widetilde{\mathcal{H}} : [\mathfrak{b}, z] \to_0$ be a $\mathcal{FNVM}$, whose $\mathfrak{e}$-cuts define the family of $\mathcal{IVM}$s $\mathcal{H}_{\mathfrak{e}} : [\mathfrak{b}, z] \to \mathcal{X}_o^+ \subset \mathcal{X}_o$ are given by*

$$\mathcal{H}_{\mathfrak{e}}(\mathfrak{w}) = [\mathcal{H}_*(\mathfrak{w}, \mathfrak{e}),\ \mathcal{H}^*(\mathfrak{w}, \mathfrak{e})], \tag{22}$$

*for all $\mathfrak{w} \in [\mathfrak{b}, z]$ and for all $\mathfrak{e} \in [0,\ 1]$. Then, $\mathcal{H}$ is upper $\mathcal{UD}$-convex (concave) $\mathcal{FNVM}$ on $[\mathfrak{b}, z]$, if and only if, for all $\mathfrak{e} \in [0,\ 1]$, $\mathcal{H}_*(\mathfrak{w},\ \mathfrak{e})$ is an affine mapping and $\mathcal{H}^*(\mathfrak{w},\ \mathfrak{e})$ is a convex (concave) mapping.*

**Remark 3.** *Both concepts "$\mathcal{UD}$-convex $\mathcal{FNVM}$" and classical "convex $\mathcal{FNVM}$, see [41]" behave alike when $\widetilde{\mathcal{H}}$ is lower $\mathcal{UD}$-convex $\mathcal{FNVM}$.*

## 3. Fuzzy Number Hermite–Hadamard Inequalities

In this section, we propose Hermite–Hadamard and Hermite–Hadamard–Fejér inequalities for $\mathcal{UD}$-convex $\mathcal{FNVM}$s, and verify with the help of nontrivial examples.

**Theorem 5.** *Let $\widetilde{\mathcal{H}} : [\mathfrak{b}, z] \to_o$ be a $\mathcal{UD}$-convex $\mathcal{FNVM}$ on $[\mathfrak{b}, z]$, whose $\vartheta$-cuts define the family of $\mathcal{IVM}$s $\mathcal{H}_\vartheta : [\mathfrak{b}, z] \subset \mathbb{R} \to \mathcal{X}_o^+$ are given by $\mathcal{H}_\vartheta(\mathfrak{w}) = [\mathcal{H}_*(\mathfrak{w}, \vartheta),\ \mathcal{H}^*(\mathfrak{w}, \vartheta)]$ for all $\mathfrak{w} \in [\mathfrak{b}, z]$ and for all $\vartheta \in [0, 1]$. If $\widetilde{\mathcal{H}} \in \mathcal{FA}_{([\mathfrak{b}, z], \vartheta)}$, then*

$$\widetilde{\mathcal{H}}\left(\frac{\mathfrak{b}+z}{2}\right) \supseteq_{\mathbb{F}} \frac{1}{z-\mathfrak{b}} \odot (FA) \int_{\mathfrak{b}}^{z} \widetilde{\mathcal{H}}(\mathfrak{w})d\mathfrak{w} \supseteq_{\mathbb{F}} \frac{\widetilde{\mathcal{H}}(\mathfrak{b}) \oplus \widetilde{\mathcal{H}}(z)}{2}. \tag{23}$$

*If $\widetilde{\mathcal{H}}(\mathfrak{w})$ concave $\mathcal{FNVM}$, then (23) is reversed.*

**Proof.** Let $\widetilde{\mathcal{H}} : [\mathfrak{b}, z] \to_o$ be a $\mathcal{UD}$-convex $\mathcal{FNVM}$. Then, by hypothesis, we have

$$2\widetilde{\mathcal{H}}\left(\frac{\mathfrak{b}+z}{2}\right) \supseteq_{\mathbb{F}} \widetilde{\mathcal{H}}(\varpi\mathfrak{b} + (1-\varpi)z) \oplus \widetilde{\mathcal{H}}((1-\varpi)\mathfrak{b} + \varpi z).$$

Therefore, for every $\vartheta \in [0, 1]$, we have

$$\begin{aligned} 2\mathcal{H}_*\left(\frac{\mathfrak{b}+z}{2}, \vartheta\right) &\le \mathcal{H}_*(\varpi\mathfrak{b} + (1-\varpi)z, \vartheta) + \mathcal{H}_*((1-\varpi)\mathfrak{b} + \varpi z, \vartheta), \\ 2\mathcal{H}^*\left(\frac{\mathfrak{b}+z}{2}, \vartheta\right) &\ge \mathcal{H}^*(\varpi\mathfrak{b} + (1-\varpi)z, \vartheta) + \mathcal{H}^*((1-\varpi)\mathfrak{b} + \varpi z, \vartheta). \end{aligned}$$

Then

$$\begin{aligned} 2\int_0^1 \mathcal{H}_*\left(\frac{\mathfrak{b}+z}{2}, \vartheta\right)d\varpi &\le \int_0^1 \mathcal{H}_*(\varpi\mathfrak{b} + (1-\varpi)z, \vartheta)d\varpi + \int_0^1 \mathcal{H}_*((1-\varpi)\mathfrak{b} + \varpi z, \vartheta)d\varpi, \\ 2\int_0^1 \mathcal{H}^*\left(\frac{\mathfrak{b}+z}{2}, \vartheta\right)d\varpi &\ge \int_0^1 \mathcal{H}^*(\varpi\mathfrak{b} + (1-\varpi)z, \vartheta)d\varpi + \int_0^1 \mathcal{H}^*((1-\varpi)\mathfrak{b} + \varpi z, \vartheta)d\varpi. \end{aligned}$$

It follows that

$$\begin{aligned} \mathcal{H}_*\left(\frac{\mathfrak{b}+z}{2}, \vartheta\right) &\le \frac{1}{z-\mathfrak{b}} \int_{\mathfrak{b}}^{z} \mathcal{H}_*(\mathfrak{w}, \vartheta)d\mathfrak{w}, \\ \mathcal{H}^*\left(\frac{\mathfrak{b}+z}{2}, \vartheta\right) &\ge \frac{1}{z-\mathfrak{b}} \int_{\mathfrak{b}}^{z} \mathcal{H}^*(\mathfrak{w}, \vartheta)d\mathfrak{w}. \end{aligned}$$

That is

$$\left[\mathcal{H}_*\left(\frac{\mathfrak{b}+z}{2}, \vartheta\right), \mathcal{H}^*\left(\frac{\mathfrak{b}+z}{2}, \vartheta\right)\right] \supseteq_I \frac{1}{z-\mathfrak{b}}\left[\int_{\mathfrak{b}}^{z} \mathcal{H}_*(\mathfrak{w}, \vartheta)d\mathfrak{w}, \int_{\mathfrak{b}}^{z} \mathcal{H}^*(\mathfrak{w}, \vartheta)d\mathfrak{w}\right].$$

Thus,

$$\widetilde{\mathcal{H}}\left(\frac{\mathfrak{b}+z}{2}\right) \supseteq_{\mathbb{F}} \frac{1}{z-\mathfrak{b}} \odot (FA) \int_{\mathfrak{b}}^{z} \widetilde{\mathcal{H}}(\mathfrak{w})d\mathfrak{w}. \tag{24}$$

In a similar way as above, we have

$$\frac{1}{z-\mathfrak{b}} \odot (FA) \int_{\mathfrak{b}}^{z} \widetilde{\mathcal{H}}(\mathfrak{w})d\mathfrak{w} \supseteq_{\mathbb{F}} \frac{\widetilde{\mathcal{H}}(\mathfrak{b}) \oplus \widetilde{\mathcal{H}}(z)}{2}. \tag{25}$$

Combining (24) and (25), we have

$$\widetilde{\mathcal{H}}\left(\frac{\mathfrak{b}+z}{2}\right) \supseteq_{\mathbb{F}} \frac{1}{z-\mathfrak{b}} \odot (FA) \int_{\mathfrak{b}}^{z} \widetilde{\mathcal{H}}(\mathfrak{w})d\mathfrak{w} \supseteq_{\mathbb{F}} \frac{\widetilde{\mathcal{H}}(\mathfrak{b}) \oplus \widetilde{\mathcal{H}}(z)}{2}.$$

Hence, the required result. □

**Remark 4.** *The following are some exceptional cases which can be obtained from inequality (23):*

If one lays $\mathcal{H}$ is lower $\mathcal{UD}$-convex $\mathcal{FNVM}$ on $[\mathfrak{b}, z]$, then one acquires the following coming inequality, see [90]:

$$\mathcal{H}\left(\frac{\mathfrak{b}+z}{2}\right) \leq_{\mathbb{F}} \frac{1}{z-\mathfrak{b}} \odot (FA) \int_{\mathfrak{b}}^{z} \mathcal{H}(\mathfrak{w}) d\mathfrak{w} \leq_{\mathbb{F}} \frac{\mathcal{H}(\mathfrak{b}) \oplus \mathcal{H}(z)}{2} \tag{26}$$

If one takes $\mathcal{H}$ is lower $\mathcal{UD}$-convex $\mathcal{FNVM}$ on $[\mathfrak{b}, z]$ and $\mathfrak{s} =$ , then one achieves the following coming inequality, see [98]:

$$\mathcal{H}\left(\frac{\mathfrak{b}+z}{2}\right) \leq_{I} \frac{1}{z-\mathfrak{b}} (IA) \int_{\mathfrak{b}}^{z} \mathcal{H}(\mathfrak{w}) d\mathfrak{w} \leq_{I} \frac{\mathcal{H}(\mathfrak{b}) + \mathcal{H}(z)}{2} \tag{27}$$

Let $\mathfrak{s} = 1$. Then, from Theorem 5, we acquire the following inequality, see [99]:

$$\mathcal{H}\left(\frac{\mathfrak{b}+z}{2}\right) \supseteq \frac{1}{z-\mathfrak{b}} (IA) \int_{\mathfrak{b}}^{z} \mathcal{H}(\mathfrak{w}) d\mathfrak{w} \supseteq \frac{\mathcal{H}(\mathfrak{b}) + \mathcal{H}(z)}{2}. \tag{28}$$

Let $\mathfrak{s} =$ and $\mathcal{H}_*(\mathfrak{w}, \mathfrak{s}) = \mathcal{H}^*(\mathfrak{w}, \mathfrak{s})$. Then, from Theorem 5, we achieve the classical Hermite–Hadamard inequality.

**Example 1.** *Let* $\mathfrak{w} \in [2, 3]$, and the $\mathcal{FNVM}$ $\widetilde{\mathcal{H}} : [\mathfrak{b}, z] = [2, 3] \to {}_0$, defined by

$$\widetilde{\mathcal{H}}(\mathfrak{w})(\theta) = \begin{cases} \dfrac{\theta - 2 + \mathfrak{w}^{\frac{1}{2}}}{1 - \mathfrak{w}^{\frac{1}{2}}} & \theta \in \left[2 - \mathfrak{w}^{\frac{1}{2}}, 3\right], \\ \dfrac{2 + \mathfrak{w}^{\frac{1}{2}} - \theta}{\mathfrak{w}^{\frac{1}{2}} - 1} & \theta \in \left(3, 2 + \mathfrak{w}^{\frac{1}{2}}\right], \\ 0 & \text{otherwise}, \end{cases} \tag{29}$$

*Then, for each* $\mathfrak{s} \in [0, 1]$, *we have* $\mathcal{H}_{\mathfrak{s}}(\mathfrak{w}) = \left[(1-\mathfrak{s})\left(2 - \mathfrak{w}^{\frac{1}{2}}\right) + 3\mathfrak{s}, (1-\mathfrak{s})\left(2 + \mathfrak{w}^{\frac{1}{2}}\right) + 3\mathfrak{s}\right]$. *Since left and right end point mappings* $\mathcal{H}_*(\mathfrak{w}, \mathfrak{s}) = (1-\mathfrak{s})\left(2 - \mathfrak{w}^{\frac{1}{2}}\right) + 3\mathfrak{s}$, *and* $\mathcal{H}^*(\mathfrak{w}, \mathfrak{s}) = (1-\mathfrak{s})\left(2 + \mathfrak{w}^{\frac{1}{2}}\right) + 3\mathfrak{s}$, *are convex and concave mappings, respectively, for each* $\mathfrak{s} \in [0, 1]$, *then* $\widetilde{\mathcal{H}}(\mathfrak{w})$ *is* $\mathcal{UD}$*-convex* $\mathcal{FNVM}$. *We clearly see that* $\widetilde{\mathcal{H}} \in L([\mathfrak{b}, z], {}_0)$ *and*

$$\mathcal{H}_*\left(\frac{\mathfrak{b}+z}{2}, \mathfrak{s}\right) = \mathcal{H}_*\left(\frac{5}{2}, \mathfrak{s}\right) = (1-\mathfrak{s})\frac{4-\sqrt{10}}{2} + 3\mathfrak{s},$$

$$\mathcal{H}^*\left(\frac{\mathfrak{b}+z}{2}, \mathfrak{s}\right) = \mathcal{H}^*\left(\frac{5}{2}, \mathfrak{s}\right) = (1-\mathfrak{s})\frac{4+\sqrt{10}}{2} + 3\mathfrak{s}.$$

*Note that*

$$\frac{1}{z-\mathfrak{b}} \int_{\mathfrak{b}}^{z} \mathcal{H}_*(\mathfrak{w}, \mathfrak{s}) d\mathfrak{w} = \int_2^3 \left((1-\mathfrak{s})\left(2 - \mathfrak{w}^{\frac{1}{2}}\right) + 3\mathfrak{s}\right) d\mathfrak{w} \approx 0.4215(1-\mathfrak{s}) + 3\mathfrak{s},$$

$$\frac{1}{z-\mathfrak{b}} \int_{\mathfrak{b}}^{z} \mathcal{H}^*(\mathfrak{w}, \mathfrak{s}) d\mathfrak{w} = \int_2^3 \left((1+\mathfrak{s})\left(2 + \mathfrak{w}^{\frac{1}{2}}\right) + 3\mathfrak{s}\right) d\mathfrak{w} \approx 3.58(1-\mathfrak{s}) + 3\mathfrak{s},$$

*and*

$$\frac{\mathcal{H}_*(\mathfrak{b},\theta)+\mathcal{H}_*(z,\ \theta)}{2}=(1-\theta)\left(\frac{4-\sqrt{2}-\sqrt{3}}{2}\right)+3\theta,$$

$$\frac{\mathcal{H}^*(\mathfrak{b},\theta)+\mathcal{H}^*(z,\ \theta)}{2}=(1-\theta)\left(\frac{4+\sqrt{2}+\sqrt{3}}{2}\right)+3\theta.$$

*Therefore,*

$$\left[(1-\theta)\frac{4-\sqrt{10}}{2}+3\theta,(1-\theta)\frac{4+\sqrt{10}}{2}+3\theta\right]\supseteq_I\left[\frac{843}{2000}(1-\theta)+3\theta,\frac{179}{50}(1-\theta)+3\theta\right]$$
$$\supseteq_I\left[(1-\theta)\left(\frac{4-\sqrt{2}-\sqrt{3}}{2}\right)+3\theta,(1-\theta)\left(\frac{4+\sqrt{2}+\sqrt{3}}{2}\right)+3\theta\right],$$

*Hence,*

$$\widetilde{\mathcal{H}}\left(\frac{\mathfrak{b}+z}{2}\right)\supseteq_{\mathbb{F}}\frac{1}{z-\mathfrak{b}}\odot(FA)\int_{\mathfrak{b}}^{z}\widetilde{\mathcal{H}}(\mathfrak{w})d\mathfrak{w}\supseteq_{\mathbb{F}}\frac{\widetilde{\mathcal{H}}(\mathfrak{b})\oplus\widetilde{\mathcal{H}}(z)}{2},$$

*and Theorem 5 is verified.*

**Theorem 6.** *Let* $\widetilde{\mathcal{H}}:[\mathfrak{b},\ z]\to_o$ *be a* $\mathcal{UD}$*-convex* $\mathcal{FNVM}$ *on* $[\mathfrak{b},\ z]$, *whose* $\theta$*-cuts define the family of* $\mathcal{IVM}$*s* $\mathcal{H}_\theta:[\mathfrak{b},\ z]\subset\mathbb{R}\to\mathcal{X}_o^+$ *are given by* $\mathcal{H}_\theta(\mathfrak{w})=[\mathcal{H}_*(\mathfrak{w},\theta),\ \mathcal{H}^*(\mathfrak{w},\theta)]$ *for all* $\mathfrak{w}\in[\mathfrak{b},\ z]$ *and for all* $\theta\in[0,\ 1]$. *If* $\widetilde{\mathcal{H}}\in\ \mathcal{FA}_{([\mathfrak{b},\ z],\ \theta)}$, *then*

$$\widetilde{\mathcal{H}}\left(\frac{\mathfrak{b}+z}{2}\right)\supseteq_{\mathbb{F}}\ \mathfrak{T}_2\supseteq_{\mathbb{F}}\frac{1}{z-\mathfrak{b}}\odot(FA)\int_{\mathfrak{b}}^{z}\widetilde{\mathcal{H}}(\mathfrak{w})d\mathfrak{w}\supseteq_{\mathbb{F}}\mathfrak{T}_1\supseteq_{\mathbb{F}}\frac{\widetilde{\mathcal{H}}(\mathfrak{b})\ \oplus\ \widetilde{\mathcal{H}}(z)}{2},\tag{30}$$

*where*

$$\mathfrak{T}_1=\frac{\frac{\widetilde{\mathcal{H}}(\mathfrak{b})\oplus\widetilde{\mathcal{H}}(z)}{2}\ \oplus\ \widetilde{\mathcal{H}}\left(\frac{\mathfrak{b}+z}{2}\right)}{2},\ \mathfrak{T}_2=\frac{\widetilde{\mathcal{H}}\left(\frac{3\mathfrak{b}+z}{4}\right)\ \oplus\ \widetilde{\mathcal{H}}\left(\frac{\mathfrak{b}+3z}{4}\right)}{2}$$

*and* $\mathfrak{T}_1=[\mathfrak{T}_{1*},\ \mathfrak{T}_1{}^*]$, $\mathfrak{T}_2=[\mathfrak{T}_{2*},\ \mathfrak{T}_2{}^*]$.

**Proof.** Take $\left[\mathfrak{b},\ \frac{\mathfrak{b}+z}{2}\right]$, we have

$$2\widetilde{\mathcal{H}}\left(\frac{\varpi\mathfrak{b}+(1-\varpi)\frac{\mathfrak{b}+z}{2}}{2}+\frac{(1-\varpi)\mathfrak{b}+\varpi\frac{\mathfrak{b}+z}{2}}{2}\right)\supseteq_{\mathbb{F}}\widetilde{\mathcal{H}}\left(\varpi\mathfrak{b}+(1-\varpi)\frac{\mathfrak{b}+z}{2}\right)\oplus\widetilde{\mathcal{H}}\left((1-\varpi)\mathfrak{b}+\varpi\frac{\mathfrak{b}+z}{2}\right).$$

Therefore, for every $\theta\in[0,\ 1]$, we have

$$2\mathcal{H}_*\left(\frac{\varpi\mathfrak{b}+(1-\varpi)\frac{\mathfrak{b}+z}{2}}{2}+\frac{(1-\varpi)\mathfrak{b}+\varpi\frac{\mathfrak{b}+z}{2}}{2},\ \theta\right)\le\mathcal{H}_*\left(\varpi\mathfrak{b}+(1-\varpi)\frac{\mathfrak{b}+z}{2},\ \theta\right)+\mathcal{H}_*\left((1-\varpi)\mathfrak{b}+\varpi\frac{\mathfrak{b}+z}{2},\ \theta\right),$$
$$2\mathcal{H}^*\left(\frac{\varpi\mathfrak{b}+(1-\varpi)\frac{\mathfrak{b}+z}{2}}{2}+\frac{(1-\varpi)\mathfrak{b}+\varpi\frac{\mathfrak{b}+z}{2}}{2},\ \theta\right)\ge\mathcal{H}^*\left(\varpi\mathfrak{b}+(1-\varpi)\frac{\mathfrak{b}+z}{2},\ \theta\right)+\mathcal{H}^*\left((1-\varpi)\mathfrak{b}+\varpi\frac{\mathfrak{b}+z}{2},\theta\right).$$

In consequence, we obtain

$$\frac{\mathcal{H}_*\left(\frac{3\mathfrak{b}+z}{4},\ \mathfrak{s}\right)}{2} \leq \frac{1}{z-\mathfrak{b}}\int_{\mathfrak{b}}^{\frac{\mathfrak{b}+z}{2}} \mathcal{H}_*(\mathfrak{w},\ \mathfrak{s})d\mathfrak{w},$$
$$\frac{\mathcal{H}^*\left(\frac{3\mathfrak{b}+z}{4},\ \mathfrak{s}\right)}{2} \geq \frac{1}{z-\mathfrak{b}}\int_{\mathfrak{b}}^{\frac{\mathfrak{b}+z}{2}} \mathcal{H}^*(\mathfrak{w},\ \mathfrak{s})d\mathfrak{w}.$$

That is

$$\frac{\left[\mathcal{H}_*\left(\frac{3\mathfrak{b}+z}{4},\ \mathfrak{s}\right),\ \mathcal{H}^*\left(\frac{3\mathfrak{b}+z}{4},\ \mathfrak{s}\right)\right]}{2} \leq \frac{1}{z-\mathfrak{b}}\left[\int_{\mathfrak{b}}^{\frac{\mathfrak{b}+z}{2}} \mathcal{H}_*(\mathfrak{w},\ \mathfrak{s})d\mathfrak{w},\ \int_{\mathfrak{b}}^{\frac{\mathfrak{b}+z}{2}} \mathcal{H}^*(\mathfrak{w},\ \mathfrak{s})d\mathfrak{w}\right].$$

It follows that

$$\frac{\widetilde{\mathcal{H}}\left(\frac{3\mathfrak{b}+z}{4}\right)}{2} \supseteq_{\mathbb{F}} \frac{1}{z-\mathfrak{b}} \odot (FA)\int_{\mathfrak{b}}^{\frac{\mathfrak{b}+z}{2}} \widetilde{\mathcal{H}}(\mathfrak{w})d\mathfrak{w}. \tag{31}$$

In a similar way as above, we have

$$\frac{\widetilde{\mathcal{H}}\left(\frac{\mathfrak{b}+3z}{4}\right)}{2} \supseteq_{\mathbb{F}} \frac{1}{z-\mathfrak{b}} \odot (FA)\int_{\frac{\mathfrak{b}+z}{2}}^{z} \widetilde{\mathcal{H}}(\mathfrak{w})d\mathfrak{w}. \tag{32}$$

Combining (31) and (32), we have

$$\frac{\left[\widetilde{\mathcal{H}}\left(\frac{3\mathfrak{b}+z}{4}\right) \oplus \widetilde{\mathcal{H}}\left(\frac{\mathfrak{b}+3z}{4}\right)\right]}{2} \supseteq_{\mathbb{F}} \frac{1}{z-\mathfrak{b}} \odot (FA)\int_{\mathfrak{b}}^{z} \widetilde{\mathcal{H}}(\mathfrak{w})d\mathfrak{w}.$$

By using Theorem 5, we have

$$\widetilde{\mathcal{H}}\left(\frac{\mathfrak{b}+z}{2}\right) = \widetilde{\mathcal{H}}\left(\frac{1}{2}.\frac{3\mathfrak{b}+z}{4} + \frac{1}{2}.\frac{\mathfrak{b}+3z}{4}\right).$$

Therefore, for every $\mathfrak{s} \in [0,\ 1]$, we have

$$\mathcal{H}_*\left(\frac{\mathfrak{b}+z}{2},\ \mathfrak{s}\right) = \mathcal{H}_*\left(\frac{1}{2}.\frac{3\mathfrak{b}+z}{4} + \frac{1}{2}.\frac{\mathfrak{b}+3z}{4},\ \mathfrak{s}\right)$$
$$\mathcal{H}^*\left(\frac{\mathfrak{b}+z}{2},\ \mathfrak{s}\right) = \mathcal{H}^*\left(\frac{1}{2}.\frac{3\mathfrak{b}+z}{4} + \frac{1}{2}.\frac{\mathfrak{b}+3z}{4},\ \mathfrak{s}\right),$$

$$\leq \left[\frac{1}{2}\mathcal{H}_*\left(\frac{3\mathfrak{b}+z}{4},\ \mathfrak{s}\right) + \frac{1}{2}\mathcal{H}_*\left(\frac{\mathfrak{b}+3z}{4},\ \mathfrak{s}\right)\right]$$
$$\geq \left[\frac{1}{2}\mathcal{H}^*\left(\frac{3\mathfrak{b}+z}{4},\ \mathfrak{s}\right) + \frac{1}{2}\mathcal{H}^*\left(\frac{\mathfrak{b}+3z}{4},\ \mathfrak{s}\right)\right],$$

$$\leq \frac{1}{z-\mathfrak{b}}\int_{\mathfrak{b}}^{z} \mathcal{H}_*(\mathfrak{w},\ \mathfrak{s})d\mathfrak{w}$$
$$\geq \frac{1}{z-\mathfrak{b}}\int_{\mathfrak{b}}^{z} \mathcal{H}^*(\mathfrak{w},\ \mathfrak{s})d\mathfrak{w},$$

$$= \mathfrak{T}_{2*}$$
$$= \mathfrak{T}_2{}^*,$$

$$\leq \frac{1}{2}\left[\frac{\mathcal{H}_*(\mathfrak{b},\ \mathfrak{s}) + \mathcal{H}_*(z,\ \mathfrak{s})}{2} + \mathcal{H}_*\left(\frac{\mathfrak{b}+z}{2},\ \mathfrak{s}\right)\right]$$
$$\geq \frac{1}{2}\left[\frac{\mathcal{H}^*(\mathfrak{b},\ \mathfrak{s}) + \mathcal{H}^*(z,\ \mathfrak{s})}{2} + \mathcal{H}^*\left(\frac{\mathfrak{b}+z}{2},\ \mathfrak{s}\right)\right],$$

$$= \mathfrak{T}_{1*}$$
$$= \mathfrak{T}_1{}^*,$$

$$\leq \frac{1}{2}\left[\frac{\mathcal{H}_*(\mathfrak{b},\,\vartheta)+\mathcal{H}_*(z,\,\vartheta)}{2}+\frac{\mathcal{H}_*(\mathfrak{b},\,\vartheta)+\mathcal{H}_*(z,\,\vartheta)}{2}\right]$$
$$\geq \frac{1}{2}\left[\frac{\mathcal{H}^*(\mathfrak{b},\,\vartheta)+\mathcal{H}^*(z,\,\vartheta)}{2}+\frac{\mathcal{H}^*(\mathfrak{b},\,\vartheta)+\mathcal{H}^*(z,\,\vartheta)}{2}\right],$$
$$=\frac{\mathcal{H}_*(\mathfrak{b},\,\vartheta)+\mathcal{H}_*(z,\,\vartheta)}{2}$$
$$=\frac{\mathcal{H}^*(\mathfrak{b},\,\vartheta)+\mathcal{H}^*(z,\,\vartheta)}{2},$$

that is

$$\widetilde{\mathcal{H}}\left(\frac{\mathfrak{b}+z}{2}\right)\supseteq_{\mathbb{F}}\mathfrak{T}_2\supseteq_{\mathbb{F}}\frac{1}{z-\mathfrak{b}}\odot(FA)\int_{\mathfrak{b}}^{z}\widetilde{\mathcal{H}}(\mathfrak{w})d\mathfrak{w}\supseteq_{\mathbb{F}}\mathfrak{T}_1\supseteq_{\mathbb{F}}\frac{\widetilde{\mathcal{H}}(\mathfrak{b})\,\oplus\,\widetilde{\mathcal{H}}(z)}{2},$$

hence, the result follows. □

**Example 2.** *We consider the* $\mathcal{FNVM}$ $\widetilde{\mathcal{H}}:[\mathfrak{b},\,z]=[2,\,3]\to{}_0$ *defined by,* $\mathcal{H}_\vartheta(\mathfrak{w})=\left[(1-\vartheta)\left(2-\mathfrak{w}^{\frac{1}{2}}\right)+3\vartheta,(1+\vartheta)\left(2+\mathfrak{w}^{\frac{1}{2}}\right)+3\vartheta\right]$*, as in Example 1, then* $\widetilde{\mathcal{H}}(\mathfrak{w})$ *is* $\mathcal{UD}$*-convex* $\mathcal{FNVM}$ *and satisfying (10). We have* $\mathcal{H}_*(\mathfrak{w},\,\vartheta)=(1-\vartheta)\left(2-\mathfrak{w}^{\frac{1}{2}}\right)+3\vartheta$ *and* $\mathcal{H}^*(\mathfrak{w},\,\vartheta)=(1+\vartheta)\left(2+\mathfrak{w}^{\frac{1}{2}}\right)+3\vartheta$*. We now compute the following*

$$\frac{\mathcal{H}_*(\mathfrak{b},\,\vartheta)+\mathcal{H}_*(z,\,\vartheta)}{2}=\frac{4+2\vartheta-(1-\vartheta)\left(\sqrt{2}+\sqrt{3}\right)}{2}$$
$$\frac{\mathcal{H}^*(\mathfrak{b},\vartheta)\,\widetilde{+}\,\mathcal{H}^*(z,\vartheta)}{2}=\frac{4+10\vartheta+(1+\vartheta)\left(\sqrt{2}+\sqrt{3}\right)}{2},$$

$$\mathfrak{T}_{1*}=\frac{\frac{\mathcal{H}_*(\mathfrak{b},\,\vartheta)+\mathcal{H}_*(z,\,\vartheta)}{2}+\mathcal{H}_*\left(\frac{\mathfrak{b}+z}{2},\,\vartheta\right)}{2}=\frac{8+4\vartheta-(1-\vartheta)\left(\sqrt{2}+\sqrt{3}+\sqrt{2}\times\sqrt{5}\right)}{4}$$
$$\mathfrak{T}_1{}^*=\frac{\frac{\mathcal{H}^*(\mathfrak{b},\,\vartheta)+\mathcal{H}^*(z,\,\vartheta)}{2}+\mathcal{H}^*\left(\frac{\mathfrak{b}+z}{2},\,\vartheta\right)}{2}=\frac{8+20\vartheta+(1+\vartheta)\left(\sqrt{2}+\sqrt{3}+\sqrt{2}\times\sqrt{5}\right)}{4},$$

$$\mathfrak{T}_{2*}=\frac{\mathcal{H}_*\left(\frac{3\mathfrak{b}+z}{4},\,\vartheta\right)+\mathcal{H}_*\left(\frac{\mathfrak{b}+3z}{4},\,\vartheta\right)}{2}=\frac{5+7\vartheta-\sqrt{11}(1-\vartheta)}{4}$$
$$\mathfrak{T}_2{}^*=\frac{\mathcal{H}^*\left(\frac{3\mathfrak{b}+z}{4},\,\vartheta\right)+\mathcal{H}^*\left(\frac{\mathfrak{b}+3z}{4},\,\vartheta\right)}{2}=\frac{11+23\vartheta+\sqrt{11}(1+\vartheta)}{4},$$

*Then we obtain that*

$$(1-\vartheta)\frac{4-\sqrt{10}}{2}+3\vartheta\leq\frac{5+7\vartheta-\sqrt{11}(1-\vartheta)}{4}\leq\frac{843}{2000}(1-\vartheta)+3\vartheta$$
$$\leq\frac{8+4\vartheta-(1-\vartheta)\left(\sqrt{2}+\sqrt{3}+\sqrt{2}\times\sqrt{5}\right)}{4}\leq(1-\vartheta)\left(\frac{4-\sqrt{2}-\sqrt{3}}{2}\right)+3\vartheta$$
$$(1+\vartheta)\frac{4+\sqrt{10}}{2}+3\vartheta\geq\frac{11+23\vartheta+\sqrt{11}(1+\vartheta)}{4}\geq\frac{179}{50}(1+\vartheta)+3\vartheta$$
$$\geq\frac{8+20\vartheta+(1+\vartheta)\left(\sqrt{2}+\sqrt{3}+\sqrt{2}\times\sqrt{5}\right)}{4}\geq(1+\vartheta)\left(\frac{4+\sqrt{2}+\sqrt{3}}{2}\right)+3\vartheta.$$

*Hence, Theorem 6 is verified.*

We now obtain some $HH$-inequalities for the product of $\mathcal{UD}$-convex $\mathcal{FNVM}$s. These inequalities are refinements of some known inequalities, see [57].

**Theorem 7.** *Let $\widetilde{\mathcal{H}}, \widetilde{T} : [\mathfrak{b}, z] \to {}_0$ be two $\mathcal{UD}$-convex $\mathcal{FNVM}$s on $[\mathfrak{b}, z]$, whose $\vartheta$-cuts $\mathcal{H}_\vartheta$, $T_\vartheta : [\mathfrak{b}, z] \subset \mathbb{R} \to \mathcal{X}_0^+$ are defined by $\mathcal{H}_\vartheta(\mathfrak{w}) = [\mathcal{H}_*(\mathfrak{w}, \vartheta), \mathcal{H}^*(\mathfrak{w}, \vartheta)]$ and $T_\vartheta(\mathfrak{w}) = [T_*(\mathfrak{w}, \vartheta), T^*(\mathfrak{w}, \vartheta)]$ for all $\mathfrak{w} \in [\mathfrak{b}, z]$ and for all $\vartheta \in [0, 1]$. If $\widetilde{\mathcal{H}} \otimes \widetilde{T} \in \mathcal{FA}_{([\mathfrak{b}, z], \vartheta)}$, then*

$$\frac{1}{z-\mathfrak{b}} \odot (FA) \int_{\mathfrak{b}}^{z} \widetilde{\mathcal{H}}(\mathfrak{w}) \otimes \widetilde{T}(\mathfrak{w}) d\mathfrak{w} \supseteq_{\mathbb{F}} \frac{\widetilde{\mathcal{M}}(\mathfrak{b}, z)}{3} \oplus \frac{\widetilde{\mathcal{N}}(\mathfrak{b}, z)}{6}. \tag{33}$$

*where $\widetilde{\mathcal{M}}(\mathfrak{b}, z) = \widetilde{\mathcal{H}}(\mathfrak{b}) \otimes \widetilde{T}(\mathfrak{b}) \oplus \widetilde{\mathcal{H}}(z) \otimes \widetilde{T}(z)$, $\widetilde{\mathcal{N}}(\mathfrak{b}, z) = \widetilde{\mathcal{H}}(\mathfrak{b}) \otimes \widetilde{T}(z) \oplus \widetilde{\mathcal{H}}(z) \otimes \widetilde{T}(\mathfrak{b})$, and $\mathcal{M}_\vartheta(\mathfrak{b}, z) = [\mathcal{M}_*((\mathfrak{b}, z), \vartheta), \mathcal{M}^*((\mathfrak{b}, z), \vartheta)]$ and $\mathcal{N}_\vartheta(\mathfrak{b}, z) = [\mathcal{N}_*((\mathfrak{b}, z), \vartheta), \mathcal{N}^*((\mathfrak{b}, z), \vartheta)]$.*

**Proof.** Since $\widetilde{\mathcal{H}}, \widetilde{T} \in \mathcal{FA}_{([\mathfrak{b}, z])}$, then we have

$$\begin{gathered}\mathcal{H}_*(\varsigma\mathfrak{b} + (1-\varsigma)z, \vartheta) \leq \varsigma\mathcal{H}_*(\mathfrak{b}, \vartheta) + (1-\varsigma)\mathcal{H}_*(z, \vartheta),\\ \mathcal{H}^*(\varsigma\mathfrak{b} + (1-\varsigma)z, \vartheta) \geq \varsigma\mathcal{H}^*(\mathfrak{b}, \vartheta) + (1-\varsigma)\mathcal{H}^*(z, \vartheta).\end{gathered}$$

And

$$\begin{gathered}T_*(\varsigma\mathfrak{b} + (1-\varsigma)z, \vartheta) \leq \varsigma T_*(\mathfrak{b}, \vartheta) + (1-\varsigma)T_*(z, \vartheta),\\ T^*(\varsigma\mathfrak{b} + (1-\varsigma)z, \vartheta) \geq \varsigma T^*(\mathfrak{b}, \vartheta) + (1-\varsigma)T^*(z, \vartheta).\end{gathered}$$

From the definition of $\mathcal{UD}$-convex $\mathcal{FNVM}$s, it follows that $\widetilde{0} \leq_{\mathbb{F}} \widetilde{\mathcal{H}}(\mathfrak{w})$ and $\widetilde{0} \leq_{\mathbb{F}} \widetilde{T}(\mathfrak{w})$, so

$$\begin{gathered}\mathcal{H}_*(\varsigma\mathfrak{b} + (1-\varsigma)z, \vartheta) \times T_*(\varsigma\mathfrak{b} + (1-\varsigma)z, \vartheta)\\ \leq (\varsigma\mathcal{H}_*(\mathfrak{b}, \vartheta) + (1-\varsigma)\mathcal{H}_*(z, \vartheta)) \times (\varsigma T_*(\mathfrak{b}, \vartheta) + (1-\varsigma)T_*(z, \vartheta))\\ = \mathcal{H}_*(\mathfrak{b}, \vartheta \times)T_*(\mathfrak{b}, \vartheta)\varsigma^2 + \mathcal{H}_*(z, \vartheta) \times T_*(z, \vartheta)\varsigma^2\\ +\mathcal{H}_*(\mathfrak{b}, \vartheta) \times T_*(z, \vartheta)\varsigma(1-\varsigma) + \mathcal{H}_*(z, \vartheta) \times T_*(\mathfrak{b}, \vartheta)\varsigma(1-\varsigma)\\ \mathcal{H}^*(\varsigma\mathfrak{b} + (1-\varsigma)z, \vartheta) \times T^*(\varsigma\mathfrak{b} + (1-\varsigma)z, \vartheta)\\ \geq (\varsigma\mathcal{H}^*(\mathfrak{b}, \vartheta) + (1-\varsigma)\mathcal{H}^*(z, \vartheta)) \times (\varsigma T^*(\mathfrak{b}, \vartheta) + (1-\varsigma)T^*(z, \vartheta))\\ = \mathcal{H}^*(\mathfrak{b}, \vartheta) \times T^*(\mathfrak{b}, \vartheta)\varsigma^2 + \mathcal{H}^*(z, \vartheta) \times T^*(z, \vartheta)\varsigma^2\\ +\mathcal{H}^*(\mathfrak{b}, \vartheta)T^* \times (z, \vartheta)\varsigma(1-\varsigma) + \mathcal{H}^*(z, \vartheta) \times T^*(\mathfrak{b}, \vartheta)\varsigma(1-\varsigma),\end{gathered}$$

Integrating both sides of the above inequality over [0, 1], we get

$$\begin{gathered}\int_0^1 \mathcal{H}_*(\varsigma\mathfrak{b} + (1-\varsigma)z, \vartheta) \times T_*(\varsigma\mathfrak{b} + (1-\varsigma)z, \vartheta)d\varsigma\\ = \frac{1}{z-\mathfrak{b}} \int_{\mathfrak{b}}^{z} \mathcal{H}_*(\mathfrak{w}, \vartheta) \times T_*(\mathfrak{w}, \vartheta)d\mathfrak{w}\\ \leq (\mathcal{H}_*(\mathfrak{b}, \vartheta) \times T_*(\mathfrak{b}, \vartheta) + \mathcal{H}_*(z, \vartheta) \times T_*(z, \vartheta)) \int_0^1 \varsigma^2 d\varsigma\\ +(\mathcal{H}_*(\mathfrak{b}, \vartheta) \times T_*(z, \vartheta) + \mathcal{H}_*(z, \vartheta) \times T_*(\mathfrak{b}, \vartheta)) \int_0^1 \varsigma(1-\varsigma)d\varsigma,\\ \int_0^1 \mathcal{H}^*(\varsigma\mathfrak{b} + (1-\varsigma)z, \vartheta) \times T^*(\varsigma\mathfrak{b} + (1-\varsigma)z, \vartheta)d\varsigma\\ = \frac{1}{z-\mathfrak{b}} \int_{\mathfrak{b}}^{z} \mathcal{H}^*(\mathfrak{w}, \vartheta) \times T^*(\mathfrak{w}, \vartheta)d\mathfrak{w}\\ \geq (\mathcal{H}^*(\mathfrak{b}, \vartheta) \times T^*(\mathfrak{b}, \vartheta) + \mathcal{H}^*(z, \vartheta) \times T^*(z, \vartheta)) \int_0^1 \varsigma^2 d\varsigma\\ +(\mathcal{H}^*(\mathfrak{b}, \vartheta) \times T^*(z, \vartheta) + \mathcal{H}^*(z, \vartheta) \times T^*(\mathfrak{b}, \vartheta)) \int_0^1 \varsigma(1-\varsigma)d\varsigma.\end{gathered}$$

It follows that,

$$\begin{gathered}\frac{1}{z-\mathfrak{b}} \int_{\mathfrak{b}}^{z} \mathcal{H}_*(\mathfrak{w}, \vartheta) \times T_*(\mathfrak{w}, \vartheta)dw \leq \mathfrak{B}_*((\mathfrak{b}, z), \vartheta) \int_0^1 \varsigma^2 d\varsigma + \mathfrak{C}_*((\mathfrak{b}, z), \vartheta) \int_0^1 \varsigma(1-\varsigma)d\varsigma,\\ \frac{1}{z-\mathfrak{b}} \int_{\mathfrak{b}}^{z} \mathcal{H}^*(\mathfrak{w}, \vartheta) \times T^*(\mathfrak{w}, \vartheta)d\mathfrak{w} \geq \mathfrak{B}^*((\mathfrak{b}, z), \vartheta) \int_0^1 \varsigma^2 d\varsigma + \mathfrak{C}^*((\mathfrak{b}, z), \vartheta) \int_0^1 \varsigma(1-\varsigma)d\varsigma,\end{gathered}$$

that is

$$\begin{gathered}\frac{1}{z-\mathfrak{b}}\left[\int_{\mathfrak{b}}^{z} \mathcal{H}_*(\mathfrak{w}, \vartheta) \times T_*(\mathfrak{w}, \vartheta)d\mathfrak{w}, \int_{\mathfrak{b}}^{z} \mathcal{H}^*(\mathfrak{w}, \vartheta) \times T^*(\mathfrak{w}, \vartheta)d\mathfrak{w}\right]\\ \supseteq_I \left[\frac{\mathfrak{B}_*((\mathfrak{b}, z), \vartheta)}{3}, \frac{\mathfrak{B}^*((\mathfrak{b}, z), \vartheta)}{3}\right] + \left[\frac{\mathfrak{C}_*((\mathfrak{b}, z), \vartheta)}{6}, \frac{\mathfrak{C}^*((\mathfrak{b}, z), \vartheta)}{6}\right].\end{gathered}$$

Thus,

$$\frac{1}{z-\mathfrak{b}} \odot (FA)\int_{\mathfrak{b}}^{z} \widetilde{\mathcal{H}}(\mathfrak{w}) \otimes \widetilde{T}(\mathfrak{w})d\mathfrak{w} \supseteq_{\mathbb{F}} \frac{\widetilde{\mathcal{M}}(\mathfrak{b},z)}{3} \oplus \frac{\widetilde{\mathcal{N}}(\mathfrak{b},z)}{6}.$$

And the theorem has been established. □

**Example 3.** *Let* $[\mathfrak{b}, z] = [0, 2]$, *and the* $\mathcal{FNVM}s$ $\mathcal{H}, T : [\mathfrak{b}, z] = [0, 2] \to {}_{o}$, *defined by*

$$\mathcal{H}(\mathfrak{w})(\theta) = \begin{cases} \dfrac{\theta}{\mathfrak{w}} & \theta \in [0,\ \mathfrak{w}], \\ \dfrac{2\mathfrak{w}-\theta}{\mathfrak{w}} & \theta \in (\mathfrak{w},\ 2\mathfrak{w}], \\ 0 & otherwise, \end{cases}$$

$$T(\mathfrak{w})(\theta) = \begin{cases} \dfrac{\theta-\mathfrak{w}}{2-\mathfrak{w}} & \theta \in [\mathfrak{w},\ 2], \\ \dfrac{8-e^{\mathfrak{w}}-\theta}{8-e^{\mathfrak{w}}-2} & \theta \in (2,\ 8-e^{\mathfrak{w}}], \\ 0 & otherwise. \end{cases}$$

*Then, for each* $\flat \in [0,\ 1]$, *we have* $\mathcal{H}_{\flat}(\mathfrak{w}) = [\flat\mathfrak{w}, (2-\flat)\mathfrak{w}]$ *and* $T_{\flat}(\mathfrak{w}) = [(1-\flat)\mathfrak{w} + 2\flat, (1-\flat)(8-e^{\mathfrak{w}}) + 2\flat]$ *Since left and right end point mappings* $\mathcal{H}_*(\mathfrak{w}, \flat) = \flat\mathfrak{w}$, *and* $\mathcal{H}^*(\mathfrak{w},\ \flat) = (2-\flat)\mathfrak{w}$, *are convex and concave mappings, respectively, and* $T_*(\mathfrak{w}, \flat) = (1-\flat)\mathfrak{w} + 2\flat$ *and* $T^*(\mathfrak{w},\ \flat) = (1-\flat)(8-e^{\mathfrak{w}}) + 2\flat$ *are convex and concave mappings, respectively, for each* $\flat \in [0,\ 1]$, *then* $\widetilde{\mathcal{H}}(\mathfrak{w})$ *and* $\widetilde{T}(\mathfrak{w})$ *both are* $\mathcal{UD}$*-convex* $\mathcal{FNVM}s$. *We clearly see that* $\widetilde{\mathcal{H}} \otimes \widetilde{T} \in L([\mathfrak{b},\ z],_{o})$ *and*

$$\frac{1}{z-\mathfrak{b}}\int_{\mathfrak{b}}^{z} \mathcal{H}_*(\mathfrak{w}, \flat) \times T_*(\mathfrak{w}, \flat)d\mathfrak{w} = \frac{1}{2}\int_{0}^{2} \left(\flat(1-\flat)\mathfrak{w}^2 + 2\flat^2\mathfrak{w}\right)d\mathfrak{w} = \frac{2}{3}\flat(2+\flat),$$

$$\frac{1}{z-\mathfrak{b}}\int_{\mathfrak{b}}^{z} \mathcal{H}^*(\mathfrak{w}, \flat) \times T^*(\mathfrak{w}, \flat)d\mathfrak{w} = \frac{1}{2}\int_{0}^{2}((1-\flat)(2-\flat)\mathfrak{w}(8-e^{\mathfrak{w}}) + 2\flat(2-\flat)\mathfrak{w})d\mathfrak{w}$$

$$\approx \frac{(2-\flat)}{2}\left(\frac{1903}{250} - \frac{903}{250}\flat\right).$$

*Note that*

$$\Delta_*(\mathfrak{b}, z) = [\mathcal{H}_*(\mathfrak{b}) \times T_*(\mathfrak{b}) + \mathcal{H}_*(z) \times T_*(z)] = 4\flat,$$

$$\Delta^*(\mathfrak{b}, z) = [\mathcal{H}^*(\mathfrak{b}) \times T^*(\mathfrak{b}) + \mathcal{H}^*(z) \times T^*(z)] = 2(2-\flat)\left[(1-\flat)\left(8-e^2\right) + 2\flat\right],$$

$$\nabla_*(\mathfrak{b}, z) = [\mathcal{H}_*(\mathfrak{b}) \times T_*(z) + \mathcal{H}_*(z) \times T_*(\mathfrak{b})] = 4\flat^2,$$

$$\nabla_*(\mathfrak{b}, z) = [\mathcal{H}^*(\mathfrak{b}) \times T^*(z) + \mathcal{H}^*(z) \times T^*(\mathfrak{b})] = 2(2-\flat)(7-5\flat).$$

*Therefore, we have*

$$\frac{1}{3}\Delta_{\flat}(\mathfrak{b}, z) + \frac{1}{6}\nabla_{\flat}(\mathfrak{b}, z)$$

$$= \frac{1}{3}\left[4\flat, 2(2-\flat)\left[(1-\flat)\left(8-e^2\right) + 2\flat\right]\right] + \frac{1}{3}\left[2\flat^2, (2-\flat)(7-5\flat)\right]$$

$$= \frac{1}{3}\left[2\flat(2+\flat), (2-\flat)\left[2(1-\flat)\left(8-e^2\right) - \flat + 7\right]\right].$$

*It follows that*

$$[\frac{2}{3}\flat(1+2\flat), \frac{(2-\flat)}{2}\left(\frac{1903}{250} - \frac{903}{250}\flat\right)] \supseteq_I \frac{1}{3}[2\flat(2+\flat), (2-\flat)[2(1-\flat)(8-e^2) - \flat + 7]],$$

*and Theorem 7 has been demonstrated.*

**Theorem 8.** *Let $\widetilde{\mathcal{H}}, \widetilde{T} : [\mathfrak{b}, z] \to_0$ be two UD-convex FNVMs, whose $\mathfrak{s}$-cuts define the family of IVMs $\mathcal{H}_\mathfrak{s}, T_\mathfrak{s} : [\mathfrak{b}, z] \subset \mathbb{R} \to \mathcal{X}_0^+$ are given by $\mathcal{H}_\mathfrak{s}(\mathfrak{w}) = [\mathcal{H}_*(\mathfrak{w}, \mathfrak{s}), \mathcal{H}^*(\mathfrak{w}, \mathfrak{s})]$ and $T_\mathfrak{s}(\mathfrak{w}) = [T_*(\mathfrak{w}, \mathfrak{s}), T^*(\mathfrak{w}, \mathfrak{s})]$ for all $\mathfrak{w} \in [\mathfrak{b}, z]$ and for all $\mathfrak{s} \in [0, 1]$, respectively. If $\widetilde{\mathcal{H}} \otimes \widetilde{T} \in \mathcal{FA}_{([\mathfrak{b}, z], \mathfrak{s})}$, then*

$$2\, \widetilde{\mathcal{H}}\left(\frac{\mathfrak{b}+z}{2}\right) \otimes \widetilde{T}\left(\frac{\mathfrak{b}+z}{2}\right) \supseteq_{\mathbb{F}} \frac{1}{z-\mathfrak{b}} \odot (FA) \int_\mathfrak{b}^z \widetilde{\mathcal{H}}(\mathfrak{w}) \otimes \widetilde{T}(\mathfrak{w}) d\mathfrak{w} \oplus \frac{\widetilde{\mathcal{M}}(\mathfrak{b},z)}{6} \oplus \frac{\widetilde{\mathcal{N}}(\mathfrak{b},z)}{3}. \quad (34)$$

*where $\widetilde{\mathcal{M}}(\mathfrak{b},z) = \widetilde{\mathcal{H}}(\mathfrak{b}) \otimes \widetilde{T}(\mathfrak{b}) \oplus \widetilde{\mathcal{H}}(z) \otimes \widetilde{T}(z)$, $\widetilde{\mathcal{N}}(\mathfrak{b},z) = \widetilde{\mathcal{H}}(\mathfrak{b}) \otimes \widetilde{T}(z) \oplus \widetilde{\mathcal{H}}(z) \otimes \widetilde{T}(\mathfrak{b})$, and $\mathcal{M}_\mathfrak{s}(\mathfrak{b},z) = [\mathcal{M}_*((\mathfrak{b},z), \mathfrak{s}), \mathcal{M}^*((\mathfrak{b},z), \mathfrak{s})]$ and $\mathcal{N}_\mathfrak{s}(\mathfrak{b},z) = [\mathcal{N}_*((\mathfrak{b},z), \mathfrak{s}), \mathcal{N}^*((\mathfrak{b},z), \mathfrak{s})]$.*

**Proof.** By hypothesis, for each $\mathfrak{s} \in [0, 1]$, we have

$$\begin{aligned}
&\mathcal{H}_*\left(\frac{\mathfrak{b}+z}{2}, \mathfrak{s}\right) \times T_*\left(\frac{\mathfrak{b}+z}{2}, \mathfrak{s}\right) \\
&\mathcal{H}^*\left(\frac{\mathfrak{b}+z}{2}, \mathfrak{s}\right) \times T^*\left(\frac{\mathfrak{b}+z}{2}, \mathfrak{s}\right)
\end{aligned}$$

$$\begin{aligned}
&\leq \frac{1}{4}\begin{bmatrix} \mathcal{H}_*(\varpi\mathfrak{b} + (1-\varpi)z, \mathfrak{s}) \times T_*(\varpi\mathfrak{b} + (1-\varpi)z, \mathfrak{s}) \\ +\mathcal{H}_*(\varpi\mathfrak{b} + (1-\varpi)z, \mathfrak{s}) \times T_*((1-\varpi)\mathfrak{b} + \varpi z, \mathfrak{s}) \end{bmatrix} \\
&+\frac{1}{4}\begin{bmatrix} \mathcal{H}_*((1-\varpi)\mathfrak{b} + \varpi z, \mathfrak{s}) \times T_*(\varpi\mathfrak{b} + (1-\varpi)z, \mathfrak{s}) \\ +\mathcal{H}_*((1-\varpi)\mathfrak{b} + \varpi z, \mathfrak{s}) \times T_*((1-\varpi)\mathfrak{b} + \varpi z, \mathfrak{s}) \end{bmatrix}, \\
&\geq \frac{1}{4}\begin{bmatrix} \mathcal{H}^*(\varpi\mathfrak{b} + (1-\varpi)z, \mathfrak{s}) \times T^*(\varpi\mathfrak{b} + (1-\varpi)z, \mathfrak{s}) \\ +\mathcal{H}^*(\varpi\mathfrak{b} + (1-\varpi)z, \mathfrak{s}) \times T^*((1-\varpi)\mathfrak{b} + \varpi z, \mathfrak{s}) \end{bmatrix} \\
&+\frac{1}{4}\begin{bmatrix} \mathcal{H}^*((1-\varpi)\mathfrak{b} + \varpi z, \mathfrak{s}) \times T^*(\varpi\mathfrak{b} + (1-\varpi)z, \mathfrak{s}) \\ +\mathcal{H}^*((1-\varpi)\mathfrak{b} + \varpi z, \mathfrak{s}) \times T^*((1-\varpi)\mathfrak{b} + \varpi z, \mathfrak{s}) \end{bmatrix},
\end{aligned}$$

$$\begin{aligned}
&\leq \frac{1}{4}\begin{bmatrix} \mathcal{H}_*(\varpi\mathfrak{b} + (1-\varpi)z, \mathfrak{s}) \times T_*(\varpi\mathfrak{b} + (1-\varpi)z, \mathfrak{s}) \\ +\mathcal{H}_*((1-\varpi)\mathfrak{b} + \varpi z, \mathfrak{s}) \times T_*((1-\varpi)\mathfrak{b} + \varpi z, \mathfrak{s}) \end{bmatrix} \\
&\quad +\frac{1}{4}\begin{bmatrix} (\varpi\mathcal{H}_*(\mathfrak{b}, \mathfrak{s}) + (1-\varpi)\mathcal{H}_*(z, \mathfrak{s})) \\ \times((1-\varpi)T_*(\mathfrak{b}, \mathfrak{s}) + \varpi T_*(z, \mathfrak{s})) \\ +((1-\varpi)\mathcal{H}_*(\mathfrak{b}, \mathfrak{s}) + \varpi\mathcal{H}_*(z, \mathfrak{s})) \\ \times(\varpi T_*(\mathfrak{b}, \mathfrak{s}) + (1-\varpi)T_*(z, \mathfrak{s})) \end{bmatrix}, \\
&\geq \frac{1}{4}\begin{bmatrix} \mathcal{H}^*(\varpi\mathfrak{b} + (1-\varpi)z, \mathfrak{s}) \times T^*(\varpi\mathfrak{b} + (1-\varpi)z, \mathfrak{s}) \\ +\mathcal{H}^*((1-\varpi)\mathfrak{b} + \varpi z, \mathfrak{s}) \times T^*((1-\varpi)\mathfrak{b} + \varpi z, \mathfrak{s}) \end{bmatrix} \\
&\quad +\frac{1}{4}\begin{bmatrix} (\varpi\mathcal{H}^*(\mathfrak{b}, \mathfrak{s}) + (1-\varpi)\mathcal{H}^*(z, \mathfrak{s})) \\ \times((1-\varpi)T^*(\mathfrak{b}, \mathfrak{s}) + \mathfrak{s}T^*(z, \mathfrak{s})) \\ +((1-\varpi)\mathcal{H}^*(\mathfrak{b}, \mathfrak{s}) + \mathfrak{s}\mathcal{H}^*(z, \mathfrak{s})) \\ \times(\varpi T^*(\mathfrak{b}, \mathfrak{s}) + (1-\varpi)T^*(z, \mathfrak{s})) \end{bmatrix},
\end{aligned}$$

$$\begin{aligned}
&= \frac{1}{4}\begin{bmatrix} \mathcal{H}_*(\varpi\mathfrak{b} + (1-\varpi)z, \mathfrak{s}) \times T_*(\varpi\mathfrak{b} + (1-\varpi)z, \mathfrak{s}) \\ +\mathcal{H}_*((1-\varpi)\mathfrak{b} + \varpi z, \mathfrak{s}) \times T_*((1-\varpi)\mathfrak{b} + \varpi z, \mathfrak{s}) \end{bmatrix} \\
&\quad +\frac{1}{2}\begin{bmatrix} \left\{\varpi^2 + (1-\varpi)^2\right\}\mathcal{N}_*((\mathfrak{b},z), \mathfrak{s}) \\ +\{\varpi(1-\varpi) + (1-\varpi)\varpi\}\mathcal{M}_*((\mathfrak{b},z), \mathfrak{s}) \end{bmatrix}, \\
&= \frac{1}{4}\begin{bmatrix} \mathcal{H}^*(\varpi\mathfrak{b} + (1-\varpi)z, \mathfrak{s}) \times T^*(\varpi\mathfrak{b} + (1-\varpi)z, \mathfrak{s}) \\ +\mathcal{H}^*((1-\varpi)\mathfrak{b} + \varpi z, \mathfrak{s}) \times T^*((1-\varpi)\mathfrak{b} + \varpi z, \mathfrak{s}) \end{bmatrix} \\
&\quad +\frac{1}{2}\begin{bmatrix} \left\{\varpi^2 + (1-\varpi)^2\right\}\mathcal{N}^*((\mathfrak{b},z), \mathfrak{s}) \\ +\{\varpi(1-\varpi) + (1-\varpi)\varpi\}\mathcal{M}^*((\mathfrak{b},z), \mathfrak{s}) \end{bmatrix}.
\end{aligned}$$

Taking integration over $[0, 1]$, we have

$$\begin{aligned}
2\,\mathcal{H}_*\left(\frac{\mathfrak{b}+z}{2}, \mathfrak{s}\right) \times T_*\left(\frac{\mathfrak{b}+z}{2}, \mathfrak{s}\right) &\leq \frac{1}{z-\mathfrak{b}} \int_\mathfrak{b}^z \mathcal{H}_*(\mathfrak{w}, \mathfrak{s}) \times T_*(\mathfrak{w}, \mathfrak{s}) d\mathfrak{w} + \frac{\mathcal{M}_*((\mathfrak{b},z), \mathfrak{s})}{6} + \frac{\mathcal{N}_*((\mathfrak{b},z), \mathfrak{s})}{3}, \\
2\,\mathcal{H}^*\left(\frac{\mathfrak{b}+z}{2}, \mathfrak{s}\right) \times T^*\left(\frac{\mathfrak{b}+z}{2}, \mathfrak{s}\right) &\geq \frac{1}{z-\mathfrak{b}} \int_\mathfrak{b}^z \mathcal{H}^*(\mathfrak{w}, \mathfrak{s}) \times T^*(\mathfrak{w}, \mathfrak{s}) d\mathfrak{w} + \frac{\mathcal{M}^*((\mathfrak{b},z), \mathfrak{s})}{6} + \frac{\mathcal{N}^*((\mathfrak{b},z), \mathfrak{s})}{3},
\end{aligned}$$

that is

$$2\widetilde{\mathcal{H}}\left(\frac{\mathfrak{b}+z}{2}\right)\otimes\widetilde{T}\left(\frac{\mathfrak{b}+z}{2}\right)\supseteq_{\mathbb{F}}\frac{1}{z-\mathfrak{b}}\odot(FA)\int_{\mathfrak{b}}^{z}\widetilde{\mathcal{H}}(\mathfrak{w})\otimes\widetilde{T}(\mathfrak{w})d\mathfrak{w}\oplus\frac{\widetilde{\mathcal{M}}(\mathfrak{b},z)}{6}\oplus\frac{\widetilde{\mathcal{N}}(\mathfrak{b},z)}{3}.$$

Hence, the required result. □

**Example 4.** *We consider the $\mathcal{FNVM}$s $\widetilde{\mathcal{H}},\ \widetilde{T}:[\mathfrak{b},\ z]=[0,\ 2]\to{}_{0}$. Then, for each $\vartheta\in[0,\ 1]$, we have $\mathcal{H}_{\vartheta}(\mathfrak{w})=[\vartheta\mathfrak{w},(2-\vartheta)\mathfrak{w}]$ and $T_{\vartheta}(\mathfrak{w})=[(1-\vartheta)\mathfrak{w}+2\vartheta,(1-\vartheta)(8-e^{\mathfrak{w}})+2\vartheta]$, as in Example 3, then $\widetilde{\mathcal{H}}$ and $\widetilde{T}$ both are $\mathcal{UD}$-convex mappings. We have $\mathcal{H}_{*}(\mathfrak{w},\vartheta)=\vartheta\mathfrak{w}$, $\mathcal{H}^{*}(\mathfrak{w},\ \vartheta)=(2-\vartheta)\mathfrak{w}$ and $T_{*}(\mathfrak{w},\vartheta)=(1-\vartheta)\mathfrak{w}+2\vartheta$, $T^{*}(\mathfrak{w},\ \vartheta)=(1-\vartheta)(8-e^{\mathfrak{w}})+2\vartheta$, then*

$$2\mathcal{H}_{*}\left(\frac{\mathfrak{b}+z}{2},\vartheta\right)\times T_{*}\left(\frac{\mathfrak{b}+z}{2},\vartheta\right)=2\vartheta(1+\vartheta),$$

$$2\mathcal{H}^{*}\left(\frac{\mathfrak{b}+z}{2},\vartheta\right)\times T^{*}\left(\frac{\mathfrak{b}+z}{2},\vartheta\right)=2\left[16-20\vartheta+6\vartheta^{2}+(2-3\vartheta+\vartheta^{2})e\right],$$

$$\frac{1}{z-\mathfrak{b}}\int_{\mathfrak{b}}^{z}\mathcal{H}_{*}(\mathfrak{w},\vartheta)\times T_{*}(\mathfrak{w},\vartheta)d\mathfrak{w}=\frac{1}{2}\int_{0}^{2}\left(\vartheta(1-\vartheta)\mathfrak{w}^{2}+2\vartheta^{2}\mathfrak{w}\right)d\mathfrak{w}=\frac{4}{3}\vartheta(3-\vartheta),$$

$$\frac{1}{z-\mathfrak{b}}\int_{\mathfrak{b}}^{z}\mathcal{H}^{*}(\mathfrak{w},\vartheta)\times T^{*}(\mathfrak{w},\vartheta)d\mathfrak{w}=\frac{1}{2}\int_{0}^{2}((1-\vartheta)(2-\vartheta)\mathfrak{w}(8-e^{\mathfrak{w}})+2\vartheta(2-\vartheta)\mathfrak{w})d\mathfrak{w}$$

$$\approx\frac{(2-\vartheta)}{2}\left(\frac{1903}{250}-\frac{903}{250}\vartheta\right).$$

$$\Delta_{*}(\mathfrak{b},z)=[\mathcal{H}_{*}(\mathfrak{b})\times T_{*}(\mathfrak{b})+\mathcal{H}_{*}(z)\times T_{*}(z)]=4\vartheta,$$

$$\Delta^{*}(\mathfrak{b},z)=[\mathcal{H}^{*}(\mathfrak{b})\times T^{*}(\mathfrak{b})+\mathcal{H}^{*}(z)\times T^{*}(z)]=2(2-\vartheta)\left[(1-\vartheta)\left(8-e^{2}\right)+2\vartheta\right],$$

$$\nabla_{*}(\mathfrak{b},z)=[\mathcal{H}_{*}(\mathfrak{b})\times T_{*}(z)+\mathcal{H}_{*}(z)\times T_{*}(\mathfrak{b})]=4\vartheta^{2},$$

$$\nabla_{*}(\mathfrak{b},z)=[\mathcal{H}^{*}(\mathfrak{b})\times T^{*}(z)+\mathcal{H}^{*}(z)\times T^{*}(\mathfrak{b})]=2(2-\vartheta)(7-5\vartheta).$$

*Therefore, we have*

$$\frac{1}{6}\Delta_{\vartheta}((\mathfrak{b},z),\ \vartheta)+\frac{1}{3}\nabla_{\vartheta}((\mathfrak{b},z),\ \vartheta)$$

$$=\frac{1}{3}\left[2\vartheta,(2-\vartheta)\left[(1-\vartheta)\left(8-e^{2}\right)+2\vartheta\right]\right]+\frac{2}{3}\left[2\vartheta^{2},(2-\vartheta)(7-5\vartheta)\right]$$

$$=\frac{1}{3}\left[2\vartheta(1+2\vartheta),(2-\vartheta)\left[(1-\vartheta)\left(8-e^{2}\right)-8\vartheta+14\right]\right].$$

*It follows that*

$$2\left[\vartheta(1+\vartheta),\left[16-20\vartheta+6\vartheta^{2}+(2-3\vartheta+\vartheta^{2})e\right]\right]\supseteq_{I}\left[\frac{2}{3}\vartheta(2+\vartheta),\frac{(2-\vartheta)}{2}\left(\frac{1903}{250}-\frac{903}{250}\vartheta\right)\right]$$

$$+\frac{1}{3}\left[2\vartheta(1+2\vartheta),(2-\vartheta)\left[(1-\vartheta)\left(8-e^{2}\right)-8\vartheta+14\right]\right],$$

*and Theorem 8 has been demonstrated.*

We now give *HH*-Fejér inequalities for $\mathcal{UD}$-convex $\mathcal{FNVM}$s. Firstly, we obtain the second *HH*-Fejér inequality for $\mathcal{UD}$-convex $\mathcal{FNVM}$.

**Theorem 9.** *Let $\widetilde{\mathcal{H}}:[\mathfrak{b},\ z]\to{}_{0}$ be a $\mathcal{UD}$-convex $\mathcal{FNVM}$ with $\mathfrak{b}<z$, whose $\vartheta$-cuts define the family of $\mathcal{IVM}$s $\mathcal{H}_{\vartheta}:[\mathfrak{b},\ z]\subset\mathbb{R}\to\mathcal{X}_{0}^{+}$ are given by $\mathcal{H}_{\vartheta}(\mathfrak{w})=[\mathcal{H}_{*}(\mathfrak{w},\vartheta),\ \mathcal{H}^{*}(\mathfrak{w},\vartheta)]$ for*

*all* $\mathfrak{w} \in [\mathfrak{b}, z]$ *and for all* $\vartheta \in [0, 1]$. *If* $\widetilde{\mathcal{H}} \in \mathcal{FA}_{([\mathfrak{b}, z], \vartheta)}$ *and* $\mathfrak{B} : [\mathfrak{b}, z] \to \mathbb{R}$, $\mathfrak{B}(\mathfrak{w}) \geq 0$, *symmetric with respect to* $\frac{\mathfrak{b}+z}{2}$, *then*

$$\frac{1}{z-\mathfrak{b}} \odot (FA) \int_{\mathfrak{b}}^{z} \mathcal{H}(\mathfrak{w}) \odot \mathfrak{B}(\mathfrak{w})d\mathfrak{w} \supseteq_{\mathbb{F}} [\mathcal{H}(\mathfrak{b}) \oplus \mathcal{H}(z)] \odot \int_{0}^{1} \varpi\mathfrak{B}((1-\varpi)\mathfrak{b} + \varpi z)d\varpi. \quad (35)$$

**Proof.** Let $\widetilde{\mathcal{H}}$ be a $\mathcal{UD}$-convex $\mathcal{FNVM}$. Then, for each $\vartheta \in [0, 1]$, we have

$$\begin{aligned} &\mathcal{H}_*(\varpi\mathfrak{b} + (1-\varpi)z, \vartheta)B(\varpi\mathfrak{b} + (1-\varpi)z) \\ &\leq (\varpi\mathcal{H}_*(\mathfrak{b}, \vartheta) + (1-\varpi)\mathcal{H}_*(z, \vartheta))\mathfrak{B}(\varpi\mathfrak{b} + (1-\varpi)z), \\ &\mathcal{H}^*(\varpi\mathfrak{b} + (1-\varpi)z, \vartheta)\mathfrak{B}(\varpi\mathfrak{b} + (1-\varpi)z) \\ &\geq (\varpi\mathcal{H}^*(\mathfrak{b}, \vartheta) + (1-\varpi)\mathcal{H}^*(z, \vartheta))\mathfrak{B}(\varpi\mathfrak{b} + (1-\varpi)z). \end{aligned} \quad (36)$$

And

$$\begin{aligned} &\mathcal{H}_*((1-\varpi)\mathfrak{b} + \varpi z, \vartheta)B((1-\varpi)\mathfrak{b} + \varpi z) \\ &\leq ((1-\varpi)\mathcal{H}_*(\mathfrak{b}, \vartheta) + \varpi\mathcal{H}_*(z, \vartheta))\mathfrak{B}((1-\varpi)\mathfrak{b} + \varpi z), \\ &\mathcal{H}^*((1-\varpi)\mathfrak{b} + \varpi z, \vartheta)\mathfrak{B}((1-\varpi)\mathfrak{b} + \varpi z) \\ &\geq ((1-\varpi)\mathcal{H}^*(\mathfrak{b}, \vartheta) + \varpi\mathcal{H}^*(z, \vartheta))\mathfrak{B}((1-\varpi)\mathfrak{b} + \varpi z). \end{aligned} \quad (37)$$

After adding (36) and (37), and integrating over $[0, 1]$, we get

$$\begin{aligned} &\int_0^1 \mathcal{H}_*(\varpi\mathfrak{b} + (1-\varpi)z, \vartheta)\mathfrak{B}(\varpi\mathfrak{b} + (1-\varpi)z)d\varpi \\ &\quad + \int_0^1 \mathcal{H}_*((1-\varpi)\mathfrak{b} + \varpi z, \vartheta)\mathfrak{B}((1-\varpi)\mathfrak{b} + \varpi z)d\varpi \\ &\leq \int_0^1 \begin{bmatrix} \mathcal{H}_*(\mathfrak{b}, \vartheta)\{\varpi\mathfrak{B}(\varpi\mathfrak{b} + (1-\varpi)z) + (1-\varpi)\mathfrak{B}((1-\varpi)\mathfrak{b} + \varpi z)\} \\ +\mathcal{H}_*(z, \vartheta)\{(1-\varpi)\mathfrak{B}(\varpi\mathfrak{b} + (1-\varpi)z) + \varpi\mathfrak{B}((1-\varpi)\mathfrak{b} + \varpi z)\} \end{bmatrix} d\varpi, \\ &\int_0^1 \mathcal{H}^*((1-\varpi)\mathfrak{b} + \varpi z, \vartheta)\mathfrak{B}((1-\varpi)\mathfrak{b} + \varpi z)d\varpi \\ &\quad + \int_0^1 \mathcal{H}^*(\varpi\mathfrak{b} + (1-\varpi)z, \vartheta)\mathfrak{B}(\varpi\mathfrak{b} + (1-\varpi)z)d\varpi \\ &\geq \int_0^1 \begin{bmatrix} \mathcal{H}^*(\mathfrak{b}, \vartheta)\{\varpi\mathfrak{B}(\varpi\mathfrak{b} + (1-\varpi)z) + (1-\varpi)\mathfrak{B}((1-\varpi)\mathfrak{b} + \varpi z)\} \\ +\mathcal{H}^*(z, \vartheta)\{(1-\varpi)\mathfrak{B}(\varpi\mathfrak{b} + (1-\varpi)z) + \varpi\mathfrak{B}((1-\varpi)\mathfrak{b} + \varpi z)\} \end{bmatrix} d\varpi, \end{aligned}$$

$$\begin{aligned} &= 2\mathcal{H}_*(\mathfrak{b}, \vartheta) \int_0^1 \varpi B(\varpi\mathfrak{b} + (1-\varpi)z)d\varpi + 2\mathcal{H}_*(z, \vartheta) \int_0^1 \varpi B((1-\varpi)\mathfrak{b} + \varpi z)d\varpi, \\ &= 2\mathcal{H}^*(\mathfrak{b}, \vartheta) \int_0^1 \varpi B(\varpi\mathfrak{b} + (1-\varpi)z)d\varpi + 2\mathcal{H}^*(z, \vartheta) \int_0^1 \varpi B((1-\varpi)\mathfrak{b} + \varpi z)d\varpi. \end{aligned}$$

Since $\mathfrak{B}$ is symmetric, then

$$\begin{aligned} &\int_0^1 \mathcal{H}_*(\varpi\mathfrak{b} + (1-\varpi)z, \vartheta)\mathfrak{B}(\varpi\mathfrak{b} + (1-\varpi)z)d\varpi \\ &\quad + \int_0^1 \mathcal{H}_*(\varpi\mathfrak{b} + (1-\varpi)z, \vartheta)\mathfrak{B}(\varpi\mathfrak{b} + (1-\varpi)z)d\varpi \\ &\leq 2[\mathcal{H}_*(\mathfrak{b}, \vartheta) + \mathcal{H}_*(z, \vartheta)] \int_0^1 \varpi B((1-\varpi)\mathfrak{b} + \varpi z)d\varpi, \\ &\int_0^1 \mathcal{H}^*((1-\varpi)\mathfrak{b} + \varpi z, \vartheta)\mathfrak{B}((1-\varpi)\mathfrak{b} + \varpi z)d\varpi \\ &\quad + \int_0^1 \mathcal{H}^*(\varpi\mathfrak{b} + (1-\varpi)z, \vartheta)\mathfrak{B}(\varpi\mathfrak{b} + (1-\varpi)z)d\varpi \\ &\geq 2[\mathcal{H}^*(\mathfrak{b}, \vartheta) + \mathcal{H}^*(z, \vartheta)] \int_0^1 \varpi B((1-\varpi)\mathfrak{b} + \varpi z)d\varpi. \end{aligned} \quad (38)$$

Since

$$\begin{aligned} &\int_0^1 \mathcal{H}_*(\varpi\mathfrak{b} + (1-\varpi)z, \vartheta)\mathfrak{B}(\varpi\mathfrak{b} + (1-\varpi)z)d\varpi \\ &= \int_0^1 \mathcal{H}_*((1-\varpi)\mathfrak{b} + \varpi z, \vartheta)\mathfrak{B}((1-\varpi)\mathfrak{b} + \varpi z)d\varpi = \frac{1}{z-\mathfrak{b}} \int_{\mathfrak{b}}^{z} \mathcal{H}_*(\mathfrak{w}, \vartheta)\mathfrak{B}(\mathfrak{w})d\mathfrak{w} \\ &\int_0^1 \mathcal{H}^*((1-\varpi)\mathfrak{b} + \varpi z, \vartheta)\mathfrak{B}((1-\varpi)\mathfrak{b} + \varpi z)d\varpi \\ &= \int_0^1 \mathcal{H}^*(\varpi\mathfrak{b} + (1-\varpi)z, \vartheta)\mathfrak{B}(\varpi\mathfrak{b} + (1-\varpi)z)d\varpi = \frac{1}{z-\mathfrak{b}} \int_{\mathfrak{b}}^{z} \mathcal{H}^*(\mathfrak{w}, \vartheta)\mathfrak{B}(\mathfrak{w})d\mathfrak{w} \end{aligned} \quad (39)$$

Then from (38), we have

$$\begin{aligned} &\frac{1}{z-\mathfrak{b}} \int_{\mathfrak{b}}^{z} \mathcal{H}_*(\mathfrak{w}, \vartheta)\mathfrak{B}(\mathfrak{w})d\mathfrak{w} \leq [\mathcal{H}_*(\mathfrak{b}, \vartheta) + \mathcal{H}_*(z, \vartheta)] \int_0^1 \varpi\mathfrak{B}((1-\varpi)\mathfrak{b} + \varpi z)d\varpi, \\ &\frac{1}{z-\mathfrak{b}} \int_{\mathfrak{b}}^{z} \mathcal{H}^*(\mathfrak{w}, \vartheta)\mathfrak{B}(\mathfrak{w})d\mathfrak{w} \geq [\mathcal{H}^*(\mathfrak{b}, \vartheta) + \mathcal{H}^*(z, \vartheta)] \int_0^1 \varpi\mathfrak{B}((1-\varpi)\mathfrak{b} + \varpi z)d\varpi, \end{aligned}$$

that is
$$\left[\frac{1}{z-\mathfrak{b}}\int_{\mathfrak{b}}^{z}\mathcal{H}_*(\mathfrak{w},\vartheta)\mathfrak{B}(\mathfrak{w})d\mathfrak{w},\ \frac{1}{z-\mathfrak{b}}\int_{\mathfrak{b}}^{z}\mathcal{H}^*(\mathfrak{w},\vartheta)\mathfrak{B}(\mathfrak{w})d\mathfrak{w}\right]$$
$$\supseteq_I [\mathcal{H}_*(\mathfrak{b},\ \vartheta)+\mathcal{H}_*(z,\ \vartheta),\ \mathcal{H}^*(\mathfrak{b},\ \vartheta)+ \mathcal{H}^*(z,\ \vartheta)]\int_0^1 \varpi\mathfrak{B}((1-\varpi)\mathfrak{b}+\varpi z)d\varpi,$$

hence
$$\frac{1}{z-\mathfrak{b}}\odot(FA)\int_{\mathfrak{b}}^{z}\widetilde{\mathcal{H}}(\mathfrak{w})\odot\mathfrak{B}(\mathfrak{w})d\mathfrak{w}\supseteq_{\mathbb{F}}\left[\widetilde{\mathcal{H}}(\mathfrak{b})\oplus\widetilde{\mathcal{H}}(z)\right]\odot\int_0^1\varpi\mathfrak{B}((1-\varpi)\mathfrak{b}+\varpi z)d\varpi.$$

Next, we construct first *HH*-Fejér inequality for $\mathcal{UD}$-convex $\mathcal{FNVM}$, which generalizes first *HH*-Fejér inequalities for classical convex mapping. □

**Theorem 10.** *Let $\widetilde{\mathcal{H}}:[\mathfrak{b},\ z]\to_0$ be a $\mathcal{UD}$-convex $\mathcal{FNVM}$ with $\mathfrak{b}<z$, whose $\vartheta$-cuts define the family of $I\mathcal{VM}s$ $\mathcal{H}_\vartheta:[\mathfrak{b},\ z]\subset\mathbb{R}\to\mathcal{X}_{\mathcal{Q}}^+$ are given by $\mathcal{H}_\vartheta(\mathfrak{w})=[\mathcal{H}_*(\mathfrak{w},\vartheta),\ \mathcal{H}^*(\mathfrak{w},\vartheta)]$ for all $\mathfrak{w}\in[\mathfrak{b},\ z]$ and for all $\vartheta\in[0,\ 1]$. If $\widetilde{\mathcal{H}}\in\mathcal{FA}_{([\mathfrak{b},\ z],\ \vartheta)}$ and $\mathfrak{B}:[\mathfrak{b},\ z]\to\mathbb{R}$, $\mathfrak{B}(\mathfrak{w})\geq 0$, symmetric with respect to $\frac{\mathfrak{b}+z}{2}$, and $\int_{\mathfrak{b}}^{z}\mathfrak{B}(\mathfrak{w})d\mathfrak{w}>0$, then*
$$\widetilde{\mathcal{H}}\left(\frac{\mathfrak{b}+z}{2}\right)\supseteq_{\mathbb{F}}\frac{1}{\int_{\mathfrak{b}}^{z}\mathfrak{B}(\mathfrak{w})d\mathfrak{w}}\odot(FA)\int_{\mathfrak{b}}^{z}\widetilde{\mathcal{H}}(\mathfrak{w})\odot\mathfrak{B}(\mathfrak{w})d\mathfrak{w}. \tag{40}$$

**Proof.** Since $\widetilde{\mathcal{H}}$ is a $\mathcal{UD}$-convex, then for $\vartheta\in[0,\ 1]$, we have
$$\begin{aligned}\mathcal{H}_*\left(\frac{\mathfrak{b}+z}{2},\ \vartheta\right)&\leq\frac{1}{2}(\mathcal{H}_*(\varpi\mathfrak{b}+(1-\varpi)z,\ \vartheta)+\mathcal{H}_*((1-\varpi)\mathfrak{b}+\varpi z,\ \vartheta)),\\ \mathcal{H}^*\left(\frac{\mathfrak{b}+z}{2},\ \vartheta\right)&\geq\frac{1}{2}(\mathcal{H}^*(\varpi\mathfrak{b}+(1-\varpi)z,\ \vartheta)+\mathcal{H}^*((1-\varpi)\mathfrak{b}+\varpi z,\ \vartheta)),\end{aligned} \tag{41}$$

Since $\mathfrak{B}(\varpi\mathfrak{b}+(1-\varpi)z)=\mathfrak{B}((1-\varpi)\mathfrak{b}+\varpi z)$, then by multiplying (41) by $\mathfrak{B}((1-\varpi)\mathfrak{b}+\varpi z)$ and integrating it with respect to $\varpi$ over $[0,\ 1]$, we obtain
$$\begin{aligned}&\mathcal{H}_*\left(\frac{\mathfrak{b}+z}{2},\ \vartheta\right)\int_0^1\mathfrak{B}((1-\varpi)\mathfrak{b}+\varpi z)d\varpi\\ &\leq\frac{1}{2}\begin{pmatrix}\int_0^1\mathcal{H}_*(\varpi\mathfrak{b}+(1-\varpi)z,\ \vartheta)\mathfrak{B}(\varpi\mathfrak{b}+(1-\varpi)z)d\varpi\\ +\int_0^1\mathcal{H}_*((1-\varpi)\mathfrak{b}+\varpi z,\ \vartheta)\mathfrak{B}((1-\varpi)\mathfrak{b}+\varpi z)d\varpi\end{pmatrix},\\ &\mathcal{H}^*\left(\frac{\mathfrak{b}+z}{2},\ \vartheta\right)\int_0^1\mathfrak{B}((1-\varpi)\mathfrak{b}+\varpi z)d\varpi\\ &\geq\frac{1}{2}\begin{pmatrix}\int_0^1\mathcal{H}^*(\varpi\mathfrak{b}+(1-\varpi)z,\ \vartheta)\mathfrak{B}(\varpi\mathfrak{b}+(1-\varpi)z)d\varpi\\ +\int_0^1\mathcal{H}^*((1-\varpi)\mathfrak{b}+\varpi z,\ \vartheta)\mathfrak{B}((1-\varpi)\mathfrak{b}+\varpi z)d\varpi\end{pmatrix}.\end{aligned} \tag{42}$$

Since
$$\begin{aligned}&\int_0^1\mathcal{H}_*(\varpi\mathfrak{b}+(1-\varpi)z,\ \vartheta)\mathfrak{B}(\varpi\mathfrak{b}+(1-\varpi;)z)d\varpi\\ &=\int_0^1\mathcal{H}_*((1-\varpi)\mathfrak{b}+\varpi z,\ \vartheta)\mathfrak{B}((1-\varpi)\mathfrak{b}+\varpi z)d\varpi=\frac{1}{z-\mathfrak{b}}\int_{\mathfrak{b}}^{z}\mathcal{H}_*(\mathfrak{w},\vartheta)\mathfrak{B}(\mathfrak{w})d\mathfrak{w}\\ &\int_0^1\mathcal{H}^*((1-\varpi)\mathfrak{b}+\varpi z,\ \vartheta)\mathfrak{B}((1-\varpi)\mathfrak{b}+\varpi z)d\varpi\\ &=\int_0^1\mathcal{H}^*(\varpi\mathfrak{b}+(1-\varpi)z,\ \vartheta)\mathfrak{B}(\varpi\mathfrak{b}+(1-\varpi)z)d\varpi=\frac{1}{z-\mathfrak{b}}\int_{\mathfrak{b}}^{z}\mathcal{H}^*(\mathfrak{w},\vartheta)\mathfrak{B}(\mathfrak{w})d\mathfrak{w}.\end{aligned} \tag{43}$$

Then from (43), we have
$$\begin{aligned}\mathcal{H}_*\left(\frac{\mathfrak{b}+z}{2},\ \vartheta\right)&\leq\frac{1}{\int_{\mathfrak{b}}^{z}\mathfrak{B}(\mathfrak{w})d\mathfrak{w}}\int_{\mathfrak{b}}^{z}\mathcal{H}_*(\mathfrak{w},\vartheta)\mathfrak{B}(\mathfrak{w})d\mathfrak{w},\\ \mathcal{H}^*\left(\frac{\mathfrak{b}+z}{2},\ \vartheta\right)&\geq\frac{1}{\int_{\mathfrak{b}}^{z}\mathfrak{B}(\mathfrak{w})d\mathfrak{w}}\int_{\mathfrak{b}}^{z}\mathcal{H}^*(\mathfrak{w},\vartheta)\mathfrak{B}(\mathfrak{w})d\mathfrak{w},\end{aligned}$$

from which, we have

$$\left[\mathcal{H}_*\left(\frac{\mathfrak{b}+z}{2},\, \mathfrak{d}\right),\ \mathcal{H}^*\left(\frac{\mathfrak{b}+z}{2},\, \mathfrak{d}\right)\right]$$
$$\supseteq_I \frac{1}{\int_{\mathfrak{b}}^{z}\mathfrak{B}(\mathfrak{w})d\mathfrak{w}}\left[\int_{\mathfrak{b}}^{z}\mathcal{H}_*(\mathfrak{w},\mathfrak{d})\mathfrak{B}(\mathfrak{w})d\mathfrak{w},\ \int_{\mathfrak{b}}^{z}\mathcal{H}^*(\mathfrak{w},\mathfrak{d})\mathfrak{B}(\mathfrak{w})d\mathfrak{w}\right],$$

that is

$$\widetilde{\mathcal{H}}\left(\frac{\mathfrak{b}+z}{2}\right) \supseteq_{\mathbb{F}} \frac{1}{\int_{\mathfrak{b}}^{z}\mathfrak{B}(\mathfrak{w})d\mathfrak{w}} \odot (FA)\int_{\mathfrak{b}}^{z}\widetilde{\mathcal{H}}(\mathfrak{w})\odot\mathfrak{B}(\mathfrak{w})d\mathfrak{w}.$$

This completes the proof. □

**Remark 5.** *From Theorem 9 and Theorem 10, we clearly see that:*

*If $\mathcal{W}(\mathfrak{w}) = 1$, then we acquire the inequality (23).*

*If $\mathcal{H}$ is lower $\mathcal{UD}$-convex $\mathcal{FNVM}$ on $[\mathfrak{b}, z]$, then we acquire the following coming inequality, see* [90]*:*

$$\mathcal{H}\left(\frac{\mathfrak{b}+z}{2}\right) \leq_{\mathbb{F}} \frac{1}{\int_{\mathfrak{b}}^{z}\mathcal{W}(\mathfrak{w})d\mathfrak{w}} \odot (FA)\int_{\mathfrak{b}}^{z}\mathcal{H}(\mathfrak{w})\odot\mathcal{W}(\mathfrak{w})d\mathfrak{w} \leq_{\mathbb{F}} \frac{\mathcal{H}(\mathfrak{b})\oplus\mathcal{H}(z)}{2}. \tag{44}$$

*If $\mathcal{H}$ is lower $\mathcal{UD}$-convex $\mathcal{FNVM}$ on $[\mathfrak{b}, z]$ with $\mathfrak{d}$ $=$, then from (35) and (40) we acquire the following coming inequality, see* [99]*:*

$$\mathcal{H}\left(\frac{\mathfrak{b}+z}{2}\right) \leq_I \frac{1}{z-\mathfrak{b}}\,(IA)\int_{\mathfrak{b}}^{z}\mathcal{H}(\mathfrak{w})d\mathfrak{w} \leq_I \frac{\mathcal{H}(\mathfrak{b})+\mathcal{H}(z)}{2}. \tag{45}$$

*If $\mathcal{H}$ is lower $\mathcal{UD}$-convex $\mathcal{FNVM}$ on $[\mathfrak{b}, z]$ with $\mathfrak{d}$ $=$, then from (35) and (40) we acquire the following coming inequality, see* [99]*:*

$$\mathcal{H}\left(\frac{\mathfrak{b}+z}{2}\right) \leq_I \frac{1}{\int_{\mathfrak{b}}^{z}\mathcal{W}(\mathfrak{w})d\mathfrak{w}}\,(IA)\int_{\mathfrak{b}}^{z}\mathcal{H}(\mathfrak{w})\mathcal{W}(\mathfrak{w})d\mathfrak{w} \leq_I \frac{\mathcal{H}(\mathfrak{b})+\mathcal{H}(z)}{2}. \tag{46}$$

*Let $\mathfrak{d}$ $=$. Then from (35) and (40), we acquire the following inequality, see* [56]*:*

$$\mathcal{H}\left(\frac{\mathfrak{b}+z}{2}\right) \supseteq \frac{1}{\int_{\mathfrak{b}}^{z}\mathcal{W}(\mathfrak{w})d\mathfrak{w}}\,(IA)\int_{\mathfrak{b}}^{z}\mathcal{H}(\mathfrak{w})\mathcal{W}(\mathfrak{w})d\mathfrak{w} \supseteq \frac{\mathcal{H}(\mathfrak{b})+\mathcal{H}(z)}{2}. \tag{47}$$

*Let $\mathfrak{d} = 1$ and $\mathcal{H}_*(\mathfrak{w},\, \mathfrak{d}) = \mathcal{H}^*(\mathfrak{w},\, \mathfrak{d})$. Then, from(35) and (40), we obtain the following classical Fejér inequality:*

$$\mathcal{H}\left(\frac{\mathfrak{b}+z}{2}\right) \leq \frac{1}{\int_{\mathfrak{b}}^{z}\mathcal{W}(\mathfrak{w})d\mathfrak{w}}\int_{\mathfrak{b}}^{z}\mathcal{H}(\mathfrak{w})\mathcal{W}(\mathfrak{w})d\mathfrak{w} \leq \frac{\mathcal{H}(\mathfrak{b})+\mathcal{H}(z)}{2}. \tag{48}$$

**Example 5.** *We consider the $\mathcal{FNVM}$ $\mathcal{H} : [0,\ 2] \to {}_I$ defined by*

$$\mathcal{H}(\mathfrak{w})(\theta) = \begin{cases} \dfrac{\theta - 2 + \mathfrak{w}^{\frac{1}{2}}}{\frac{3}{2} - 2 - \mathfrak{w}^{\frac{1}{2}}} & \theta \in \left[2 - \mathfrak{w}^{\frac{1}{2}},\ \frac{3}{2}\right], \\ \dfrac{2 + \mathfrak{w}^{\frac{1}{2}} - \theta}{2 + \mathfrak{w}^{\frac{1}{2}} - \frac{3}{2}} & \theta \in \left(\frac{3}{2},\ 2 + \mathfrak{w}^{\frac{1}{2}}\right], \\ 0 & \textit{otherwise}, \end{cases}$$

*Then, for each* $\mathfrak{s} \in [0,\ 1]$, *we have* $\mathcal{H}_{\mathfrak{s}}(\mathfrak{w}) = \left[(1-\mathfrak{s})\left(2-\mathfrak{w}^{\frac{1}{2}}\right)+\frac{3}{2}\mathfrak{s},(1+\mathfrak{s})\left(2+\mathfrak{w}^{\frac{1}{2}}\right)+\frac{3}{2}\mathfrak{s}\right]$. *Since end point mappings* $\mathcal{H}_*(\mathfrak{w},\mathfrak{s})$, *and* $\mathcal{H}^*(\mathfrak{w},\mathfrak{s})$ *are convex and concave mappings, respectively, for each* $\mathfrak{s} \in [0,\ 1]$, *then* $\mathcal{H}(\mathfrak{w})$ *is* $\mathcal{UD}$*-convex* $\mathcal{FNVM}$. *If*

$$\mathfrak{B}(\mathfrak{w}) = \begin{cases} \sqrt{\mathfrak{w}}, & \sigma \in [0,1], \\ \sqrt{2-\mathfrak{w}}, & \sigma \in (1,\ 2], \end{cases}$$

*then* $\mathfrak{B}(2-\mathfrak{w}) = \mathfrak{B}(\mathfrak{w}) \geq 0$, *for all* $\mathfrak{w} \in [0,\ 2]$.

*Since* $\mathcal{H}_*(\mathfrak{w},\mathfrak{s}) = (1-\mathfrak{s})\left(2-\mathfrak{w}^{\frac{1}{2}}\right)+\frac{3}{2}\mathfrak{s}$ *and* $\mathcal{H}^*(\mathfrak{w},\mathfrak{s}) = (1+\mathfrak{s})\left(2+\mathfrak{w}^{\frac{1}{2}}\right)+\frac{3}{2}\mathfrak{s}$. *Now we compute the following*:

$$\begin{aligned}
\frac{1}{z-\mathfrak{b}}\int_{\mathfrak{b}}^{z}[\mathcal{H}_*(\mathfrak{w},\mathfrak{s})]\mathfrak{B}(\mathfrak{w})d\mathfrak{w} &= \frac{1}{2}\int_0^2[\mathcal{H}_*(\mathfrak{w},\mathfrak{s})]\mathfrak{B}(\mathfrak{w})d\mathfrak{w} \\
&= \frac{1}{2}\int_0^1[\mathcal{H}_*(\mathfrak{w},\mathfrak{s})]\mathfrak{B}(\mathfrak{w})d\mathfrak{w} + \frac{1}{2}\int_1^2 \mathcal{H}_*(\mathfrak{w},\mathfrak{s})\mathfrak{B}(\mathfrak{w})d\mathfrak{w}, \\
\frac{1}{z-\mathfrak{b}}\int_{\mathfrak{b}}^{z}[\mathcal{H}^*(\mathfrak{w},\mathfrak{s})]\mathfrak{B}(\mathfrak{w})d\mathfrak{w} &= \frac{1}{2}\int_0^2[\mathcal{H}^*(\mathfrak{w},\mathfrak{s})]\mathfrak{B}(\mathfrak{w})d\mathfrak{w} \\
&= \frac{1}{2}\int_0^1[\mathcal{H}^*(\mathfrak{w},\mathfrak{s})]\mathfrak{B}(\mathfrak{w})d\mathfrak{w} + \frac{1}{2}\int_1^2 \mathcal{H}^*(\mathfrak{w},\mathfrak{s})\mathfrak{B}(\mathfrak{w})d\mathfrak{w},
\end{aligned}$$

$$\begin{aligned}
&= \tfrac{1}{2}\int_0^1\left[(1-\mathfrak{s})\left(2-\mathfrak{w}^{\frac{1}{2}}\right)+\tfrac{3}{2}\mathfrak{s}\right](\sqrt{\mathfrak{w}})d\mathfrak{w} + \tfrac{1}{2}\int_1^2\left[(1-\mathfrak{s})\left(2-\mathfrak{w}^{\frac{1}{2}}\right)+\tfrac{3}{2}\mathfrak{s}\right](\sqrt{2-\mathfrak{w}})d\mathfrak{w} \\
&= \tfrac{1}{4}\left[\tfrac{13}{3}-\tfrac{\pi}{2}\right]+\mathfrak{s}\left[\tfrac{\pi}{8}-\tfrac{1}{12}\right], \\
&= \tfrac{1}{2}\int_0^1\left[(1+\mathfrak{s})\left(2+\mathfrak{w}^{\frac{1}{2}}\right)+\tfrac{3}{2}\mathfrak{s}\right](\sqrt{\mathfrak{w}})d\mathfrak{w} + \tfrac{1}{2}\int_1^2\left[(1+\mathfrak{s})\left(2+\mathfrak{w}^{\frac{1}{2}}\right)+\tfrac{3}{2}\mathfrak{s}\right](\sqrt{2-\mathfrak{w}})d\mathfrak{w} \\
&= \tfrac{1}{4}\left[\tfrac{19}{3}+\tfrac{\pi}{2}\right]+\mathfrak{s}\left[\tfrac{\pi}{8}+\tfrac{31}{12}\right].
\end{aligned} \tag{49}$$

*And*

$$\begin{aligned}
&[\mathcal{H}_*(\mathfrak{b},\ \mathfrak{s})+\mathcal{H}_*(z,\ \mathfrak{s})]\int_0^1 \varpi B((1-\varpi)\mathfrak{b}+\varpi z)d\varpi \\
&= \left[4(1-\mathfrak{s})-\sqrt{2}(1-\mathfrak{s})+3\mathfrak{s}\right]\left[\int_0^{\frac{1}{2}}\varpi\sqrt{2\varpi}d\varpi+\int_{\frac{1}{2}}^1\varpi\sqrt{2(1-\varpi)}d\varpi\right] \\
&= \tfrac{1}{3}\left(4(1-\mathfrak{s})-\sqrt{2}(1-\mathfrak{s})+3\mathfrak{s}\right), \\
&[\mathcal{H}^*(\mathfrak{b},\ \mathfrak{s})+\mathcal{H}^*(z,\ \mathfrak{s})]\int_0^1 \varpi\mathfrak{B}((1-\varpi)\mathfrak{b}+\varpi z)d\varpi \\
&= \left[4(1+\mathfrak{s})+\sqrt{2}(1+\mathfrak{s})+3\mathfrak{s}\right]\left[\int_0^{\frac{1}{2}}\varpi\sqrt{2\varpi}d\varpi+\int_{\frac{1}{2}}^1\varpi\sqrt{2(1-\varpi)}d\varpi\right] \\
&= \tfrac{1}{3}\left(4(1+\mathfrak{s})+\sqrt{2}(1+\mathfrak{s})+3\mathfrak{s}\right).
\end{aligned} \tag{50}$$

*From (49) and (50), we have*

$$\left[\frac{1}{4}\left[\frac{13}{3}-\frac{\pi}{2}\right]+\mathfrak{s}\left[\frac{\pi}{4}-\frac{7}{6}\right],\ \frac{1}{4}\left[\frac{19}{3}+\frac{\pi}{2}\right]+\mathfrak{s}\left[\frac{\pi}{4}+\frac{25}{6}\right]\right]$$

$$\supseteq_I \left[\frac{1}{3}\left(4(1-\mathfrak{s})-\sqrt{2}(1-\mathfrak{s})+3\mathfrak{s}\right),\ \frac{1}{3}\left(4(1+\mathfrak{s})+\sqrt{2}(1+\mathfrak{s})+3\mathfrak{s}\right)\right], \text{for all } \mathfrak{s} \in [0,\ 1].$$

*Hence, Theorem 9 is verified.*

For Theorem 10, we have

$$\begin{aligned}
\mathcal{H}_*\left(\frac{\mathfrak{b}+z}{2},\ \mathfrak{s}\right) &= \mathcal{H}_*(1,\ \mathfrak{s}) = \frac{2+\mathfrak{s}}{2}, \\
\mathcal{H}^*\left(\frac{\mathfrak{b}+z}{2},\ \mathfrak{s}\right) &= \mathcal{H}^*(1,\ \mathfrak{s}) = \frac{3(2+3\mathfrak{s})}{2},
\end{aligned}$$

$$\int_{\mathfrak{b}}^{z}\mathfrak{B}(\mathfrak{w})d\mathfrak{w} = \int_0^1\sqrt{\mathfrak{w}}d\mathfrak{w}+\int_1^2\sqrt{2-\mathfrak{w}}d\mathfrak{w} = \frac{4}{3}, \tag{51}$$

$$\frac{1}{\int_{\mathfrak{b}}^{z}\mathfrak{B}(\mathfrak{w})d\mathfrak{w}}\int_{\mathfrak{b}}^{z}\mathcal{H}_{*}(\mathfrak{w},\vartheta)\mathfrak{B}(\mathfrak{w})d\mathfrak{w}=\frac{3}{8}\left[\frac{13}{3}-\frac{\pi}{2}\right]+\frac{3\vartheta}{2}\left[\frac{\pi}{8}-\frac{1}{12}\right],$$
$$\frac{1}{\int_{\mathfrak{b}}^{z}\mathfrak{B}(\mathfrak{w})d\mathfrak{w}}\int_{\mathfrak{b}}^{z}\mathcal{H}^{*}(\mathfrak{w},\vartheta)\mathfrak{B}(\mathfrak{w})d\mathfrak{w}=\frac{3}{8}\left[\frac{19}{3}+\frac{\pi}{2}\right]+\frac{3\vartheta}{2}\left[\frac{\pi}{8}+\frac{31}{12}\right]. \quad (52)$$

From (51) and (52), we have

$$\left[\frac{2+\vartheta}{2},\ \frac{3(2+3\vartheta)}{2}\right]\supseteq_{I}\left[\frac{3}{8}\left[\frac{13}{3}-\frac{\pi}{2}\right]+\frac{3\vartheta}{2}\left[\frac{\pi}{8}-\frac{1}{12}\right],\ \frac{3}{8}\left[\frac{19}{3}+\frac{\pi}{2}\right]+\frac{3\vartheta}{2}\left[\frac{\pi}{8}+\frac{31}{12}\right]\right].$$

Hence, Theorem 10 has been verified.

## 4. Conclusions

This paper provides the introduced class $\mathcal{UD}$-convex concept for $\mathcal{FNVM}$s. The H.H. and Jensen-type inequalities were developed utilizing this idea and a fuzzy-inclusion relation. This study expands on several recent findings made by Zhao et al. [56,57] and the writers who came after them, Refs. [61,62]. Furthermore, some nontrivial cases are provided to verify our primary conclusions' accuracy. In the future, it will be fascinating to look into how analogous inequalities are established for other convexity types and by employing various integral operators. Our study of interval integral operator-type integral inequalities will broaden their practical applications because integral operators are widely used in engineering technology, such as various forms of mathematical modeling, and because different integral operators are suitable for different forms of practical problems. Convex optimization theory may take a new turn as a result of this idea. Other researchers working on a range of scientific subjects may probably find the idea useful.

**Author Contributions:** Conceptualization, M.B.K.; methodology, M.B.K.; validation, A.M.A.; formal analysis, H.A.O. and A.M.A.; investigation, M.B.K.; resources, H.A.O. and A.M.A.; data curation, M.G.V.; writing—original draft preparation, M.B.K.; writing—review and editing, M.B.K. and A.M.A.; visualization, M.G.V.; supervision, M.B.K. and L.A.; project administration, M.B.K. and L.A.; funding acquisition, A.M.A. and M.G.V. All authors have read and agreed to the published version of the manuscript.

**Funding:** This research received no external funding.

**Institutional Review Board Statement:** Not applicable.

**Informed Consent Statement:** Not applicable.

**Data Availability Statement:** Not applicable.

**Acknowledgments:** The authors would like to thank the Rector, COMSATS University Islamabad, Islamabad, Pakistan. The authors would like to thank the Deanship of Scientific Research at Umm Al-Qura University for supporting this work by Grant Code: 22UQU4330052DSR11. This research was also supported by Office of Research Management, Universiti Malaysia Terengganu, Malaysia.

**Conflicts of Interest:** The authors declare no conflict of interest.

## References

1. Sarikaya, M.Z.; Saglam, A.; Yildirim, H. On some Hadamard-type inequalities for h-convex functions. *J. Math. Inequal.* **2008**, *2*, 335–341. [CrossRef]
2. Bombardelli, M.; Varoşanec, S. Properties of h-convex functions related to the Hermite-Hadamard-Fejer inequalities. *Comput. Math. Appl.* **2009**, *58*, 1869–1877. [CrossRef]
3. Noor, M.A.; Noor, K.I.; Awan, M.U. A new Hermite-Hadamard type inequality for h-convex functions. *Creat. Math. Inform.* **2015**, *2*, 191–197.
4. Khan, M.B.; Santos-García, G.; Treanță, S.; Noor, M.A.; Soliman, M.S. Perturbed Mixed Variational-Like Inequalities and Auxiliary Principle Pertaining to a Fuzzy Environment. *Symmetry* **2022**, *14*, 2503. [CrossRef]
5. Khan, M.B.; Santos-García, G.; Noor, M.A.; Soliman, M.S. New Class of Preinvex Fuzzy Mappings and Related Inequalities. *Mathematics* **2022**, *10*, 3753. [CrossRef]
6. Khan, M.B.; Macías-Díaz, J.E.; Treanță, S.; Soliman, M.S. Some Fejér-Type Inequalities for Generalized Interval-Valued Convex Functions. *Mathematics* **2022**, *10*, 3851. [CrossRef]

7. Liu, Z.-H.; Sofonea, M.T. Differential quasivariational inequalities in contact mechanics, Math. *Mech. Solids.* **2019**, *24*, 845–861. [CrossRef]
8. Zeng, S.-D.; Migórski, S.; Liu, Z.-H.; Yao, J.-C. Convergence of a generalized penalty method for variational-hemivariational inequalities. *Commun. Nonlinear Sci. Numer. Simul.* **2021**, *92*, 105476. [CrossRef]
9. Li, X.-W.; Li, Y.-X.; Liu, Z.-H.; Li, J. Sensitivity analysis for optimal control problems described by nonlinear fractional evolution inclusions. *Fract. Calc. Appl. Anal.* **2018**, *21*, 1439–1470. [CrossRef]
10. Liu, Z.-H.; Papageorgiou, N.S. Positive solutions for resonant (p,q)-equations with convection. *Adv. Nonlinear Anal.* **2021**, *10*, 217–232. [CrossRef]
11. Dragomir, S.S.; Mond, B. Integral inequalities of Hadamard type for log-convex functions. *Demonstr. Math.* **1998**, *31*, 355–364. [CrossRef]
12. Dragomir, S.S. Refinements of the Hermite-Hadamard integral inequality for log-convex functions. *RGMIA Res. Rep. Collect.* **2000**, *3*, 219–225.
13. Niculescu, C.P. The Hermite–Hadamard inequality for log-convex functions. *Nonlinear Anal.* **2000**, *3*, 219–225. [CrossRef]
14. Khan, M.B.; Zaini, H.G.; Santos-García, G.; Noor, M.A.; Soliman, M.S. New Class Up and Down $\lambda$-Convex Fuzzy-Number Valued Mappings and Related Fuzzy Fractional Inequalities. *Fractal Fract.* **2022**, *6*, 679. [CrossRef]
15. Khan, M.B.; Zaini, H.G.; Macías-Díaz, J.E.; Soliman, M.S. Up and Down -Pre-Invex Fuzzy-Number Valued Mappings and Some Certain Fuzzy Integral Inequalities. *Axioms* **2023**, *12*, 1. [CrossRef]
16. Khan, M.B.; Noor, M.A.; Macías-Díaz, J.E.; Soliman, M.S.; Zaini, H.G. Some integral inequalities for generalized left and right log convex interval-valued functions based upon the pseudo-order relation. *Demonstr. Math.* **2022**, *55*, 387–403. [CrossRef]
17. Khan, M.B.; Noor, M.A.; Zaini, H.G.; Santos-García, G.; Soliman, M.S. The New Versions of Hermite–Hadamard Inequalities for Pre-invex Fuzzy-Interval-Valued Mappings via Fuzzy Riemann Integrals. *Int. J. Comput. Intell. Syst.* **2022**, *15*, 66. [CrossRef]
18. Khan, M.B.; Santos-García, G.; Noor, M.A.; Soliman, M.S. New Hermite–Hadamard Inequalities for Convex Fuzzy-Number-Valued Mappings via Fuzzy Riemann Integrals. *Mathematics* **2022**, *10*, 3251. [CrossRef]
19. Khan, M.B.; Treanţă, S.; Soliman, M.S. Generalized Preinvex Interval-Valued Functions and Related Hermite–Hadamard Type Inequalities. *Symmetry* **2022**, *14*, 1901. [CrossRef]
20. Dragomir, S.S. On the Hadamard's inequlality for convex functions on the co-ordinates in a rectangle from the plane. *Taiwan J. Math.* **2001**, *5*, 775–788. [CrossRef]
21. Zhao, D.; Zhao, G.; Ye, G.; Liu, W.; Dragomir, S.S. On Hermite–Hadamard-Type Inequalities for Coordinated h-Convex Interval-Valued Functions. *Mathematics* **2001**, *9*, 2352. [CrossRef]
22. Faisal, S.; Khan, M.A.; Iqbal, S. Generalized Hermite-Hadamard-Mercer type inequalities via majorization. *Filomat* **2022**, *36*, 469–483. [CrossRef]
23. Faisal, S.; Adil Khan, M.; Khan, T.U.; Saeed, T.; Alshehri, A.M.; Nwaeze, E.R. New "Conticrete" Hermite–Hadamard–Jensen–Mercer Fractional Inequalities. *Symmetry* **2022**, *14*, 294. [CrossRef]
24. Dragomir, S.S. Inequalities of Hermite–Hadamard type for functions of selfadjoint operators and matrices. *J. Math. Inequalities* **2017**, *11*, 241–259. [CrossRef]
25. Stojiljković, V.; Ramaswamy, R.; Ashour Abdelnaby, O.A.; Radenović, S. Riemann-Liouville Fractional Inclusions for Convex Functions Using Interval Valued Setting. *Mathematics* **2022**, *10*, 3491. [CrossRef]
26. Stojiljković, V.; Ramaswamy, R.; Alshammari, F.; Ashour, O.A.; Alghazwani, M.L.H.; Radenović, S. Hermite–Hadamard Type Inequalities Involving (k-p) Fractional Operator for Various Types of Convex Functions. *Fractal Fract.* **2022**, *6*, 376. [CrossRef]
27. Wang, H. Certain integral inequalities related to $(\varphi,\varrho^{\alpha})$–Lipschitzian mappings and generalized h–convexity on fractal sets. *J. Nonlinear Funct. Anal.* **2021**, *2021*, 12.
28. Tam, N.; Wen, C.; Yao, J.; Yen, N. Structural convexity and ravines of quadratic functions. *J. Appl. Numer. Optim.* **2021**, *3*, 425–434.
29. Khan, M.B.; Alsalami, O.M.; Treanţă, S.; Saeed, T.; Nonlaopon, K. New class of convex interval-valued functions and Riemann Liouville fractional integral inequalities. *AIMS Math.* **2022**, *7*, 15497–15519. [CrossRef]
30. Saeed, T.; Khan, M.B.; Treanţă, S.; Alsulami, H.H.; Alhodaly, M.S. Interval Fejér-Type Inequalities for Left and Right-λ-Preinvex Functions in Interval-Valued Settings. *Axioms* **2022**, *11*, 368. [CrossRef]
31. Khan, M.B.; Cătaş, A.; Alsalami, O.M. Some New Estimates on Coordinates of Generalized Convex Interval-Valued Functions. *Fractal Fract.* **2022**, *6*, 415. [CrossRef]
32. Santos-García, G.; Khan, M.B.; Alrweili, H.; Alahmadi, A.A.; Ghoneim, S.S. Hermite–Hadamard and Pachpatte type inequalities for coordinated preinvex fuzzy-interval-valued functions pertaining to a fuzzy-interval double integral operator. *Mathematics* **2022**, *10*, 2756. [CrossRef]
33. Macías-Díaz, J.E.; Khan, M.B.; Alrweili, H.; Soliman, M.S. Some Fuzzy Inequalities for Harmonically *s*-Convex Fuzzy Number Valued Functions in the Second Sense Integral. *Symmetry* **2022**, *14*, 1639. [CrossRef]
34. Moore, R.E. *Interval Analysis*; Prentice Hall: Hoboken, NJ, USA, 1966.
35. Snyder, J.M. Interval analysis for computer graphics. In Proceedings of the 19th Annual Conference on Computer Graphics and Interactive Techniques, Chicago, IL, USA, 27–31 July 1992; pp. 121–130.
36. Rahman, M.S.; Shaikh, A.A.; Bhunia, A.K. Necessary and sufficient optimality conditions for non-linear unconstrained and constrained optimization problem with interval valued objective function. *Comput. Ind. Eng.* **2020**, *147*, 106634. [CrossRef]
37. Qian, Y.; Liang, J.; Dang, C. Interval ordered information systems. *Comput. Math. Appl.* **2008**, *56*, 1994–2009. [CrossRef]

38. De Weerdt, E.; Chu, Q.P.; Mulder, J.A. Neural network output optimization using interval analysis. *IEEE Trans. Neural Netw.* **2009**, *20*, 638–653. [CrossRef]
39. Gao, W.; Song, C.; Tin-Loi, F. Probabilistic interval analysis for strucqrres with uncertainty. *Struct. Saf.* **2010**, *32*, 191–199. [CrossRef]
40. Wang, X.; Wang, L.; Qiu, Z. A feasible implementation procedure for interval analysis method from measurement data. *Appl. Math. Model.* **2014**, *38*, 2377–2397. [CrossRef]
41. Mizukoshi, M.T.; Lodwick, W.A. The interval eigenvalue problem using constraint interval analysis with an application to linear differential equations. *Fuzzy Sets Syst.* **2021**, *419*, 141–157. [CrossRef]
42. Jiang, C.; Han, X.; Guan, F.J.; Li, Y.H. An uncertain structural optimization method based on nonlinear interval number programming and interval analysis method. *Eng. Struct.* **2007**, *29*, 3168–3177. [CrossRef]
43. Wang, C.; Li, J.; Guo, P. The normalized interval regression model with outlier detection and its real-world application to house pricing problems. *Fuzzy Sets Syst.* **2015**, *274*, 109–123. [CrossRef]
44. Zhao, T.H.; Castillo, O.; Jahanshahi, H.; Yusuf, A.; Alassafi, M.O.; Alsaadi, F.E.; Chu, Y.M. A fuzzy-based strategy to suppress the novel coronavirus (2019-NCOV) massive outbreak. *Appl. Comput. Math.* **2021**, *20*, 160–176.
45. Zhao, T.H.; Wang, M.K.; Chu, Y.M. On the bounds of the perimeter of an ellipse. *Acta Math. Sci.* **2022**, *42B*, 491–501. [CrossRef]
46. Zhao, T.H.; Wang, M.K.; Hai, G.J.; Chu, Y.M. Landen inequalities for Gaussian hypergeometric function. *RACSAM Rev. R. Acad. A* **2022**, *116*, 1–23. [CrossRef]
47. Wang, M.K.; Hong, M.Y.; Xu, Y.F.; Shen, Z.H.; Chu, Y.M. Inequalities for generalized trigonometric and hyperbolic functions with one parameter. *J. Math. Inequal.* **2020**, *14*, 1–21. [CrossRef]
48. Zhao, T.H.; Qian, W.M.; Chu, Y.M. Sharp power mean bounds for the tangent and hyperbolic sine means. *J. Math. Inequal.* **2021**, *15*, 1459–1472. [CrossRef]
49. Chu, Y.M.; Wang, G.D.; Zhang, X.H. The Schur multiplicative and harmonic convexities of the complete symmetric function. *Math. Nachr.* **2011**, *284*, 53–663. [CrossRef]
50. Chu, Y.M.; Xia, W.F.; Zhang, X.H. The Schur concavity, Schur multiplicative and harmonic convexities of the second dual form of the Hamy symmetric function with applications. *J. Multivariate Anal.* **2012**, *105*, 412–421. [CrossRef]
51. Hajiseyedazizi, S.N.; Samei, M.E.; Alzabut, J.; Chu, Y.M. On multi-step methods for singular fractional q-integro-differential equations. *Open Math.* **2021**, *19*, 1378–1405. [CrossRef]
52. Jin, F.; Qian, Z.S.; Chu, Y.M.; Rahman, M. On nonlinear evolution model for drinking behavior under Caputo-Fabrizio derivative. *J. Appl. Anal. Comput.* **2022**, *12*, 790–806. [CrossRef]
53. Wang, F.Z.; Khan, M.N.; Ahmad, I.; Ahmad, H.; Abu-Zinadah, H.; Chu, Y.M. Numerical solution of traveling waves in chemical kinetics: Time-fractional fisher's equations. *Fractals* **2022**, *30*, 2240051. [CrossRef]
54. Chalco-Cano, Y.; Flores-Franulic, A.; Román-Flores, H. Ostrowski type inequalities for interval-valued functions using generalized Hukuhara derivative. *Comput. Appl. Math.* **2012**, *31*, 457–472.
55. Costa, T.M.; Román-Flores, H.; Chalco-Cano, Y. Opial-type inequalities for interval-valued functions. *Fuzzy Sets Syst.* **2019**, *358*, 48–63. [CrossRef]
56. Román-Flores, H.; Chalco-Cano, Y.; Lodwick, W. Some integral inequalities for interval-valued functions. *Comput. Appl. Math.* **2016**, *37*, 22–29. [CrossRef]
57. Zhao, D.; An, T.; Ye, G.; Liu, W. New Jensen and Hermite-Hadamard type inequalities for h-convex interval-valued functions. *J. Inequalities Appl.* **2018**, *2018*, 302. [CrossRef]
58. Ibrahim, M.; Nabi, S.; Baz, A.; Alhakami, H.; Raza, M.S.; Hussain, A.; Salah, K.; Djemame, K. An In-Depth Empirical Investigation of State-of-the-Art Scheduling Approaches for Cloud Computing. *IEEE Access* **2020**, *8*, 128282–128294. [CrossRef]
59. Talpur, N.; Abdulkadir, S.J.; Alhussian, H.; Hasan, M.H.; Aziz, N.; Bamhdi, A. A comprehensive review of deep neuro-fuzzy system architectures and their optimization methods. *Neural Comput. Applic.* **2022**, *34*, 1837–1875. [CrossRef]
60. Alsaedi, A.; Ahmad, B.; Assolami, A.; Ntouyas, S.K. On a nonlinear coupled system of differential equations involving Hilfer fractional derivative and Riemann-Liouville mixed operators with nonlocal integro-multi-point boundary conditions. *AIMS Mathematics* **2022**, *7*, 12718–12741. [CrossRef]
61. Khan, M.B.; Noor, M.A.; Al-Bayatti, H.M.; Noor, K.I. Some New Inequalities for LR-Log-h-Convex Interval-Valued Functions by Means of Pseudo Order Relation. *Appl. Math.* **2021**, *15*, 459–470.
62. Khan, M.B.; Noor, M.A.; Abdeljawad, T.; Mousa, A.A.A.; Abdalla, B.; Alghamdi, S.M. LR-Preinvex Interval-Valued Functions and Riemann-Liouville Fractional Integral Inequalities. *Fractal Fract.* **2021**, *5*, 243. [CrossRef]
63. Bhunia, A.K.; Samanta, S.S. A study of interval metric and its application in multi-objective optimization with interval objectives. *Comput. Ind. Eng.* **2014**, *74*, 169–178. [CrossRef]
64. Zhao, T.H.; Bhayo, B.A.; Chu, Y.M. Inequalities for generalized Grötzsch ring function. *Comput. Meth. Funct. Theory* **2022**, *22*, 559–574. [CrossRef]
65. Zhao, T.H.; He, Z.Y.; Chu, Y.M. Sharp bounds for the weighted Hölder mean of the zero-balanced generalized complete elliptic integrals. *Comput. Meth. Funct. Theory* **2021**, *21*, 413–426. [CrossRef]
66. Zhao, T.H.; Wang, M.K.; Chu, Y.M. Concavity and bounds involving generalized elliptic integral of the first kind. *J. Math. Inequal.* **2021**, *15*, 701–724. [CrossRef]

67. Zhao, T.H.; Wang, M.K.; Chu, Y.M. Monotonicity and convexity involving generalized elliptic integral of the first kind. *RACSAM Rev. R. Acad. A* **2021**, *115*, 1–13. [CrossRef]
68. Chu, H.H.; Zhao, T.H.; Chu, Y.M. Sharp bounds for the Toader mean of order 3 in terms of arithmetic, quadratic and contra harmonic means. *Math. Slovaca* **2020**, *70*, 1097–1112. [CrossRef]
69. Zhao, T.H.; He, Z.Y.; Chu, Y.M. On some refinements for inequalities involving zero-balanced hyper geometric function. *AIMS Math.* **2020**, *5*, 6479–6495. [CrossRef]
70. Zhao, T.H.; Wang, M.K.; Chu, Y.M. A sharp double inequality involving generalized complete elliptic integral of the first kind. *AIMS Math.* **2020**, *5*, 4512–4528. [CrossRef]
71. Zhao, T.H.; Shi, L.; Chu, Y.M. Convexity and concavity of the modified Bessel functions of the first kind with respect to Hölder means. *RACSAM Rev. R. Acad. A* **2020**, *114*, 1–14. [CrossRef]
72. Zhao, T.H.; Zhou, B.C.; Wang, M.K.; Chu, Y.M. On approximating the quasi-arithmetic mean. *J. Inequal. Appl.* **2019**, *2019*, 42. [CrossRef]
73. Zhao, T.H.; Wang, M.K.; Zhang, W.; Chu, Y.M. Quadratic transformation inequalities for Gaussian hyper geometric function. *J. Inequal. Appl.* **2018**, *2018*, 251. [CrossRef] [PubMed]
74. Chu, Y.M.; Zhao, T.H. Concavity of the error function with respect to Hölder means. *Math. Inequal. Appl.* **2016**, *19*, 589–595. [CrossRef]
75. Qian, W.M.; Chu, H.H.; Wang, M.K.; Chu, Y.M. Sharp inequalities for the Toader mean of order −1 in terms of other bivariate means. *J. Math. Inequal.* **2022**, *16*, 127–141. [CrossRef]
76. Othman, H.A. On fuzzy θ-generalized-semi-closed sets. *J. Adv. Stud. Topol.* **2016**, *7*, 84–92. [CrossRef]
77. Elghribi, M.; Othman, H.A.; Al-Nashri, A.H.A. Homogeneous functions: New characterization and applications. *Trans. A. Razmadze Math. Inst.* **2017**, *171*, 1–10. [CrossRef]
78. Khan, M.B.; Noor, M.A.; Abdullah, L.; Chu, Y.M. Some new classes of preinvex fuzzy-interval-valued functions and inequalities. *Int. J. Comput. Intell. Syst.* **2021**, *14*, 1403–1418. [CrossRef]
79. Khan, M.B.; Santos-García, G.; Noor, M.A.; Soliman, M.S. Some new concepts related to fuzzy fractional calculus for up and down convex fuzzy-number valued functions and inequalities. *Chaos Solitons Fractals* **2022**, *164*, 112692. [CrossRef]
80. Zhao, T.H.; Chu, H.H.; Chu, Y.M. Optimal Lehmer mean bounds for the nth power-type Toader mean of $n = -1, 1, 3$. *J. Math. Inequal.* **2022**, *16*, 157–168. [CrossRef]
81. Zhao, T.H.; Wang, M.K.; Dai, Y.Q.; Chu, Y.M. On the generalized power-type Toader mean. *J. Math. Inequal.* **2022**, *16*, 247–264. [CrossRef]
82. Huang, T.R.; Chen, L.; Chu, Y.M. Asymptotically sharp bounds for the complete p-elliptic integral of the first kind. *Hokkaido Math. J.* **2022**, *51*, 189–210. [CrossRef]
83. Zhao, T.H.; Qian, W.M.; Chu, Y.M. On approximating the arc lemniscate functions. *Indian J. Pure Appl. Math.* **2022**, *53*, 316–329. [CrossRef]
84. Liu, Z.H.; Motreanu, D.; Zeng, S.D. Generalized penalty and regularization method for differential variational- hemivariational inequalities. *SIAM J. Optim.* **2021**, *31*, 1158–1183. [CrossRef]
85. Liu, Y.J.; Liu, Z.H.; Wen, C.F.; Yao, J.C.; Zeng, S.D. Existence of solutions for a class of noncoercive variational-hemivariational inequalities arising in contact problems. *Appl. Math. Optim.* **2021**, *84*, 2037–2059. [CrossRef]
86. Zeng, S.D.; Migorski, S.; Liu, Z.H. Well-posedness, optimal control, and sensitivity analysis for a class of differential variational-hemivariational inequalities. *SIAM J. Optim.* **2021**, *31*, 2829–2862. [CrossRef]
87. Liu, Y.J.; Liu, Z.H.; Motreanu, D. Existence and approximated results of solutions for a class of nonlocal elliptic variational-hemivariational inequalities. *Math. Method Appl. Sci.* **2020**, *43*, 9543–9556. [CrossRef]
88. Liu, Y.J.; Liu, Z.H.; Wen, C.F. Existence of solutions for space-fractional parabolic hemivariational inequalities. *Discrete Contin. Dyn. Syst. Ser. B* **2019**, *24*, 1297–1307. [CrossRef]
89. Nanda, N.; Kar, K. Convex fuzzy mappings. *Fuzzy Sets Syst.* **1992**, *48*, 129–132. [CrossRef]
90. Khan, M.B.; Noor, M.A.; Noor, K.I.; Chu, Y.M. New Hermite–Hadamard–type inequalities for (h1, h2)-convex fuzzy-interval-valued functions. *Adv. Differ. Equ.* **2021**, *2021*, 149. [CrossRef]
91. Kulish, U.; Miranker, W. *Computer Arithmetic in Theory and Practice*; Academic Press: New York, NY, USA, 2014.
92. Khan, M.B.; Noor, M.A.; Shah, N.A.; Abualnaja, K.M.; Botmart, T. Some New Versions of Hermite–Hadamard Integral Inequalities in Fuzzy Fractional Calculus for Generalized Pre-Invex Functions via Fuzzy-Interval-Valued Settings. *Fractal Fract.* **2022**, *6*, 83. [CrossRef]
93. Bede, B. *Mathematics of Fuzzy Sets and Fuzzy Logic. Studies in Fuzziness and Soft Computing*; Springer: Berlin, Germany, 2013; p. 295.
94. Diamond, P.; Kloeden, P.E. *Metric Spaces of Fuzzy Sets: Theory and Applications*; World Scientific: Singapore, 1994.
95. Kaleva, O. Fuzzy differential equations. *Fuzzy Sets Syst.* **1987**, *24*, 301–317. [CrossRef]
96. Costa, T.M.; Roman-Flores, H. Some integral inequalities for fuzzy-interval-valued functions. *Inf. Sci.* **2017**, *420*, 110–125. [CrossRef]
97. Breckner, W.W. Continuity of generalized convex and generalized concave set–valued functions. *Rev. Anal. Numér. Théor. Approx.* **1993**, *22*, 39–51.
98. Sadowska, E. Hadamard inequality and a refinement of Jensen inequality for set-valued functions. *Result Math.* **1997**, *32*, 332–337. [CrossRef]

99. Khan, M.B.; Treanţă, S.; Soliman, M.S.; Nonlaopon, K.; Zaini, H.G. Some Hadamard–Fejér Type Inequalities for LR-Convex Interval-Valued Functions. *Fractal Fract.* **2022**, *6*, 6. [CrossRef]
100. Khan, M.B.; Santos-García, G.; Treanţă, S.; Soliman, M.S. New Class Up and Down Pre-Invex Fuzzy Number Valued Mappings and Related Inequalities via Fuzzy Riemann Integrals. *Symmetry* **2022**, *14*, 2322. [CrossRef]
101. Khan, M.B.; Macías-Díaz, J.E.; Soliman, M.S.; Noor, M.A. Some New Integral Inequalities for Generalized Preinvex Functions in Interval-Valued Settings. *Axioms* **2022**, *11*, 622. [CrossRef]
102. Aubin, J.P.; Cellina, A. *Differential Inclusions: Set-Valued Maps and Viability Theory, Grundlehren der Mathematischen Wissenschaften*; Springer: New York, NY, USA, 1984.
103. Aubin, J.P.; Frankowska, H. *Set-Valued Analysis*; Birkhäuser: Boston, MA, USA, 1990.
104. Costa, T.M. Jensen's inequality type integral for fuzzy-interval-valued functions. *Fuzzy Sets Syst.* **2017**, *327*, 31–47. [CrossRef]
105. Zhang, D.; Guo, C.; Chen, D.; Wang, G. Jensen's inequalities for set-valued and fuzzy set-valued functions. *Fuzzy Sets Syst.* **2020**, *2020*, 1–27. [CrossRef]
106. Liu, Z.H.; Loi, N.V.; Obukhovskii, V. Existence and global bifurcation of periodic solutions to a class of differential variational inequalities. *Int. J. Bifurcat. Chaos Appl. Sci. Eng.* **2013**, *23*, 1350125. [CrossRef]
107. Ashpazzadeh, E.; Chu, Y.-M.; Hashemi, M.S.; Moharrami, M.; Inc, M. Hermite multiwavelets representation for the sparse solution of nonlinear Abel's integral equation. *Appl. Math. Comput.* **2022**, *427*, 127171. [CrossRef]
108. Chu, Y.-M.; Ullah, S.; Ali, M.; Tuzzahrah, G.F.; Munir, T. Numerical investigation of Volterra integral equations of second kind using optimal homotopy asymptotic methd. *Appl. Math. Comput.* **2022**, *430*, 127304.
109. Chu, Y.-M.; Inc, M.; Hashemi, M.S.; Eshaghi, S. Analytical treatment of regularized Prabhakar fractional differential equations by invariant subspaces. *Comput. Appl. Math.* **2022**, *41*, 271. [CrossRef]
110. Zeng, S.-D.; Migórski, S.; Liu, Z.-H. Nonstationary incompressible Navier-Stokes system governed by a quasilinear reaction-diffusion equation. *Sci. Sin. Math.* **2022**, *52*, 331–354.
111. Deveci, M.; Gokasar, I.; Castillo, O.; Daim, T. Evaluation of Metaverse integration of freight fluidity measurement alternatives using fuzzy Dombi EDAS model. *Comput. Ind. Eng.* **2022**, *174*, 108773. [CrossRef]

MDPI
St. Alban-Anlage 66
4052 Basel
Switzerland
www.mdpi.com

*Mathematics* Editorial Office
E-mail: mathematics@mdpi.com
www.mdpi.com/journal/mathematics

www.ingramcontent.com/pod-product-compliance
Lightning Source LLC
LaVergne TN
LVHW070140100526
838202LV00015B/1856
* 9 7 8 3 0 3 6 5 7 3 7 4 8 *